CHARIOTS
IN ANCIENT EGYPT
The Tano Chariot, A Case Study

EDITED BY
ANDRÉ J. VELDMEIJER
SALIMA IKRAM

WITH CONTRIBUTIONS BY
OLE HERSLUND
LISA SABBAHY
LUCY SKINNER

© 2018 A.J. Veldmeijer

Published by Sidestone Press, Leiden
www.sidestone.com

Lay-out: A.J. Veldmeijer
Cover Design: Sidestone Press
Photograph cover: Sculpture: combat de Ramsès-Meïamoun contre les Khétas sur les bords de l'Oronte (Thèbes -- Ramesseum -- XIXe. dynastie) Retrieved from http://digitalcollections.nypl.org/items/510d47d9-68d4-a3d9-e040-e00a18064a99 The Miriam and Ira D. Wallach Division of Art, Prints and Photographs: Art & Architecture Collection, The New York Public Library (1878). Colour details: photography by André J. Veldmeijer. Courtesy of the Ministry of Antiquities/ Egyptian Museum Authorities.

Printed and bound in Great Britain by Marston Book Services Ltd, Oxfordshire

ISBN 978-90-8890-466-0 (softcover)
ISBN 978-90-8890-467-7 (hardcover)
ISBN 978-90-8890-468-4 (PDF e-book)

CHARIOTS
IN ANCIENT EGYPT

Sidestone Press

To Khalid Ikram and our ancestor, Mian Nuru Khan,
the *chabuk sawar* of Raja Ranjit Singh

Contents

Part I. Analysis

I. Introduction (André J. Veldmeijer & Salima Ikram)   12

    I.1. Scope of the Project   12
    I.2. The Chariot in Ancient Egypt   13
    I.3. Sources of Evidence   13
    I.4. Methodology   13
    I.5. Introduction to the Archaeological Evidence   14
       I.5.1. Maiherpri   14
       I.5.2. Tomb of Amenhotep II (Cat. Nos. 1-11)   14
       I.5.3. Tomb of Thutmose IV (Cat. Nos. 12-27)   15
       I.5.4. Tomb of Amenhotep III (Cat. Nos. 28-42)   16
       I.5.5. Amarna   17
       I.5.6. Tomb of Tutankhamun   18
       I.5.6. Tano Chariot (Cat. Nos. 43-167)   20

II. Deconstructing and Construction:
Identifying the Parts of a Chariot (André J. Veldmeijer & Salima Ikram)   22

    II.1. Chariot Body   22
       II.1.1. Main Casing   22
       II.1.2. Siding Fill   28
       II.1.3. Support Straps   30
       II.1.4. Nave Hoops   34
    II.2. Accessories   35
       II.2.1. Bow-Cases and Quivers   35
       II.2.2. Pouches   46
       II.2.3. Holder(?)   48
    II.3. Harness   49
       II.3.1. Neckstrap   49
       II.3.2. Girth   52
       II.3.3. Yoke Saddle Pad   54
       II.3.4. Headstall (including blinker and bridle boss)   56
       II.3.5. Enigmatic Bands   60
    II.4. Charioteer's Accessories   60
       II.4.1. Wrist Guards   60
    II.5. Discussion: Piecing the Tano Leather Together   62
       II.5.1. Main Casing and Siding Fill   62
       II.5.2. Support Straps   67
       II.5.3. Bow-Case   67
       II.5.4. Nave Hoops   69
       II.5.5. Neckstrap and Girth   69
       II.5.6. Various   69

III. Looking at Skin: Analysis of the Leather (Lucy Skinner)   72

   III.1. Introduction   72
   III.2. The Raw Material: Skin   73
      III.2.1. Structure   73
      III.2.2. Areas Within a Skin   75
      III.2.3. Species   75
   III.3. Skin Processing   80
   III.4. The Degradation of Skin   83
   III.5. The Tano Leather   84
      III.5.1. Condition   84
      III.5.2. Skin Type   86
      III.5.3. Evidence for Leathering or Tanning   90
      III.5.4. Colour Identification   93
   III.6. Handling and Conservation   95
   III.7. Conclusions   95

IV. Dressing a Chariot:
Leatherwork Technology (André J. Veldmeijer & Salima Ikram)   97

   IV.1. Manufacturing Chariot and Chariot Related Leathers   97
      IV.1.1. Glue, Stitching and Seams   97
      IV.1.2. Constructional Features   102
      IV.1.3. Decoration   108

V. Moving Pictures:
Context of Use and Iconography of Chariots in the New Kingdom
(Lisa Sabbahy)   120

   V.I. Introduction   120
   V.2. Pre-Amarna 18th Dynasty   121
      V.2.1. Royal Scenes: Warfare, Victory, and Sport   121
      V.2.2. Non-Royal Scenes: Officialdom at Work, Hunting,
and Funerals   125
   V.3. Amarna Period   131
      V.3.1. Royal Scenes: Karnak *Talatat*   131
      V.3.2. Amarna   133
   V.4. Post-Amarna 18th Dynasty   138
      V.4.1. Royal Scenes of Battle, Victory, Procession and Hunting: Kings
Tutankhamun, Ay, and Horemheb   138
      V.4.2. Elite Scenes   139
   V.5. Ramesside Period   142
      V.5.1. Royal Scenes   142
      V.5.2. Non-Royal Depictions   148
   V.6. Conclusion   149

VI. Chronicling Chariots:
Texts, Writing and Language of New Kingdom Egypt (Ole Herslund) 150

    VI.1. Introduction 150
    VI.2. Chariots in War 151
    VI.3. Chariots as Booty and Tribute 156
    VI.4. Chariots as Gifts for the King 159
    VI.5. Chariot Workers, Production and Materials 159
    VI.6. Private Ownership and Daily Use of Chariots 162
    VI.7. Ideology, Kingship and Meanings of Chariots 165
    VI.8. Chariots in the Lexicon and Writing Systems 169
        VI.8.1. General 169
        VI.8.2. Lexicological Catalogue of Chariot Part Names 177
    VI.9. Discussion 194

VII. Discussion and Conclusions (André J. Veldmeijer & Salima Ikram) 199

    VII.1. Chariot Leather Craftsmanship 199
    VII.2. The Tano Leather 200
        VII.2.1. Provenance and Ownership 200
        VII.2.2. Dating the Tano Material 201
        VII.2.3. Shape 202

Part II. Catalogue
(André J. Veldmeijer & Salima Ikram)

Tomb of Amenhotep II   (Cat. No. 1-11) 206

Tomb of Thutmose IV   (Cat. No. 12-27) 256

Tomb of Amenhotep III   (Cat. No. 28-42) 288

Tano 317
    Main Casing   (Cat. No. 43-49) 317
    Siding Fill   (Cat. No. 50-80) 350
    Suspension Straps   (Cat. No. 81-87) 402
    Nave Hoops   (Cat. No. 88-90) 416
    Bow-Case   (Cat. No. 91-95) 422
    Harness   (Cat. No. 96-119) 442
    Unidentified   (Cat. No. 120-167) 475

Appendix 523
    I. Concordance 524
    II. Chariot Leather from Amarna (facsimile) 542
    III. What's in a Stitch (facsimile) 562

Abbreviations 565

Glossary 566

Chronology of Egypt 570

Bibliography 574

Part I

Analysis

I. Introduction

André J. Veldmeijer & Salima Ikram

I.1. Scope of the Project

As leather had been little studied in the ancient Egyptian context, the authors (AJV & SI) instigated a holistic inter-disciplinary project to study this versatile and essential material, the Ancient Egyptian Leatherwork Project (AELP).[1] The word 'leather' in English modern language terminology is usually only used to refer to hide or skin which has been made non-putrescible in moist conditions, through 'tanning' (Thomson, 2006b: 1). However, in the context of ancient Egyptian material, there is no consensus of opinion on how hide and skin was processed. Therefore, the word 'leather' is used more generally in this publication, to describe skin or hide which has been processed in some way, allowing it to survive for over three thousand years, even when the preservative effects of this processing can be reversed through exposure to water (see also Veldmeijer, Submitted).

During the course of this research, in a book by Forbes (1957: 30, fig. 6) a reference was found to horse trappings kept in the Egyptian Museum (Cairo). Intrigued, we instigated a search for this assemblage, and in collaboration with Ibrahim Abd el-Gawad, the curator in charge of the section, the material was found. Instead of merely consisting of horse trappings and harnessing, we discovered that the assemblage was actually the leather from a chariot, complete with accessories and fragments of the harness, all catalogued under a single number (JE 88962; SR 14530). It was purchased from a dealer named Georges Tano in 1932.[2] This changed the direction of the AELP, creating a sub-project, the Egyptian Museum Chariot Project (EMCP).[3] The focus of this project was to document and conserve the Tano materials, provide secure storage for them (Veldmeijer & Ikram, 2009; 2012a; 2012b; Veldmeijer *et al.*, 2013), and compare the fragments with those coming from other chariots, in some cases fully documented in this volume for the first time. Images, iconography, and textual material complemented the study.

---

1   See www.leatherandshoes.nl.
2   See Merrillees (2003) on the Tano family.
3   We are grateful to the Ministry of Antiquities and the Egyptian Museum Authorities for allowing us access to the material. The work was made possible due to a grant of ARCE's Antiquities Endowment Fund (backed by USAID). The material is under curatorship of Ibrahim Abd el-Gawad, to whom we are grateful, as we are to the directors of the Egyptian Museum (Cairo): Wafaa el-Seddik, Tarek el-Awady, Lotfi Abdel Hamid, Sayed Amer, Mohammed Ali, Sabah Abelrazek. We are indebted to the wonderful colleagues of the Conservation Department of the Egyptian Museum (Cairo) for collaboration and providing the venue to work on conservation. We thank Katja Broschat, Joost Crouwel, Christian Eckman, Kathy Hansen and Martin Moser for useful discussions. We thank Maria Cristina Guidotti for allowing us to study the Florence chariot. We are grateful for the Metropolitan Museum of Art, New York to allow us to study and include the so-called Amenhotep III chariot leather.

I.2. The Chariot in Ancient Egypt

It is generally accepted that chariots were introduced into Egypt by the Hyksos in the Second Intermediate Period (c. 1650-1549 BC), together with horses and a variety of weapons, including the double bow, sickle swords and daggers (Crouwel, 2013; Shaw, 1999; Spalinger, 2005: 4-31; Darnell & Manassa, 2007: 63-65, 77-80; Littauer & Crouwel, 1985, but see section VI.2. 'Chariots in War'). Initially the preserve of royalty, chariots were soon adopted by the high elite, but remained a more expensive form of transport, especially due to the cost of obtaining and keeping horses. Royalty and the elite used chariots in processions, battle, on hunts, as well as for rapid transportation in the desert (*e.g.* Cotterell, 2004; Köpp-Junk, 2015b; Partridge, 1996; Raulwing, 2002; Littauer & Crouwel, 1979). Chariots varied somewhat in size and form, depending on their purpose, with additional changes over time, as the design improved.

I.3. Sources of Evidence

Sources of information for the study of chariots include depictions from tombs, temples and small objects, such as stelae, ostraca, and boxes, dating from the late Second Intermediate Period and continuing thereafter (Chapter V). For the study of chariots and iconography, these images are useful. However, given the profile representations and the myriad of issues associated with using artistic representations to decipher reality, these can be a challenging source of information to use in chariot reconstruction. Mentions of chariots appear in texts from that time onward, and range from references in royal annals to being exalted in long poems (Chapter VI), providing practical information about their use in battle, as well as an idea of the metaphoric role they came to play in literature. In addition to images, the actual remains of these vehicles have been found in tombs, notably the six chariots from the tomb of Tutankhamun (Carter's Numbers 120, 121, 122, 332, 333, 161; Carter, 1927: 54-63; Littauer & Crouwel, 1985), the processional chariot of Thutmose IV (CG 46097; Carter, 1904), the chariot of Yuya and Tjuiu (CG 51188; Quibell, 1908; Carter & Newberry, 1904: 24-33), and the unprovenanced chariot in the Florence Museum (Inv. No. 2678; Guidotti, 2002). None of these chariots was completely intact, as in most cases the leather casing was missing or had disintegrated, leaving only the wooden frame. Thutmose IV's chariot is an exception as it is made entirely of wood (as are the so-called 'State Chariots' from the tomb of Tutankhamun), and some fragments of the casing of Yuya and Tjuiu survived, but the chariot is heavily restored, and is curiously low, thus raising questions of its own.

The Tano leather, which was investigated initially in 2008, is the first complete chariot casing, together with some of its accessories, such as (parts of) the bow-case, support straps, and horse harnessing, found, to date. Although some other examples of chariot accessories exist, the Tano material is unique in that it includes a complete chariot body cover.

I.4. Methodology

Although the present work focuses on chariots in Egypt, it is, by no means, an exhaustive study of the subject, as the focus is more on the associated leather, highlighting the Tano material, rather than providing a complete history of these vehicles. Each leather object has been examined, described verbally (using the terminology listed in the Glossary), photographed, drawn, and entered into a catalogue (Part II). In some instances, conservation was necessary, and the information garnered during this process is included in this publication (Chapter III). In order to understand the role of chariots and to contextualise the Tano find, evidence from art, literature, and archaeological parallels were used. Thus, the book is divided into two parts. Part I consists of archaeological parallels and their contexts, identification of chariot parts using images, texts, and archaeological material, chariot leatherwork technology, iconographic and textual studies. Part II is the catalogue of archaeological remains, with photographs, drawings and diagrams (all by A.J. Veldmeijer/E. Endenburg, with a scale bar of 50 mm unless mentioned otherwise, and courtesy of the Ministry of Antiquities/ Egyptian Museum Authorities; the images for Cat. Nos. 28-41 are courtesy of the Metropolitan Museum of Art, New York, unless stated otherwise).

I.5. Introduction to the Archaeological Evidence

In addition to the Tano assemblage, other archaeological chariot leather has survived from the Valley of the Kings and the settlement at Amarna.

I.5.1. Maiherpri

The earliest group of leather comes from the largely intact tomb of Maiherpri (KV36), child of the royal nursery and royal standard or fan-bearer (Carter, 1903: 46-47; Daressy, 1902: 1-61; Orsenigo, 2016; Reeves, 1990: 140; Schweinfurth, 1900; Orsenigo & Piacentini, 2004: 214-221, 271-281; Reeves & Wilkinson, 1996: 178), dating to the reigns of Hatshepsut/Thutmose III (c. 1472-1424 BC). Although this tomb did not yield a full chariot, it did contain leather quivers (JE 33772, JE 33775; Daressy, 1902: 32-33) and wrist guards (JE 33773, JE 33776; Daressy, 1902: 33; Figure I.1). Unfortunately, the material was not available for detailed study, so it does not appear in Part II, although it is referred to in this volume.

I.5.2. Tomb of Amenhotep II (Cat. Nos. 1-11)

The tomb of Amenhotep II (KV35) contained not only the king's body, but that of several other individuals, together with a collection of grave goods, most of which seem to be royal (Daressy, 1902; Loret, 1898; Reeves, 1990: 192). It is probable that the leather objects were part of the king's burial as it is unlikely that fragmentary material would have been brought into the tomb with the other mummies who do not seem to have any clearly identified personal grave goods. The finds related to chariotry (Daressy, 1902: 76-78, CG 24144-24155; Littauer & Crouwel, 1985: 67, 87-88) that are in the Egyptian Museum (Cairo) and that have been studied are: CG 24144 (Cat. No. 8); CG 24145 (Cat. No. 7); CG 24147 (Cat. No 4); CG 24148 (Cat. No. 5); CG 24149 (Cat. No. 3, 9, 11); CG 24150 (Cat. No. 2); CG 24151 (Cat. No. 1), CG 24252 (Cat. No. 10) and CG 24155 (Cat. No. 6). The condition of the material has severely deteriorated since they have been excavated and many of the objects are now (severely) fragmented (compare for example CG 24147, Cat. No.4). Conservation interventions are evidenced by the reinforcement cloth on the backs of the artefacts.

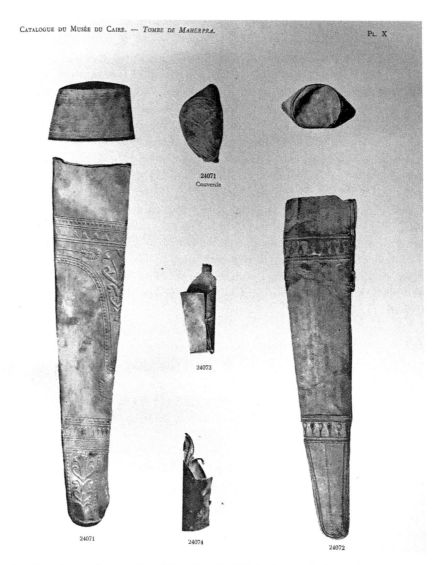

Figure I.1. Two of the quivers (CG 24071 and CG 24072), including the lid, and two wrist guards (CG 24073 and CG 24074) from the tomb of Maiherpri. From: Daressy (1902: pl. X).

I.5.3. Tomb of Thutmose IV (Cat. Nos. 12-27)

When Howard Carter cleared Thutmose IV's tomb (KV43) in 1903 (Carter, 1904), he found that though it had been looted, it still contained some of its original burial equipment. The deposition of objects in the burial chamber allowed for hypotheses about their original locations (Reeves, 1990: 35). The most unusual find in the tomb was the king's wooden chariot body covered with plaster and gilt, and moulded decoration (not part of the present work; see instead Calvert, 2013: 45-71; Carter & Newberry, 1904: 24-33). It is significant for its uniqueness as well as for the images of the chariots that decorated it (Figure II.17). Although Carter does not mention the exact position of any of the other equipment except that it was all found in chamber 3 (the burial chamber, Chamber J in Reeves, 1990: 34-38), Reeves (1990: 35) concludes that "the south end of the burial chamber seems to have been intended for the king's chariotry equipment – hence the term 'chariot hall' encountered in later documents" that identify the different sections of a royal tomb. The chariot equipment, all housed in the Egyptian Museum (Cairo), consists of 51 objects, besides the wooden chariot body. Carter and Newberry (1904: 34-38; Littauer & Crouwel, 1985: 67, 87-88) described 21 leather objects (CG 46098-46118), including a scabbard (CG 46115, Cat. No. 27), wrist guards (SR 3387, Cat. No. 23 and CG 46112, Cat. No. 24) and a wood and leather saddle(?). One single entry, without a CG-number (Carter & Newberry, 1904: 38), lists: "Thirty-one miscellaneous pieces of harness, trappings, sandals, leather bindings, etc." Of these, only those that the present authors believe to have belonged to chariots have been included in this volume (JE 97803, Cat. No. 13; SR 3385, Cat. No. 15; SR 3387, Cat. No. 23; JE 97827, Cat. No. 17; JE 97824, Cat. No. 26; JE 97825, Cat. No. 26; JE 97826, Cat. No. 21; JE 97827, Cat. No. 18). These pieces were identified as being part of this group because they did not conform to any of the other, more fully described, objects published by Carter and Newberry (1904: 34-38). Unfortunately, not all elements listed by Carter and Newberry that were associated with chariots were available for study (missing were: CG 46098; CG 46099; CG 46100; CG 46101; CG 46104; CG 46105; CG 46107; CG 46116; CG 46117; CG 46118).[4]

I.5.4. Tomb of Amenhotep III (Cat. Nos. 28-42)

The looted tomb of Amenhotep III (WV22) yielded very few remains (Reeves, 1990: 38), including the hub of a chariot wheel, found by Carter in 1915 (Western, 1973; Reeves & Wilkinson, 1996: 111). The exterior of the tomb also yielded some chariot-related leather, now housed in the Metropolitan Museum of Art (New York; MMA 24.8 A-T, Cat. No. 28-41). These were probably discovered in the rubbish heaps below WV 22 and seem to be connected to the leather that was recovered by Chassinat (Reeves, 1990: 40, citing Carter; Chassinat, 1904-1905). Additionally, the material in WV A, possibly a storage room for WV22 and some 100 meters away from it (Letter of E. Thomas to W.C. Hayes, 5-10-1962; Reeves & Wilkinson, 1996: 113), might have been washed/thrown in here from these spoil heaps (Reeves, 1990: 40). Another object that seems to be associated with this group was a small piece of wood with leather cladding, purchased by Carter in Luxor in 1912 (Carter MS. I.A.138, card 10-11) and given by him to the Metropolitan Museum of Art (New York; MMA 24.8 D, Cat. No. 28). Carter suggested that this came from Burton's clearance of tomb WV A (Letter E. Thomas to W.C. Hayes, 5-10-1962) and, on the basis of the colour and workmanship of the leather matching those of the other leather fragments, that they belonged together. It is still uncertain from which of these tombs the leather originated, while the source of the piece of clad wood is even more obscure. The colour combinations are common in chariot (and other) leather of the period, and is also seen in the Amarna and Tano material.[5] Notably, the backstitching seen in the cladding, although not uncommon in footwear made of vegetal material (*e.g.* Veldmeijer, 2009b; 2010), is not seen in leatherwork.

---

4 The material was studied during 2011-2013, when it was in a reasonable condition, although some objects had clearly withstood the ravages of time less well than others.

5 As well as other leatherwork, such as footwear, with the piece of red and green upper (note 6) as good example.

The leather finds from this tomb consisted, according to Hayes (1953: 244) of "nineteen pieces of elaborately decorated chariot harness, made up of layers of pink, green, and white leather stitched together to from a variety of elements" all of which are in good condition. Of these, 18 fragments were studied, some of which join one another (see Part II 'Catalogue'). One piece, although described in the present work, is actually a piece of a shoe's upper, rather than from a chariot (MMA 24.8 F, Cat. No. 31).[6] The pieces were thought to include "parts of girths, chest bands, back pads, and blinkers, as well as a bridle strap of pink-dyed calfskin overlaid with green and white appliqués and adorned with a row of large, brightly gilded metal studs" (Hayes, 1953: 244). Closer study of these has revised some of these identifications (see Part II). In addition to the finds in the Metropolitan Museum of Art, the Egyptian Museum (Cairo) has two well preserved pieces, both with the same number (SR 4/10676; Cat. No. 42), also originating from this tomb.

I.5.5. Amarna

The bulk of the decorated leather from the city of Amarna (Veldmeijer, 2011b: 26-27, 93-143; Appendix II), the short-lived capital of Egypt in the time of Akhenaten (c. 1352-1335 BC) was recovered by the German Mission, directed by Ludwig Borchardt between 1911 to 1914 (listed by Veldmeijer, 2011b: 93-143: house P 49, 2[?]; Q 47,7; N 50, 8; N 50, 13; N 50, 1; M 50, 11; O 49, 20; N 50, 5; N 51, 3). Some of these finds were recovered in association with remnants of chariots and harnesses (Borchardt & Ricke, 1980: 330). The leather is kept in the Ägyptisches Museum und Papyrussammlung (Berlin), but, during the Second World War, the material was hastily gathered up and stored in various places out of central Berlin for protection (see also Loschwitz, 2009: 192-193). Although this move preserved much of the material, many objects were misplaced or destroyed, while others lost their numbers and thus their provenance. Ever since then, scholars have been working to re-establish their provenance, with varying degrees of success. The leather was in good condition when excavated, judging from the fortuitous find of several old photographs (see Veldmeijer & Endenburg, 2007: 36). However, the foray outside of the museum during the Second World War as well as a following period of moving and storage under varying conditions (Loschwitz, 2009: 193) has caused the leather to decay and the collagen to turn to gelatin, while several pieces have fragmented.[7] The excavation photographs have been key in identifying some of the degenerated pieces (Veldmeijer, 2011b: 26, 41, 93-143; Cat. Nos. 31-49).

An additional seven fragments, excavated by the Egypt Exploration Society in the 1920s and 1930s, when it took over the concession from the German Mission after the First World War, are currently in the Petrie Museum of Egyptian Archaeology University College London (Veldmeijer, 2011b: 257-261). These were found in the North City, House U 25, 7 (Frankfurt & Pendlebury, 1933: 119). According to Pendlebury (1951: 136), other fragments came from the Central

---

6   Although it is usually referred to as chariot leather (Elnaggar *et al.*, 2016; Littauer & Crouwel, 1985: 68, 87), it is clear that this fragment is actually a piece of the upper of a Curled-Toe Ankle Shoe (discussed in more detail by Veldmeijer, 2009a: 2-11; 2011a: 187-192; In Press).

7   ÄM AM 013b-d; 026a-h; 030k, l; 031a, b, e-g; 032a-g; 034; 035; 053; 065c; 068c; 072a-f; 073a-f; 074a-c; 075; 076a-ac; 077; 078a-t; 079.

City, the Police Barracks, and House R 42, 10 (south rooms in the west section and the central court). These were divided between the Manchester Museum and the Egyptian Museum (Cairo). The objects in the Petrie Museum (London) (UC 35939a-g, Cat. No. 276) also show signs of degeneration.

At the time of preparing the Amarna leather volume (Veldmeijer, 2011b), little work had been carried out on Egyptian leatherwork in general, hence the paucity of identifications of the objects. Subsequent studies have enabled possible identifications of some of the Amarna material (Table I.1), which will be discussed below in detail (Chapter II).[8]

Specialist Number	Identification	Publication
AM 034	Bottom of bow-case	Veldmeijer (2011b: 103-105)
AM 035	Bottom of bow-case	Veldmeijer (2011b: 105-106)
AM not numbered	Yoke saddle pad	Veldmeijer (2011b: 142-143)
AM 079	Bow-case flap	Veldmeijer (2011b: 140-152)
AM 074	Support strap	Veldmeijer (2011b: 113-116)
AM 013b	Support strap(?)	Veldmeijer (2011b: 93)

Table I.1. Identification of chariot leather from Amarna (see Appendix II).

I.5.6. Tomb of Tutankhamun

Tutankhamun's tomb (KV62), discovered by Howard Carter in 1922, yielded six chariot bodies, some with portions of their leather covering (Carter, 1927: 54-63[9]; Littauer & Crouwel, 1985). In addition, a large number of embossed sheet gold, recovered from the Antechamber, are clearly associated with the chariots (Carter & Mace, 1923: 121; Figure I.2). The majority of the material was found in the vicinity of the chariot bearing Carter's Number 122 (122v-122qqqq), but Carter (Card No. 122i) warns that it is "Impossible to assign the parts of the harness to any chariot in particular, so they are treated here under this number, as most of it was found in neighbourhood of body 122". Additional fragments were associated with other chariots found in the Antechamber (Carter's Numbers 117b [chariot 120]; 150 [close to wheels 133 and 134, in front of chariot 122]; Carter's Number 151 [under wheels 133 and 134]). Additionally, leather coming from a chariot but without any indication which one (Carter's Numbers 085e; 095c; 119a), or thought possibly to be from chariots but without a clear association (Carter's Number 046ll) were also noted. Carter's Numbers 332 and 333 include chariot remains as well as various fragments of leather with embossed sheet gold. All this material is now in the Egyptian Museum (Cairo)[10] and is being studied by an international team of specialists – it is awaiting publication,[11] thus it will be mentioned here only in passing, and as comparanda used to identify chariot pieces.

---

8 Another example of such identifications is the typology of leather sandals from Amarna (Veldmeijer, 2011e).
9 See also http://www.griffith.ox.ac.uk/discoveringTut/.
10 Dd. 21 August 2017.
11 See http://www.dainst.org/projekt/-/project-display/63504 for the project's description. This interdisciplinary project is being led by Christian Eckmann.

Figure I.2 (continues on next page). Several examples of embossed gold sheet from the tomb of Tutankhamun (Carter's Number 122). Some still include remains of leather. Photographs by H. Burton. Courtesy of the Griffith Institute, University of Oxford.

Figure I.2 (continued from previous page).

The Tutankhamun material had degenerated due to the high humidity of the tomb (Lucas, 1927: 175-176): "Originally there had been a considerable amount of leather in the tomb, for example, for horse trappings, for the seats of stools and for sandals, but when found most of this leather was unrecognizable except from its position and by chemical analysis, as it had become a black brittle, pitch-like mass, parts of which at some period had been viscous and had "run," and in several instances had dropped on to objects below, which it had cemented together. [...] This destruction of the leather had been brought about by the combined heat and humidity of the tomb." This is a common phenomenon (Chapter III; see also Veldmeijer, 2011a: 35; Veldmeijer *et al.*, 2013: 259; the Amarna material mentioned above). The process was so distinct that it is still possible to identify examples of 'melted' leather having dropped down on other objects (Personal Observation, but see also Carter & Mace, 1923: 121, 132).[12] The gold sheets covering a few of the leather pieces has contributed to the survival of some of them (several are mentioned and illustrated by Littauer & Crouwel, 1985: 34-47, 87-88, pl. XLI-XLIX, LXI; see Figure I.2. for examples). It should be noted that there are many more fragments in the museum than those registered by Carter – some might be the result of the fragmentation of material due to the ravages of time (Ch. Eckmann, Personal Communication, 2017).

I.5.6. Tano Chariot (Cat. Nos. 43-167)

The Tano chariot, named after the antiquities dealer who sold the assemblage to the Cairo Museum (recorded in Dossier du Service 32-2/101), was kept in magazine R2S on the Ground Floor[13] of the Egyptian Museum (Cairo) in 2008. Only a

---

12 See Veldmeijer (2011a: 36, fig. 2.1) for another clear example of this process but of a leather open shoe from the tomb.
13 Moved to Room 19, Ground Floor in early 2009.

photograph had been published by Forbes (1957: 30, fig. 6), leading the Ancient Egyptian Leatherwork Project (AELP) to seek it out for study (Veldmeijer & Ikram, 2012b: 36-37). Unfortunately, the find is unprovenanced. The *Journal d'Entrée* only states that it was purchased from the well-known dealer in antiquities, [Georges] Tano, probably in February of 1932, with no mention of any wooden chariot frame.

Tano came from a long line of antiquities dealer of Cypriot-Greek origin. Their shop, initially located across the street from the old Shepheard's Hotel in Cairo and moving at some point to 53 Sharia Ibrahim Pasha Street, was founded in 1870 by Marious Panayiotis Tano(s), who supplied not only private collectors, but also museums like the Louvre, the Nicosia Museum, as well as the museums of Marseilles, Rouen, and Lyon. His nephew, Nicolas Tanos continued the tradition, followed by his son Georges Tano, responsible for this assemblage, and ultimately his nephew, Phocion Jean Tano. In addition to selling objects, the Tano family also donated artefacts to several museums. No further information about the leathers' provenance and date have come to light as no records belonging to Tano, if they ever existed, survive/have been found.[14]

However, given its condition, it is safe to assume that the chariot leather originated from a place with a regular and stable environment, low in humidity, with no direct contact with soil or sand, suggesting that it came from a tomb, possibly in Upper Egypt, maybe even Luxor (Veldmeijer *et al.*, 2013: 259-269).

The Tano group consists of numerous pieces of leather, of varying sizes, all under a single JE and a single SR number (JE 88962; SR 14530) (Veldmeijer & Ikram, 2012a). It includes the main casing, siding fill as well as fragments of the bow-case, nave hoops and straps and ties to connect the chariot to the horses. Almost all portions of the chariot are present: the rawhide tires (in general, there is nothing among the group of anything different than the leather) as well as the floor, which is usually woven from leather or rawhide strips, are absent. There are a number of straps but some of these are impossible to identify with certainty. The leather falls into two categories based on colour and robustness: red and green fine leather, and beige and green robust leather (Veldmeijer *et al.*, 2013).

It is curious to have a chariot find consisting only of leather pieces. As thus far there are no records of Tano (or any other dealer) selling a chariot body, it would seem that only the leather had been found and put on the market. Of course, it might have been associated with a body whose wood was in such poor condition due to environmental reasons that it was left behind. However, an environment that affected the wood would surely have also affected the leather. Insect infestation could have been a(nother) reason: insects such as termites only eat wood, leaving the leather intact. It is also possible that the wooden frame was used for some other purpose, like a fire, or that the chariot itself was sold separately, but has never been investigated by scholars and remains unpublished. Another scenario is that only the leather was placed in the tomb, with the part symbolising the whole. Alternatively, this could be a spare leather cover, maybe one that was old and of less value and use to the deceased's heirs, or perhaps one of many such covers. The absence of information from Tano makes it challenging to more precisely situate the leather in context.

---

14   More on the Tano family can be found in Merrillees (2003). See also Hagen & Ryholt (2016).

II. Deconstructing and Construction

Identifying the Parts of a Chariot

André J. Veldmeijer & Salima Ikram

Chariots consist not only of the vehicle and its casing/siding fill, but also of the attachments to the animals, the accoutrements of the animals and the chariot itself, such as quivers, bow-cases, wrist guards, scabbards, housing, saddle pads, pouches, blinkers, nave hoops, straps of different varieties, bosses, and decorative elements (see the image in the Glossary). The sections below present the actual remains of the different parts of chariots that have been identified from archaeological material and their use, based on other archaeological remains and imagery. Of course, there are problems in using images to determine details. These include the fact that certain parts of the chariot can be shown in a very stylised manner, some portions could be omitted due to issues of representation, elements that were originally depicted are now missing as they were executed in paint, the change in tomb decorative programmes in the 19th Dynasty (Dodson & Ikram, 2008: 139), as well as the accident of survival.

II.1. Chariot Body

Chariots consisted of a body made of slender bent wooden parts that were connected by mortises and rawhide lashings. Depending on the type of chariot, the body was enclosed with leather, either completely or partially. Different layers of leather, decorated or not, could be used to enclose varying amounts of the body, thereby making it possible to adjust the way in which the chariot was used and/or perceived. Of course, some chariots, presumably processional ones, were enclosed in wood rather than in leather, such as that of Thutmose IV (Carter & Newberry, 1904: 24-33), and Tutankhamun's so-called 'State Chariots' (see Carter, 1927: 54-63).

II.1.1. Main Casing

Introduction

Two-dimensional representations show variations in the casing of the chariot body (Figure II.1A): some are almost completely open with large fenestrations, while others are completely closed, with no or only very small openings in the side. The entire covering of the chariot body seems to have consisted of two parts, although from the images of the closed bodies, one cannot always tell whether it

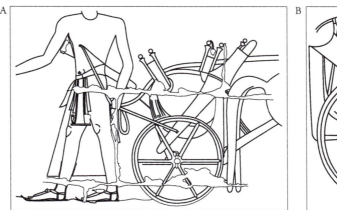

Figure II.1. Chariot bodies could be entirely closed (A) (with or without apertures for weapons) or nearly entirely open (B). Usually, the main casing is heavily decorated (C). Note the aperture in A with quiver sticking out; the support straps in B, and the hand-grip in C. A) Luxor. Temple of Karnak. Battle reliefs of Seti I. After: The Epigraphic Survey (1986: pl. X); B) Luxor. Temple of Karnak. Battle reliefs of Seti I. After: The Epigraphic Survey (1986: pl. XXXV); C) Luxor. Tomb of Huy (TT40). From: Davies & Gardiner (1936: pl. LXXXI). See also Figure V.9.

is one complete cover, which appears different due to its decoration, or a cover made up of two separate elements. In the present work, a division in the covering is made: the main casing and the siding fill. The main casing follows the lower part of the body, going upwards at the corners as well as the in the centre at the front (Figure II.1B) – a minimalist upside-down 'T'; it is always present. This can vary somewhat in its width, but never completely covers the larger areas of the sides. The siding fill covers the remaining open areas. Usually the main casing is heavily decorated (Figure II.1C), while the siding fill less so, perhaps with the edges of small fenestrations and grips enhanced. Notably, the chariot depicted on the Thutmose IV chariot seems heavily decorated as well; perhaps this was a feature of particular royal vehicles (see below Figure II.17).

In imagery, the shape of the main casing on the wooden chariot frame changes over time, and variations occur in the Amarna period. The shape of the main casing changes in that the end of the top of the inverted 'T' increases in size slightly (Davies, 1903: pls. X, XIX; Davies, 1905a: pl. XIII; Davies, 1905b: pl. XII [3rd and bottom registers]; Redford, 1988: TS 45). It is interesting to note that Yuya and Tjuiu's chariot (CG 51188; Carter & Newberry, 1904: 24-33; Davis, 1907: pls. XXI, XXXII) from the reign of Amenhotep III presages the imagery of the Amarna period – possibly similar depictions antedating the Amarna corpus have not survived or been noted.

Identifications

Two chariots from the tomb of Tutankhamun were clad in leather (Carter's Numbers 332 and 333; Figure II.2), with a third possibly also having some (Carter's Number 161; Littauer & Crouwel 1985: 72-74). However, the unfavourable climatic conditions in the tomb (see above) resulted in the deterioration of nearly all of it. However, the tiny fragments and other features still visible on two chariots allowed Carter to reconstruct the leather casing (Figure II.2). This reconstruction is curious in that the front central part of the chariot is uncovered, and the leather does not connect along the entire length of the frontal rods.

The main casing of the Tano chariot is the only complete example of leather casing that is known to have survived thus far, albeit in a fragmentary state, and is coloured red and green (L3 #001, L3 #002, L3 #003, L3 #004A-E; Cat. No. 43-46)[15] (Figure II.3). It consists of two layers of leather, the red verso and the green recto. The casing, however, was reversible, perhaps depending of the occasion,[16] as the red verso of the central, vertical element shows the impression of the central rod of the body but, albeit far less clearly, comparable impressions can be seen on the green recto. Additionally, the tripartite top of the central vertical part of the casing (L3 #002, Cat. No. 44) shows similar wear marks (L3 #003, Cat. No. 45) on both sides, caused by being attached to the upper railing of the body or, possibly, a cross-shaped extension of the central rod, as is shown in Figure II.29. Again far less clearly, such a feature can also be seen on the reverse of this tripartite top. Although one would, perhaps, have expected a chariot to show the striking and solar red colour on the outside, it should be noted that the decorative edge bindings are positioned at the green side except for the tripartite top (L3 #002, Cat. No. 44), where the decorative binding faces the red surface.

The bottom back corners (L3 #004A & D, Cat. No. 46) go upwards at a 90-degree angle, terminating in a short rectangular section. The corners themselves are not straight, but rather form two scallops which meet in a point in the middle. Each corner is finished with a binding. A reinforced hole is located at the junction of this decorated edge and the straight edge of the end of the casing. It was used to further secure the casing to the wooden frame.

---

15 Of course, small non-descript fragments of leather found in a variety of contexts might have originated from a main casing as well, but are unidentified, or indeed, unidentifiable.
16 Contrasting what is suggested by the fastening of the leather to a wooden rod that is ascribed to Amenhotep III (MMA 24.8.D., Cat. No. 28) and which was tentatively identified as part of the siding frame (Littauer & Crouwel, 1985: 73), showing a permanent fastening of the casing.

Figure II.2. A) Remnants of chariots Carter's Number 332 and 333 in situ; B) Carter's sketch of the leather covering chariots 332 and 333. The accompanying text reads (Card No. 333-02): "Sketch of body to show (approximately) the details of the leather covering that were upon the bodies of the Chariots Nos. 332 & 333 [Littauer & Crouwel, 1985 Nos. A5 & A6]. From the few fragments that remain of this leather covering show that it was highly coloured & decorated. The sheet gold & bark decoration upon the parts of the upper frame work, suggest that the above was the form the leather took." If the covering looked indeed as reconstructed, such a shape is not clearly identified in two-dimensional art. All images courtesy of the Griffith Institute, University of Oxford.

C

D

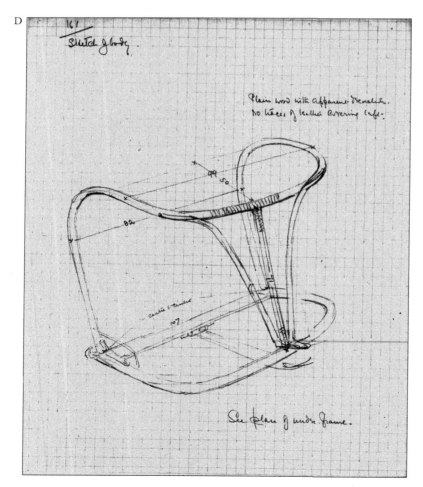

Figure II.2. C) Chariot Carter's Number 161 reassembled; D) Carter's sketch of the body of chariot 161. The accompanying text reads (Card No. 161-3): "Sketch of body. Plain wood with apparent decoration. No traces of leather covering left [but see Littauer & Crouwel, 1985: 72-74). Courtesy of the Griffith Institute, University of Oxford.

Figure II.3. The complete main casing (put together from several parts, see Catalogue). Impressions and discolouration suggests that both sides could have been turned outwards, but the fact that these features are more prominent at the red surface, suggests this surface was tied to the body more often/for longer periods of time; thus, the green surface is regarded as 'recto' (A).

A leather tube is attached to the bottom of the main casing (*e.g.* L3 #004E, Cat. No. 46). A drawstring of thick leather, deliberately folded lengthwise probably to give it additional strength, runs through this. The tube follows the shape of the casing, but at the centre it separates from it, to go beneath the pole, while the casing goes above, in order to accommodate the pole.

II.1.2. Siding Fill

Introduction

A siding fill is the leather that covers the space above the main casing (the fenestration), thus enclosing all but the back of the chariot completely, and is not always present. In imagery, at least, siding fill seems to appear first in the Amarna period, with the depiction on the body of the chariot of Thutmose IV as an exception (Davies, 1903: pl. XIX; Davies, 1905a: pls. XIII, bottom register, at outer edge of the page; pl. XII, all; pls. XXXIII, XXXVI). It can include grips (holes close under the upper railing as to allow the person in the chariot to hold on; Figure II.1C; II.4), which started to be used in the Amarna period, and/or bigger apertures further down (either more towards the back upper corner or more in the centre of the siding fill) through which quivers or other items can be thrust, or both (Figure II.1A). These apertures were introduced during the time of Seti (*e.g.* The Epigraphic Survey, 1986: pl. X; Figure II.1A) and appear intermittently in chariots thereafter. Cut out hand-grips become extremely rare after the Amarna period. Siding fills continue to be used from the Amarna period onward (for example from the reign of Tutankhamun see Johnson, 1992: 186, 187, 189; Ockinga, 1997: pl. 36; reign of Horemheb, *e.g.* Manassa, 2002: 259, 263; Bologna Museum 1889; Seti I at Karnak see The Epigraphic Survey, 1986: pls. V, XIII, XXXI; Ramesses II at Beit el Wali see Ricke *et al.*, 1967: pls. VIII, XIII; and for Ramesses III see *e.g.* The Epigraphic Survey, 1930: pls. XIX, XXXV), but often chariots are shown, after the Amarna period, without them. As with the main casing, there is no suggestion from the pictorial evidence as to how it was attached to the chariot body.

Identification

A fair number of variously sized fragments have been identified as pieces of siding fill (L1 #001-003, Cat. No. 50-52; L1 #005, Cat. No. 68; L1 #008A, B, Cat. No. 69 [Figure II.4]; L1 #010A, B, Cat. No. 70; L1 #012, Cat. No. 71; L1 #014, Cat. No. 72; L1 #016, Cat. No. 73; L1 #018, Cat. No. 53; L1 #020, Cat. No. 75; L1 #023, Cat. No. 54; L2 #001, Cat. No. 79; L2 #002, Cat. No. 55; L2 #008A-C, Cat. No. 56; L4 #001-003, Cat. No. 67, 73, 63 resp.; L4 #006, Cat. No. 78; L4 #013, Cat. No. 58; L4 #014, Cat. No. 64; L4 #018, Cat. No. 65; L5 #003, Cat. No. 80; L6 #001-004, Cat. No. 60, 59, 61, 62 resp.; L6 #007, Cat. No. 57; L6 #017, Cat. No. 77; L6 #027; Cat. No. 63). All of these are red with green decoration, the colour being far brighter on the stained side. Some of these pieces have leather tubes containing drawstrings, similar to what is seen in the main casing, to secure the pieces to the chariot body, such as L1 #001 (Cat. No. 50) and L1 #002 (Cat. No. 51), L2 #008A (Cat. No. 56), and L1 #023 (Cat. No. 54; see the catalogue for more examples). The ends of many of these tubes were decorated with an edge binding (tripartite: L1 #002, Cat. No. 51; L2 #008A, Cat. No. 56;

Figure II.4. Example of siding fill fragment of the Tano assemblage (L3 #008B, Cat. No. 69). The arrow indicates the hand-grip that would have been situated immediately below the top railing.

single: L1 #016, Cat. No. 73; L1 #020, Cat. No. 75; L6 #017, Cat. No. 77); thus, these would not have been placed somewhere in the middle, but rather at a corner. Other fastening systems also existed, as will be discussed below.

Two pieces of this single layered leather (L2 #008A, B, Cat. No. 56) have features that are seen in representations of chariot bodies, and were thus identified as siding fill. The other fragments are assigned to this category because they fit together, and/or on the basis of similarity in decoration and technology (see Chapter IV). In general, the leather of the siding fill is in much worse condition than that of the main casing. This is not only because it consists of only one layer, but also because it had more wear and tear prior to interment. The main wear is seen at the edges, giving an indication of how the leather was attached to the frame. Fragment L1 #001 (Cat. No. 50), for example, has a tube with drawstring; the seam is hidden by the triple green/red/green appliqué, visible to the viewer. The area below the triple appliqué has tears from wear, and is distinctly discoloured and abraded, which is due to the edge of the leather being folded over the top railing, secured by the drawstring in the attached tube, with the discoloration being augmented by the sweat and oils from hands holding on to the railing for dear life. This has also helped to determine which side was on top, and which on the bottom. The leather is still partially folded from storage in this area. Such wear is seen to various degrees in many pieces that are identified as siding fill. Another piece of the siding fill, the badly preserved large sheet L2 #008B (Cat. No. 56), was expertly unfolded by the AELP's conservator Lucy Skinner in close collaboration with the Conservation Department of the Egyptian Museum (Cairo) (see section III.6. 'Handling and Conservation'). It shows an oval cut out, with a green edge binding, just below the tube with drawstring. There is no question that this was made intentionally. The hole can be identified as a hand-grip, which is shown sometimes in imagery at the side of the chariot (Figure II.1C, see also Figure II.4), particularly from the Amarna period onward. Usually, the grips are positioned more toward the back of the chariot.

Fragment L2 #008A (Cat. No. 56) consists of two pieces of leather that are secured with a double row of stitching. This seam runs at an angle relative to the top edge. A tube with a drawstring was attached to the top of the piece, of which a portion survives. There is noticeable wear at the side of the tube and drawstring (see above), suggesting that it too was draped over the top railing. Below, there is a circular aperture with edge binding (L1 #003, Cat. No. 52 fits with this fragment). This is an aperture to hold a quiver or some comparable object. The bottom half of a similar hole survives in the piece that is on the other side of the seam. However, in this case, one would expect some sort of fastening mechanism for the quiver and further reinforcement of the aperture: though leather is strong, here it has a single thickness that is fairly thin. The weight of a quiver, especially filled with arrows or spears, surely would deform the edges of this opening (such features are not identified with the Tano leather), increasing the chance of tearing. An absence of such fastening would also be curious, because when the chariot was in motion, the object would move about within the aperture. Presumably, the quiver was secured to the chariot body in some way, possibly by means of a holder (see below) placed inside the chariot. The positions of the apertures, flanking the seam, and the overall shape of the piece suggests that the seam would have been placed over the front/centre of the chariot body, and would have been covered by the upright central section of the main casing. Thus, the apertures would have been situated along the sides, as is seen in representations of chariots with quivers.

II.1.3. Support Straps

Introduction

Chariots with bodies that are mainly open (chariots without siding fill) often, in imagery from the 19th Dynasty onwards (starting with the reign of Seti I, The Epigraphic Survey, 1986: pl. XXXV, possibly also pl. XXXIV, and are a common feature thereafter; Breasted, 1903: pl. 3; The Epigraphic Survey, 1930: pls. XXXIII, XXXV; 1932: pl. LXVIII), show an oval (Figure II.5A) or rectangular (Figure II.5B) piece of leather folded over the top railing at the sides, with two (rare; Figure II.5C) or three straps (Figure II.5A, B) emerging from it and extending to the bottom of the frame (see also Figure II.1B). These are also sometimes found in conjunction with siding fill (Figure II.5B).[17] Furthermore, there are a few representations where the oval or rectangular piece is visible, but without straps (Figure II.5D) – is this due to issues/conventions of representation and depiction, or do these pieces serve a different function? The straps provided extra support to the framework, and could possibly have helped in the stabilisation of quivers and bow-cases. It is unlikely to have supported the leather casing directly, as has been suggested for the chariot from Populonia (Emiliozzi et al., 2000: 10).

---

[17] In which case they were not visible. Actually, it seems likely that they were present in all chariots, as perhaps suggested by the rare example in Figure II.5B, combining the support straps with a siding fill.

Figure II.5. Support straps and their variation as shown in imagery (in grey). A) Oval without siding fill. Luxor. Temple of Karnak. Battle reliefs of Seti I. After: The Epigraphic Survey (1986: pl. XXXV); B) Rectangular with siding fill. Luxor. Medinet Habu I. Ramesses III. After: The Epigraphic Survey (1930: pl. XVI); C) A rare example of support strap consisting of two extensions (cf. the Tano leather, Figure II.6A; enemies are not illustrated here). Luxor. Ramesseum. Asiatic campagne (Dapur). After: Heinz (2001: pl. IX.I); D) Oval without siding fill but also without the extensions. Luxor. Temple of Karnak. Battle reliefs of Seti I. After: The Epigraphic Survey (1986: pl. XXXIV).

Identification

BI-001 and BI-006 (Cat. No. 81 and 82[18]; Figure II.6A), made of beige, thick leather enhanced with green and stitched through thoroughly, consist of a rectangular element and two long, narrow straps emerging from one short end. The opposite end, at the verso, has two loops of beige leather, sewn onto it. The straps were threaded through these two loops (the measurements of the straps and the loop holes support such interpretation), and pulled tight, while the rectangular element was folded around something – presumably the upper railing of the chariot body frame. The diameter that is created by pulling the straps through the loops is approximately three centimetre and fits the diameters of the siding frame given for Tutankhamun's chariots (Littauer & Crouwel, 1985: 9, 18, 23, 26, 53) which vary from 2.5 to 3.3 centimetre in diameter. This would confirm the identification of BI-001 and BI-006 (Cat. No. 81 and 82) as support straps. The ends of the two Tano support straps are curled several times (apparent in the old images in Forbes, 1957: 30), suggesting that it was wound around the frame several times before being tied. BI-001 (Cat. No. 81) has a hole in the terminal end with another piece being pulled through, suggesting a toggle closure of some sort (or knotted), but it is incomplete and thus could not be securely reconstructed. Remarkably, no slits were observed in the other support strap, suggesting the terminal end was simply knotted (which also would have secured the strap tighter).

Comparable objects, thought different in detail, have been noted as coming from Amarna (Table II.1; Figure II.6B, C; Veldmeijer, 2011b: 113-116; Appendix II). These incomplete (hence the difference in measurements) objects, are now badly decayed but were in fairly good condition when discovered. The two Amarna objects are elliptical in shape rather than rectangular and they are decorated with appliqué decoration of strips, zigzag and inward curling spiral motifs (only indicated by the stitching: the appliqué itself is lost). The verso has a transverse band rather than two loops as seen in the Tano examples. This narrow band is approximately two centimetre wide. Probably, the rectangular object with a rounded top from the tomb of Thutmose IV (JE 97803, Cat. No. 13) is part of support straps as well, although no loops are seen at the back (but these could have been situated at the lost end).

Object	Provenance	Measurements (in cm)	Shape	Source
JE 97803	Thutmose IV	L: 8; W: 6 (but incomplete)	Rectangular with one edge rounded	Present work (Cat. No. 13)
ÄM AM 074	Amarna	L: 13.5/12.5; W: 8.5; 12.5 (approximate; see source)	Rectangular with one edge rounded	Veldmeijer (2011b: 113-116); Figure II.6B, C; Appendix II
BI-001	Tano	L: 16.5; W: 6	Rectangular	Present work (Cat. No. 78)
BI-006	Tano	L: 17; W: 5.5	Rectangular	Present work (Cat. No. 79); Figure II.6A.

Table II.1. Support straps compared.

---

18 Focus will be on these to fragments as they include the rectangular elements; the other fragments are only piece of straps, of which most belong to BI-006 (Cat. No. 82).

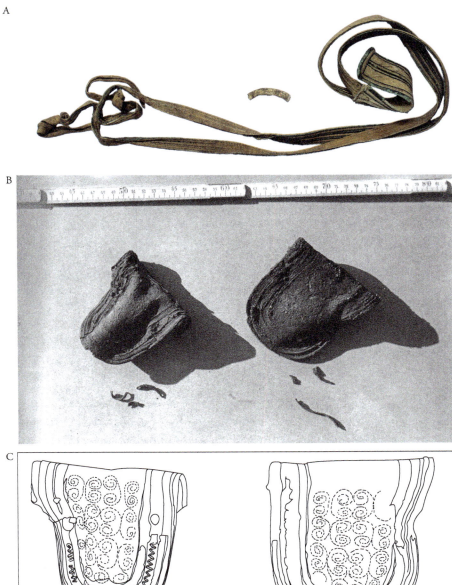

Figure II.6. A) Example of a support strap from Tano (BI-006, Cat. No. 81); B) Two elliptical, incomplete, elaborately decorated objects from Amarna (ÄM AM 074) that were part of support straps; C) Line drawing. Photograph (B) courtesy of the Ägyptisches Museum und Papyrussammlung (Berlin).

II.1.4. Nave Hoops

Introduction

Nave hoops are covers "on the outer ends of the naves [which] would have given protection against wear caused by friction with the linch pins, and would have helped to prevent the nave from splitting" (Littauer & Crouwel, 1985: 76). Two-dimensional art is not always helpful in identifying the nave hoop, but a fair number of archaeological specimens made of various materials survive, as well as remnants of nave hoops still *in situ* on chariots (see below).

More leather can be expected related to wheels: tires of rawhide or leather (*e.g.* Littauer & Crouwel, 1985: 76-79) but these are not idenified or recognised among the finds described here. Good wheels are of utmost importance (*e.g.* Sandor, 2013) and it is thus no surprise that the most obvious changes occur in the number of wheel-spokes. The earliest images of chariot wheels, both royal and non-royal, show four spokes, through the reign of Amenhotep II (for example, TT42, TT11, TT78, TT73, TT84, Luxor Museum J. 129). The change from four-spoked wheels to six-spoked wheels occurs during the reign of Thutmose IV and is normalised during the reign of Amenhotep III (for example, TT69, TT89, TT57), continuing thereafter into the subsequent dynasties. Presumably these wheels were sturdier and would be better for faster movement over more varied terrain. There are also some rare images of eight-spoked wheels. The first surviving example is the depiction on the state/processional chariot of Thutmose IV (Carter & Newberry, 1904: 26, pls. 10, 11; Figure II.17). The eight spokes, with strong reinforcements at the wheel-edge, in this case might be indicative of wheels that had to support a heavier chariot body, such as the wooden one that the image itself adorns. The spokes might also be indicative of divinity (ogdoad), suggesting that the king here was divine, as well as being accompanied, in one image on the right proper side of the chariot by Montu (Calvert, 2013; Carter & Newberry, 1904: 26; Figure 11.17B). Another published image of a chariot from the tomb of Kenamun (TT93, reign Amenhotep II) appears to have eight spokes (Aldred, 1969: 79), but on closer examination, this appears to be an error on the part of the copyists as the wheel is very poorly preserved in the original. However, an image from the tomb of Khaemhat (TT57; Pinch-Brock, 2001) shows not only four- and six-spoked wheels, but also an eight-spoked chariot wheel. An ostracon in the Egyptian Museum (Cairo) (CG 25125) depicts Nefertiti wielding bow and arrow while riding in a chariot with eight-spoked wheels, and from Amarna there is a representation of Akhenaten driving an eight-spoked wheeled chariot with a falcon/raptor hovering above him (Davies, 1905a: pl. XXXVIII). From the reign of Tutankhamun comes an image of the king in his chariot with eight-spoked wheels, with the first chariot in the royal entourage also having the same number of spokes (Ockinga, 1997: pl. 36). After this there is a hiatus in eight-spoked wheeled chariots (ostraca are excluded here), though it is possible that some are shown in representations of the Battle of Qadesh on the Ramesseum's Second Pylon (Breasted, 1903: pl. III), though these images are not very clear. The next instances of such wheels occur late in Egyptian history on stelae, often when chariots are being pulled by griffons, again an allusion to the divine (Sternberg-El Hotabi, 1999: 243, Abb. 36a, b; it should be noted that a seven-spoked wheel also appears in Abb. 36c). A rare image of an eight-spoked wheel being made in a workshop scene comes from the tomb of Aba in Thebes (Davies, 1902: pl. XXV), dating to c. 664 BC. One final Ptolemaic example of such a wheel is found in Edfu (Leclant, 1960: pl. 4), used to convey Astarte.

Based on the extant evidence, it is clear that the eight- (and even seven-) spoked wheel was a rarity. It is possible that such wheels were associated with heavier or speedier vehicles, or they might have had divine connotations as eight was a sacred number in ancient Egypt, due to the Ogdoad, and, for the most part (save the Qadesh images and the tomb of Aba), such wheels only appear on chariots conveying the king or a deity.

Identification

The two flaring tubes (#33 and #34, Cat. No. 88; Figure II.7A) can be identified as the nave hoops and BI-023, and BI-025 (Cat. No. 89 and 90) as the straps that secured them to the naves. Several examples of nave hoops are known from the archaeological record. Tutankhamuns chariot Carter's Number 333 had bronze nave hoops and nave hoops for chariots with Carter's Number 120, 121 and 122 are assumed too (Littauer & Crouwel, 1985: 76-77). Chariot Carter's Number 332 has leather nave hoops (Littauer & Crouwel, 1985: 76; Figure II.7B). The nave hoop from the chariot of Yuya and Tjuiu was made of bronze (suggested by Carter, see Littauer & Crouwel, 1985: 76) but Quibell (1908: 67) suggests otherwise: "Covering the inner half of the nave and guarding the bearing to some extent from the entry of dust was a kind of sheath or sleeve of red leather, attached tightly to the axletree and covering the nave up to the spokes with a loose cover in which it could turn freely. The fixed part of this sleeve is gilt and the free edge is adorned with the same pattern of green leather appliqué [...]. The two edges in the free part are not stitched together." A bronze nave hoop was found at Qantir (Herold, 1999: 26-30). It is of comparable shape as the leather Tano examples and has comparable measurements (Table II.2).

Tano (#33, #34, Cat. No. 88)	Qantir (FZN 86/0280a; after Herold, 1999: 26)
L: 180	L: 160
W: 80-120	W: 85-125

Table II.2. Measurements (in mm) of the Tano and Qantir nave hoops compared.

II.2. Accessories

II.2.1. Bow-Cases and Quivers

Introduction

Leather bow-cases[19] are often seen in the pictorial record: they hang at one or either side of the chariot but are also featured in leather workshops, complete, or in the process of being made by the leatherworkers. The leather workshop scene in TT66 (Hepu, reign of Thutmose IV, Figure II.8) shows two complete,

---

19   The present work focuses exclusively on bow-cases and quivers made of leather, leaving aside those made of wood, basketry and textile, although a wooden bow-case (Carter's Number 335; JE 61502) was recovered from the tomb of Tutankhamun. Its size and weight, however, makes it an unlikely candidate for being attached to a chariot.

A

Figure II.7. A) One of the Tano nave hoops (#33, Cat. No. 88); B) Carter's Card 333-08, illustrating the wheel and nave of chariot 333, including the leather nave hoop. Courtesy of the Griffith Institute, University of Oxford.

B

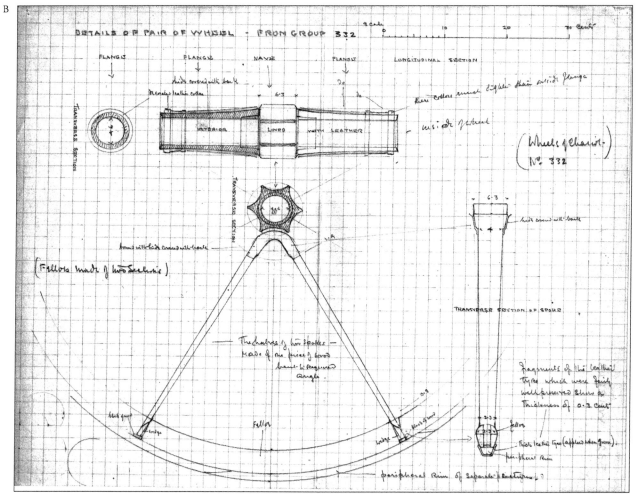

isolated bow-cases (A & B) and one attached to the chariot (C). The isolated two are closed; the one at the chariot, however, is open and the top part (slightly less than half of the entire length) is hanging down at the pseudo-hinged opening. The triangular bow-cases are asymmetrical lengthwise, with a rounded bottom and top: one long edge is straight whereas the other runs slightly diagonally, resulting in a triangular container. These top and bottom halves are of about the same size in the bow-case depicted at the top. But in the bow-case shown at the bottom, the lower part of the container is slightly narrower. At the point where these two portions meet, a semi-circular element can be seen, which is the flap that closes the bow-case (but see below with II.2.2. 'Pouches'). That this is the opening is clear from the container attached to the chariot. The two parts of the bow-case are

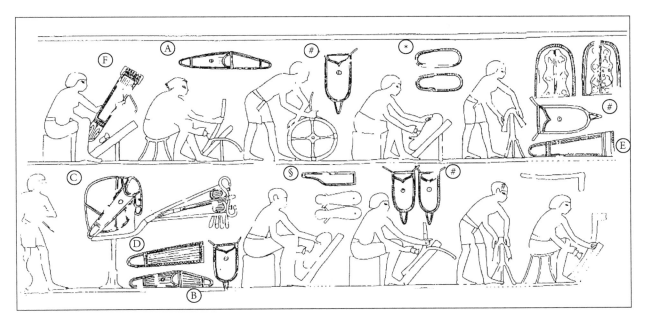

Figure II.8. Leather workshop from the tomb of Hepu (TT66). The numbers are explained in the text. # indicate pouches; * yoke saddle pads and § wrist guard (see below). From: Davies (1963: pl. VIII).

actually two individually made elements, which are sewn together, rather than one piece of leather cut out from a single sheet. At the bottom in Figure II.8, above the complete bow-case, an asymmetrical object with rounded base is seen (D & E in Figure II.8), which equals a bottom half of a bow-case.[20]

Bow-cases, made to hang from the chariot, have an elaborate suspension system (see below), but only very little can be learned from the imagery for the exact technique of securing them to the body since it is situated at the back of the bow-case and thus largely obscured. These containers are much larger than quivers and, if the bows are stored, heavier.

Both the top and bottom half of a leather bow-case possibly consists of two parts: the oval top, the bottom piece and a flaring body part. This is indicated by horizontal lines in bow-case A in Figure II.8, but sometimes even with decoration bands to obscure the seam,[21] as in the bow-case suspended from the chariot (C). From the imagery it cannot be determined whether or not these are two individual elements or that the parts are only seemingly individual elements due to the different decoration. Often, images show that the different parts of a bow-case were differentiated not only by shape, but also by the decoration or lack thereof. The top can be substantially smaller than the bottom part, but is often depicted of comparable size (compare bow-case 'A' with bow-case 'B' in Figure II.8).

The two isolated bow-cases in Figure II.8 are elaborately decorated, but in different ways. Bow-case A has decorated edges, marked by two parallel lines following the edge (possibly edge bindings), but the composition is not clear. The interior is plain (unless paint is missing), although the short lines immediately below the flap and only on this half, suggests lengthwise running lines, as seen in container B and D. A circular decorative unit, possibly a roundel, is added at two thirds of the length of the lower half. Note that, remarkably, the two halves (D & E) do not have a roundel, which suggests, if these are bow-case parts, that the

---

20 It is possible that the images show parts of other containers, possibly for spears.
21 Also seen in the Tano bow-case.

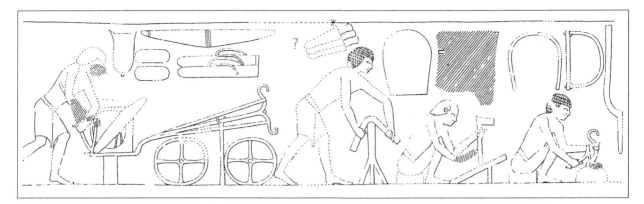

Figure II.9. Leather workshop from the tomb of Puyemre (TT39). From: Davies (1922-1923: pl. XXIII).

circular elements are added late in the manufacturing process, perhaps reflecting the identity or allegiance of the owner. Alternatively, these bow-cases simply did not have such roundels (not all bow-cases in the pictorial record have roundels). In bow-case B, both halves are decorated with lengthwise parallel lines, and the edges are enhanced as well. Flaps also show signs of edging.

In the same scene (Figure II.8), a leatherworker is finishing a quiver (F). These types of containers can be symmetrical lengthwise, with a slightly flared opening, or are shown as tubes without flaring (see *e.g.* the tomb of Puyemre, TT39, reign of Thutmose III; Figure II.9). In the archaeological record quivers are known to have separately made circular lids (quivers CG 24071 & CG 24072 from the tomb of Maiherpri, Figure I.1; see also below). Quivers are often elaborately decorated. In the pictorial evidence, they are always narrower than the tubular part of a bow-case, as is confirmed by the measurements of the Tano bottom of the bow-case (#31, Cat. No. 92) and Maiherpri's quivers (Daressy, 1902: 32-33), which helps in their identification. The two quivers of Maiherpri (CG 24071 & 24072, Figure I.1) are made of two pieces of leather that are secured at the sides[22]; the bottom part is not, as seen in the Tano bow-case, a separate element. A quiver, possibly from Khizam (near Luxor, Egypt) in the British Museum (London) (EA48985), is one such undecorated, non-tapering example. In addition, it has a cord attached to it, not seen in Egyptian bow-cases, so that the owner could carry it over his shoulder rather than hanging it on the chariot.

Identification

The Tano material includes at least four parts of a bow-case: top (#30, Cat. No. 91), flap (L1 #015, Cat. No. 93), bottom (#31, Cat. No. 92; Figure II.10), and elements of the closing system (L5 #034, Cat. No. 94; L5 #035, Cat. No. 95). The identification of the bottom part is without question: it has the shape familiar from two-dimensional images, as well as Tutankhamun's wooden bow-case (Carter's Number 335), and the back shows the various points of attachment to secure it with straps to the chariot frame. Moreover, the object's thickness (approximately three centimetres) is appropriate for the storage of (a) bow(s), particularly when unstrung.

---

22 It is possible, but unlikely, that this was made with one piece of leather; however, due to the brevity of time available for its study, we could not ascertain this.

Figure II.10. Three of the fragments of the Tano bow-case. A) Top part; B) Flap; C) Bottom. All showing the recto.

Two objects from the tomb of Amenhotep II have a similar shape and dimensions (CG 24146, Cat. No. 4 and CG 24149, Cat. No. 3) (Table II.3). According to Daressy (1902: 76), CG 24146 (Cat. No. 4) is made of plaster, lined with skin, gilded, and elaborately decorated. At the time of the authors' examination, it had deteriorated somewhat and the gilding had vanished. It belongs to the same bow-case as the flap discussed below (CG 24147, Cat. No. 4), as it is made in the same way and has comparable decoration. If, as discussed previously, it is accepted that bow-cases were made of different parts, then CG 24149 (Cat. No. 3; Daressy, 1902: 77) can be identified as the bottom of a bow-case as well.

Two objects from Amarna, AM 034 and 035 (Table II.3; Figure II.11; Veldmeijer, 2011b: 103-106; Appendix II) are comparable in their elongated semi-circular shape, as well as in the measurements. They are made of at least two layers of leather, the outermost one of which is decorated at the edges in both objects. An impressed line runs from top to bottom in both: it is not clear what this means, but possibly it is just decoration. AM 035 clearly, and AM 034 less distinctly, shows, at the left and right margins, that originally the objects must have been rather thick.

Several finds from the tomb of Tutankhamun (Figure II.12) have a comparable shape. However, the measurements vary, and one is substantially smaller (Table II.3). This could be because these elements do not actually belong to bow-cases, or they might be for smaller bows, used by the king when he was a child, and included in his tomb, just as were the smaller chairs and clothes. Alternatively, they might be for special diminutive bows used to hunt small birds or similar game. However,

Bow-Cases				
Object	Provenance	Measurements (in cm)	Decoration	Source
#31	Tano	W: 14; H: 24.2	Green/red; appliqué: stair-step overlapping strips, icicles/petals	Present work (Cat. No. 92); Figure II.10C
CG 24146	Amenhotep II	W: 16; H: 20	Gilt, red; Impressed running palmette	Daressy (1902: 76); Cat. No. 4
CG 24149	Amenhotep II	W: 16; H: 25	Different colour appliqué	Daressy (1902: 77); Cat. No. 3
ÄM AM 34	Amarna	W: 14; H: 21	Different colour(?) appliqué	Veldmeijer (2011b: 103-106); Figure II.8; Appendix II
ÄM AM 35	Amarna	W: 14; H: 21	Different colour(?) appliqué	Veldmeijer (2011b: 103-106); Figure II.8; Appendix II
Quivers and Tutankhamun's possible quiver bottom parts				
CG 24071	Maiherpri	W: 6.5; H:	Colour and impressed decoration	Daressy (1902: 32)
CG 24072	Maiherpri	W: ?	Different colour appliqué, paint	Daressy (1902: 32-33)
CN 122ff (G.11)	Tutankhamun	W: 12; H: 22.5	Gold foil, embossed	Carter's Card 122bbff; Figure II.9
CN 122gg (G.12)	Tutankhamun	W: 12; H: 20	Gold foil, embossed	Carter's Card 122ggnn; Figure II.9
CN 122hh (G.13)	Tutankhamun	W: 9.5; H: 19.5	Gold foil, embossed	Carter's Card 122ggnn; Figure II.9
CN 122ii (G.14)	Tutankhamun	W: 8.5; H: 16	Gold foil, embossed	Carter's Card 122ggnn; Figure II.9
CN 122jj	Tutankhamun	W: 8.5; H: 16	Gold foil, embossed	Carter's Card 122ggnn; Figure II.9
CN 122kk	Tutankhamun	No measurements	Gold foil, embossed	Carter's Card 122ggnn; Figure II.9
CN 122ll	Tutankhamun	W: 8.5; H: 18	Gold foil, embossed	Carter's Card 122ggnn; Figure II.9
CN 122mm	Tutankhamun	Not given	Gold foil, embossed	Carter's Card 122ggnn; Figure II.9
CN 122oo	Tutankhamun	W: 8.5; H: 18	Gold foil, embossed	Carter's Card 122ggnn; Figure II.9
CN 122pp	Tutankhamun	W: 8.5; W: 18	Gold foil, embossed	Carter's Card 122ggnn; Figure II.9

Table II.3. The various bottom parts of bow-cases and quivers compared. The probable gold sheet quiver cladding with the same shape from the tomb of Tutankhamum is referred to by the Carter Number (but see also Littauer & Crouwel, 1985: 34-47). Key: ÄM = Ägyptisches Museum und Papyrussammlung (Berlin); AM = Amarna; CG = Catalogue General; CN = Carter's Number; Preface 'G' refers to the numbering system used by Littauer & Crouwel (1985). The measurements of ÄM AM 34 and 35 were taken from the old photograph, as the objects are in such a bad condition that the measurements of the individual pieces were not reliable for comparison (see Appendix II).

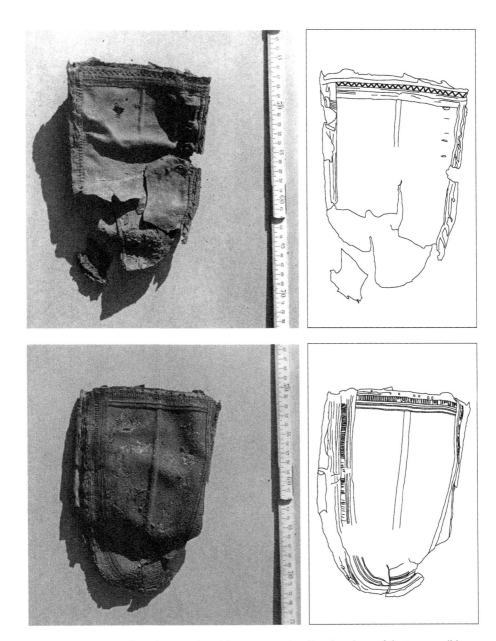

Figure II.11. Excavation photographs with accompanying line drawings of the two possible bottom parts of bow-cases from Amarna (ÄM AM 034 & 035 respectively). Photographs courtesy of the Ägyptisches Museum und Papyrussammlung (Berlin).

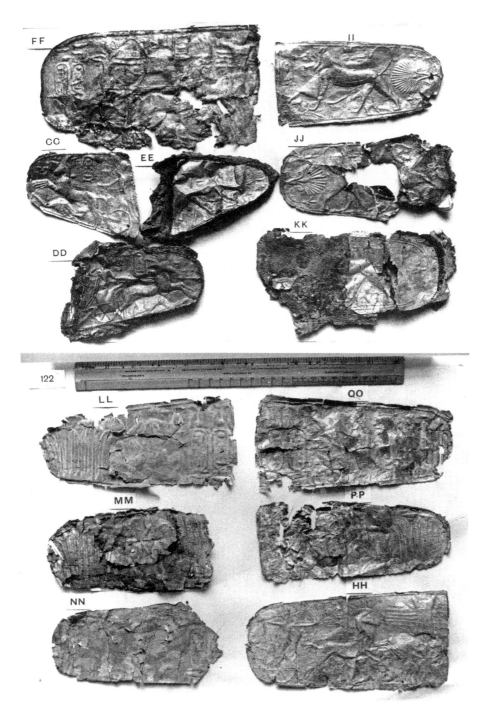

Figure II.12. Embossed gold sheet from the tomb of Tutankhamun, identified as bow-case or quiver elements (cf. Table II.3). Photographs by H. Burton. Courtesy of the Griffith Institute, University of Oxford.

Figue II.13. The bow-case flap (recto) from Shaft 3 and its related burial, just outside the court of TT65 in Luxor. Courtesy of the TT65 Project (Eötvös Loránd University, Budapest).

the objects are a bit closer to the measurements of the quivers of Maiherpri, and it is not beyond the realm of possibility that these fragments are actually from quivers, albeit of an unusual shape. Of course, the gold cladding would have been smaller than the object to which it was attached, and it is impossible to estimate the original size of the containers.

The semi-circular object from Tano, L1 #015 (Cat. No. 93; Figure II.10B; Table II.4), is a bow-case flap, with its closing system. Although pouches also have flaps (see below), they are usually different in shape, although some rare depictions show them with semi-circular flaps as well (Figure II.15). Given the fact that the Tano material contains both the top and bottom sections of a bow-case, it is logical to assume that the flap is from one and the same bow-case. The dimensions provide additional support to this hypothesis. The only two known archaeological parallels of a semi-circular flap thus far is the specimen from Shaft 3, just outside the court of TT65, immediately north of its northern court wall (Bács, 2009: 30), excavated by the Hungarian mission directed by Tamás Bács (Figure II.13[23]; Table II.4), and the example from the tomb of Amenhotep II (CG 24147, Cat. No. 4; Table II.4), of which, unfortunately, only very little is preserved (*cf.* the black and white photograph in the catalogue with the recent photographs). Three possible flaps were recovered from the tomb of Tutankhamun, consisting of gold sheet only. The measurements of the objects (Table II.4) are comparable, although the example from TT65 is slightly smaller. The Tano example is the only one in which the closing system is (partially) preserved.[24]

The bow-case flap from the tomb of Amenhotep II (CG 24147, Cat. No. 4; Table II.4) consists, according to Daressy (1902: 76-77), of gilt over a thin layer of plaster, with a leather lining (but currently, only the leather remains). The

---

23 Under study by the AELP.
24 The flax stitch at approximately the same position in the Luxor example seems to be a repair of a crack in the leather.

DECONSTRUCTING AND CONSTRUCTION | 43

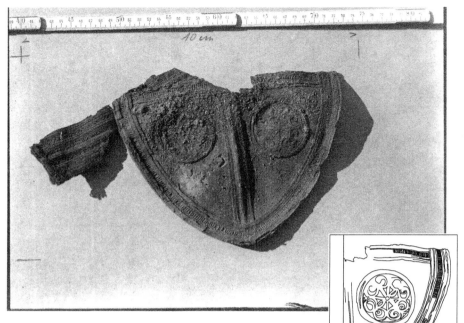

Figure II.14. The possible Amarna bow-case flap with accompanying line drawing (ÄM AM 079) with the two emblems. Photograph courtesy of the Ägyptisches Museum und Papyrussammlung (Berlin).

impressed running palmettes are also seen in the part of the bottom of, probably, the same bow-case (CG 24146), previously discussed, to which Daressy (1902: 76-77) refers as a quiver. The flap clearly differs from the other two discussed here, which are both made of leather only, and might be more comparable to the material from the tomb of Tutankhamun.

One object from Amarna, AM 079 (Veldmeijer, 2011b: 142-143; Figure II.14; Table II.4), has been tentatively identified as a bow-case flap. It differs from other flaps in that it is more triangular rather than semi-circular (AM 072 & AM 073; Veldmeijer, 2011b: 109-113). Piece AM 079 has a roundel on either side of a transverse appliqué division of differently coloured(?), stair-step overlapping strips of leather, so its decoration also differs somewhat from what is seen in images.

An object from the tomb of Tutankhamun with a comparable shape to AM 079 is Carter's Number 122w (Figure I.2). It is also semi-triangular, and the overall dimensions would fit the 'average' bow-case. Gold foil is added directly on top of the leather.[25] The imagery is elaborate, showing, according to Carter (Card No. 122waa) an "Ibex, or some similar animal, attacked by a dog below and by a four legged winged animal above. Plants and trees. Scroll on rounded edge." The scene is orientated transversely, so if the bow-case was closed when hanging diagonally from the chariot, it would have been in the correct plane. Two additional semi-circular pieces of gold foil on leather (Carter's Numbers 122x & y; Figure I.2)

---

25 This will be discussed in detail in the aforementioned project of the DAI "Restaurierung der Goldbleche aus dem Grab des Tutanchamun" (note 11).

might also be parts of bow-case flaps; these are, as with Carter's Number 122w, higher than wide, in contrast to the leather flaps from the other provenances, but unlike 122w, semi-circular. The imagery on both (the king slaying prisoners with his khepesh) is orientated in the same way as Carter's Number 122w. Note that fans from the tomb, such as Carter's Number 242, have a semi-circular palm, which too is covered in gold foil. The presence of leather in some of the semi-circular gold foil elements suggests, however, that they did not come from fans as none of those were reported to have included leather.

The identified bow-case flaps show different decoration and motifs, suggesting a large variation. The size would have been more or less comparable, as this is dictated by practicalities, such as suspending it from the chariot, and the dimensions of the bow. Focussing on the Tano flap (L1 #015, Cat. No. 93; Figure II.10B); it has stair-step overlapping strips applied along the edge and, from top to bottom, through the centre, in alternating green and red. This technique as well as the decoration compares well with the Tano casing, as well as with objects from Amarna and the tombs of Thutmose IV and Amenhotep III. However, the Tano bottom part (#31, Cat. No. 92; Figure II.10C) as well as the top (#30, Cat. No. 91; Figure II.10A) show more elaborate decoration, including zigzag patterns and icicles/petals.

Object #30 (Cat. No. 91; Figure II.10A) is interpreted as the top part of the bow-case. The design of the decoration, including icicles/petals, zigzag and overlapping strips of green and red, is the same as the design of the bow-case bottom, and the shape is commensurate with a bow-case top. It cannot be part of a quiver as no known examples of quivers have such a piece, and this object is too narrow to serve as a quiver. Finally, the extension seen in #30 (Cat. No. 91) might have played a role in opening the the bow-case to store or retrieve the bow.

Curiously, the Tano material does not seem to include a quiver. Either it has deteriorated to such a degree that it has lost any distinctive features, or was not part of the lot acquired/sold by Tano. Certainly from images of workshops chariots together with the bow-case and quivers are made in sets (Figure II.8). Of course, Maiherpri's tomb, that contained three quivers, had no bow-case.

Table II.4. Bow-case flaps compared. Key; AM = Amarna; CG = Catalogue General; CN = Carter's Number; The number with preface 'G' refers to the numbering system used by Littauer & Crouwel (1985).

Object	Provenance	Measurements (in cm)	Decoration	Source
L1 #015	Tano	W: 23.3; H: 10.6	Green/red; appliqué: stair-step overlapping strips	Present work (Cat. No.93); Figure II.10B
TT65	Hatshepsut/ Thutmose III to Amenhotep II (Bács, 2009: 31)	W: appr. 14; H: 8.3	Red/black (but see description); painted bands of dots, lines and line with triangles	Under study (Figure II.13)
CG 24147	Amenhotep II	W: 21; H: 12	Gilt, red; Impressed running palmette	Daressy (1902: 76); Cat. No. 4
AM 079	Amarna	W: 23; H: 12	Different colour(?) appliqué	Veldmeijer (2011b: 140-142); Figure II.11; Appendix II
CN 122w (G.2)	Tutankhamun	W: 19.5; H: 13.8	Gilt, impressed imagery	Card No. 122waa; Figure I.2
CN 122x (G.3)	Tutankhamun	W: 14; H: 12	Gilt, impressed imagery	Card No. 122waa; Figure I.2
CN 122y (G.4)	Tutankhamun	W: 14; H 11	Gilt, impressed imagery	Card No. 122waa; Figure I.2

II.2.2. Pouches

Introduction

Carter and Newberry (1904: 26) mention that "a leather pocket or pouch with embossed flap to cover it" was attached to the inside of Thutmose IV's chariot body, and thus would not be seen from outside, or indeed in depictions. Unfortunately, they provide no further details about this, and certainly no form of attachment, which most probably was part of the pouch construction, is visible on the chariot.[26] In the leather workshop in the tomb of Hepu (TT66, Figure II.8, indicated by #), five objects are shown that are identified as pouches. The pictured pouches are elongated half-ovals, with closing flaps with triangular lower parts. They are adorned with a roundel on the body of the pouch, slightly below the flap. However, in the tomb of Amenmose (TT42; Davies, 1933a: pl. XXXIII) semi-circular pouch flaps are shown, which are rare (see also TT65, Figure II.15). These might cause some confusion with bow-case flaps. There has been some debate about the interpretation of these objects (Müller, 1989: 24). The identification of some of these as shield cover, as explained by Müller (1989: 24), is very unlikely. Müller's identification as yoke saddle pad can be dismissed as well, since these can be expected to be symmetrical, either oval or rectangular (see below section II.3.3. 'Yoke Saddle Pad'), and without closing flaps and attachment straps and loops. It is possible that such pouches contained spare parts for weaponry (or even the chariot itself) or in some cases letters that needed to be sent, and served as the equivalent of a 'glove compartment' found in modern automobiles.

Identification

The flap from the tomb of Thutmose IV (JE 97820, Cat. No. 22; Table II.5) is identified by Carter and Newberry (1904: 35) as a pouch flap, which has a more pronounced triangular end flap than seen in some images. Carter's Number 122z from the tomb of Tutankhamun (Figure I.2; Table II.5) is more in keeping with images of chariot pouches (Figure II.8). Tutankhamun's tomb has also yielded two pieces of gold sheet that can be identified as covering pouch flaps (Figure I.2; Table II.5), and which are closer in shape to the flap from the tomb of Thutmose IV: Carter's Numbers 122aa and 122bb. Note that the lid of the wooden bow-case (Carter's Number 335) has a central panel with the same shape as the two small examples from the tomb of Tutankhamun (Carter's Numbers 122aa & bb). The presence of leather in at least 122bb suggests that it originates from a leather object rather than a comparable wooden bow-case.

The pouch flaps all have complex imagery, including the king's titulary. This contrasts with the pouch flaps in two-dimensional art, however, as although they might show some decoration along the edge, they do not show any other decoration except for, occasionally, a roundel.

---

26 Did they see connecting points or was there actually a pouch attached, which fell off or was removed at some point after discovery?

Figure II.15. Depiction of a pouch with remarkably small flap(?). Tomb of Nebamun (TT65). Courtesy of T.A. Bács.

Object	Provenance	Measurements (in cm)	Decoration	Source
JE 97820	Thutmose IV	W: 22; H: 17	Bird with outstretched wings, cartouches	Present work (Cat. No. 22); Carter & Newberry (1904: 35)
CN 122z (G.5)	Tutankhamun	W: 27; H: 11.5	"Two representations of the King holding up lions by their tails and transfixing them with a lance. Both cartouches of Tutankhamen & that of Ankhsenamen" (Card No. 122waa)	Card No. 122waa & 122zkk; Figure I.2
CN 122aa (G.6)	Tutankhamun	W: 16; H: 11	"King slaying prisoner with a mace. Queen stands behind him." (Card No. 122waa)	Card No. 122waa & 122vgg; Figure I.2
CN 122bb (G.7)	Tutankhamun	W: 12; H: 8.5	"Two figures of King seated, with cartouches between." (122bbff)	Card No. 122bbff; Figure I.2

Table II.5. The pouch flaps compared. Key: CG = Catalogue General; CN = Carter's Number; The number with preface 'G' refers to the numbering system by Littauer & Crouwel (1985).

II.2.3. Holder(?)

Introduction

There are no clear indications from pictorial evidence or archaeological material of suspension/attachment mechanisms connecting bow-cases and quivers to the chariot. This might be due to the fact that a series of simple straps were used, or that a more elaborate holder was positioned inside the chariot, or perhaps not clearly defined if external.

Identification

Although the Tano leather was taken out of the package in the museum at least one time (judging from the photograph published by Forbes, 1957: 30), an enigmatic piece of leather (L3 #004F, Cat. No. 46; Figure II.16) was stored with the main casing in the same box, possibly suggesting that they belonged together. The undecorated, bottom edge of the enigmatic object from the Tano leather is intact: it is folded, sandwiching a single layer of leather, and thus is three layers thick. The only other item in the assemblage that has three layers of red leather is a tapering fragment (L1 #011, Cat. No. 47) and a group of small fragments (L5 #009, Cat. No. 48; L1 #022, Cat. No. 49). The top edge of L3 #004F is intact too, secured with edge binding. Thus the object has two complete sides, and two broken ones. The remnant of another enhanced edge (Figure C in Cat. No. 46), though largely incomplete, could very well be of the same composition as the decorated edge binding at the top of the object, which would suggest that these were attached, forming some sort of holder in the form of a large loop. It has a roundel that is frequently seen on quivers and bow-cases in the artistic record. Fragment L1 #011 (Cat. No. 47), which consists of the same number of layers of leather as L3 #004F (Cat. No. 46), as well as having the same design of the enhanced edge, might belong to L3 #004F. The strap protruding from one side of the (near) vertical elongated decorated element is of comparable composition as the support straps (*cf.* above II.1.3. 'Support Straps'; Cat. Nos. 78-84), and must have been used to secure it, diagonally, to the wooden framework of the body of the chariot. Thus, the loop would have been toward the inside of the chariot, with the decorated side facing outward. This situation might suggest that it was more

Figure II.16. Possible holder of the Tano leather (F3 #004F, Cat. No. 46).

commonly used with the main casing only. Plausible as this may seem, holders such as L3 #004F (Cat. No. 46) are not clearly identifiable in images of open chariots.[27] A holder like this could have been used to put another object in, such as the large quivers for spears, bow-cases, and even other quivers. If quivers etc., were put through apertures in the siding fill, this holder would have been a solution for when the chariot had no siding fill. It could also act as reinforcement when a siding fill was present and the object was inserted through one of the apertures in it. Certainly, such a detachable accessory would make the chariot more versatile.Alternative to this intepretation is that it was used as holder to further secure the bow-case at the outside of the chariot, in which case it would only have been used with the main casing. This would better explain the roundel, so often shown on bow-cases in depictions. Another possible function might be that it supported the top of a bow-case on the left side of the chariot is currently under study and the hypothetical reconstruction being tested by experimental archaeology.

II.3. Harness

The harnessing system in a chariot is made up of several components, many of which have been identified in the Tano material, and include the girth (#40 and #41, Cat. No. 96), neckstraps (#37 and #39, Cat. No. 103) and possibly the two broad straps (#35 and #36, Cat. No. 97), whose function has not been established. Fragments of the headstall and reins might be present, but none can be identified securely.

II.3.1. Neckstrap

Introduction

The neckstrap is, following Littauer and Crouwel (1985: 6): "a strap passing around the neck and attached at either end to the lower ends of the yoke saddles or to the yoke itself. Its purpose is to hold the yoke in place." Pictorial evidence does not show precisely how it connects to the yoke or yoke saddles, and how it is secured. In some cases, the neckstrap runs under the girth. Shortly before it runs under the girth, the belt-strap transition area is sometimes shown with a taper, after which the neckstrap continues as a much narrower strap towards the attachment area of the harness. This can be seen in the depiction on the left exterior of the chariot body from the tomb of Thutmose IV (Figure II.17A). Neckstraps, however, do not always taper, although in some cases the shape of the terminal ends cannot be determined since they disappear under the yoke saddle pad (see below) and/or the girth (Figure II.17B). Sometimes a sort of loop can be seen at the hole in the girth, with strands hanging down from it: the neckstrap is pulled through the girth, turned into a loop that functions as a terret for the reins (Figure II.17C) and the end dangle down (Figure II.17D). In other depictions, it seems that the girth has a loop at its end. The reins are being led to this same spot and either pulled through the loop (functioning as a terret) or, seemingly, run through the hole in the girth itself. Decoration can be seen in the transitional area, usually tear-shaped.

---

27 Although of different design, chariots in the Ashurnasirpal's relief in Berlin (Littauer & Crouwel, 1979, Fig. 53) show sort of bags hanging from the side of the chariot, containing quivers and bows, suggesting such items were not unheard off.

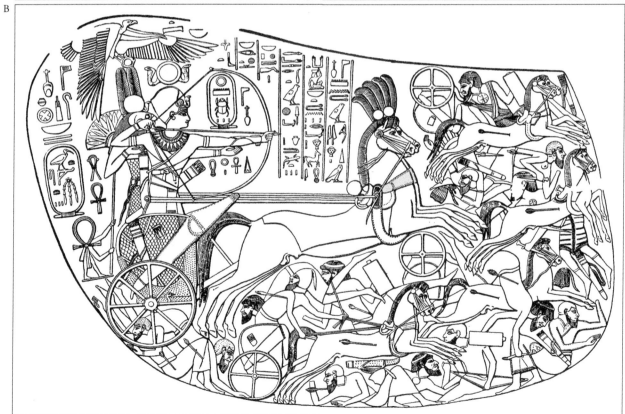

50 | CHARIOTS IN ANCIENT EGYPT

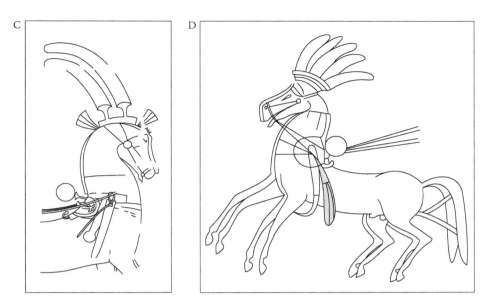

Figure II.17. Neckstraps (in grey). C) The end of the neckstrap is pulled through the girth and tied into a loop, functioning as terret. Luxor. Medinet Habu. After: The Epigraphic Survey (1932: pl. LXVIII); D) The ends of the neckstrap have a decorative finishing. Tomb of Ahmes (Amarna, T3). After: Davies (1905b: pl. XXXII).

Fairly often images show that the neckstrap even runs under the yoke saddle pad, suggesting it would have gone through it in order to connect it with the girth (if it was always connected) that runs over it (*e.g.* tomb of Panehesy; Davies, 1905b: pl. XV). Alternatively, it was connected to the harness in a different way, which cannot be determined from the imagery.

Identification

Tano objects #37 and #39 (Cat. No. 103; Figure II.18) can be recognised as neckstraps due to their shape, seen in the Thutmose IV chariot as well (Figure II.17). In the Tano leather, the neckstrap would have run under the girth, because otherwise the decoration of the girth would have been obscured. Surely, the two slits, set close together and fairly close to the belt-strap transition, played a part in the attachment of the neckstrap to the rest of the harness, but exactly how this was achieved is unclear, although a toggle closure seems plausible. An alternative way would be that another strap was pulled through the hole in the girth and through one of the slits, thus securing them together; this strap must have been prevented from slipping through the girth hole, and judging from the use of toggles in the casing of the body, this could have been done here with a toggle too. A good candidate for such an element would be BI-028 (Cat. No. 117): it is slightly bigger than the size of the hole and could not be pulled through. In addition, the width of the strap going through the ball is (slightly) less than the length of the slits in the neckstrap, allowing for it being pulled through, yet attaching it securely.[28] Unfortunately, the strap of BI-028 (Cat. No. 117) is broken off,

Previous page: Figure II.17. Neckstraps (in grey). The left (A) and right (B) exterior of the body of a chariot from the tomb of Thutmose IV. From: Carter & Newberry (1904: pl. XI).

---

28   Diameters of the holes in the girth: 16.5 mm & 19.5 mm; length of the slits: 24 mm; diameter of the toggle: 24.6 mm x 32.2 mm; width of the strap going through the toggle: 18.5 mm.

Figure II.18. One of the two Tano neckstraps (#37, Cat. No. 103), showing the decoration that would be visible for the viewer when used (the other end has no decoration)..

although it might have been connected to BI-024 (Cat. No. 116), a strap with the same design and measurements, thus making it difficult to determine how it was secured at the inner side of the construction, *i.e.* against the horse's body. If, however, BI-024 (Cat. No. 116) and BI-028 (Cat. No. 028) connect, the toggle only served to prevent slipping from the hole in the girth: the other end of this attachment strap would, seemingly, be knotted judging by the tapering, rolled up end. A problem with the system of using toggles is that a toggle closure is never depicted in imagery or not recognisable. What is suggested sometimes in imagery, as mentioned above, is that the narrow extension of the neckstrap was pulled through the hole in the girth, and made into a loop that functions as a terret (Figure II.17C). In depictions, this loop is often fairly big, but if in the Tano neckstrap the two slits were used for making a loop, it would have been fairly narrow. Still, it needs to be secured, but precisely how this was done is not shown in art, although the aformentioned examples suggest it was simply knotted – the slits in the Tano neckstrap might not have been used for this. The end of the narrow neckstrap extension seems to hang loose. In the tomb of Ahmes in Amarna (T3; Figure II.17D), the loose hanging part widens into an aesthetically pleasing end, but this is not always the case (see Figure II.17C) and also was not so with the Tano strap. In this construction, the neckstrap is not connected directly to the yoke, which might be the reason why the remainder of the narrow extension of the neckstrap (as far as it is preserved) show no signs of slits. However, possibly the dangling end did not always hang lose at the horse's side, but was pulled back and secured to the yoke, hence the fairly long length of the extensions. The decoration on the transition area between the belt and its strap differs between the two sides: one side has an elaborate floral design (Figure II.18), whereas the other is plain. This suggests that the end with the floral design was facing outwards toward the viewer, and the plain ends faced one another, on the sides of the horses flanking the pole. No archaeological parallels are known.

II.3.2. Girth

Introduction

The girth, or belly strap, is the strap that encircles the horse's belly immediately behind the front legs (J. Crouwel, Personal Communication, 2016; Figure II.19). Although it is used to secure the harness saddle, it can act as backing element but is usually more bulky than a backing element (Littauer & Crouwel, 1985: Fig. 2).

The end has a big hole for the attachment to and with other harness elements. In the more detailed imagery, such as the depiction on the chariot body from the tomb of Thutmose IV (Figure II.17), one can also see decorated reinforcement at the end, which can have various shapes (oval or tear-shaped for example). The girth can have a rounded end as well as a straight terminal one.

Identification

The shape and size of #40 and #41 (Cat. No. 96; Figure II.20) suggest they are the horse's girths.[29] It is, however, not clear whether the fragments belong to one girth or two, but most likely two, if we assume that, as seen with the neckstraps, the ends that would face inside, between the horses, was un- or barely decorated. However, if this were the case and these were two girths, only fairly short pieces are preserved. This is rather remarkable considering the fact that both neckstraps

Figure II.19. Two span of horses with different rendering of neckstrap and girths. Saqqara. Tomb of Horemheb.

Figure II.20. One of the two girth fragments (#40, Cat. No. 96), showing the decoration that would be visible for the viewer when used.

---

29 See II.3.1. 'Neckstrap' for information on the attachment of the two elements (girth and neckstrap).

survived nearly entirely, as did two enigmatic belts (#35 and #36, Cat. No. 97; see below). A fragment from Amarna can now also be identified as the terminal end of a girth (ÄM AM 031, Veldmeijer, 2011b: 98-100; Appendix II).

II.3.3. Yoke Saddle Pad

Introduction

The yoke, the wooden bar that joins the two horses and allows them to pull the chariot in tandem, rests on their backs, and was involved in securing the girth and neckstraps, as is sometimes suggested in imagery (Figure II.21). A yoke saddle pad protected the horses' bodies from the weight of the yoke and from abrasion (Littauer & Crouwel, 1985: 81-83, 102). Most often it is depicted as being oval (only one side is visible on the horse's back, but it is assumed that the pad was symmetrical; Figure II.21A) but sometimes a pad is rectangular (Figure II.21B), or seems even to widen at the ends at either side of the horse (Figure II.21C). In some instances, there is another, larger and usually rectangular, element underneath the pad. Oval pads are sometimes shown in the workshops where chariots and leather are produced (Figure II.8, marked with *). If there is horse housing present, it could run under the yoke and its pad (*e.g.* Figure II.17). Although housing could have been made of leather, remnants found in Tutankhamun's tomb, which are said to be housing, are made of linen (Littauer & Crouwel, 1985: 88, pl. LXII), though it is not clear exactly why this fragment was identified thus. Initially, caparisons for horses seem to largely be restricted to royalty. The first example of housing on chariot horses is found pictured on the chariot of Thutmose IV (Carter & Newberry, 1904: pls. 10, 11; Figure II.17); this is also the first instance of horses wearing feathered headdressess (see below), and sporting a solar disk on their back. These elements appear on Amenhotep III's horses, insofar as one can make them out with the addition of the captives on their backs (Petrie, 1896: pl. X). All these elements, feathers, housing, disk, are very common on royal chariots (king, queen, princesses) from the Amarna period onward, although they do not appear in every image of royal chariots. Of course, when chariots are shown without their riders, in the absence of texts it is sometimes difficult to determine if a chariot is royal or belongs to a high elite (Davies, 1905b: pl. XIV). Variations in the use of housing occurs during the reign of Ramesses II, when it seems that non-royal chariot horses sometimes also wear housings, but only in depictions of the Battle of Qadesh (Breasted, 1903: pls. III [top], VI [middle and right in the area of XXVI], XXXI-XXXIII [bottom]). After Ramesses II's reign, housings revert to being the purview of royalty.

In images from the tombs at Amarna, the disk on the horse is more commonly found on the animals associated with chariots conveying the royal family, though there are examples of smaller disks on the back of horses with chariots devoid of royalty (for example, Davies, 1905a: pls. XI, XIII; 1905b: pl. XIV). There are a few possible examples of disks on non-royal chariots featured in the Qadesh reliefs (Breasted, 1903: pl. 6, bottom, and another to the side, though these might be royal chariots), but after the reign of Ramesses II, these disks are exclusive to horses pulling royalty.

Figure II.21. Yoke saddle pads (in grey). A) Example of oval yoke saddle pad. Tomb of Menna (TT69). From: Davies & Gardiner (1936: pl. L); B) A rectangular yoke saddle pad. Temple of Karnak. Battle reliefs of Seti I. After: The Epigraphic Survey (1986: pl. XXXV); C) A large, rectangular pad which widens at the ends. Luxor. Horemheb mortuary temple. After: Ray (1992: fig. 15.69).

Identification

An unnumbered object, excavated by the German mission to Amarna in the early part of the 20th century, was unfortunately not among the material that was available for study and was, therefore, described only from an old photograph (Veldmeijer, 2011b: 142-143; Appendix II; Figure II.22). The oval shape, the size and the combination of leather with textile, which would have been appropriate protection of the horse's skin against rubbing of the yoke, suggests that this is a yoke saddle pad. The Tano material in the Egyptian Museum (Cairo) contained no such item.

Figure II.22. A large object of decorated, but badly worn leather, which is interpreted as yoke saddle pad. Courtesy of the Ägyptisches Museum und Papyrussammlung (Berlin).

II.3.4. Headstall (including blinker and bridle boss)

Introduction

The cheekstrap, one of the elements of the headstall, usually consists of two strips that form a V (Figure II.23A), but three strips are also known (Figure II.23B), as are rare images showing a single strip (Figure II.23C) (see also Rommelaere, 1991: 99-100). A bridle boss (Figure II.23A; II.24) covers the point where the cheekstrap connects with the crownpiece, the element that crosses the crown of the head behind the ears (Littauer & Crouwel, 1985: 6). Bridle bosses are always circular, albeit of varying sizes, and decorated.

Horses usually wore blinkers (Figure II.24) to prevent them from seeing to the rear and side, and thus avoiding distraction. Littauer and Crouwel (1985: 86) suggest two further functions for them: protecting the eyes from flying objects and discouraging interaction between the two horses that pulled the chariot. Blinkers can have various shapes, but the spade-shape seems most common in ancient Egypt. They are made of different materials, including wood, ivory and rawhide (*e.g.* the six examples from the tomb of Amenhotep II; Daressy, 1902: 70-71, pl. XX; see also Littauer & Crouwel, 1985: 85) and are generally decorated using a variety of motifs (Littauer & Crouwel, 1985: 85-86). Blinkers are also known from outside of Egypt (*e.g.* National Archaeological Museum in Athens, X 15070, coming from the sanctuary of Apollo Daphnephoros in Eretria; Metropolitan Museum of Art 54.117.1, from Nimrud, which is one of many pairs).[30]

---

30 Interestingly, sometimes Egyptian motifs were favoured in their decoration (see for an example 54.117.1 in the Metropolitan Museum of Art, New York).

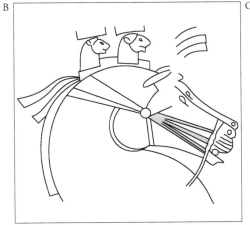
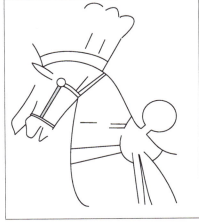

Figure II.23. Cheekstraps (in grey in B, C). A) Example of a cheekstrap consisting of two straps. Luxor. Medinet Habu. After: The Epigraphic Survey (1932: pl. CX); B) Three-piece cheekstrap. Ibidem. After: The Epigraphic Survey (1932: pl. CXVI); C) Example of fairly rare one-piece cheekstrap. Amarna. Tomb of Huya (T1). After: Davies (1905b: pl. VIII).

Figure II.24. Bridle boss and blinkers (in grey). Luxor. Medinet Habu. After: The Epigraphic Survey (1930: pl. XXIII).

Headstalls included more items than are discussed here. These, although not among the material discussed in the present work, provide some additional information on their use and dating. Feathered headdresses (*e.g.* Figure V.7 & 14) seem to be exclusively royal, save for a few instances, from the reign of Tutankhamun on (Johnson, 1992: 189, first and second registers; The Epigraphic Survey, 1994: pl. XCV), with a few possible examples also coming from Ramesses II's Qadesh scenes (Breasted, 1903: pl. VI, bottom, and another to the side, though these might be royal chariots). Ribbons attached to the horses' headdress first appear in the reign of Amenhotep III (Petrie, 1896: pl. X), and continue to appear but only in a limited fashion at Amarna (Davies, 1903: pl. XXXIV), which is surprising as ribbons are a common feature of Amarna art, whether fluttering in the breeze, or hanging from clothing. The ribbons almost become de rigeur during the reign of Tutankhamun (Carter's Nos. 021, 242, 335; Johnson, 1992: 187, 189), with one possible non-royal example (together with the disk and feathered headdress) occurring in Luxor temple, dating to the reign of Tutankhamun or Ay (The Epigraphic Survey, 1994: pl. XCV). Ribbons continue to appear on headdresses through the 20th Dynasty, and are seemingly still restricted to royalty. Interestingly, though Ramesses II's horses have them in the Beit el-Wali depictions (Ricke *et al.*, 1967: pls. VIII, XIII), they do not seem to feature in the Qadesh images unless they were added in paint.

There does not seem to be any particular preference for when the horse is covered by a housing, wears a headdress, and has a sun disk on its back. One might have thought that all of these items would have been a hindrance in battle or hunting, but this does not seem to be the case as such accoutrements are commonly shown when the king is carrying out these activities. Of course, the images might not necessarily reflect reality. Ramesses II tends to eschew the housing in the heat of battle (Breasted, 1903: pl. 6), and Ramesses III has bare horses in the Nubian campaign (The Epigraphic Survey, 1930: pl. IX); perhaps it was too hot to have the horses thus clad on this particular campaign. On the whole, it seems that at least the headdress and sun disk are commonly worn by royal horses from the reign of Thutmose IV onward.

Figure II.25. A) A possible piece of cheekstrap from the Tano chariot (BI-003, Cat. No. 85); B) Blinker from the tomb of Amenhotep II (JE 32506, Cat. No. 8); C) Bridle boss from the tomb of Amenhotep II (JE 32525, Cat. No. 7); D) Bridle boss from the tomb of Thutmose IV (JE 97801, Cat. No. 12).

Identification

One fragment of the Tano leather can tentatively be identified as a cheekstrap: BI-003 (Cat. No. 85; Figure II.25A). It consists of three composite straps that are secured at an angle, resulting in a tripartite element. The components and decoration of the cheekstrap matches that of the support straps.

In contrast to much of the chariot related leatherwork, many more blinkers are preserved, possibly because these were made in a variety of materials. The Tano material has no blinkers, but a pair of rawhide (with gypsum or plaster) blinkers, possibly once covered with gold come from the tomb of Amenhotep II (JE 32506, Cat. No. 8; Daressy, 1902: 76, pl. XXII; Figure II.25C).[31] Rawhide/leather covered with gold foil examples, of which only the gold survives, were found in the tomb of Tutankhamun (Carter's Numbers 122ccc and ddd, see Littauer & Crouwel, 1985: 85). In addition to the rawhide blinker, Amenhotep II's tomb yielded wooden examples (Daressy, 1902: pl. XX). The rawhide blinker is slightly larger than the wooden examples and those from Tutankhamun's tomb.

Several bridle bosses are also preserved, as, like blinkers, they are not always made of rawhide, but also from wood, such as the examples from the tomb of Tutankhamun (Littauer & Crouwel, 1985: 33-34, 86) and from the tomb of Amenhotep II (Daressy, 1902: 71, pl. XX; see also Littauer & Crouwel, 1985: 86). Furthermore, their diminutive size, shape, and solid construction also aid

---

31 Although Daressy (1902: 76) and Littauer and Crouwel (1985: 85) state that the rawhide blinker (JE 32506, Cat. No. 8) had "a sticky surface that probably indicates that they had been covered with gold foil", we observed no such stickiness – instead, the object had a yellow hue, suggesting that the surface was painted to imitate gold. Note that Littauer and Crouwel (1985: 85) mention a pair of leather blinkers, but only one was among the material studied.

their survival. The tomb of Amenhotep II (JE 32625, Cat. No. 7) and the tomb of Thutmose IV (JE 97801, Cat. No. 12; Figure II.25C) yielded two rawhide bosses. Some of those from the tomb of Tutankhamun showed means of attachment, while others did not, which is more in keeping with the rawhide bosses. These were secured with stitching along the edge. However, the example from the tomb of Thutmose IV has a circular hole in the middle, which might have been used to further secure the boss to the headstall, possibly with a sort of toggle.

II.3.5. Enigmatic Bands

Two relatively wide bands (#35 and #36, Cat. No. 97; Figure II.26) remain unidentified. The bands, tapering at one end, have asymmetrical vegetal appliqué decoration (comparable to that seen on the neckstrap and girth) that, when the two bands are put together, complement each other and create a symmetrical whole. There are stitch holes at the thickness, suggesting that the two were, indeed, secured together with a buttseam. One of the straps still has a small loop *in situ*, but no further features hint to their function. Imagery is not helpful in identifying these two straps.

II.4. Charioteer's Accessories

II.4.1. Wrist Guards

Introduction

The charioteer, and especially the king, was well equipped with weaponry (such as bows and arrows) and armour (which might even include a cuirass, *e.g.* such as the example from the tomb of Tutankhamun, Carter's Number 587a; see Hulit, 2002: 86-99; 2006; Hulit & Richardson, 2007),[32] and other objects, such as wrist guards (Müller, 1989), which are often depicted (Müller, 1989: 20-38). Thutmose IV

Figure II.26. One of the two enigmatic bands (#35, Cat. No. 97), which might have been part of the harness.

---

32 The cuirass will not be discussed in the present work, as it has been dealt with exhaustively in the aforementioned publications. Note that a comparable scale to those identified in Tutankhamun's cuirass is described from Amarna (Veldmeijer, 2011b: 179).

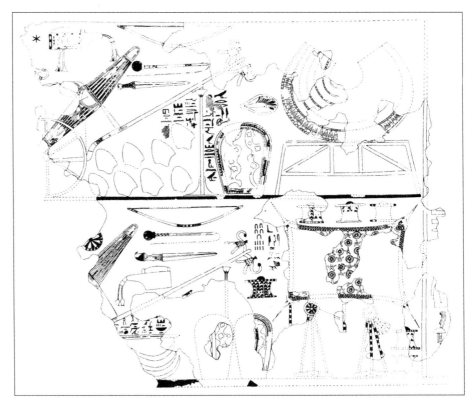

Figure II.27. Chariots and related equipment, such as blinkers, headstalls and housing as well as a highly decorated wirst guard, marked with *. Tomb of Kenamun (Luxor, TT93). After: Davies (1930: pl. XXII).

is shown wearing a wrist guard on his chariot body (Figure II.17A, B), but they are also shown as product of the leather workshop (TT66; Davies, 1963: pl. VIII; Figure II.8, marked with §), and the elaborately decorated wrist guards in the tomb of Kenamun (Figure II.27, marked with *).

Identification

Based on its shape, the identification of CG 46112 (Cat. No. 24) from the tomb of Thutmose IV as wrist guard is beyond any doubt (see Müller, 1989: 22). Müller suggests that the guard was closed by a metal ring or band that had been torn off by robbers. Indeed, large tears are present in the position where a closing system would be expected. There are several comparable examples from the archaeological record, which are depicted and discussed by Müller (1989: 21).[33] Two examples from the tomb of Maiherpri (Daressy, 1902: 33) have a protruding, narrow element to protect the thumb from the bowstring, as seen in CG 46112 (Cat. No. 24), although shaped slightly differently. Thutmose IV's tomb also yielded a more simple wrist guard (SR 3387, Cat. No. 23).

---

33   The other two comparable guards, as mentioned by Müller (1989: 21-22), are from Abd el-Qurna (JE 31166; Daressy, 1898: 73; McLeod, 1982: 63) and one from an unnumbered tomb of Se-aa (JE 31390).

II.5. Discussion: Piecing the Tano Leather Together

II.5.1. Main Casing and Siding Fill

Understanding how the different pieces of leather were attached to the chariot body or to one another is challenging, and not altogether clear, with several options being possible, based on the archaeological remains and common sense. Additional clues are found in the coloration of the leather, and also matches that were made between pieces. The red and green leather that is more refined and is exclusively decorated with geometric patterns is used on the chariot body itself, while the more robust beige and green leather with vegetal patterns is used on the horses and to secure the structure of the body and nave hoops. There are rare instances when the two colour groups overlap, such as the red and green ball toggle (BI-028, Cat. No. 117), which is attached to a beige and green piece of leather, and indeed might have been used to secure the girth.

The Tano main casing is almost complete (Figure II.3; Figure II.28 & II.29). The tube on the bottom edge that also bracketed the pole, together with the height of the casing, suggests that the main casing would have been stretched tautly over the wooden frame, and secured by the drawstring. This scenario fits well with the construction of the chariot body in Florence, and the dimensions of the main casing, including the diameter of the aperture for the pole, are in keeping with those of the Florence chariot. An alternative way of attaching the tubes with drawstring would be that the tube was folded under the wooden frame and then secured. However, if this were the case, the height of the main casing would be very low indeed, and, more importantly, there are no wear marks on the tube to support such a reconstruction. Unfortunately, the ends of the tube and the drawstring are not preserved, making it difficult to interpret how it was finally attached to the chariot. Most probably, however, the drawstring ended in a toggle similar to that of BI-034 (Cat. No. 74; Figure IV.1A), which is also seen in the siding fill (L1 #016, Cat. No. 73; see below), and this system was used to secure the main casing to the frame. The fastening would nonetheless have resulted in a fairly loose casing, since the drawstring runs freely through the tube and securing it with toggle-hole fastenings does not allow for pulling the leather very tight and keeping it that way.

A reinforced hole is located at the junction of the decorated edge and the straight edge of the end of the casing (Figure II.28A). It was used to further secure the casing to the wooden frame, possibly (together) with the drawstring of the front part of the casing (see below), or with a separate strap (perhaps a strap with a large toggle, such as BI-028, Cat. No. 117). The reinforced hole shows stress from pulling, so whatever system/technique was used, the casing was pulled tight to the frame. Strangely, as with the tripartite top of the central part, the top of the rectangular end does not show clear indications of having been secured to the frame, but it is hard to believe that it would have been loose, and there are the vestiges of toggles and slim straps on opposing sides, which might have served to further secure them (L3 #004D, Cat. No. 46; Figure II.28B).

How the vertical and tripartite section on top were secured is more difficult to determine. No attachments are visible on the vertical section, which bears the impression of the central strut on both the recto and verso, and there are no variations in colour that would indicate that straps had been used on any part of

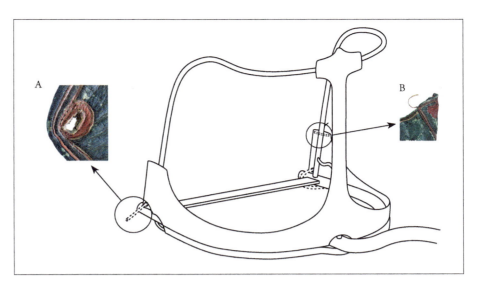

Figure II.28. Reconstruction of the main casing, showing the exterior, with details. A) The bottom corner of the side with reinforced hole for securing it to the body. Possibly, the drawstring leading through the tube played a role in securing the corner as well; B) The extension might have been loosely secured simply by means of a narrow strap.

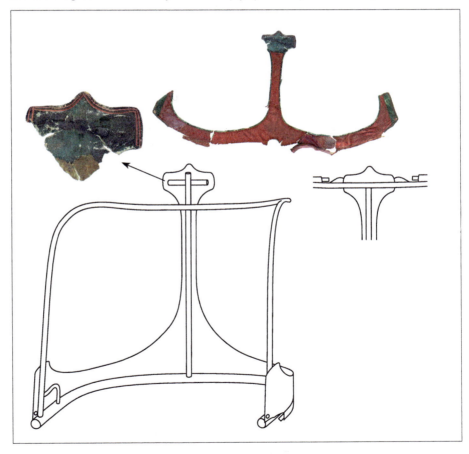

Figure II.29. Reconstruction of the main casing, showing the interior, with two suggestions as how the centre part would have been attached to the top railing. The cross-shaped extension of the central rod to support the tripartite section of the central upgoing part is hypothetical: there are no archaeological parallels to such a construction.

it. It is probable that the tripartite section rested on a cross piece, based on the discoloration on the verso (Figure II.29), which would make this piece visible. However, it is possible that the side portions were supported by the upper railing, and that the small protruding central element stuck out above the railing (Figure II.29B), and was able to move back and forth a bit (although the two layers of leather would have prohibited extreme movement). There are no examples known of chariot bodies that have special extensions to the wooden frame to support the tripartite top of the main casing. The back of the tripartite piece has pieces of red leather emerging from it (L3 #002, Cat. No. 44). These are made by the pushing through of the decoration on the recto, and form toggles. Possibly additional straps were wound around these, or secured in some other way, affixing this piece to the chariot frame.

The main casing was reversible. One side is red with green accents, and a green tripartite top, with red accents; the central section is discoloured, probably due to contact with the strut. The other side is entirely green, with red accents, and only faint discolouration on the central vertical section. Based on the finish of the decorated edge-binding, the green side should have been more visible; indeed, used with the red siding fill (below), it would have made a striking contrast. However, the possible connection points for the tripartite section discussed above only occur on the green side of the main casing, and the seam that connects the tubes to the green side protrudes more than it does on the red side. Both sides show evidence for having been the exterior side and the more distinct impressions on the red side suggests that the other side, the green one, might have been favoured.

The siding fill (Figure II.30) is harder to reconstruct because there are so many pieces of red leather that might belong to it, and many are quite fragile, particularly as they are only one layer thick. This, like the main casing, was secured using a system of tubes and drawstrings, both at the top, sides, and bottom. The tubing at the top was folded over the frame (arrow in figure II.30), as indicated by wear marks and discoloration. The drawstrings were tied using toggle closures (for example, L1 #016, Cat. No. 73; Figure IV.1; II.30A). Whether the drawstrings were tied to the top railing, the central strut(s), or both, cannot be determined. Additional means of securing the siding is suggested by a series of slits in, for example, L1 #023 (Cat. No. 54). The area above the slits is much darker in colour, while the slits are located in areas that are discoloured, worn and torn. This suggests that this darker area was covered by another band of leather, and secured through these slits either by a series of individual lashings (Figure II.30B) or extensions emerging from the piece of leather covering (Figure II.30C). Despite the fact that the slits have no bindings or edgings, they are deliberate. As they are not reinforced like so many other openings, they do not seem to be part of the original design, but might have been made shortly after the initial installation in order to solve a problem; the bright colour and the absence of wear in the area under the band also support this idea. It is hard for us to judge why and when the Egyptians chose to use edge bindings and reinforcements around holes; certainly, the edges of these slits do not seem to have suffered due to an absence of binding. Curiously, the leather is not wrinkled, suggesting that the overlying piece was not tied very tightly. As the edges of the slits show only slight stress on their top edges, it is probable that the connection that was being made did not require too much tension.

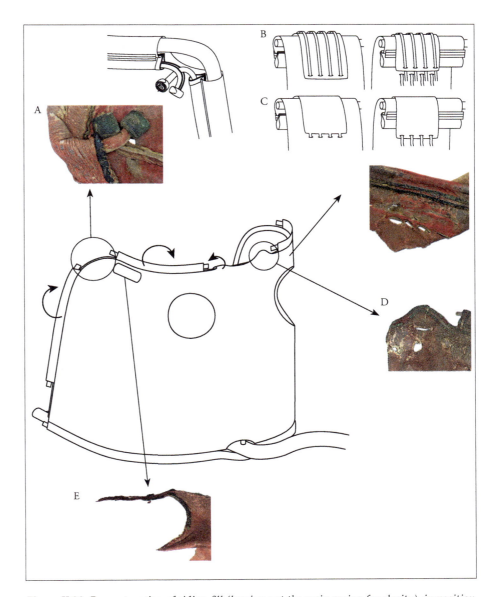

Figure II.30. Reconstruction of siding fill (leaving out the main casing for clarity), in position at the body of the chariot. A) The attachment of the corner between the upper horizontal part and the vertical back part, seen from the interior; B, C) The two possibilities of secondary attachment areas, seen from the exterior and interior respectively. The example with the four slits could have been positioned at the floor railing instead of the top railing; D) The scallop-shaped extension of the siding fill flanking the vertical centre part of the main casing; E) The cut out hand-grip.

The bottom of the siding fill was also secured by a tube and drawstrings, with a passepoil between the casing and the tube, giving strength to the join. The tube was probably folded around the floor frame too (for example, L1 #016, Cat. No. 73), as is attested by their discoloration. Indeed, one piece of tubing (L6 #001, Cat. No. 60) was possibly repaired using (possibly) re-used leather, and reinforced with a passepoil, which suggests that it was not visible to the viewer. The top of the siding, flanking its centre (L2 #008A, Cat. No. 56), has two scallops, with a horizontal slit (which is intended as opposed to the perforation below this slit, which, like others nearby, seems to be due to damage; *cf.* above L2 #008B, Cat. No. 56), beneath it. Through these a strap could pass, after the scalloped portion was folded over the top railing (Figure II.30D). The slit clearly shows stress from a strap that was pulled through to secure it to the wooden frame. Remarkably, the decorative rounded top must have been folded over the railing and secured with a strap that ran through the slit, rendering it invisible (Figure II.30D). The edges have no (reinforcement) bindings, as seen with original holes in the main casing as well as in the case of the apertures in the siding fill. Thus, this system of attachment does not seem original to the construction of the chariot, but a secondary solution to a problem that was noticed after the chariot's fabrication and use, with a simple strip of leather being used to secure this piece to the chariot body. If this is true, the scallops were, possibly, meant to stand up straight.

Two fragments of tubes set at right angles to each other, separated by a space, and attached to a large piece of red leather form fragment L6 #001 (Cat. No. 60; Figure II.30). This spacing enables both tubes to be folded around the framework. A slit, not reinforced and comparable to the ones discussed before (L1 #023, Cat. No. 54), is positioned slightly below the horizontal tube. The long fragment of tube was probably folded around the horizontal top railing of the chariot frame, and the smaller one around the vertical rod marking the back corner of the chariot (Figure II.30). Note that a short length of the horizontal tube, at the end, has an extension that retains its bright red colour. This might have been because it was replaced shortly before the leather was buried – it is impossible for the colour to be due to the fact that this area had been covered and protected by a fold, as the area directly adjacent to it is much worn and faded. Overall, this piece shows less wear than others, such as L1 #001 (Cat. No. 50) and L1 #023 (Cat. No. 54).

A curious feature of the siding fill is the fenestration, which appears to be asymmetrical, based on the measurements that could be made without damaging the piece (Figure II.29). The asymmetry might be indicative of different usages for each aperture: one might have held a large quiver, suitable for spears, while the other might have been for a quiver for arrows.

One piece of the siding fill shows evidence of having an opening that served as a hand-grip (Figure II.30E), a feature that is found on chariots from the Amarna period onward. These are located at the sides and, usually, more towards the back, of chariots.

The question arises whether or not the main casing and siding fill were used together. If they were used simultaneously, each with tubes and drawstrings, then how were they attached to the body or to one another without interfering with each other? It is probable that the siding fill was folded *around* the frame, both at the top and bottom, while the main casing might have been placed over the siding fill and resting on (rather than folding over) the floor frame, which would make the placement of the latter over the former possible. The space between the two scalloped parts on top of the siding fill would be admirably filled by the tripartite section of the main casing. It is also possible that the two coverings were used independently. Certainly, the construction of both made it fairly easy to remove and re-fix them, and different coverings might have depended on whatever use the chariot was pressed into at any given time. Of course, there is the question as to why the siding fill was of a single layer of leather, and the main casing was double layered. Perhaps this indicates that the latter was the more permanent and usual covering of the chariot, which also would have served to reinforce the framework of the chariot body.

II.5.2. Support Straps

The most difficult elements to identify in terms of specific location on the chariot are the straps. There are several strips of red leather of different widths (such as BI-005, Cat. No. 104 and BI-014, Cat. No. 107 and BI-012, Cat. No. 109), that could have been used to secure various elements, which were kept in reserve for repairs.

Some pieces, however, have been identified as a pair of support straps (Figure II.28; BI-001, Cat. No. 81 is a complete example; the second near complete one is BI-006, Cat. No. 82 with various fragments probably belong to this one, Cat. No. 83-87) that are made of sturdy beige leather with green accents, and figure frequently in representations of chariots from the 19th Dynasty onwards (but, thus, the archaeological remains, see section II.1.3. 'Support Straps', suggests that they were used before this too). The solid, broad section was wrapped around the top railing (Figure II.31A), the two emerging strands were pushed through loops, and stretched to the floor frame, to which they were tied, as is attested by the way in which the ends are bunched (Figure II.31B). The diameter of the solid piece, when folded, matches that of the top railing of Tutankhamun's chariots.

II.5.3. Bow-Case

Parts of the red and green bow-case (top #30, Cat. No. 91; #31, bottom Cat. No. 92, flap LI #015, Cat. No. 90; Figure II.31) are relatively straightforward to identify, although no portions of the body that would fit between these parts have been recognised. The bottom part of the bow-case is secured to the chariot by a strong, thick piece of beige leather, with a green reinforcement, passing through a tunnel with an aperture (its continuation might be #38, Cat. No. 111). The aperture in the tunnel, and the reinforcement of the leather band might have provided additional stability to the bow-case. Another set of narrow green and beige straps attached to a pair of reinforced ovals flanking the main tunnel strengthen the bow-case's attachment to the chariot frame. The most suitable position of such a bow-case, which would have been fairly big relative to the chariot, is with the bottom in the far back corner (Figure II.31C), which would offer enough possibilities to fasten it, diagonally over the side towards the top front. It is not entirely impossible that somehow the support straps were invovled in (further) securing the bow-case, but only when the siding fill was not installed, unless the support straps would go over it (imagery, however, does not show such a construction).

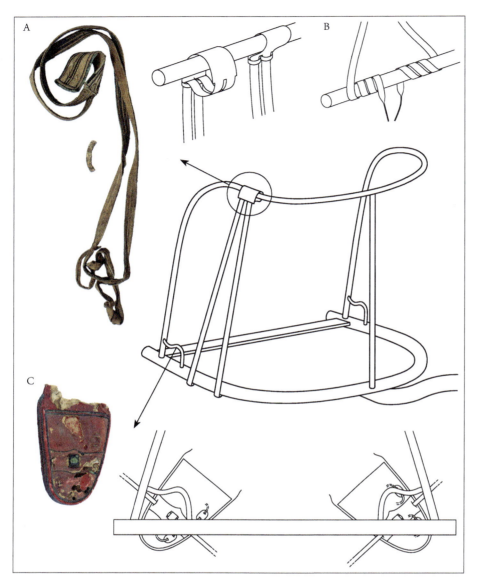

Figure II.31. The support straps that reinforces the wooden frame of the body of the chariot and bow-case. The straps in A are shown from the interior; B) Suggestion how the straps were attached to the floor frame; C) The bottom of the bow-case, seen from the interior, and how it might have been attached to the chariot.

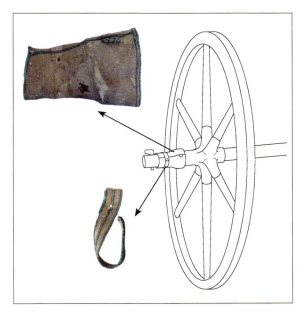

Figure II.32. The nave hoop and the strap that secures it around the wheel.

II.5.4. Nave Hoops

The nave hoops (#33 and #34. Cat. No. 88; Figure II.32) are easily identifiable, and also made of beige and green leather. The seams closing the nave hoops are sewn with interlocking or double running stitch, with a passepoil, making the connection very strong. The nave hoops were further secured by straps (for example, BI-024, -025, Cat. Nos. 86, 87) that have left their shadow on them. This combination of beige and green leather is used for the more functional portions of the ensemble.

II.5.5. Neckstraps and Girths

The beige and green neckstraps are clearly identifiable as well (#37, #39, Cat. No. 103). These might have been connected to the girths (#40, #41, Cat. No. 96; incomplete) using a toggle (BI-028, Cat. No. 117). This is a secure means of fastening, and its brilliant red and green colouring would complement the reinforced floral motif on the girth.

II.5.6. Various

One enigmatic piece (L3 #004F) is particularly difficult to situate, but might be some sort of holder to stabilise the bow-case, quiver, or spear container. The roundel that decorates it is a feature that is often seen on bow-cases and quivers in representations. It would have been secured to the top railing and floor frame with the strap that were attached to the decorated elongated centre part (Figure II.33).

There are several fragments of both beige and red leather straps of different widths and thicknesses that were presumably used to reinforce joins/connections in the chariot, or served as straps to secure weapons or other items to the chariot. One is wrapped up tidily (BI-027, Cat. No. 161), perhaps because it was meant to be used thus, rather than because it was stored in this manner. Some of the thick, beige leather ones might even have served as reins.

The roles of some pieces have yet to be clarified. A pair of beige and green decorated bands (#35, #36, Cat. No. 97) might be placed on the horse itself as their decoration echoes that of the neckstrap and girth. A red piece of leather with slits at one edge (L1 #009, Cat. No. 121) might be related to the body of the chariot, and be part of some sort of attachment feature. A unique piece of red leather with a repoussé line and circle that surrounds the holes (#32, Cat. No. 134), appears to have slid over some hard object. This might have had a ridge on it, which was the source for the repoussé.

The assemblage lacks a quiver and clearly identified reins, headstall, and yoke saddle pads. The absence of a quiver is particularly odd, as the bow-case is present. However, Maiherpri, whose tomb was found intact, had three quivers, but no bow-case. Possibly, the quiver was worn by the charioteer as the small size of the chariot might not have had enough space after the bow-case would have been attached (Figure II.34).

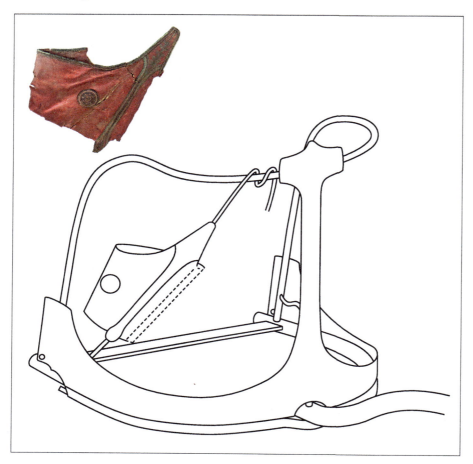

Figure II.33. Hypothetical reconstruction of the enigmatic holder(?) in the chariot. A) A big quiver (for spears) could be put in with its bottom resting on and sticking out from the top railing. The dashed line indicates uncertainty (the closing of the tube). Cf. Figure VI.7 where a big quiver is shown hanging diagonally along the side, though pointing towards the back (and resting on the top railing?). Alternative to this interpretation is the use to further secure the bow-case at the outer side of the chariot.

Figure II.34. Artist's impression of the Tano chariot. Top, the chariot with main casing only; bottom, also with the siding fill.

DECONSTRUCTING AND CONSTRUCTION | 71

III. Looking at Skin

Analysis of the Leather

Lucy Skinner

III.1. Introduction

In the course of documenting the Tano chariot leather pieces, analyses of the leather itself were made, including studies on how it was produced and coloured. Questions also arose as to whether the hide of a particular animal might have been favoured, as well as which particular parts of the hide, depending on where and how the leather was being used.

Leather is not a homogenous material. It varies considerably between animal species, even over the area of one hide, in terms of thickness, appearance, strength, stretch and drape. Once the hide has been selected, the type of processing used and the skill of the leatherworker will change the properties of the final material. The processing stages involved in creating a sheet of durable leather include dehairing and defleshing the skin, tanning or leathering (pseudo-tannages that do not impart a permanent preservative effect on the skin) it to render it non-putrescible, dressing the leather with fats or oils to protect and make it supple, and finally colouring it using dye or stains.

Thus, the Tano leather provides an opportunity to investigate the technological choices that were made by the ancient leatherworkers to create the leather for a chariot, such as the cladding and harnessing. The work is also a first step towards extrapolating a broader view of ancient trade, animal husbandry, agriculture and social contexts. However, such investigations rely on comparative material from contemporary archaeological sources. The Tano leather, despite now consisting of well over 300 fragments, is in fact all from one single group (chariot leather and its accoutrements) and it is of unknown provenance and date, and thus wider inferences may not be possible.

Moreover, it is known that skin preparation techniques greatly influence the degree of preservation of an archaeological leather object. Therefore, in order to devise a conservation treatment protocol for the chariot leather, a thorough understanding of the micro-structure of skin and the chemistry and materials involved in turning it into leather, is vital. It is also necessary to identify the additional factors that may have influenced the leather's condition – such as the original archaeological milieu and the storage environment in the Egyptian Museum (Cairo). Before discussing the Tano leather directly, the first section of this chapter gives an overview of the raw material (skin) and leather making in ancient Egypt, including the stages of manipulation to create a durable and attractive material and the appropriate methods to investigate it.

III.2. The Raw Material: Skin

The raw material of leather is animal skin. Most vertebrate animal skins can be converted into leather, including mammals, reptiles, birds and fish, but typically mammal hides and skins are used.

Technical and chemical analyses of the Tano leather provide significant information about its working properties and function, as well as the technologies used to produce it and why in particular these might have been chosen. Analyses also contribute to understanding the leather's original appearance. For instance, one can better understand the degree of specialisation and skill of the craftsmen and quality of the chariot leather by determining how much importance was given towards selection of a certain animal species (or even choosing different parts of one hide) for different parts in the chariot and its accompanying harnessing and accoutrements.

III.2.1. Structure

'Hides' (the skin of large animals, such as cattle) and 'skin' (referring typically to smaller animals such as sheep or goat) of mammals, are similar in structure to each other, but vary in size of overall area, thickness and the proportion of their different components and as a result, properties such as strength, stretch and flexibility.

The fibrous network of animal skin is composed of a protein, collagen, which is a long chain polypeptide that twists into a helical shape (Figure III.1). The collagen molecule is formed of three of these helices that coil together to form a triple helix and is further stabilised by hydrogen bonds between the adjacent chains in the triple helix. Collagen molecules will bunch together forming fibrils,

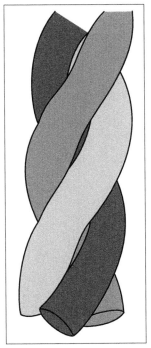

Figure III.1. A collagen molecule. After: Haines (2006a: Figure 2.6).

which in turn group to form fibre bundles, all of which are held together by electrostatic salt-links and covalent intermolecular bonds (Haines, 2006a). The twisting and splicing together of ever-increasing strands of collagen gives the fibres similar properties to a rope – flexible yet very strong, until deterioration makes the strands become frayed and begin to unravel (Michel, 2014: 24).

The cross section of mammalian skin changes throughout its depth (Figure III.2). These features are small and generally only clearly visible microscopically. The surface layer of skin, before it is converted into leather, is the epidermis. This lies over the grain layer. Hair, deriving from the grain, grows upwards at a slight angle through the epidermis. In full grained leather, hair follicle holes remain preserved and visible on the grain surface, usually even after processing (Haines, 1981: 9; Michel, 2014). This is the main feature that archaeologists use to identify species, since the distribution of these follicles is characteristic for each different species (see below). Sometimes the grain surface is removed from the leather in order to create a buff 'new-buck' appearance to the skin, which also means that the hair follicles are completely removed (Skinner & Veldmeijer, 2015).

Other structures in the grain layer include blood vessels, sweat and sebaceous glands and erector pili muscles. The greater the number of structures in the living skin, the 'looser' the grain layer will be in the finished leather, because during processing, epidermal structures are removed leaving behind voids. The grain merges into the corium, which contains the collagen fibre bundles of larger size, interwoven at a higher angle than in the grain, and hence is much stronger than the grain layer (Haines, 2006b: 20).

The flesh layer is located at the base of the corium. It contains fat cells and divides the skin from the flesh and muscles. The flesh layer does not form part of finished leather and is removed during processing, in order to allow solutions involved in tanning and leathering to enter into the fibrous collagen network.

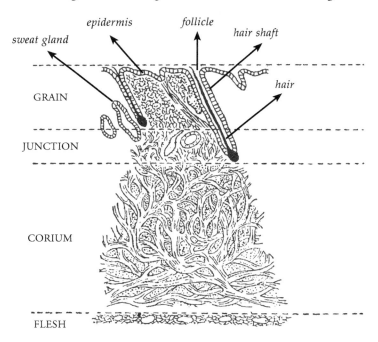

Figure III.2. The skin cross section. After: Haines (2006b: Figure 3.2).

III.2.2. Areas Within a Skin

Animal hides are not homogenous and there are wide differences between the butt, belly, neck and axilla region in terms of thickness, strength, hair follicle density and grain texture (Figure III.3; Michel, 2014: 27-30). For instance, the belly area of a hide is thin, hair is sparse and projects at a low angle from the skin, and collagen fibres are loose – allowing for expansion of the belly when the animal breathes, eats and, if female, is pregnant. Leather made with belly skin is loose, and unsuitable for many functions because it easily becomes stretched and baggy (Michel, 2014: 28). Similarly, the axillae areas of a hide, *i.e.* the area where the limbs meet the body, is at a low angle of weave and the skin is at its thinnest and stretchiness (Haines, 1981: 13). This part produces the poorest quality leather of the entire hide and consequentially leatherworkers try to avoid using it, except for backings and linings where these adverse properties do not matter (Michel & Daniels, 2009). Skin from the neck is at its thickest and tends to develop deep creases and wrinkles during the animal's life, which are perpetuated in the hide (Michel, 2014: 27). The butt area of a hide has a particularly compact fibre structure and the smoothest grain. It will withstand abrasion, impact and the greatest weight, especially in the long-direction – following the length of the animal and is considered the part of the skin with the highest quality (Michel, 2014: 27).

There is a certain degree of directionality in the way the collagen fibres are orientated within an animal hide, which influences the strength and ease with which the finished leather stretches. The identification of the region of a hide from which (part of) a leather object originates provides some insights into the knowledge of the ancient leatherworker, as well as the use of an object. Even today, leatherworkers give great importance to selecting leather from a particular part of the hide for different purposes, and in cutting from a hide in a certain orientation in line with, or against, the direction of hair growth (Figure III.4). This is particularly important with straps and edgings – any piece that is going to be put under force or subjected to abrasion. The strongest straps are made from strips of leather taken from the area running along the length of the animal, in line with the backbone as in such an orientation the leather will have the minimum stretch (BLMRA, 1957: 339; Michel, 2014: 31).

III.2.3. Species

After the hairs have been removed during processing of the skin, the last vestiges of hairs – the follicles – retain their shape and arrangement, a record of the density and pattern of hair growth on the skin grain surface (Haines, 1981: 17; Michel, 2014: 30-39). The follicle pattern, usually referred to as 'grain pattern' is, as mentioned, specific for animal species.[34] Reference microphotographs of grain surface patterns of leather from different animal species in various publications (BLMRA, 1957; Haines, 1981; 2006; Michel, 2014; Waterer, 1968) offer images with which to

---

34 Species ID is also a process that can be executed analytically. Zooarchaeology by Mass Spectrometry (Zoo-MS) is a technique developed at York University for the identification of animal species by protein mass fingerprinting using a MALDI-TOF mass spectrometer (Collins *et al.*, 2010). Unfortunately, Zoo-MS is not available yet as a technique in Egypt and the current ban on the exportation of samples precludes any possibility of using this on the Tano leather to confirm the identifications that were made based on a visual study of the follicle pattern.

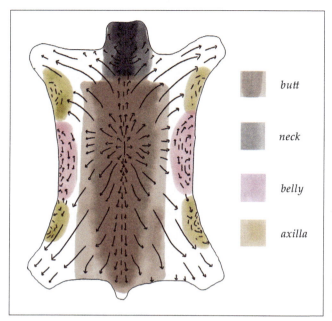

Figure III.3. Variations in the hide. Diagram by L. Skinner.

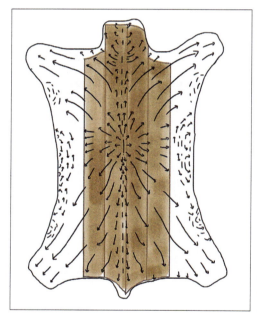

Figure III.4. The optimal way to cut strips from a hide to maximise strength. Diagram by L. Skinner.

compare the grain pattern of an unknown leather and enable identification. This method is not always straightforward, with differences in magnification and lighting making identification more complicated, and variations in the appearance of follicle patterns from different areas of the hide (see above), as well as the age of the animals possibly causing confusion. The best way to use this method is to have a collection of leather samples of known species, from different parts of the body (such as the neck, back and belly) and if possible to examine as many parts of the object as possible (Y. Fletcher, Personal Communication, 2017).

Cattle

Cattle were used in ancient Egypt for their meat, milk, as draught animals, and for their hides (Ikram, 1995: 8-15). Cattle hides have an average thickness of 4-6 mm and can be up to 4 m² in area. In comparison, a calf skin is a lot smaller, varying dependent on the animal's age. The hide of a six-month old calf is about 1.3 mm thick and covers approximately 1 m² in area (Haines, 2006b: 14).

In modern leather production, full thickness cattle hide is usually split through the corium, using a splitting machine. Splitting is done not only to double the yield by creating a flesh split and a grain split, but also to create two sheets of leather of more manageable and useful thickness. In antiquity, the technology to split a hide did not exist and thinning could only be achieved by shaving away the flesh surface using a sharp knife, a time-consuming and wasteful process which probably was only used to reduce the thickness of small pieces, cut from a full hide (Haines, 2006b: 13; Figure III.5A, B). Mature cattle skin has relatively large follicle holes, all of a similar diameter, which are spaced in roughly equidistant rows over the grain surface. Calf skin is like a miniature version of adult cattle hide – with a similar follicle pattern but the holes are smaller and closer together.

Goat/Sheep

Herds of goat and sheep were kept as livestock in ancient Egypt, for their milk, meat and hair/wool used to manufacture textiles; the skin was used to make leather (Ikram, 1995: 16-19). Goatskin typically ranges in thickness from 1-3 mm with collagen fibre bundles even in texture, and a medium angle of weave. There is a gradual increase in thickness of fibres from the grain to the corium of the skin, creating leather with strong and even texture throughout the full depth. It has compact fibres, but not as much drape as sheepskin, which tends to have a looser fibre network.

Sheepskin from woolbearing varieties produces skin of 2-3 mm thickness, which is fatty and loose textured with a weak network of collagen fibres. The fat concentrated at the grain junction (associated with the large number of hair follicles in wool sheepskin) can cause delamination (Reed, 1972: 42). Defleshing such fatty, loose-fibred skins is difficult, possibly resulting in flay cuts in the processed skin. This kind of sheepskin is better suited for 'hair-on' sheepskins than leather making. Modern domesticated sheep in Egypt are 'hair sheep', the descendents of the Asiatic mouflon, *Ovis orientalis*. Being adapted to a hot climate, they do not have wool-bearing coats. Rather, a large proportion of the coat is made up of straight hair and coarse kemp fibres (Clutton-Brock, 1989, 52-54; Ryder, 1958, 781-783). In appearance hair sheep look much like goat, but with hair that is finer (Michel, 2014: 37). Hair sheepskins are around 0.8-1 mm in thickness, so thinner than goatskin, with a fine and compact grain merging smoothly into the corium, which is not liable to delamination. The skin is of high quality, smooth and strong relative to its thickness and well suited for gloving or garment leather. Nevertheless, goatskin is more hardwearing than hair sheepskin.

Goatskin appears to be quite textured on the back, neck and flank area with deep troughs in which the follicles are found, but the belly is smoother and the hair follicles orientated at a more acute angle (Figure III.5C). There are paw-print-like rows of primary and secondary hair follicles, grouped together. Wool sheepskin has fine follicle holes that are more closely grouped together than in

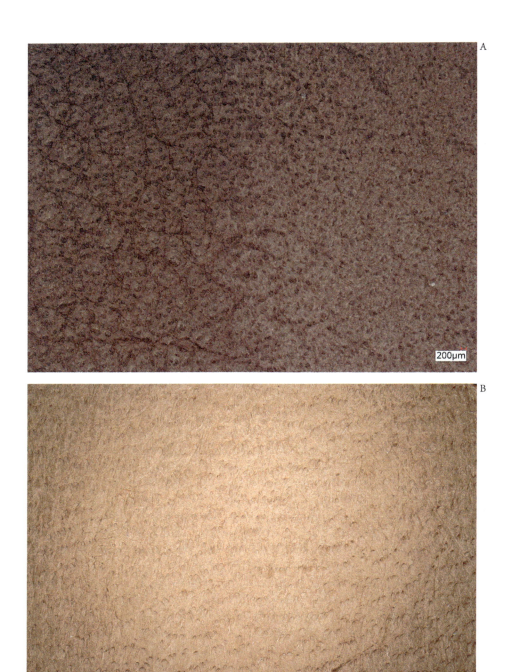

Figure III.5. Grain patterns: A) Cattle; B) Calf; C) Goat; D) Hair sheep. Photographs by L. Skinner.

C

D

goatskin, and the density of follicles is bigger (Figure III.5D). Hair sheepskin has primary and secondary hair follicles which group together in the same manner as goat. However, the grain appears to be smoother and the hair density is higher.

Calf, kid or lamb skin is much less likely to be scarred and scratched than leather made from adult hide or skin, because it has had less time to get hurt or attacked by other animals or insects (J. Vnouček, Personal Communication, 2017).

Other Animals

Other animals that could have been exploited for leather production in ancient Egypt include those from the Equus genus (horse and donkey). However, even though horse hide is known to make a superior quality leather (A. Covington, Personal Communication, 2017), draught animals are worth more to the owner alive than dead, and would only be slaughtered and used in leather production if they died from disease or exceeded their age of usefulness. Ancient Egyptian leatherworkers could also have had access to a wide array of wild animal species, which were hunted for meat (Ikram, 1995: 19-23) and for fur (the objects made from leopard skin from the tomb of Tutankhamun, Carter's Number 044q and 545 & 566, are good examples). The former group might include gazelle, oryx, ibex, or hartebeest. The skin of gazelle is reported on various objects, including the edging of a mummy brace in the Petrie Museum (London), musical instruments (Van Driel-Murray, 2000: 302) and cut leather loincloths (Van Driel-Murray, 2000: 302; Vogelsang-Eastwood, 1993: 16-31). However, it has not yet been scientifically proven that gazelle skin was used for loincloths, despite repeated claims, and every example examined by the present author of this kind of loincloth is lacking a grain surface (having been removed during processing). Consequently, there are no follicle patterns remaining with which to confirm species. Wild animal skin would be more heavily marked on the grain surface by, for example, scratching by thorny bushes, or scars caused by fighting with other animals. Skin biting or burrowing insects such as ticks or warble fly will also frequently leave their mark on leather (A. Lama, Personal Communication, 2017). Male animals – which tend to be more prone to fighting – produce the toughest but also the most scarred leather, while young animals are less likely to have scarred and scratched skin as they have had less time to be injured or attacked by other creatures (J. Vnouček, Personal Communication, 2017).

III.3. Skin Processing

Due to the lack of archaeological evidence for leather processing sites from ancient Egypt (see also IV.1. 'Manufacturing Chariot and Chariot Related Leathers'), our current knowledge about this first stage of the ancient Egyptian leather industry is mainly based on images in tombs, leather production from other parts of the world (especially Medieval Europe) or modern analogies (Schwarz, 2000). Unfortunately, tomb images tend to suggest a rather simplified version of the process, and therefore there are some notable gaps in the depictions, such as the unsavory processes of skinning or defleshing the animal (Schwarz, 2002; Van Driel-Murray, 2000: 301). The famous scene in the tomb of Rekhmire (TT100; Davies, 1943: LI-LIV) is the most elaborate example of a depiction of skin processing known from antiquity but it lacks explanatory inscriptions and so there is ambiguity in the interpretation of some pictured activities (Schwarz, 2002: 484). For example, in one part of the scene, a skin is held taught by the craftsman's feet and is being scraped with a small tool, held in both hands over a low block on the ground. This could show the dehairing of the skin, although there is no surviving sign of colour variation and/or texture on the skins being scraped to indicate that the hair is still attached (Schwarz, 2000: 46) – so it is possible that this part of the scene in fact illustrates defleshing.

It is rare for a sheet of leather to be produced completely devoid of damage on the grain surface from insect bite bumps or scratches and scars from thorns and fighting. Flaying cuts are frequently inflicted when the animal is skinned and these will expand in size when the skin is stretched. Scrapes and grazes can occur when a skin is dehaired and defleshed. Other signs left from skin preparation include incomplete dehairing of the grain. All these signals can be found on a leather artefact, although, if the leatherworker can cut around the flaw, and use unblemished skin, he is likely to do so, and the damaged leather is discarded or used as a rag.

In modern leather processing, hair is released from the epidermis of the skin by opening up the fibres using lime, and allowing the hairs to be easily pulled out, but lime seems not to have been used in ancient Egypt for this purpose (Van Driel-Murray, 2000: 304). Perhaps hair slippage was induced by controlled rotting of the hide in flowing water, or by sweating a pile of hides to bring on hair slippage, as was done in Medieval and post-Medieval periods (Thomson, 2006c: 68). The above-mentioned scene in Rekhmire's tomb does not show this part of skin processing, but there is one relief fragment in Berlin (ÄM 19782; Schwarz, 2000: 47, Cat. C, No. 22, 24 [no page numbers]) showing men scraping a hide with a half-moon shaped knife while it is stretched on a frame. It is possible to dehair and deflesh a hide by tying the raw skin to a frame, and then wet or dry scraping it. This technique is still used sometimes by Native Americans for tanning (especially deer) skin, which results in soft grain-off leather (Baillargeon & Canadian Museum of Civilization, 2010). Another possibility is that the actions depicted in ÄM 19782 is the preparation of parchment, not leather. Drying frames are still used to this day in the production of parchment. The frame hold the skin taught for defleshing, dehairing, stretching and thinning, with a half-moon shaped knife (called a lunette or lumella; Waterer, 1956) to produce a flat paper-like sheet (Reed, 1972). There are examples of thin parchment and parchment-like materials from ancient Egypt that were used as painting surfaces (*e.g.* Elnaggar *et al.*, 2016: 137; Kemp, 2012: 278, pl. XLV) and also stretched over instruments as a soundboard (Veldmeijer, 2017: 71, 164-168; Veldmeijer & Skinner, In Press).

The next stage of skin processing, leathering or tanning, provides the skin or hide with durability and resistance to microbiological attack, ensuring that it does not easily revert back to the raw state (Thomson & Kite, 2006), while also imparting beneficial qualities to the skin, such as softness and flexibility by preventing the collagen fibres in the skin from sticking together once it is dried (Covington, 2006). The types of preservative materials available to the ancient leatherworker would have included various oils and fats of animal and plant origin, alum, and vegetal materials that are rich in polyphenolic tannins (Reed, 1972; Schwarz, 2000: 25-35; Skinner, 2007: 125-127; Thomson, 2006c: 66-68; Van Driel-Murray, 2000: 302, 306).

Leathering processes are those that do not impart a permanent preservative effect on the skin. The two most relevant leathering processes to ancient Egyptian material include alum tawing and fat/oil dressing. Potash alum alone reacts weakly with collagen, but when the alum is applied to skin in combination with flour, water, salt and egg yolk, the fibre structure of the skin is filled and fibres lubricated, creating a soft white 'tawed' leather. Tawing works very effectively as a process unless the leather gets wet, in which case the preservative effects are reversed (Covington, 2006). Ancient Egyptians had access to alum (Lucas & Harris, 2012: 258) and it is possible that leather was prepared by alum tawing, but there has never been any reliable scientific analysis carried out to confirm this (Van Driel-Murray, 2000: 304). Moreover, alum was used as mordant for organic dyes (Van Driel-Murray 2000; Ikram *et al.*, 2018), complicating its identification as leathering agent.

Oil tanning involves the use of unsaturated fatty acids such as brain or fish liver oil. The curing effect of oil tanning on the skin is due to an aldehydic reaction and oxidation of the fats when they are manipulated and exposed to warmth and air (Covington, 2006: 30). Oil dressing, distinct from oil tanning, simply involves the application of fatty or oil based materials to a skin or hide and working this deeply into the skin to coat the fibrous collagen structure (Thomson, 2006b: 1), a procedure probably used in pharaonic Egypt (Schwarz, 2000: 31-32; Van Driel-Murray, 2000: 303). Another vignette that is part of the leatherworking scene in Rekhmire's tomb (Davies, 1943: LII-LIV) shows an animal hide, hair still attached, being dipped into a large vessel, possibly containing oil as part of oil dressing the leather (Schwarz, 2000: 60). If this is oil dressing, there is nothing to identify the oils used but if one looks at what was available in Egypt during the New Kingdom (Hepper, 2009: 19) the most likely suspects are sesame oil or castor oil (Moreno Garcia, 2018) but to date, only one analytical study is known which identifies fats or oils used to tan or dress hides from ancient Egypt (Trommer, 2005: 144; concerning oils from the tomb of Tutankhamun, see Carter, 1927: 176-178).

Polyphenols, contained in many plant materials, can be used in leather tanning. Seed pods of one of the most common trees in Egypt – the Egyptian mimosa (*Acacia nilotica* sp.) (Boulos, 1999: 367-368; Springuel, 2006: 74) provide an excellent local source of a condensed type of vegetable tannin known locally as 'sunt' or 'garad', which is rich in polyphenols (for more information on vegetable tanning using acacia tree pods see Knew, 1947: 1-8; Lamb, 1981: 58-62; Skinner, 2011: 49-57). Leather tanned with vegetable tannins is extremely durable and will have, if tanned with mimosa, a pale beige colour when first produced but will darken over time. The existence of vegetable tanned leather in Egypt from the pharaonic era, however, is uncertain (Schwarz, 2000: 49-50; Van Driel-Murray 2000, 304). Records of a 1st millennium BC Sumerian text recording the use of 'gall nuts' for tanning hides in Mesopotamia has been found to be wrongly translated and is in fact describing the use of madder for colouring (Soldt, 1990: 347). In recent decades scholars have come to generally believe that vegetable tanning was not introduced to Egypt until the Greco-Roman period but that the field is in need of reassessment using analytical science (Van Driel-Murray, 2000: 305-306). Some recent research has found the presence of hydrolysable vegetable tannins in Middle Kingdom leather from Nubian contexts (in the Metropolitan Museum of Art; MMA 31.3.88), using High Performance Liquid Chromatography (HPLC;

Elnaggar *et al.*, 2016: 139). Though it is a very interesting result, the impact of this research is limited by there only being a small number of objects investigated in the study.

A simpler method for indicating the presence of vegetable tannins does exist, using a micro-chemical spot test involving ferric chloride (for further details about this test consult, see Thomson, 2006a; Van Driel-Murray, 2002). It should be noted that the chemical spot tests used to detect vegetable tannins can give unreliable results if the leather is contaminated with soil minerals or coloured with vegetable dyes (see for more results as well as a discussion on the problems related to this test Thomson, 2006a: 59; Van Driel-Murray, 2002: 19-20; Veldmeijer, 2012: 29-30; 2016: 18; Van Roode & Veldmeijer, 2005). Clearly, until further research is carried out, it cannot be ascertained for certain whether the ancient Egyptians or Nubians really used vegetable tannins or not.[35]

III.4. The Degradation of Skin

The reason for the apparent heavy chemical degradation of ancient Egyptian leather has not been thoroughly studied (Loschwitz, 2009) but there have been several in depth studies of the degradation of historic leather (Larsen, 2008; 2012; Larsen *et al.*, 1994; 2005). Their conclusions are that the age of the leather is certainly a factor in the level of degradation, as fats and oils in the leather can, over time, catalyse the oxidation of proteins. Oxidation as well as hydrolysis are sped up by heat, air pollution and acidic microenvironments.

Heating raw skin or leather in water has a damaging effect on the collagen. This is because, at a certain temperature, the hydrogen bonds will break in a process known as 'hydrolysis', causing untwisting and shrinkage of the triple helix (Haines, 2006a: 9). The 'shrinkage-temperature' (T_s) has been exceeded and the leather is 'denatured'. If the denatured leather continues to boil, eventually the collagen will become gelatinised and dissolve in water, forming hide glue. In fact, this is the method used to manufacture animal hide glue (Kite, 2006: 192). In the case of vegetable tanned leather animal hide, it can take several hours to hydrolyse collagen completely to form glue. In contrast, shrinkage temperature tests that have been carried out on ancient Egyptian leather samples shows that even at room temperature, collagen can dissolve in water, and elevated humidity will cause the leather to become sticky, a situation also identified in the leather from the tomb of Tutankhamun (Figure III.6; Carter, 1933: 164; Lucas, 1927: 175-176; Veldmeijer, 2011a: 35-41; see Veldmeijer, 2011b: esp. 93-143, 257-261) and from Amarna (see Appendix II), to name a few examples. This is a reaction that does not normally happen to leather in arid environments (Larsen, 2012: 61). Other types of degradation witnessed in ancient Egyptian leather includes powdering and stiffening and general loss of strength and integrity, resulting in breakage. In the author's personal experience, it can at times be a challenge to distinguish between defects in the leather caused by insect bites, scars and flaying cuts and faults caused by deterioration of the leather over time.

---

35 New research exploring the technology of skin processing, including animal species identification, colour analysis and identification of materials and methods, from ancient Egypt and Nubia (on the basis of objects in the British Museum, London), is ongoing by the author, the results of which will be expected in the near future.

III.5. The Tano Leather

III.5.1. Condition

The first impression of the leather, as the layers of card and brown paper folders were removed from the original wooden trays, and opened, was that it was incredibly well preserved. However, it was soon noticed that there was an accumulation of powdered leather at the bottom of the paper folders. Moreover, in the case of the red and the green stained leather, the vibrant coloured layer on the surface, so rarely seen preserved to this extraordinary extent and with a general impression of suppleness and softness to the leather, disguised its immense fragility (Figure III.7B). The upper (grain) surface of the red and green leather, which is the side to which the colour is applied, continues to hold together well (partly due to cohesion provided by the applied coloured layer). The layer, however, is thin, and beneath it the corium and flesh layers are powdery (Figure III.7A), and the fibrous network of leather fibres have very little strength remaining. The visible effect of this degradation is significant breakage and tearing of the main casing and siding fill, embrittlement in some small areas, while in other cases entire sections are fragmented into hundreds of pieces. At what point in time the coloured parts of the Tano leather became broken into so many pieces remains unclear, though some damage must have occurred at the time it was removed from its find spot, and when it was subsequently boxed up, transported and sold on the antiquities market. It is likely, however, that the leather suffered most, including becoming misshapen and significantly broken, after it was placed in storage in the museum, suffering from the elevated and fluctuating humidity levels and pollution, as well as years of periodic handling and being compressed inside the tightly packed wooden trays and paper folders. The beige leather of the harnessing and nave

Figure III.6. Degraded leather from Amarna (ÄM AM 032c), showing gelatinisation of the leather. Scale bar is 10 mm. Courtesy of the Ägyptisches Museum und Papyrussammlung (Berlin).

hoops is in a better state of preservation. This leather is stiff and cannot be flexed. It is not powdering and on the whole is not broken either. It is likely that little if any additional oils were applied to the beige leather, because it was not necessary or desirable for it to be particularly soft and flexible. As noted above, it is known that the oxidation of proteins is catalysed by fats and oils, and if the beige leather contains less, this might explain why it is in better condition. The beige leather also lacks the same degree of surface sheen as the green and red leather and so was perhaps not 'dressed' or polished in the same way (for further description of these finishes, see below).

Other indications of chemical degradation are the dark and glossy spots or splashes located on several of the coloured and beige fragments. These appear to be caused by water, which has dripped or splashed onto the leather at some point

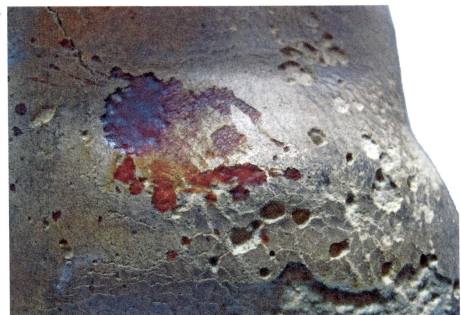

Figure III.7. Degradation of the Tano leather. A) Broken fragments and leather powder as it was found in the bottom of L5; B) Gelatinisation from water splash on the nave hoop. Insect grazing damage (the pits and holes on the surface) is also visible. Photographs by L. Skinner.

after recovery, and has caused gelatinisation of the collagen (Figure III.7B). This is irreversible damage but conservation intervention as part of this project focused on stopping any further deterioration from occurring.

The flesh surface of the Tano leather is almost always smooth, fine-fibred, thoroughly scraped and cleaned, without any traces remaining from the flesh. The exception to this is where the leather was (originally) double sided, *i.e.* the main casing (two sheets stitched together back-to-back to create a red side and a green side), but now sections of the flesh surface have been revealed after the two layer have become detached, showing the interior surface. Figure III.8A shows part of the green side that has detached, revealing the flesh surface of the red leather. Compared to Figure III.8B, the difference in appearance is clear. For pieces where the flesh surface would be hidden from sight, the degree of cleaning and finishing seems not as high as where it is visible, indicating that the leatherworker knew that this surface would be hidden and hence spent less time scraping and cleaning it. On the other hand, it is possible, though less likely, that it looks rougher merely because it was protected from abrasion whereas other, exposed parts have been rubbed smooth meaning they have lost any of the remaining flesh surface.

III.5.2. Skin Type

The Red/Green Leather

The leather varies quite considerably in quality. For instance, L1 #005 (Cat. No. 68) shows leather of deep and uneven texture in the grain that suggests that leather from the flanks/belly of an animal was used. Some sections examined have extremely smooth grain surfaces, for example, in the centre of L3 #004 (Cat. No. 46). The main portion probably comes from the butt and back of the animal and is smooth in texture on the grain, with regular follicle holes. L2 #008 (Cat. No. 56) has curved cuts in the corners which appear to correspond to the axilla region of the hide – meaning that the leatherworkers were careful when cutting the leather to conceal or remove the substandard sections at the edges of the skin.

The photomicrograph in Figure III.9A of the follicle pattern shows wave-like rows, with larger holes (where primary hairs originally grew) next to a few smaller follicle holes left by the underfur – in a paw print-like pattern. This follicle pattern is typical for goatskin.

As can be seen in Figure III.9B, when compared to III.9A, there is considerable variation in the appearance of grain patterns between differently coloured parts of the Tano leather. These variations can be due to the skin preparation techniques (such as the amount of scraping and stretching that took place while the skin was still wet), stretching and wear from use (as explained, large parts, especially the siding fill, are heavily worn) and/or it is of the remains of the appearance and function of the skin while the animal was still alive. Figure III.9C shows characteristics of leather from the belly or flank, with hair follicles lying quite flat against the grain, whereas Figure III.9D shows large rounded follicles at a high angle, which is suggestive of hair that stuck up from the grain. This is what one would expect to see on the skin running along the spine of a goat (where the hair stands upright), for example. The follicle holes in cattle skin are similarly rounded but there is less variation in the size of the follicles on cattle hide and when the thickness of the skin is taken into account it is usually possible to tell them apart.

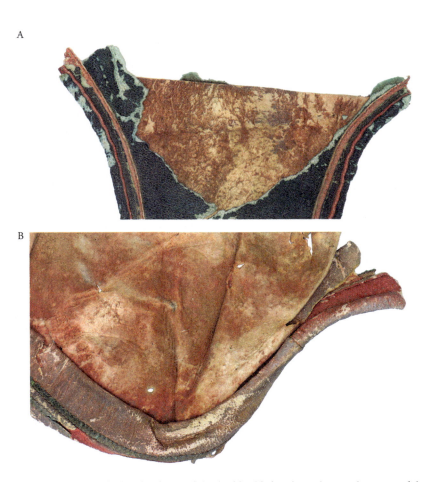

Figure III.8A) This flesh side of part of the double sided main casing retains more of the flesh surface than the flesh side in other parts (L3 #003, Cat. No. 45) – the leatherworker new it would not be visible because of the other (here: green) layer covering it; B) The smoother flesh surface of a part of the siding fill that has always been exposed (L1 #001, Cat. No. 50).

In the case of the tubes with drawstrings where there is occasionally appliqué of three strips of red and green leather, it was found that, in general, there is not always consistency in the direction in which the leather is cut from the hide (one can tell this by the orientation of the follicles). For example, in L2 007 (Cat. No. 137) the green edging has rows of follicle holes running in line with the length of the strip, meaning that stretch in the lengthwise direction is minimised, whereas the red strip next to it has large and clear follicles (now better visible because they are full of dirt) in rows running across the leather (Figure III.10A, B). Both appear to be made from goatskin. L1 #009 (Cat. No. 121) is a piece of a double-side leather with three slits along one edge which are stretched, suggesting that this piece was under some tension during use, possibly to further secure the siding fill to the wooden body of the chariot. At least eight wide parallel lines, which run across this section (especially visible on the recto of the object), look very much like the creases that run around the back of the neck of the animal. Neck leather is known to be the strongest section of the entire hide and so it seems the leatherworker carefully selected this piece of leather to ensure maximum strength. In L1 #014 (Cat. No. 72) a cross section through the drawstring can be seen. The leather is folded lengthwise to increase thickness and strength, but

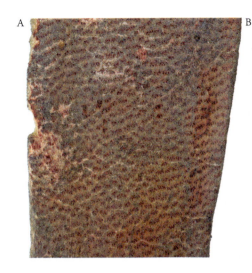

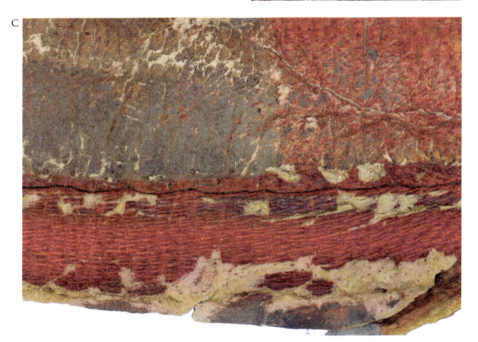

Figure III.9A. Details of the red leather (L2 #004, Cat. No. 167); B) The red and green leather in L3 #003 (Cat. No. 45) shows a fuller grain pattern; C) Leather from the belly with hair follicles lying flat in L1 #018 (Cat. No. 53); D) More rounded and larger follicles, possibly from the back, where there are more primary hairs along the spine of the animal (L2 #007, Cat. No. 137). Scale bar is 5 mm.

III.10A) L6 #004 (Cat. No. 62). Skin orientated to minimize stretch and maximize strength of the tubing; B) L6 #017 (Cat. No. 77). Skin is orientated in a way which does not maximize strength of this piece of tubing. Scale bar is 10 mm.

even one layer of this leather is over two times thicker than the tube through which it is fed. Nevertheless, the drawstring is composed of fine collagen fibres that are woven at a high angle, quite even across the depth of the hide and not too compact. This suggests that the leather comes from a thick part of a goatskin, and probably not calf or adult cattle, which would have larger fibre bundles that would be more compact. From a technological point of view, goatskin would be more practical than cattle hide for making pull cords because it is almost as strong (provided it is from larger, potentially male animals and from the thicker portions of the skin), but it is more flexible – meaning it can be pulled and fastened more easily and securely. The compact weave of cattle and calf leather means it could not have been easily stretched over and around edges or manipulated into soft and decorative edgings (Haines, 1981: 4). The only sections of the Tano chariot leather where the properties of a thick stiff hide such as cattle or even calf being used is for the nave hoops (#33 & 34, Cat. No. 88), harnessing such as girths (#40 & #41, Cat. No. 96) and neckstraps (#37 & #39, Cat. No. 103).

In terms of the thickness and softness, the main casing and siding fill leather (Cat. No. 43-79) could be made from either goatskin or hair sheepskin: as it is quite fine – generally a single layer is less than 1 mm thick. Even though the leather is relatively well preserved, the grain follicle pattern is quite difficult to see on these panels because of the red stain coating the surface. There are some areas where the fullness of the grain suggests goatskin, but where the grain surface is smooth it looks more like the skin of hair sheep.

The grain surface of the green and the red leather sections varies slightly: The surface of the green leather appears to be more textured and 'full' (plump). This is due, not necessarily to a difference in the animal species (where grain pattern is discernible, goatskin seem to be preferred) or processing of the skin, but the properties of the green stain which forms a thicker layer over the grain than the red stain and seems to enhance the contours of the grain surface. Apart from the difference in the grain, both the red and the green leather is fine and thin; the flesh surface is soft and spongy. The even thickness and texture suggests that the skin was expertly processed from high quality hides. Most of the red and green leather was evidently flexible and stretchy when it was first manufactured, suitable for tying over a wooden chariot frame. Only the bow-case, made of the same type of skin, is stiff, but this is due to the use of several layers as well as constructional features. It is possible that a different processing method was used, such as avoiding staking the leather, which makes a skin stretchy and supple, when it was important that the leather remain stiff.

Beige Leather

Chariot pieces such as the the beige girth (#40 & #41; Cat. No. 96) and nave hoops (##33 & #34; Cat. No. 88), are clear examples where careful selection of hide to suit the purpose can be demonstrated. They are made of thick leather – over 3 mm in cross section. The surface colour layer making the follicle pattern is clearly visible (Figure III.11A). On the main part of the girth, the large round and even spacing of follicles indicates that it is made from cattle hide. The decorative appliqué at the top end of the strap is much thinner, only 1 mm, and the grain pattern is quite different (Figure III.11B). The surface texture is smoother too, and has an attractive appearance. The paw-print like clustering of slightly slanted follicle holes, strongly suggesting goatskin was used. It would be very difficult to achieve such a delicate effect using cattle hide.

III.5.3. Evidence for Leathering or Tanning

Due to the rules governing sampling, it has not been possible to test the Tano leather to identify the materials that were originally used for leathering or tanning it to make the skin durable, although some other tests have been possible.

There are only a few possibilities for the leathering or tanning techniques that could have been used (see Section III.3. 'Skin Processing'). These include oil dressing or oil tanning, alum tawing and vegetable tanning, and each technique affects the properties of the skin in a different way. The differences are manifested in changes in the characteristics of the skin in terms of fibre colour and density, softness and handle. With this knowledge, there is potential by simply observing the skin of the Tano leather, to make some inferences on the nature of the leathering or tanning technique used. The Tano leather is pale buff, cream in colour, soft and fibrous in the cross section. It is possible that a variation on alum (potassium aluminium sulphate) tawing was used, which produces a white leather, soft and supple in texture, and retains the skin grain surface (Covington, 2011: 268). Alum 'tawed' skin is an excellent base for the application of colours, because the alum doubles up as a mordant, to chemically fix a colour applied to the fibres (Covington, 2011: 268). Alum is known to have been used thus in ancient Egypt (Van Driel-Murray, 2000: 304). Darkening of the white coloured alum tawed skin to a buff cream colour can occur with age, caused by oxidation of the fats or oils used as lubricants (A. Elnaggar, Personal Communication, 2016). The presence of alum may be identified by scientific analysis using Scanning Electron Microscopy (SEM) or X-ray fluorescence spectroscopy (XRF; Thomson, 2006a: 59). Alternatively, a simple micro-chemical spot test can be applied, which indicates the presence of aluminium using aluminium ammonium hydroxide and sodium alizarin sulphonate (Odegaard *et al.*, 2000: 36). A positive result is yielded if the solution on the glass microscope slide turns the colour red.

On the two small samples studied from the Tano leather, there was a positive result for aluminium from two samples – each of fibres from the corium of the green leather and from the red leather. With the red leather, the colour change was

Figure III.11A) A photomicrograph of the thick part of the girth (#40 & #41, Cat. No. 96). Magnification x12; B) A photomicrograph of the thin decorative appliqué on the girth (#40 & #41, Cat. No. 96) showing clearly the paw-print like follicle pattern of goatskin. Magnification x12. Photographs by L. Skinner.

more difficult to see because the fibres are already pink/red in hue. In contrast, the beige leather appeared to produce a negative result for aluminium but it was only tested once. This result would suggest that alum was applied in some form to the red and green leather, but we might deduce from the negative result given for the beige leather that alum was probably not used to 'leather' the skin, rather it was applied as a preparation for the application of the red or green colour (for further discussion of this see below). So, even though the Tano leather does have the appearance of alum tawed goat or hair sheep skin, the negative result for aluminium in the uncoloured beige leather, would suggest otherwise. It must be stated, however, that spot testing is a crude and simple method for testing for alum and without robust scientific analysis, it is impossible to confirm either the positive or the negative results. Furthermore, alum tawing might also be distinguished from a mordant (see above) were it possible to detect the presence of egg or of flour that are traditionally a part of the tawing method to make the skin soft. However, to identify this would require analysis of the leather using High Performance Liquid Chromatography-Mass Spectrometry (HPLC-MS) (R. Stacey, Personal Communication, 2017), which was unavailable to us in Egypt.

If the Tano leather had been oil tanned, this may be discovered if the fats or oils could be identified analytically, using Gas Chromatography – Mass Spectrometry (GC-MS) (also currently unavailable). However, every kind of leather tanning involves the application of oils in the final stages – for softening and lubricating the skin – and so it may be difficult to distinguish one from another. The natural colour of oil tanned leather is light beige (Tuck, 1983: 14). The texture of skin after oil or lipid tanning is usually very soft and flexible because of all the physical manipulation that is necessary to ensure even penetration and coating of the collagen fibres throughout the thickness of the skin. Oils and fats are hydrophobic and so will not enter the wet skin without assistance and encouragement. Commonly, the grain surface of oil tanned skin is removed during processing, and the result is soft and flexible leather such as chamois or native tanned buckskin (Sharphouse, 1985; Tuck, 1983: 14). The grain surface of the Tano leather, however, has been retained and is well preserved. Therefore, if it was oil tanned, the leatherworkers who carried out the process did an extremely skilled job by making the skin durable while also retaining the strength and appearance of the grain surface.

In terms of the 'true' tanning processes, until scientific analysis is possible, vegetable tanning of the Tano leather cannot be ruled out. However, although freshly vegetable tanned leather may be pale beige in colour, aged vegetable tanned leather is usually brown and has a 'full', not loose texture but with a relatively stiff handle (Haines, 2006b: 20). The micro-chemical spot test to determine whether leather has been vegetable tanned (introduced in section III.3) has been adapted for small leather samples, and carried out on tiny samples of the red, the green and beige coloured leather. This involved removing several fibres, placing them individually at either end of a glass slide. Distilled water was applied to fibres on one side (as a control) and a 1% ferric chloride solution in water applied to those on the other end. The fibres were observed under magnification. If vegetable tannins are present, the fibres will be stained blue/black in colour and although in all cases the results were negative, one still cannot automatically rule out vegetable tanning, because the test has been found to be unreliable in some cases, giving false results (see above) probably as a result of soil contamination.

III.5.4. Colour Identification

The natural colour of the harnessing pieces appears to be light beige, as can be seen in the corium (the centre of the cross section) of the skin. Some parts, for example the nave hoops and harness pieces, have green edgings but on the whole, they are beige coloured on the surface, the same hue as the corium. It is likely that these parts naturally have this colour, without the additional application of colour. This is confirmed by observing the grain surface under magnification and finding an absence of colour film or any pigment grains. Originally the beige leather may have been lighter in colour but darkened with age (see above).

The remainder of the Tano leather is either red or green in colour. Although it continues to appear bright and fresh, there is visible evidence that the colours, the red in particular, are not as vibrant as they were when first applied. Where edging strips or the top layer of leather in layered sheets have become detached, the original vivid colour is exposed underneath. The reduction in vibrancy, or fading of the colours, is due to photochemical fading and mechanical damage. The Tano leather shows a lot of evidence for use – stretching and rubbing in select areas, dirt and grease deposits forming accretions, and abrasion of the coloured leather surface causing pieces of the grain enamel to flake away. For an example of flaking away, fading and dirty accretions on the leather, see L6 #003 (Cat. No. 61).

The bright red stain of the Tano leather is a lot brighter than the pink colour which is seen so often in pharaonic leatherwork, such as EA36678 in the British Museum (London) (Figure III.12a). A recent visual survey in the galleries at the Egyptian Museum (Cairo) found that, with a few exceptions such as the pair of shoes (SR 5174/5175, see Veldmeijer, 2009a: 2-9) and the tent of Isemkhet (JE 26276; Brugsch-Bey, 1889), none of the pink/red coloured leather is of such a vibrant red colour as the Tano leather – almost all of it is pink. This includes the pink edging around mummy braces (for example object JE 3947). The red leather edgings around the mummy braces housed in the British Museum (London; EA36678), is a much deeper pink/red than those in the Egyptian Museum (Cairo). An explanation for this difference in colour might be photo-oxidative fading. Madder lake pigments are sensitive to photo-oxidation and will fade, becoming lighter if exposed to sunlight and the mummy braces on display in the Egyptian Museum (Cairo) are illuminated by natural sunlight on a daily basis (E. Zidan, Personal Communication, 2017). Mummy brace EA36678 is now stored in the magazines of the British Museum (London), where it is dark, and not on display anymore but it was on display in the Egyptian galleries for an unknown length of time, suspended inside a two-sided glass mount so that the front and back were visible and exposed to sunlight from the skylights, probably causing the red to fade.[36] The Tano leather has never been on display and so the colour has been protected from fading during modern times.

Colour was applied to the grain surface of the Tano leather exclusively as a topcoat rather than as a dip-dye that would have resulted in uniform colouration throughout the leather, on the recto and verso. The correct terminology for describing this superficial application method is 'staining'. To attain such an even tone the stain must have been applied liberally as a viscous liquid and rubbed or

---

36 The technology of this object will be subject of investigation in 2018, including the colouring methods and materials employed (see note 35).

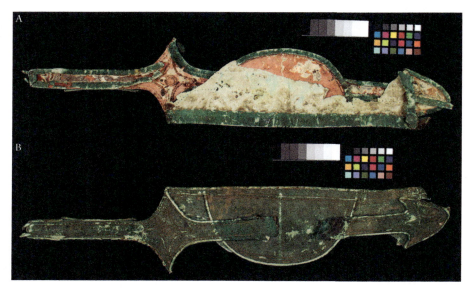

Figure III.12A) The recto of EA36678, possible a part of horse harnessing, in the collection of the British Museum (London). The bright green colour compares well the Tano leather; B) The verso of same object. Note the faded red colour. Photographs by L. Skinner. © Trustees of the British Museum (London).

padded over the surface of the leather using a rag or something similar. A faint hint of green and red colouration evident throughout the corium and on the verso of many of the fragments is likely due to the liquid medium of the stain soaking through the leather when it was first applied, drawing the smallest pigment grains through to the flesh surface.

Neither the colourant, nor the binding media have yet been definitively identified. Red textiles from this period have been analysed and found typically to be dyed using red ochre (Vogelsang-Eastwood, 1993: 278) or madder (Daniels *et al.*, 2014), an organic colorant derived from plant roots (Eastaugh *et al.*, 2012: 50; Vogelsang-Eastwood, 2000: 279). It seems to have been introduced to Egypt during the 18th Dynasty and produces an intense red dye for textiles, if bound to a mordant such as alum (Chenciner, 2003: 229). If an aqueous solution of the colourant is absorbed or 'complexed' with a white, inorganic substrate and precipitating, then a pink pigment is formed which can be added to a binder and applied like a paint. It is also possible to form the colourant *in situ* by applying the substrate (such as chalk or alum) and the colourant to the surface to be coloured and co-precipitating them (Daniels *et al.*, 2014)

At the Metropolitan Museum of Art (New York), Surface Enhanced Raman Scattering (SERS) has successfully identified madder lake as a surface colorant on a Middle Kingdom leather object, tentatively identified as quiver, from the collection (Leona, 2009: 14759). This suggests that madder lake pigments were being manufactured seven centuries earlier than previously thought.

The green colourant on the Tano leather forms a homogenous and intense coloured surface layer, with a slight sheen and no graininess at all. It has penetrated through the grain layer into the corium of the leather enough that there is a slight green tint even on the flesh surface. The red stain by contrast, is a thinner layer although no less glossy or intense in colour and this also has tinted the corium of the leather through to the flesh surface. The green is stiffer, more 'scale-like' and has flaked off more readily than the red. There are strong similarities between the green coloured leather of the Tano find and numerous other pieces, of which EA36678 (an enigmatic object, which is currently under study) in the British Museum (London) is only one example (Figure III.12b).

The green leather has a very deep rich colour, similar to malachite (copper carbonate) or Egyptian green (copper-wollastonite). Copper test-strip papers were used to detect whether copper was present, with positive results (Veldmeijer *et al.*, 2013: 271). Copper based colorants can take many forms: malachite, organic salts of copper including copper formates, and copper acetates (also known as verdigris – of which there are many variants), copper resinates and copper proteinates (which are verdigris-protein complexes), and copper oleates and stearates (which are oils or waxes that have reacted with cupric salts) (Oddy & Scott, 2002: 270-298). One might venture to say that in order to produce such glossy finish, and thick, semi-opaque appearance to the grain surface of, in particular the red and the green parts of the Tano leather, that the surface was waxed and polished, perhaps regularly, in antiquity. Exactly what could have been used is unknown but a mixture of beeswax with an oil or fat such as lanolin or castor oil, all of which were available in ancient Egypt, would provide the suitable properties. As well as enhancing the appearance of the leather, this coating would have helped to protect the skin too, making it more long-lasting (Tuck, 1983).

III.6. Handling and Conservation

The majority of Tano leather pieces are under 20 cm^2 in size. Most are flat sheets, while some are creased or partly folded at the edges. These smaller fragments have been photographed, drawn and occasionally turned over without risk of further damage. The largest, flat sheets of the leather were supported on flat boards while they were moved and have posed no great issues for documentation on one side. Turning them over, however, proved much more of a challenge. There are a few sections, for example, the large pieces of siding fill, which are heavily creased, split and folded multiple times in some parts, making viewing, drawing and photographing them particularly difficult (hence the occasional lack of photographs of verso's in the catalogue). A high level of physical and chemical degradation of the leather is evidenced by spots in the leather, which have completely converted to hide glue or gelatine – probably due to drops of liquid falling onto the surface at some point subsequent to the Tano leather's discovery. The conservation program for the leather took place in small blocks of time, over the autumn of 2011, through to the summer of 2012. In summary, the treatment involved consolidation of several sections, some gentle reshaping, repairing cracks and supporting broken edges with Japanese tissue backing supports. The conservation treatment is described in detail elsewhere (Veldmeijer *et al.*, 2013: 261-262).

III.7. Conclusions

The investigation and analysis of this unique object group has been executed gradually over a ten-year period. A huge amount of technical information has been recovered, frequently using quite basic techniques and careful observations. Yet, there remains a number of unknown facts about the leather, such as the kind of leathering or tanning technique that was used to make the skin durable enough to survive over three thousand years, and confirmation of the details of techniques used to colour the skin and create the surface sheen which still persists, preserving the vibrant surface colour. Hopefully these will be resolved in the future when more sampling is permitted, and the variety of in-house analytical equipment increases.

Although it is now fairly certain that goatskin was predominantly used for the Tano leather, there may be some instances where the smoother-grain of hair sheep was preferred. In some cases, if thick and sturdy leather was required, for instance the girth straps and nave hoops, cattle leather was used, although even here the applied decoration was executed using goatskin. Clearly very high quality, unblemished, hides were used and the skins were skillfully and carefully processed to avoid damage to the grain surface. The leatherworkers made a careful selection of materials to maximise functionality and strength, while at the same time, wasting very little leather. They made sure to orientate the leather to maximise the yield while also not be wasteful, meaning that in some cases an element of compromise was necessary. It would be beneficial to confirm what we suspect regarding species identification, using protein mass finger-printing (Zoo-MS) and add a level of completeness to the study of the leather technology. This will be the focus of future work, together with further consolidation and conservation (including the unfolding and reshaping of the leather).

IV. Dressing a Chariot

Leatherwork Technology

André J. Veldmeijer & Salima Ikram

IV.1. Manufacturing Chariot and Chariot Related Leathers

Images provide the majority of evidence concerning the production of chariots and their accoutrements (for example Luxor tombs TT39 [Puyemre], TT66 [Hepu], TT75 [Amenhotep-sise], TT86 [Menkheperraseneb], TT95 [Mery], TT100 [Rekhmire] and TT276 [Amenemipet]). However, these are not comprehensive, and generally unaccompanied by texts that might elucidate any details of the process. Chariot production workshops have not been identified in the archaeological record, save for one at Qantir (Raedler, 2007) and another possible example of a leatherworking area at Akoris (Hanasaka, 2004: 9-10, but see Veldmeijer, In Press on the identification as workshop); no doubt more will be found or recognised in future excavations. Thus, the objects themselves are the best source for understanding their production. A variety of techniques were used in the production of chariot leather: gluing, stitching, appliquéing, painting, scraping and stamping/impressing. The preference for or use of different techniques seems to have depended on the function of the object, possibly the workshop, and maybe changing trends in leatherwork.

Below, different techniques are discussed, by assemblage. Choices of particular technologies, and changes therein over time appear in Chapter VII.

IV.1.1. Glue, Stitching and Seams[37]

Different techniques were used for attachment, mainly gluing and stitching (Table IV.1). The most commonly used stitch was the running stitch, closely followed by the whip stitch.

---

37 A detailed analysis of the technology of the (possible) chariot leather from the tomb of Tutankhamun will be presented elsewhere as part of the gold foil project, see note 11. Note that only very little leather is preserved from this tomb and the condition of this preserved remains is often too bad to identify small details such as stitching.

Provenance	Stitch type	Material thread	Glue	Edge binding	Passepoil	Appliqué technique
Tomb of Amenhotep II	- Running stitch - Whip stitch	Twisted sinew	Yes: +++	No?	-	- 'Single stitch' (serrated motif) - Appliqué with running stitch - Glue
Tomb of Thutmose IV	- Running stitch - Whip stitch - Sailor stitch - Double running stitch	Twisted and plied sinew	Yes: +	- Folded strip over edge - Folded edge	-	- Pre-stitched appliqué added with double running stitch - Appliqué with running stitch - Two 'single' stitches (icicles/petals) - Glue
Tomb of Amenhotep III	- Running stitch - Whip stitch - Back stitch (functional and decorative) - Double running stitch	Z and S twisted sinew	Yes: +	- Folded strip over edge - Folded edge	-	- Appliqué with running stitch - 'Single' stitch (zigzag motif) - Pre-stitched appliqué added with double running stitch: only 24.8.1 - Split pin of bosses
Amarna	Running stitch (only?)	S twisted sinew	?	- Folded strip over edge - Folded edge (incl. towards recto)	-	- 'Single' stitch (zigzag motif) - Running stitch
Tano	- Running stitch - Whip stitch - Double running stitch - Interlocking running stitch(?)	- zS$_2$ sinew - zS$_2$ flax	Yes: +	- Various, see diagrams below	Yes	- Appliqué with running stitch - Pre-stitched appliqué added with double running stitch - Appliqué with whip stitch

Table IV.1. Summary of the technological details of the chariot leather, with, below, the large variety of edge bindings identified in the Tano leather.

Tomb of Amenhotep II

The material from Amenhotep II's tomb (Cat. No. 1-11) relies heavily on glue. There was some stitching involved, but only in a limited way (Table IV.1). This was especially the case for the decorated objects (particularly the appliqué), which were either glued, or with stitches augmenting the glue at strategic points in the object; only in a few instances were only stitches used. Unfortunately, no tests on the glue could be carried out, but it is likely that it was derived from animals rather than being vegetal in origin (Newman & Serpico, 2000: 475-494). Glue, less sturdy than stitching, might have been used as these are decorative rather than functional pieces. The top part of a bow-case/quiver (JE 32435C, Cat. No. 3) is made with running stitch, secured by a leather thong, which is rare, and seems to have been only used to secure an object to a lower layer, or as a (layman's?) repair. In addition to the stitching, glue was used to secure the decoration. The stitches were the same in the lower part of the object (JE 32435B, Cat. No. 3), and only glue was used to attach the vertical decoration.

Running stitch was predominant (CG 24145, Cat. No. 7; JE 32506, Cat. No. 8, JE 32435, Cat. No. 9). The spacing of the stitches (indicated by the holes, when the thread was missing) varied, either because larger or smaller stitches were needed, dependent on the use of the object, or due to the individual hand. Tacking, using sinew, is used to secure the row of serrated strips in JE 32435C (Cat. No. 3). Thus, a single stitch, made of S-spun sinew, pierces every two triangles: it is secured with a single sinew stitch vertically through every two triangles, following its shape (Figure F in Cat. No. 3). The long connecting threads are visible at the verso.

Two pieces of the red lining of a rawhide quiver (JE 32400B, Cat. No. 5) are secured with whip stitches, while the lining itself is glued to this – again, an example of the combined use of glue and stitching. A start(?) of the sewing, visualised by a knot in the sinew, can still be seen. The quiver also shows another interesting feature: an unusual example of a buttseam (grain[?]-edge stitching) (Figure S & T in Cat. No. 5), is used the close the quiver. This type of stitching is not often seen in such early leatherwork (indeed, the only other example comes from the Tano leather; #35 and #36, Cat. No. 97); the use of piercing the leather's thickness is much more common in the Roman period and thereafter.

Tomb of Thutmose IV

Little glue was noted in the materials coming from Thutmose IV's tomb (Table IV.1; JE 32435, Cat. No. 11, JE 97802, Cat. No. 14), sometimes occurring with additional stitching. Running stitch, used without glue, was omnipresent (Cat. Nos. 12-27). An interesting example of the use of this stitch is seen in the wrist guard (SR 3374, Cat. No. 24), in which the holes for the running stitch used to secure the appliqué layers within an edging are re-used to attach it to an undersurface (Veldmeijer, 2011c), in the present work referred to as 'double running stitch' (see 'Glossary').

Sailor stitch is, in contrast to the running and whip stitch, used sparsely in pharaonic leatherwork.[38] An example of it is seen in the scabbard (CG 46115, Cat. No. 27), where sailor stitches closes the tapering tube (Figure C in Cat. No. 27). Despite the suitability of the sailor stitch to repair tears, as it pulls the edge together very tightly, the crack in the object of unknown use CG 46110 (Cat. No. 19) is closed very neatly with whip stitch, rather than sailor stitch.

Stitches were also used to secure some of the decoration. The icicles/petals on CG 46108 (Cat. No. 16) are secured with two stitches: a vertical one in the centre and a diagonal one at the tip (or near the tip).

Tomb of Amenhotep III

The leatherwork allegedly from the tomb of Amenhotep III (Cat. Nos. 28-42) is of high quality (Table IV.1). Glue was involved in 24.8.E (Cat. No. 30), and possibly, on the basis of the absence of stitching, in 24.8.P (Cat. No. 38) but it is clearly a less favoured means of assembling the leather objects, as opposed to the finds from the tombs of Amenhotep II and even Thutmose IV.

Running stitch is used commonly. The stitching is done with Z-twisted sinew, seen in the appliqué work in SR 4/10676 (Cat. No. 42). It is very fine and regular and equals the quality of some of the leatherwork from the tomb of Thutmose IV (especially the appliqué on the wrist guard, CG 46112, Cat. No. 24).

A technique not registered in other pharaonic leatherwork is seen in MMA 24.8.D (Cat. No. 28) if allowing for the identification of this piece of wood as part of a chariot (see I.5.4 'Tomb of Amenhotep'). The red with green and white leather cladding is secured only at one side by back stitch using a green thong, which also creates a pleasing pattern. Its use in pharaonic leather is rare; only two sandal straps from Adindan in Nubia use it, though it is common in footwear made of vegetal material (Veldmeijer, 2009b; 2010; 2013).

In MMA 24.8.A-C (Cat. No. 29), the zigzag appliqué was secured with a continuous thread making single stitches horizontally over the tips to attach it. However, the zigzag in MMA 24.8.H (Cat. No. 33) is attached by small vertical stitches following the orientation of each tip. This is also seen at Amarna (see below). This diversity of style might reflect different workshops, hands, or diachronic change.

The technique of adding appliqué in two phases by means of double running stitching is clearly seen in MMA 24.8.I (Cat. No. 34), in MMA 24.8.H (Cat. No. 33), and MMA 24.8.O (Cat. No. 37).

Amarna

The Amarna chariot leather is in a very poor state, and what can be analysed shows that it was characterised by a predominant use of running stitches of different qualities (Table IV.I), comparing well with the material putatively from the tomb of Amenhotep III. The zigzag motif in AM 076k, r and AM 075 (and possibly AM

---

38 Other examples are seen in the closure of the leather cover of a harp's soundbox from Dra Abu el-Naga (FN1065) (Veldmeijer, 2017: 164-168; Veldmeijer & Skinner, In Press); a bag (FN1064) from the same assemblage is mended with sailor stitch (Veldmeijer, 2017: 139-145; Veldmeijer & Skinner, In Press), and the loincloth from the tomb of Maiherpri in Boston (03-1035; Veldmeijer, 2017: 60) also utilises this stitch.

034; Veldmeijer, 2011b: 22-23, 103-105, 116-120, 126-127, 130-132; Appendix II) is secured in the same way as that coming from the tomb of Amenhotep III. The open work circles (AM 032, Veldmeijer, 2011b: 100-103; Appendix II) are secured in a comparable way too: one stitch through the circle. Even the tiny floral motif in AM 013c (Veldmeijer, 2011b: 94; Appendix II) is secured with one stitch in the centre and one through the tip of the side leaf, rather than glued, indicating the high level of craftsmanship. Whip stitches have not been registered, nor were sailor stitches. As far as the condition allowed identification, the stitching was done with sinew.

No pre-manufactured sets of appliqué, such as were seen in the Amenhotep III material, were identified, suggesting that the appliqué was added individually. This is remarkable, as this is a much more laborious and time consuming method of creating appliqués. Again, this might reflect different workshops, hands, local preferences, or diachronic change.

Tano

The great variety in constructions and use of seams in the Tano leather (Table IV.1) is partially due to the fact that much more and varied leather (in terms of elements, such as support straps, nave hoops and casing) survives than from any other assemblage, even though it is unlikely that the Tano leather is royal. Moreover, it is most probable that the diversity of techniques reflects increased experience in leatherworking. Despite the larger variety in seams and bindings, the most common stitches to be used are the running and whip stitch; the stitching is very regular and straight. The nave hoops (#33 & #34, Cat. No. 88, Figure O) are closed with either double running stitch or interlocking stitch, which is not possible to identify (see the explanation of the term in the Glossary). Also notable is the fact that the stitching is done with plied sinew thread and the seam includes a passepoil. The Tano material is unique in the use of the passepoil. Both flax and sinew were used to sew the Tano chariot leather, while all the other assemblages exclusively use sinew.

Running stitch is used in a constructional way as well as to secure appliqué, as is the case for whip stitch. In some cases, the usage might dictate the type of stitch chosen. As one might expect, running stitch is used to close elements (*e.g.* L6 #001, Cat. No. 60), to connect layers (*e.g.* L1 #009, Cat. No. 121), including various layers of straps that are obtained by folding a strip of leather two or three times lengthwise, and secured with up to four rows of running stitching (such as the neckstraps, #37 & #39, Cat. No. 103). Applied decoration is secured with running stitches, mainly made with flax zS_2 thread. An unusual use of running stitch to secure an edge binding is found in one instance when a repair is being made (L6 #001, Cat. No. 60). Two rows of whip stitch are seen in a fragment where two pieces of body leather are secured without a passepoil (L2 #008, Cat. No. 56), and whip stitch is almost always used to secure edge bindings (L1 #024, Cat. No. 120). The whip stitch is also used to secure rolled up strap ends, when the edges are folded inwards, with the stitching piercing the folds. Alternately, the edges are not folded, thus creating what is more or less a buttseam (*cf.* BI-038, Cat. No. 119 with BI-029, Cat. No. 118). Furthermore, it is employed to create the tripartite strip decoration that hides the seams between the body of the leather and the tube found throughout the siding fill when there is no passepoil between the body leather and the tubes. Here, most likely, the three strips were first secured to each other, after which it was fixed to the object with whip stitches of flax thread. The use of whip stitch indicates that the appliqué was attached after the tube and body were secured, since whip stitch is easier to use in such a situation than other types of stitching (Veldmeijer, 2009a: 14-15). In some examples, running stitch is combined with whip stitch to secure the edge with the folds (such as BI-033, Cat. No. 114),[39] as well as in the creation of edge bindings.

A rare feature is seen in two bigger fragments of harness (#35, #36, Cat. No. 97): they have stitch holes at the edge, suggesting a buttseam. Their decoration is asymmetrical but if the two are put together and secured at these stitch holes, the design becomes symmetrical. The only other example of such a seam is found in the quiver from the tomb of Amenhotep II. Threads were prevented from slipping simply by tying an overhand stopper knot.[40]

IV.1.2. Constructional Features

Assembling the different leather parts of a chariot involves a variety of constructions. These include edge bindings, reinforcement methods, and diverse ways of connecting different components, including passepoils, split pin attachments, drawstrings and toggles.

Edge Binding

An edge binding not only aesthetically finishes an edge, but also reinforces and protects it.

Tomb of Amenhotep II

Amenhotep II's tomb yielded no true edge binding (Table IV.1): the appliqué runs until the edge of the under surface, but is not folded over it.

Tomb of Thutmose IV

In contrast to the material from the tomb of Amenhotep II, the leatherwork from Thutmose IV's tomb (Table IV.1) uses fairly simple edge bindings consisting of a strip of leather folded over the edge. Additional strips sometimes overlap the binding, to enhance its decorative aspect, but are not part of the binding themselves. The stitching that attaches these strips often further secures the binding, but sometimes just misses it (for example in CG 46110, Cat. No. 19). CG 46108 (Cat. No. 16) shows yet another way of securing an edge: a seam of running stitches connects the complex appliquéd strip to the main piece of

---

39 A combination of running and whip stitching is also seen in the straps that are extended and secured at an overlapping area (*e.g.* BI-005, Cat. No. 104): the edges along the length are sewn with running stitches whereas the edges transversely to the length are sewn with whip stitches (both are made of sinew).

40 L1 #005 (Cat. No. 68) shows the start of sewing with whip stitches: the protruding end of the thread that secures a green, lengthwise folded passepoil has an overhand stopper knot. Shortly thereafter the passepoil is broken, and one end of the sewing thread that sticks out is tied into an overhand stopper knot. This suggests that the damage occurred in ancient times and the thread was not repaired but rather it was prevented from slipping by tying a knot in the loose hanging ends. Another example of the start of sewing (also by tying an overhand knot) is seen in L4 #006 (Cat. No. 78).

leather, which is then folded over at the edge and, using a running stitch, binds the appliqué to it. This second seam fills in the gaps left by the seam that attached the appliqué to the undersurface (so-called 'double running stitching').

Tomb of Amenhotep III

In the material from the tomb of Amenhotep III (Table IV.1), edge bindings consist of strips folded over the edge (*e.g.* MMA 24.8.G., Cat. No. 32) and few examples of the unusual folded edge construction as was seen in the Thutmose IV material (MMA 24.8.I., Cat. No. 34; 24.8.M., Cat. No. 36; MMA 24.8.P., Cat. No. 38; note that the other edge of this object has a separate strip folded around the edge). A red backing piece of leather is attached by whip stitch to the green edge binding of fragment MMA 24.8.I. (Cat. No. 34). Attaching a backing to the binding is unusual. This backing protected the main object from being damaged by the split pins securing the bosses that decorate the object.

Amarna

Besides the use of isolated strips folding around the edge, as seen with the older examples, the Amarna material (AM 073, AM 076l; Veldmeijer, 2011b: 111-113, 127 respectively; Appendix II; Table IV.1) also shows the simple folding of the edge, and securing it with running stitch.

Tano

There is a large variation in edge bindings in the Tano leather, including both simpler and more complicated examples that not only protect the edge proper, but also the stitching close to the edge (Table IV.1). Especially, but not exclusively, in the harness (for example B1-001 and BI-006, Cat. No. 81 and 82), edges are simply folded and secured together with the appliqué. Another form of edging is seen in, *e.g.*, L2 #008B (Cat. No. 56, G). Here, lengthwise folded strips of leather, with the folded edges lining up with the edge of the backing, are attached to the backing with whip stitch. Such a binding is also seen in the ends of tubes, but is rare as usually the ends of the tubes have a binding consisting of the applied tripartite strip decoration of which the outermost whip stitching is simply sewn over the edge of the tube's leather (*e.g.* L2 #008B, Cat. No. 56). More complicated bindings that reinforce and strengthen the edge are noted in the main casing and siding fill (*e.g.* L2 #008B, Cat. No. 56). Here, a strip of leather is whip stitched to the edge of the body of the piece. It is then folded over, going towards the body and secured with running stitch, which also secures strips of appliqué (*e.g.* L2 #008B, Cat. No. 56). It has no parallel among the other chariot leather or any other contemporary leatherwork studied thus far.[41] It elegantly combines protection with decoration as it not only covers the edge, but also protects the vulnerable whip stitching at the edge. A comparable technique is seen in the main casing[42] (for example, see L3 #002, Cat. No. 44), but here the edge binding strip

---

41   Several unidentified fragments shows such bindings too, which therefore seem to be pieces of siding fill (and not of the main casing as they are a single layer of leather and the described edge binding has not been identified in the main casing).

42   And some unidentified fragments, which might therefore be parts of the main casing.

is integrated into the stair-step applied decoration, forming its topmost strip, all of which are attached to one another with running stitch. It is then pulled over the edge and secured with whip stitch. According to Veldmeijer (2009a: 14) securing the strip at the verso is easier with whip stitching.

Connections

Tano

The Tano material is the only chariot leather that shows the use of passepoils (Table IV.1): these are used in the attachment of the tubes to the body leather, but only in some pieces of the siding fill (*e.g.* L1 #016, Cat. No. 73). The tubes in the main casing are secured without such an element. The lengthwise folded, red strip of leather in L1 #010A (Cat. No. 70, figure A) might have been intended as a passepoil rather than part of a stair-step overlapping decoration, serving to reinforce this attachment. In L2 #008B (Cat. No. 56) a lengthwise folded green strip is seen between the body and a small piece of red leather, suggesting a function as a passepoil, but the fragment is fairly damaged so this identification is uncertain. The nave hoops also use passepoils in closing the cylinder (#33 & #34, Cat. No. 88).

Leather pieces are enlarged by sewing two pieces together with one or double rows of whip stitch, as in L2 #008A (Cat. No. 56) and L3 #001 (Cat. No. 43).

Other Techniques

Split Pin Attachment

One object from the tomb of Amenhotep III (MMA 24.8.I., Cat. No. 34) is enhanced with gilded bronze bosses that are attached to the leather with split pins. It is the only example of such practice in the chariot leather discussed in the present volume.[43]

Drawstrings and Toggles

The drawstrings found in the tubes in the main casing and siding fill that secure the Tano leather to the frame terminate in toggles. These reinforce the ends of the drawstrings, hinder them from slipping through the tube, and provide secure closing mechanisms, either by tying or by being pulled through a small slit in the drawstring.

The toggles seen in the Tano leather are made in different ways. In one, a strip of leather is wrapped around the end of the drawstring and secured by stitching the wrapped leather through the drawstring (*e.g.* L1 #016, Cat. No. 73; Figure IV.1A).[44] In another, a strip is rolled over itself, passing through a slit, which

---

[43] Comparable bosses are used in a pair of leather sandals from the tomb of Tutankhamun (Carter's Number 021h, i; Veldmeijer, 2011a: 98-105). Split pins, however, are also used to attach the gold floral decoration on the straps in shoes found in the tomb (Carter's Number 021f, g; Veldmeijer, 2011a: 109-121).

[44] A common technique; even most of the sticks from the tomb of Tutankhamun are made in a comparable way: the straight stick is at the top wrapped around with a leather strip (in stair-stap overlap) as to make a knob (AJV/SI Personal observation). Also the next discussed type of toggle is common in leatherwork. See Veldmeijer (2017: 63-65).

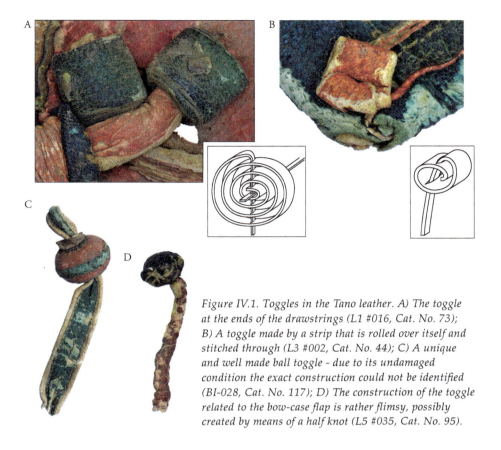

Figure IV.1. Toggles in the Tano leather. A) The toggle at the ends of the drawstrings (L1 #016, Cat. No. 73); B) A toggle made by a strip that is rolled over itself and stitched through (L3 #002, Cat. No. 44); C) A unique and well made ball toggle - due to its undamaged condition the exact construction could not be identified (BI-028, Cat. No. 117); D) The construction of the toggle related to the bow-case flap is rather flimsy, possibly created by means of a half knot (L5 #035, Cat. No. 95).

secures it (L3 #002, Cat. No. 44; Figure IV.1B). A unique ball toggle is seen in BI-028 (Cat. No. 117; Figure IV.1C) of the Tano chariot. Its manufacture is impossible to determine without taking it apart: inside, it could have been built up in the same way as the coiled toggles and covered with the leather, but it is more likely that it was stuffed with material to attain this shape, comparable to toy balls. Possibly, the strap with this toggle was used to fix the girth and neckstrap. A toggle of this size would secure the girth firmly, and also satisfy aesthetics. Two tiny toggles are part of the bow-case flap (one isolated: L5 #035, Cat. No. 95 [Figure IV.1D], with one still attached to the flap, L1 #015, Cat. No. 93). Their construction is also not clear. They might have been created by tying a half knot around the strap, and sewn. No toggles have been identified in the other chariot leatherwork.

Reinforcement

Different ways of strengthening and reinforcing are used in leatherwork, but only the Tano material provides examples of these in the chariot leather corpus presented here. Extra layers of material appliqués, reinforcing seams, and bindings[45] all contribute to maintaining the integrity of an object.

The bottom corners of the main casing of the Tano leather (L3 #004A, Cat. No. 46 and L3 #004D, Cat. No. 16) have holes, which are reinforced with leather rings on the verso (Figure IV.2A). They are secured with a row of running stitches of zS_2 sinew at both the outer and inner edge. The reinforcement clearly was necessary as attested by the distortion of the hole due to stress, probably from a leather or rawhide strap with which it was tied to the chariot frame. The reinforcement ring was added to the leather before the decorative edge, as the latter covers it.

The holes in the ends of the girth (#40 and #41, Cat. No. 96; Figure IV.2B), which is made of fairly thick beige leather, are reinforced with green appliqué. This appliqué is stitched on with running stitches along the edges. Here, the appliqué's function is twofold: reinforcement and decoration.

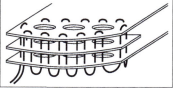

Figure IV.2. Reinforcements in the Tano leather. A) Hole, reinforced with a ring of leather (L3 #004A, Cat. No. 46); B) Combined reinforced and enhanced hole in the girth (#41, Cat. No. 96); C-E) Several examples of holes that are simply reinforced with stitches (BI-012, Cat. No. 109; #31, Cat. No. 92 and L1 #009, Cat. No. 121 respectively).

---

45 Edge bindings are, basically, also reinforcement. A good example is fragment L2 #008A (Cat. No. 56), which has another hole close to the tube. This near-rectangular hole, probably a hand-grip, is reinforced with a green edge binding. Larger fenestrations in the siding fill (such as seen in L1 #002, Cat. No. 51 and L1 #003, Cat. No. 52) have edge bindings comparable to this hand-grip. They will not be discussed here – see 'Edge Binding' above.

Another technique of reinforcement is seen in BI-009 and BI-012 (Cat. No. 110 and 109 respectively; Figure IV.2C): the tear-shaped slit is reinforced with sinew stitching. Such a technique is also seen in the slits in the narrow extension of the neckstraps (# 37 and 39, Cat. No. 103). The bottom of the bow-case (#31, Cat. No. 92) has three points for its attachment to the chariot. The two oval patches (Figure IV.2D) have slits at either short side from which the remains of a strap protrude. These are reinforced by stitches that might also have helped to secure the straps. Three slits in a row, parallel to the edge in L1 #009 (Cat. No. 121; Figure IV.2E), are reinforced by the stitching that encircles them. Also the tube-shaped quiver JE 32400 (Cat. No. 5) has a similarly reinforced hole.

Some pieces that one would expect to be reinforced, are not. Strap BI-023 and BI-025 (Cat. No. 89 and 90 respectively; Figure IV.3A) were clearly used, as evidenced by by discoloration which also attests to its use to secure the nave hoops to the wheels. However, the small holes in the straps that were used to secure them around the hoops are not reinforced. Several other holes/slits are not reinforced, such as L2 #008A (Cat. No. 56; Figure IV.3B), L2 #008B (Cat. No. 56), L6 #001 (Cat. No. 60), and L6 #009 (Cat. No. 148). Fragment L1 #023 (Cat. No. 54)

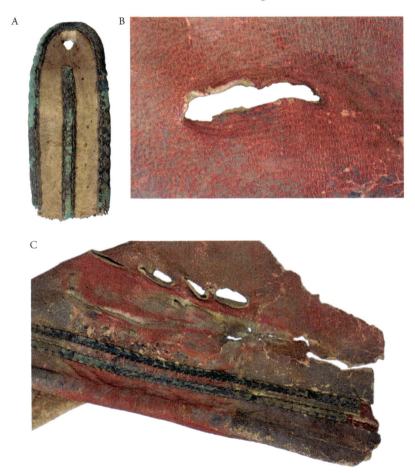

Figure IV.3. Several examples of holes that one would expect to have been reinforced in the Tano leather but are not. A) Strap to secure the nave hoop (BI-023, Cat. No. 89); B) Siding fill (L2 #008A, Cat. No. 56); C) Siding fill (L1 #023).

has four slits in a row parallel to the tube's length (Figure IV.3C), through which straps were pulled – none of these slits were reinforced.

Appliqué

Appliqué is a complicated subject as it can both adorn and serve as reinforcement. A discussion of its construction is often dependent on its form, and thus all appliqué will be covered in IV.1.3 'Decoration'.

IV.1.3. Decoration (Table IV.2)

Painted Decoration

Decorating leather with paint exists, but is infrequently found in ancient Egyptian leatherwork, and appears to be confined to the 18th Dynasty, prior to the Amarna period.[46] Within painted designs, dots are most common. For example, the bow-case element JE 96912A-C (Cat. No. 1) from the tomb of Amenhotep II is stained pinkish-red,[47] and enhanced with two painted parallel lines (Figure IV.4A), which are filled in with dots that form a repeating diamond pattern. This is paralleled by CG 46108 (Cat. No. 16), from the tomb of Thutmose IV (Figure IV.4B). Dots between lines or bands, both horizontal and vertical also feature, such as on the quiver CG 24072 from the tomb of Maiherpri (Daressy, 1902: 32-33) and the red bow-case flap from TT65 (Figure II.13). Lines, bands, and scallops are seen too (for example on the flap from TT65, which has the most elaborate monochrome painted decoration seen in leatherwork thus far).

A far more elaborately painted design is seen in the trapezoidal fragment JE 97809 (Cat. No. 20) from the tomb of Thutmose IV (Figure IV.5). The leather was first stained white, then bands with various motifs – zigzag, running spirals, icicles/petals, and vegetal – were added in green and red, separated by green horizontal lines. The motifs are familiar from ancient Egyptian art and several, such as the icicles/petals and the zigzag motif, are common in appliqué that enhance much of the chariot leather as well. The only other example of painted zigzag on leather is seen on the body of the chariot from the tomb of Yuya and Tjuiu (Figure IV.6). The zigzag pattern is always green.

Gold Foil and Sheet

Two ways to enhance leather with gold foil or thin gold sheet have been registered: the quiver from the tomb of Amenhotep II (JE 32400, Cat. No. 5) has applied rosettes, a beadnet design, and diamonds, all of which are gilded. Some other material from the tomb of Amenhotep II was thought to have been gilded as well (for example, CG 24146, Daressy, 1902: 76); only a fragment of this survives, and it is impossible to see any evidence of this here. The only other example of

---

46 Not included is the staining of the leather itself (see III.5.4. 'Colour Identification'). The blue paint trimmings of the gold foil from the tomb of Tutankhamun will be discussed elsewhere (see note 11).

47 This is due to fading: it was bright red originally. In the Tano leather, some areas are still much darker, indicating it was covered for most of the time and thus not exposed to the sun. In a more extreme case, an originally green shoe has completely faded to beige: the original colour could only still be noted deep between the sole/upper seam (Veldmeijer, 2009a: 7-8).

Figure IV.4. A) Detail of the painted design in JE 96912 (Cat. No. 1) from the tomb of Amenhotep II; B) Detail of the painted design in CG 46108 (Cat. No. 16).

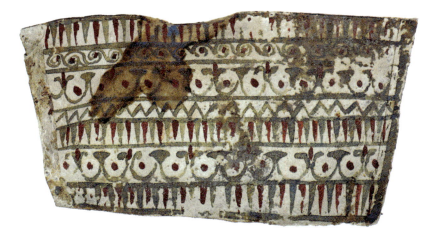

Figure IV.5. Fragment JE 97809 (Cat. No. 20) from the tomb of Thutmose IV is elaborately enhanced with painted design, including familiar motifs such as zigzag, running spirals and icicles/petals.

DRESSING A CHARIOT | 109

Figure IV.6. The chariot from the tomb of Yuya and Tjuiu. The inside part of the casing is painted green and has a painted border which imitate the delicate appliqué work seen elsewhere (and on the axle of Yuya's chariot), consisting of red, white, blue, green zigzag, blue, white and finally a red line.

chariot related leather that is enhanced with gold, is the leather from the tomb of Tutankhamun (Figure I.2; II.12), which includes the gold sheet cladding of not only bow-cases and quivers, but also other chariot related objects yet to be identified.[48] The sheer quantity of gold foils from his tomb suggests that nearly all chariot related leather was embellished with gold.

Appliqué

Appliqué is the most common technique used to decorate chariot leather, as well as other leatherwork. In addition to straight appliqué, there is also relief appliqué and stuffed appliqué, although the use of the latter has only been noted in vegetal motifs.

By far the most common design is the use of strips of leather in different colour, mainly red and green, and occasionally white, which are overlapped in stair-step fashion, thus producing thin lines of alternating colour (many examples, but see MMA 24.8.H, Cat. No. 33 from the tomb of Amenhotep III, or CG 46112, Cat. No. 24, from the tomb of Thutmose IV; Figure IV.7). Besides overlapping in stair-step fashion, a narrow strip can be placed lengthwise in the middle of a wider one.[49] Both methods are often combined. Occasionally, strips are folded lengthwise. Adding straight appliqué is fairly simple: the strips were cut and sewn onto the object or a set was sewn together first and added later to an object, using double running stitch.

Bands made of different widths and colours, without using stair-step overlapping are also known from the tomb of Amenhotep II (JE 96912, Cat. No. 1). In JE 32435 (Cat. No. 3) such appliqué is combined with an 'edge binding', which is simply a strip that follows the edge on one side only. Here, all strips are of single thickness: none was folded lengthwise. The use of a set of strips that are composed in such a way is rarely seen in chariot leather: it is more common to add one final, very narrow strip on top of another which is part of a series of stair-step overlapping strips.

---

48 See note 11.
49 Note that a series of strips of alternating colour that are secured on top of each other lengthwise through the centre is not uncommon in leather composite sandals (Veldmeijer, 2009c).

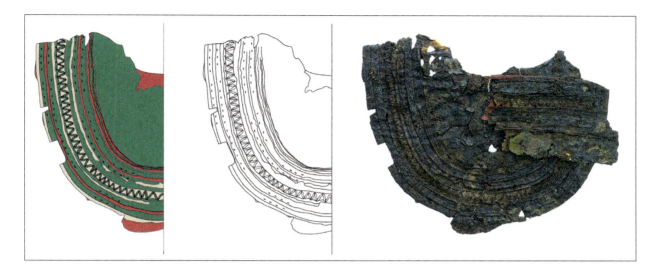

Figure IV.7. Example of Amarna leather (ÄM AM 075), elaborately embellished with appliqué in different colours.

Figure IV.8. Appliqué combining single layer strips with folded ones. A) First occurence of such combination is seen in the leather from the tomb of Thutmose IV (SR 3375, Cat. No. 24), seen from recto and in cross section; B) Example of the Tano leather (L5 #009, Cat. No. 48).

The material from the tomb of Thutmose IV, with the wrist guard (SR 3374, Cat. No. 24; Figure IV.8A) being the clearest example, is the first use of appliqué that consists of a combination of lengthwise folded strips with thin, non-folded bands. Stair-step overlapping appliqué in the Amarna leather (Veldmeijer, 2011b: 93-143; Appendix II) seems to have been made exclusively with single strips,[50] as was the case in the Amenhotep III material.

---

50 In ÄM AM 032, the edge of the topmost, openwork strip might have been folded, but this is not beyond doubt: overall the condition of the material is too bad to be absolutely sure about this, although the use of single strips only in one of the larger and better preserved pieces, ÄM AM 075 (Veldmeijer, 2011b: 116-120; Figure IV.7) is certain.

 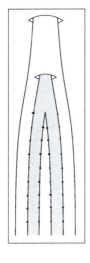

Figure IV.9. The appliqué of the side of the bottom of the Tano bow-case (#31, Cat. No.89) is made of two strips of different colour, which are cut in and the separated strips attached alternatingly.

In the Tano leather, the appliqué of stair-step overlapping strips often include (a) lengthwise folded strip(s) (Figure IV.8B). In L1 #015 (Cat. No. 93) several folded strips follow on top of each other in stair-step fashion without non-folded strips, which is a rare exception.

A type of appliqué unique to the Tano leather gives the effect of parallel strips (three or six) in alternating colours (for example, the bottom of the bow-case, #31, Cat. No. 92; Figure IV.9). This was achieved by making vertical slits in a wide piece of leather (green in the example), and pulling the leather apart a bit in order to insert the strips of the other colour (red).

In several examples, the overlapping strips are combined with bands of different shapes (zigzag [Figure IV.7], scallops, triangles, icicles/petals) and other forms of decoration (scraped).[51] Scallop bands of different sizes are seen, notably in the Amenhotep II tomb material (JE 32435, Cat. No. 3).

One of the most commonly occurring motif is the zigzag, secured by means of stitching but in different ways (Figure IV.10). In the leather from the tomb of Amenhotep III, the zigzag motif in the triangular fragment (SR 4/10676, Cat. No. 42) is cut in shape, rather than folded at the edges (which is also registered in the Metropolitan pieces from the tomb), and stitched at the tips. In the Amarna leather a strip is folded at the tips, rather than cut as a zigzag, but stitched in a comparable way. The zigzag in the Tano leather, however, is cut in a zigzag and sewn along the edges with running stitches, thus a distinctly different technique than seen in the older material.

The icicles/petals in the rectangular object from the tomb of Thutmose IV (CG 46108, Cat. No. 16; Figure IV.11A) were cut out of a strip of leather, the top of which was cut off after it was applied to the object, indicated by a clearly visible cut mark.[52] They are secured with a single stitch in each icicle/petal. This differs

---

51 In several cases these represent elements of garlands.
52 Also in other leatherwork, strips of which one edge is worked into a serrated edge, shows the opposite edge cut *in situ* (Veldmeijer, 2009c: 7-8). It is difficult judge whether or not this way of working was intended, but anyway the strip was too wide to be inserted completely and had to be cut off.

Figure IV.10. Various ways of applying zigzag appliqué. A) Folded strip, sewn at the tips (Amarna); B) Cut zigzag sewn more or less lengthwise down the centre (Amenhotep III); C) As B, but sewn at the tips (Amenhotep III); D) As B but sewn along both edges (Tano); E) Diagrams of the zigzag shown in A-D.

Figure IV.11. Various ways of applying icicles/petals. A) A strip, of which the icicles/petals were cut off in situ (Thutmose IV, CG 46108, Cat. No. 16); B) Strip, cut from one side, secured with running stitches along the entire edge (Tano, #30, Cat. No. 91); C) A strip, cut from one side, which is secured with glue (Amenhotep II, JE 32509A, Cat. No. 2). The arrows point to the opposite edge.

DRESSING A CHARIOT | 113

from other, comparable appliqué in the Tano bow-case (#30, Cat. No. 91 and #31, Cat. No. 92; Figure IV.11B), where the non-cut edge was not cut *in situ* but left intact. The strip is, in contrast to the previous example, applied with running stitches along the edge of the icicles/petals rather than with a single stitch. The icicles/petals in CG 46108 (Cat. No. 16) are secured with two stitches: a vertical one in the centre and a diagonal one at the tip (or near the tip). The icicles/petals in the example from the tomb of Amenhotep II are glued (Figure IV.11C). These are also left uncut after adding to the object.

From Amarna a strip of leather is cut into almost complete circles with central holes at one edge, leaving the other edge integrated in the stair-step overlapping appliqué (Veldmeijer, 2011b: 100-103; Appendix II). This compares well with the way other appliqués were made, such as the icicles/petals in CG 46108 (Cat. No. 16) from the tomb of Thutmose IV just discussed, and from Tano (#30, Cat. No. 91; #31, Cat. No. 92), and the strips with scalloped edge in leather from the tomb of Amenhotep II (*e.g.* JE 32509, Cat. No. 2).[53]

Relief appliqué is not uncommon in leatherwork in general, but is especially common in the Tano leather (Figure IV.12). One technique, the bulging of thicker appliqué strips, is very distinct in the bow-case bottom and top (#30, Cat. No. 91 and #31, Cat. No. 92; Figure IV.12A, arrow) but is also seen, a bit more subtly, in other parts such as the support straps.

Appliqués with vegetal motifs are common, especially in the Tano leather, and are constructed in a variety of ways: straight appliqué, relief appliqué, and stuffed appliqué (Figure IV.12B, C), in which a stuffing of plant material was used. Stuffed appliqué in combination with relief appliqué is seen in the vegetal appliqué on the girth (#40 & #41, Cat. No. 96; Figure IV.12B, C) and the possible holder among the Tano leather (L3 #004F, Cat. No. 46). Further relief is obtained due to the folding of the green lining of the motif – stitching it slightly away from the edge proper results in lifting the edges of the motif a bit above the undersurface (Figure IV.12C, arrow). It is questionable, though, that this was an intended feature.

In the rectangular, incomplete object JE 97802 (Cat. No. 14) from the tomb of Thutmose IV, the vegetal motif (in green with details picked out in red) is made of a single, unfolded strip of leather. The appliqué was first secured to the white undersurface and subsequently to the red backing. Another interesting detail is that the tendrils of the plant are not separated from the stalk leading to the triangular flowers. A comparable motif is seen in ÄM AM 078a (Van Driel-Murray, 2000: 311, but see Veldmeijer, 2011b: 137-140; Appendix II), though the technology is a bit more elaborate as it is secured at either edge with running stitches of sinew. The relief in the Amarna example, especially in the centre part, suggests that the motif was made using the stuffed appliqué technique, in order to convey a sense of three-dimensionality.

---

53 Interestingly, the scallops are standing free from the under surface and came loose: these ends were not glued. In this, it is not that different from the Tano appliqué mentioned below in which the green lining that defines the floral appliqué is stitched on away from the edge with the result that the edge is slightly lifted from the undersurface as well.

Figure IV.12. Relief in chariot leatherwork. A) Some strips in the Tano leather (here the bow-case, #30, Cat. No. 92) were pushed from one edge to one edge to make it a bit bulging and accentuating the relief (arrow); B) Vegetal motif of the girth (#40, Cat. No. 96), with a detail (C) showing remnants of the stuffing. A green edging is lifted from the undersurface (arrow) accidentally(?) creating relief too.

The glued appliqué on the fragments of a quiver from the tomb of Amenhotep II (JE 32400, Cat. No. 5; Figure IV.13 is extraordinary.[54] Two fragments of quiver fit together, and at first glance both pieces seem to have the same decoration. Strangely, there is a distinct difference in the quality and, in part, in the detailing. The rectangular fragment is decorated with a beadnet pattern made of bark with gilded diamond insets, and the connection points emphasized by gilded circles, and the whole further enhanced by gilded rosettes (Figure IV.13A, C). The long section is similarly decorated, except the net pattern is coarser, there are no circles at the connecting points of the mesh, and the rosettes are more coarsely made (Figure IV.13B, D). Although the beadnet pattern is a fairly common decorative motif, this is the only example in chariot related leatherwork.

---

54 This technique of applied decoration, however, is common in other objects, such as the sticks and staves from the tomb of Tutankhamun, currently under study by the authors.

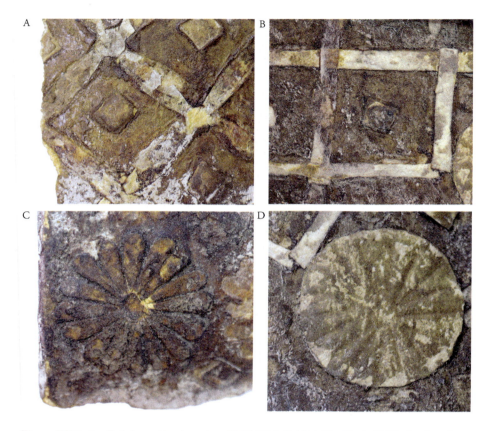

Figure IV.13. Applied decoration in quiver JE 32400A, B (Cat. No. 5). A, B) The beadwork and lattice pattern; C, D) The detailed rosette versus the coarsely made example.

A rare appliqué is the roundel seen in the enigmatic Tano fragment L3 #004F (Cat. No. 46). It is, together with a roundel with vegetal motif from Amarna (Veldmeijer, 2011b: 140-142; Figure II.11; Appendix II) the only archaeological example of this kind, though it appears on images of chariots.

Scraping

Scraping (removing the topmost layer of the background leather with a knife) has been tentatively identified in the Amarna material (AM 076g, k, m, s; Veldmeijer, 2011b: 125-128, 130; Appendix II), taking the form of scallops and running spirals. The technique has been used as a way of providing a different colour, as seen in CG 46108 (Cat. No. 16) from the tomb of Thutmose IV.

Stamping/Impressing

Impressed decoration in chariot related leather exists, and is noted particularly in harnessing elements, such as blinkers and bosses.[55] It is seen in the material from the tomb of Amenhotep II (running palmettes, rosettes and flowering plants) and Thutmose IV (bird with outstretched wings and sun-disc accompanied by

---

55 With the exception of the gold foils from the tomb of Tutankhamun (see below and note 11).

cartouches, elaborate vegetal motif[56]), as well as from the tomb of Tutankhamun.[57] In the Thutmose IV pouch-flap (JE 97820, Cat. No. 22), the impressed bird is rather shallow and poorly visible but it is assumed that it was stamped as a whole rather than each element separately. Stamping/impressing is seen in other chariot related objects too, such as the quivers of Maiherpri (CG 24017; Daressy, 1902: 32, pl. X; Figure I.1). These are impressed with bands of running spirals, wavy lines as well as vegetal motifs.

On the whole, it seems as if the designs were stamped on the verso, giving the recto a repoussé effect (for example, the running palmettes in the bow-case flap, JE 32513, Cat. No. 4, and the decoration on Maiherpri's quiver, CG 24071). All bridle bosses (Amenhotep II: JE 32625, Cat. No. 7; Thutmose IV: JE 97801, Cat. No. 12) and blinkers (Amenhotep II: JE 32506, Cat. No. 8; Figure II.25), have deeply impressed floral motifs. The motif in both bridle bosses must have been made from the recto. Although it is tempting to suggest a comparable technique for the blinker, the verso is obscured prohibiting clear vision.

Running spiral stamped motifs are especially common in the gold foil that once covered the leatherwork from the tomb of Tutankhamun (Littauer & Crouwel, 1985: pl. XLI-XLVII; Figure I.2; II.12).[58] Unfortunately, only a very small piece of the leather is preserved, which make it difficult to be sure about the way it was impressed, but likely one stamp was used repetitively.[59]

Motifs

A variety of motifs are used to decorate chariot and chariot related leather. Most common are parallel lines, zigzags bands, bands of scallops, icicles/petals, triangles, running spirals, and vegetal motifs (Table IV.2). Dots are found in paint in the earlier material. Vegetal motifs are plentiful, including rosettes, and variations on emblematic plants, which is not unsurprising in royal material. The container's beadnet pattern, from the tomb of Amenhotep II (JE 32400, Cat. No. 5), is unique, as is the bird on the pouch-flap from the tomb of Thutmose IV (JE 97820, Cat. No. 22). In some cases, the motif is integrated with functionality, as evidenced by the stylised *ankh*/flower, in the girth (#40 and #41, Cat. No. 96), surrounding the aperture for the closing mechanism.

---

56 Daressy (1902: 35) also noted other objects with elaborate royal iconography and texts, but these were unavailable for study.
57 Predominantly showing scenes of different nature, including hunting scenes and inscriptions, in gold foil which covered leather. See note 11.
58 It is a common motif in the decoration of the chariots with Carter's Number 120 and 122 as well, where this motif covers large parts of the body. Could the leather casing of the other chariots have shown comparable motifs?
59 The research is ongoing, see note 11.

Provenance	Decoration	
	Type	Motif
Maiherpri	Appliqué	- Stair-step overlapping strips - Strips lengtwise through centre - Layered teardrop
	Colours	- Red (faded to pink) - Green - White
	Paint	- Dots between lines (black)
	Impression/Stamping	- Vegetal - Scallops - Row alternating lily/papyrus - Running spirals - Teardrop
Tomb of Amenhotep II	Appliqué	- Stair-step overlapping strips - Strips lengtwise through centre - Icicles/petals - Scallops - Beadnet with diamonds - Vegetal (rosettes)
	Colours	- Gold - Green - Red - White - Black - Beige/brown (yellow originally?)
	Impression/Stamping	- Vegetal - Running palmettes
	Paint	- Dots between lines (black)
Tomb of Thutmose IV	Appliqué	- Stair-step overlapping strips - Strips lengtwise through centre - Thicker/thinner strips (relief) - Folded lengthwise/single (relief) - Vegetal - Icicles/petals
	Colours	- White - Black - Green - Red
	Impression/Stamping	- Floral - Horus falcon
	Incision	- Zigzag - Diamonds
	Paint	- Dots between lines (black) - Icicles/petals (red/green) - Running spirals (red/green) - Row alternating lily/papyrus (red/green) - Zigzag (green)
Tomb of Amenhotep III	Appliqué	- Stair-step overlapping strips - Strips lengtwise through centre - Strips folded lengthwise/single (relief) - Zigzag - Vegetal - Running spirals
	Colour	- White - Green - Red
	Gilded bronze bosses	

Provenance	Decoration	
Amarna	Appliqué	- Stair-step overlapping strips - Vegetal - Vegetal - Running spirals - Roundel - Stuffing (relief)
	Openwork	Included in the appliqué: - Row of circles - Vertical slits
	Scraping(?)	- Scallops - Running spirals
	Colours	- White - Green - Red
Tano Chariot and related	Appliqué	- Stair-step overlapping strips - Parallel strips - Bulging (relief) - Thicker/thinner strips (relief) - Folded lengthwise/single strips (relief) - Vegetal - Icicles/petals - Zigzag - Roundel
	Colours	- Green - Red
Tano Harness and related	Appliqué	- Stair-step overlapping strips - Parallel strips - Bulging (relief) - Stuffing (relief) - Vegetal
	Colours	- Green - Red - Beige

Table IV.2. Distribution of decoration techniques and motifs/designs. Remarks: - 'Lengthwise through the centre' refers only to those cases in which it is not combined with stair-step overlapping strips.

V. Moving Pictures

Context of Use and Iconography of Chariots in the New Kingdom

Lisa Sabbahy

V.I. Introduction

The ancient Egyptians probably obtained the chariot when the Theban kings of the 17th Dynasty launched attacks against the Hyksos to drive them out of Egypt's Delta at the end of the Second Intermediate Period, about 1650-1549 BC. The earliest evidence of the chariot used by Egyptians is actually textual, and found in the autobiographical inscription of Ahmose, Son of Ebana, who mentions "following the chariot of His Majesty", in the reign of King Ahmose (Sethe, 1961: 3, 6; see Chapter VI). There are fragments of battle scenes from Ahmose's temple at Abydos, but it is not clear from the fragments of bridled chariot horses whether or not they belong to the Hyksos or the Egyptians (Harvey, 1998: figs. 76-79). The initial use of the chariot may well have been slightly earlier, in the reign of Kamose, since he boasts of taking away chariots from the Hyksos in the text on his Second Stela (Habachi, 1972: 36; Malek, 1989: 71-72; discussed in detail in Chapter VI).

Once the chariot has been introduced into Egypt, it is used throughout the period of the New Kingdom, particularly by the king, who is depicted riding in a chariot in scenes of war, hunting, and procession. Elite officials also adopt the use of chariots, and are depicted riding in them for work-related activities, and while hunting. Often a parked chariot with a waiting attendant is shown as a subsidiary detail to a scene of official business, particularly associated with the examination of the fields. Only in the Amarna Period, and in processional scenes, are females shown in chariots. These females are royal, the queen or her daughters, although sometimes women accompany them who might have been non-royal. By the time of the later New Kingdom (19th and 20th Dynasties), with some exceptions, only royal chariot scenes are known, and they are limited to displays of warfare, victory and hunting. The war scenes include depictions of the chariotry divisions of the king's army, but they are never shown outside of these royal scenes, all of which are carved on cult and funerary temple walls.

V.2. Pre-Amarna 18th Dynasty

V.2.1. Royal Scenes: Warfare, Victory, and Sport

Textual evidence shows that the kings of the early 18th Dynasty captured chariots in war (see Chapter VI). For example, Ahmose, Son of Ebana, captures a chariot with horses and charioteer in a battle in Retjenu, or Syro-Palestine, and presents them to Thutmose I (Sethe, 1961, Vol. 1: 9-10, section 39). There is also written evidence for the king of Egypt riding into battle on a chariot: Thutmose III appears at dawn on a chariot of fine gold for the attack on Megiddo (Sethe, 1961, Vol. 3: 657, section 85; see Chapter VI). Unfortunately, representations of royal chariots at this time are minimal. Rediscovered pieces of a lost temple of Thutmose I on the West Bank (Barakat, 1981) give fragmentary evidence for a battle scene with a chariot, but they only show hooves with part of a chariot wheel, and small parts of the chests and throats of two horses (Iwaszczuk, 2011: 24; 2012). A green jasper scarab in the British Museum (EA17774), dating to the 18th Dynasty, depicts Thutmose I in a chariot shooting arrows at a wounded Nubian (Hall, 1913: 50, no. 475; Heinz, 2001: 235; Figure V.1).

Similar to the scene fragments from Ahmose's temple at Abydos are portions of scenes from the funerary temple of Thutmose II, which was either built or finished by his son, Thutmose III, on the West Bank of Thebes (Jaeger, 1982: 344, note 849). The decoration may well date to late in the reign of Thutmose III (Gabolde, 1989; 2009: 175-176). The fragments show horse hooves and chariot wheels, horse heads and bodies with bridle equipment (Bruyère, 1926: pls. II-IV). The largest fragment shows parts of the wheels of four superimposed chariots. The wheels appear to have eight spokes, and the body of the chariot is very open (Bruyère, 1926: pl. III, 7), but it is not clear whether Egyptians or foreigners were in them. Johnson (1992: 96) suggests that these fragments come from two scenes, one on each side of a columned court, with the Egyptian king attacking retreating Asiatic chariots.

Figure V.1. Jasper scarab (EA17774) depicting King Thutmose I in a chariot. © Trustees of the British Museum (London).

The upper part of a broken granite block in the Egyptian Museum (Cairo) (JE 36360), discovered in the Fourth Pylon at Karnak, depicts Amenhotep II victorious, smiting and presenting tied up captives to the god Amun (Zayed, 1985: pls. 1-2; Janzen, 2013: 120-122). In the lower part of the block, the king is depicted tying up captives, and then, mounted on a chariot, he leads them away. His chariot and horses also have bound captives on them. Three captives sit on the backs of the horses, two stand in front of the king, tied to the railing of the chariot body, and one other captive, on his back, is tied to the chariot pole (Figure V.2).

A scene similar to that of Amenhotep II with captives tied on his chariot is found on a limestone stela from the mortuary temple of his grandson, Amenhotep III, which was later reused in the mortuary temple of King Merenptah (Petrie, 1896: pl. X). The upper and lower parts of the stela are divided in half by the way that the scenes are laid out. In the top half, figures of Amun stand back-to-back in the centre of the stela, while on one side the king offers a figure of Ma'at to him, and on the other side, jars of wine. Below, the lower part depicts two back-to-back figures of the king in a chariot. On the left proper, the king drives over foreigners from the south, although the bottom part of this scene with the horses' legs is missing. On the right he drives over foreigners from the north, but here the body of the chariot, and those of the horses, are broken away. It is clear on the left side, however, that four captives are tied and seated on the chariot horses, while another is tied kneeling on the chariot pole. A sixth face can be seen protruding from the bottom front of the chariot (Johnson, 1992: 104; Saleh & Sourouzian, 1987: no. 143).

Figure V.2. A block, found in 1904 in the Fourth Pylon at Karnak, showing Amenhotep II with captives. After: Zayed (1985: pl. 1). Drawing by L.D. Hackley.

Figures tied to royal chariots are not seen often after this stela. Johnson (1992: 29) suggests that the depiction of prisoners on the chariot horses was somewhat awkward, and so the scene was 'discontinued'. There are some Ramesside examples, discussed below, but they only have figures of foreign captives tied under or behind the chariot, and in one case, there seems to be a head on the top railing; captives are not found placed on the horses.

A granite block in the Luxor Museum (J. 129), found in pieces in the fill of the Third Pylon of Karnak Temple in 1927, may come from the same monument as the Amenhotep II block with tied up captives on his chariot, discussed above. On this block, Amenhotep II is shown shooting arrows through a pillow-shaped copper ingot, as he rides in his chariot, reins tied around his waist (Der Manuelian, 1987: 206; Romano, 1979: 68). In both scenes on these two blocks in the Egyptian and Luxor Museum, the king's chariot has largely open sides, *i.e.* it lacks a siding fill.

The driving and manipulating of the chariot has been a topic of discussion, particularly with regard to tying the reins around the waist of the chariot's royal occupant. Is tying the reins around the waist merely artistic license so that the king can be shown alone in the chariot, or could someone actually drive a chariot in this position? As seen in the tomb of Userhet (TT56), Userhet is also shown thus. Did artistic license extend to the elite depictions as well? Looking at other chariot scenes with archers in chariots supplies further evidence. In the Battle of Qadesh, as depicted in Ramesses II's temple at Abu Simbel, two men are shown in each Egyptian chariot: A shield-bearer and an archer (Figure V.3). The shield-bearer grasps the shield with one hand, and holds onto the chariot with the other. In other scenes, the shield-bearer's free hand reaches out and holds the reins that are tied around the archer's waist, who is drawing his bow and shooting. Another scene from the battle shows the royal princes arriving in chariots. Each prince drives the horses while also holding his bow in one hand. A shield-bearer accompanies them in the chariot, and helps with the reins. In the poem about the battle, Ramesses II refers several times to his charioteer and shield-bearer (Lichtheim,

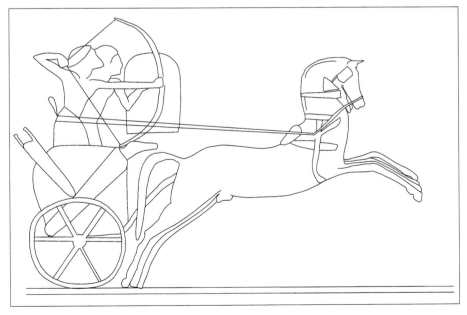

Figure V.3. Shield-bearer and archer. Abu Simbel. Great Temple. After: Oriental Institute P2345, Photographic Archives, Nubia. Drawing by L.D. Hackley.

1976: 68-70). In the action described in the poem, it is clear that wielding the shield to protect the king is this man's main responsibility, but obviously, he could help drive as well. In all of these examples, the archer drives the chariot, but when busy shooting, he ties the reins around his waist. These depictions with reins tied around the waist do appear to reflect reality (Hansen, 1992: 176-77; Heagren, 2010: 74-75; Crouwel, 2013: 87; Sabbahy, 2013: 193).

Another, similar depiction of King Amenhotep II in a chariot, shooting, is found in the tomb of Rei on the West Bank of Thebes (TT72). Rei was a priest at the mortuary temple of King Thutmose III, father of Amenhotep II (Radwan, 1969: 101). Although the tomb wall is badly damaged by burning, it is clear that the king is in his chariot, pursuing wild animals, with his arm in position to be shooting an arrow. There are also hunting dogs, and some accompanying soldiers, as well as a fragmentary text stating that the kill from the hunt would be "presented by the king for sacrifices in the mortuary temple of his father" (Davies, 1934-1935: 50). The only other depiction of Amenhotep II in a chariot is on a small, rectangular, green jasper plaque in the Louvre (E 6256) in which the king is shown in battle shooting arrows from his chariot (Desroches-Noblecourt, 1950; Heinz, 2001: 235), which, like the scarab of Thutmose I mentioned above, dates to the 18th Dynasty (Jaeger, 1982: 2000).

The chariot body of King Thutmose IV, found in his tomb at the Valley of the Kings, is decorated with scenes of the king in a chariot (Figure II.17). The body has a wooden frame with paneling that was covered with cloth, and then stucco, carved with scenes and ornamental decoration (Carter & Newberry, 1904: 26; see also Calvert, 2013; Johnson, 1992: 100-102). It has been suggested that it was probably also covered with silver or gold (Littauer & Crouwel, 1985: 72, but see Calvert, 2013: 47, note 2), but that this was pulled off by tomb robbers. On the outside right proper of the chariot the king is shown driving his chariot, reins tied around his waist, shooting arrows into a mass of fleeing and dying enemies, also in chariots, but only with four spokes and not as elaborate as the king's. Beside the king, and helping him aim his bow, is the hawk-headed god Montu, wearing his insignia of disc and two feathers on his head. Montu stands next to and slightly behind the king, so it is clear the god is there, but also merged with the king. The hieroglyphic inscription in front of the king begins by stating that the king is 'beloved of Montu'. The chariot body that is depicted on the real body has, obviously, a main casing but also a siding fill. A bow-case and quiver are attached to the side. The wheel has eight spokes, which is unusual, and may indicate the heaviness of the chariot body. There is an interesting detail on the body of the chariot, just above the spoke of the wheel, and parallel with the base of the chariot body: the small head and neck of a duck or goose. There is at least one other example of a small figure in that position. A part of a limestone block from the Great Aten Temple at Amarna depicts a chariot wheel with a small kneeling captive in exactly the same position (Whitehouse, 2009: 75). However, a *talatat* block from Karnak might also show this type of kneeling figure (Ertman, 1998: 59-60). These small figures at the bottom of the chariot are perhaps related to small heads of foreigners that can be found as decorations on the top of chariot linchpins, and serving as symbols of the king's destruction of his enemies (Ritner, 1993: 130-131). This decorated linchpin appears first in the Amarna Period, on a *talatat* from the Great Aten Temple at Amarna (Aldred, 1973: 151; Ertman, 1998: 51-60), and they are common on chariots in military scenes of the 19th and 20th

Dynasties (The Epigraphic Survey, 1930: pls. XXI, XXX, XXXI; 1986: pls. V, X, XXII, XXXV). Note that the small head can also be shown being bitten by a lion whose head appears to be on top of the human head (The Epigraphic Survey, 1930: pl. XVII). On the left side of the chariot body Thutmose IV is shown alone in a chariot riding into a group of foreign enemies who are also in chariots. The king is not shooting, but grabbing enemies by the hair with one hand, while holding his bow, and dispatching them with his war axe, held in his other hand. The reins are tied around his waist. The side of the depicted chariot shows the Horus falcon spreading a wing across the opening. A quiver hangs on the chariot's side (Carter & Newberry, 1904: pl. XI; Figure II.17).

V.2.2. Non-Royal Scenes: Officialdom at Work, Hunting, and Funerals

Officials of the 18th Dynasty are often depicted in their tombs using chariots in their work. In fact, the earliest complete, surviving New Kingdom scenes featuring chariots are non-royal and non-military. The tomb of Renni, (T7) at El Kab, dating to the reign of Amenhotep I, depicts his chariot parked in the field, as part of a harvest scene (Tylor, 1900: pl. II). This is the earliest known example of a chariot standing empty in the fields, which becomes more popular in the 18th Dynasty, particularly in tombs of officials connected to grain, as was Renni, who held the titles of mayor and counter of the grain. The chariot is accompanied by an attendant, probably the chariot driver, who waits, holding the reins, or, rarely, sitting in the chariot. In Renni's scene, the attendant stands behind the chariot, holding the reins and a whip. The body of the chariot is damaged, but a bow-case seems to point up from the side. The wheel has four spokes.

A similar scene appears in the El Kab tomb of Paheri (T3), from the reign of Thutmose III (Tylor & Griffith, 1894: pl. 3). Paheri was mayor as well as scribe of the granary. His chariot is also shown waiting in the fields, with an attendant standing behind it holding reins and whip (Figure V.4). The chariot wheel has four spokes; the chariot body only has a main casing. In the bottommost scene on the wall, a boat is shown twice, once with its sail down for traveling downstream, and once with the sail up for tacking upstream. In each boat a chariot with four-spoke wheels is shown lying on the roof of the cabin. In the boat with the sail up, the chariot horses are standing in the front of the boat. The boats are connected to a scene of Paheri "receiving the tribute of gold for the king" (Tylor & Griffith, 1894: 12). A similar boat scene is found in the tomb of Ka'emhet in Thebes (TT57), reign of Amenhotep III, who was a scribe and overseer of granaries. A chariot is lying on the roof of a boat being rowed, and the chariot horses are standing in the very rear of the boat (Decker, 2006: fig. 28). This chariot has six-spoke wheels, but the details of the chariot body are somewhat amorphous.

The tomb of Amenemopet (and Djehutynefer; TT297), who was a scribe and counter of the grain of Amun, has two very similar scenes of chariot teams waiting by a tree, under which is a round-topped boundary stone (Strudwick, 2003: pl. 3, 6.2 b-c). Only fragments of either chariot can still be seen, but the chariot teams, trees, and boundary stones make the type of scene clear. This scene development showing detailed field measuring, appears in the scenes from the tomb of Nebamun (tomb location unknown, but in Thebes) and Menna (TT69). Nebamun was scribe of the grain accounts of Amun, active probably during the

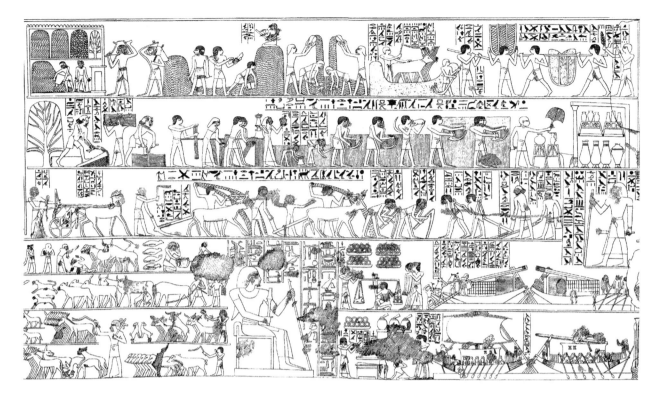

Figure V.4. Scene from the Tomb of Paheri (T3) at El Kab. From: Tylor & Griffith (1894: pl. III).

reign of Thutmose IV. A beautiful fragment from his tomb depicting two chariots waiting by a sycamore tree is housed in the British Museum (London) (Parkinson, 2008: 110) (Figure V.5). Nearby, although not completely preserved, officials measure fields of grain. In the top register, the attendant of the chariot stands behind the vehicle, holding the reins with both hands. In the register below, the chariot attendant sits on the floor of the chariot body, dangling his legs off the back. The reins are looped casually over the top railing, and the attendant holds them as they hang down. The horses of this chariot seem to be drinking from a trough of some kind, although the paint on this part of the wall is not well preserved. Both chariots have bluish or faded green colored leather or wood as main casing, and no siding fill; the wheels have six spokes.

A very similar scene occurs in the aforementioned tomb of Ka'emhet (TT57). A bored, or possibly sleeping, chariot attendant sits backward in the chariot while the horses, like in the Nebamun scene, face a tree and seem to be eating (Wreszinski, 1915: pl. 192). In the field measuring scene in this tomb, four chariots are shown waiting with their attendants or drivers (Wreszinski, 1915: pl. 191). The first chariot has his driver standing behind the chariot holding the reins. In the next two chariots the drivers are looking backwards, and their heads are at a lower level, so they must be seated backwards in the chariot. The driver of the last chariot stands in it, bending forward, pulling on the reins and holding a whip. Only the details of the first chariot can be seen: the siding is filled and the wheel has eight spokes.

Menna was scribe of the fields, during the period of Thutmose IV to that of Amenhotep III. In his tomb in Luxor (TT69) a chariot stands ready, reins held by the attendant behind it, while a large pile of grain is being measured (Campbell, 1910: 86; Hodel-Hoenes, 1991: fig. 54; Parkinson, 2008: 111). The main casing

Figure V.5. Scene from the tomb of Nebamun (EA37982), showing two chariots waiting by a sycamore tree. © Trustees of the British Museum (London).

of the chariot has a dark bluish hue, and the chariot has a siding fill. A bow-case is attached to the side and the wheels have six spokes.

There are a few other types of work scenes where an official is depicted in or with his chariot. Meeting Puntites on the Red Sea shore is shown in TT143 of an unknown owner (Davies, 1934-1935: 48, fig. 3; Hallman, 2006: pl. 9), but tentatively dated to the period of Thutmose III to Amenhotep II (Hallman, 2006: 24, note 829). There are two registers, the upper one showing the arrival of the Puntites by water, and offering of goods to the Egyptians, and then below, the departure of the Puntites, while the Egyptian official makes offerings, before they leave as well. Behind the official, an attendant holds the reins of the chariot horses (Wreszinski, 1915: pls. 347-348). The Egyptians are armed with shields, spears, axes and quivers, and a bow-case is on the side of the chariot.

In the tomb of Amenmose (TT89), Chancellor of the King, who had a long career spanning the reigns of Thutmose III to that of Amenhotep III, Amenmose is depicted with his soldiers, leaving the shore of the Red Sea where the Puntites have brought him exotic goods (Davies & Davies, 1940: pl. XXV). After a scene of the tribute of Syria and Nubia, there are two registers of Puntites presenting piles and sacks of gum, followed by two registers below showing the Egyptian soldiers heading away with their loaded donkeys. None of these men are shown with weapons. Among them is Amenmose in his chariot, shown large enough to span both registers. Unfortunately, Amenmose's figure has been completely damaged, along with much of the chariot.

Two more scenes of officials in chariots from the reign of Thutmose IV are known. In TT90, the tomb of the Standard-Bearer and Troop Commander Nebamun (not to be confused with the Nebamun mentioned previously), there is a fragment showing a man in a chariot beside the river, next to the royal boat

(Davies, 1923: pl. XXIV, XXV). Amenhotep-sise, Second High Priest of Amun (TT75), is shown driving his chariot with attendants walking in front of him, and four others, one with scribal equipment, following behind him (Davies, 1923: pls. VI, XVIII).

Offering of chariots to the temple of Amun as gifts for the New Year is sometimes depicted. One such scene is seen in the tomb of Amenhotep (TT73), who was an overseer of works for Hatshepsut's obelisks at Karnak (Aldred, 1969: 78; Porter & Moss, 1960: 143). There are three registers of offerings on the northwest wall: One chariot is offered in the top row, while two are shown in the bottom register (Säve-Söderbergh, 1957a: pl. 3). All three chariots have low and narrow main casings only and thus are largely open. Two of the chariots clearly show two support straps on the side. All the chariots have an empty quiver on the side; the wheels have four spokes. Another such scene is found in the tomb of Kenamun (TT93), Chief Steward of King Amenhotep II. Incuded with weapons and shields given as New Year gifts for the king, are two chariots on stands (Aldred, 1969: 79). Their images are not completely preserved, but it is clear that they both have a bow-case attached (Davies, 1930: pl. XXII; Littauer & Crouwel, 1985: pl. LXXV). A similar scene in (TT92) the tomb of Suemniwet, the Royal Butler of Amenhotep II (Bryan, 2009: 25, pls. 10-11), shows registers of objects offered to Amenhotep II, which include at least four chariots.

A common scene in 18th Dynasty Theban tombs belonging to high officials, such as the vizier, or a High Priest of Amun, is of foreigners, invariably Syrians, presenting tribute including chariots and horses, to the king. This scene is first known from the period of the co-regency of Hatshepsut and Thutmose III (Morkot, 2007: 172), and perhaps the earliest example is found in the tomb of the vizier Rekhmire (TT100; Davies, 1943: pls. XXII-XXIII; Hallman, 2006: pl. 2). On the southwest wall of the north-south hall, a Syrian wheels a chariot, holding the chariot pole and yoke. An empty bow-case is attached to the side, attached by straps. There is only a main casing and the wheel has four spokes. A similar scene appears in the tomb of Intef (TT155) the Great Herald of the King, dating to the co-regency of Hatshepsut and Thutmose III (Säve-Söderbergh, 1957a: pl. 13). One man pulls a chariot, holding the yoke with one hand and the chariot pole with the other. The bow-case on the side of the chariot is open, and a man following the chariot carries a bow and quiver for arrows.

Menkheperraseneb, High Priest of Amun under Thutmose III, has a five-register tribute scene on the northwest wall of the north-south hall of his tomb (TT86), where in the third register a chariot with team of horses is brought in. In the register just below, a man carries a chariot pole with yoke and chariot body attached, on his shoulder, and holds a wheel in one hand (Davies, 1933a: pl. VII; Wreszinski, 1915: pls. 273, 276-277). Two contemporary tombs, TT84 of Amenedjeh, the Royal Herald of Thutmose III (Davies & Davies, 1941: pl. 13), and TT42, of Amenmose, Captain of the Troops (Davies, 1933a: pl. XXXV), each has a two-register scene of Syrian tribute. In TT84, a man wheels in a chariot, pulling it by the pole, and holding a quiver in his other hand. The chariot body has a low main casing and support straps are visible. A bow-case is on the side of the chariot; the wheel has four spokes. The chariots in TT42 are the same in every detail. There are two of them, presented by a Syrian kneeling on the ground. The chariots are not attached to horses, but standing with a stick supporting the chariot pole; the horses are being held behind the chariots by attendants.

Two additional Syrian tribute scenes with chariots are somewhat later. Sobekhotep (TT63), from the reign of Thutmose IV (Dziobek & Raziq, 1990), only has a fragment of a chariot wheel visible on a piece from the tomb currently housed in the British Museum (London) (EA37987). Two horses are depicted behind the wheel fragment, so it has been suggested that one man was pulling the chariot by its pole, and the reins of the horses were tied to the chariot railing (Hallman, 2006: pl. 4; Dziobek & Raziq, 1990: pl. 33). The tomb of Amenmose (TT89), from the reign of Amenhotep III, depicts a row of Syrians presenting tribute, two of whom have chariots that they hold with both hands upright by the chariot pole (Davies & Davies, 1940: pl. XXIV). The scene is somewhat damaged, but one chariot wheel clearly has six spokes.

A related scene-type in tombs of high officials is the production of chariots, or parts thereof, often depicted along with scenes of leather making (discussed in more detail in Chapter II). The earliest scene of chariot production seems to occur in the tomb of Hepusonb (TT67), First Prophet of Amun in the time of Hatshepsut, from which a fragment of a scene is preserved (Davies, 1963: 9, note 6). After that, is a scene of chariot manufacturing in the tomb of Intef (TT155). Although only fragments remain, one of them clearly shows the work being done to shape a chariot pole (Säve-Söderbergh, 1957a: pl. 10, 5). The tomb of Menkheperraseneb (TT86), shows the finishing of the wheels and one man seems to be finishing the attachment of a chariot body and pole (Davies, 1933a: pl. 12).

A similar scene is found in the tomb of Puyemre (TT39), who was the Second High Priest of Amun in the reign of Thutmose III. A craftsman is shown working on the body of a chariot, set on a stand, with its two wheels shown, but not yet attached (Davies, 1922-1923: pls. XXIV, XXVIII). A virtually identical scene is seen in the tomb of Mery (TT95), who was High Priest of Amun during the reign of Amenhotep II (Wreszinski, 1915: pl. 307). In one register a man makes finishing touches on a chariot body with pole, while in the register below, two wheels are finished, and a yoke is being attached to a pole.

Two tombs from the reign of Thutmose IV have manufacturing scenes that include chariots: the tomb of Hepu (TT66; Figure II.8), the vizier, and the tomb of Amenhotep-sise (TT75), Second Prophet of Amun. Hepu is depicted seated, watching the work of three registers of craftsmen (Davies, 1963: pl. VIII). In the top register leather is being worked for quivers and bow-cases, and a strip of leather or rawhide is being put on a chariot wheel to serve as a tire. In the register below is a completed chariot body with pole and yoke on a stand awaiting wheels. This scene is repeated in the tomb of Amenhotep-sise; a man in exactly the same position is putting a leather or rawhide tire onto a wheel, while a completed chariot, minus the wheel, is on a stand behind him (Davies, 1923: pl. X; Wreszinski, 1915: pls. 241-242).

Hunting scenes in tombs of elite officials also feature chariots. A fragment of such a scene is preserved in the tomb of User (TT21), in the reign of Thutmose I (Davies, 1913: pl. XXII). The fleeing animals, shot with arrows, are preserved, but only part of the wheel of the chariot pursuing them is. Another fragment from a hunting scene is preserved from the tomb of the Intef (TT155; Säve-Söderbergh, 1957a: pl. 16). The bottom half of the chariot wheel and the horses' legs are shown, facing a man with a gazelle over his shoulders. Behind the chariot is a foot pushing off the ground; perhaps this individual is stepping up into the chariot. Other assorted fragments show bits of sandy ground, parts of various wild animals, and arrows.

A fragmentary chariot scene, which is suggested to belong to a scene of bringing the catch from a hunt, was found in the tomb of Djehuty (TT11), the overseer of the treasury in the time of Hatshepsut and Thutmose III (Säve-Söderbergh, 1958: 287, fig. 5), although the actual hunting is on foot, and shown in another room (Säve-Söderbergh, 1958: 290, fig. 7). An empty chariot is preserved, along with the legs of the chariot team, a man next to the horses, and one in front. Another scene of a man in a chariot shooting his bow is found in the just mentioned tomb of Amenedjeh (TT84), from the reign of Thutmose III. The scene is complete but the paint and plaster are badly damaged. The man stands in a chariot that is clad with only a main casing, shooting his bow and driving with the reins around his waist, and a quiver on his back (Porter & Moss, 1960: 169, 15; Virey, 1891: 355, fig.5; Wegner, 1933: pl. IXa).

The first completely preserved hunting scene is that in the tomb of Userhet (TT56), reign of Amenhotep II (Beinlich-Seeber & Shedid, 1987: pl. 12). Userhet stands in the chariot, reins tied around his back, shooting arrows at the fleeing desert animals. Userhet's stance in his chariot is modeled on that of King Amenhotep II, discussed above, as he shoots arrows through copper ingots.

One last type of elite tomb scene that includes a chariot is that of the funeral. A few scenes, seemingly all belonging to the period of Thutmose III to Thutmose IV/Amenhotep III, show a chariot being carried or pulled to the tomb along with other possessions of the deceased. In the tomb of Userhet (TT56) one man pulls a chariot, holding the yoke in one hand and the chariot pole in the other. Another man walks beside the chariot, holding the reins of a single horse that walks behind. The chariot only has a main casing, two support straps attached to the side, as well as a bow-case and the wheels have four spokes (Beinlich-Seeber & Shedid, 1987: pls. 14, 27). A similar scene is seen in the tomb of Haremheb (TT78), dating to the period of Thutmose III to Amenhotep III. A register depicting objects being brought to the tomb shows one chariot being carried, followed by a second chariot pulled by a team of horses. No one is in the chariot; an attendant walks behind it, pulling on the reins (Brack & Brack, 1980: pls. 54, 61). Chariots being brought in a procession of funerary goods for the burial are shown as well in the tomb of Mentiywy (TT172), reign of Thutmose III (Porter & Moss, 1960: 280, 5-6); Ahmose (TT121), reign of Thutmose III (Porter & Moss, 1960: 235, 8); Hety (TT151), reign of Thutmose IV (Porter & Moss, 1960: 261, 8), and that of Sobekhotep (TT63), reign of Thutmose IV (Porter & Moss, 1960: 125, 11).

A related funerary scene can depict a river boat pulling or accompanying a smaller papyriform funeral boat that is taking the deceased and his wife on the pilgrimage to Abydos (Assmann, 2001: 305-308; Settgast, 1963: 80). Such a scene appears in the tomb of Ka'emhet (TT57), mentioned before. He and his wife are shown seated in a papyriform boat being pulled by a larger ship with rowers. A chariot lies on the roof of the cabin, along with a bed and headrest. The horses can be seen on the deck at the front (Wreszinski, 1923: 207). Sometimes the horses are shown on the boat, but the chariot is not, for example in the 19th Dynasty tomb of Tia, an official of Ramesses II, and his sister, Tia, at Saqqara (Martin, 1997: pl. 47).

V.3. Amarna Period

V.3.1. Royal Scenes: Karnak Talatat

There is an abundance of pictorial evidence for chariot use in the Amarna Period, which can be basically divided into three different categories: *talatat* blocks from Karnak; the *talatat* blocks from Amarna that were removed and taken to Hermopolis in Ramesside times (particularly by Ramesses II), and scenes in the elite rock cut North and South Tombs at Amarna. The Karnak *talatat* blocks depict chariots of the king and queen in procession, accompanied by military or police personal, also in chariots. Those taken from Amarna depict this same subject as well. In addition, the scenes in the elite tombs contain royal processions, and, moreover, some tombs show the tomb owner carrying out the duties of his office, as well as being rewarded for such by the king.

That royal chariot scenes are so abundant in the Amarna Period, especially in terms of processions, begs the question of what happened before that to bring about this seemingly new development. Other than the stela of Amenhotep III with the captives on his chariot, discussed above, there are no other known chariot depictions from his reign. In fact, little evidence is preserved of everyday use by royalty of chariots in the earlier part of the 18th Dynasty; what is preserved does not shown royal use of chariots for processions or travel, but rather for war or sport. This might reflect the new landscape of Amarna, with its complex system and importance of roads (Kemp, 2008: 8), or an increase in production and use of chariots.

The *talatat* blocks from Karnak with chariot scenes come from the *Rwd-mnw*, one of the four sun temples Amenhotep IV built at Karnak. The chariot scenes seem to indicate that this structure had long walls, with the decoration focusing on processions by the royal family, accompanied by military attendants (Redford, 1984: 72). These scenes have been discussed in great detail by Hoffmeier (1988: 35-40), so only the most important details that were actually present on the *talatat*s in the greatly restored scenes are discussed here. The largest scene that could be identified depicts Amenhotep IV and Nefertiti standing together in a chariot pulled by galloping horses, with the king holding the reins. The queen grasps a handle attached to the top of the top railing with her right hand (Hoffmeier, 1988: pl. 37). It is an actual handle, a rare feature and only seen in the Amarna period, and different from the cut out hand-grips seen on chariots at Amarna (see Section V.3.2 'Royal Processions'). A bow-case is on the side. The wheel has six spokes. Behind them, and on a much smaller scale, are three registers of attendants in chariots, three chariots to a register. Each chariot has a driver, bending over and holding the reins, and a second man who stands, also bending over.

This scene displays another development in the Amarna Period: the appearance of a female member of the royal family in a chariot. This type of scene first appears here in the Karnak *talatat*, but it is much more common in the Amarna tomb scenes depicting royal processions in the city. At Amarna the queen can be shown in a chariot with the king, or driving her own chariot behind him. The royal daughters can be shown in these two ways, as well. Hoffmeier (1988: 36, and pl. 18) suggests a reconstructed scene based on Karnak *talatat* blocks TS 1465 and TS 1441, of the king in a large chariot followed by the queen, driving alone in a much smaller chariot, but this is, according to him, "very tentative".

A number of new and unusual chariot scenes appear in the *talatat* blocks from Karnak. One partially restored scene depicts King Akhenaten stepping into his chariot with the help of a stool (Figure V.6). This is the first known scene of a king mounting his chariot, but one that will be repeated numerous times in Ramesside temple relief scenes of the king setting off on campaign (*e.g.* The Epigraphic Survey, 1930: pl. XVI), and returning in victory to Egypt (such as The Epigraphic Survey, 1986: pl. XXXV).

A number of *talatat* that were found reused in the interior of the Ninth Pylon have scenes from a first *heb-sed* of Amenhotep IV, which must have taken place very early in his reign. The reconstructed blocks show the king, and also his family, coming and going from the palace to the celebration, and being carried in the jubilee procession (Redford, 1984: 116-18). All of them are carried, in carrying chairs, or in the case of the king, on a large palanquin (Gohary, 1992: pl. I). There is one scene of two small, waiting chariots with attendants, but the chariots might well belong to a man labeled Mayor of Thebes and Vizier, standing nearby (Gohary, 1992: pls. 2, 19). There is no evidence of chariot use by the royal family during any of the movement connected to the *heb-sed*. There is also no evidence of a *heb-sed* having been depicted in the Amarna tombs, so there is no comparative evidence.

The ceremonial setting created by Akhenaten at Amarna may have been influenced by that created by his father, Amenhotep III, at Thebes, which became "a stage for enacting kingship" (Baines, 2001: 299). Amenhotep III built or added to a series of very traditional cult temples on the East Bank of Thebes, connected by processional avenues set up north-south (O'Connor, 2001: 155-157). In addition, there were approaches to the temples by water, such as the canal that led up to the quay before the entrance into the Karnak Amun Temple. On the West Bank, the king built his extensive funerary temple, and to the south a palace complex including another Amun temple (Malqata). A large harbor known as the Birket Habu was cut south of the palace, and opposite on the East Bank, was a smaller, matching harbor (O'Connor, 2001: 77). It is known that during ceremonies, such

Figure V.6. King Akhenaten with stepping-stool. After: Redford (1976: pl. 12). Drawing by L.D. Hackley.

as his *heb-seds*, Amenhotep III traveled in barques in these harbors (Kemp, 2006: 277), reenacting the travels of the sun god Ra "through the day sky and then the netherworld" (O'Connor, 2001: 162) in the god's day and night barques. In the tomb of Kheruef (TT192), who was the Steward of Queen Tiye, is a text describing part of the ceremony at the king's first *heb-sed*, which states: "(They) were directed to the lake of His Majesty to row in the bark of the king. They grasped the towropes of the evening bark and the prow rope of the morning bark, and they towed the barks at the great place" (The Epigraphic Survey, 1980: 43).

V.3.2. Amarna

Royal Processions in Elite Tomb Scenes

The city of Amarna was set up on a north-south axis alongside the river. The royal family lived at the far north, and the largest ceremonial palace and the Great Aten Temple were in the center of the city. A straight road, called the Royal Road, started in the north and passed straight south through the city. On a daily basis, the royal family left the North Palace, and galloped down the Royal Road to the Great Temple of the Aten in central Amarna in the morning, and returned in the evening, perhaps in a recreation of a tradition temple procession in which divine images would have been carried through the populace (Kemp, 2006: 284). Or, it has been suggested, Akhenaten, appearing like the sun (in his electrum covered chariot), traveled through the city on the Royal Road as if, like the sun, he brought creation to life each day (Aldred, 1988: 131). The processions of his father Amenhotep III were based on boat travel, in the tradition of the ancestors. The inscription of Kheruef (TT192), mentioned above, says that the king insisted the barks were towed "in accordance with writings of old" (The Epigraphic Survey, 1980: 43). "From time immemorial the gods in Egypt had travelled over the waters of heaven in ships" (Aldred, 1988: 130). Akhenaten continued his father's predilection for processions, but he 'modernized' them with chariots, which were also more practical in his new city.

In the rock cut tomb of Ahmes at Amarna (T3), Royal Scribe and Fan-Bearer, there is a badly damaged scene depicting Akhenaten, Nefertiti and one of their daughters, together in a chariot being driven by the king (Davies, 1905b: pl. XXXVa). There had been no evidence of royal daughters in any of the chariots in the Karnak *talatat*, perhaps because they may have been too young at that point. This scene in the tomb of Ahmes, then, is the earliest example of a royal daughter riding in a chariot. The king faces forward, and the queen, slightly in front of him and on his far side, turns to face him. The Aten is directly above them, and one ray holds an *ankh*-sign between their faces. The small princess stands in the very front of the chariot with just her head over the bar, while her left arm rests on a quiver. The reconstruction of the scene clearly shows an object resembling three strands of beads, or decorated leather that looks similar to beads, hanging down from the neckstrap of the horse. In his discussion of the chariots on the Karnak talatat, Hoffmeier (1988: 37) pointed out several *talatat* that he said have a *menat* hanging down on the side of the horse. The present author does not see a *menat* in the relevant block in TS 45, and what Hoffmeier refers to in scene TS 1464 is something different than what seems to be on T45, and also not a *menat*. Ikram and Veldmeijer (Personal Communication, 2017) suggest that these are just beads and are decorative, similar to what is found on horses pulling carriages in Egypt today. In fact, a string of faience decorative beads, with eyes, *wadjet* eyes, and an *ankh*, which functioned to protect the horse, was found in the stable belonging to house N 51.3 at Amarna (Weber, 2012: 214; Markowitz, 1999: 261).

The tomb of the High Priest of the Aten, Meryre I (T4), has a scene of the daily procession from the palace in the north, with the king driving a large chariot, and the queen behind, driving a much smaller one (Davies, 1903: pl. X). Both of their chariots have a circular aperture in the siding fill, and a double front support going from the chariot body to the chariot pole. Their chariots, like all the others in the scene, have a closed bow-case on the side, and the wheels have six spokes. Behind the queen's chariot, two much smaller registers show their daughters and attendants in chariots. The first group in each of the registers is a chariot with two princesses. One drives, holding the reins and whip, while the other stands beside her, right hand grasping a hand-grip which sticks out of the top railing of the chariot, and left arm around her sister. The inscriptions in the tomb of Meryre I have the late epithets given the Aten, and so the princesses may have been older at that time, and able to drive their own chariot, although Redford (1988: 87) warns against believing that the "artist would always faithfully depict the age of his royal subjects". Behind each chariot with the princesses are three chariots with attendants. These chariots are driven by charioteers, who are depicted on the far side of the chariot, hunched over, protruding from a kind of cabin, separating them from the two attendants. Each attendant holds a tall feather fan in the right hand, and holds onto a sticking out handle on the chariot with the left hand (encircled in Figure V.7). This is the only representation of the people in chariots who hold on in such a way and it is not entirely without doubt if the sticking out objects are truly purpose-made hand-grips or not. A partition separating the driver from the other occupants of the chariot is not depicted in any other scenes of chariot drivers from Amarna, however. All of the chariots with the daughters and attendants have siding fill, and there is a small circular cut out hand-grip in the center of the side of the vehicle, just below the top railing. Hand-grips first appear in the chariots at Amarna and are seemingly meant for passengers. Though common in the Amarna Period, they appear only occasionally afterwards. Since the Amarna Period is also when females are first seen in chariots, perhaps hand-grips and female use of chariots are related, although there are images, Amarna Period and just after, showing males using the hand-grips too (see below). At the very bottom of the scene is a register with running military personnel and standard-bearers, as well as five chariots, which seem to be carrying high officials,

Figure V.7. Royal daughters and their attendants in a chariot procession. Amarna. Tomb of Meryre I (T4). From: Davies (1903: pl. XIX).

although the details are not well preserved (Davies, 1903: pl. XX). After the royal family arrives at the temple, Meryre I accompanies them inside. Two drivers are shown waiting with chariots from the retinue traveling with the royal family, and other attendants hold the chariots of the king and queen (Davies, 1903: pl. XXVI). The drivers stand behind the chariot, holding the ends of the reins and bowing toward the king, while two other men stand at the horses' heads, holding the reins by the horses' head. Finally, a scene follows of the royal chariots waiting at the riverside, again with attendants holding the horse at the headstall (Davies, 1903: pl. XXIX). These same two minor scenes are shown in the tomb of Pentu (T5), Royal Scribe and Chief Physician. Four chariots of officials and one royal chariot wait outside the temple, each with one attendant at the back, holding the reins (Davies, 1906: pl. V). Another scene has four chariots waiting near boats on the river (Davies, 1906: pl. VIII).

A somewhat similar procession leaving from the palace can be found in the tomb of Panehsy (T6), the Second Prophet of the Aten, whose tomb inscriptions also have the late Aten epithets (Davies, 1905a: pl. XIII). The king is driving his own chariot, which has a large circular opening in the siding fill. The queen drives behind in a smaller chariot with a closed side panel. One small chariot with princesses, and attendants following is right behind the chariot of the queen, and another is shown below (Davies, 1905a: pl. XV). As in the tomb scene just discussed above, one princess drives and another stands beside and slightly behind her. The attendants are two to a chariot, and the charioteer driver is hunched over, but clearly not separated by a partition. A *talatat* block found at Hermopolis has a similar grouping of attendants (Cooney, 1965: 57), with the driver leaning forward on the far side, but also in this case, there is no partition separating him from the attendants. Redford (1976: 89) has suggested from inscriptional evidence that the *talatat* from Hermopolis seem to have come from a "sunshade of Ankhesenpaaten" and "a house of Meretaten", so processions with attendants would probably be an expected scene type. Note that there are *talatat* blocks depicting attendants restraining waiting chariots with horses (Cooney, 1965: 54, 58). An interesting detail of Panehsy's tomb scene is that in the lower right corner there is a chariot with three individuals: a driver, and two attendants holding sunshades (Davies, 1905a: pl. XVIII). One of the chariots in front of this group has the man standing next to the driver holding on to the hand-grip. On the east side of the south wall of Panehsy's tomb are four registers with minor scenes, each having a waiting chariot; the chariot details are not well preserved (Davies, 1905a: pl. XI).

Elite Work and Reward Scenes

The Chief of Police at Amarna, Mahu, is depicted in other scenes in his tomb (T9) involved with his responsibility for security at the city. In the first scene, on the north-east wall, the king and queen, with one of their small daughters, leave the temple in their chariot, and then are greeted and adored by Mahu as they pass through an area in which Davies (1906: pls. XX-XXII) suggests are gate-like structures with sentries. Other, different interpretations have been put forth, including that these odd structures are platforms with standards (Healey, 2012: 34-37), or else the actual boundary stelae of the city (O'Connor, 1988: 41-52). The royal chariot is entirely closed, has a bow-case at the side, and a single front support. The wheels have six spokes. Another scene, on the south-west wall, depicts Mahu's role in capturing three criminals, and taking them to the vizier (Davies, 1906: pl. XXVI). In the upper registry Mahu is listening to the news brought by men running up to him on foot. His chariot and driver are waiting. In the lower register, Mahu drives up to the vizier's office in his chariot, reaching out with his left hand to pull on the reins along with his driver (Figure V.8). The chariot is entirely closed, and there is a bow-case on the side. Two other minor scenes with waiting chariots show Mahu and his attendants in front of the palace, and Mahu visiting the temple (Davies, 1906: pls. XVII, XIX).

Huya (T1) was the Overseer of the Royal Harim and Steward of the Great Wife Tiye. One scene in his tomb depicts him accompanying Queen Tiye when she visits the temple with her son, Akhenaten (Davies, 1905b: pl. VIII). A small register showing waiting royal chariots runs under the temple scene (Davies, 1905b: pl. XII). Huya was present at Akhenaten's receiving of foreign tribute from Syria and Kush in regnal year 12. Soldiers are shown bringing in two chariots as part of the tribute. Royal chariots waiting with their drivers are depicted amid the scenes of the foreigners and tribute (Davies, 1905b: pl. XIV). This same scene of foreign tribute in year 12 is depicted in the tomb of Meryre II (T2) (Aldred, 1988: 178-179). In the top register a chariot is shown along with other weapons and armaments, and three registers below, a chariot is shown being carried in and presented (Davies, 1905a: pl. XXXIX). Like in Huya's tribute scene, waiting royal chariots are included as part of the scene (Davies, 1905a: pl. XL). On the back wall of the shrine in Huya's tomb, funerary objects are depicted around his statue, sculpted in the rock. Along with other furniture, in the top left is a chariot (Davies, 1905b: pl. XXIV).

Figure V.8. Mahu chasing criminals, from his tomb at Amarna. After: Davies (1906: pl. XXVI). Drawing by L.D. Hackley.

During the Amarna Period, rather than a single scene displaying the Gold of Honour (*shebu*) being given by the king to the official, the occasion becomes a sequence of scenes. The rock cut tomb of Meryre II (T2), Royal Scribe and Overseer of the House of Nefertiti, contains a good example of such a sequence (Davies, 1905a: pl. XXXIII). Meryre II is standing under the Window of Appearance while King Akhenaten leans over and hands him down the Gold of Honour. Other gold collars are already around his neck. The royal chariots are depicted in two small registers up at the level of the king and queen. They both are entirely closed with a hand-grip as the only aperture. The upper chariot clearly has a decorative band of uraei with discs on their heads along the bottom of the main casing. Both chariots have a bow-case at the side. The wheels are six-spoked. In the register below this, Meryre II, greeted by cheers, returns to his chariot, driver holding the reins. Then in the next register below, amid a jubilant crowd, Meryre II is driven home, standing in the chariot holding the top railing, while a bending over charioteer drives. The chariot has a main casing and siding fill and is thus entirely closed, and the wheels have six spokes.

A similar reward scene appears in the tomb of Parennefer (T7), the Royal Craftsman. Parennefer is shown below the Window of Appearances wearing several Gold of Honour collars (Davies, 1908b: pl. IV). The royal chariots are shown waiting in registers above, opposite the large window. Parennefer's waiting chariot may have been shown, but the scene is badly damaged. However, there is enough preserved to see that he is driven away amid celebrating people (Davies, 1908b: pl. V).

Similarly, in the tomb of Tutu (T8), Gold of Honour necklaces are given by the king, and then Tutu moves away from the Window of Appearances, driving away in his chariot and holding onto the hand-grip (Davies, 1908b: pls. XIX-XX). There are numerous small scenes with chariots in the registers above and below him. For example, in the top register, horses are shown eating out of troughs, with their chariots parked nearby. Two chariots, each with driver and passenger, are galloping along; another scene has a driver starting up a chariot, while another man jumps on.

The reward scene in the tomb of Ay (T25) is also similar to that of Parennefer and Tutu. Ay's chariot is not shown waiting – only those of the king and queen (Davies, 1908b: pl. XXIX). Then Ay is shown being congratulated when he has left the palace. Three waiting chariots with drivers are depicted above this scene, but it is not clear if one of the chariots belongs to Ay (Davies, 1908b: pl. XXX).

A much simpler version of the award of the Gold of Honour is depicted on the stela of Any, found at Amarna (Davies, 1908a: pl. XXIII; Freed, 1999: 173). The stela simply depicts Any returning after receiving the award. He is shown being driven by his charioteer. He stands, wearing four gold collars, holding on to the left side of the chariot, and resting his right hand on the bar of the chariot. The chariot is entirely closed, and there is a bow-case on the side. The wheels have six spokes. In the inscription above him, it states: "I come in peace as the favored one of the king".

Saqqara: Elite Scenes

Two tombs from the New Kingdom necropolis south of the Unas causeway date to the reign of Akhenaten, and both have scenes including chariots. The tomb of Meryneith, Royal Scribe and Steward of the Temple of Aten in Memphis has a 'sub-scene' of six chariots with attendants as part of the scenes of the funeral ritual (Raven & Van Walsem, 2014: 96, 15). The nearby tomb of Ptahemwia, the Royal Butler, depicts his waiting chariot and driver in a scene of an encampment by the river, probably during an inspection tour (Raven et al., 2007: 26, fig. 8).

V.4. Post-Amarna 18th Dynasty

V.4.1. Royal Scenes of Battle, Victory, Procession and Hunting: Kings Tutankhamun, Ay, and Horemheb

Large and small sized blocks from the interior of the Second Pylon of Karnak Temple, originally part of a structure built by Amenhotep IV were reused by Tutankhamun to build a temple of 'Nebkheprure in Thebes', probably on the East Bank at Karnak (Eaton-Krauss, 2016: 95-101; Johnson, 1992: 34-47). There are fragments of depictions from two battle scenes, one Asian and one Nubian, which were probably placed opposite each other on the walls of an open court. Sixteen blocks have preserved portions of chariots (Johnson, 1992: 156-182), mostly parts of wheels, except for Blocks 50 and 66, which preserve the chariot body. Johnson has reconstructed two scenes: one, the battle with Egyptian chariots against an Asiatic city, including the king in his vehicle and two, the presentation of the spoils of the battle to King Tutankhamun, including his waiting chariot, and three smaller registers of waiting chariots (Johnson, 1992: 187-190).

The procession to Luxor Temple for the Opet festival was carved in relief on the inner walls of the Colonnade Hall during the reign of Tutankhamun. Attendants with the royal chariots are shown among those on the side of the river, accompanying the procession of the sacred barques from Karnak Temple, and then they are being driven in the scene of the return to Karnak from Luxor (The Epigraphic Survey, 1994: pl. LXVIII). The chariots are those typical of the Amarna Period: main casing and siding fill, circular cut out hand-grip just below the top railing, and attached bow-case (The Epigraphic Survey, 1994: pls. XVIII, XXII).

A procession scene with King Tutankhamun driving his chariot was carved on the façade of a tomb at Akhmim, belonging to a man who held the title of Overseer of Tutors (Eaton-Krauss, 2016: 14-15; Ockinga, 1997: pls. 36-39). Although badly preserved, there appears to be a second figure in the chariot, holding a fan. Ockinga (1997: 35) suggests that this person might be Ay, God's Father under Tutankhamun. If the reconstructed drawing of the king's chariot, and the five smaller ones following behind are correct, they all have eight spokes, which is unusual, as six spokes is "the standard with occasional eight-spoked exceptions" (Littauer & Crouwel, 1979: 115). There are only two other examples of eight-spoked chariots wheels in the present work (see the decoration on the chariot body of King Thutmose IV, Section V.2.1. 'Royal Scenes: Warfare, Victory, and Sport', and the field scene in T57, tomb of Ka'emhet, section V.2.2. 'Non-Royal Scenes: Officialdom at Work, Hunting, and Funerals').

After the hunting and sporting scenes of King Amenhotep II, the next known hunting scenes are those of King Tutankhamun. For the most part Tutankhamun's hunting scenes are on objects from his tomb, but there are also two blocks that were found in the Ninth Pylon at Karnak preserving portions of a bull-hunting scene attributed to Tutankhamun (Lauffray, 1979: pl. 120; Sa'ad, 1975: pl. 34). Other blocks possibly show a desert hunt (Eaton-Krauss, 1983; Johnson, 1992: 17). Only parts of the front of the chariot body can be seen. Both the obverse and reverse of Tutankhamun's wooden bow-case (Carter's Number 335; Carter, 1933: 94-97; pl. XXVIII-XXIX) depict the king in his chariot, reins tied behind his back, shooting at fleeing desert game (McLeod, 1982: pls. 9, 14). One side of Tutankhamun's fan (Carter's Number 242; Carter, 1927: pl. LXI-LXII) represents him shooting bustards (Reed & Osborn, 1978: 273-276), usually referred to as ostriches (Houlihan, 1986: fig. 1), in the same manner (James, 2000: 78-79), and on the other side he drives his chariot behind the bearers taking back the kill (Edwards, 1978: 110-113). His chariot has a large, circular aperture in the siding fill and double front supports going to the chariot pole. The lid of Tutankhamun's painted box (Carter's Number 021) has two parallel scenes of hunting game in the desert – lions on one side, and gazelles and other animals on the other. The king is alone in his chariot, shooting with the reins tied behind his back (Carter & Mace, 1923: pls. L-LI; Edwards, 1978: 76- 77). The king's chariot has a large circular opening in the siding fill, while the chariots of his attendants, in two small registers behind him, have entirely closed chariots with hand-grips. The king's horse wears a housing.

From the reign of King Ay is a piece of gold leaf showing the king in a chariot shooting arrows through a copper ingot. The chariot is of the Amarna type with entirely closed body and circular hand-grip. The king drives the chariot with the reins tied around his waist (Davis, 1912: 127, fig. 3).

V.4.2. Elite Scenes

Huy was the King's Son of Kush under King Tutankhamun. In his tomb (TT40) is a scene on the west wall of the Nubian Prince Hekanefer, along with the other Princes of Wawat and Kush, coming with tribute for the king (Davies & Davies, 1926: pl. XXIX). Included in his retinue is a Nubian royal woman brought in a chariot pulled by a pair of oxen (Figure V.9), a mixture of Egyptian conveyance and Nubian animals, discussed by Van Pelt (2013: 536) as an example of "relational entanglement". The chariot is clearly one like those used in Egypt at the time: six spokes, main casing (here elaborately decorated) and siding fill with round cut out hand-grip just below the top railing, and a bow-case attached to the side. The driver bends forward in good Amarna style. One other chariot shown in Huy's tomb appears to be a model one in gold that can be seen in the small registers of offering (Davies & Davies, 1926: pl. 26).

The Gold of Honour rewarding scene in the Theban tomb of Neferhotep (TT49), dating to the reign of King Ay near the end of the 18th Dynasty, is perhaps the most interesting of all these scenes of royal gifting (Figure V.10). It shows that when a chariot was the conveyance of choice, even in an elite, ceremonial setting its use does not extend to non-royal females. Neferhotep is seen below the Window of Appearance, having been given the Gold of Honour (Davies, 1933b: pl. I). Then he is seen driving away in his chariot, in the same pose as Meryre II in his Amarna tomb (see above), with a charioteer doing the driving. In the scene in the registers

Figure V.9. A Nubian royal woman in a chariot. Luxor. Tomb of Huy (TT40). From: Davies & Gardiner (1936: pl. LXXXI). See also Figure II.1C.

above this, the queen gives Neferhotep's wife the Gold of Honour collar from her own Window of Appearance. When the wife turns to go, an attendant takes her arm, and she is escorted away on foot. She does not share her husband's chariot, nor does she have her own. Females driving and riding in chariots seem to be a prerogative of the Amarna royal family (Köpp-Junk, 2015a).

The tomb of Horemheb at Saqqara was built in the period when he served as Commander of the Army under Tutankhamun. The Saqqara scenes from the time of his military career come from the second court, behind in the statue room, and innermost court. The chariot scenes all come from the second court and fall into two groups: the theme of attendants waiting with chariots in a military setting, and then, on the north wall of the court chariots and their drivers in a westward procession as part of the funeral (Martin, 1976: 15;1989: pls. 120-123; 1991: 79). This funeral scene is very much like the one in the Saqqara tomb of Meryneith (see V.3.2. 'Saqqara: Elite Scenes'). In the military scenes there are a total of six chariots in four small scenes. On a block in the Berlin Museum (AM 20363), which came from this part of the tomb, an attendant sits backward on the floor of a chariot parked on a stand (Martin, 1989: pls. 28-29). Three other blocks, one in Bologna (1889) and two still preserved on the tomb wall, depict attendants, holding reins and whips, standing with chariots attached to their teams of horses (Martin, 1989: pls. 32, 94). All of these chariots have closed bodies, circular aperture (the position relatively far below the top railing rules out it is a handgrip), bow-cases and six spoke wheels (Figure V.11).

Figure V.10. Neferhotep (TT49) and his family after receiving the Gold of Honour. After: Davies (1933b: pl. II). Drawing by L.D. Hackley.

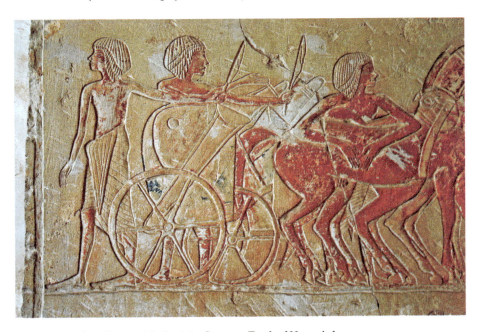

Figure V.11. Attendants with chariots. Saqqara. Tomb of Horemheb.

There are two blocks in the Yale Art Gallery that are likely to have come from Saqqara, and have been dated to the late 18th Dynasty, based on the similarity of the carving style to that in the tomb of Horemheb (Manassa, 2002: 257, note 8, pls. 14-17). Each block has a fragment of registers with offering bearers; one depicts a man pulling a chariot by its pole, with another chariot in front of him, and the other just preserves a chariot body. The chariots have bodies with decorated edges of the main casing, and a small hand-grip at the usual spot. Each has a bow-case and quiver on the side, so these chariots are probably part of a military-related scene.

V.5. Ramesside Period

V.5.1. Royal Scenes

Extensive narratives of ancient Egyptian military expeditions and victories decorated temple walls in the Ramesside Period. The entire story of a military expedition unfolded in carved and painted relief portraying the march, the battle itself, the resulting slaughter of the enemy, the victorious king, and the return home with booty. Johnson (2009: 31) concludes that the Ramesside narratives were "the culmination and final flowering of a much longer tradition, which was in full flower by the end of the Eighteenth Dynasty". The bulk of these scenes belong almost, if not entirely, to Kings Seti I, Ramesses II, and Ramesses III, and they are very stereotypical showing the king and his soldiers in chariots attacking and the victorious king returning in his chariot (often dragging along captives). The discussion that follows will focus on presenting particular scenes or details in these larger battle narratives, many of which seem to be innovations of Ramesside Period artists.

One such scene is the motif of the smiting king, who steps over the front bar of the chariot and onto the chariot pole. The earliest evidence known for this is in the reign of Seti I of the 19th Dynasty. In his battle against the Libyans, depicted on the north outer wall of the Hypostyle Hall at Karnak Temple, Seti has caught a Libyan by the neck with his bow, and is stepping and swinging with his *khepesh* sword (The Epigraphic Survey, 1986: pl. XXVIII), and he also steps over onto the chariot pole in his attack on Yenoam (The Epigraphic Survey, 1986: pl. XI). There is a similar scene in the temple of Beit el-Wali, carved in year 13 of Seti I, while Ramesses II was still crown prince (Figure V.12). Ramesses II steps onto the chariot pole while grasping his bow and the hair of two Bedouins in one hand, swinging his *khepesh* with the other (Ricke *et al.*, 1967: pl. 13). Ramesses II is shown doing this in the damaged war scenes on the south outer wall of the Hypostyle Hall at Karnak as well (Gaballa, 1969: 17-18).

Ramesses III is also depicted in this stance. He steps onto the chariot pole swinging his *khepesh* when storming the town of Tunip (The Epigraphic Survey, 1932: pl. LXXXVIII), and when spearing wild bulls in the swamp as well, which can be seen on the back of the south wall of the First Pylon at Medinet Habu (The Epigraphic Survey, 1932: pl. CXVII, CXXX). The latest known example of this scene is found on an ostracon from the reign of Ramesses IV of the 20th Dynasty (Heinz, 2001: 323). The king is stepping onto the chariot bar while grasping foreigners with his left hand. His right arm is down by his side, but it is not clear if he is holding anything in it.

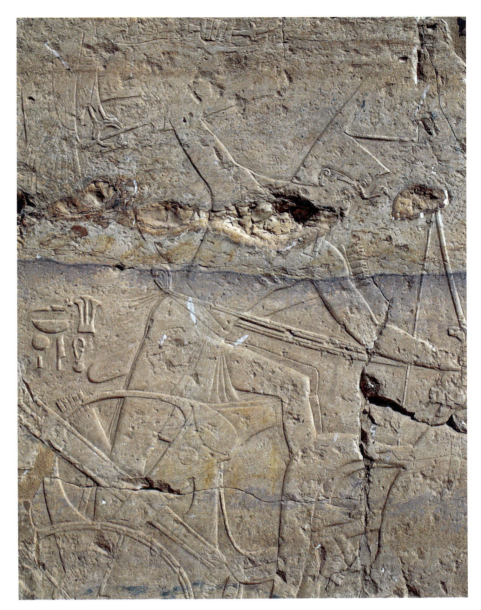

Figure V.12. King Ramesses II stepping onto the chariot pole. Temple of Beit el-Wali. Photograph by L. Sabbahy.

Another type of scene that first appears in the Ramesside Period is that of the king watching the 'counting of the hands' after a battle. Near an Egyptian outpost, such as on the Way of Horus, the king stands in what appears to be a portable Window of Appearance. Out on a battlefield in foreign territory, the king uses his chariot as a throne, and sits in it backward. He is not sitting on the floor of the chariot, but up at the level of the top railing (Sabbahy, 2016: 321-328). The first completely preserved example of such a scene is of Ramesses II after the Battle of Qadesh (Desroches Noblecourt *et al.*, 1971: pl. III, d). The king is shown sitting backward in his chariot, left hand holding reins and bow, while resting on the top railing of the chariot. He gestures with his right hand down to the cut-off hands being piled before him, in three small registers. Two attendants with sunshades stand on the far side of his chariot team, while two other attendants stand in front of the horses, controlling them. The line of the king's long garment and his foot below, are clear. The bottom of the king's foot is horizontal with the wheel spoke just below it. The latest depiction of such a scene appears to be that of Ramesses III after his first Libyan battle (The Epigraphic Survey, 1930: pl. XXIII). On the south wall of the second court of his mortuary temple at Medinet Habu, Ramesses III sits backward in his chariot (Figure V.13) in front of four registers; three depict prisoners and piles of hands, and one has prisoners and a pile of phalli (Figure V.14).

The sitting backward in a chariot scene is one that can be recognized just by the detail of a backward foot extending down over a chariot wheel. This is clear in a fragmentary scene from the north exterior wall of the Ramesses II temple at Abydos; only the chariot wheel with the king's feet can still be seen in front of the piles of hands (Naville *et al.*, 1930: pl. 21; Iskander & Goelet, 2015: pl. 2.2.23). Sometimes the addition of a captured foreigner, or his head, is part of this 'counting of the hands' scene. On the interior south wall of the second court of the temple of Seti I at Abydos, decorated in the time of Ramesses II, the preserved relief breaks along the top of a chariot wheel, before which a pile of hands is being counted. A sandaled left foot, slanting down from above, can be seen through the spokes of the wheel. Just under the king's foot, is the head of a foreigner, seemingly attached under the chariot (Figure V.15).

A detail similar to this can be found in the earlier scene of Seti I's return from a Libyan campaign on the north exterior wall of the Hypostyle Hall at Karnak. A rectangular section is marked off on the bottom of the chariot body, and from it, two heads can be seen between the spokes, and a third head stretches up above the wheel. In addition, there is a small head on the top of the linchpin (The Epigraphic Survey, 1986: pl. XXI; see above section V.2.1). A later parallel is found in the captives tied under the chariot of Ramesses III at Medinet Habu when he is shown returning from his Libyan campaign. Not just the heads, but entire figures of captives are shown under the chariot, as discussed previously. Ramesses II's chariot wheel in the Seti I Abydos temple scene is depicted with an axle whose linchpin top is carved with the head of a lion biting the head of a foreigner. This same motif decorates the linchpin of his chariot in the scene at his own Abydos Temple, discussed just above, as well as in the chariot of Ramesses III at Medinet Habu, when he is shown setting out on his Libyan campaign, following the chariot bearing the standard of Amun (The Epigraphic Survey, 1930: pl. XVII) (Figure V.16). The chariot is driven by one of the royal princes, and the king follows along behind, driving his own chariot. The two chariots are exactly the same size, and the king and the god's standard are exactly the same height. The inscription accompanying the standard's chariot reads in part: "Words spoken by Amun-Re, King of the God's: Behold, I am before you, my son...I open for you the ways of the Tjemehu" (The Epigraphic Survey, 1930: pl. XVII). The god Montu was shown in a chariot with Thutmose IV, discussed above, helping the king with steadying his aim with the bow, but this scene at Medinet Habu is the only known example of a divine standard driven in a chariot. The only other scene of a deity in a chariot is possibly the god Shed, the 'protector' or 'savior', known from the beginning of the 18th Dynasty (Brunner, 1983: 547-549). A small limestone fragment from the Amarna Period preserves the figure of a nude young man with a side lock, in a chariot with reins around his waist, pulling back a bow (Brooklyn Museum Acc. No. 36.965). Brunner (1984: 49-50) has identified the

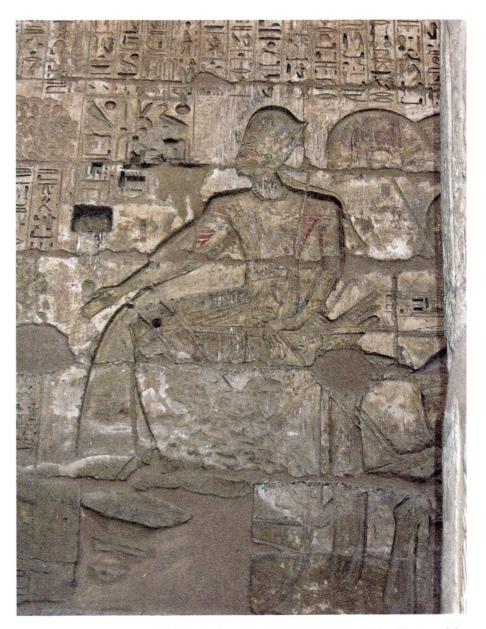

Figure V.13. King Ramesses III sitting backward in his chariot. Medinet Habu. Photograph by L. Sabbahy.

figure as Shed, rather than as a young prince, such as Tutankhamun, as Romano (1983; 1991) has claimed. Indeed, there are other depictions of Shed from Amarna on stelae from the tomb chapels east of the Workman's Village (Peet & Woolley, 1923: 97, pl. XXVIII).

One last, rather small detail about chariots dating from the period of Ramesses II to his successor Merenptah should be mentioned: the use of a chariot umbrella or canopy. The most outstanding example of such an umbrella appears in the Battle of Qadesh scene at the temple of Abu Simbel. Behind and below Ramesses II sitting in his camp near Qadesh, an attendant stands behind the king's chariot, holding the reins (Desroches Noblecourt *et al.*, 1971: pl. IV). On a single pole,

Figure V.14. Ramesses III seated backwards in his chariot, counting trophies. Medinet Habu. After: The Epigraphic Survey (1930: pl. LXXVI). Drawing by L.D. Hackley.

Figure V.15. A wheel of Ramesses' II chariot in the temple of Seti I at Abydos. The king's foot shows that he is sitting backwards. Note the head and foreigner and linchpin with a lion biting a human head. Photograph by B. Taylor Woodcock.

Figure V.16. Standard of the god Amun in a chariot. Medinet Habu. After: The Epigraphic Survey (1930: pl. XVII). Drawing by L.D. Hackley.

which seems to come from the center front of the chariot body, is a round-topped umbrella topped by a vulture holding feathers in her claws. A fringed edge hangs down from the umbrella cloth. A comparable umbrella can be seen in a similar scene on the west wall of the temple of Ramesses II at Abydos (Iskander & Goelet, 2015: pl. 2.1.13) although the vulture cannot be seen. Brock (2013: 39, fig. 10) published a photo of a similar umbrella on the west wing of the First Pylon of the Luxor Temple, another place Ramesses II decorated with scenes from his Battle of Qadesh. There is one last example this author knows of from the war scenes of Merenptah on the west wall of the *Cour de la Cachette*. There is a block with Merenptah's son, Crown Prince Seti, driving a chariot with a similar umbrella shading him (Brand, 2004-2005: 5).

Brock suggests that the wooden frame and bars from the tomb of Tutankhamun (Carter's Number 123 [and 095b]; JE 60705), generally accepted as a stand to hold up a canopy over the king, was actually to be put on the so-called 'State Chariot' (Carter's Number 122) (Brock, 2013: 35-36). This chariot was probably only used in slow moving processions, or as an "impromptu audience pavilion" (Brock, 2013: 41). Certainly this rather cumbersome frame, if it was associated with a chariot, could not have functioned in the same way that the Ramesside umbrellas on a single pole, discussed just above, did.

V.5.2. Non-Royal Depictions

There is only very limited representational evidence for chariots in non-royal contexts in the Ramesside Period, because in this period tomb decoration focuses on religious scenes (Dodson & Ikram, 2008: 252). However, there are a few tombs that still include scenes of the official's professional life. The tomb of Chief Steward of Amun in Thebes and Overseer of the Granaries, Amenemopet (TT41), dates to the very late 18th or the early 19th Dynasty (Binder, 2008: 119). A scene on the top of the northeast wall depicts him amid standing in a chariot with a bow-case on the side. He holds on to the railing, while a much smaller figure drives (Assmann, 1991: pl. 31). He arrives and enters his home.

The Theban tomb of the High Priest of the cult temple of Thutmose I, User-het (TT51), dates to the early 19th Dynasty. User-het is depicted leaving the temple while being greeted by members of his family (Binder, 2008: 120). In a small upper register, his chariot driver waits, standing and holding the reins while in discussion with another man. The chariot seems to have a completely closed body, with round hand-grip, and a bow-case is on the side.

Blocks from Saqqara from lost or unknown tombs of the early Ramesside Period have scenes of chariot production or use. One example is that of Kairy, Chief of Chariot-Makers (Grajetzki, 2001; Herold, 2003), known from blocks found by Quibell in a church foundation. There are workshop scenes with finished chariots being carried, pulled, and lined up. Other blocks found by Quibell, from a lost tomb of Apuia, show a workshop scene with a chariot wheel being made, and a possible scene of military training including a chariot (Quibell & Hayter, 1927: pls. 12-13). A miscellaneous block shows a finished chariot on a stand (Martin, 1987: pl. 10, 32). Another block, also from Saqqara, shows a king's [royal?] Scribe Tjay, being driven by a charioteer, while he holds onto the top railing with his left hand, and the charioteer's arm with his right (Cooney, 1965: 52; Martin, 1987: pl. 26, 72).

V.6. Conclusion

Chariot depictions first appear in Egypt in the beginning of the 18th Dynasty. Although both kings and elite officials used chariots, until the reign of Amenhotep II, there are only a few damaged, representations of chariots at the royal level. An elite tomb scene with a chariot is known from the reign of Amenhotep I, and by the time of Thutmose III, scenes of officials' chariots are numerous. These scenes with elite chariots have a fairly wide range of subjects, such as: inspection of fields, meeting Puntites on the Red Sea coast, loaded on a boat to travel with their owner, being made in workshops, brought as tribute to the crown, carried with other funerary objects to be placed in their owner's tomb.

It is really not until the reign of Amenhotep IV/Akhenaten that royal scenes with chariots become common, and then it is almost always in the context of a procession, not only of the royal family, but also with a myriad of attendants and military personal. Perhaps it was the importance of roads in the layout of the city of Amarna, along with Akhenaten's seeming fixation on ceremonial procession that brought about this change. The scenes in elite tombs at Amarna, although focused on the activities of the royal family, depict a wide variety of elite chariot use: accompanying the royal family's procession, returning from being rewarded with the Gold of Honour, getting about on official business, as well as two tribute scenes including chariots as gifts, and one of the chariot as a funerary object.

Depictions of royal chariot use become extensive in the cult and mortuary temple battle scenes of the Ramesside Period, while their appearance in elite contexts, in terms of scenes, wanes. This, of course, must have been influenced by the change in elite tomb decoration, which becomes almost entirely religious. Particularly under Ramesses II of the 19th Dynasty, and Ramesses III of the 20th, battle scenes predominate in the exterior decoration of temples. Since Medinet Habu, the mortuary temple of Ramesses III, is the last major pharaonic temple structure of the New Kingdom, this fact itself probably explains the disappearance of large scale military scenes, including depictions of chariots, but should not be taken as evidence that, therefore, chariots disappeared from the lives of the Egyptians either.

VI. Chronicling Chariots

Texts, Writing and Language of New Kingdom Egypt

Ole Herslund[60]

VI.1. Introduction

Although chariots are iconic pieces of technology in ancient Egyptian culture, only limited work has been carried out on the textual evidence; indeed, this has never been studied as a whole and synthesised in one publication. The written record provides two forms of evidence: literary and lexicological. It comprises an uneven distribution of battle inscriptions, royal stelae inscriptions, and often fragmentary tomb inscriptions, together with literary works, such as model letters and tales, which makes synthesising the material in an overview challenging and the conclusions tentative. However, it is possible to follow a number of trajectories that allow one to study chariots in battle, as booty, as tribute, as royal gifts and, in daily life, including their manufacture. Furthermore, texts elucidate the symbolism of these vehicles in both sacred and secular contexts, and help establish the socio-economic status of their owners and the craftsmen who manufactured them.

The lexicological study focuses on the words for chariots and chariot parts, as well as determinatives depicting chariots. This study revisits the three lexemes that the standard dictionaries translate as 'chariot' by bringing together the lexicological studies and observations made after the Berlin dictionary project (http://aaew.bbaw.de), for a more accurate understanding of the meaning of these words. By examining the writing system itself, through the characters most commonly referred to as 'determinatives', or more accurately 'graphemic classifiers and repeaters', the chariot presents a case of how changes in technology could have a direct impact on the shaping of hieroglyphic signs, and thereby changes in otherwise deeply rooted conceptions of the chariot itself. The most substantial contribution to the lexicological examination of chariots offered here is a collation of the many studies in English, German and French, that were carried out on the more technical words in the Egyptian lexicon for the different parts of the chariot. Since this corpus consists of many extremely rare or uniquely attested words, as well as a great number of foreign loanwords without clear etymologies, most of

---

[60] I am grateful to Rune Nyord and Heidi Köpp-Jung for critically reading the text and their remarks and suggestions.

the meanings remain obscure, or can at best be translated tentativey. Possibly, this situation can never be improved, unless a group of chariot parts labelled with their names were to be discovered in some future excavation. In spite of the great difficulties presented to scholars by these technical words for chariot parts, they have received a great deal of attention in a number of studies. For the sake of overview and access, the many different studies have been brought together in the present work, synthesised, and presented in one updated lexicological catalogue where each lexeme is treated individually, with sources as well as with the observations and discussions of the suggested translations provided by the different Egyptological studies.

VI.2. Chariots in War

The ancient Egyptian chariot of the New Kingdom was intimately linked with warfare and the establishment of an Egyptian empire expanding into both Africa and Western Asia. Like most aspects of the ancient Egyptian chariot, two-dimensional art and archaeological sources are often the most informative relative to the textual record. However, a few texts contribute to the understanding of the chariot's use in warfare, including lists of casualties, prisoners or war booty that feature chariots. Unfortunately, the tactical use of chariots is not clarified in texts, though consensus and common sense dictate that these war vehicles were used on level ground, and served as mobile firing platforms for shooting arrows and throwing spears, terrifying the enemy and subsequently pursuing a broken and fleeing enemy.

The Hyksos Wars are the earliest theatres in which Egypt used chariots but as far as can be inferred from the textual record, chariots only played a minor role in the late 17th and early 18th Dynasty. The early New Kingdom biography of the marine veteran Ahmose, Son of Ebana, provides the very first mention of the word for chariot in the Egyptian language, as well as a few glimpses of chariots in battle. Ahmose tells how he followed Kamose on foot during his siege of the Hyksos capital Avaris, while "his majesty rode about on his chariot (*wrry.t*)" (Sethe, 1906: 3, 5). From Kamose onward, pharaohs appear on the battlefields riding in chariots, which provided the basis for changes in both royal iconography and the ideology of Kingship in New Kingdom Egypt (see below).

It is still uncertain whether only the Egyptians had chariots or that the Hyksos also had chariots (as explained in the discussion of *ḥtri* below, there is no archaeological, pictorial or textual evidence demonstrating that the Hyksos even had chariots, although they have long been credited with their introduction to Egypt, see Section I.2). The text from the tomb of Ahmose, Son of Ebana relating to the Hyksos Wars of Kamose and Ahmose (Sethe, 1906: 1-11) present the Egyptian leaders as charioteers, but in the accounts chariots do not feature prominently, perhaps because they are concerned with siege battles, which would not make use of these brand new war machines yet. This oft-cited Biography does not mention the use of chariots by King Ahmose during his expansion of the Egyptian borders into Nubia (Sethe, 1906: 5-6), although the newly acquired chariots, bronze weapons and the associated tactics gave the royal army and navy a clear advantage over their southern neighbours. Chariots were not mentioned in the sections relating to Amenhotep I's Nubian campaign either (Sethe, 1906: 6-8), where Thutmose I, in Nubia, is described as becoming "enraged like a leopard. His Majesty shot and his first arrow pierced the chest of that foe" (Sethe, 1906: 8, 13-14), after which the Nubians forces are broken and slaughtered. If Thutmose I lived up to the warrior ethos presented in later sources from the New Kingdom, he would be shooting his arrows from a chariot. Perhaps the equation between the king's rage and a leopard also plays on the image of speed evoked by that dangerous animal and the king's power in a chariot. The iconography on the chariot body of Thutmose IV shows, on the interior, the king as a sphinx trampling Asiatic enemies, which parallels the imagery on the exterior, where the king as a charioteer likewise crushes his Asian enemies (Calvert, 2013: 52, fig. 8; 55, fig. 13; Figure II.17A), imagery that is seen on other royal objects (see *e.g.* the front and back side of Tutankhamun's painted box Carter's Number 021; Davies, 1962; Carter & Mace, 1923: pl. LII-LIII). In Ahmose, Son of Ebana's last battle against the Naharin (Mitanni), the war veteran relates how he captured an enemy chariot, the horses and its owner as living captives, a mighty deed for a footsoldier, which earned him a reward of gold from King Thutmose I (Sethe, 1906: 9-10).

Although Thutmose II only ruled for a few years, according to an inscription from Year 1 that is located between Aswan and Philae, he fought in Nubia. Unfortunately the text contains no reference to the potential use of chariots by the army (Sethe, 1906: 137-141). Thutmose II's northern campaign in Asia, however, is illustrated with representations in his temple at Thebes that clearly show the presence of chariots in battle, although the relevant reliefs have been reduced to fragments (Bruyère, 1926: pls. III & IV; Porter & Moss, 1972: 456). His successor and wife, Hatshepsut, furthered the development of Egyptian imperialism in Nubia. There are only a few and scattered references to the campaign she personally led and fought in Nubia (see now Redford, 1967: 57ff; Spalinger, 2005: 59 note 31), but there is no mention or depiction of chariots. However, Amenhotep, Hatshepsut's High Steward, records in his tomb that he gave her a great chariot made from "Kushite thorn acacia" and "wrapped with gold", but whether this vehicle was intended to be used in warfare or other royal functions is unknown (Herslund, 2013: 125; Säve-Söderbergh, 1957b: 2, pl. III). Both the wood for the frame and possibly the gold wraps are of Nubian origin, so making them into a chariot with which Egypt could have subjugated the Nubians would have carried a further material symbolic expression of Egyptian dominance over Nubia (Manassa, 2013: 151).

It is, however, not until the reign of Thutmose III, notably in his Karnak Annals concerned with the Battle of Megiddo, that texts listing large numbers of chariots used in warfare are found. One should of course always be careful when dealing with numbers presented in Egyptian war inscriptions, which are often exaggerated and presented as round numbers, but this account is based on the army's own war records, compiled just after the battle was over. The booty list states that the victorious Egyptians won "2041 horses and 191 young ones, 6 stallions, an unknown number of colts and 924 chariots" (Sethe, 1907: 663-664). As noted by Spalinger (2005: 36), the 924 chariots would each have had a two-man crew, thus a total of 1848 men. The discrepancy between the number of horses and vehicles can simply be explained as the result of casualties or units having been broken and scattered (Spalinger, 2005: 36).

Based on the Megiddo account, it would seem that, by the reign of Thutmose III, chariots in the armies of the different groups inhabiting Western Asia could be counted in their thousands. Sandor (2004: 158) suggests that at any given time in the New Kingdom, a few thousand vehicles could have existed. There can be no doubt that the Egyptian armies, in order to be successful in their military campaigns abroad, had to match, if not outnumber, those figures. In fact, the ability to maintain and expand the chariot branch of the Egyptian army consistently has been emphasised as one of the reasons for Thutmose III's military successes in Asia and the expansion of Egypt's borders far to the north (Spalinger, 2005: 51). From Amenhotep II's reign through the Late Bronze Age untill the reign of Ramesses III, the army's chariotry became a fixed and highly important part of the Egyptian armed forces, and the officers belonging to the chariot divisions could attain high offices of state (Spalinger, 2005: 55-56; 70-17; 178-179; Excursus 182-183).

The only textual insights into how massed chariot units could be used tactically during battles come from the often-cited Qadesh Bulletin and Poem of Ramesses II, found at his temples in Abydos, Thebes and Abu Simbel (Kitchen, 1979: 2-147). The numbers presented are not only rounded up, but are also possibly exaggerated, claiming the Hittite forces included more than 3500 chariots (Spalinger, 2005: 36). In fact, it is only the actions of the chariotry of the Egyptian and Hittite coalition forces, *mš3 nt ḥtri* that are highlighted, besides those of the pharaoh. The footsoldiers of the infantry are only mentioned by numbers, thereby emphasising the high cultural and strategic importance of having chariot regiments available at the battlefields of the time. The Qadesh texts inform us how chariot regiments, with the required strategic intelligence and reconnaissance regarding the enemy's movements and whereabouts, could be used tactically to stage surprise attacks by outflanking enemy army divisions on the march, break their lines and make them scatter. While marching towards the camp set up by Ramesses II to the north, the Egyptian army's, Second Division of Pre, is charged by the chariotry of the Hittite king and his allies in a surprise attack: "crossing the ford to the south of Qadesh, they charged into his majesty's army as it marched unaware" (Kitchen, 1979: 118, §78-80). The Poem informs us further how the Hittite chariots had "three man to a chariot and equipped with all weapons of warfare" (Kitchen, 1979: 25, §68-69; 32, §87) and how the flanking ambushers "came forth from the south side of Qadesh and attacked the division of Pre in the middle as they were marching unaware and not prepared to fight" (Kitchen, 1979: 26-27, §71-73). Having 'weakened' (*bdš*) the Second Division of Pre, presumably meaning broken and scattered (Kitchen, 1979: 27, §74), the Hittite army pushes onwards to attack the camp of Ramesses by encircling it: "thereupon the forces of the foe from Khati surrounded (*inḥ*) the followers of his majesty who were by his side" (Kitchen, 1979: 119, §82). Again, the high mobility of the chariotry is used tactically to rapidly redeploy for engagement with the enemy and encircle them to create a killing field.

The first examples of chariots that were used in warfare inside Egyptian territory since the Hyksos Wars come from the late Ramesside Period wars against invading Libyans and their Sea People allies during the reigns of Merenptah and Ramesses III, as for example shown in the temple of Karnak and Medinet Habu. In the battles fought in the western Delta, both the Egyptian and the Libyan armies used chariots. The chariots belonging to the Libyans are relatively few in number compared to the armies the Egyptians fought in Western Asia. The Libyan chariots are only mentioned indirectly in the Karnak Inscriptions relating to Merenptah's war against the Libyans in Year 5 (Kitchen, 1982: 9. 5-6), whereas both, chariots (*mrkbt.w*) and twin spans of horses, are counted in the booty list in

Medinet Habu from Ramesses III's war against the Libyans in his Year 11. Pictorial evidence from both Egypt (such as Medinet Habu) and Sahara (for example Nah Kolorodna) likewise makes the identification of the existence of war chariots in the Libyan arsenal secure (Manassa, 2003: 89-90). The Karnak Inscription on Merenptah's war against the Libyans in his Year 5, mentions that the enemy ruler and his sons had 12 spans (*ḥtri.w*) of horses (Kitchen, 1982: 9. 5-6). In addition to these, according to the booty list on the Victory Column from Heliopolis, Merenptah captured an additional 18 horses from the Libyu, Kehekyu and (?) Meshweshyu resulting of a total of 42 horses (Kitchen, 1982: 38, 5). O'Connor (1990: 57) suggests that some, if not all, of these additional 18 horses may have been ridden, as practiced by mounted scouts of Egyptian army in the late New Kingdom, but the even number might indicate pairs, making for a maximum of 21 Libyan chariots. In any case, the total number of chariots possessed by the Libyan and their allies' was considerably less than those encountered by the Egyptians in the Near East, which at times were encountered in several hundreds.

More impressive is the count of Libyan chariots and horse spans captured by Ramesses III from the Libyan and coalition forces in his regnal Year 11. The booty lists recorded in Medinet Habu (The Epigraphic Survey, 1932: pl. LXXV) claim the capture of 92 chariots (*mrkbt.w*) and 184 spans (*ḥtri.w*) of horses (Kitchen, 1983: 53, 8). In the accompanying relief scene, one can even see Libyans carrying their 'out of date' chariots with four-spoked wheels after their defeat by Ramesses III (The Epigraphic Survey, 1932: pl. LXXV; see also Manassa, 2003: 90 note 81).

Although the textual record is minimally informative with regard to the actual use of chariots in war, a few glimpses are offered, perhaps symbolically rather than literally, in how the royal war chariot was used to transport living prisoners of importance, or the cut-off hands of fallen enemies taken as war trophies after the battle. Notwithstanding the debate of the textual problems with the account of Amenhotep II's Syrian campaigns, presented on two royal stelae from Memphis and Karnak (Der Manuelian, 1987; Helck, 1955: 1300-1316; 1977: 241-256), the pharaoh is said to have placed 16 captured living Mariannu warriors on the side of his chariot. A royal emissary of Mitanni is likewise placed on his chariot as a living prisoner, and 20 hands hung on the foreheads of Amenhotep's horses (Helck, 1955: 1304, 12-19; 1311, 11). Given the weight and space required, it would surely have been impossible to place 17 prisoners on the chariot, and the 20 hands hung on the horses' forehead likewise seems exaggerated. Nonetheless, the practice of tying living captives to the royal chariot and bringing them back to Egypt can be found mirrored in a battle relief from Amenhotep's reign showing bound prisoners placed on the chariot sides, pole and horses, whereas the rest are walking with their hands tied to their backs with a rope anchoring them to the royal chariot (Figure VI.1; Zayed, 1985: pl. II).

In the much later Late Egyptian Miscellany texts, we find a similar motif in the so-called 'More Praise to Merenptah' text, where it is said about the victorious warrior king returning from a battle "How sweet is your going to Thebes, your chariot bowed down with hands and chiefs pinioned before you! You will present them to your noble father, Amunkamutef" (P. Anastasi II, 5,3-5,4; Gardiner, 1937: 15). Different parts of the king's panoply is mentioned in The Hymn to the King in His Chariot (also known as the Poem to the Royal Chariot), which is a text that is preserved on two ostraca (oEdinburgh O. 916 = National Museum of Scotland A.1956.310; oTurin S. 9588, formerly CG 57365) and is comprised of

Figure VI.1. Amenhotep II with captives. Temple of Karnak, Fourth Pylon. From: Zayed (1985: pl. I).

stanzas in which parts of the king's chariot and the associated panoply appear in, often obscure, word plays (*i.e.* in paronomasia). It should also be noted that the texts on the two ostraca do not overlap, but each seem to represent a different part of a larger composition (Dawson & Peet, 1933: 168; see also Manassa, 2013: 144; Schulman, 1986: 19).[61] One of these many obscure word plays addresses: "the *mḫ3*-bindings of your chariot, it binds those who are evil" (oEdinburgh 916, vs. 14-15; Dawson & Peet, 1933: pl. XXVIII). Although *mḫ3*-bindings cannot be identified more precisely than a type of leather strap (see below), the word play on the chariot leather straps (*mḫ3*) and the binding (*mḫ3*) of evil doers seem directly related to the practice of tying prisoners or the hands of dead enemies to the king's war chariot. Prisoners strapped to the royal war chariot can also be found in iconography, exemplified by the carvings and reliefs on Tutankamun's chariots (Carter's Number 122 and 120 – A1 and A2 in Littauer & Crouwel, 1985: pl. XIII, XX, XXI, XXIV) or in the Medinet Habu relief showing Ramesses III returning from the first Libyan campaign with prisoners strapped underneath his chariot's floor (The Epigraphic Survey, 1930: pl. XXIV).

---

61 In 1933 Dawson and Peet made a philological edition of the two ostraca with The Hymn to the King in his Chariot in which a number of chariot parts were identified. This was followed by a dedicated lexicographical study by Schulmann (1986) including an analysis of the frequently occurring loanwords. Hofmann (1989: 208-215) has studied the chariot terminology found in the hymn in other textual contexts, and the many foreign loanwords in the hymn are included in a number of lexicographical studies (Hoch, 1994; Jéquier, 1922; Meeks, 1997; Schneider, 2008; Ward, 1989). Popko published an online compilation of previous commentaries on the text (Popko, 2012a; 2012b). Most recently, Manassa (2013) has revisited the poem and offered a combined study of the lexicographical potential of the text for understanding chariot part terminology, the use of paronomasia and technological terms to create works of art, literary aspects and intertextuality, as well as providing suggestions for a socio-historic context in which the hymn could have been performed.

VI.3. Chariots as Booty and Tribute

Thus, the written sources and the pictorial evidence suggest that chariots were introduced into Egypt during the Hyksos era, but were of lesser importance in the early 18th Dynasty than in the later New Kingdom, especially the 19th and 20th Dynasties. By or during the reign of Thutmose III chariots gained importance in warfare, and at the battle of Megiddo the Egyptians fought against hundreds of chariot teams with thousands of warriors. However, judging from most booty lists of the New Kingdom, the numbers of chariots captured range roughly from 15 to 60. Egypt's engagements in Asia against the chariot-based armies of the local rulers led to an increased ability to fight on land by adding large numbers of war chariots to its arsenal (Spalinger, 2005: 4-5, 16-19). During the period of Thutmose III to Thutmose IV, the army grew and became increasingly professional. From the reign of Amenhotep II onward, officers with a background in the army's chariotry could cross over into offices of civil administration or priestly duties of high status and importance (Spalinger, 2005: 55-56, 70-17, 178-179; Excursus 182-183).

A few earlier examples of chariots depicted in private tombs in Thebes (*e.g.* TT21, tomb of User and TT11, tomb of Djehuty) are known, but the period between Thutmose III and Thutmose IV saw an increase in the number of private elite tombs with depictions of chariots (see below). The increased focus on chariots in war, and the increasing importance of chariot divisions within the army, and the spread of chariots in daily life (for hunting and transport) among the elite from the middle of the 18th Dynasty onward (see also Chapter V) all emphasize the high status and cultural importance that was attributed to this vehicle. Clearly, the chariot impacted Egyptian New Kingdom society on multiple levels, including royalty, military, daily life of the elite, the language and even the writing system. From the reign of Thutmose III onward, there was an increased demand for chariots, horses and raw materials for their production (for the impact on the leather industry, see Chapter IV). In order to meet this increased demand, the Egyptian state pursued mainly two strategies. One was simply to capture chariots, horses and materials along with weapons and armours from vanquished enemies from both Asia and Libya. This practice not only increased the number of war chariots in the Egyptian army, but also simultaneously weakened the enemies' battle strength. Indeed, chariots and horses appear frequently in the booty lists of the New Kingdom, and even features in private listings of personal booty, exemplified in Ahmose, Son of Ebana's biography, where he claims the mighty feat of a footsoldier capturing a chariot warrior, his chariot and two horses (this earned him a reward in gold when presented to the pharaoh) (Sethe, 1906: 9-10, 36). Chariots, horses and related materials also feature frequently in the war booty and '*inw*-tribute' lists in the Karnak Annals of Thutmose III. The single biggest capture are the 924 chariots and 2041 horses after the battle of Megiddo, including the "perfect chariot covered in gold" belonging to the ruler of Megiddo himself along with the many "chariots of his army" (Sethe, 1907: 663f). In the aftermath of a battle over the port city of Ullaza (*inrṯw*) against Syrian rebels in regnal Year 31, 7th campaign, Thutmose captured 26 horses and 13 chariots and from the battle in Year 34, 9th campaign, he earned an additional 15 chariots and 40 horses – these were taken from the Djahy. In Year 35, 10th campaign against Mitanni (Naharin) Pharaoh took 60 chariots, 180 horses and 15+ reins/harnesses, and in Year 38, 13th campaign, an unknown number of chariots and horses from the

Nuḫašše Iniwgš. Furthermore, in Year 42, Thutmose's last campaign, he captured 48 horses from cities in the Qadesh area. In total, according to the Karnak Annals of Thutmose III, the war booty included a total of at least 1012 chariots and 2335 horses (Sethe, 1907: 704, 711, 717, 731).

Subsequently, Amenhotep II claims to have captured a total of 730 chariots and 820 horses during his first campaign in Asia, according to the Memphis Stela (Helck, 1955: 1305), and a total of 300 chariots and 210 horses are recorded among the war booty of the Second Campaign on the Karnak Stela (Helck, 1955: 1315). That is a suspicious total of 1030 chariots and 1030 horses, where one would expect a higher number of horses, if not double, relative to the chariots, as chariots are generally driven by pairs. This is one of many problems with the Amenhotep II war inscriptions and the numbers presented therein, as noted by Helck (1977: 241-256). On a stela fragment erected by the Viceroy of Kush during the reign of Amenhotep IV in the temple of Buhen, an unknown Viceroy claims to have ended a Nubian rebellion and subsequently sent captives and tribute to the king, including no less than 361 *nfr.w* 'foals' (Randall-Maciver & Woolley, 1911: 92, 4). It is to this author's knowledge the only example of horses being sent from Nubia to Egypt. In the earlier war annals of Thutmose III, chariots or horses never feature among the entries of the *inw*-tribute lists relating to Nubia.

With a hiatus in textual sources regarding war booty, it is not until the Libyan Wars of Merenptah and Ramesses III that information is offered about captured chariots and horses from battles, albeit in more modest numbers than those presented by the earlier kings of the mid-18th Dynasty. Merenptah captured 42 horses according to his Karnak Inscription and Victory Column in Heliopolis (Kitchen, 1982: 9, 5-6; 38, 5), while Ramesses III claims to have won 92 chariots and 184 spans (*ḥtri.w*) of horses in a Medinet Habu list of booty (Kitchen, 1983: 53, 8).

The second strategy for acquiring more chariots from abroad was through what will here be loosely referred to as tribute and gifts to the Egyptian state, in which chariots, horses and related materials often feature among the entries in listings and letters. As noted by Spalinger (2005: 133), in the *inw*-lists of goods sent from the conquered areas of the Near East to Egypt in the Karnak Annals of Thutmose III, chariots and horses are both key features. According to these lists, the conquered areas in Syria (Retjenu) shipped chariots ranging between 10 and 90 in number (Sethe, 1907: 669, 690, 692, 706, 712, 717, 721, 722, 809). These Syrian chariots brought to Egypt are often listed as being 'worked with gold and silver', or labelled as being 'painted' (*nˁˁ.w*). *Inw*-shipments from Syria to Egypt could also contain parts for chariots like an unknown number of harnesses (Sethe, 1907: 669), 343 yokes (Sethe, 1907: 672), or the much needed types of 'wood for chariots' for production in Egypt including *ḅgꜣ*, *ssndm* and *knkwt* (Sethe, 1907: 707). In the private elite tombs in the Theban area that date to the reign of Thutmose III to Thutmose IV, such as Intef (TT155), Menkheperraseneb (TT86), Rekhmire (TT100), and Nebamun (TT90), scenes showing foreigners bringing chariots and horses to Egypt feature as part of the tomb decoration programs, mirroring the situation drawn up by the *inw*-lists (Hofmann, 1989: 294-295, pl. 89-96; Figure VI.2).

From the late 18th Dynasty, the Amarna letters shed some light on deliveries of chariots and horses to Egypt from the Near East and Mesopotamia, during the reigns of Amenhotep III and Akhenaten. Although the deliveries are referred

Figure VI.2. Foreigners bringing chariots and horses to Egypt. Tomb of Amenedjeh (TT84). From: Hofmann (1989: Taf. 091).

to here as gifts or tributes, the exact nature of these diplomatic and economic transactions remains somewhat elusive for modern scholars. In the letters addressed to Amenhotep III from King Tushratta of Mitanni, three occurrences of chariots, chariot parts and horses being sent from Syria to Egypt are noted in addition to other valuable items. As a "gift of praise for my brother" the Mitanni king sent Pharaoh "five chariots and five teams of horses", and a second time "10 chariots of wood and 10 teams of horses with all their paraphernalia" (EA 17, 39; Moran, 1987: 111; EA 19, 84; Moran, 1987: 116). Among the many entries in the somewhat damaged clay tablet, labelled EA 22, of items sent from Mitanni to Egypt are: "four horses, one chariot", "10 poles, 10 frames, x chariot yokes, x chariot floors" (I, 1; Moran, 1987: 123; IV 37-38; 131-132). From Kadashman Enlil I, the Kassite king of Babylon, Amenhotep III was presented a "gift of praise" of "10 chariots of wood and 10 teams of horses" (EA 3, 32-34; Moran, 1987: 67). On two different occasions, his son, Amenhotep IV, received the same number of chariots and horses from the Kassite king of Babylon, Burnaburiash II (EA 7, 58; Moran, 1987: 75; EA 9, 37; 81). The correspondence between Amenhotep IV and Burnaburiash II also attest to the reciprocal, or *do ut des*-nature of gift giving between the kings, indicated by a total of "four chariots of wood, wrapped with gold" sent by pharaoh to the king of Babylonia (EA 14 II, 15; Moran, 1987: 95). Ashuruballit, the king of Assyria, gave Amenhotep IV "a beautiful chariot with two horses" on one occasion, and another time a vehicle and horses explicitly stated to be fit for an Assyrian king: "a beautiful chariot equipped for me [*i.e.* Ashuruballit], with two white horses, also equipped for me" (EA 15, 12; Moran, 1987: 105; EA 16, 9; 106). Even from Cyprus (Alashiya), the king of Egypt received a "chariot with gold and two horses" along with 100 talents of copper and other valuable items, as attested in a letter from an anonymous king (EA 34, 16-25; Moran, 1987: 198). Scenes showing deliveries of chariots from abroad are depicted in the contemporary Amarna tombs belonging to Meryre (II) and Huya (Davies, 1905a: pl. XXXVII; 1905b: pl. XIV; See also Hari, 1964: fig 36; see also Chapter V).

The textual sources regarding the influx of chariots and horses through gifts or tribute in the Ramesside Period are all but non-existent, and mostly it is horses that are emphasized in the few relevant texts. This might indicate that by the 19th and 20th Dynasty Egypt relied primarily on its own local production of chariots to fill up its arsenals and the economizing of the manufacturing of the Tano leather can be seen a supporting such a suggestion. In the inscriptions about the First Hittite Marriage of Ramesses II, we hear how the chiefs of Khati are bringing gifts to the pharaoh including: "gold, silver and many flocks of horses" (Kitchen, 1979: 247). The motif of foreigners bringing chariot parts and horses to Egypt as gifts or tribute also features in the Ramesside Miscellanies (Caminos, 1954; Gardiner, 1937). A group of chariots being prepared for the king's arrival is said to have elements brought from Palestine and Syria: "their spokes are from Pher, their poles are from of Iupa" and "horse teams and fine young steeds (*nfr.w*) of Sangar, top stallions of Khatti, and cows of Alyshiya are in the charge of their masters who bow down beneath the [window]" (P. Anastasi IV, 16, 11-17, 8-9; Gardiner, 1937: 53-54).

VI.4. Chariots as Gifts for the King

The written record provides some insights into the distribution of chariots within the Egyptian society that cannot be directly related to booty or tribute. This can be detected in a number of different textual contexts, especially gifts presented to the pharaohs on the occasion of accession to the throne, royal jubilees and New Year's celebrations, in which not only the kings and their reigns were rejuvenated, but also a whole range of royal and cultic statuary and equipment (Aldred, 1969: 73-81).

The tomb of Amenhotep in Luxor (TT73), the High Steward of Hatshepsut, a chariot is shown amongst the gifts presented to the pharaoh. It is labelled "great chariot of Kushite thorn acacia (?), wrapped with gold" (Säve-Söderbergh, 1957b: 2, pl. III). The same theme of presenting gifts to the king appears in the Theban tomb of Kenamun (TT93; Figure II.27), High Steward of Amenhotep II, who lists a substantial quantity of objects, such as statuary, collars, and weapons, as well as ornamented horse covers and chariots. The inscriptions state that the goods were "the work of all craftsmen of the Delta Towns", and hence produced in the north where Kenamun served as High Steward, but they were destined to become presents before the king in Thebes. The chariots are generically described as "being of silver and gold", but two chariots, one of which is named "The One of Syria" (*t3-m3w rn=s*), are specified as being made of wood brought from Naharin (*i.e.* Mitanni). Thus we can follow a supply line from the wood being cut and brought from Mitanni to the workshops in the Delta and finally presented to Pharaoh in Thebes (Davies, 1930: 24, pl. XIII, XXII). In the later miscellany text that was composed as an instruction to a chariot workshop, the *mrkbt* 'chariot' of the pharaoh is said to be constructed, or possibly repaired, for the feast of New Year's Day (P. Anastasi III, vs. 1, 2; Gardiner, 1937: 30). In an instruction, likewise from the Ramesside Miscellanies, the scribe of the armoury, called Mahu, commissions the scribe Pewehem to arrange the construction of chariots for the second celebration of the king's *heb-sed* (P. Bologna 1094, 4, 1-4, 5; Gardiner, 1937: 4). Hence, the combination of several texts, inscriptions and representations testify to the cultural significance of creating and presenting specially made coronation and jubilee chariots for the pharaoh.

VI.5. Chariot Workers, Production and Materials

Our primary knowledge concerning chariot production and materials in Egypt itself is mainly derived from archaeological studies with a largely technological perspective (*e.g.* Herold, 2006; Littauer & Crouwel, 1985: 92-95). To this can be added a number of New Kingdom reliefs in which scenes of the manufacturing of chariots are often found in connection with larger multipurpose workshops, including leatherworkers (Drenkhahn, 1976: 130-132; Herold, 2006: 51-78; Schwarz, 2000: esp. 143-146, 169-267; Figure II.8 and II.9). Philological investigations into chariot workers and production have been limited to a single cataloguing of New Kingdom titles of workers, which simply provides a few examples of dedicated 'chariot maker' titles (Steinmann, 1980: 151). Yet, a number of stelae and tomb inscriptions provide some socio-historical insights into the craft of a specialised group of people, who built and performed maintenance on chariots.

Chariot makers can be identified by the compound title ḥmw-wrry.t 'chariot maker' (Florenze Stela 1568; Schiaparelli, 1887: 290; Leiden Ushabti P 109; Schneider, 1977: 13), with the variant ḥmw mrkbt from the 20th Dynasty (Gardiner, 1947: 68*), ranked beneath a ḥry ḥmw wrry.t 'chief chariot maker' in some form of hierarchical organisation. The earliest evidence for a dedicated chariot maker stems from a stela of the Amarna Period belonging to the 'chief chariot maker' Ptah-mai, which also indicates that two of his sons, Nakht and Rija, worked as ḥmw.w wrry.t 'chariot makers'. Hence, we get a glimpse of the well-known anthropological phenomenon in which craft specialisation is made hereditary (Florenze Stela 1568; Schiaparelli, 1887: 290). Only two additional New Kingdom occurrences of the title ḥry ḥmw wrry.t 'chief chariot maker' are known from the later 19th Dynasty (Herold, 2006: 52-53; Schneider & Raven, 1981: 94).

In the Ramesside Period, chariot workers can also be refered to generically as ḥmw.w 'craftsmen' (P. Anastasi I, 26, 4; Fischer-Elfert, 1986: 227; P. Anastasi III, vs. 1, 2; Gardiner, 1937: 30). In two instances we also find additional types of specialised craftsmen working on chariots. In one example in the Satirical Letter of P. Anastasi I a chariot is being repaired by both ḥmw.w 'craftsmen' and tbw.w 'leather workers': "You make your way into the armoury; workshops surround you; craftsmen and leather-workers are all about you. They do all what you wish. They attend to your chariot, so that it may cease from lying idle" (P. Anastasi I, 26, 4-6; Fischer-Elfert, 1983: 130; 1986: 227).

The miscellany text on the verso of P. Anastasi III is formed as an instruction given to a workshop with ḥmw.w 'craftsmen', working on a mrkbt-type chariot, and ḥmty.w 'smiths' working on a bronze clad tprt-type vehicle (P. Anastasi III, vs. 1, 3; Gardiner, 1937: 30). The terminology of the sources indicate that in addition to dedicated chariot builders, certain parts of the construction, or possible repair phases, required additional types of craftsmen with a specialised knowledge of certain materials and their properties.

Coincidentally, material qualities of chariots are one of the few topics through which they are frequently specified in inscriptions and texts. It is not uncommon to find references to both Egyptian and Asiatic chariots covered in gold or electrum (Davies, 1930: pl. XIII, XXII; Säve-Söderbergh, 1957b: pl. III; Sethe, 1907: 657-659, 663, 669, 690, 692, 704, 706, 712, 717, 809), to which can be added different types of wood such as 'ꜥg.t-wood (?)' (Sethe, 1907: 669, 7), brry 'ash-tree (?)' (Gardiner, 1937: 53, 116; Hoch, 1994: 101), Asiatic wood types called ssndm and knkwt (Sethe, 1907: 707), wood from Mitanni (Davies, 1930: pl. XXII), Nubian wood called šnd.t kš 'Kushite-Acacia (?)' (Säve-Söderbergh, 1957b:

pl. III), or *bg3* 𓎁𓂋𓆭𓏥 wood from Egypt (Sethe, 1907: 707; P. Lansing, 13a, 1; Gardiner, 1937: 112; P. Koller, 2,1; Gardiner, 1937: 117). Sadly, like most plant terminology, the ethnobiological semantics underlying these terms for types of wood remain largely unknown.

In the Ramesside Miscellany text of P. Anastasi IV, which details the preparations for the arrival of Pharaoh, the chariots that are being readied are described at length with an emphasis on their visual and wealthy splendour through the listing of a multitude of expensive and imported materials that were used in their manufacture. In addition, the text mentions that various chariot parts could be imported into Egypt as tribute and assembled to make complete vehicles at home: "Fine chariots of *brry*-wood more resplendent than lapis lazuli, their *ᶜmdy* being wrought in gold, the *ḫtr*-piece of gold and their *thr* having the hue of red cloth and being carved with blossoms; the board wrought in *dšr-wood,* their *tst*-piece of ivory, their skin (*inm* + wood det.) of *sḫt*, their reins in one set, their spokes from Pher, their poles from Iupa. They are washed, trimmed (?), leather fitted, finished off, oiled and polished (?); Their *mḫt* being set with six-fold alloy, their *gs-dbw* of gold, and their *swr* with the workings of a cloth covering" (P. Anastasi IV, 16, 7-17, 1; Caminos, 1954: 201; Gardiner, 1937: 53).

Although the lexemes for chariot parts, investigated in detail below, are exceedingly challenging in terms of lexicography and translation, for the production and materials of chariots and related objects, it is still possible to identify a number of relevant material categories, and thereby, indirectly, gain some insight into the craft specialisations of Egyptian chariot production. The list includes wood, gold and leather, which matches the craft specialisations seen in the worker titles discussed previously. One can also speculate on the extent of specialised ivory and bone workers as well as weavers for producing not only *swr* 𓏞𓈖𓆭𓏥𓏥 'bindings/coverings of cloth' of P. Anastasi IV (17, 1; Gardiner, 1937: 53), but also textile *ḥbs* 𓎛𓃀𓋴𓏥 'covers' for chariots known from elsewhere (P. Turin B, vs. 1, 9; Gardiner, 1937: 126; P. Salt 124 rt. 1, 7; Černý, 1929: pl. XLII). The description of the leather *thr* 𓏏𓉔𓂋𓏥 'side panelling' as having a red hue and decorated with blossoms instantly reminds one of the Tano leather with its red-coloured leather casing and the neckstrap embellished with a leather appliqué work in a stylised floral motif (present work, but see also Veldmeijer & Ikram, 2014: 118, fig. 4 Veldmeijer *et al.*, 2013: 258, fig. 1).

In the List of People section of the Onomasticon of Amenemope we get a clue to the overall organisation of chariot workers and their place within the broader society. In this classificatory text of 'that which exists in the world', the 'chariot makers' are listed after the *tbw.w* 𓍿𓃀𓅱𓏥 'leather workers' and the *irw-tryn* 𓇋𓂋𓅱𓏏𓂋𓇋𓈖𓏥 'armourers', while the 'chariot makers' themselves are followed by the *ḥmw.w-ᶜḥ3.w* 𓇅𓅓𓏥𓉔𓂝𓎛𓄿𓏥 'weapon/arrow makers' and *ir.ty pdt.w* 𓂋𓏏𓏭𓏸𓏸 'bow makers' – in effect a small nomenclature of the personnel working within the New Kingdom military industry (Gardiner, 1947: 68*). We know from titles that an armoury was called a *ḫpš* 𓐍𓊪𓈙, and in at least one instance from the 19th Dynasty we find a man of high status, called Kairy, who was both 'chief chariot maker' as well as 'overseer of a workshop in the armoury' (Drenkhahn, 1976: 131-132; Herold, 2003; Quibell, 1912: pl. 76, 3; 78, 4). A reconstructed scene from his Saqqara tomb gives insight into how the production of chariots was indeed set within a larger multifunctional armoury that, in addition to chariots, displays metal working and the production of projectiles, while rows of men in the lower registers bring forth bow-cases and quivers, swords, helmets, chariots and chariot parts (Herold, 2003: 198, Abb. 2; Figure VI.3). The hierarchical organisation of the workers, the military workshop setting, the degrees of craft specialisation and the employment of expensive and imported materials are all indicative of an institutionalised nature of chariot production in New Kingdom Egypt.

VI.6. Private Ownership and Daily Use of Chariots

Although the textual sources for private ownership and use of chariots are less informative than those derived from the pictorial and archaeological record, tomb inscriptions and literary works enhance our understanding of these issues. The tomb of Kenamun (TT93) contains an additional reference to a chariot in an inscription stating that it was given to Kenamun by the king as a reward (ḥsiwt.w) at some point during his career (Davies, 1930: 47). The inscription that mentions this chariot appears in the context of a damaged depiction of a weeping Nephthys following a bier, as well as a possible sacrifice and offering scene, so the chariot itself may have been depicted amongst the now vanished display of funerary equipment.

The group of Ramesside Miscellany texts (Caminos, 1954; Gardiner, 1937) offer some glimpses of chariots in daily life as well. The miscellanies cannot be taken to be accurate historical documents, but there is no reason to doubt that they draw on what would have been recognisable imagery of elite life in Egypt for the reader, listener or copyist. In the literary P. Anastasi III (6, 7-8; Gardiner, 1937: 27) an army officer buys a chariot pole for three *deben* and a chariot for five *deben*. Janssen (1975: 329) remarks that these prices seem extremely doubtful, when compared to the price of a bed for instance, which ranged between 15 and 20 *deben*. Conversely, if the *deben* price is taken to refer to silver *deben*, to which the text makes no reference, the price seems unreasonably high. In any case, the passage in P. Anastasi III (6, 7-8) suggests that in addition to chariots given to individuals by the king, like the one given to the High Steward Kenamun, chariots could be bought through private means.

Figure VI.3. Workmen producing chariots and weapons. Saqqara. Tomb of Kairy. From: Herold (2003: 198, Abb. 2).

In the so-called School Text of P. Lansing the scribe of the army and overseer of the cattle of Amun Nebmare-nakht, called Raia, has built himself a richly furnished mansion owing to a successful scribal and teaching career. Raia's lavish elite residence is here described as having, among many other things, "...horses in the stable" (P. Lansing, 12, 4; Gardiner, 1937: 111) and gardens that provide the wood for not only the construction of his boats, but also of a chariot (P. Lansing, 13a, 1; Gardiner, 1937: 112). The metonymy between ownership of an expensive vehicle to express a relatively abstract concept like 'success in life' is of course easily recognisable even today, when one thinks about the embodied status that is associated with super sport cars. That some elite men in the Ramesside Period owned private chariots is also indicated in a more indirect way – the generic dream literature. According to the Beatty Dreambook, "should a man see himself in a dream yoking (?)/attaching a chariot, (then) It is Bad! (it means that) insults are hurrying against his very flesh" (P. Chester Beatty III, rt. 9, 7; Gardiner, 1935: pl. 7).

The two-horse lightweight chariot was quintessentially a weapon system, but its mobility, speed and function as mobile firing platform found a number of uses in daily life, by both men and women. In the tomb decoration programs of the elite in Thebes of the 18th Dynasty, four different types of scenes invoke the otherwise military chariot in daily life, or afterlife, of the tomb owners (for an overview, see Hofmann, 1989: 311-312; see also Chapter V). The scene types show chariots being used for hunting (TT21, TT123, TT155, TT342, TT56 & TT276), the chariot in full speed (TT39, TT42, TT75 & TT89), the chariot parked after transport to the fields (TT11, TT80, TT84, TT69 & TT57), or simply depicted in object scenes showing burial goods (TT121, TT85, TT172 & TT63). In the later and often more vivid Amarna tomb art, chariots continued to be a popular element, showing the king, queen and the elite in everyday transport, in processions or simply going about their business in the capital city of Akhetaten.

The well-known motif of the active and masculine king in ancient Egypt (Decker, 1971), finds a few attestations in the textual sources documenting Pharaoh hunting dangerous animals in his chariot. In the Temple of Hatshepsut at Deir el-Bahari, a badly damaged inscription relates how Thutmose I hunted elephants in Syria in a chariot and later offered the tusks to Amun in Thebes (Sethe, 1906: 104). On the Dream Stela of Thutmose IV, the setting for the story is a desert hunt on the Giza plateau: "hunting lions and desert game, driving in his chariot, his horses being swifter than the wind; together with two of his followers" (Helck, 1957a: 1541). In the corpus of commemorative scarabs of Amenhotep III, the inscription concerning the wild bull hunt emphasises how the hunt was done by chariot (Helck, 1957b: 1739), whereas the one concerning the lion hunt makes no references to chariots or horses (Helck, 1957b: 1740). The royal chariot hunt is often presented in the Egyptological literature among the group of sport and leisure activities of Egyptian kings in daily life contexts, but as Spalinger (2005: 108, note 4) notes, both Xenophon and Machiavelli emphasise the value of hunting in military education. The ability to aim and shoot arrows from a moving chariot would have required training and practice, which, as the Great Sphinx Stela of Amenhotep II from Giza relates, could also be done with fixed targets to aim and shoot at while driving the vehicle at high speed (Helck, 1955: 1279-1280; Porter & Moss, 1974: 39).

In addition to the image of the active king using his chariot for hunting, training and leisure purposes, a few texts of the New Kingdom allow for glimpses of how chariots were simply used for personal transport over land (otherwise known from tomb scenes in the first part of 18th Dynasty, as well as from the Amarna rock tombs, as discussed in Chapter V). According to the group of Later Proclamations on the Boundary Stelae of Akhenaton, the king and his attendants drove in chariots around the vast desert plain area laid out for the royal city of Akhetaten to inspect the demarcations laid out for his new capital (Murnane & Van Siclen, 1993: 86, A1-A2; 88, A4).

The corpus of literary texts from the Ramesside Period includes a few additional examples of chariots that were used for locomotion in civilian contexts. In the Tale of Woe, written in the style of a letter, the author Wermai laments the circumstance that he had to walk on his feet in unknown places as both his horses and his chariot had been stolen (P. Pushkin 127, 3, 4-7; Caminos, 1977: 25, pl. 7). In the Tale of Two Brothers, a passage relates how both the king and queen drive out of the palace in their chariots to visit the two big persea trees that have marvellously grown over one night: "Then he <mounted> a golden chariot and came out of the palace to view the persea trees. Then the Lady came out on a chariot behind Pharaoh" (P. d'Orbiney 17, 4-5; Gardiner, 1932: 27). This is just one of many examples of high-status women riding in chariots in ancient Egyptian sources, though it is the only direct textual reference, besides the case of the warrior Queen Hatshepsut (see Köpp-Junk, 2008: 34-44; 2013: 134-135).

The most substantial textual evidence of chariots as means of transportation for persons over longer distances comes from the Satirical Letter of P. Anastasi I, where the *mhr* 'messenger' traverses the mountainous and hostile landscape between Egyptian institutions and town centres in the Near East (P. Anastasi I: 18, 5-20, 6; 23, 1-24, 6; 25, 8-26, 1; Fischer Elfert, 1983: 123-130, 137-143, 146-147; 1986: 159-161, 196-203, 224-225). Since the paths being travelled with chariots pass through rough and dangerous terrain that can damage the vehicle, it is emphasised how knowledge of the correct routes is key to successfully moving between destinations (P. Anastasi I: 19, 2-6; 24, 2-26, 6; Fischer Elfert, 1983: 125-127, 141-148; 1986: 160, 203). The Ramesside Love Poetry provides a glimpse of a chariot-based fast message system, with a *wpw.ty nsw.t* 'royal envoy' moving between dedicated chariot stations with fresh horses. The stanzas emphasise the inherent limitation of chariot transportation over distances and the dependence on dedicated way stations, given the stamina and physiology of the horses (P. Chester Beatty I: vs. G 1-2; Gardiner, 1931: pl. XXIXa). Although featured in literary passages, the *mhr* 'messenger' and *wpw.ty nsw.t* 'royal envoy' moving in chariots between way points with stables and facilities, both seem to indicate an institutionalised fast message system, relying on chariots and dedicated way stations, reminiscent of the Pony Express of 19th century America. Though not concerned with an institutionalised fast message system as such, an additional example of 'sending messages by chariot' is found in the Taking of Joppa on P. Harris 500, where general Djehuty dispatches a *kdn* 'charioteer' to announce, deceitfully, to the besieged town that the Egyptians have surrendered (P. Harris 500: vs. II, 10-11; Gardiner, 1932: 84).

To these few examples, one can add further textual insights into more long-distance travel by chariots during everyday life of the Ramesside Period. As noted by Köpp-Junk (2013: 136), the textual corpus of inscriptions relating to expeditions into the Eastern Desert indicates the presence and use of chariots during such endeavours. An inscription on a rock stela in Kanais, dating to the reign of Seti I, mentions the presence of "the charioteer of his majesty, *Twny*" (Kitchen, 1975: 304, 1-3). In Wadi Hammamat, a short inscription commemorates the visit of the charioteer *Pn-iri-rʿw-ms-sw* during the reign of Ramesses IV (Coyat & Montet, 1912: 108, No. 223), while a roughly contemporary inscription relates to the largest known expedition to the wadi in the New Kingdom, said to have consisted of no less than 8361 people, including a royal chariot driver, 20 stable masters and 50 charioteers (Coyat & Montet, 1912: 37, No. 12).

VI.7. Ideology, Kingship and Meanings of Chariots

The growing cultural importance of chariots from the early to mid-18th Dynasty society directly impacted the ideological portrayal of the king as ruler and warrior in art and texts throughout the New Kingdom. In art, the eternal warrior pharaoh changed from a footsoldier wielding a mace, club or axe to a superhuman charioteer, who drives the chariot himself while shooting arrows that kill the enemy and break through their lines, scattering them in chaotic disarray. The warrior pharaoh is depicted as a footsoldier only in the traditional 'smiting of the enemy' scenes on the temple pylons. The clearest example in texts of the re-interpretation of the warrior aspect and qualities of pharaoh is the Great Sphinx Stela of Amenhotep II from Giza. The narration portrays the king as the chariot warrior *par excellence*, though he also possesses superhuman mastery of the more traditional naval warfare. The ideological portrayal of the qualities of Amenhotep II, as the ideal warrior king, makes several references to horsemanship, archery and chariotry: "He had no equal on the battlefield. He was one who knew horses; there was not his like in this numerous army. Not one among them could draw his bow; he could not be approached in running" (Helck, 1955: 1279), and "He also came to do the following, which is brought to your attention. Entering his northern garden, he found erected for him four targets of Asiatic copper, of one palm in thickness, with a distance of 20 cubits between one post and the next. Then his majesty appeared on the chariot like Montu in his might. He drew his bow while holding four arrows together in his fist. He rode northward shooting at them like Montu in his panoply, each arrow coming out at the back of its target" (Helck, 1955: 1280). In addition to the superhuman strength and aim of the king, the Great Sphinx Stela narration portrays Amenhotep as a horsemaster from youth: "he loved his horses, he rejoiced in them. He was stout-hearted (*rwd-ib*) in working with them, who knew their nature (*qi*), skilled in turning them about (*pḫr*), who understands their ways (*sḫr.w*)" (Helck, 1955: 1281). As a young man his qualities as horse master is said to have earned the later King Amenhotep II the task of being in charge of the best chariot horses of the royal stables in Memphis: "He trained (*sḫpr*) horses that were unequalled. They did not tire when he held the reins (*ḫnr*); they did not drip sweat when running at high speed (*šsš k3i*). He would yoke (*nḥb*) (the horses) with the bit (*tmit*) in Memphis and would stop at the resting place of Harmakhis. He would spend time turning them over and over (*pnʿnʿ*)" (Helck, 1955: 1282-1283). The text draws up an image of the ideal chariot warrior as being one who can gain high speed, aim steadily while driving, has strength of his bow shot, knowledge of the horses' physiology and their inherent limits, how to control the horses and make sharp turns, which would have been key for successfully using the chariot as mobile firing platform and hit-and-run tactics.

From the Ramesside Period we gain additional insights into the prowess of the ideal charioteer. The inscriptions for the Ramesseum scene depicting the Siege of Dapur, relate that "His [Ramesses II] grip of the reins does not slip" (Kitchen, 1979: 173, 10). The Satirical Letter of P. Anastasi I emphasises the knowledge required of the *mhr* 𓅓𓉔𓂋𓀀 'messenger' concerning the proper routes through the landscape. Failing to navigate correctly could result in being ambushed at night, or simply crashing the chariot in the dangerous, rocky terrain (P. Anastasi I 25, 8-26, 1; Fischer Elfert, 1983, 146-147; 1986, 224-225). In the Late Egyptian 'Sufferings of an Army Officer', an incompetent chariot driver ends up crashing in the undergrowth and the reins cut his legs (P. Anastasi III, 6, 9; Gardiner, 1937: 27).

As well as the physical prowess, knowledge and skills required in handling chariots, riding chariots was directly related to the notion of speed. It was simply the fastest vehicle and mode of transport in the New Kingdom and thus was used as the embodiment of speed in both image and text. In tomb decoration of the mid- to late-18th Dynasty, one can find examples of chariot scenes that invoke this notion of speed with the horses in full gallop (*e.g.* TT39, TT42, TT75 & TT89; Hofmann, 1989: 311-312). Amenhotep II is said to be the fastest charioteer of anyone in his army "he could not be approached in running (*i.e.* driving fast)" (Helck, 1955: 1279). The Dream Stela tells how Thutmose IV hunted lions and desert game while "driving in his chariot, his horses being swifter than the wind" (Helck, 1957a: 1541). The topic of the chariot messenger moving swiftly through the landscape from waypoint to waypoint can be found in the Ramesside Love Poems of P. Chester Beatty I (see above). The Chester Beatty Love Poems (I-III) consist of metaphorical stanzas expressing the speed by which a man moves to his longing lover with 'chariot riding' and 'the gazelle' as sources for the 'speed' metaphors; the 'fastest vehicle' and the 'fastest animal' in Late Bronze Age Egypt. Poem I is of particular interest, because in addition to the metaphorical relation between 'chariots' (source) and 'speed' (target) we get a glimpse of a fast message system with a chariot rider moving between dedicated chariot stations with fresh horses: "O! That you may come to your sister (*i.e.* female loved one) swiftly! Like a swift messenger of the king ... all stables are held ready for him, he has horses at the stations. The chariot is harnessed in its place; he may not pause on the road" (P. Chester Beatty I: vs. G 1-2; Gardiner, 1931: pl. XXIXa).

The re-interpretation of the warrior aspects of the king from footsoldier to charioteer in the 18th Dynasty is also traceable in a number of more or less standardised formulaic expressions concerning the charioteer king within the interwoven ideological complex of Egyptian Kingship and religion. As in the Great Sphinx Stela inscription of Amenhotep II mentioned above, most of these phrases follow the pattern "the king is on his chariot like the god NN". Conveniently, Hofmann (1989: 264-270; see also Calvert, 2013: 60-61, 67) has collected and studied these formulaic statements concerning the king in his chariot, and has shown how different aspects and qualities of the charioteer king could be sacramentally interpreted to be those of gods and goddesses throughout the New Kingdom. There is no evidence from the New Kingdom for gods and goddesses riding into battle in their own chariots aside from Pharaoh, but divinities like

Montu and Sakhmet can appear alongside the king in his chariot, as pictured on Thutmose IV's chariot (see Figure II.17). The king, however, is portrayed as the active charioteer whereas the divinities only hold supportive roles (Hofmann, 1989: 264-272; Manassa, 2013: 150). The exception to the rule is when we see the image of the goddess Astarte riding in her own chariot in the much later Ptolemaic Temple of Edfu (see Köpp-Junk, 2013: 134-135).

From its earliest occurrence in the reign of Thutmose III to the end of the New Kingdom, the charioteer king is said to be "Unshakeable (*mn*) in the chariot like the Lord of Thebes" (Gardiner & Peet, 1952: Nr. 198; 1955: pl. 61; Littauer & Crouwel, 1985: pl. LXIV, C; P. Anastasi II 3, 7; Gardiner, 1937: 14; Kitchen, 1979: 173, 195, 206). The focus on the warrior king as being unaffected by the moving and shaking chariot is said to mirror the prowess of the Lord of Thebes. The remarkableness of remaining steady in a chariot while driving at high speed is notable, and attests to the idea of physical core strength required to balance and to aim steadily and shoot arrows with deadly accuracy while driving over the battlefield terrain. Another epithet of the kings as chariot warrior is "Strong (*tnr*) in the chariot", which in the case of Thutmose IV is "like Astarte" (Helck, 1957a: 1559: see also Littauer & Crouwel, 1985: pl. LXIV, C; Hölscher, 1929: pl. 68). Strength and prowess seems to be a universal part of warrior ethos across cultures, but is in this case described as goddess-like – a goddess who sometimes rides in a chariot herself in Ptolemaic Period imagery (see above).

On the battlefield, as well as in civilian contexts such as royal spectacles and appearances, gilded chariots embellished with solar iconography were used to frame the kings symbolically as a manifestation of the sun god (Calvert, 2013; 57-59, 67; Hartwig, 2007: 122; Martinez, 2012; Darnell & Manassa, 2007: 39). This is correspondingly evident from a number of inscriptions following the schema "His majesty appeared (*ḫʿi*) on his chariot like the god NN". In the Great Sphinx Stela of Amenhotep II, the charioteer king is equalled to the god of war and the scorching sun Montu who shoots arrows (quoted above).

On the Theban Victory Stele of Amenhotep III, the warrior king is described as "Golden [Horus] shining on the chariot, like the rising sun" above a scene in which Asiatic enemies are crushed underneath his chariot (Petrie, 1896: pl. X). Texts also describe Amenhotep III as "speedy like the sun disc, an electrum star when he flashes by, chariot-mounted, and strong-armed bowman, deadly shot", "a runner like the sun disc when he moves, a star of electrum when he shines in a chariot" (Redford, 1994: 169-170). We find a similar statement about Akhenaten on the Early Boundary Stelae of Tell el-Amarna, though this time during a peaceful event: "...His Majesty, Life, Prosperity, Health, appeared on a great chariot of electrum, like Aton when he rises in the horizon" (Murnane & Van Siclen, 1993: 86, A1-A2). Later in his reign, Akhenaten is famous for having ridden his chariot during a daily procession through his capital city Akhetaten in a micro-cosmic imitation of the sun disc's journey across the sky, creating the world anew each day (O'Connor, 1994: 289-290; Redford, 1984: 178-179). An inscribed whip handle belonging to Tutankhamun (Carter's Number 50ss) shows how the event of the king appearing publicly on a chariot was continued to be equated to the sun god in the post-Amarna Period: "He (the king) appears on his chariot like Re, everybody gathers to see him" (Kakosy, 1977: 58; Littauer & Crouwel, 1985: pl. LXV, A).

In the later Battle of Qadesh Inscriptions, Ramesses II appears from his tent "like the rising of Re" and when fighting all alone in his chariot against the Hittites attacking his camp "all his ground was ablaze in fire; he burned all the countries with his fiery blast" (Kitchen, 1979: 103, 120). The poem accompanying the scene showing Ramesses fighting the enemies in his camp shows more examples when the king relates how he "arose against them like Montu, equipped with my weapons of war" and "I was like Re when he rises at dawn, my rays they burned the rebels' bodies" (Kitchen, 1979: 85-86; Figure VI.4).

In Ramesses II's Battle of Qadesh Inscriptions (Kitchen, 1979: 85-86) Montu, as a sun god, represents the scorching and burning aspect of the sun (Calvert, 2013: 61), and the multiple arrows fired by the king in his gold clad chariot, pierce the skin with burning pain like the rays of the sun. In other Ramesside Period examples of pharaoh in his chariot being likened to divinities Seti I appears (ḫʿi) on the chariot as Horus in the form "Son of Isis" (Kitchen, 1975: 204) and Ramesses III is said to "appear in his chariot like Min" (Kitchen, 1980: 203). Calvert (2013: 57-58) notes that the link between sun god and the royal chariot might explain why chariots followed the kings into their afterlives and were placed in the tombs: to aid in defeating the chaotic rebels against the sun god. The chariots were even placed in dedicated tomb sections labelled 'Chariot Hall' or the 'Hall of Repelling Rebels' (Calvert, 2013: 57-58).

According to Hofmann's survey, the appearance-formula was eventually replaced with the formula "the king is beautiful (ʿn) in the chariot", as is said about Ramesses II in a Ramesseum inscription (Kitchen, 1979: 173). In Medinet Habu, the formula equates the beauty of the charioteer pharaoh with that of the war and sun god Montu (Hölscher, 1929: pl. 18, 62, 98). Unlike modern warfare with camouflage and covered positions, warriors in traditional societies focus on battlefield splendour through dress and equipment that accentuates height and visibility in order to frighten the enemy as is evidenced by the ethnographic and

Figure VI.4. Ramesses II in his chariot shooting arrows during the Battle of Qadesh. Luxor. Ramesseum. From: Leblanc & Sesana (2006: 67).

historic records: The royal chariot and horses were themselves highly embellished with colourful ribbons and plumes, while the gold elements would have reflected the sunlight. The visibility of the chariot of the war leader would enable his army to identify and protect their king on the field, while the overall image of the Egyptian chariot army charging towards the foe while shooting arrows and reflecting sun beams would surely have been a terrifying vista for any footsoldier on the receiving end. We can only speculate why the Egyptians, or their Asiatic neighbours, placed expensive gold elements on war chariots, but if nothing else, it would have served the function of enhancing their visibility and thereby the potential to terrorise the enemy and make them break.

VI.8. Chariots in the Lexicon and Writing System

VI.8.1. General

Anyone going through the standard dictionaries to look up ancient Egyptian words for 'chariot' will note how the lexicon apparently contains not one, but three different lexemes that could be used: *wrry.t*, *mrkbt* and *ṯprt* (Wörterbuch I: 334.1-3; Faulkner, 2002: 65; Lesko & Lesko, 1982: I, 121; Wörterbuch II: 113.4; Lesko & Lesko, 1982: I, 229; Wörterbuch V: 364.9). There is, however, reason for caution as the three lexemes seem to possess a varying degree of inclusiveness or specificity on the level of taxonomy. More specifically, *wrry.t* could be used for chariots but also for other types of wheeled vehicles, but *mrkbt* seems only ever to signify chariots, whereas *ṯprt* probably signifies a type of Ramesside Period supply cart or wagon rather than a (Hittite) type of chariot as implied by the dictionaries. The chariot, or rather the use of chariots, could also be signified through the metonymical expression of being *ḥr ḥtri*, litterally "on top of the twin (span)" meaning to ride 'on' a chariot (see below).

To this set of basic terms and metonymies for the chariot itself, one can add a number of technological terms for the different parts of such vehicles, along with descriptions of materials and (possibly) names for specific types of chariots. Given the multifaceted vocabulary relating to chariots, their parts and other kinds of wheeled vehicles, it is not surprising that this group of lexemes has received a significant amount of attention from philologists, socio-historians, and lexicographers. The early works on foreign loanwords in the Egyptian language by Bondi (1886) and Burchardt (1909) both include a number of chariot-part terms. Following these pioneering works, both Helck (1971) and Hoch (1994) have included some of the names of chariot parts in their studies of foreign loanwords in Egyptian texts and language. In his materials for an archaeological dictionary, Jéquier (1922) likewise collected some of the chariot-part names, whether with a foreign or Egyptian etymology, as well as providing identifications between words and vehicle parts.

The majority of the chariot part names are known from literary works from the Ramesside Period written in hieratic, but the corpus also includes a few occurrences in hieroglyphic inscriptions of the 18th Dynasty in *Inw*-tribute lists of the Karnak Annals of Thutmose III (Sethe, 1907: 663, 669, 671, 708, 732) as well as the Great Sphinx Stela (Helck, 1955: 1282) and Karnak-Memphis Stelae of Amenhotep II (Helck, 1955: 1304, 1311). There are additional references to chariot parts in 19th Dynasty texts: the List of Objects for the First Jubilee of Ramesses II (Kitchen, 1979: 382, 10), and the inscriptions for the Siege of Dapur scene in the Ramesseum (Kitchen, 1979: 173, 10).

The New Kingdom composition The Hymn to the King in His Chariot provides some key insights into the names for the different technological parts that constituted a chariot (Manassa, 2013). The text is also characterised by the frequent use of foreign loanwords, which, together with the paronomasia, makes it rather challenging in terms of the lexicographical study of chariot part names. Generally speaking, chariot terms are very rare in the textual record or even uniquely attested, so the overall nomenclature of names for chariot parts remains somewhat obscure.

In addition to the aforementioned Hymn a few other literary texts of the Ramesside Period provide analogous passages that contain names for chariot parts. In the Satirical Letter dealt with by Gardiner (1911) and later Fischer-Elfert (1983; 1986), a chariot is wrecked and subsequently different parts are repaired (P. Anastasi I, 24, 5-7; 26, 4-9). The Ramesside Miscellany Texts, translated by Caminos (1954), includes passages dealing with the purchase of a chariot pole (P. Anastasi III 6, 7), the preparations made for the arrival of Pharaoh (P. Anastasi IV, 16, 7-71) and a record of equipment for an expedition to Syria (P. Koller, 1, 1-2, 2).

In the following section, the individual words for chariots and their parts will be discussed and presented in a lexicological catalogue, as well as a discussion of the 𓍁 'chariot' sign in the hieroglyphic and hieratic writing systems. As mentioned, the nomenclature is challenging in terms of lexicography, identification and translation, level of inclusiveness and taxonomy, as well as the fact that in the case of foreign loanwords, most do not have a clear etymology. Another problem is seen with the tentative translations by philologists: these do not follow a standardised and common terminology for chariot parts. To this can be added the circumstance that the names of the parts of the vehicle and categories do not always match across the main European languages of Egyptology in which the texts have been published and translated. Only a few lexemes of the nomenclature are securely identified, while the meaning of the vast majority remains unknown. Therefore most translations of the names of chariot parts still rely on the Egyptologists' interpretation, which is based on textual contexts, determinatives in the writing system, suggested root etymologies, foreign etymologies, or the straight-forward, though problematic, method of exclusion.

Chariot parts were never represented in the writing system in hieroglyphic signs or as specific determinatives, so the generic determinatives featuring in the nomenclature such as 𓏏 'wood', 𓍯 'leather' or 𓎸 'copper/bronze' can only provide schematic information on meronymic 'made of' relationships between vehicle parts and materials. The relationship between word and determinative does not show if the part was entirely, only partly or simply prototypically made of the material in question, and the occurrences with more than one generic determinative do not offer additional insight into the meaning of the preceding word.

Regardless of the challenges, a number of lexicological observations and insights by Egyptologists and lexicographers who have studied the ancient Egyptian chariot and chariot part terminology is put forward below. Even though the nomenclature is presented as a lexicological catalogue, the collection of words for chariots and their parts provide a number of cultural, technological and socio-historic insights in addition to ones presented above: lexicon and knowledge organisation, foreign loans and Egyptian etymologies, imports and materials, motor interactions, donkeys and mules, production and repairs.

wrry.t 'chariot, wagon'

The earliest basic lexeme signifying a chariot in Egyptian is *wrry.t*, written: , , , or alternatively . It is seen in the early 18th Dynasty tomb of Ahmose, Son of Ebana (Sethe, 1906: 3, 6; 9, 17) from which it can be traced diachronically through a number of texts to the temple inscriptions of the Roman Period (*e.g.* Sauneron, 1963: #190, 310). *Wrry.t* is mostly encountered in monumental inscriptions written in hieroglyphs, but is also known from some instances in hieratic (P. Anastasi I, 19, 4; 24, 4; P. Anastasi II, 3, 7; 5, 3-4; P. Harris 500, ro. 4, 13; P. D'Orbiney [P. BM EA 10183], 17, 3-5; P. Chester-Beatty I, G, I, 3; P. Chester Beatty III, 9, 4; P. Lansing 13a,3; P. Pushkin 127, 3, 5). It is, however, entirely absent from both Demotic and Coptic sources, as the term was gradually replaced during the New Kingdom by more specific chariot, cart and wagon terms (see below).

Several scholars have tried to explain the introduction of the lexeme *wrry.t* in the lexicon as a matter of borrowing a word from a foreign language. Suggestions for a predecessor include the Hurritic word *waratu-šhu* (Helck, 1971; Speiser, 1933), though the meaning of this Hurritic word remains unknown. Others have looked for an Indo-European origin (Raulwing, 1994), or more specifically, a Hittite origin (Schneider, 1999). The latter, however, was dismissed on orthographical, linguistic and chronological premises (Groddek, 2000: 109; Simon, 2010: 87; Zeidler, 2000: 97). In short, there is no cogent evidence to suggest that *wrry.t* was anything but an indigenous Egyptian word, which could be derived from the well-known root *wr* for 'big' or 'great'.

wrry.t should be translated 'chariot' in the vast majority of occurrences, yet evidence suggests that the lexeme was more generic and could also be used for other types of vehicles like a four-wheeled 'wagon' pulled by oxen, or possibly even a two-wheeled (donkey) 'cart'. According to the Gebel Barkal Stela, during a campaign against Mitanni, Thutmose III orders that ships be built in the cedar forests of the Lebanese mountains and subsequently put on 'wagons' (*wrry.t.w*), which are 'drawn by oxen' (*iḥw ḥr stȝ*) so the ships can be brought down to the banks of the Euphrates. Surely, the meaning of the *wrry.t.w* must here be something like 'wagons', *i.e.* a four-wheeled vehicle with two axes to distribute and balance the weight of the ships, emphasised by the use of oxen, rather than horses, as draught animals (Edel, 1983: 104; Faulkner, 1946: 40; Helck, 1955: 1232, 4). Later, on the same monument, *wrry.t* , in an identical writing, is used for silver and gold covered 'chariots' in a list of booty in between references to (other) kinds of weapons and horses (Helck, 1955: 1235, 7).

There is one other example in which *wrry.t* is used for transporting an object: a divine statue of 'Khons-who-Exercises-Authority' (*Khons-Pȝ-ʾIr-šḥr*) to Bactria, on the much discussed Bentresh Stela (Louvre C 214) from the second half of the first millennium BC, written in classical Egyptian. The monument imitates a New Kingdom stela and is pseudepigraphically attributed to the reign of a king whose name is partly that of Ramesses II and partly that of Thutmose IV. Hence, the example is highly problematic for the lexicology of *wrry.t* as it is not only mentioned in a fictive story of a legendary king, but is also from a period in which the lexeme only seems to have existed in writing and archaic language (Louvre C 214; Kitchen, 1979: 286, 4; 15). The GSL T17 'chariot' determinative is rendered rather crudely and schematised, simply showing wheel, pole and a stroke for the yoke/yoke-saddle like a 'stick-man chariot', although the stela is otherwise inscribed with quality hieroglyphs (see 'The Chariot Sign' below). It would seem that the scribe knew the basic technology of a chariot, but otherwise did not know what the chariots of old looked like, as they had vanished from daily life and the battlefields had become dominated by phalanx warfare.

Indirect evidence from a 19th Dynasty Deir el-Medinah ostracon (oCairo 25543, rt. 4-5; Černý, 1930: pl. 39*) suggests a more generic meaning of *wrry.t*. It records the sale of *t3 ꜥ3.t n wrry.t* 'the female chariot donkey'. As Janssen (1975: 170-171) remarks, it is unknown what kind of animal a '(female) chariot-donkey' really was but the employment of a donkey to pull a vehicle seems better suited for heavier types of wagons or carts, rather than the speedy, usually horse-drawn and prestigious chariot. In his later work on donkeys in Deir el-Medinah, Janssen (2005: 74, note 5) translates the text as 'the she-ass of the wagon'. The 'she-ass of the wagon' from oCairo 25543 can be related to another example from a later Ramesside letter, dated to year 10 of Ramesses XI, mentioning *ꜥ3.t.w n mrkbt.w* 'chariot donkeys' (BM. 10326, vs. 6-7 = Černý, 1939: 19, 10 [vs. 6-7] VIII and XVI [description], 17-21 [transcription]; Janssen, 1991: pls. 37-38 [photographs]). Wente (1967: 40, n. w) suggests that the absence of an article before *mrkbt.w* makes it possible that *ꜥ3.t.w n mrkbt.w* 'chariot donkeys' should be understood as a type of donkey, as opposed to 'donkeys of the/a chariot'. He also notes that the Semitic and common loanword *mrkbt* can only ever signify a 'chariot' whereas *wrry.t* can refer to both war chariots and transport wagons, and in the Miscellany Text dealing with the equipment of a Syrian expedition (P. Koller 1, 3) donkeys are listed right before the description of the chariots.

Hofmann (1989: 44-46) remarks that the price of three *deben* for 'the she-ass of the wagon' from oCairo 25543 is remarkably high, and speculates if the animal in question could be an equine hybrid like a mule or hinny for which no specific names in the Egyptian lexicon seem to exist. Equine hybrids are generally more powerful, and possibly therefore more expensive than a donkey, and could be used to pull even heavier vehicles (Janssen, 1975: 171). Indeed, in a scene from the Asasif tomb of Amenemopet (Djehutynefer; TT297), Overseer of Fields, from the early 18th Dynasty, mules are shown as pull animals for a chariot, distinctly separated from the register above showing a chariot with a span of horses (Hofmann, 1989: 287, Taf. 054-56).

mrkbt 'chariot'

In the text from the Karnak Stela of Amenhotep II, a second lexeme for 'chariot' appears for the first time in the Egyptian lexicon, *mrkbt*, or alternatively — a word that is otherwise encountered in hieratic texts of the later Ramesside Period. Unlike *wrry.t*, *mrkbt* is clearly a common Semitic word, known from Ugarit: *markabtum*; Akkadian: *narkabtu*; Hebrew: *merkaba*; and Arabic: *markabat*. Contrary to *wrry.t* this lexeme survives into both Roman Period Demotic as *mkw.t*, and in Coptic as βερεγωογτ, but seems otherwise entirely absent in the textual record of the Third Intermediate Period, Late Period and Ptolemaic Period (Hoch, 1994: 145-147).

It is interesting to note that in its earliest occurrence, on the Karnak Stela of Amenhotep II, *mrkbt* is used to denote the chariot of an Asiatic prince, whereas the chariot of the pharaoh is called a *wrry.t* (Helck, 1955: 1311, 11-12). So, in this earliest attestation of *mrkbt* in an Egyptian text, an Asiatic chariot is linguistically, and orthographically, differentiated from an Egyptian one by writing it phonetically. When *mrkbt* is found in later attestations it always denotes a 'chariot' in general without any cultural, technological reference or specifications.

When comparing the distribution of *wrry.t* and *mrkbt* through time and contexts there is a clear tendency to show how *mrkbt* became the most frequently used word for chariot through its frequent employment in hieratic texts of the Ramesside Period, where it features in a wide range of diverting and often secular textual genres. *Wrry.t*, on the contrary, retained an archaic, normative status and continued to be used in monumental hieroglyphic inscriptions of the New Kingdom, as well as in hieroglyphic inscriptions of the first millennium BC, though only in rare instances due to the chariot's lessening and changing cultural significance. *Mrkbt* is only found written in New Kingdom hieroglyphs twice, in its first appearance on the afore-mentioned Karnak Stela of Amenhotep II, while the second example comes from the late New Kingdom where it is used in a list of booty from Ramesses III's Second Libyan War in the temple of Medinet Habu: (Kitchen, 1983: 53, 8).

tprt 'cart, wagon'

The third lexeme in the ancient Egyptian lexicon which the dictionaries translate as 'chariot' *tprt* is much rarer than the dedicated chariot terms *wrry.t* and *mrkbt*, and only attested twice. One example comes from Ramesses II's temple in Abydos, where it appears in an inscription preceding a Qadesh-scene showing the Hittite chariot warriors, infantry and four wheeled supply wagons: *thr n tprt p3-ihy n p3-hrw n ht* "The thr-troops of the *tprt*-chariots belonging to the camp of the enemy lord of Khati" (Kitchen, 1979: 140, 12). Here, *tprt* is written with the GSL T17 'chariot' determinative and if one understands it as a specific determinative in this context, and considers the accompanying reliefs showing Hittite army scenes including chariots, it seems straightforward to follow the main translation provided by the Wörterbuch 'Streitwagen der Hethiter' (Wörterbuch V: 364, 10). *tprt* cannot be verifiably related to Hittite words for 'chariot', because it is consistently written with the Sumerio-grams *giš-gigir* and the Hittite pronunciation is hence unknown. We simply do not know what the Hittite lexeme for 'chariot' is and there is no evidence that *tprt* is derived from Hittite (Edel, 1983: 99; Simon, 2010: 85, 19).

In a second occurrence, *tprt* refers to a vehicle in a royal Egyptian workshop. The example comes as part of a model instruction given to woodworkers working on a *mrkbt* 'chariot' whereas it is metalworkers that work on a *tprt* 'chariot' (P. Anastasi III, vs. 1, 3; Gardiner, 1937: 30). The technological differences between the two vehicles are further emphasised by the employment of the generic 'wood' determinative GSL M3 in the writing of *mrkbt* [hieroglyphs], whereas *tprt* [hieroglyphs] features with the generic [hieroglyph] 'copper/bronze' determinative GSL N34, thus indicating that part of the *tprt* [hieroglyphs] was 'made of' [copper/bronze]. For the example of *trpt* written with the 'metal'-determinative (P. Anastasi III, vs. 1, 3; Gardiner, 1937: 30), Edel (1983) wonders whether this refers to supporting metal elements like brackets that would enable the cart to carry considerable loads when compared to the *mrkbt* 'chariot' [hieroglyphs] written with the wood-determinative. Hoch (1994: 365), notices that *tprt* could possibly be derived from the Akkadian *saparru* 'cart' and notes that *tprt* is also very likely connected with a word for 'bronze' *siparru* attested in several Semitic languages. He therefore translates *tprt* with 'bronze covered chariot'.

However, in a study of Semitic names and loanwords in the hieroglyphic Battle of Qadesh texts, Edel (1983) has furnished evidence that strongly implies that the *tprt* [hieroglyphs] was not a chariot-type vehicle at all, but rather a kind of wagon or cart for transport and cargo. Edel, like Hoch (1994), also believes that the Egyptian *tprt* could very likely be derived from the Akkadian *sappuru* for a 'cart'. Both the inscription and the image make it clear that the '*thr*-troops of the *tprt*-vehicles' belong to the army camp (*p3 ihy*). The chariot soldiers of the battlefield have their own label inscription that refers to them as *thr*-troops of the shield carrier (*kr'w*) – a chariot warrior title (Yoyotte & Lopez, 1969: 11). In short, there are logistical troops with four-wheeled wagons in the Hittite army's supply train and camps (*thr n tprt*) separate from the chariot warriors on the battlefield (*thr n kr'w*). The Hittite supply wagons can be seen flanked on all sides by the infantry on the Abydos temple in the scene headed by the inscription in question (Naville *et al.*, 1930: pl. XVII), and when looking at depictions of the camp of Ramesses II, one can likewise see two-wheeled carts for transport and cargo used by the Egyptian army (*e.g.* the camp of Ramses at Shabtûn, Figure VI.5, Abu Simbel and Ramesseum; Hofmann, 1989: Taf. 087-088; Darnell & Manassa, 2007: 80).

It should be noted that, if Edel is correct in regarding *tprt* [hieroglyphs] as the word for a two-wheeled cart, by the 20th Dynasty, the Egyptian language would have moved from using one word (*wrry.t*) for both chariots and wagons in the 18th Dynasty, to a later New Kingdom situation in which there existed specific names for various vehicles: two-wheeled vehicles, which one stands or sits on, *mrkbt* 'chariot' and *tprt* 'cart' respectively, and four-wheeled vehicles *ʿgr.t* (Coptic αγολτε) 'wagon'. This in effect mirrors the vehicle designations of modern English.

The *ḥr ḥtri* [hieroglyphs] Metonymy

In addition to the basic words for chariot and cart discussed above, the textual record contains a secondary mode of referring to chariots, through the metonymic expression of being *ḥr ḥtri* [hieroglyphs] 'on the twin span (of horses)'. The twin span of horses, being part of the overall concept of a 'chariot', stands metonymically for the whole chariot, while the preposition *ḥr* 'to be upon' encapsulates the embodied notion of standing upon a chariot while driving it. It can be written [hieroglyphs], [hieroglyphs] or [hieroglyphs]. The latter writing, [hieroglyphs], is sometimes mistakenly read *ḥr šsm.t* and translated 'on horse', rather than *ḥr ḥtri* 'on twin span/chariot' (Decker, 1971: 142, note 953). In the New Kingdom, the expression *ḥr ḥtri* [hieroglyphs] always refers metonymically to a chariot, and when Egyptian or enemy soldiers are referred to as being *nt ḥtri* [hieroglyphs] 'of the twin span' it signifies that they are

Figure VI.5. Chariots and carts in the camp of Ramesses II at Shabtûn. Abu Simbel. Great Temple. From: Desroches-Noblecourt et al. (1971: pl. 5).

chariot warriors (Wörterbuch III: 200. 3-4; Decker, 1971: 142-144; Schulman, 1986: 34, note 134). The metonymic use of *ḥtri* for 'chariot' can also be found in the compound *mš3 n ḥtri* 'chariot army' (Wörterbuch III: 200.5).

According to Helck (1978: 337; see also Habachi, 1972: 36 n. g; Spallinger, 2005: 11; Darnell & Manassa, 2007: 63 note 35) the mentioning of *t3-nt-ḥtri* 'that which belong to the twin span' among the goods and resources claimed as war booty following the fall of the Hyksos capital Avaris, as commemorated on the Second Victory Stela of Kamose, perhaps suggesting that the Hyksos had chariots, but the text part could be interpreted differently. Since there is no archaeological, pictorial or other further textual evidence to prove that the Hyksos even had chariots, it is thus worth revisiting the context to determine if the term is actually a metonymic reference to chariots besieged by the victorious Kamose after the battle: "Look! I drink of the wine of your vineyards that the Asiatics whom I captured pressed out for me. I have smashed up your rest house, I have cut down your trees, I have forced your women into ships' holds, I have seized **that which belong to the twin span**; I haven't left a plank to the hundreds of ships of fresh cedar which were filled with gold, lapis, silver, turquoise, bronze axes without number, over and above the moringa-oil, incense, fat, honey, willow, box-wood, sticks and all their fine woods – all the fine products of Retenu. I have confiscated all of it! I haven't left a thing to Avaris to her (own) destitution: the Asiatic has perished!" (Habachi, 1972: 36 [emphasis added]).

The list is arranged according to some overall conceptual categories under which the entries in the list are grouped. First the list mentions the place of events (the vineyard and rest house), then living things (the tress, the captured women, and the twin spans), and finally non-living objects in the form of materials (cedar, gold, lapis, silver, etc.). Unlike the later war booty lists of the 18th Dynasty ennumerating chariots among other kinds of war equipment, such as weapons and armours, the emphasis of the Kamose list is on resources and materials for production and consumption without which the Hyksos nation would not function. The only direct reference to weapons is the 'bronze axes without number', but as they feature after precious metals and minerals, it seems likely that their value should be found in the material (bronze), rather than their function as weapons, although there are several ways in which the value or type of these different objects could be organised. Traditionally, going back to at least the Old Kingdom, the *ḫtri* [hieroglyphs] always referred to twin spans of animals pulling ploughs (Wörterbuch III: 199.8). The determinative is simply the generic 'hide and tail' used in the writing of words and names for quadrupeds (Goldwasser, 2002: 57-89). Only later, in the New Kingdom proper, do we find *ḫtri* used metonymically for chariots, especially during the Ramesside Period (Decker, 1971: 142-144; Schulman, 1964: 14ff). It therefore seems more logical to understand [hieroglyphs] 'that which belong to the twin span', as pertaining to plough spans rather than chariots.

The Chariot Sign [hieroglyph]

The writing of the words for chariots and the use of the chariot sign as a determinative provide some interesting insights into the ancient Egyptians' conceptions of what constituted a prototypical chariot through time. According to the GSL, the chariot sign [hieroglyph] T17, can serve as an ideogram for *wrry.t* 'chariot' or as specific determinative for *wrry.t* 'chariot' (Gardiner, 1957: 513). Based on a complete survey of the total number of attestations from the Wörterbuch Zettelarkiv and the dictionaries by Faulkner (2002) and Lesko & Lesko (1982), in roughly 50% of all hieroglyphic instances of *wrry.t* [hieroglyphs] 'chariot' it is written with a specific determinative depicting a two-horse light-weight chariot, whereas the writing of *wrry.t* and *mrkbt* in hieratic will only ever show the generic [hieroglyph] wood-sign when written with a determinative: [hieroglyphs], [hieroglyphs]. The use of generic [hieroglyph] 'wood'-determinative, relates to the preceding word for 'chariot' through the meronymic 'made of'-relationship between the core material wood and the chariots – a relationship attested in examples spanning the New Kingdom to the end of the hieroglyphic writing system in the Roman Period (Wörterbuch I: 334.1-3). In the hieratic writing system, words for chariots (*wrry.t* and *mrkbt*) are only ever written with the generic [hieroglyph] wood determinative, following the general trend of using the often simpler and more quickly written generic determinatives rather than the particular, and often more detailed, specific determinatives found mainly in hieroglyphic writing.

The feature of the hieroglyphic writing system known as specific determinatives provides a form of pictorial tautology of the word they appear with: a pictorial tautology, which theoretically displays a culturally selected prototype or 'best example', like when a [hieroglyph] lotus adds further visual information about the possible shape of such a flower to the word [hieroglyphs] 'lotus', or when reading about [hieroglyphs] 'sandals', we get an example of what Egyptian sandals looked like (Goldwasser, 2002: 15, 28-29). In New Kingdom hieroglyphic inscriptions, the specific determinative consistently depicts a [hieroglyph] light two-horse Egyptian chariot, but in a few instances from the second half of the first millennium BC, it is possible to trace changes in the conception of what constituted a prototypical chariot.

The first example comes from the above-mentioned Bentresh Stela. The specific determinative for *wrry.t* is in this, otherwise elaborately written text, shaped rather schematically (see above). The second example is perhaps an even clearer case of how the iconicity of the Egyptian writing system gives insights into changed conceptions of what constituted a prototypical chariot through time. In an example from the Ptolemaic Period, in which Egypt had become part of the Hellenistic world, the specific determinative depicts a Hellenistic type four-horse-powered racing-chariot, which shows a driver sporting a whip. Hence the writing system offers a cognitive glimpse into how the conception of chariot prototypes went from the light-two-horse drawn type of the Late Bronze Age, to being forgotten in the Iron Age, before being changed to a *tetrippon* in the early Ptolemaic Period (Figure VI.6). It is a case of what Gardiner (1957: 439) describes as "bringing a sign up to date" in the introduction to his sign list for the cases in which developments in technology and material culture gave input to new hieroglyphic sign forms and related concepts. That leaves the problem of the GSL T17 'chariot'-determinative when used in the writing of words that signifies other types of vehicles than a 'chariot', where the sign cannot serve as a specific determinative that simply reiterates the preceding word visually. As Edel (1983) is surely correct in identifying the meaning of the word *tprt* as a two-wheeled supply cart rather than a 'Hittite chariot', the 'chariot' sign must in this case function as a generic determinative, marking a broader and more superordinate category of (wheeled vehicles), indicated by the sign depicting the most prototypical member, *i.e.* the light two-horse Egyptian chariot. Edel (1983) reminds us of another example of such a use when *wrry.t* refers to a four-wheeled wagon for transporting heavy ship parts on the Gebel Barkal stela (Helck, 1955: 1232, 4; Edel, 1983: 99-105). The latter, however, could simply be because it shares, as ideogram, the same root value as the preceding word it appears with.

VI.8.2. Lexicological Catalogue of Chariot Part Names

im 'floor' (?)

According to Helck (1971: 507, 3) *im* is of Semitic origin though the etymology remains obscure (see also Hoch, 1994: 22-23). Schneider (2008: 185, 187) proposes that the Egyptian *im* could be derived from the Semitic root *umm* for 'mother' to 'mother piece, main body' and onto the 'standing space within the chariot body (?)'. The supposed Semitic origin of *im* is not indicated by the Wörterbuch, which simply defines it as 'part of a chariot' (Wörterbuch I:

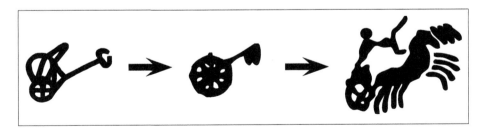

Figure VI.6. Bringing the chariot sign 'up to date'. 18th Dynasty: Light two-horse chariot; Late Period: 'Stickman' Chariot; Ptolemaic Period: **Tetrippon**. *Drawing after original by T. Jakobsen.*

78.6). As a word for a chariot part, *im* 𓂝𓏛 is attested both in a pun in the Edingburgh Hymn to the King in His Chariot (rt. 2-3) "The floor (*im*) of your chariot: gracious (*im3*) towards you do they become, the (foreign) chiefs" (transl. Manassa, 2013: 144), and in an equally obscure passage in P. Anastasi IV (16, 10) concerned with the description of chariots for an expedition to Syria: "Their *im.w* (floors (?)) are of *sḫt*". In this case *im* is written with the wood-determinative whereas it is hesitantly transcribed with a leather determinative in the Edingburgh Hymn to the King in His Chariot (Gardiner, 1937: 53; Dawson & Peet, 1933: pl. XXVI).

The word *sḫt* is significant in understanding the meaning of *im*, though the Wörterbuch does not contain an entry for the spelling of *sḫt* as it is written in P. Anastasi IV, (16, 10; Gardiner, 1937: 53). Jéquier (1922: 153-154) connects it with *sḫt* 'to weave' (Wörterbuch IV: 263.6-16) and relates the *im* of the chariot to the D-shaped floor frame and the interwoven leather straps creating the floor surface of the chariot box. Caminos (1954: 214) did not accept this reading since it is written with the ° 'pellet, granulated materials' determinative like in the medical texts. It is, of course, not uncommon that root determinatives are employed in the spelling of different words based on the same root, so Jéquier's idea cannot be dismissed on the premise of determinative used in the writing of *sḫt*. The only part of a chariot, which is of both wood and leather, and could conceivably be described as 'woven' is the D-shaped floor made from leather or rawhide thongs (Hofmann, 1989: 216; Manassa, 2013: 144-145; Schulman, 1986: 40; Littauer & Crouwel, 1985: 70).

iwn-kfkf.t 'clamp' (?)

It is extremely problematic to identify and subsequently relate *iwn-kfkf.t* to any part of a chariot or the belonging equipment. The Wörterbuch simply gives 'part of a chariot' (Wörterbuch I: 101.12). It is attested only once, in the episode from P. Anastasi I mentioned above in which Amenemope, the driver, has to perform emergency repairs after having crashed his vehicle. It is written with the wood-determinative and features in a somewhat problematic passage: *t3 iwn-kfkf.t ḫ3ꜥ.ty n st=s p3 ḥtr dns r 3tp.st* "The *iwn-kfkf.t* is left where it is, for the team is too overburdened to support it." As Schulman (1986: 39) notes the passage follows the sentences dealing with repairing the yoke and yoke saddle (P. Anastati I 24, 5-7), but otherwise does not offer much help in identifying what part it is or why the horses cannot move it after the accident. Helck (1971: 507, nr. 5) viewed *iwn-kfkf.t* as a Semitic loanword for 'to circle', whereas Schulman (1986: 39-40) argues for an Egyptian etymology partly based on *iwn* for 'pillar, column, support' (Wörterbuch I: 53.10-14) and partly on *kfkf* 'cult vessel' (Wörterbuch V: 33.5) and concludes hesitantly that the only part associated with the yoke and draught pole, which is both made of wood and relatively heavy, and for which no name has been identified, is a large disk, supported on a pillar-like base affixed to the centre of the yoke where the two arms meet. Wente & Meltzer (1990: 108) translate 'clamp (?)', but whether this translation is connected to Schulman's observations and suggestion is unknown.

ꜥ 'pole'

As stated by Gardiner (1911: 28* note 6): "the ꜥ is certainly the pole" – a fact which is widely accepted (Wörterbuch I: 159.3; see also Hofmann, 1989: 219-220; Jéquier, 1922: 1-2; Manassa, 2013: 149; Schulman, 1986: 28). The root meaning of an 'arm' for a chariot pole encapsulates the embodied notion of a long, slender and strong limb, trimmed with leather (see below), which projects from the vehicle. The determinative employed in writing ꜥ 'pole' is consistently found to be 'wood', and texts inform us that this could either be the hitherto unidentified wood type called *ꞮŞgꞮŞ* (P. Koller 2,1; Gardiner, 1937: 117) or the pole is imported, partly prefabricated, from Syria, specifically the land of Upe (P. Anastasi IV, 16, 11; Gardiner, 1937: 53). In both cases, the pole was *tby/dby* 'fitted with leather' (Caminos, 1954: 215; Gardiner, 1911: 38* note 9, of which, possibly, #32, Cat. No. 134, is an example).

From the Miscellany Text 'The Sufferings of An Army Officer' (P. Anastasi III, 6, 7; Gardiner, 1937: 27) insight is obtained about the value of an ꜥ 'pole', set at the cost of three *deben* whereas the chariot (*mrkbt*), presumably the body, costs five *deben*. The relatively high cost for the pole compared to that of the body, should perhaps be sought in the costly nature of producing it and the wood types required to withstand the strain and forces put on the pole when driving a chariot as well as the production. As the Miscellany Text cannot be taken as a strictly historical document, the prices might be fictitious altogether as explained previously. In fact, Janssen (1975: 329) remarks that these prices are extremely doubtful, when compared to the prices of a bed for instance, which ranged between 15-20 *deben*, compared to the three and five *deben* for pole and chariot (body). On the other hand, if the *deben* price for the pole and body is understood as referring to silver, to which the text makes no reference, the price seems unreasonably high as already noted above.

ꜥbii(.t) 'rein'

The Late Egyptian ꜥbii(.t) for 'rein' is derived from the Middle Egyptian ꜥbꞮŞyt 'bond, (steering) rope' (Anm. 726&862; Osing, 1976: 195; Westendorf, 1978: 153). It continues in Coptic as αβε 'fetter' (Westendorf, 1965-1977: 1). ꜥbii(.t) is known from two occurrences in the Late Egyptian Miscellany Text 'The Sufferings of An Army Officer'. Here, an incompetent chariot driver seizes tꞮŞ ꜥbii(.t) 'the reins' and put them on his horses, only to end up in the undergrowth and *"the ꜥbii(.t) 'reins' cut his legs, while his flank is pierced by bites"* (P. Anastasi III, 6, 9; Gardiner, 1937: 27).

ꜥmd 'central upright support' (?)

For this entry, the Wörterbuch simply provides the translation 'a part of a chariot' (Wörterbuch I: 187.9). It is, however, argued by Jequier (1922: 16-17, Fig. 12), and later Ward (1963: 428-429, but see Hofmann, 1989: 221; Manassa, 2013: 151; Schulman, 1986: 28), that ꜥmd probably signifies the main upright support, which braces the upper and lower frame (here: top railing and floor frame resp.) of the chariot body. It is a Semitic loanword that corresponds to Akkadian *imdu* 'support' (Hoch 1994, 70; Schneider, 2008: 188). pꞮŞ ꜥmd 'the upright support' is only attested twice, written one time with a meronymic determinative for objects made of wood ⌒𓆱⌒ⁿ𓏛𓏥, and with the determinative for objects made of leather in the second instance: ⌒𓎡𓆱𓏛𓏲𓏛𓏥. In P. Anastasi IV (16, 8; Gardiner, 1937: 53) an ꜥmd 'support' is described as being 'worked/ wrapped with gold'. Schulman notes that even though it is written with the singular article in The Hymn to the King in His Chariot, surviving chariots and pictorial representation of chariots show how they could be fitted with one, two or several upright supports (Schulman, 1986: 29).

ꜥrḳ ⌒𓂝𓏤𓎡𓍢𓏛 'front support, chariot box, horses' housing' (?)

There is some controversy centred on the meaning of the term ꜥrḳ, and the Wörterbuch simply lists the lexeme as "part of a chariot" (Wörterbuch I: 213.9). Jéquier (1922: 218) related the noun to the verb ꜥrḳ 'to tie/to attach' and understood ꜥrḳ as the front support which drops down from the chariot body and connects to the draught pole, thereby creating support for the body and reinforcing the joint between the two main parts of the vehicle. Dawson and Peet (1933: 172) suggest ꜥrḳ should be related to the noun ꜥrḳ 'basket/container' (for measuring fruit) and tentatively translates ꜥrḳ 'basket', which they believe could be "the large weapon case carried at the side of the chariot?".

Schulmann (1986: 29), however, rules out this identification as the names for quivers (ỉspt) and bow-case (š3k) are well known. Conversely, it can be argued that the Egyptian language, like any other, contains complementary lexemes that just exist on different levels of taxonomy and inclusion. Thus Schulman's method of exclusion is problematic. In the single occurrence of ꜥrḳ ⌒𓂝𓏤𓎡𓍢𓏛 as a term for a chariot part it is clearly written with the hieratic 'cattle-hobble' determinative that corresponds to GSL 𓍢 V19 and with a second determinative tentatively transcribed by Dawson and Peet (1933: 172) as 'leather', corresponding to GSL 𓏛 F27. Based on the container and possible leather determinative, Schulman (1986: 29-30) suggests ꜥrḳ ⌒𓂝𓏤𓎡𓍢𓏛 to be understood as the 'chariot box [= body]', which often was clad with leather. According to Hofmann, the body of the chariot was made of wood and stucco, not leather, and therefore ꜥrḳ written with the GSL F27 'leather' determinative cannot signify a chariot body. This, however, is only partly true as most bodies of chariots were clad with leather. Hofmann (1989: 221) simply translates ꜥrḳ-band without further technological specification or function. Manassa (2013: 148) proposes that the term could be related to ꜥrḳ 'to put on (clothing)' (Wörterbuch I: 211.19-23) and makes the conjecture that ꜥrḳ ⌒𓂝𓏤𓎡𓍢𓏛 could signify the horses' housing, known from depictions and the tomb of Tutankhamun (Littauer & Crouwel, 1985: 88, pl. LXII). The appearance of the 'cattle-hobble' determinative (GSL 𓍢 V19) could simply have been influenced by, and derived from, the writing of the more common term ꜥrḳ 'fruit basket' (Manassa, 2013: 148).

ꜥdr.w ⌒𓂝𓂧𓂋𓏤𓆱𓏥 'yoke braces, front support, strut' (?)

A number of scholars have related ꜥdr.w (oEdingburgh 916, rt. 4; Dawson & Peet, 1933: pl. XXVI) to the Semitic root for 'helper' (Burchardt, 1909: 303; Darnell, 1986: 17-18; Fischer-Elfert, 1986: 204; Helck, 1971: 510 nr. 49-50; Hoch, 1994: 88-90; Jéquier, 1922: 158). Schulman suggests the translation 'yoke braces' as the function of a 'helper' in a technical context would be 'supporting' or 'bracing'. The yoke braces are shown in depictions as extending from the middle of the pole to the middle of each yoke arm, thereby keeping the horse team in step while relieving the stress from the traction of the chariot on the yoke and its pole (Schulman, 1986: 30). The identification of ꜥdr.w with 'yoke braces' is problematic as these are consistently made of leather and therefore do not fit the writing with the 'wood' determinative (Hofmann, 1989: 222-223). Hoch (1994: 90, note 109) argues for a kind of leather strut *"that secures the top front rail of the chariot box [= body] to the pole"* and later Schneider (2008: 188) provided the tentative and more generic translation *"auxiliary (strut)?"* (i.e. '*Hilfs(verstrebung)*'?). Manassa tentatively suggests ꜥdr.w should be related to the wooden supports, which connects the body to the pole (referred to by Littauer & Crouwel, 1985 as front or triple support). If ꜥdr.w signify these 'front supports' that connect the railing of the body with the pole at an angle, it therefore differentiates from the main and vertical ꜥmd 'upright support' of the body's front (Manassa, 2013: 145).

bt.w 'sides, decorative tassels' (?)

The term *bt.w* occurs only once, in the Edinburgh ostracon of the Hymn to the King in His Chariot (rt. 7-8). It is written in plural with a 'leather' determinative (?) and spelled out phonetically indicating it is a foreign loanword, which should probably be connected to the Akkadian *bîtu* for 'house, container, repository' (Manassa, 2013: 146; Schulman, 1986: 40). Hoch (1994: 115) notes that in the Amarna Letters, the Akkadian *bîtu* is used for leather containers. In the chariot terminology of Mesopotamia *bit* can be used for the whole 'chariot box [= body]', but since the word is written in plural, in what he calls a 'wild guess', Schulman (1986, 40; but see also Hoch, 1994: 115, no. 145; Manassa, 2013: 146; Schneider, 2008: 188) proposes that *bt.w* are the often decorated leather cladding of the body. Hofmann (1989: 223 and Taf.019) remarks that it seems impossible to identify the form or function of *bt.w*, but notes that Akkadian also contains a *bîtu* for 'tassels' and wonders if the tassels, which can sometimes be seen hanging from the yoke ends for decorative purposes in some Egyptian depictions, are the signified of *bt.w*.

pḫ3 'side panel [called 'siding fill' in the present work]'

The basic meaning of *pḫ3* is a thin board or plank, and is known in the context of ship building (Glanville, 1932: 12). Dawson and Peet (1933: 170) propose, with great hesitation, the meaning 'block'. In ship building, *pḫ3* was used for the decking of the ships, but this does not correspond to the floors of the chariot bodies, as suggested by Caminos (1954: 213), as they are made of a tightly woven mesh of leather or rawhide thongs with a hide or cloth cover placed over it like a mat. Based on the context of the single occurrence in which *pḫ3* appears in relation to chariots, Schulmann (1986: 30-31) thinks that the *pḫ3* was used for the breastwork or side panelling of the chariot body: *n3y.sn tḥr.w m inm n ins(y) iw.w t3 ḥr dd iw pḫ3 b3k m dsr* "Their *tḥr.w* have the hue of red cloth, being carved with rosettes, and the *pḫ3*-board is made from djeser-wood" (P. Anastasi IV, 16, 8-9; Gardiner, 1937: 53). Hofmann (1989: 223-224) notes that some Egyptian chariots were fitted with a board or plank attached to the rear of the axle and propose to equate the signified of *pḫ3* with this rear board. However, he does not refer to any concrete examples of such a board or plank attached to the axle, so one is left to wonder what element he is actually thinking of when consulting the schematic overview and standardised terminology for chariot parts, put forth by, for example, Littauer and Crouwel (1985: 4, fig. 1; see the figure in the Glossary).

m3wt.w 𓌴𓄿𓌙𓀔𓏛𓏥 'wheel spokes, axle'(?)

m3wt.w is based on the same root as the words for staff, shaft and spear shaft as well as the rays of the sun when written in plural and with the 𓌴𓄿𓌙𓇳 'sunshine' determinative (GSL N8) and thus it is probable that *m3wt.w* 𓌴𓄿𓌙𓀔𓏛𓏥 signifies 'wheel spokes' (P. Anastasi IV, 16, 11; Gardiner, 1937: 53). Like the rays emanating from the sun, the spokes of the chariot wheel emanate from the nave (Caminos, 1954: 214; Schulman, 1986: 31). Hofmann (1989: 224-225), on the contrary, argues that *m3wt.w* 𓌴𓄿𓌙𓀔𓏛𓏥 should be understood as the axle as *m3wt* in other contexts signifies a 'staff' or rounded shaft of worked wood as part of tribute (*e.g.* Sethe, 1907: 708, 732), or the staffs carried by Nubians (P. Anastasi III, A 7-8; Gardiner, 1937: 33), which could be embellished with inlays and red leather (P. Anastasi IV, 6-7; Gardiner, 1937: 53). Caminos (1954: 214), however, in dealing with P. Anastasi IV, rules out the possibility of *m3wt.w* 𓌴𓄿𓌙𓀔𓏛𓏥 meaning 'axle' by stating "it is clear from the passage in P. Anastasi IV (16, 11) that each chariot has a plurality of *m3wt*". In addition to the meronymic 𓆱 'wood'-determinative, P. Anastasi IV informs us how *m3wt.w* could be imported from Pher in Palestine (16, 10-11; Gardiner, 1937: 53; Gauthier, 1925: 39).

mḫ3.w 𓌳𓐍𓄿𓍱𓏥 '(leather) bindings'

It seems impossible to identify exactly what chariot part the *mḫ3.w* 𓌳𓐍𓄿𓍱𓏥 'bindings' is. Burchardt (1910: nr. 490) and Helck (1971: 514, 107) view *mḫ3* as being of Semitic origin, but given the 'cord' determinative there can be little doubt it is related to the Egyptian *mḫ3* for 'to tie, bind' known from the Middle Kingdom onwards. When *mḫ3.w* 𓌳𓐍𓄿𓍱𓏥 'leather bindings' is used for a chariot part it must refer to one of the numerous rawhide lashings used for binding and tying the vehicle together (Schulman, 1986: 41) or perhaps even the leather support straps (see Chapter II). The single occurrence features in one of the word plays in the Edinburgh text (oEdinburgh 916, vs. 14-15; Dawson & Peet, 1933: pl. XXVIII) where the *mḫ3*-bindings are said to "bind (*mḫ3*) evil doers" in a passage following a word play on the yoke saddles (*dr.t*). This leads Schulman (1986: 41; but see also Hofmann, 1989: 225-226; Manassa, 2013: 149) to suggest that the *mḫ3*-bindings could be those used to tie the yoke saddles and the yoke together.

mš3y.w 𓌳𓈙𓄿𓏭𓍱𓏥 'leather thongs, container' (?)

Defined simply by the Wörterbuch as "a leather part of a chariot" (Wörterbuch II: 154.20), the meaning of *mš3y.w* 𓌳𓈙𓄿𓏭𓍱𓏥 remains unknown. Both Burchardt (1910: 505) and Helck (1971: 514, 116) believe the lexeme to be of Semitic origin, but neither are able to provide any etymology or cognates for it (see also remarks by Simon, 2010: 85). It features in the somewhat obscure passage in P. Anastasi I in which a chariot is being repaired in a workshop (26, 6-7; Gardiner, 1911: 37): "*They place n3 mš3y.w* at your *dr.t* (yoke saddle) and *ḫ3*, and tighten up your yoke". The context and the employment of the leather determinative in the writing of *mš3y.w* indicate it could signify some kind of leather binding (Fischer-Elfert, 1986: 227 e; Schulman, 1986: 34; Spiegelberg, 1928: 112 n.3; Wente & Meltzer, 1990: 109). In his treatment of *p3 mḫ3* '(leather) bindings' Schulman notes how *mḫ3* could have been the same as *mš3y*: "its writing with *ḫ* derived from *š>ḥ>ḫ?*". If so, then the *mḫ3/mš3y* would have been the leather thong or binding which secured either the yoke saddles to the yoke arms, or those which secured the yoke to the draught pole, or both (Schulman, 1986: 41). Along the same line of thought, Schneider (2008: 184) proposes "leather tapes" or similar, by comparing *mš3y.w* with Hittite *maššiya* "type belt or scarf".

Mš3y.w occurs once in P. Koller (2,1; Gardiner, 1937: 117), but in the context of bows rather than chariots: [*nʿy*].*sn mšw m mtri wʿb* "[Th]eir leather bindings are of neat webbing", which, according to Schulman (1986: 41), were used as a grip, and could also be bound around a grip on a chariot. There is, however, no known examples of such a feature on chariots from ancient Egypt whereas there are plenty examples of leather 'webbing' in axes and adze. We cannot rule out, however, the possibility that hand-grips were lashed with webbing for better grip. Caminos (1954: 435) looked to the Demotic *mšy* for a type of container in his treatment of P. Koller but states that the meaning of *mš3y.w* is unknown.

mḫti.w 'thin, metal wraps' (?)

Although attested in two different texts, we do not know what *mḫti.w* refers to. It is believed to be a Semitic loanword by Burchardt (1910: 495) and Helck (1971: 514, 110) although they offer no etymology. Hoch (1994: 152) speculates whether *mḫti* is derived from the root *ḫwt* 'needle, pin'. Hofmann (1989: 226; see also p. 217) rules out the Akkadian *maḫitu* for 'whip', as the well-known Egyptian word *isbr* for 'whip' is mentioned in the same two texts as *mḫti.w*. The word is written with a metal determinative and occurs once in the stanzas on the repair of Amenemope's chariot in the Satirical Letter: (P. Anastasi I, 26, 7; Gardiner, 1911: 38). Apart from the metal determinative, the preceding sentence hints that *mḫti.w*, as a chariot part, could be part of the yoke assembly. In the second occurrence, *mḫti.w* is written with the wood determinative and said to be *w3ḥ m sm3 n šrsw* "set with six fold alloy" (P. Anastasi IV, 16, 12; Gardiner, 1937: 53). Schullman (1986: 41f; see also Fischer-Elfert, 1986: 229f) suggests the metal sheeting found on some chariot parts, like the gold sheeted segments on at least one of Tutankhamun's chariots, or the three plaster-gilded segments of the pole of the Yuya and Tjuiu tomb chariot, imitating the earlier true metallic sheeting.

msšt3 'pole'

The lexeme *msšt3* is only known from the War Annals of Thutmose III (Sethe, 1907: 671, 15) where the *msšt3* 'pole' of a chariot is said to be made of the best wood (*m tpi n ḫt*). The single attestation is strangely written with the 'book roll' determinative where one would expect the 'wood' determinative given the text itself. However, Hofmann (1989: 226) notes that the use of the determinative could be influenced by the writing of *sšt3* 'secret' and related words. Given *msšt3* is very close to the Akkadian *mašaddu* 'pole' he translates *msšt3* with 'pole'. Another Egyptian term for pole is ʿ discussed above.

nḥb 𓍊𓏌𓏲𓏤 'yoke'

Within the nomenclature of chariot part terminology *nḥb* 𓍊𓏌𓏲𓏤 'yoke' is the only one that has been securely identified beyond any doubt. Before the introduction of chariots in Egypt *nḥb* 𓍊𓏌𓏲𓏤 was used for the 'yoke' for cattle and later also for the yoke of the horses pulling chariots (Hofmann, 1989: 219-220; Manassa, 2013: 149; Schulman, 1986: 28).

ḥ3 𓎛𓄿𓅱𓏤 'unknown'

The signified of *ḥ3* 𓎛𓄿𓅱𓏤 in the nomenclature of chariot part terminology is rather obscure as mentioned by Gardiner (1911: 28*, note 10), but from its single occurrence (P. Anastasi I, 26, 6; Gardiner, 1911: 37) the textual context indicates it is a part related to, or in the vicinity of the yoke saddles (*dr.tw*). The determinative 𓏤 shows that the object in question was made of wood. Schulman (1986: 34-35) hesitantly proposes to identify *ḥ3* 𓎛𓄿𓅱𓏤 as a wooden dowel or brace placed behind the yoke saddle, believing that *ḥ3* 𓎛𓄿𓅱𓏤 is "surely related to the preposition "behind"". According to Fischer-Elfert (1986: 228 note e), however, *dr.t ḥ3* should be understood as "the rear *dr.t*" that could be the part of the pole that went under the body and was fixed to the axis with rawhide straps. Manassa (2013: 149) suggests that *dr.t* 'yoke saddle' in the singular refers to that of the lead horse, whereas the *ḥ3* 𓎛𓄿𓅱𓏤 could refer to the yoke saddle of the second horse of the team, or, alternatively *ḥ3* 𓎛𓄿𓅱𓏤 could refer to the backing elements that prevented the horses from backing out of the yoke. However, such backing elements consisted of leather rather than wood as indicated by the determinative in writing but is, according to Littauer and Crouwel (1985: 5) in antiquity "often lacking and, when present, […] relatively inefficient […] passing beneath the belly" [*i.e.* comparable to the girth presented in the present work, which can act as a backing element, J. Crouwel, Personal Communication with AJV/SI, 2016]. Hofmann (1989: 228) simply remarks *"Bedeutung unbekannt"*.

ḥ3ry.w 𓎛𓄿𓂋𓇋𓇋𓅱𓎡𓏤𓏥 'rein cords' (?)

The term *ḥ3ry.w* 𓎛𓄿𓂋𓇋𓇋𓅱𓎡𓏤𓏥 is only known from a single occurrence in the very end of the Hymn to the King in his Chariot where it is shown with 𓎡 'leather' and 𓍲 'cord' determinatives. According to Helck (1971: 517 nr. 165), *ḥ3ry.w* 𓎛𓄿𓂋𓇋𓇋𓅱𓎡𓏤𓏥 should be considered as a Semitic loanword, but offers no etymology for it. It features in one of the obscure word plays so characteristic of the overall composition: "With regards to the *ḥ3ry.w* of your chariot – the sky (*ḥr.t*) with its four supports" (oTurin 9588, 8-9; Dawson & Peet, 1933: pl. XXIX).

Schulman (1986: 42) could not make sense of the passage and relied solely on the determinatives (*i.e.* 𓎡 leather + 𓍲 cord) for a translation of *ḥ3ry.w* 𓎛𓄿𓂋𓇋𓇋𓅱𓎡𓏤𓏥, which he argues could signify one of the many leather or rawhide bindings somewhere in the chariot, without any further specifications. Hofmann (1989: 229) speculates whether the *ḥ3ry.w* 𓎛𓄿𓂋𓇋𓇋𓅱𓎡𓏤𓏥 refer to the individual leather cords that comprised the reins, there being four in total, like the supports of the sky (see also Manassa, 2013: 151).

ḥbs 𓎛𓃀𓋴𓈖𓍱 'cover'

The well-known lexeme for 'cover' ḥbs 𓎛𓃀𓋴𓈖𓍱 can be found in Late Egyptian Miscellany texts as referring to cloth covers for both chariots and horses. In the Letter from two Royal Scribes to their Superior a shipment of goods and equipment is said to include: "12 covers for twin spans (ḥbs n ḥtri) and 5 coverings for chariots (ḥbs n mrkbt)" (P. Turin B, vs. 1, 9; Gardiner, 1937: 126). The parallel between the covers for horses and those for the chariot exclude the possibility that the ḥbs n mrkbt should be understood as the leather covering of the chariot body rather than covers of cloth, though such covers are unknown from the pictorial and archaeological records (Hofmann, 1989: 229). In a second occurrence from the Impeachment of the Chief of Workmen Paneb, the cloth cover of a chariot has allegedly been stolen (iṯȝ) from a royal tomb (P. Salt 124 rt. 1, 7; Černý, 1929: pl. XLII). It is unknown what exactly the meaning of a ḥbs 𓎛𓃀𓋴𓈖𓍱 'cloth cover' for a chariot was, but perhaps it refers to a mat lying on the rawhide woven floor of the chariot as alternative to a skin (Littauer & Crouwel, 1985: 70).

ḥr šfiit 𓎛𓂋𓈙𓆑𓇋𓇋𓂝𓁶 'Ram's Head, yoke, standard' (?)

In the first preserved line of the Hymn to the King in his Chariot on oEdinburgh 916, we read about a part referred to as ḥr šfiit 𓎛𓂋𓈙𓆑𓇋𓇋𓂝𓁶 'Ram's Head': "… seeing every land, its Ram's Head is (like) iron" (rt. 1-2; Dawson & Peet, 1933: pl. XXVI). For Schulman (1986: 46-49), the identification of the meaning of the ḥr šfiit 𓎛𓂋𓈙𓆑𓇋𓇋𓂝𓁶 'Ram's Head' can be found on a Medinet Habu scene (see The Epigraphic Survey, 1930: pl. XVII; Sabahy, 2013: 195, fig. 5; Figure VI.7) in which a ram-headed standard of Amun (actualising the god on the battlefield) features in a chariot next to an army charioteer preceding Ramesses III and his war host on their way to the battlefield.

Schulman's suggestion is problematic. The text is addressing the king, not Amun, and there is no textual or pictorial evidence to suggest that Amun, or gods and goddesses in general, ride into battle on chariots. There are examples like Month and Sakhmet who can appear alongside the king in his chariot, but the king is portrayed as the active charioteer whereas the divinities hold supportive roles only (Manassa, 2013: 150).

The only divinities that are regularly found to ride and fight from a chariot is Horus-Shed, with griffons as draught animals, and some rare examples with Bes, known from the magical cippi stelae of the Third Intermediate Period through the Late Period (Berlandini, 1998: 31-55; see also Köpp-Junk, 2013: 134-135, fig. 5 for the goddess Astarte riding on a chariot; see also Section V.5.1. 'Royal Scenes'). Conversely, the chariot of the king itself could frame him as manifestations of a divinity, or divine powers, in the New Kingdom (Calvert, 2013: 60-61; Herslund, 2013: 125; and above). When viewing a chariot from the front, the curved yoke-arms project out from the centre pole, which is reminiscent of a ram's head with its swirling horns. So it would seem much more plausible to view ḥr šfiit 𓎛𓂋𓈙𓆑𓇋𓇋𓂝𓁶 'Ram's Head' as an embodied metaphor for the yoke of the chariot (Hofmann, 1989: 230; Manassa, 2013: 150). The mentioning of iron remains enigmatic, as no part of a chariot is known to have been made from it.

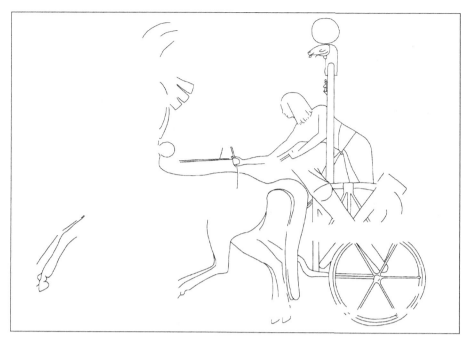

Figure VI.7. Standard of Amun in a chariot. Luxor. Medinet Habu. After: The Epigraphic Survey (1930: pl. XVII). Drawing by L.D. Hackley.

ḫ3b 𓎛𓄿𓃀𓏏𓏭 'tire' (?)

According to Ward (1989: 429; see also Hoch, 1994: 240) the Egyptian word ḫ3b 𓎛𓄿𓃀𓏏𓏭 'tire' is connected to the Akkadian word for 'tire' ḫuppu (alt. ḫubbu). It has, however, later been argued by Meeks (1997: 46) that ḫ3b for 'tire' is not a loanword but derived from the Egyptian ḫ3b for a 'curved element' (see also Schneider, 2008: 186). In the Wörterbuch (III: 229.13) ḫ3b 𓎛𓄿𓃀𓏏𓏭 'tire' is shown with a 𓏭 'wood'-determinative. In the belonging slip note from the Wörterbuch Zettelarkive, the determinative is marked with a question mark. In the primary publication of the oEdinburgh, Dawson & Peet (1933: 172) transcribe, with hesitation, the determinative as the 'rib' corresponding to GSL 𓄹 F42.

The rim of an Egyptian chariot wheel consists of several curved elements joined together in a circular form. This could also explain the employment of the 𓄹 'rib'-determinative GSL F42 in the writing of ḫ3b 𓎛𓄿𓃀𓏏𓏭 'tire' as its shape mirrors that of the curved elements making up the tire (Hofmann, 1989: 230-231; Manassa, 2013: 148; see also remark by Schulman, 1986: 31). However, the use of GSL 𓄹 F42 'rib' determinative, if that transcription is correct, could simply have been influenced by the writing of ḫ3b/ḫ3b 'neck'/'collar bone', which likewise can be written with a GSL 𓄹 F42 'rib' determinative (Wörterbuch III: 229; 362.2).

ḫnr 𓎛𓈖𓂋𓏭 'reins, harness'

According to the Wörterbuch (Wörterbuch III: 298.2), ḫnr 𓎛𓈖𓂋𓏭 signifies the 'reins or similar'. That we are dealing with a word relating to the chariot harness that fixed the horses to the vehicle and made it possible for the charioteer to control them is certain, though it can be questioned whether it is a basic word for a single object like 'rein', or rather a superordinate, collective term for the overall harnesses including the reins.

In royal inscriptions *ḥnr* is sometimes listed among war booty or tribute. In the Annals of Thutmose III we find the *ḥnr* listed twice after *ḥsmn* 'bronze' though the determinative written after *ḥnr* clearly shows 'leather' (Sethe, 1907: 669, 16; 711, 15). In a list of objects for the first jubilee of Ramesses II, *ḥnr* features directly after chariots: *mrkbt 30 ḥnr 30* (Kitchen, 1979: 382, 10). In a third occurrence *ḥnr* appears in the listing of chariot parts where the *ḥnr* of the chariots are said to be arranged in one set: *n3y=sn ḥnr.w m sbwt wˁ* (P. Anastasi IV, 16, 10; Gardiner, 1937: 53; see also Caminos, 1954: 214; Erman, 1911: 35, a).

From the textual record, we also get some glimpses of some of the actions and skills involved when using the *ḥnr*. As part of the praise of the king and his qualities as a horseman on the Great Sphinx Stela of Amenhotep II it is said: "They (the horses) did not tire (*wrd*) when he held (*t3y*) the *ḥnr*" (Helck, 1955: 1282, 17). In the inscriptions accompanying the Ramesseum scene depicting the Siege of Dapur it is said about Ramesses II on his chariot: "His grip (*t3y*) of the *ḥnr*, does not slip (*wḥy*)" (Kitchen, 1979: 173, 10). That the *ḥnr* is something that the charioteer holds (*t3y*) in order to drive the vehicle can also be found in the hieratic Satirical Letter: "you let go of (*wḥy*) the *ḥnr* and seize (*t3y*) the bow" (P. Anastasi I, 18, 5-6; Gardiner, 1911: 30). Later, the relationship between the object *ḥnr* and the action to 'seize, grasp' can be found once again, when it says: "I know how to seize (*t3y*) the *ḥnr*" (P. Anastasi I, 28, 2; Gardiner, 1911: 39).

From the contexts we learn that the *ḥnr* was an object of leather the driver would hold (*t3y*) in his hands, so translating 'reins' seems plausible. When featuring in descriptions of war booty, however, *ḥnr* is preceded by the label *ḥsmn* 'bronze' and the only part of a harness made of bronze would be the bit. So it would seem the term could be used to indicate the overall harness, including reins and bits, and possibly also the bridle. Or perhaps the bit and rein only, the parts that connected directly to the horses to control them rather than the entire harness comprising an aggregate of various straps, like neckstrap and girth, which attach the animal to the traction elements of a vehicle. In the later texts from the Ramesside Period, *ḥnr* is said to be arranged in 'one set' and when they are counted separately alongside the 30 chariots in an object list with a total of 30 *ḥnr*, one would expect the double amount if the term only referred to the 'reins' rather than the overall 'harness' (Hofmann, 1989: 89-92), thus seemingly supporting the identification as overall chariot harness (*i.e.* for two horses) unless the two sets of reins and bits are seen by the ancient Egyptians as *one* set for one chariot rather than an entire harness (also since there seem to be words for other parts).

ḥtr 'rail'(?)

The term *ḥtr* (*ḥtr-ḥt* ?) is only known from a single occurrence in an erroneous writing, making the transcription somewhat uncertain. The possessive pronoun is plural (*n3i=sn*) but the word itself is written without plural strokes below the presumed determinative. The determinative corresponds to GSL M3 'wood' but the text says they are *m nb* 'of gold': *n3i=sn ḥtr.wt m nb* (P. Anastasi

IV, 16, 8; Gardiner, 1937: 53). The transliteration provided by the Wörterbuch, suggests to read ẖtr-ḥt, or simply ẖtr, but offers no translation beyond "parts of the chariot" (Wörterbuch III: 342.5). In his collection of words for objects, Jéquier (1922: 17, fig. 12) transliterates ḥt-ir-ḥt 𓊽𓏤𓊽𓏤 and translates *"bandage en bois"*, but exactly which element of a chariot he was thinking of is unclear, and the accompanying figure of a chariot body is uninformative in this regard.

Since ẖtr 𓊽𓏤𓊽𓏤 features in the description of fine and elaborate chariot bodies and their parts, Schulman (1986: 42-43) suggests that ẖtr 𓊽𓏤𓊽𓏤 could signify the upper framework, or top railing, rising at an angle from the rear to about hip height, enclosing the front and side. This suggestion is based on exclusion, but this method is highly uncertain since most of the terms in question are unknown, or their translations highly uncertain. Schneider (2008: 184) reads ḥrḥ 𓊽𓏤𓊽𓏤, and likewise believes it means the 'railings' of the chariot frame (*i.e. Brüstungsstangen des Wagenkastens*). Another possible lexeme for the 'rail' is ṭ 𓂝𓏏𓂝 'hand grip; rail', discussed below.

swr.w 𓇋𓆑𓄿𓂝𓏤𓏛 'bindings, coverings' (?)

Among the group of terms of seeming Semitic origin, identified by Helck (1971: 519 nr. 190), swr.w 𓇋𓆑𓄿𓂝𓏤𓏛 belong to those for which no etymology was suggested. The Wörterbuch simply translates "part of a chariot" but makes no mention of swr being a loanword (Wörterbuch IV: 71.2). From the single context of swr.w 𓇋𓆑𓄿𓂝𓏤𓏛 (P. Anastasi IV 16, 12-17, 1), it seems that whatever object swr was, it could be part of the ḏbw/ḏbȝ 𓂧𓃀𓄿 'wheel'/'decorative appliqué' given the circumstantial iw: nȝy=sn gs-ḏbȝ.w m nb iw nȝy=sn swr.w m bȝkw ktt "Their ḏbȝ are of gold, their swr.w are the works of a covering (ktt)". Here the covering ktt 𓎡𓏏𓏏𓏛 (Wörterbuch V: 148.18) is determined with the hieratic determinative equivalent to GSL 𓏛 V6 'cord', which made Schulman (1986: 43) to suggest that the swr.w 𓇋𓆑𓄿𓂝𓏤𓏛 are the bindings that secured the decorated appliqués to the siding or framework of the chariot body. However, these were an integral part of the leather casing and siding fill, so perhaps the swr.w 𓇋𓆑𓄿𓂝𓏤𓏛 should be understood as the lashings that went over the leather at the top railing (*e.g.* seen in L1 #023, Cat. No. 54) or maybe even the drawstring system (?) seen at the top and bottom of the main casing and siding fill (*e.g.* L1 #016, Cat. No. 70; for both suggestions see Chapter II.V. 'Discussion: Piecing the Tano Leather').

In the Ramesside Period, however, the cord/loop determinative was also used in the writing of textile names and related terms (Herslund, 2011: 159-174), and Hofmann (1989: 231, 234) in his work on chariot terminology, points to two lexemes for textile objects srw 𓇋𓂝𓏛 and srw.t 𓇋𓂝𓏏𓏛 (Wörterbuch IV: 193.4-5). ktt 𓎡𓏏𓏏𓏛 can also be used for a kind of garment (Albright, 1934: XVII, C.10, 61; Hoch, 1994: 257). Therefore, Janssen and Janssen (1990: 56-58) wonder if swr.w 𓇋𓆑𓄿𓂝𓏤𓏛 could be the cloth padding under the yoke saddle.

sd 𓊃𓂧𓏤 'tail' (?)

This word for a chariot part is highly problematic as well and no one has convincingly shown which element the sd 𓊃𓂧𓏤 'tail' should refer to. In the transcribed publication of the single occurrence, Dawson and Peet (1933: pl. XXVIII, 4; see also Popko, 2012a) had great difficulty in identifying the three obscure determinatives that appear in the writing and suggest, tentatively, GSL 𓏛

T19 'bone harpoon', a stroke, and the GSL N34 for 'metal'. Seeing that there is no apparent part of a chariot made of bone and metal, the three determinatives offer no assistance in translating the meaning of *sd* 'tail' when used for a part of a chariot.

Schulmann (1986: 31-32) identifies a possible 'tail' projecting from the back of Ramesses III in a Medinet Habu hunting scene, which he relates to a pendant-like object known from Assyrian chariots, but as noted by Manassa (2013: 148), this element is simply a continuation of the reins tied around the king's waist. Given the root-terminology of *sd* 'tail', Manassa (2013: 148) provides a list of objects and features to be found at the rear part of the chariot as possible candidates. One element that protrudes from the back of some chariot bodies are figurative heads of enemies, but Manassa dismisses this possibility and goes on to tentatively suggest that *sd* 'tail' could refer to the 'axle' as it is found towards the very back of the chariot and the single occurrence of the word is found in conjunction with *ḥ3b* 'tire'. Hofmann (1989: 232-233) looks beyond the organic chariot parts and tentatively suggests that the meaning of *sd* 'tail' could be the 'fly whisk'. Popko (2012a: *sd*), however, suggests that the term might not be a derivation *sd* 'tail' at all, but derived from *sd* 'to clothe, to adorn' (Wörterbuch IV: 365.1-6), which occasionally is determined by phonetic similarities with the tail. Therefore, conceivable, *sd*, could refer to a kind of metal ornamentation.

kwšn 'girth, leather covering, leather bag' (?)

The *kwšn* is only attested once (P. Anastasi I 24, 5; Gardiner, 1911: 36) and from the context it seems to be an object associated with or located near to the yoke saddle (*i.e. dr.t* 'hand', see below): "Your chariot is upon its side; you fear to press your horses. If it is thrown to the pit, your "hand" will lie exposed, your *kwšn* fallen" (Manassa, 2013: 148). It features the hieratic equivalent to the GSL F27 'leather' determinative, which together with the context led Gardiner (1911: 26*, note 14 & 15; see also Hoch, 1994: 314-315) to translate *kwšn* as 'girth' (?), though as purely conjectural explanation. Schulman (1986: 34-35; see also Manassa, 2013: 149; Schneider, 2008: 189) likewise offers a conjectural explanation for the leather object *kwšn*, and suggests it signifies the leather coverings on the curved parts of the yoke found on one of Tutankhamun's chariots.

There is, however, some evidence that *kwšn* means a leather sack or container since the root *k-š-n* is near to the Akkadian *gušanu* (Von Soten, 1965: 299), also written *kušanu* as *g* and *k* are interchangeable in Mitanni-Akkadian (Helck, 1971: 522; Hoch, 1994: 315; Hofmann, 1989: 234). Fischer-Elfert (1986: 205, l) follows Helck and translates *kwšn* as '*Ledersack*'. Finds of possible pouch flaps from the tomb of Tutankhamun, the identification of pouches in workshops that produce chariot leather, as well as the mentioning of a pouch in the body of the chariot from the tomb of Thutmose IV (for discussion of these items see section II.2.2. 'Pouches'), suggests that the vehicles could be outfitted with bags on the inside of the body, and common sense dictates that messengers, *e.g.* carrying clay tablet letters like those found in Amarna, would have needed containers for them.

ktt 𓎡𓏏𓏏 — see *swr.w* 𓋴𓅱𓂋𓏥 'bindings, coverings' (?)

tḥr/t(i)ḥ 𓏏𓎛𓂋 'Side panelling, bridle boss' (?)

There is a general consensus that the term *tḥr* 𓏏𓎛𓂋, seen in P. Anastasi IV (16,9; Gardiner, 1937: 53) is identical to the word *tḥ* 𓏏𓎛, found in the Hymn to the King in his Chariot (oTurin 9588, 2; Dawson & Peet, 1933: pl. XXIX), though it lacks the final consonant (Caminos, 1954: 213; Schulman, 1986: 43). Burchardt (1910: nr. 1127) and Helck (1971: 524 nr. 282) identify the lexeme as a Semitic loanword for 'armour', being a cognate with the Egyptian *dḥr* (var. *dḥꜥ*) 𓂧𓎛𓂋 'leather (armour)' (Hoch, 1994: 363; but see Schneider, 2008: 189). The Wörterbuch (V: 328.2) defines *tḥr* 𓏏𓎛𓂋 simply as "leather part of the chariot", but does not include the Turin example without the final *r* where the determinative is the hieratic equivalent to GSL 𓆱 M3 'wood'. We can therefore assume that whatever element of the chariot the *tḥr* 𓏏𓎛𓂋 was, it could be made of leather or wood, or a combination of the two materials.

Caminos (1954: 213) remarks in his notes to his translation of the passage in which *tḥr* occurs that the meaning is unknown, though from the context it seems clear that we are probably dealing with a red-coloured leather siding fill, decorated with carved rosettes: *n3y.sn tḥr.w m inm n ins(y) iw.w t3 ḥr dd iw pḥ3 b3k m dsr* "Their *tḥr.w* 𓏏𓎛𓂋 have the hue of red cloth, being carved with rosettes, and the *pḥ3*-board is made from djeser-wood" (P. Anastasi IV, 16, 8-9; Gardiner, 1937: 53). The second textual context likewise indicates how *tḥr* could indicate the siding or panelling of a chariot, even though it features in the obscure word plays comprising the Hymn to the King in His Chariot: "As for the *tḥ* 𓏏𓎛 of your chariot – the one who tramples (*ḥnd*) in Syria" (oTurin 9588, 2; Dawson & Peet, 1933: pl. XXIX). Indeed, the body of the Thutmose IV chariot body shows scenes of the king as a sphinx, who tramples or overthrows Asiatic enemies, as well as decorative rosettes (which are also common in some chariots from the tomb of Tutankhamun as well as the chariot from the tomb of Yuya and Tjuiu), thereby graphically mirroring the literary statements found in P. Anastasi IV and the Hymn to the King in his Chariot (Manassa, 2013: 150-151; Schulman, 1986: 43-44).

The word *bt* 𓃀𓏏, discussed above, is also believed to refer to the sidings or panelling of the chariot body. The relationship between *tḥr* 𓏏𓎛𓂋 and *bt* 𓃀𓏏 is uncertain, but it could be that *bt* 𓃀𓏏 refers to the wooden framework of the sides, whereas *thḥ/tḥ* 𓏏𓎛𓂋 is the wood and leather casing of the framework (Manassa, 2013: 151).

In Hofmann's (1989: 235) treatment of *tḥr* he does not include the variation *tḥ* 𓏏𓎛, which is dealt with separately and classified as 'meaning unknown'. For the meaning of *tḥr*, Hofmann notes that in addition to the decorated side panels, coloured leather and embellishing rosettes can also be found on the bridle bosses (litt. *Riemenverteiler*) and other parts of the harness as known from the material coming from the tombs of Amenhotep II and Tutankhamun (Hofmann, 1989: 213 & Fig. 3; Littauer & Crouwel, 1985: pl. XL, LX), as well as from images in tombs and temples (see Chapter V).

ṯt ḥnr 'part of harness' (?)

In the miscellany text listing equipment for an expedition in Syria, the obscure compound *ṯt ḥnr* for a part of a chariot harness is mentioned without any additional qualifications amongst the descriptions of weapons and other chariot elements (P. Koller 1, 6; Gardiner, 1937: 117). The literal meaning of *ṯt ḥnr* is 'rein-looser', so it must have been some part of the harness (Caminos, 1954: 434). The 'rein/harness-looser' should probably be understood as a kind of '*Riemenschnalle*' (a toggle or spacer) or some similar object (Hofmann, 1989: 235).

ṯꜣ 'hand grip, railing' (?)

For the lexeme *ṯꜣ* the Wörterbuch (V: 349.4) and, later, Dawson and Peet (1933: 171), do not provide any translation beyond 'part of a chariot'. Schulman (1986: 32) relates the noun *ṯꜣ* to the verb *ṯꜣy* for 'to take; bear; grip; hold' and suggests tentatively that *ṯꜣ* signifies the 'hand grips' situated in the upper areas of the siding fill, and which have been cut out to allow for grasping the top rail (see section II.1.2. 'Siding Fill'; L3 #008B, Cat. No. 69) or a separate attached element (see Section V.3.2. 'Amarna'). Manassa (2013: 145), however, argues that *ṯꜣ* should be understood as the entire top railing of the chariot body seeing that the rail (*ṯꜣ*) is what a driver would 'seize' (*ṯꜣy*) while driving. If Manassa is correct in this identification of the *ṯꜣ* as the overall 'railing', it also solves the problem noted by Schulman as the chariots often have more than one handgrip and *ṯꜣ* is written in the singular definite as *pꜣ ṯꜣ*. In the Tano leather, the worn upper area of the siding fill that was draped over the upper railing, indeed, suggests that the railing was hold on to, also where there were no cut out handgrips (*e.g.* L1 #001, Cat. No. 47). The rail was either made of one horseshoe shaped piece of wood, or two pieces fitted together.

ṯmit 'bit' (?)

From the single context in which *ṯmit* occurs, it seems to refer to a part of the harness. Towards the end of the narrative part of the Great Sphinx Stela of Amenhotep II, the charioteer king is said to yoke (*nḥb*) with *ṯmjt* in Memphis (Helck, 1955: 1282). According to Helck (1961: 27, Anm. 6), *ṯmit* is derived from *ṯꜣm* 'bandages' (Wörterbuch V: 354.15-18), though written with a metal determinative, and translates, with hesitation: "curb bit". The curb bit, however, is apparently unknown in ancient Egypt, but that *ṯmit* signifies a 'bit' is likely as this is the only part of the overall harness that is made of metal (Hofmann, 1989: 236).

ṯst 'knob' (?)

The chariot term *ṯst* is only known from P. Anastasi IV (16, 10; Gardiner, 1937: 53) and signifies a chariot part made of ivory (*m ꜣbw*). In his translation of the text, Caminos (1954: 214) gives none other than '*ṯst*-piece' but notes that it could be a boss or knob made of ivory. He relates it to *ṯs.t* for 'tooth' or, alternatively to *ṯs* for 'to tie together; bind' for some kind of joint or binding (Caminos, 1954: 214: *ṯs.t* 'tooth', Wörterbuch V: 401.1, 409.9-12). Schulman (1986: 33) follows the former suggestion and relates *ṯst* to the knobs that serve as terminals on the butt of yoke saddles or the curved ends of the yoke arms, known from both images and the archaeological record (Littauer & Crouwel, 1985: 80-81; pl. XXIV, LXXXIV [top left]). The definite article employed in P. Anastasi IV *t3* indicates that a chariot only had one *tst*, but seeing that the very beginning of the line is damaged, Schulman (1986: 33) wonders if the scribe did not write *n3* rather than *t3*. The identification of *tst* as 'knob' remains problematic, as it is written with a wood-determinative, which indicates it was prototypically made of wood but in this case ivory.

dby.wt 'yoke arms' (?)

For the term *dby.wt*, the Wörterbuch offers no translation beyond 'parts of the chariot pole' (Wörterbuch V: 435.4). Schulman (1986: 33) remarks how *dby.wt* could be related to *db* for 'horn' (Wörterbuch V: 434.3-7) and when written with the wood-determinative seems to signify the 'yoke arms', being curved wooden objects, which were connected to the pole and whose form is hornlike (see also Manassa, 2013: 149; Hofmann, 1989: 237). The connection between *dby.wt* and the *ꜥ* 'pole' is clear from the single occurrence in P. Anastasi I (26, 5-6; Gardiner, 1911: 37) in which a wrecked chariot is brought to the workshop where its pole is "planned anew, then its yoke arms (*dby.wt*) attached" (Manassa, 2013: 149).

ḏbw 'wheel, decorated appliqué' (?)

It is hard to identify what part of the chariot *ḏbw* refers to. In his treatment of the Satirical Letter of P. Anastasi I, where the chariot of Amenemope is being repaired, Gardiner (1911: 28* note 12) remarks that "The *ḏbw* must be an important part of the chariot". The Wörterbuch defines *ḏbw* as "an essential part of the chariot" and "also in the compound *gs-ḏbw.w*" (Wörterbuch V: 553.5-6).

ḏbw is consistently found written with the wood determinative and its importance is partly due to its appearance in the lists of war booty of the Annals of Thutmose III, "a chariot worked in gold, the *ḏbw* in gold" taken from the ruler of Qadesh after the battle of Megiddo (Sethe, 1907: 663, 12) and the tribute received from Retjenu in year 40 that included "five chariots worked in gold, the *ḏbw* in gold (and) five chariots worked in gold, the *ḏbw* in Aget-wood" (Sethe, 1907: 669, 6-7). We also find *ḏbw* mentioned in the repair scene of Amenemope's wrecked chariot in P. Anastasi I (26, 7; Gardiner, 1911: 37) and in the description of fine chariots in P. Anastasi IV (16, 12; Gardiner, 1937: 53) where their "*gs-ḏbw.w* are of gold".

Zimmern (1917: 42) connects the Egyptian *ḏbw* to the Akkadian *sumbu(m)*, *subbu* for 'wheel' (see also Schneider, 2008: 184-185; Von Soten, 1965: 1111). The chariots of Tutankhamun show how those belonging to the elite could be fitted with golden, or partly golden, wheels. Schulman takes a different etymological path and connects *ḏbw* with the verb *ḏbꜥ* 'to adorn, to dress' (Wörterbuch V: 556.11-558.5; but see Schneider, 2008: 184-185), and speculates whether the *ḏbw* was a kind of wooden and gold worked adornment, or the decorated appliqué, intergrated into the leather casing of elite chariots (Schulman, 1986: 43-44). Fischer-Elfert (1986: 227, 229 e) translates 'side walls' (litt. *Wagenaufbau*)

so regard *dbw* as signifying some constructional element rather than a word for 'wheel'.

dr.wt 'the hands, yoke saddles' (?)

As far as we know, *n3 dr.wt* 'the hands' probably refers to the two yoke saddles, attached to the yoke arms for keeping the horses in formation. As such, *n3 dr.wt* 'the hands' provide the embodied notion of two outspread hands projecting downwards, grasping the horses and thereby making them conform to the yoke (Schulman, 1986: 34-35; but see Hofmann, 1989: 228). Zayed (1985: 10-11) presumed the meaning to be 'drawbar'. He refers to the relief of Amenhotep II on a chariot surrounded by bound prisoners. Three of the prisoners are sitting on the horses, one of them is seated on the pole, two others are standing in the car, and seven are walking behind them. The accompanying inscription reads: *3tp.n=f ssm.t=f m skr(.w) ʿnh w3h.n=f m dr.wt tm rdi hr mw=f* "He loaded his team with living prisoners, he put the illegitimate on the *dr.wt*". However, Zayed's parallelisation of *dr.wt* with ʿ 'pole' seems impossible as a chariot only ever had one pole and not more as implied by the writing of 'chariot hands' in plural. Ritter (1990: 60-62) proposes that *n3 dr.wt* 'the hands' refer to the wheel spokes, consisting of two V-shaped components, which thereby could be equated visually with cupped hands. Gardiner (1911: 26* note 14 and 28*), and later Wilson (1969: 478), do not equate *n3 dr.wt* 'the hands' to 'yoke saddles' and translates it as collar pieces. It is unknown exactly what chariot part Gardiner and Wilson meant by 'collar pieces'. Manassa (2013: 148-149) follows Schulman's suggestion 'yoke saddles' and reiterates the evidence that points to the meaning of the *n3 dr.wt* 'the hands' as indeed 'yoke saddles'.

P. Anastasi I (24, 5-7; Gardiner, 1911: 35-36) relates how the horses need to be unharnessed in order for the driver to perform emergency repairs after having crashed in a *wadi* inside hostile territory. That the horses need to be unyoked in order to perform repairs on 'the hands' seems to exclude references to parts of the body or the wheels as that would not strictly require the unyoking of the horses, especially during a dangerous emergency situation (Manassa, 2013: 148; Schulman, 1986: 34-35). In a later passage in the same text (P. Anastasi I, 26, 5-6; Gardiner, 1911: 37) on chariot repairs and parts replacement, *n3 dr.wt* 'the hands' is seen in relation with the front structure of the chariot: "your pole (ʿ) will be planned anew, then its yoke arms (*dby.wt*) attached, leather set down for its "hand" (*dr.t*) and *h3*; they will prepare your yoke" (Manassa, 2013: 149). When *dr.wt* 'hands' refers to a chariot part, it is consistently found written with the 'wood' determinative (Schulman, 1986: 34) and the mentioning of leather in the repair situation just quoted could be the pad of the yoke saddle or maybe the straps to tie (?). Another important indicator that *n3 dr.wt* 'the hands' signifies the two yoke saddles is that the word can be found written in plural in the Edinburgh ostracon, or in single when just one of them is damaged in P. Anastati I: .

When featuring in the puns (*i.e.* paronomasia) found in the Hymn to the King in His Chariot, *n3 dr.wt* 'the hands' are equated to two Asiatic goddesses: "As to the hands of your chariot, they are Anat and Astarte" (oEdingburgh 916, vs. 12-14; Schulman, 1986: 34; Dawson & Peet, 1933: pl. XXVIII). Manassa made a sagacious observation that the association between the two yoke saddles and the

Asiatic goddess could very well be understood as a metaphor. It is well known from Egyptian iconography that the goddess Astarte regularly appears mounted on a horse. Since the yoke saddles are the only chariot parts that ride directly atop of the horses, they could be seen as metaphors for the two Asiatic warrior goddesses (Manassa, 2013: 149; but see Quack, 1994: 125, note 3 referring to Levantine axle nails with depictions of goddesses).

ḏrw 'side'

The term ḏrw for the 'side' of a chariot known from the Karnak and Memphis stelae of Amenhotep II (Helck, 1955: 1304, 12; 1311, 11) is certainly identical with P. Turin (PuR 103, 2, 17) of the 20th Dynasty as identified by Hofmann (1989: 238-239; Wörterbuch V: 602.19). Helck (1961: 35, 37), however, translates 'Ende' for ḏrw, whereas Edel (1953: 128, 131) follows the Wörterbuch and translates "*16 lebende Mariannu an der Seite seines Streitwagens*" and "*Er führte nun den Asiaten weg an der Seite [seines Wagens]*". Common sense dictates that trying to fit 16 prisoners of war into the chariot would simply be impossible, and whether the Amenhotep story is truly historical or rather fictional, the correlation with the root ḏrww for the 'side' of an animal or human body make the reading ḏrw for the 'side of the chariot' secure.

VI.9. Discussion

It has been argued here that in spite of the uneven distribution of an already fragmentary textual record concerning chariots, certain details and contexts provide a number of socio-historic glimpses into the role, status, meaning and cultural importance of chariots throughout the New Kingdom, whether on the battlefield, for hunting, processions or in daily life, as well as in the language and the writing system. The contextual settings for battle inscriptions and narratives give insight into the deployment of chariots in war as well as the kind of settings and landscapes in which they were used. Battle inscriptions and the associated booty lists reveal the presence of chariots in both the armies of Western Asia and, more rarely, of Libya, whereas Nubian war chariots are never mentioned, the only text of which might hint to chariots is a single mention of 361 horses captured after a rebellion. By paying attention to details in the Qadesh texts, information concerning military tactics involving chariots in battle can be garnered. These include outflanking, ambushing and pincher manoeuvres to encircle the foe. After the battles were over, the royal chariot could serve as a trophy rack for the cut-off hands of defeated enemies or as a mobile tying pole for parading living prisoners.

Following its probable introduction during the Hyksos wars, the chariot grew in cultural importance, changing modes of warfare and transport, as well as the world of symbolism and semantics. During the New Kingdom the state pursued two overall strategies to obtain more chariots and horses to meet an increased demand as neither the required materials nor the draught animals were indigenous to Egypt. Thus, chariots and horses were captured from the enemy after battles, and tribute (among which chariots and horses) was sent from vassal states, as well as parts and materials for domestic production, thereby restricting the arsenals of the conquered peoples while increasing those of the Egyptian army. It can be questioned, though, how much of a negative effect it really would have had on the resources of the Syrian city state vassals as the numbers presented in the written sources range between roughly 10 to 60 chariots per year. Texts and inscriptions reveal chariots as a type of gift that was exchanged between the great kings of the Late Bronze Age where Pharaoh could receive expensive chariots from Mitanni, Babylonia and Assyria. The latter even sent a royal Assyrian chariot, so Akhenaten could ride around Akhetaten in the manner of the king of Ashur. Chariots are also found in relation to the culturally significant event of presenting the king with new equipment as part of royal and New Year's festivals in which the Kingship and parts of the associated paraphernalia were renewed and replaced. The commemoration of chariots given to the king by high-ranking courtiers shows not only gift-giving and thereby some of the relationship between the king and his/her courtiers, but the inscriptions also enable us to follow the supply of long-distance import of wood from Nubia or Mitanni in Syria, to workshops in the Nile Delta, and on to the presentation in Thebes. Conversely, chariots could also be given by the king to high ranking courtiers as in the case of the chariot mentioned in an inscription in the tomb of Kenamun (TT93) and the chariot that was given by Amenhotep III to his father-in-law.

From the late 18th Dynasty and through the Ramesside Period a number of texts provide evidence for the production of chariots within New Kingdom society, augmenting what is known from archaeological and pictorial sources. The evidence suggests that chariot workers were organised in some form of loose hierarchical organisation, and are consistently encountered in contexts where other types of craft specialists also appear. The descriptions and qualifications of chariots in texts attest to the variety of materials used such as wood, leather, ivory, pigments and metals, some of which were of high value and imported into Egypt from faraway places. Furthermore, some of the materials mentioned correlate directly to the craft specialists we can identify in the textual record with chariot workers, leatherworkers and metal workers. Inscriptions also show how the craft of chariot making could be hereditary when title and job passed on from father to son. The corpus of worker and overseer titles, literary texts and the Ramesside Onomasticon's listing of the 'chariot makers' between other kinds of weapon makers situate chariot production firmly within a larger institutionalised setting of a multifunctional armoury, which was largely dependent on a number of materials that had to be imported on state level.

When looking for the chariot in daily-life settings, the textual record of the New Kingdom creates a picture that could suggest that the use of chariots and private ownership of such vehicles were perhaps not uncommon among elite men and possibly women in the civic sector of society. The king could reward individuals by giving them these costly and high-status vehicles, chariots could be purchased if one could afford the price (especially the costs of maintaining horses), while others would have been able to provide the required materials from their personal estates. Even in dreams the chariot was seen as part of daily life, though featuring in a, for us, highly elusive dream interpretation. Through the rare occurrences of chariots being mentioned in a variety of royal and private inscriptions as well as miscellanies, letters, love poetry and dream literature, the role and status of chariots is often found to parallel the iconographic material concerning these vehicles of the battlefield. The strong and athletic king hunts dangerous animals like elephants, lions, and wild bulls, or practices his skills as a bow-shooting charioteer and horsemaster. We meet the chariot as a mode of locomotion for royalty and the elite over relatively short distances as well as personal transport over longer distances for messengers, royal envoys and participants in mining expeditions. Travel over longer distances, however, was dependant on a logistic setup for the chariot and, especially, the draught animals. The texts provides glimpses of the existence of repair facilities set within multifunctional workshops and dedicated way stations with fresh horses in stables. The inherent limitation of the lightweight chariot technology and physiology of the horses restricted the use of this type of vehicle to roads and paths, and certain types of landscapes when going off-road. Texts even emphasise the knowledge of routes to avoid being assaulted or crashing the chariot. In spite of the impact the chariot had on so many levels of society, language and thought, we cannot evaluate the degree to which it led to any kind of mobile revolution beyond the existence of a fast message system based on chariots. We can only speculate further on such a system, but if it was a purely literary phenomenon without a basis in the real world of experience, it seems highly unlikely that it would have become a source domain for (speed) metaphors as in the case of late Ramesside love poetry.

Certain texts shed light on some of the multifaceted meanings the ancient Egyptians associated with chariots. The chariot became a key feature in the reinterpretation of the king as warrior, who went from being portrayed as the club wielding footsoldier of old to the arrow shooting chariot warrior, which became the prototype for New Kingdom royal iconography. Different aspects of the 'chariot warrior' ideal are correspondingly evident in royal inscriptions and religio-ideological formulaic expressions, emphasising a number of qualities and divine prowess of the charioteer king. The amalgamation of examples portray the ideal chariot warrior as being a fast driver, having a firm grip of the reins, steady aim, strong in body and bow arm as well as knowledgeable concerning the horses, their inherent physiological limitations and stamina, how to control them and make challenging manoeuvres like sharp turns at speed. Thus, he is in control of the natural and the man-made world. In formulaic expressions, aspects of the charioteer king's qualities such as being unshakeable in the chariot, strong and beautiful are sacramentally interpreted and likened to solar and warlike divinities. Several written sources provide evidence for how the golden chariots, embellished with solar iconography, framed the king as a manifestation of the shining, life-giving sun during public displays and appearances, while the chariot king in war was likened to the scorching and burning qualities of the sun gods when shooting his arrows like burning sun rays.

The New Kingdom texts also enable us to detect some deep-rooted cognitive semantic structures relating to chariots. Their relative costliness in terms of ground transportation made them an obvious conceptual source to express the otherwise abstract notions of conspicuous consumption, high status, royal praise or a successful career. Chariots can also be found as the embodiment of speed and moving with utmost haste, when serving as source domain for metaphor paralleled by one of the fastest animal in the world, the gazelle, and the fastest domesticated animal, the horse, as well as the powerful and fast-moving phenomenon in nature and landscape, the wind.

The parts concerned with the lexicology of chariot terminology add another aspect to the study of chariots in texts, inscriptions and the writing system itself. By revisiting the scholarly discourse and sources for the three basic lexemes the standard dictionaries translate as 'chariot', it is shown that each of these lexemes in fact carries different meanings and degrees of inclusiveness on the level of taxonomy. The original word for chariot could also be used for wagons and was later replaced by a dedicated, foreign loanword that only ever refers to chariots, while the third lexeme in question signifies a type of wagon or cart. Thus, we see wheeled vehicle terminology developing through the New Kingdom with words for chariots, carts and wagons respectively, mirroring the designations and taxonomy that we know from, for example, modern English. There is, however no evidence to suggest that the original term prototypically signifying chariots, and one time wagons, was a superordinate and overarching word for 'vehicles' in general, as such terms for whole categories of material culture are rare in the Egyptian language and consistently found written in plural.

The determinative depicting the two-horse light-weight chariot of the New Kingdom retained its strong iconicity and consistently depicted an Egyptian-style chariot. It is, however, only found in the writing of the traditional word *wrry.t* for 'chariot' where it serves as a specific determinative that offers a pictorial tautology of the preceding word. When found employed in the writing of the word *wrry.t* for a 'wagon' and *tprt* 'cart' the chariot determinative must be perceived as a generic determinative that functions as a graphemic classifier, which visually assigns the preceding word to an overall category of 'wheeled vehicles'. The ancient Egyptians may not have possessed a word for the category 'wheeled vehicles' in their lexicon, but the employment of the chariot determinative as classifier in the writing of the word for 'cart' shows not only the existence of a wheeled vehicle category in the minds of the ancient people, but simultaneously how the chariot was conceived as the best example, or best member of that category for the elite in the New Kingdom. When following the chariot determinative through time, we are faced with a clear case of what Gardiner described as 'bringing a sign up to date' in the introduction to the sign list of his grammar. The long-term change from the chariot of the Late Bronze Age, to the 'stick-man' chariot of the Iron Age and on to the four-horse racing chariot of the Hellenistic Period, directly reflects changes in more deep-rooted cultural and conceptual categories through time. This is an evident example of the agency of material culture, when developments and changes in technology, or the forgetting and out-phasing of technology, impact other cultural systems and codes.

The final section revisited the lexicographical literature and sources for the nomenclature of words for chariot parts, providing additional insights and information regarding chariots in texts and language. The nomenclature is well-known for being challenging and has continuously presented the lexicographers with a number of trials with regards to identifying etymologies and finding a suitable translation and identification of individual parts of the vehicle. Even words for significant parts of the chariot *e.g.* the 'wheel' remain elusive. The examples providing the evidence for the nomenclature are very rare and often the lexemes are only ever known from a single occurrence.

It is, nonetheless, possible to draw up some general observations and trends regarding the words for chariot parts. One group of terminology is based on old Egyptian words for objects that already existed in the material culture. These objects possessed enough family resemblance to characteristic elements of the chariot that old words for the 'yoke', 'pole' and 'reins' of the plough could effortlessly be applied to the resembling yoke, pole and reins of the new chariot. The many evidently foreign loanwords for chariot, cart and chariot parts emphasise the intimate connection between this field within the Egyptian material culture, its origin in Western Asia, and Egypt's technological, economic and material dependence on the civilisations in the Near East to first establish and later maintain a chariot culture. Even if the foreign loanwords mostly feature in obscure and propagandistic stanzas based on word plays, they must have been somewhat familiar for the writer, reader or listener in addition to whatever political connotations and associations the paronomasia carried and expressed. As shown, chariot part names also feature in inscriptions, instructions and tales. The use of embodied metaphors to name parts attests further to some of the deep-rooted meanings that the ancient people related to individual chariot parts. The swirling end pieces of the yoke evoked the image of a 'ram's head' (*i.e.* yoke) with its horns as well as the case of the yoke-saddles, referred to as the 'hands' of the chariot, which again could be further equated to horse-riding goddesses in a word play. The chariot even had a 'tail', though that term remains elusive.

The author hopes that the present contribution to chariot studies in text, language and writing of the New Kingdom will serve as a useful tool and inspiration for future philological and text-based research into not only chariots, but the broader study of material culture. The few dedicated studies of material culture that do exist in Egyptology have proved fruitful for the study of ancient Egyptian economy, rituals and religion, but, as was demonstrated in the present work, the study of material culture in texts and writing system can be productive beyond those fields. Such an approach reveals not only the material culture's setting in a socio-historic framework, but contexts, metaphor and writing system all provide the empirical evidence for some of the deep-rooted meanings carried by material culture, and contribute to a clear empirical case showing how technological developments and changes in the material culture can directly impact other cultural systems and codifications.

VII. Discussion and Conclusions

André J. Veldmeijer & Salima Ikram

This work has presented the Tano assemblage of chariot leather, in conjunction with portions of other, similar assemblages, augmented by discussions on chariots in two-dimensional art as well as in texts. These different sources complement each other, allowing for a better understanding and interpretation of the Tano leather, as well as aspects of chariot craftsmanship, construction, their use, terminology, and role in the ancient Egyptian society, culture, and economy.

VII.1. Chariot Leather Craftsmanship

The technologies employed in the Tano leather can help flesh out how leatherwork technology changed and production of these objects evolved diachronically.

Leather has featured in Egypt's material culture from Predynastic times onward (for a short overview of leatherwork in time, see *e.g.* Van Driel-Murray, 2000), as evidenced by finds and depictions of objects. Unfortunately, the archaeological record is scanty prior to the New Kingdom, and it is, as yet, impossible to estimate the scale and significance of leather and the leatherworking industry. It is clear, however, that it increased after the Second Intermediate Period's introduction of the horse and chariot. The Egyptians' adoption, particularly for the military, of these vehicles and animals would have necessitated the large-scale production of chariot bodies, their accoutrements (including more quivers and bow-cases), harnessing, and other horse trappings. This possibly would have engendered a more complex and industrial-scale production of leather. An increased familiarity and experience with a material, as well as the pressure of producing larger numbers of objects (*i.e.* chariots and related objects) triggers efficiency and resource-saving technologies,[62] as well as innovations (some possibly introduced from abroad), which would improve the mode of production as well as the end product (see below).[63]

---

62 Besides this new weapon technology, these foreign people seem to have been responsible for introducing other leather objects and accompanying technology as well: shoes (Veldmeijer, In Press). Here too a clear development and merging of indigenous and foreign design and technology can be seen.

63 We should, however, keep in mind that, although all leather presented in this volume is chariot leather, they are to some extent different objects and the Tano leather is the most complete assemblage. Thus, for example, harnessing related to the chariots from Amenhotep II or Thutmose IV, might have had a comparable technology to the technology seen in the Tano harnessing but although comparison is as much as possible limited to comparable objects, still differences (and comparable features) are clearly visible.

Quite possibly the chariot leather was made by people who worked solely on these objects (the sheer number of chariots as well as their maintenance would have been enough to keep a fair number of people occupied full-time), rather than by general leatherworkers. Of course, it is also possible that the military, at least, had leather workshops with a few chariot construction specialists who oversaw the basic cutting and assembly of chariot leather. The professionalism is also apparent in the choices of the type of leather as well as the more specific parts of a skin that was used for different parts of the chariot, such as the use of the thicker and stronger neck skin for, among others, drawstrings, the use of goat for the casing and the thicker and stronger bovine leather for the harnessing and trappings. Choices in stitching materials (flax or sinew), also reflect a deep technical knowledge of the materials and their properties. Moreover, the care taken in cleaning and colouring the Tano leather, keeping the grain largely intact, equally shows the high degree of professionalism and expertise of the ancient Egyptian leatherworker as well as the types of seams and edge bindings used.

VII.2. The Tano Leather

While the technologies employed in the Tano material are fairly understandable, although certain observations related to skin processing and colouring need confirmation by analytical techniques, there are several questions concerning the find as a whole. These include provenance, ownership, date, and chariot type, and are discussed below.

VII.2.1. Provenance and Ownership

The chariot leather described in the present volumes comes from royal tombs (if we accept the provenance of the Amenhotep III leather). However, the origin of the Tano leather is unknown: it arrived in the Egyptian Museum in Cairo in 1932, and was purchased, not excavated. The condition of the leather, though far from perfect, indicates that it was never in contact with, or buried directly in soil or sand. Thus, it must originate from a tomb or a similar context with a stable environment, continuously arid, which would have ensured the preservation of organic materials, with some degree of suppleness preserved. This excludes the Delta and situates the find geographically in the drier areas of the south. Furthermore, it rules out an urban context such as Amarna, which has yielded leather finds, but these are almost always (very) fragmented, brittle and overall in poorer condition than leather found in Theban tombs (except that of Tutankhamun). There is also no argument to support the idea that the leather came from an ancient workshop located in a settlement, as such sites are rarely accessible because modern habitations frequently cover the ancient ones. Furthermore, they are also less likely to have been the target of antiquities' thieves as they require more digging, and yield less desirable material, unless a temple is being looted. Thus, the Tano leather more probably originates from a Theban or some other Upper Egyptian tomb.

So, to whom might the chariot have belonged? Pictorial and textual evidence indicates that chariots were used by royalty, the military, and the wealthy or favoured elite. Even if chariot bodies were affordable, training and sustaining the horses would have been a somewhat costly business, thus making chariots an untenable form of transport for the majority of Egypt's population. Thus, the Tano material must have belonged to either a royal or an elite/military chariot.

Pictorial evidence shows far more elaborate decoration on royal chariots than on those of the elite. Examples of royal chariots are often enhanced with gold, silver and inlays of various materials, as seen on the so-called 'State Chariots' found in Tutankhamun's tomb, as well as those that are mentioned in the Amarna letters (*e.g.* EA 14, EA 22, Moran, 1992: 30, 51). Even the scanty remains on the wooden frames of Tutankhamun's other chariots (Carter's No. 332 and 333; see Figure II.2B), are described by Carter as probably having been "highly coloured and decorated", although it is unclear as to what precise form this elaborate decoration took. If he meant that the leather was multi-coloured, with appliquéd designs, then the Tano leather would fit such a description. Some of the other royal leather objects associated with chariots are also without gold or other precious items, so it is not impossible that the Tano leather comes from a simple, every-day chariot that royalty might have used for hunts or for moving about in less formal and non-processional contexts.

However, the Tano leather seems to have more in common with elite chariots than royal chariots, as is attested by depictions of noblemen's chariots, particularly in terms of the zigzag and linear patterns that adorn their chariot leather (Figure 11.21 shows just one example as opposed to the far more elaborately decorated chariot in Figure V.9, which is a chariot of Nubian royalty). The Tano material is also similar to the Amarna leather, found in areas associated with the police (Borchardt, 1911: 26; Borchardt & Ricke, 1980: 292, 330). This material is slightly more elaborately decorated than the Tano material having more and different layers of appliqué. The streamlined technology used to create the Tano chariot (flax and sinew, prefabrication of sections, standarized and simple design), might also support the idea of a police/military chariot that was 'mass' (for the time period) produced.

In light of the textual evidence, one should also explore the idea that the leather comes from a foreign, confiscated or tribute chariot. The use of the passepoil, for example, in leatherwork is not reported in Egyptian pharaonic leatherwork but is seen in the so-called Persian leather from Elephantine (Kucketz, 2006; Veldmeijer, 2016: 102-136). The more complex edge bindings might argue for foreign influence or knowledge, too. But, many of the Tano materials, technologies, workmanship and decoration are in keeping with both the physical and pictorial evidence from Egypt, and thus it is more likely that the Tano material was produced in Egypt for an elite individual, but possibly one who had experience of foreign technology. However, without comparative material from securely identified non-Egyptian (chariot) leather it is impossible to know what role, if any, foreign technology played in creating the Tano material.

VII.2.2. Dating the Tano Material

In the progress report (Veldmeijer *et al.*, 2013) a date of not earlier than the 18th Dynasty was proposed on the basis of historical and pictorial evidence. Since the Tano chariot is thought to have belonged to an elite individual, it is more likely to date from the latter part of the reign of Tuthmose III onward, when, at least in the pictorial record, an increasing number of images show elite individuals using chariots, although a few earlier examples are known (see Chapter V for details). It should also be noted that in Amarna tombs, royalty, nobility, and the police are shown riding chariots, and perhaps, due to the nature of the site, the use of chariots became increasingly common among the elite. The presence of hand-grips in the Tano material suggests that it is of the Amarna-period or later, as these, in the pictorial record, only start to appear then. After the Amarna period, these cut out hand-grips become very rare in depictions of chariots but they do exist (for example, chariots shown in Luxor temple's Opet festival, dating to the reign of Tutankhamun/Ay, in the Memphite tomb of Horemheb (Martin, 1989: pls. 28-29), and in the Seti I reliefs at Karnak; The Epigraphic Survey, 1986: pl. III).

The Tano siding fill has additional apertures for quivers, which are rarely depicted in the 18th Dynasty (see for example Figure V.7, cf. Figure 11.1A), and if they are present, they are situated more towards the back and are small in size. Such apertures become far more common in the Ramesside Period (e.g. Breasted, 1903, 6; The Epigraphic Survey, 1986: pl. X; Figure II.1A), where they are positioned in a variety of places, but often more toward the front and relatively large in size, which compare better to the Tano siding fill.

The technologies used to produce the Tano material contribute to its dating. The use of stitching, with little gluing, is more in keeping with the leatherwork of and after the reign of Thutmoses IV, and finished, rather than folded edges are indicative of a date of Amenhotep III and beyond. The increasing complexity of these finished edges, incorporating the appliqué as well as protecting the edge and the stitching, as seen in the Tano leather, stands in big contrast to the other leatherwork. The possibility of pre-fabricated parts joined together is also a phenomenon in keeping with the reign of Amenhotep III and later (although it has not be identified for the leatherwork from Amarna, possibly indicative of a different workshop/tradition), suggesting a change in leatherwork technology and its organisation, with parts being made in advance, perhaps by separate specialists. The use of flax for securing the decorative elements and sinew for the functional portions might also be indicative of a post-Amenhotep III production (it is only attested in the Tano leather), as the leatherwork dating to that king's reign and earlier tends to be secured exclusively with sinew. The use of passepoils, an innovation to create stronger seams between two (larger) sheets of leather, has also not been seen in the non-Tano material. Perhaps the use of both flax and sinew (together with pre-fabrication of appliqué and a more standardized, simple decoration) attest to a more streamlined, almost assembly-line, process for making chariots, indicative of an increased production, such as might have started in the Amarna period and could have existed in the Ramesside era when chariot production for military use seems to have increased.

Thus, pictorial, textual, technological, and physical evidence in terms of shape, decorative motifs, and technology, all indicate an Amarna or, more likely, a post-Amarna date for the Tano material, while the changing nature of elite burials by the Third Intermediate Period, with few grave goods, provides a terminus for dating the material.

VII.2.3. Shape

Reconstructing the shape of chariot leather and the type of chariot it fit is difficult based on the extant information. Imagery is only partially helpful for reconstructing the form of complete chariots, as they are, save rare exceptions of chariots on the battlefield, depicted in profile, leaving the rear and frontal details to the imagination. Standardisation or abstraction for a quick visual understanding and identification also make images hard to interpret in terms of details. Moreover, the depictions of elite chariots wanes during the Ramesside period as tomb decoration changes (Dodson & Ikram, 2008: 139). During this time, images of chariots in royal or military contexts predominate. Physical remains of chariot leather shed little light on the problem as they are few and fragmentary, and do not include elements of the chariot body, although some ideas can be garnered from the chariots from the tombs of Thutmose IV, Yuya and Tjuiu, and Tutankhamun. Although texts might provide words for parts of the chariot, their appearance is not detailed in a practical manner. Thus, within the confines of the extant pictorial, archaeological and textual evidence, it remains difficult to be sure of how, in general, the leather was secured to the chariot and what shapes the main casing and siding fill took, particularly in terms of knowing whether a tripartite end piece commonly crowned the central part of the main casing, whether the apertures truly were asymmetrical, if the siding fill had scalloped corners, and if/how the siding fill and the main casing were used separately or only together.

That the chariot's casing might have been distinctly different from depictions is also suggested by two of Tutankhamun's chariots: if the reconstruction made by Carter on the basis of the remaining scraps of leather is correct, the shape is clearly different from what is usually shown, with diagonal running edges at the front and holes at the back upper and lower corners (Figure II.2B). Possibly, there was a greater variation in the way that bodies of ancient Egyptian chariots were clad than we know on the basis of imagery. From the extant evidence, the main casing of the Tano leather fits well with the Florence chariot size and type with a more dramatically curving of the top railing. This was established by making a 1:1 paper print of the Tano leather and fitting it onto the Florence chariot in the summer of 2015. A life-scale reproduction of the Tano material made in leather, a project that is in progress, might shed further light on the possibilities.

The Florence chariot is the smallest extant vehicle from ancient Egypt and one wonders if the Tano casing belonged to this vehicle originally. However, as discussed elsewhere (Veldmeijer *et al.*, 2013: 269), it is unclear why the leatherwork would be separated from the frame. The Tano material has substantial wear marks: places along the upper railing are discoloured, and the upper surfaces of the leather are rubbed off due to grasping the railing. The leather is faded and abraded in many places, indicating that it was exposed to the elements and was actively used. Furthermore, the presence of secondary slits cut into the leather suggest that these were made to adjust the leather during use. Thus, it is clear that it was not made specifically as a funerary offering, but rather, was chariot leather that was used in real life. It is possible that, instead of giving an entire chariot, the old leatherwork was placed in a tomb – a part symbolic of the whole. Alternatively, this might have been a spare leather cover, perhaps the second class version, which was interred with the deceased

Thus, although there is no clear attestation for the ownership of the Tano material, based on archaeological remains, imagery, and technological details, it would seem that it belonged to a small chariot, which dates to the Amarna period or more likely the early Ramesside period as it has both a main casing and siding fill, holes for handgrips, (an) extra apertures for (a) quivers, and support straps. It was clearly the possession of an elite individual, and saw active service before its interment in an Upper Egyptian sepulchre. Its workmanship is a testament to the talent and expertise of the ancient Egyptian craftsmen. The study of the Tano material has not only afforded an unparalleled opportunity to learn about ancient Egyptian leather technologies, but also has provided an example of hitherto missing crucial components of chariots: the leather casing and horse trappings. Thus, the Tano material has allowed for a better understanding of the key vehicle of the ancient world, the chariot.

Part II

Catalogue

TOMB OF AMENHOTEP II

CATALOGUE NUMBER 1

Id. No. JE 96912A-C [-W] (SR 2502A-C; CG 24151); See 'Remarks'.

Object Container (bow-case/quiver).

Measurements
A) Length: 217. Width: 160. Thickness: 1.
B) Length: 130. Width: 196. Thickness: 1.8.
C) Length: 240. Width: 105. Thickness: 0.6-3.
D) Length: 80. Width: 48. Thickness: 0.8.
E) Length: 33. Width: 84. Thickness: 0.9.
F) Length: 66. Width: 23. Thickness: 0.7.
G) Length: 55. Width: 50. Thickness: 1.
H) Length: 45. Width: 54.3. Thickness: 0.5.
I) Length: 2.3. Width: 51.5. Thickness: 0.9.
J) Length: 28. Width: 38.9. Thickness: 0.9.
K) Length: 28. Width: 19. Thickness: 0.8.
L) Length: 28.5. Width: 7. Thickness: 0.8.
M) Length: 31.2. Width: 19. Thickness: 0.8.
N) Length: 55. Width: 38. Thickness: 1.
O) Length: 6.2. Width: 2.2. Thickness: 0.3.
P) Length: 4.3. Width: 5. Thickness: 0.75.
Q) Length: 37. Width: 10.5. Thickness: 1.1.
R) Length: 37.2. Width: 15.5. Thickness: 0.8.
S) Length: 18.2. Width: 14. Thickness: 0.8.
T) Length: 35.4. Width: 17.2. Thickness: 0.8.
U) Length: 23. Width: 13.6. Thickness: 0.5-1.1.
V) Length: 24.4. Width: 9. Thickness: 0.9.
W) Length: 14.9. Width: 10.8 Thickness: 0.8.

Remarks Various fragments have pieces of modern cloth as backing, indicating previous conservation interventions (2502A-C), probably early 20th century. The material is (also due to this intervention) in very poor condition and deteriorating ('melting').

A-C are the larger pieces and have JE numbers thus: SR 2502A = JE 96912A; SR 2502B = JE 96912B; SR 2502C = JE 96912C. The remainder are numbered in the present work, but do not have a JE-number. These pieces probably flaked off from fragments A-C.

Description
A) A large piece of brittle leather, with one side that has a finish of sorts. The whole is coloured red, which has faded to pink (figure A, B) and is decorated by a series of vertical painted bands (figure C; width: average 4 mm; space between the bands: approximately 5 mm). These bands consist of black, narrow parallel lines which are filled in with dots that form a repeating

Cat. No. 1, JE 96912A. *Overview of recto (A) and verso (B). The textile reinforcements are modern-day conservation intervention. The black discolouration at the recto is due to the deterioration of the leather.*

Cat. No. 1, JE 96912A. *C) Detail of painted design at the recto, consisting of bands of dots with repeated diamond pattern. Scale bar is 5 mm.*

Cat. No. 1, JE 96912A. *D-E) Details of the edge. Note the paired, slightly larger stitches holes, more triangular in shape, of the innermost stitching row. Scale bars are 10 mm.*

diamond pattern with dots being shared between subsequent 'diamonds'. The dots look dark red but might have been originally black or even green. The edge of the piece (figure D, E) is reinforced by narrow strips of leather that were stitched onto the recto (see fragment C, below, for a more complete example). Only one (width: 5.5 mm), possibly out of three or four, remains partially intact. The colour has largely worn away. It probably was secured with running stitches, but the material of the threads could not be determined as the stitch holes are empty. A discoloration at the recto, exactly on the area a strip might have been attached, suggests that the strip was also glued in place.

B) A piece of leather (figure A, B) attaching to fragment A, see above, and C, see below. It is decorated with painted bands of dots in repeating diamonds (figure C; width: 3.2-4 mm). The plain bands in between are approximately 2.5-4 mm wide. One edge (at least 24.5 mm wide) shows evidence of applied decoration (figure C; see fragment C, below, for a more complete example) consisting of strips of leather onto the reddish foundation layer with the painted dots. They are secured by means of running stitches and glue, the latter evidenced by a band of darker colour. Three rows of stitch holes are visible, as in fragment A, two of which clearly set in the described edge. The innermost, however, is placed more inwards, penetrating a band of dots. These holes are clearly in pairs (the holes in the other two rows are not), triangular in shape and bigger. Note, however, that between the first and second row of stitching, seen from the edge, another row of comparable stitching is visible (see the description of fragment C, below, for an interpretation).

C) A piece of leather with edging on one side (figure A, B). The recto is decorated with painted bands of dots in repeating diamond pattern (*cf.* above; width: 4 mm; plain bands in between: ap-

Cat. No. 1, JE 96912C. F) Detail of the inner two rows of the enhanced edge of the recto; G) Detail of the verso, showing the stitch holes of the enhanced edge. Scale bars are 10 mm.

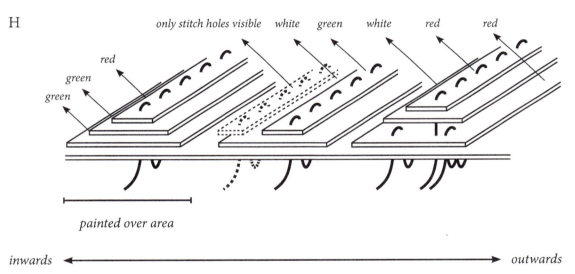

Cat. No. 1, JE 96912C. H) Diagram of the enhanced edge of the recto.

running stitches lengthwise down the centre. A 3.1 mm wide band of the red foundation (note the tiny spots of the original dark red colour) separates the final set of decoration. The bottom one, which is the widest (width: 11.6 mm) is red. Lengthwise down the centre a white/beige strip (width: 9 mm) is added. On top of this a narrow red strip (width: 2.5 mm) is attached with widely spaced running stitches of sinew. The topmost set of two obscures most of the red strip beneath, leaving only a very narrow strip visible. They also cover the stitching that secures the red one. At one broken edge, at right angle to the described decorated edge, stitch holes with sinew zS_2 thread *in situ* (especially at the verso) are visible. Note the difference in stitch hole sizes (figure F) as well as the start of stitching of the applied decoration at the verso by means of a reef(?) knot (arrow in figure D).

The body of the piece was once further decorated with a circular or semi-circular attachment of which only a portion remains in negative. It is 43.8 mm at the widest preserved point. It consisted of a narrow band of leather glued to the edge of the circular area (width: 4 mm) followed by a wider leather strip that was glued on and may have been stitched in one place (width: 20-25 mm). The verso shows that the edge, *i.e.* the enhanced edge of the recto, is distinctly darker than the rest and nearly black in colour. Possibly, this is due to the use of animal based glue to further secure the applied decoration.

D) Small piece of faded red leather with bands of dots in repeating diamond pattern on the recto (width: 4 mm; plain bands in between: 5.8 mm).

E) As fragment D (width dotted bands: 4.3 mm; plain bands in between: 3.2-3.6 mm).

F) Fragment of edge as described for fragment C. Only tiny bits of the applied decoration survives. Four rows of stitch holes are visible.

G) As fragment D with faintly visible painted decoration (but too unclear to measure).

H) Small piece with painted dotted decoration (see for example fragment C; width dotted bands: 4 mm; plain bands in between: 4 mm) and piece of the edge. One discoloured glue band is visible at the edge (width: 8 mm).

***Cat. No. 1, JE 96912C.** I) Close up of recto. Note the remains of the circular shape.*

I) As fragment D (width dotted bands: 4.8 mm; plain bands in between: 7.2 mm).

J) As fragment D. Decoration too faint to measure.

K) As fragment D. Decoration too faint to measure.

L) As fragment D (width dotted bands: 4 mm; plain bands in between: 4.5 mm).

M) Piece of glued edge (width glue band: 10.5 mm).

N) As D (width dotted bands: 5.4 mm; plain bands in between: 4.8 mm; width glue band: 8.5 mm).

O) Folded piece of red leather that seems to have been used as edge binding. Stitch holes suggest it was applied by stitching rather than glue (only?).

P) Featureless, except for a small sign of glue.

Q) As fragment O but with two rows of stitch holes.

R) As fragment D (measurements of decoration not possible).

S) As fragment D (width dotted bands: 4.5 mm; plain bands in between: 5.2 mm).

Cat. No. 1, 2502D. *Overview of recto (A) and verso (B).*

Cat. No. 1, 2502E. *Overview of recto (A) and verso (B).*

Cat. No. 1, 2502F. *Overview of recto (A) and verso (B); C) Detail of the enhancement of the recto. Scale bar is 10 mm.*

Cat. No. 1, 2502G. *Overview of recto and verso.*

Cat. No. 1, 2502H. *Overview of recto (A) and verso (B).*

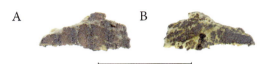

Cat. No. 1, 2502I. *Overview of recto (A) and verso (B).*

Cat. No. 1, 2502J. *Overview of recto (A) and verso (B).*

Cat. No. 1, 2502K. *Overview of recto (A) and verso (B).*

Cat. No. 1, 2502L. *Overview of recto (A) and verso (B).*

Cat. No. 1, 2502M. *Overview of recto (A) and verso (B).*

Cat. No. 1, 2502N. *Overview of recto (A) and verso (B).*

Cat. No. 1, 2502O. *Overview of recto (A) and verso (B).*

CATALOGUE

T) As fragment D (measurements of decoration not possible).
U) Small piece of red leather with tiny remnants of green strips of applied leather, attached by glue and running stitches (no thread remaining), suggesting it is a fragment of edge as described for fragment C.
V) Small fragment of red edge as described for fragment C. Two lines of stitch holes of different sizes run parallel to each other.
W) Small fragment with vestiges of a glued strip that is discoloured from the original red foundation.

Cat. No. 1, 2502P. Overview of recto (A) and verso (B).

Cat. No. 1, 2502Q. Overview of recto (A) and verso (B). Scale bar is 10 mm.

Cat. No. 1, 2502R. Overview of recto (A) and verso (B). Scale bar is 10 mm.

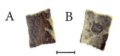

Cat. No. 1, 2502S. Overview of recto (A) and verso (B). Scale bar is 10 mm.

Cat. No. 1, 2502T. Overview of recto (A) and verso (B). Scale bar is 10 mm.

Cat. No. 1, 2502U. Overview of recto (A) and verso (B). Scale bar is 10 mm.

Cat. No. 1, 2502V. Overview of recto (A) and verso (B). Scale bar is 10 mm.

Cat. No. 1, 2502W. Overview of recto (A) and verso (B). Scale bar is 10 mm.

CATALOGUE NUMBER 2

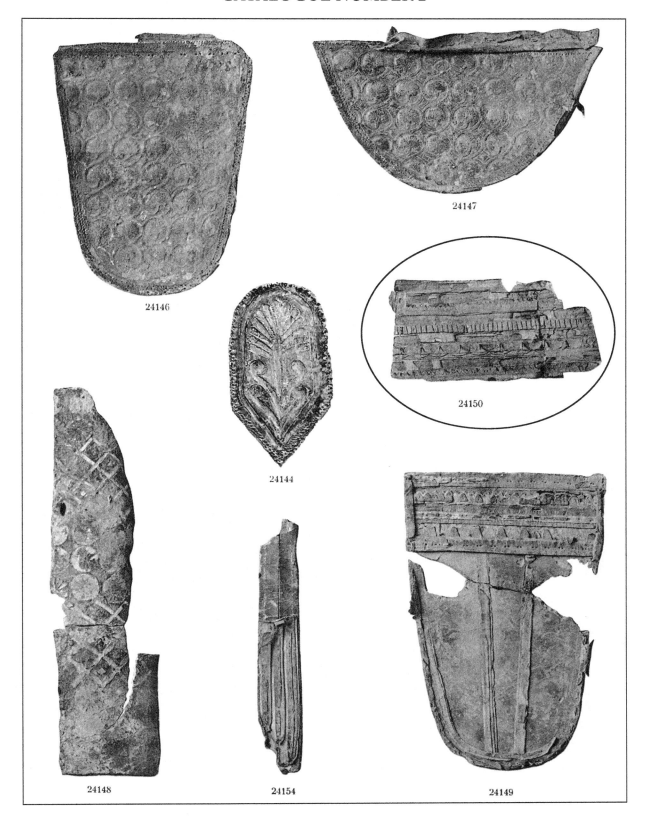

Cat. No. 2, JE 32509A *(encircled), as published by Daressy (1902: 78, pl. XXII). When this photograph was taken, the fragment was not yet restored (see the V-shaped cut at the top) and small fragments have fallen off since.*

Id. No. JE 32509A, B (SR 2505A-E; CG 24150).

Object Container (bow-case/quiver).

Measurements A) Width: 165. Height: 78.5. Thickness: 1.1-2.3.

B) Width: 128. Height: 78. Thickness: 2-2.3.

C) Width: 27.2. Height: 19. Thickness: 2.

D) Width: 18.6. Height: 24.7. Thickness: 2.3.

E) All: Width: appr. 20. Height: appr. 10. Thickness: 1.

Remarks Modern (early 20th century?) conservation intervention consisting of a narrow strip of cloth backing along a joint, probably glued with animal glue. Fragile. Fragment A) = JE 32509A; B) = JE 32509B. Daressy (1902: 78, pl. XXII). Fragment Cat. No. 3, H, is a small piece that was torn off from B and apparently stored at some point wrongly with JE 32435. Fragment A has only been photographed at the recto only as it was too fragile to turn over.

*Description**

A) This highly decorated piece (figure A, B) was connected to a large piece of leather that was coloured red. Probably there was more leather on one side of this broad decorative band (*cf.* JE 32435, Cat. No. 3). One side of the width might be a genuine terminal point of the piece, as it sports a clean edge. The whole piece is nearly rectangular, with the short side to the viewer's right broken off; the side to the viewer's left is slightly diagonal and intact. This has a strip of leather (rawhide?), 7.6 mm wide, sewn along the top of the decoration (figure C, D) with fairly big stitches of leather, which must have played a part in securing JE 32509 to a larger object.

The foundation is of rawhide. On this rests a piece of leather, 58.5 mm wide, that overlaps another, narrower piece of leather. This one, in turn, runs along and on top of the other side of the rawhide. It is 22.4 mm wide. Both these leather pieces are coloured red and they act as the foundation to the whole piece. The decoration, top to bottom (based on the orientation of the pendent pieces), is executed in red, green and white (now discoloured to gray or yellow) leather (figure C-G). In some cases the colour has been compromised and is not clear. The decoration consists of a series of thin strips, some with pendentives that overlap, and are secured to the foundation exclusively by gluing. It starts with a set of green (width: 5.5 mm) on top of a plain strip that protrudes (0.2 and 1 mm respectively) from the green on either side (1). Remnants suggest that a narrow, possibly red, strip ran lengthwise down the centre of the green. Beneath is another plain strip whose bottom part is cut in sharp scallops that has a beige colour (2a; the total width, *i.e.* including the part hidden under the previous set, is 8.5 mm). Above this, and thus sandwiched between it and the plain bottom strip of the previous set, a red strip of sharper and shorted scallops (2b) is inserted. These double layers of scallops rest on a set of strips, consisting of a top layer of green (width: 5 mm) that overlap in stair-step fashion, a wider beige one (3). All this rests on the foundation of red leather that shows through in a band here (4; width 3 mm). Another set of strips follows, consisting of a bottom plain one, almost entirely covered by a green one (width: 6.4 mm) in stair-step fashion, leaving a narrow plain strip protruding at either side (5: 0.2 and 0.2-0.5 mm respectively). A narrow red strip (width: 1.5 mm), which is mostly missing, runs lengthwise down the centre of this green strip. The opposite edge of this plain strip is made of a series of icicles/petals that now are grayish-white in colour, but probably white originally (6; width: 5.5 mm). The icicles/petals are cut from a strip, solid on one side and icicles/petals on the other (arrow in figure E). The band with icicles/petals are stuck onto another, fairly wide, thin leather band (width: 6.5 mm). At the tips of the icicles/petals, covering the bottom of the plain band on which they rest, is a strip of green leather (width:

---

* The figures refer to the described part in the diagram. The orientation as visible in the old photographed is followed.

A

Cat. No. 2, JE 32509A. *Overview of the recto.*

B

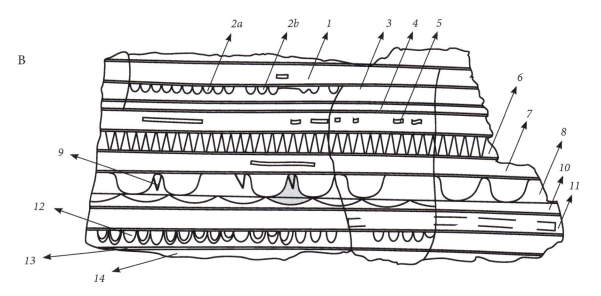

Cat. No. 2, JE 32509A. *Diagram of the recto, including the sequence of the appliqué. The numbers refer to the description in the text. One of the composite umbells is marked in gray (see figure F).*

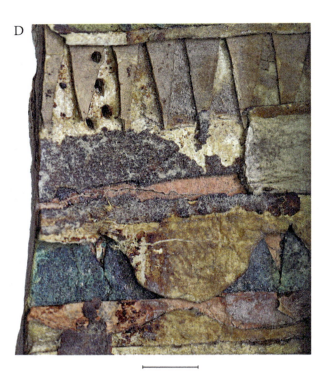

Cat. No. 2, JE 32509A. *C) Details of the appliqué at the recto (numbers 1-6 in the description, cf. figure B). Note the strip of rawhide at the edge; D) Details of the appliqué at the recto (numbers 6-10 in the description, cf. figure B). Scale bars are 10 mm.*

Cat. No. 2, JE 32509A. *E) Details of the appliqué at the recto (numbers 3-6 in the description, cf. figure B). The pendentives are cut from one edge of a strip (arrow). Scale bar is 10 mm.*

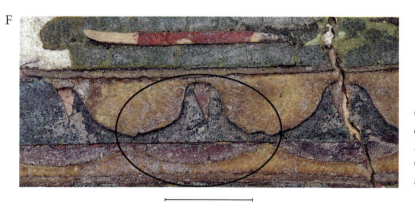

Cat. No. 2, JE 32509A. *C-G) Details of the appliqué at the recto (numbers 7-10 in the description, cf. figure B). One of the row of composite umbells is encircled. Scale bar is 10 mm.*

Cat. No. 2, JE 32509A. G) Details of the appliqué at the recto (numbers 9-14 in the description, cf. figure B). Scale bar is 10 mm.

6 mm) adorned by a narrow red strip running lengthwise through the centre. The green strip is stuck to a plain wide one that protrudes from either side (7; 0.3-0.8 and 0.3-0.5 respectively). This set slightly overlaps a broad layer of loose scallops that are yellow (8; width: 7 mm). Below these scallops is a green strip that shows through (max. width: 6.8 mm). The green negative space between them, together with the red scalloped leather strip following it, creates a papyrus umbell in flower. This green strip is cut with V-shaped cuts in the top side, thus the scallops show the V's between them (9), representing the petal of the papyrus. This is followed by a red strip (width: 1.2 mm) whose bottom ends are scallops, created by a yellowy leather strip that is cut and added on top of the red one (10; max. width: 2 mm). This creates the rounded top of the papyrus plant when it bears fruit. Numbers 8-10 form green and red umbells. Overlapping in stair-step fashion is the next set, consisting of a beige strip with a green on top, and lengthwise through the centre (width: 6.5 mm). Darker spots (from the glue?) proceeding lengthwise down the centre suggest that a narrow strip once adorned the green one (11). This set also overlaps, at the other side, two sets of scallops on top of each other, the bottom one slightly larger than the red top one (12; *cf.* the row on top, 2; width: 4 mm). This rests on top of a green strip (width: 4 mm), which makes a set together with a plain strip that slightly protrudes at either side from under the green (13; width: 0.3-0.5 mm). Projecting from this set is the red foundation (14). The entire object must have been glued as no stitches could be detected.

B) A roughly rectangular, wide piece adorned with a complex pattern in leather (figure A-C). It is incomplete from the top as one can see where it has been torn. The decoration (figure D-G) follows the same pattern as JE 32509A, and it could very well be the counterpart of the same container. The incompleteness allows for additional observations and better understanding the construction. It starts with a green strip (1; width: 7.2 mm) which might have had a narrow red strip on top of it, lengthwise down the centre, as is suggested by smears of glue. The green rests on an uncoloured strap that peeks out on either side (0.8 and 2.5 mm respectively). Beneath this is a strip that ends in pendentive icicles/petals (2; visible width: 8 mm) that point downward and protrude from the set of three. They might have been yellow or uncoloured (white). The background does not appear to be red, like the general background of the piece. This is followed by a green strip (3; width: 6.5 mm) resting on a plain one that peeks out on either side (width: 1.0 mm). A red strip possibly was superpositioned lengthwise down the centre on the green, but of this only some glue remains. Beneath this set rests a band of scallops in yellow leather (but this colour is almost certainly due to age and probably was white originally; 4; width: 7.5 mm), which overlaps the foundation as well as another green strip (5; width: 8.5

CATALOGUE | 219

Cat. No. 2, JE 32509B. *Overview of the recto (A) and verso (B).*

Cat. No. 2, JE 32509B. *C) Diagram of the recto, including the sequence of the appliqué. The numbers refer to the description in the text.*

Cat. No. 2, JE 32509B. D) Details of the appliqué at the recto (numbers 1-3 in the description, cf. figure B); E) Details of the appliqué at the recto (numbers 4-10 in the description, cf. figure B). Scale bars are 10 mm.

Cat. No. 2, JE 32509B. F) Detail of the appliqué of the recto, showing the remnants of the composite umbells (numbers 4-5 in the description, cf. JE 32509A, Cat. No. 2, figure B. Scale bar is 10 mm.

Cat. No. 2, JE 32509B. G) Detail of the appliqué of the recto, showing the remnants of the row of double scallops (numbers 7-8 in the description, cf. JE 32509A, Cat. No. 2, figure B). Scale bar is 10 mm.

mm). The green strip has V-shaped cuts in the top side, thus the scallops show the V's between them, which represents leaves. A red strip (6; width: 5.8 mm) is applied following down from the green; the top of the plants would have been glued on this strip (remnants of glue remains in one; *cf.* 8-10 in the description of JE 32509A, Cat. No. 2, figure F). It is followed by a broad strip of yellowish leather (7; width 11.5 mm; the visible part is 6.6 mm wide) but the bottom part is cut into scallops, which once had a strip of red scallops superimposed on them. The upper portion of this band was once covered by another, now lost, strip as is evidenced by the lack of discoloration, *i.e.* it shows the original colour. The scallops rest on a green strip (8) beneath which lies a strip of white leather that provides and edge (9; width: 1.2 mm). This is followed by a strip where the red background shows (10; width: 3.1 mm). The final strips of decoration are missing – only a discoloured band indicates where it/they were glued on.

C, D) Small fragment with pendentive icicles/petals and remnants of sets of strips at either side.

E) Several scraps.

Cat. No. 2, 2505C. Overview of recto (A) and verso (B). Scale bar is 10 mm.

Cat. No. 2, 2505D. Overview of recto (A) and verso (B). Scale bar is 10 mm.

Cat. No. 2, 2505E. Overview. Scale bar is 10 mm.

CATALOGUE NUMBER 3

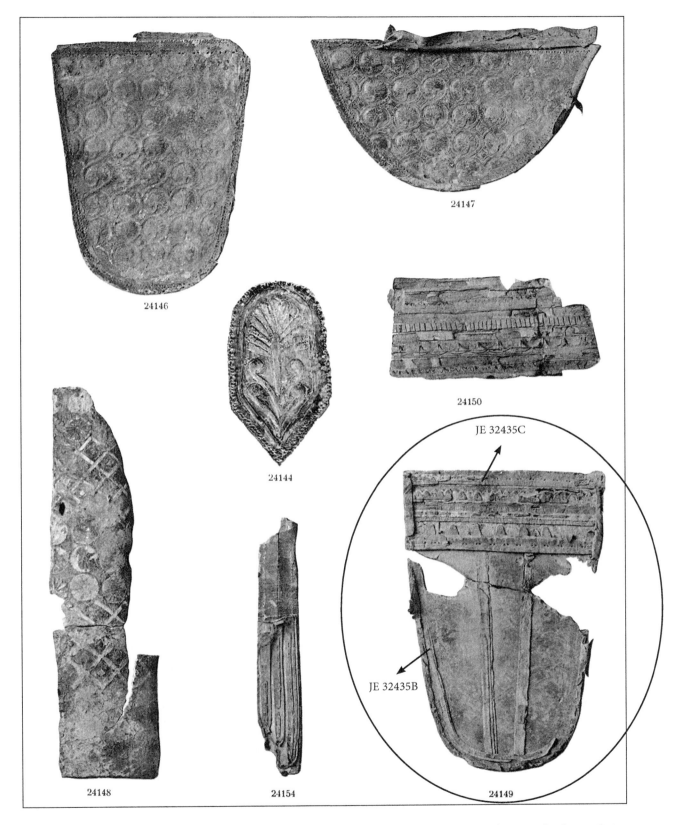

Cat. No. 3, JE 32435 *(encircled), as published by Daressy (1902: 78, pl. XXII). Since this photograph, the condition of the object seriously deteriorated, resulting in many small fragments.*

Id. No.	JE 32435A-D (SR 2506A-C, G, H. CG 24149). See remarks.
Group	2506A-I.
Object	Container (bow-case/quiver).
Measurements	JE 32435A) Length: 76.6. Width: 80. Thickness: 1.7.
	JE 32435B) Length: 141. Width: 128. Thickness: 2.6.
	JE 32435C) Length: 73. Width: 160. Thickness: 2-3.8.
	2506G).
	2506H) Length: 16. Width: 38.4. Thickness: 2.5.
	2506I) Length: 63. Width: 20. Thickness: 1.1.
Remarks	Group of objects of varying origin but with the same JE and CG numbers. See also Cat. No. 9 and 10. Number '2506D' does not exist. 2506A = JE 32435B; 2506B = JE 32435C; 2506C = JE 32435A; 2506E = JE 32435D. Various fragments have pieces of reinforcement cloth at their back, indicating modern conservation interventions, probably early 20th century (JE 32435A, D). Fragment H is a small piece that was torn off from JE 32509B, Cat. No. 2 and apparently stored at some point wrongly with JE 32435. See Daressy (1902: 77, pl. XXII).

Description[**]

A) A roughly rectangular piece of faded red leather (recto) that has broken off from a larger fragment (figure A, B). Parallel to the only finished edge, which would connect to fragment B, are two lines of paired stitch holes. The stitch holes that are closest to the edge (5.9 mm away) are smallest (0.1 mm or less) while the ones that are further from the edge (12 mm away) are larger (0.7 mm). A band of slightly darker colour, comparing to the white band at the verso, suggests the fragment was secured with glue in addition to stitching. It matches the appearance of fragment B: two vertical, parallel lines of decorated leather are glued to the recto. One of the two is lost, its presence indicated by a damaged surface. Still visible are several stitch holes, suggesting that, as in fragment B, the bottommost strip was secured with stitches before the other two strips were added. The bottom strip of the other, more intact line, is plain (width: 9.7 mm) upon which is glued (by absence of stitching) a green one lengthwise through the centre (width: 7.5 mm). This, in turn, is decorated with a narrow red strip, also glued (width: 1.5 mm). The verso shows a red brown colour save for a band along the edge.

[**] The figures refer to the described part in the diagram. The orientation as visible in the old photograph is followed.

Cat. No. 3, JE 32435A. *Overview of the recto (A) and verso (B)*

B) A piece of leather that is broken off from a larger piece (JE 32435C, see below; figure A-C). It forms the bottom part of a bow-case. The finished edges indicate an oval shape. The recto is reddish (faded) with decoration consisting of overlapping strips of leather of different colour. The simple edge at the bottom consists of a narrow strip of leather that is secured to its faded red foundation with sinew zS_2 thread in running stitch. Halfway up the edge of the oval, the sinew seems to vanish and the leather strip itself goes in and out of the foundation (figure D-H). At the end, it is knotted into a Z-overhand stopper knot (figure I). This leather 'thong' is damaged. Note the distinctly redder colour underneath this strip, confirming that the red of the foundation is faded into the current, pinkish hue. The construction is a rather sloppy repair, which was made in ancient times; the objects must have stayed in use for a long time, considering the aformentioned discoloration. At the top, the leather thong secures an even thinner strip of leather here. However, this extra thin thickness was not intended but torn off: remnants of it are still clearly visible in the old images. Both strips have a width of 4.2 mm; the top one is 5.3. mm. Following in from this, after a space of approximately 3 mm, which narrows at the bottom of the fragment to 1.7 mm, the appliqué starts with a yellowish (originally the strip was white – the yellow colour, also seen elsewhere, is due to discoloration) strip of leather (figure D-F; width: 5.8 mm), which was secured to the foundation by sewing, as suggested by empty, paired stitch holes (but at the verso also the sewing threads are still visible in some holes, figure I). This strip is, due to preservation, only clearly visible at the bottom and along part of the side (figure A). Lengthwise down the centre, a green strip is superimposed that must have been glued to it, as is suggested by the absence of stitching. The strip obscured the stitching of the first band. Going inward (approximately 17.5 mm inwards from the oval bottom edge) is another row of paired stitch holes (figure G, H) but no indication remains as to what this is from; however, as with the previous set of appliqué, the verso shows remains of very fine sinew running stitching, which would have been small at the recto with large interstitch spaces (figure I). The central area of this object has two vertical lines of leather originating from the yellow band at the bottom edge (figure J, K). One is very damaged and only a little of it is preserved: it is discoloured and distinctly yellower than the other one. The lines consists of a white lower strip (width: 10.5 mm) upon which is secured a strip of green leather lengthwise down the centre (width: 6.5 mm), which, in turn, is adorned with a narrow strip of red leather (width: 2 mm). All strips are glued: there is no stitching to be seen. The verso is reddish-brown in colour.

Cat. No. 3, JE 32435A-D. C) Diagram of the construction of the appliqué. The row of empty stitch holes, inwards from the set of decoration at the edge, is not included. The overviews (figure A, B) can be found on the next page.

Cat. No. 3, JE 32435B. Overview of the recto (A) and verso (B).

226 | CHARIOTS IN ANCIENT EGYPT

Cat. No. 3, JE 32435B. *D-H) Details of the edge at the recto (see figure C for the diagram of the technology); I) Detail of the edge at the verso. Note the remnants of the fine sinew stitching (arrows) that secure(s)d the next two rows of appliqué (cf. figure D). Scale bars are 10 mm.*

Cat. No. 3, JE 32435B. *J, K) Details of the sets of appliqué at the body's recto (see figure C for the diagram of the technology). Scale bars are 10 mm.*

C) The top part of a larger piece, connecting to fragment B (figure A-C). The recto is elaborately decorated. The decoration (figure D-F) starts with a band of beige leather, originally white (1; width: 11.2 mm) along whose centre is affixed (only small remnants at the edges remaining) a narrower white strip (2; width: 5 mm) which was topped by a red strip lengthwise down the centre (width: 1.8 mm). This tripartite set is secured with zS_2 sinew thread running stitching – at the recto, the interstitch spaces are larger than the length of the stitches (thus the stitch holes are 'paired'). A strip with a straight bottom edge but of which the top is shallowly scalloped follows (3; width: 11 mm). Over this beige strip is a smaller green piece that echoes this scalloping pattern (4; width: 6.5 mm). The two are secured together with the red foundation that protrudes from it above and below (5; width: 4.5 and 3.2 mm respectively), with single stitches of zS_2(?) sinew thread at right angle to the scallops (figure F). Large stretches of this very fine thread is clearly visible at the verso (arrow in figure B). Note the insertion of a second piece of red (dashed arrow in figure F) as well as the still visible knife cuts (arrow in figure F). A wide strip (6; width: 13.1 mm) of beige follows. It is adorned lengthwise down the centre by a narrower (width: 5.8 mm) yellowish band, which, in turn, is covered by a red strip (7; width: 3.1 mm), also applied lengthwise down the centre. This design equals the top and bottommost decorative band. Following is a yellowish strip of 11.2 mm wide (8) that forms the basis from which emerges a row of long petal-like pendentives in beige/yellow alternating in, probably, red (9; width: 7.8 mm). At several spots, the red foundation is visible through holes in the beige/yellow layer on top

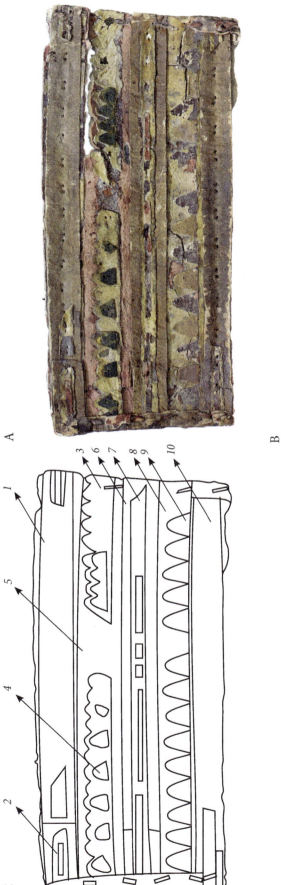

Cat. No. 3, JE 32435C. *Overview of the recto (A) and verso (B). The arrow indicates the fine sinew stitches that secures the scallops at the recto.*

Cat. No. 3, JE 32435C. *C) Diagram of the recto, including the sequence of the appliqué. The numbers refer to the description in the text.*

CATALOGUE | 229

of which the decoration is secured. The bottom is adorned with a band equivalent to the top band (10; width: 10.5, 5.4 and 1.2 mm respectively). The left short edge has a narrow leather strap covering it (figure G-J). This, in turn, is fixed with a narrow leather thong. A comparable construction can be seen on the right side. These are the remnants of the attachment of this rectangular element to the rest of the container. The verso is reinforced with a vertical strip of leather, 25.5 mm wide, and once had a series of horizontal strips running along, two of which remain (one 18 mm and the other 14 mm wide). The vertical strips seem to have been secured by a narrow leather strip, acting as 'thread'.

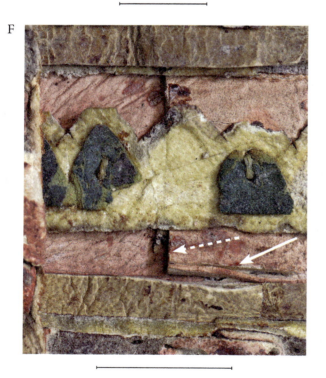

Cat. No. 3, JE 32435C. *D-F) Details of the appliqué at the recto. F) Note the tiny, single stitches that secures the two layers of scallops. The red foundation underneath shows the overlap of two different pieces (dashed arrow). The arrow indicates a cut by the leatherworker. Scale bars are 10 mm.*

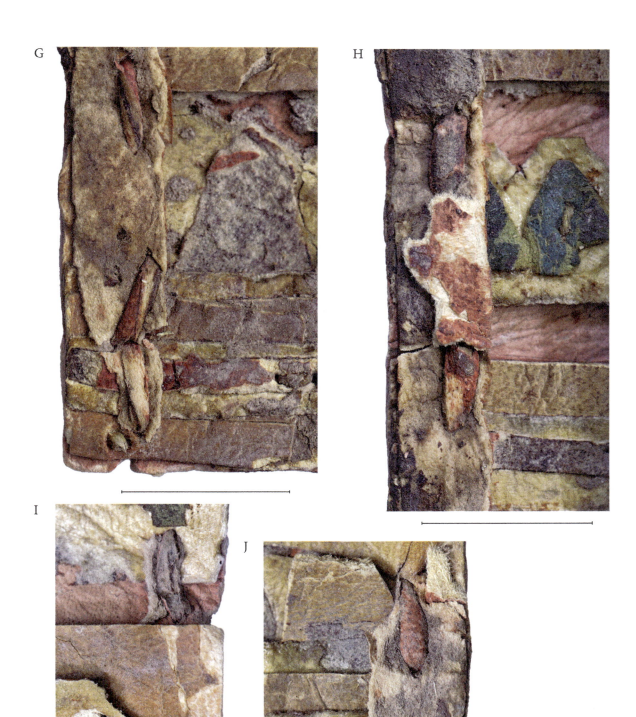

Cat. No. 3, JE 32435C. G-J) Details of the short, vertical edges, with remnants of the attachment of this element to the rest of the container; G, H) Right; I, J) Left. Scale bars are 10 mm.

G) Small fragment torn off from fragment 32435B (see above for description; figure A, B).

H) Small piece of elaborately enhanced leather with icicles/petals, scallops and strips, torn off from fragment 32509B (see above for description; figure A, B).

I) Strip of red leather (figure A, B). The top edge (figure C) has another narrow red strip (width: 3.3-3.8 mm) coarsely sewn to it in running stitches made of zS_2 sinew. Beneath it is another strip of indeterminable colour (width: 2.4 mm), overlying a narrow strip of red(?) leather (width: 1.2 mm). The verso is coloured dark brown/red.

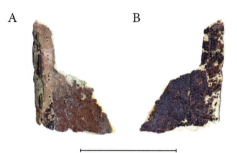

Cat. No. 3, 2506G. *Overview of recto (A) and verso (A).*

Cat. No. 3, 2506I. *Overview of verso (A) and recto (B); C) Detail. Scale bars are 10 mm.*

Cat. No. 3, 2506H. *Overview of recto (A) and verso (B). Scale bar is 10 mm.*

CATALOGUE NUMBER 4

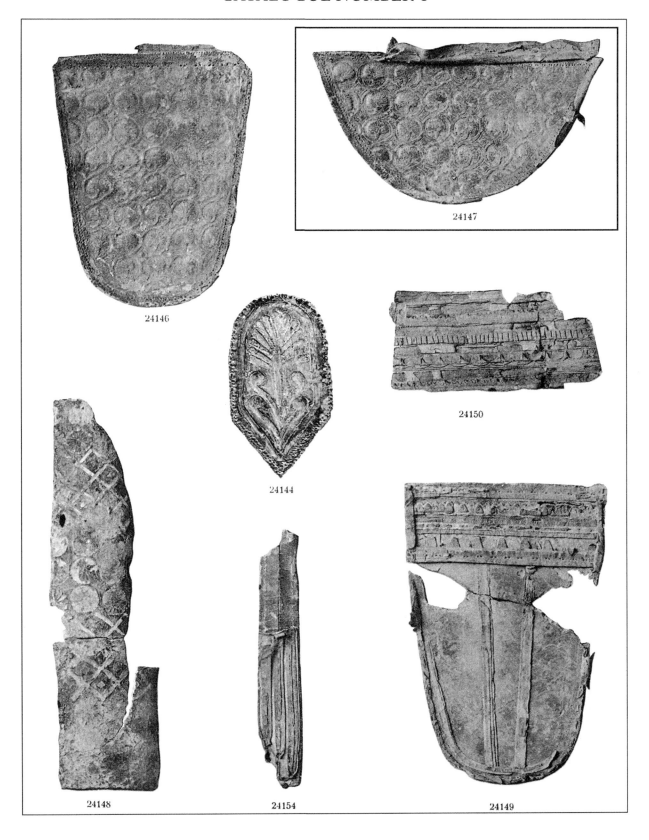

Cat. No. 4, JE 32513 *(encircled), as published by Daressy (1902: 78, pl. XXII).*

Id. No.	JE 32513 (SR 2500; CG 24147).
Object	Bow-case flap.
Measurements	Length: 81.7. Width: 73.5. Thickness: 2.1.
Remarks	According to Daressy (1902: 76-77, pl. XXII), it entered the museum as JE 32513; the JE number on the back must me a mistake (see below for the bridle boss with this number). As can be seen in the black and white photograph, large parts of CG 24146 and 24147 are lost: the fragment described here is, to the best of our knowledge, the only one preserved (at least, it is the only fragment we have found and studied). Currently, the fragment is too small to be unequivocally sure that it belongs to CG 24146 or 7, although the number in red on the verso indicates CG 24147.

Description

A roughly pear-shaped fragment (figure A, B) of beige-grey rawhide that is broken on one side. Originally it consisted of gilt over plaster with leather lining (Daressy, 1902: 76-77) but the leather is only what remains. This sturdy piece is decorated with an impressed (stamped) pattern of six palmettes (figure C) and remnants of additional motifs. There are a few stitch holes on its right proper side; several larger and more irregularly-shaped holes seem due to insect activity. Some darkening at the edges of the pieces might be indicative of glue.

A

B

Cat. No. 4, JE 32513. *Overview of the recto (A) and verso (B).*

Cat. No. 4, JE 32513. *C) Diagram of the impressed motif.*

CATALOGUE NUMBER 5

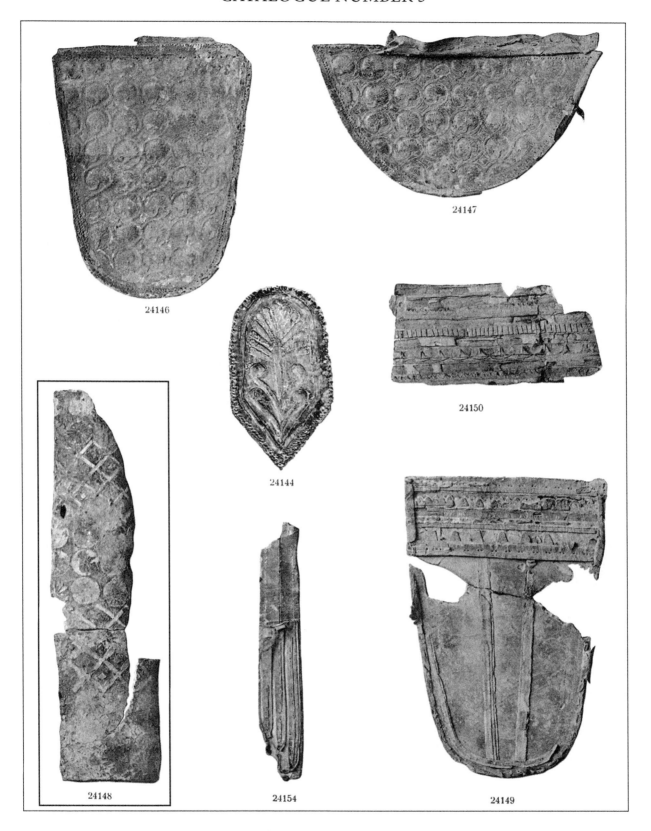

Cat. No. 5, JE 32400 *(encircled), as published by Daressy (1902: 78, pl. XXII). The description is done with the object turned around 180º, as it is believed to be upside down in the black and white image.*

Id. No.	JE 32400A, B (SR 2507A, B; CG 24148).
Object	Tube-shaped quiver.
Measurements	A) Length: 123. Width: 83. Thickness at top: 34.5. Width one leather strip verso: appr. 32.1. Diameter rosettes: 22-23.8.
	B) Length: 200. Width: 77.2. Thickness total: 3.7; Thickness rawhide: 3.2-3.4. Diameter roundel: 21.2-21.5. Width of white strips making the lattice work: 3.2.
Remarks	Has '15' in circle written in pencil on the verso. The description is of the two fragments together; Daressy (1902: 77, pl. XXII).

Description

JE 32400A (figure A, B; E-K) is the upper, rectangular (nearly square) part of the object and fits perfectly with JE 32400B (figure C, D, L-T; note that in the old black and white photograph the object is shown rotated 180⁰), which is longer and slightly curved lengthwise. JE 32400B is pierced by a hole midway down its length on one side (figure P), possibly as a button or tie-hole (length: 11.5 mm. Width: 4.7 mm). There is a faint outline of a circle of small holes (arrow in figure P), probably reinforcement by means of stitching, surmounting the hole. Also, 76.3 mm up from this one, there are faint traces that suggest the presence of a second hole.

The recto and verso decoration and treatment of the two fragments are the same. However, the top (JE 32400A; figure E-H) differs from the lower part (JE 32400B; figure L-M) insofar that the rosettes are all made of stamped out petals that were glued to the base. Obviously, the top part is the best decorated part as it is more visible and thus requires higher quality of craftsmanship. Lower down the craftsmenship deteriorates. The rosettes in the top part differ too (compare figure E with F: in one version, the petals are much more pronounced and centred around equally pronounced centres [note that only one comparable rosette is seen in JE 32400B, figure L], whereas in the other, the petals are not individually rendered and no centre can be seen). The rosettes were gilded. It is only in the lower part (fragment JE 32400B) that the stamped roundel rosettes were used (figure L-O). Each has, although barely visible anymore, a small diamond as the centre (encircled in figure M), like those in the centre of the lozenges.

At the top part (JE 32400A), a true beadnet pattern is visible (figure G, H). It is also made of strips of bark connected at the centre with yellow (gilded) circles, imitating tubular and circular beads. In the centre of each diamond, created by the net, are bark diamonds, that are also gilded. The network in JE 32400B, at either side of the rows of rosettes, might imitate a bead netting as well, but if so, it is not as neat and detailed as the one at the top of the object (JE 32400A; compare for example figure E, F with O) and might perhaps best be referred to as lattice work: three rows of latticing are visible that are made with narrow strips of bark, which are even in width, creating lozenge-shapes with diamond-shaped bark (or possibly leather) pieces at their centre (figure O). The strips run over each other rather than have been cut to size to fit between the strips at either side (figure Q, R). The overall effect is of a lattice or trellis supporting flowers.

The top of the recto of JE 32400A is treated with something and pushed over the verso (figure I); the red leather on the verso is glued on and the strips are secured together by means of whip stitches of sinew. In one spot it looks as if the leather was stained *in situ*, as some red colouring is visible between the two long pieces of leather, staining the rawhide. The red leather might have been cut lengthwise after being glued in place. At the verso, along the top edge of JE 32400A, there is a band of darker colour (width: 12.8 mm). This is probably due to a layer of glue and the attachment of another strip of leather here. The intact edge shows stitch holes in the thickness of the object: the stitches went through them, through the thickness of the opposite layer (now lost) and appear in the edge of the recto at both sides (figure P, S, T).

***Cat. No. 5, JE 32400A, B**. Overviews of recto (A, C) and verso (B, D). The two fragments fit together perfectly.*

CATALOGUE | 237

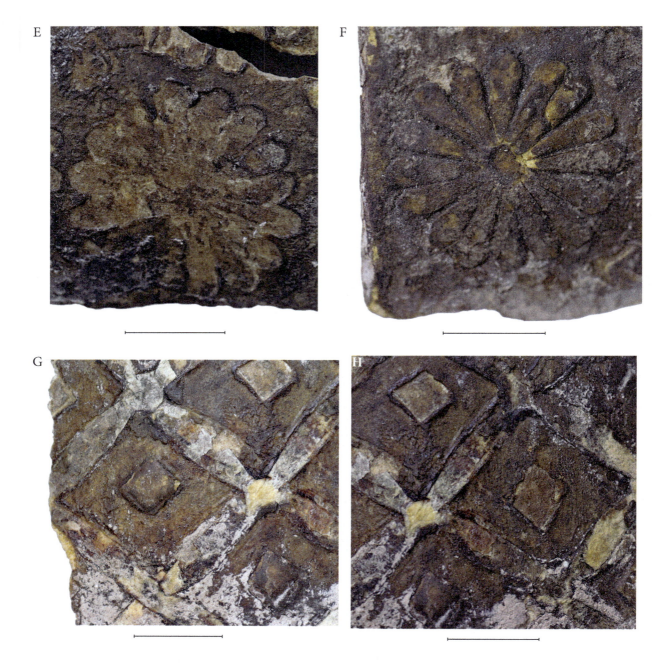

Cat. No. 5, JE 32400A. *E-H) Details of the decoration on the recto. Two differently executed rosettes (E, F) and the bead network in gilded bark (G, H). Scale bars are 10 mm.*

Cat. No. 5, JE 32400A. *I) Detail of top edge of the fragment seen at the verso. Scale bar is 10 mm.*

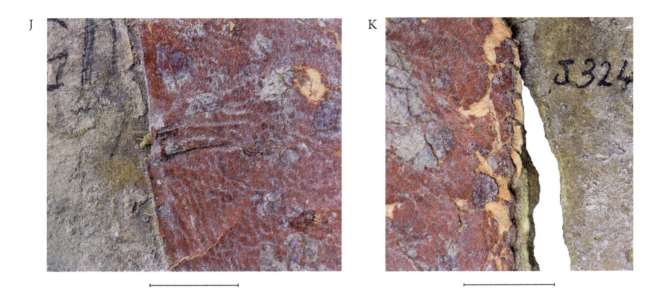

Cat. No. 5, JE 32400A. *J, K) Detail of the verso, showing the stitching that secures the strips of red leather. Scale bars are 10 mm.*

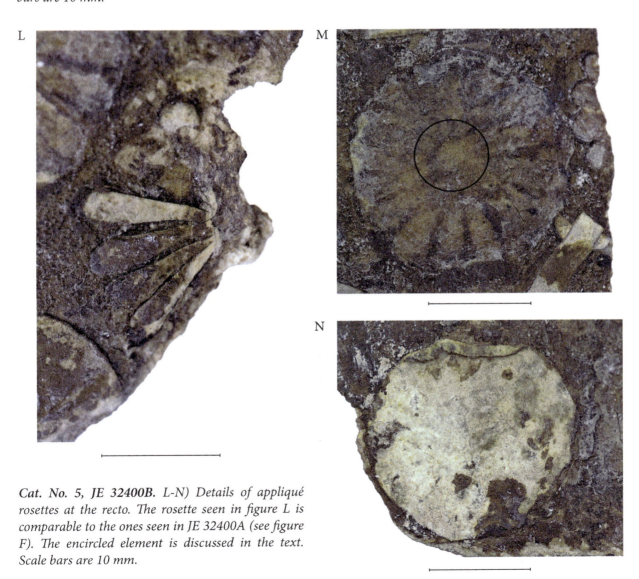

Cat. No. 5, JE 32400B. *L-N) Details of appliqué rosettes at the recto. The rosette seen in figure L is comparable to the ones seen in JE 32400A (see figure F). The encircled element is discussed in the text. Scale bars are 10 mm.*

Cat. No. 5, JE 32400B. *O, P) Detail of the strips of bark that make the lattice work, a rosette and the diamonds that are in the centre of the lattice-mazes (encircled in figure O); P) The hole, which likely had a strap pulled through to further secure closing of the tube, was probably reinforced with stitching (arrow). The stitches at the edge (encircled in figure P) were sewn through the thickness of the leather (see figure S, T). Scale bars are 10 mm.*

Cat. No. 5, JE 32400B. *Q, R) Details of the appliqué lattice work at the recto, including the diamonds in their centres. Scale bars are 10 mm.*

Cat. No. 5, 32400B. S) Edge, showing the stitch holes. Note the wavy line of the cross section. Indication of size: the thickness is approximately 3.2 mm; T) Diagram of the construction.

CATALOGUE NUMBER 6

Id. No.	JE 32559 (SR 2508; CG 24155).
Object	Axe-binding.
Measurements	Length overall: 130. Width overall: appr. 50. Thickness overall: 1.2-1.6. Average width strips: 11.5-14.8.
Remarks	Several isolated pieces of strips. Daressy (1902: 78, pl. XXIV). as can be seen in the old black and white photograph (next page), the wooden handle has been removed but is not clear when this was done.

Description

Narrow strips of rawhide, stained red at one side (display surface), that are woven together (figure A, B). The strips have been cut with no measuring tool or straight edge involved, as is evidenced by the irregularity of their width. Such bindings are known to hold together axes, adzes and other tools. Note the polished and darker stained areas resulting from the oils and sweat from hands (?; figure C).

Cat. No. 6, JE 32559. Overview of recto (A) and verso (B).

CATALOGUE | 241

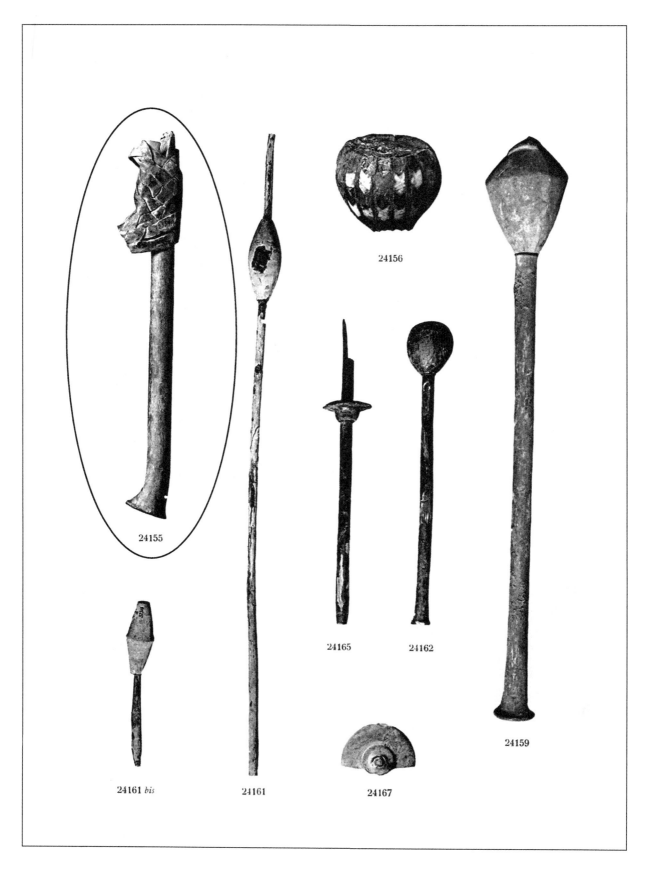

Cat. No. 6, JE 33559 *(encircled), as published by Daressy (1902: 78, pl. XXIV). The object was taken off from the wooden handle.*

Cat. No. 6, JE 32559. C) Detail showing discoloration due to contact. Scale bar is 10 mm.

CATALOGUE NUMBER 7

Id. No.   JE 32625 (SR 2501; CG 24145).
Object   Bridle boss(?)
Measurements Diameter: 73.3. Thickness: 2.1-2.6.
Remarks   Daressy (1902: 76).
Description

Rawhide roundel, partially preserved and with black discolouration due to deterioration (figure A, B). Impressed with a rosette pattern, which has at least 23 petals, radiating off the central boss (diameter: 9.5 mm). The rosette is encircled by a raised edge of uneven width that varies between 3.2-7.6 mm. This border is pierced by holes that are used for securing it to a foundation with a row of continuous holes and, between it and the edge proper, paired stitch holes (figure C). The verso is darkened in places and might have had glue on it. It still has a reddish scrap of leather surviving over an edge (figure D), covering the stitch holes, possibly from the foundation on to which the object was sewn.

Cat. No. 7, JE 32625. Overview of the recto (A) and verso (B).

Cat. No. 7, JE 32625. *C) Detail of the recto, showing two sets of stitch holes: a continuous row slightly inwards of the edge and paired stitch holes more closely to the edge proper; D) Detail of the verso, showing a fragment of the red foundation to which the boss was attached. Scale bars are 10 mm.*

CATALOGUE NUMBER 8

Id. No.	JE 32506 (SR 2504; CG 24144).
Object	Blinker.
Measurements	Length: 127.6. Width: 69.2. Thickness: 2.5. Thickness with gypsum: 4.8.
Remarks	Daressy (1902: 76, pl. XXII, see black and white photograph with JE 32400, Cat. No. 5).

Description

An oval piece of rawhide that terminates in a point on one end (figure A, B). This pointed part goes at the bottom, as indicated by the design. The object is painted or coloured yellow to imitate gold. The piece is decorated with a central design in high relief on the recto (figure C, D), consisting of a flowering plant with 13 petals, emerging from a double set of leaves that curve inward. A raised line (width: 2.8-3.1 mm) frames the design: it follows the shape of the object. The edge, starting at the right proper side, is pierced by stitch holes (figure C, D-F). A large one alternating with two small ones, which becomes a series of single large holes near the rounded top and then, on the left proper side, becomes a parallel row of punctures, the outermost one being larger than the inner one. This continues onto the point. The central part of the verso seems to have been covered with a layer of gypsum and then paint, glue or varnish.

Cat. No. 8, JE 32506. Overview of the recto (A) and verso (B).

Cat. No. 8, JE 32506. C) Detail of the deeply impressed motif (recto). Scale bar is 10 mm.

D

CATALOGUE | 245

Cat. No. 8, JE 32506. D) *Detail of the stitch holes at the edge (recto). Scale bar is 10 mm.*

Cat. No. 8, JE 32506. E, F) *Detail of the stitch holes at the edge (verso). Scale bar is 10 mm.*

CATALOGUE NUMBER 9

Id. No.	JE 32435D (SR 2506E; CG 24149).
Group	2506A-I.
Object	Support strap(?).
Measurements	Length: 80. Width: 56. Thickness: 1.5.
Remarks	Group of objects of varying origin but with the same JE and CG numbers. See also Cat. No. 3 and 11. Number 'D' does not exist. The fragment has a piece of reinforcement cloth at the verso, indicating previous conservation interventions, probably in the early 20th century. See Daressy (1902: 77).

Description

The end of a strip with part of the leather securing band still present (figure A, B). Broken on one end but oval on the other. The piece is enhanced at the edge (figure C-E), starting with a wide (at least 11.5 mm), folded strip (the extend of which could not be determined) on top of which is a wide red leather strip (width: 11 mm). This in turn is adorned, lengthwise down the centre, with another strip of indeterminable colour (width: 7.5 mm). The set is secured with running stiches of sinew (figure D, E). Concentrically is a strip of yellowish leather (width: 7.6 mm) further enhanced by a narrow strip of green that runs lengthwise down the centre (width: 3.2 mm). This set is glued on rather than sewn as there are no stitch holes visible. A horizontal slit (width: 15 mm) is cut between the two sets of decoration (figure F, G), used to attach the red strap (width: 8-11 mm; length cannot be determined anymore as it broke off short), the attachment of which is still *in situ*. It goes through the slit twice.

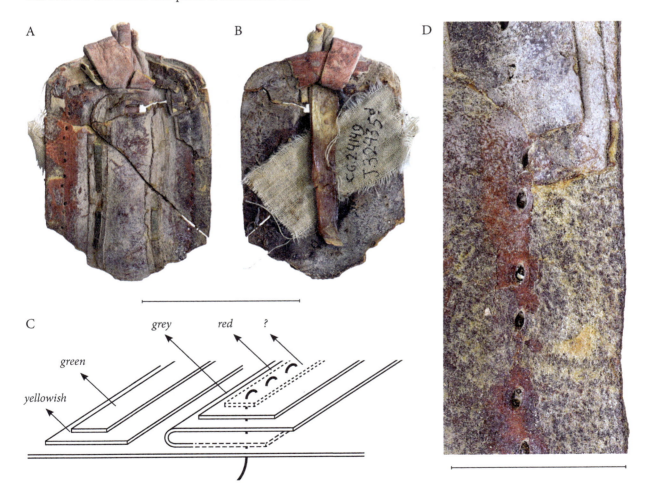

Cat. No. 9, JE 32435D. *Overview of the recto (A) and verso (B); C) Diagram of the construction; D) Detail of the right proper edge (recto). Scale bar C is 10 mm.*

Cat. No. 9, JE 32435D. E) Detail of the left proper edge (recto). Scale bar is 10 mm.

Cat. No. 9, JE 32435D. Details of the edge (recto, F, and verso, G), showing the slit with attachment and decorative sets of appliqué. Scale bars are 10 mm.

CATALOGUE NUMBER 10

Id. No. SR 2503A-C (CG 24152).
Object Unknown.
Measurements A) Length: 413. Width: 42. Thickness white foundation: 0.2. Thickness total: 2. Thickness red strip: 0.15. Thickness green strip: 0.4.
B) Length: 210. Width: 34. Thickness white layer: 0.2. Thickness total: 1.4.
C) Width: 164. Height: 70. Thickness red foundation: 0.7. Thickness total: 2.3.
Remarks SR 2503A has pieces of reinforcement cloth at the back, indicating previous conservation interventions. Daressy (1902: 78).

Description

Two bands and one triangular fragment of leather with appliqué decoration.

A) White leather background with folded over edges on either side (figure A-C, G). These edges are secured with widely spaced running stitches of sinew, which also secures the outer set of applied decoration. The recto is decorated with a symmetrical design of a series of appliqué coloured leather strips made up of two strips on top of each other. The lower one being slightly wider and thus protrudes from under the narrower top one, which is placed lengthwise down the centre. At either side, the set consists of a green band (width: 6.6 mm) on top of which is a red one (width: 2.4 mm) that is affixed with the running stitches that secures the folded edges of the foundation as well. Possibly, the green was glued and the red stitched through for better adhesion. At either side, approximately 2.3 mm inwards from the described edge with decoration, a further set of strips is fixed to the foundation, consisting of a wider red one (width: 6 mm) on top of which is placed, lengthwise down the centre, a narrower green strip (width: 2 mm). The set is glued; stitching has not been used. The 10 mm space between these two sets shows signs of having once been covered with something, undoubtedly applied strip decoration (figure D). At the end of one long side a red piece of leather (length: 37.3 mm; width: 4.5 mm) protrudes. At one end, a row of stitch holes can be seen at right angle to the decoration (arrow in figure F), which might have been used to attach the strip to another object in order the enhance it. Some features suggests repair (arrow in figure E).

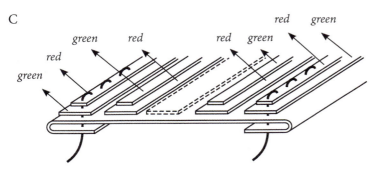

Cat. No. 10, SR 2503A. *Overview of the recto (A) and verso (B); C) Diagram of the construction.*

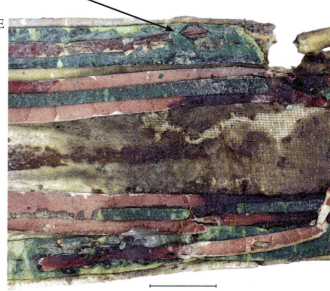

Cat. No. 10, SR 2503A. *D-G) Details. D) Detail of the recto, showing the appliqué decoration. Note the discolouration in the centre, probably due to the glue used to attach another (set of) appliqué; E) As D; note the red strip 'sewn' into the green strip underneath (arrow), probably as repair; F) As D; one end shows stitch holes (slits) to attach the strip to a surface (arrow); G) Detail of the verso, showing the folded edges as well as several red strips of leather glued onto it, the function of which is unclear. Scale bars are 10 mm.*

B) Piece of strap (originally part of a larger piece) of red to pinkish leather that is folded onto itself equally lengthwise (figure A-C). The fold is hidden by a thin piece of white leather (width: 30 mm), which is decorated with three sets of decorative strips: a wider green one (width: 7.5-8 mm) surmounted lengthwise centrally by a narrower red one (width: 1.5-2 mm). The set is secured to the pinkish foundation with small but widely spaced running stitches that are made of sinew (figure D; note the start of a new piece of red), with the stitch holes fairly regularly distributed at the verso (figure F). At the recto is a transverse cut visible in the pinkish foundation layer (figure E). At one side the white with decoration is still there, but it is absent at the other side of the cut: was the cut the result of the removal of this layer with decoration? The remnant of a diagonal cut is visible at the verso, at the break of the fragment. Probably glue was used to further secure the various layers.

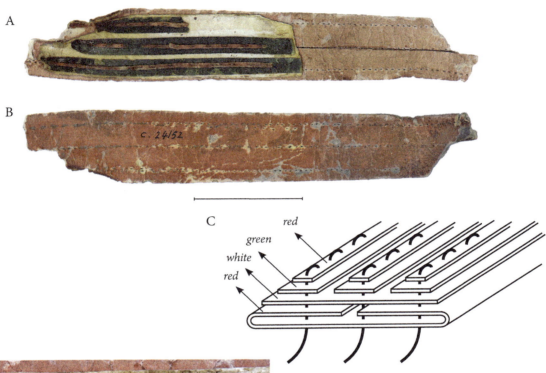

Cat. No. 10, SR 2503B. Overview of the recto (A) and verso (B); C) Diagram of the construction; D) Detail of the recto, showing the sinew stitching and start of another piece of red strip. Scale bar D is 10 mm.

E

Cat. No. 10, SR 2503B. *E) Detail of the recto, showing the cut at right angle to the length; F) Detail of the verso, showing the three rows of running stitching.*

F

C) A roughly triangular fragment of red leather that is torn off at the long edge and also partially at the diagonal edges (figure A-C). At the torn horizontal edge, the fragment has applied decoration consisting of a white foundation on top of which is attached three sets of strips of leather (figure D). The lower set is not preserved but the discoloration suggests it was once part of the design. The stitch holes might have been used to attach this decoration as well, although the rest of the decoration is glued. Additional rows of stitch holes can be seen at the intact diagonal edge (arrow in figure E); at one corner, two parallel rows are visible, suggesting this was the case for the entire edge. The subsequent set of decoration consists of a wider, red bottom strip (width: 6 mm) with a green strip (width: 2 mm) lengthwise down the centre. The last set consists of a wider, green bottom strip (width: 5.5 mm) with a red strip (width: 2 mm) lengthwise down the centre. Neither of these last two sets show stitching: they are secured with glue. Two strips, separated about 10 mm, run diagonally towards the first of the previously described sets of applied decoration; the widest of the two is green and the smaller one, on top of a white foundation, might have been red.

A

B

C

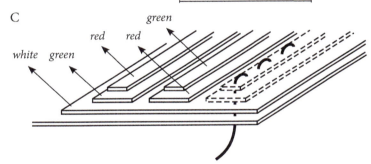

Cat. No. 10, SR 2503C. *Overview of the recto (A) and verso (B); C) Diagram of the construction; D) Detail of the recto, showing the appliqué and the emtpy stitch holes. Scale bar D is 10 mm.*

D

Cat. No. 10, SR 2503C. E) Detail of the recto, showing the two rows of stitch holes at one edge. Scale bar is 10 mm.

CATALOGUE NUMBER 11

Id. No. JE 32435 (SR 2506F; CG 24149).
Group 2506A-H.
Object Unknown.
Measurements Length: 42. Width: 31.6. Thickness: 1.5. Thickness edge: 7.
Remarks Group of objects of varying origin but with the same JE and CG numbers. See also Cat. No. 3 and 9. Probably part of Cat. No. 9, JE 32435D. See Daressy (1902: 77). Number 'D' does not exist.

Description
A small, roughly rectangular piece of red leather with an edge binding (figure A-C). A red strip of leather is folded over the edge and secured with stitching along the top. On the recto, parallel to the tip, is a strip of white leather (width: 12.4 mm), partially overlapping the red binding. On top of this, lengthwise down the centre, is a green strip of leather (width: 7.8 mm) stitched into place. A piece of leather, originally perhaps coloured yellow (width: 11 mm), crosses over the binding and the set of white and green strips, at right angle and is secured with big leather stitches (figure D). Beneath the binding (6.4 mm) is a horizontal line of glue (width: approximately 5 mm).

Cat. No. 11, JE 32435. Overview of the recto (A) and verso (B). Scale bar is 10 mm.

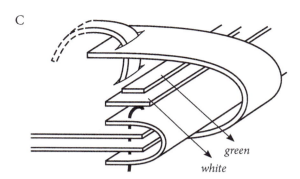

Cat. No. 11, JE 32435. *C) Diagram of the construction; D) Detail of the recto, showing the crossing over piece of leather. Note the remnants of glue below it. Scale bar is 5 mm.*

TOMB OF THUTMOSE IV

CATALOGUE NUMBER 12

Id. No.   JE 97801 (SR 3367; CG 46106).
Object   Bridle boss.
Measurements   Diameter: 84. Thickness: 3.5.
Remarks   Carter & Newberry (1904: 36).
Description

A nearly complete, circular boss (figure A-C), which is made of a fairly thick layer of rawhide, backed by a layer of what appears to be gesso and completed by a layer of coarse linen that serves as the backing. The layers are held together with an edge binding that consists of a strip of green leather (extending about 3-4 mm) on top of which is placed, at the recto, lengthwise down the centre, a red strip with a width of about 2.5 mm (figure D, E). The binding is secured with widely spaced running stitches of sinew (possibly only spun). At four parallel points, are sets of two bigger holes that seems to have been used to attach the boss to another surface (arrow in figure D). The centre is pierced by a hole (diameter: 9.0 mm).

The recto is decorated by an embossed floral motif (figure B, F). Radiating out from the central hole, it consists of four clumps of papyrus/lotus, each framed by incurving leaves/tendrils.

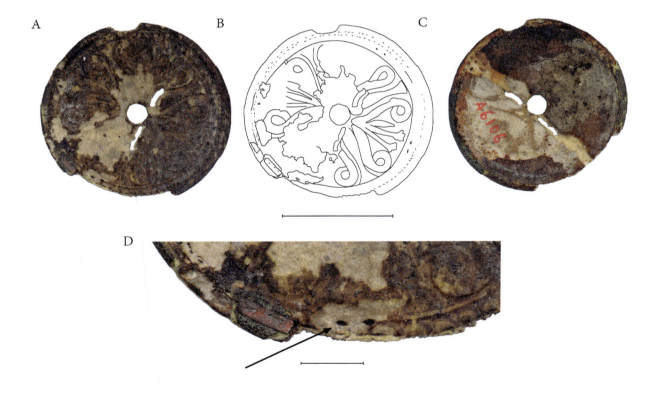

Cat. No. 12, JE 97801. *Overview of recto (A, B) and verso (C); D) Detail of the edge (recto) showing part of the binding and one set of larger stitch holes to attach the boss to another surface. Scale bar D is 10 mm.*

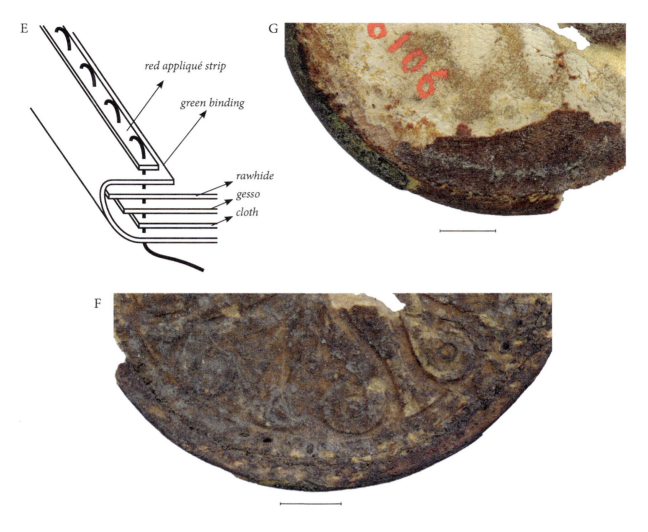

Cat. No. 12, JE 97801. *E) Diagram of the edge construction; F) Detail of the embossed floral motif at the recto; G) Detail of the verso showing the binding and the gesso with cloth. Scale bar F-G is 10 mm.*

CATALOGUE NUMBER 13

Id. No.	JE 97803 (SR 3369; TR 21 3 21 3).
Object	Support strap.
Measurements	Length: 80. Width: 60. Thickness: 2-4.
Remarks	Probably part of the "Thirty-one miscellaneous pieces of harness, trappings, sandals, leather bindings etc." (Carter & Newberry, 1904: 38) from chamber 3. The verso has, in ink, "81" or "18" written on it, as well as "R6J" in pencil.

Description

Broken piece of oval red leather (faded to pink), consisting of three layers in between which is sandwiched the extension of a protruding loop (figure A, B). This loop is situated at the oval end of the object and might have functioned as a toggle closure. It is inserted in a hole in the edge and is sandwiched with a relatively long extension between the thin backing and the second, thicker layer (arrow in figure F). The three layers of which the object is made are secured by a green leather binding that also forms a decorative edge on the recto (figure C, D). The visible layer at the verso (figure E, F) actually is a backing. It is attached after the white-with-green decoration strips at the recto, which is evident from the fact that the stitching that secures this decoration does not include the backing (figure

C). At the verso, the binding is secured with whip stitching. At the recto, the green binding is secured with running stitching, but includes a lengthwise folded white leather strip, which slightly protrudes from the binding (figure C, D).

The recto is decorated by a series of applied bands of leather (figure D). The outermost, as mentioned, is in green leather (formed by the binding, including the folded white strip, now lost for the most part). The next line is actually formed by the red background leather (3 mm wide), followed by a separate band of green (1.5 mm). Partially overlapping this strip lengthwise is a set of strips consisting of a broad white band with folded edges, on top of which are secured several other strips. Of this white strip, only about 0.3 mm shows. The first strip is a relatively wide (about 3 mm) green strip that is secured along one edge only with running stitches made of sinew. This is followed by a white band (the white strip mentioned before) of about 1.5 mm width. The next band is an applied strip of green (1.6 mm wide) that is secured lengthwise down the centre with sinew running stitches. Finally, the terminal edge of the white strip is visible (width about 1.5 mm).

Cat. No. 13, JE 97803. Overview of the recto (A) and verso (B).

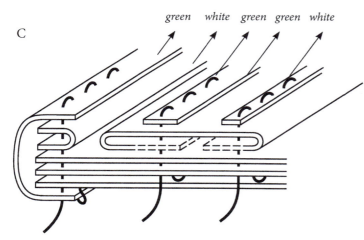

Cat. No. 13, JE 97803. C) Diagram of the construction; D) Detail of the enhanced edge (recto). Scale bar D is 10 mm.

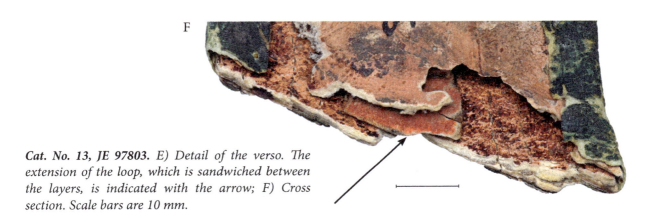

Cat. No. 13, JE 97803. E) Detail of the verso. The extension of the loop, which is sandwiched between the layers, is indicated with the arrow; F) Cross section. Scale bars are 10 mm.

CATALOGUE NUMBER 14

Id. No. JE 97802 (SR 3368; CG 46109).
Object Support strap.
Measurements Length: 100. Width: 82. Thickness: 3.
Remarks The verso has, in ink, "16" or "91" written on it. The fragment is incomplete so we are not sure about the relative position of the original object but the description has the intact short edge on top. Carter & Newberry (1904: 36).

Description
Rectangular fragment (figure A, B), consisting of two layers: the verso is red whereas the recto is white with applied decoration (figure J). The two layers are secured by a green leather binding that also forms a decorative edge on the recto (figure C, E). The binding overlaps, in stair-step fashion, a lengthwise folded red strip, which, in its turn, overlaps a single green strip of leather in stair-step fashion. The binding is relatively wide (9 mm), the red strip is relatively narrow (only 1 mm) and the bottom green strip is 2 mm wide. The entire construction is secured with stitches of sinew (two threads, S-twisted), which seems to be interlocking running stitching on the recto, but since the verso clearly shows (intact) running stitches (encircled in figure F, G), the object must have been sewn in at least two different stages: the folded green first and added to the white recto, and the binding afterwards. Note that large areas of the binding at the verso are, accidentally, not included in the stitching. The binding seems, as with the following square (see below), to consist of a separately attached element at each edge, rather than being folded at the corners to continue along the next

edge. The long vertical sides are made first as they go under the binding of the short sides.

The fragment is further decorated with a square that is made of a green leather strip, inwards of the edge decoration, which in its turn frames a motif described below. This strip consists of four separate pieces for each length, rather than one long strip that is folded at the edges. It is secured in the same way as is the binding. It appears to have been secured to the white recto first, before this set was secured to the red backing of the verso (figure D, E).

The space within the square is further enhanced by a floral motif (figure H) that is made of thin strips of green leather, which is punctuated with red. It consists of a central cross with one set of ends terminating in triangles that are made of small inset pieces of red leather representing the flowers; the other sets, ovals, represent the flower buds. These are placed underneath the green and at some points protrude from underneath (arrow in figure H). The cross pieces are flanked by green spirals, resembling the tendrils of plants. On top of the central point of the cross is a squarish piece of red leather, secured by a wide, single 'stitch' of green leather that passes through all layers. This must be a reinforcement, because at the same spot at the verso is an attachment of a lengthwise folded, relatively thick strip of leather (see below). The motif is secured with comparable stitching as for the edge and the green square (figure D). The space below this green square with floral motif, separated by the horizontal green band of the square, combines several techniques (figure I). Vertically, it is divided in wider, deeper lying areas that are filled with green strips of leather running under the green square and secured with it (most likely also glued). These are separated from each other by higher lines, which seems to have been left undecorated (*i.e.* showing the white colour of the recto). It is unclear whether the areas that accommodate the green decoration was impressed from the, now, recto or that the separating areas were impressed from the other, now invisible, surface. The bands with green leather measures between 4 and 5 mm; the intermediate bands are about 2.5-3.5 mm.

The verso has, approximately at the length of the fragment, three small pieces of lengthwise folded, relatively thick (1.5 mm) leather attached transversely (width: 6 mm). Two are secured at either side, at the edge; in the middle (arrow in figure B), at the recto complying with the centre part of the floral motif, is another one. These might have served as attachment of the object to another surface, but, more likely, it functioned as loops for pulling through straps (now lost), as seen in the Tano leather (BI-001, Cat. No. 81) and several Amarna examples (see Chapter 2 'Identification of Parts'). The object has several other holes but no surviving material hints at its use.

Cat. No. 14, JE 97802. *Overview of the recto (A) and verso (B).*

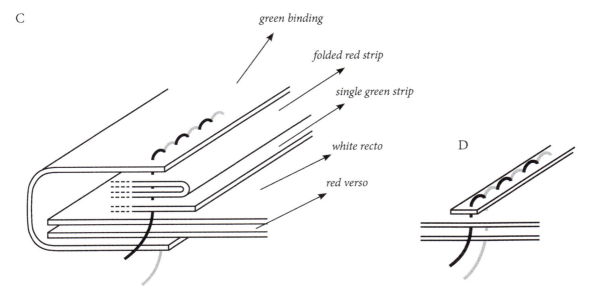

Cat. No. 14, JE 97802. Diagrams of the construction of the edge (C) and inner appliqué (D).

Cat. No. 14, JE 97802. Details. E) The edge at the recto. Note the large stitch holes at the green binding (arrow); F, G) The recto shows intact running stitches (examples are encircled). Scale bars are 10 mm.

Cat. No. 14, JE 97802. *Details. H) Vegetal motif. The arrow points to the protruding red filling of the motif; I) Detail of the lower part of the object; J) Cross section, cf. figure C. Scale bars are 10 mm.*

CATALOGUE NUMBER 15

Id. No. SR 3385 (TR 21 3 21 10).
Object Unknown.
Measurements Length: 108.2. Width: 36.9. Thickness: 3.9. Width binding: 6.0-7.4 (incl. approximately 4 mm wide white inner layer).
Remarks Probably part of the "Thirty-one miscellaneous pieces of harness, trappings, sandals, leather bindings etc." (Carter & Newberry, 1904: 38) from chamber 3. "18" or "81" written on it in black ink and "225" in pencil. The orientation of the object is unknown but we describe it with the intact rounded side at the top.

Description
An object (figure A-C) that is made of two thicknesses of leather, which were bright red originally but have faded to a pale pink. The object is incomplete: it is an elongated oval with one intact, short side. The long sides are straight. The two layers are secured with a green edge binding, which is folded over the edge of the two thicknesses and overlap, at the recto, a lengthwise-folded white strip (figure C-E). Only tiny remnants of the stitching survives, showing that the layers are secured with running stitching of sinew (figure D). Twenty millimetres inwards of the binding a set of two strips is added, consisting of a wider red one (width: 5.2 mm) with a green one running lengthwise along the middle on top (width: 2.2). These too are secured with running stitches of sinew. The stitching is relatively coarse, showing different lengths of stitches and interstitch spaces. Vague pairing of the stitch holes of the edge binding can be noticed.

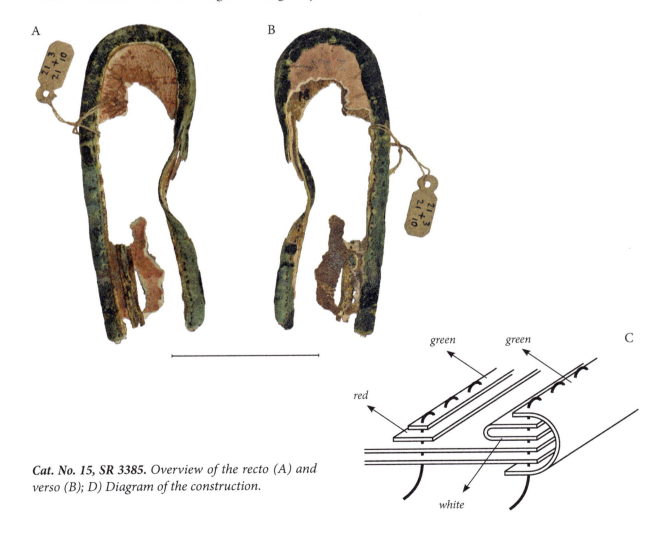

Cat. No. 15, SR 3385. *Overview of the recto (A) and verso (B); D) Diagram of the construction.*

D

E

Cat. No. 15, SR 3385. *Details. D) The edge on the recto and the appliqué. Note the intact stitches; E) Edge of the verso. Scale bars are 10 mm.*

CATALOGUE NUMBER 16

Id. No.	CG 46108 (SR 3386).
Object	Unknown.
Measurements	Width top: 135.6. Width bottom: 113.4. Length: 248. Width painted vertical lines with dots: 3.5. Thickness: 3.2.
Remarks	The verso has, in ink, "19." written on it in black ink and "R Iv" in pencil. The orientation of the object is unknown but we assume that the icicles/petals were orientated downwards. Thus, the horizontal applied decoration was at the top of the object. Carter & Newberry (1904: 37).

Description
Rectangular object with concave vertical sides (figure A, B). The shorter, horizontal sides are straight but the corners slightly protrude from the edges, which is probably due to tightly pulling the attachment. Narrow leather straps protrude from holes in all intact corners (figure C–E), no doubt to attach the object. The horizontal top edge is intact; the bottom edge, however, lacks the left corner as well as a small rectangular part of the edge decoration further towards the right hand corner. The left vertical edge misses a near-rectangular part of the decoration, including a small bit of the horizontal band of decoration. The recto shows a cracked surface, resulting in the loss of the topmost layer of the leather in various places. Horizontal splitting of a layer is a common feature in archaeological leather. The cracking is caused by use and age. The verso shows large gaps that are caused by decay. Darker spots suggest that bacterial decay is ongoing.

The edges of the recto are folded around the edges of the verso (figure H, I). This is done in such a way that, at the corners, the folding of the long edges overlap those of the vertical edges. The stitching, which secures this binding (figure F), secures, at the recto, another set of strips as well, consisting of a white bottom one, on top of which is placed, lengthwise and in stair-step fashion, a green strip. The edge binding, including the set of strips next to it (see below) is pre-fabricated and attached with running stitches to the red recto, after which it was added to the verso and secured by using the interstitch spaces, resulting in a seemingly interlocking running stitch. However, at the verso the stitches clearly have interstitch space, suggesting that half of the stitches visible at the recto do not penetrate all layers (double running stitch; figure F, H). The stitches are made with sinew (two threads, S-twisted). These stitches are close to the edge of the upper green strip rather than the centre so as to include the, probably narrower, white strip (which protrudes 1.1 mm from the inside edge of the green strip). The total width of this enhanced binding is 6.5 mm. Slightly inwards (approximately 1.8 mm), at all sides, is a comparable set of white and green strips of leather, but narrower (width: 4.2 mm; figure G). Here, the top green strip is placed lengthwise down the centre of the white bottom one and secured in a comparable procedure as described previously for the edge (also made of sinew – two threads, S-twisted). In both sets of decoration the strips are either folded to make the angle between the horizontal and vertical sides (arrow in figure C) or simply turned around the corner (double arrow in figure C).

The horizontal band of decoration has some surprising combination of techniques, which necessitates a detailed step-for-step description (figure I, J, K. The numbers refer to the various elements in figure K). The first horizontal band is of white leather (2), which slightly protrudes from the wide green one on top (1; width: 6.7). This green band is secured with stitching as described above (*i.e.* the two-step procedure of the decoration and adding the two layers to the object). The next white horizontal line (3) is probably obtained by cutting away a strip of the green, due to which the white layer (2) became visible again. This means that the next green horizontal band (4) was part of the first mentioned, which might be the reason that it is secured with one row of stitches rather than two (total width: 5.0 mm). Next follows a white band (5; total width: 7.7 mm), again obtained by cutting away part of the green layer on top. However, here also the surface of the underlying white layer was cut away, most likely accidentally (arrow in figure J). This seems to indicate that this green decoration was applied as one, to be separated by the cutting after it was applied. Thus the icicles/petals, which follows (6: width: 7.7 mm) seems to have been attached individually, secured with two stitches (one in the centre and one at the tip), but actually were not: it was a strip with the icicles/petals cut from one edge, after which the top part was cut off. How far the white layer continues is not clear. What follows is a lengthwise folded, relatively thick strip of red leather (7), on top of which is placed, lengthwise down the centre, a strip of green (8; total width: 5.8 mm). The two are secured with the previously discussed two-step stitching at either side. The last part of this decoration is rather unclear. There are two strips of green (9, 11), in between which is a strip of white (10; total width: 6.4). It is clear from the cut marks that something was cut away but it is not at all clear what the white layer is; likely, only the green upper surface was removed. Below the last green strip again a narrow white strip is visible (12), which seems to have been made by removing the red upper surface of the recto. It is remarkable that this last green strip is secured with true, evenly-spaced running stitches, rather than the two-step stitching seen in the rest of the object. This transverse band of decoration was applied before the edge decoration because it runs under it. It is not certain when the binding was attached, but since the binding is simply the folded edge of the recto over the verso, it is plausible that this was done first.

The painted decoration (figure L; dots between vertical lines with an average width of 3.5 mm) was added before the edge decoration (but not before the binding was made), evidenced by the fact that the appliqué set runs over the paint. The horizontal decoration was applied before the painted decoration, because the latter always terminates distinctly from the applied decoration.

Cat. No. 16, CG 46108. Overview of the recto (A) and verso (B).

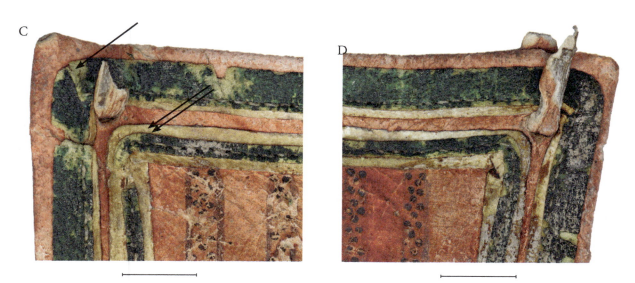

Cat. No. 16, CG 46108. Details. C) Left top corner of the recto; D) Right top corner of the recto. The arrows point to the different ways the decoration was applied at the corners. Scale bars are 10 mm.

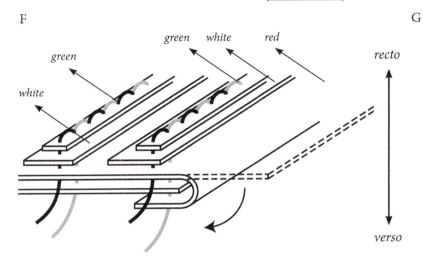

Cat. No. 16, CG 46108. *Details. E) Right lower corner and part of the edge of the recto; F) Diagram of the the enhanced edge binding. Black line: Phase I - prefabrication of the appliqué; Grey line: Phase II - putting appliqué in place; G) The edge binding and inward set of appliqué decoration; H) Broken corner of the verso; I) Top (seen from verso) with the intact corners. Scale bars are 10 mm.*

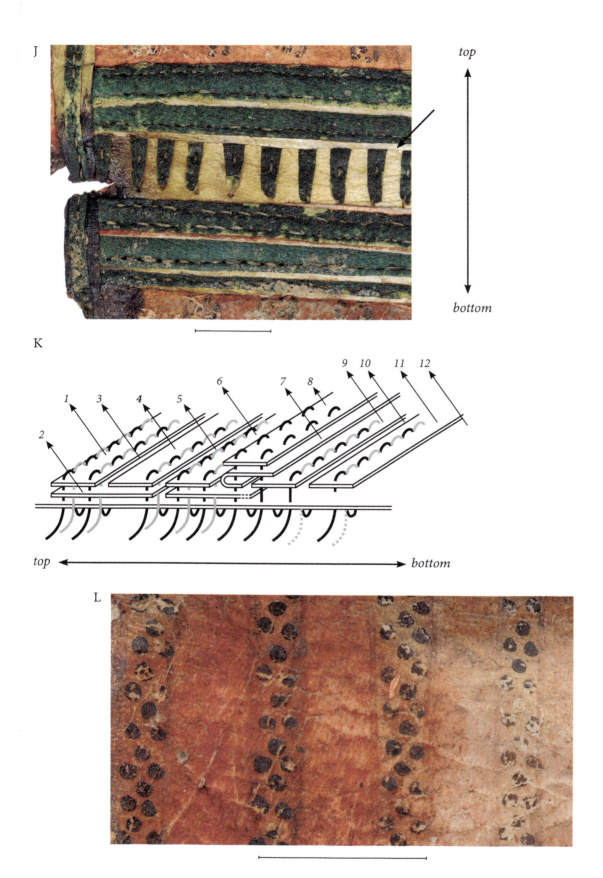

Cat. No. 16, CG 46108. Details. J) Transverse band of decoration on the recto. The arrow point to the cut away underlying white layer, as explained in the text); K) Diagram of J (uncertainty is expressed by dashed lines); L) Painted decoration of the recto. Scale bars are 10 mm.

CATALOGUE NUMBER 17

Id. No. JE 97827 (SR 3388; TR 21 3 21 2).
Object Fragment of wrist guard(?).
Measurements Length: 90. Width: 32-57. Thickness: 1-1.2.
Remarks Probably part of the "Thirty-one miscellaneous pieces of harness, trappings, sandals, leather bindings etc." (Carter & Newberry, 1904: 38) from chamber 3. The verso has, in pencil, "R 26" written on it.

Description
A tongue of red leather with a green binding (approximately 4.5 mm wide; figure A, B). The binding (figure C-E) is secured with zS_2 widely spaced running stitching, which are made of sinew. The fragment was ripped off. There are signs of being cut on one side. Note the strange angle the tip of the fragments makes at one side. This tip is darker in colour than the rest, which might be due to handling.

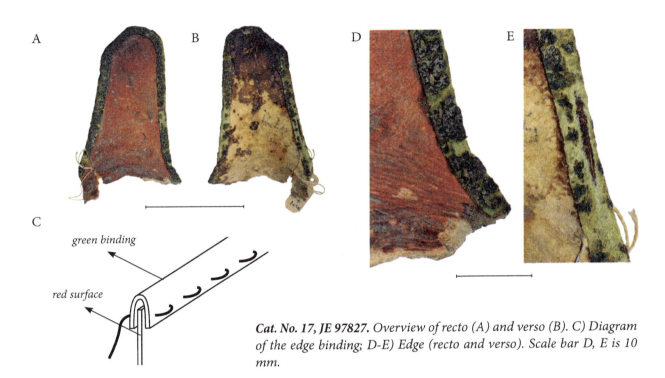

Cat. No. 17, JE 97827. Overview of recto (A) and verso (B). C) Diagram of the edge binding; D-E) Edge (recto and verso). Scale bar D, E is 10 mm.

CATALOGUE NUMBER 18

Id. No. JE 97827 (SR 3394; TR 21 3 21 7).
Object Unknown.
Measurements Length: appr. 180. Width: 27.5-62.7. Thickness edge: 5.
Remarks Probably part of the "Thirty-one miscellaneous pieces of harness, trappings, sandals, leather bindings etc." (Carter & Newberry, 1904: 38) from chamber 3. The verso has, in ink, "18" or "81" written on it.

Description
The object is roughly rectangular, of which one end is curved (figure A, B). Lengthwise, it is incomplete, leaving the original shape indeterminable (but most likely oval). Although the colours have somewhat changed through time, they are still identifiable.
The object consists of three thin layers of leather, of which the recto is white and the verso is light brown/reddish in colour. The layer in between is darkish brown. At one end, a small patch of cloth adheres to the verso, but it does not seem to have been part of the original construction.

Along the edge, a green leather binding secures the three layers (figure C-E). This binding is further enhanced, at the recto, with an edging of white leather (width: 8.8 mm) with, lengthwise down the middle, a green strip stitched onto it (width: 6.5 mm), thus obscuring the edge of the binding. The binding, together with the white/green set is secured along with two parallel lines of running stitches at the edges of the topmost and narrowest strip (figure F). These, and all other stitches, are made of sinew, consisting of two thin parts that are twisted S-wise. The innermost of these two rows, however, does not include the green binding at the reverse, but just misses it. The stitches are largely intact at the recto, but they are far less complete at the verso and often show fibrous ends. The presence of several intact stitches suggest that this was caused by rubbing of the object with the under surface, to which it might have been attached rather than that it was caused by being torn off.

Inwards from the set of strips is another row of densely packed running stitches, the distance to the edge of which slightly varies (average of 3.5 mm). A vague pattern of pairing of the stitch holes can be seen in some areas, but it is less distinct at other points. Almost all stitches are broken on both sides of the object, in contrast to the ones securing the enhanced edge binding, but remnants remain in some stitch holes. Possibly, these stitches secured the object to another surface (of which the less well organised arrangement might also be an indication?) and were taken off. There is no indication that this was done by force; the smooth cross section of the stitches contrasts with the cross section of the edge stitches at the verso (which are fibrous), suggesting that they have been cut off (but not other signs of the use of a knife, such as cuts, are seen in the object). Also, there are no torn stitch holes, which would have been the case if it were removed by force without using a knife.

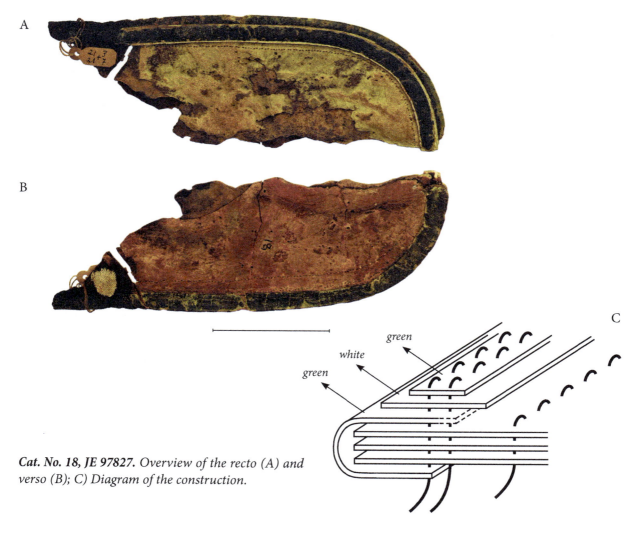

Cat. No. 18, JE 97827. *Overview of the recto (A) and verso (B); C) Diagram of the construction.*

Cat. No. 18, JE 97827. *Details. D) The enhanced edge at the recto; E) The edge at the verso; F) The row of running stitching at either side of the green top most strip. Scale bars are 10 mm.*

CATALOGUE NUMBER 19

Id. No.	SR 3375 (CG 46110).
Object	Unknown.
Measurements	Length: 220. Height: 140.5-85.4-149.5. Thickness top edge: 5.9-13.8. Thickness overall: 4.7. Width edge binding total: 11.
Remarks	The verso has, in black ink, "10" written on it. Possibly recovered from chamber 3 (the number of the room is between brackets in the publication by Carter & Newberry, 1904: 37). The orientation of the object is uncertain, but the description is done as the object is depicted in the figure.

Description

A piece of leather that is roughly vase-shaped (figure A, B) consisting of two thicknesses that are secured by a decorative green edge binding. The recto is plain and made of uneven pieces of beige/white leather, which are stitched together with whip stitches that are made of sinew (figure J). A curious feature is the various paired stitch holes at the recto (some are, as example, encircled in figure A). Although they seem random, they clearly follow the edge of the object too, mainly at the rounded lower part. Most of these stitch holes are small but there is a set of larger ones more or less in the centre. The bottom of the vase is damaged through human agency rather than the result of natural decay (figure E). Shortly below the top there is a modern restoration with textile and glue(?). The verso is made of thinner leather that had a bright red colour but has faded, albeit irregularly, to a dusky pink. Moreover, the upper part is lighter than the lower part. This side is much more destroyed; a small piece of ancient linen adheres to it (arrow in figure B). At the top, at either end, is a slit situated diagonal in the corner (figure G, H). On the left proper a knotted (overhand knot), narrow strip of red leather cord survives (figure I), which probably extended along the top and helped to affix this piece to something else, although the red side would have faced the object. At the flaring points of the vase are small vertical slits that presumably were made to attach this object to something else (figure D).

The edge binding (figure C-F) consists of a wide strip of green that is folded over the edge of the object proper. At the recto, a set consisting of a wider white strip on top of which is added a narrower green strip lengthwise through the centre, is secured over the edge binding. Thus the binding does not protrude from the set; in fact, the inner row of running stitches go through the layers but do not include the green binding as the stitches are situated slightly inwards from its edge proper. Probably this is accidental, the original idea being that this row of stitching also would pierce the strip. Interestingly, at the top, none of the rows of stitches include the edge binding at the verso. The stitches, made with sinew, are regular with fairly big interstitch spaces. The binding at the right flaring point is incomplete, but it is not clear whether this is original or damage, possibly due to use. The decorative set at the top is separate from the comparable set at the rest of the object, which is folded at the flaring edges in order to follow the outline adequately.

Cat. No. 19, SR 3375. *Overview of the recto (A) and verso (B). The encircled features are explained in the text. The arrow points to a small fragment of ancient linen.*

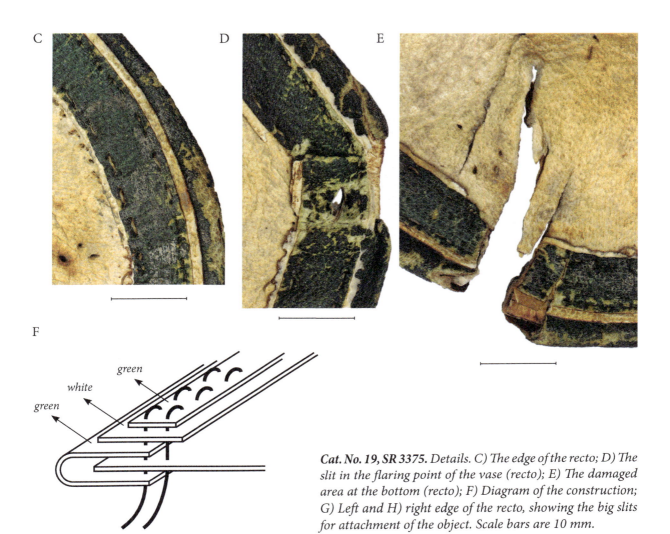

Cat. No. 19, SR 3375. Details. C) The edge of the recto; D) The slit in the flaring point of the vase (recto); E) The damaged area at the bottom (recto); F) Diagram of the construction; G) Left and H) right edge of the recto, showing the big slits for attachment of the object. Scale bars are 10 mm.

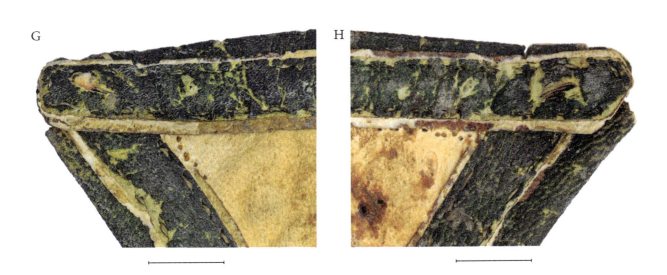

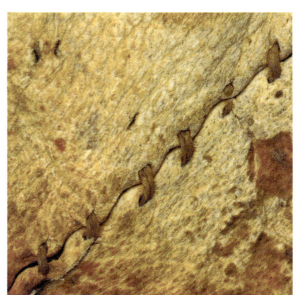
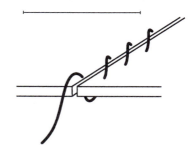

Cat. No. 19, SR 3375. Details. I) The remnant of the red strap for attachment of the object; J) The whip stitching that secures the two pieces of white leather of the recto with a diagram of the construction. Scale bars are 10 mm.

CATALOGUE NUMBER 20

Id. No.	JE 97809 (SR 3389; CG 46111).
Object	Unknown.
Measurements	Length: 103-113. Width: 170-207. Thickness: 1.1.
Remarks	The verso has, in ink, "21" written on it besides the CG number in red. Note the worsened condition relative to time of publication by Carter & Newberry (1904: 37). The description is done with the orientation of the piece resulting in pendentive icicles/petals and floral motifs. Thus the wider of the two long edges is regarded as the top edge.

Description

Trapezoidal piece of thin leather (figure A, B), the recto of which is painted white with additional coloured, painted decoration, rather than further leather enhancement. The verso is brown-red. One of the sloping sides has a strip of leather (width: 7.3-9.7 mm), which might have been folded around the edge, but the strip is clearly torn off at the edge and no clear evidence of such a construction is visible at the verso. The strip is secured with narrow, but widely spaced running stitches: the stitch holes are in pairs and of triangular shape, which is due to the pulling of the thread in the corner of the, originally oval or slit-like, stitch hole (figure F). The opposite edge had a strip too, but it is entirely lost.

There is no indication that a comparable strip was attached to the top and bottom edge. However, the top edge has stitch holes, also in pairs, which might have been used to attach the object to a surface. Remarkably, these stitch holes are more oval in shape, rather than triangular. At the bottom edge two small patches of gold foil are visible (encircled in figures D, E).

The painted decoration consists of repeating bands of various motifs (figure G, H; these are numbered in figure A to clarify the description). The painting is rather coarse without continuity in the width of the lines and shape of the motifs. The right, top and bottom edges have a green band; this is not visible at the left because the strip of leather is lost here and the painting ran over the strip, as is the case with the opposite side. Undoubtedly, it too would have been decorated with a green band. The horizontal bands of decoration are separated from one and another by green register lines (width between 1.2-2.5 mm). The decoration starts with a band of triangles (1; width: 11.0 mm) or icicles/petals, alternating in red and green, which are directed with their point downwards. Below this is a band of green running spirals (2; width: 9.0 mm) with red dots in their centres, which is followed by stylized lotuses (3; width: 17.0 mm), in green and red, and papyrus umbells in green only. The blooms are separated by red dots. The centre band (4; width: 9.0 mm), dividing the decoration in two parts of three bands, consists of a zigzag line in green. The following band (5; width: 10.5 mm) consists again of icicles/petals, disrupting symmetry with the top half. The triangles in this band are more densely packed in contrast to those of the top strip. Another band of lotuses and papyrus flowers follow (6; width: 18.0 mm), similar to the previous band (3). Finally, at the bottom, there is again a band of icicles/petals (7; width: 9.0-16.1 mm). These, however, differ greatly in height from one side to the other, due to the fact that the height of the object is not the same at either side: it is clear that the craftsman started painting at the longest side since that band of decoration is parallel to this edge.

Cat. No. 20, JE 97809. Overviews of the recto (A) and verso (B). The numbers are used in the description.

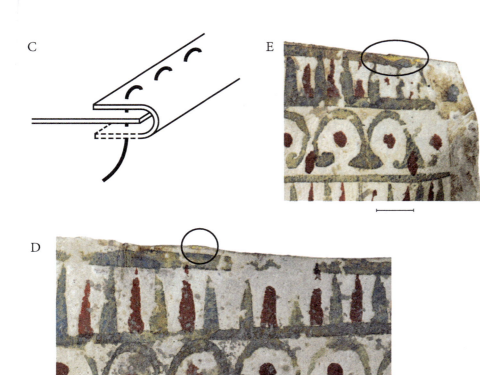

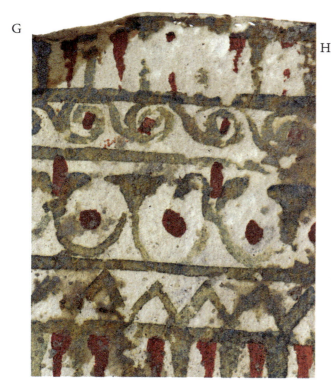

Cat. No. 20, JE 97809. *Details. C) Diagram of the edge; D, E) Small remnants of gold foil on the edge (recto; encircled); F) Detail of the edge (recto); G, H) Details of the painted design of the recto. Scale bars are 10 mm.*

CATALOGUE NUMBER 21

Id. No. JE 97826 (SR 3393; TR 21 3 21 8).
Object Unknown.
Measurements Length: 67. Width: 38. Thickness: 18.
Remarks Probably part of the "Thirty-one miscellaneous pieces of harness, trappings, sandals, leather bindings etc." (Carter & Newberry, 1904: 38) from chamber 3. "SR 3393" is written on in pencil.

Description

A roughly rectangular end of a longer object (figure A, B). The sides might have been reinforced originally, but currently only the stitch holes at one edge are visible. At the recto, there are two rows at the only intact long edge, which flank an incised line (thus not visible at the verso; figure C). Further evidence of decoration is provided by one of the short edges, which still shows remnants of an edge binding (but nothing remains of this at the verso). The stitch holes are in pairs. Some impressed vegetal design seems to adorn the recto, but it is too vague to identify it. Remnants of gypsum adhere to the verso.

Cat. No. 21, JE 97826. *Overviews of the recto (A) and verso (B); C) Detail of the edge (recto). Note the paired stitch holes. Scale bar C is 10 mm.*

CATALOGUE NUMBER 22

Id. No. JE 97820 (SR 3376; CG 46103).
Object Pouch flap.
Measurements Width: 212-220. Height: 17. Thickness: 3.7.
Remarks The verso has "6" or "9" written on it in black ink and "R4" in pencil. Carter & Newberry (1904: 35).

Description

A trapezoidal piece of leather resembling the flap and starting point of an envelope (figure A, C). The object suffered considerably, resulting in three holes. The long, straight edge shows features of having been torn off. It probably went around a corner of some sort as is indicated by the slightly curled

Cat. No. 22, JE 97820. *Overview of the recto (A) and verso (B).*

long edge. The tip of the triangle shows two holes (figure D), the function of which seems to be to close the flap (*cf.* the closure system in the Tano flap, L1 #015, L5 #034, C5 #035, Cat. No. 93-95). The recto is decorated with impressed motif. The edges are blank, then a raised line frames the internal decoration (partially damaged), showing a bird, according to Carter and Newberry (1904: 35) a falcon, with outstretched wings and sun-disc on its head. They indentified that the talons of the bird rest on "the head of a crouching figure of a Northerner on the one side and a Southerner on the other". Below the bird is a *nb*-sign, possibly followed by a R^c-symbol. The bird's head is flanked by two cartouches, both facing inwards. The left one contains the prenomen; the right one the nomen of the king. Note the (ancient?) fingerprints on the tip of the recto (figure E).

Cat. No. 22, JE 97820. *Details. C) The wing of the bird; D) The tip, showing the two holes for closing the flap. Scale bars are 10 mm.*

Cat. No. 22, JE 97820. *Details. E) The ancient(?) finger print. Scale bar is 10 mm.*

CATALOGUE NUMBER 23

Id. No.   SR 3387 (TR 21 3 21 4).
Object   Wrist guard.
Measurements   Length: 243. Width: 103-119.3-105.1. Thickness: 2.2.
Remarks   Probably part of the "Thirty-one miscellaneous pieces of harness, trappings, sandals, leather bindings etc." (Carter & Newberry, 1904: 38) from chamber 3. "14" in pen, black ink inside. The TR is added in pencil outside.

Description
A rectangular piece of rawhide that curves around as to enclose the wrist (figure A-C). It comes to a point more towards one of the short ends, rather than in the the centre of the length.

***Cat. No. 23, SR 3387.** Overviews (A, B) and from aside (C).*

CATALOGUE NUMBER 24

Id. No.   SR 3374 (CG 46112).
Object   Wrist guard.
Measurements   Length: 343. Width at elbow: 292. Width of extension: 35. Thickness: 2.
Remarks   Found beside the chariot body in room 3. "5" written in ink, besides the CG number in red. Carter & Newberry (1904: 37). Schwarz (2000: Catalogue C, no. 38 [no page numbers given]).

Description
A wrist guard in red leather (figure A, B). At one side, the lower half is broken off but still available for study. There are several cut marks from a knife or sword at one side only (figure I); this side is also missing a small portion of the edge of the front. Moreover, there is a horizontal band of about 70-80 mm wide at the wrist area (arrow in figure A, B), which shows discoloration, suggesting the presence of another element.
The wrist guard is made of one long piece of leather that is folded over and stitched closed. The portion

at the wrist was cut to a rounded point at one end to guard the thumb. The edge at this end has a green, leather binding (3 mm wide), which is secured with widely spaced running stitches of sinew (two threads twisted S-wise; figure G).

The opposite edge (*i.e.* at the elbow) is straight and has a binding of green leather too. This, however, is further enhanced by overlapping sets of leather strips, in stair-step fashion (figure C-F). The first set consists of a lengthwise folded strip of white leather (1 mm wide) on top of which a green strip (4 mm wide) is applied in stair-step fashion. These are secured with sinew stitching (two threads, twisted S-wise). This stitching, instead of widely spaced running stitches, as seen with the edging at the front, is closely spaced at the recto using the same stitch hole twice. As described previously (*e.g.* JE 97802, Cat. No. 14), the edge binding is pre-fabricated and sewn together, after which it was added to the recto and secured by using the interstitch spaces, resulting in a seemingly interlocking running stitch. However, at the verso the stitches clearly shows interstitch space, suggesting that half of the stitches visible at the recto do not penetrate all layers (double running stitch; figure D). The same type of stitching is used for the subsequent sets.

Note that parts of the enhanced edge are secured with normal running stitching (*cf.* figure C1 with C2). The next set consists of a thicker, lengthwise folded strip of red leather (still showing 1.5 mm) with a green strip on top (2 mm wide). This green strip sometimes protrudes from under the final set of strips, consisting of a white bottom strip (4 mm wide) on top of which is placed, lengthwise through the centre, a green strip (2 mm wide). This last set is secured with a single row of stitches lengthwise through the centre. All strips except one have about the same thickness: the second folded red one, however, is substantially thicker and seems to have been cut from the same sort of leather as the wrist guard proper (figure E).

The long edges show stitch holes, in some of which are still remnants of the stitches (figure H), which were used to close the wrist guard. This seems to have been done with running stitches and an overlapping seam. At either edge is a round notch that was cut into the band. It marks the difference in diameter of the wrist and elbow, and might have had a function in securing the wrist guard and providing for a better fit of the wrist part by means of the additional piece, now lost, that was obviously tied around it judging from the discolouration.

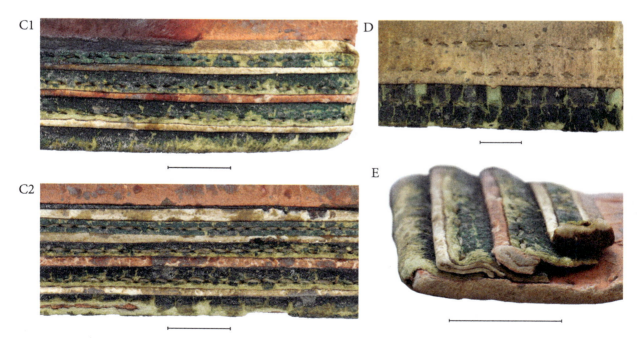

Cat. No. 24, SR 3374 *(for overviews see next page). Details. C) Enhanced edge of the recto, showing two different types of stitching (C1, 2); D) The stitching of the edge at the verso; E) Cross section to show how the appliqué is built up. See next page for the diagram of the construction. Scale bars are 10 mm.*

Cat. No. 24, SR 3374. *A, B) Overviews. The arrow points to the band of discolouration, suggesting another strap was used to secure the guard.*

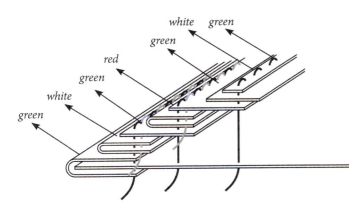

Cat. No. 24, SR 3374. *F) Diagram of the construction of the enhanced edge; G) Detail of top part. Scale bar is 10 mm.*

Cat. No. 24, SR 3374. *H) Detail of edge, showing stitch holes to close the wrist guard (inset). Scale bar is 10 mm.*

Cat. No. 24, SR 3374. *I) Detail the cut marks of a sward or dagger. Scale bar is 10 mm.*

CATALOGUE NUMBER 25

Id. No.	SR 3390 (CG 46113).
Object	Fragment of wrist guard(?).
Measurements	116 x 120. Thickness: 2.3.
Remarks	Carter & Newberry (1904: 38).

Description

Red leather fragment (figure A, B) of possibly a wrist guard. The red is partially faded to pink. It is folded over at the edges and secured with running stitches of sinew (figure C). The stitch holes are pre-pricked. The narrow part seems to have been bound around with something. The darker colour is due to deterioration. If it is part of a wrist guard, it either differs from SR 3374 (Cat. No. 24) or has been repaired/re-used; the folded parts and the protruding part that winds around is not recognised in the complete wrist guard.

Cat. No. 25, SR 3390. *For overviews see next page. C) Detail of the stitching. Scale bar is 10 mm.*

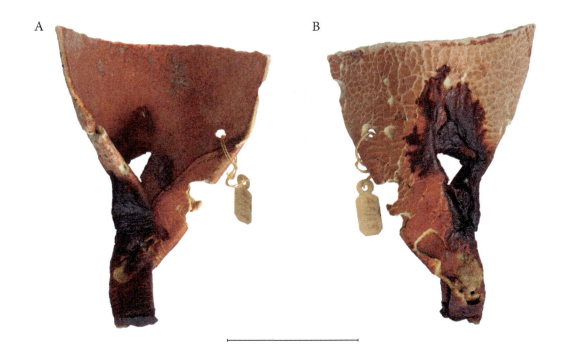

Cat. No. 25, SR 3390. *Overviews of the recto (A) and verso (B).*

CATALOGUE NUMBER 26

Id. No.	JE 97824 (SR 3391; TR 21 3 21 6).	*Id. No.*	JE 97825 (SR 3392; TR 21 3 21 5).
Object	Rawhide axe binding.	*Object*	Rawhide axe binding.
Measurements	Length: 122. Width: 53. Width thongs: 12.5-15. Thickness thongs: 2.5.	*Measurements*	Length: 117. Width: 39-48. Thickness: 39-48. Width strips: 11-11.7. Thickness thongs: 2.
Remarks	Probably part of the "Thirty-one miscellaneous pieces of harness, trappings, sandals, leather bindings etc." (Carter & Newberry, 1904: 38) from chamber 3. At one side is "12." written on it in ink.	*Remarks*	Probably part of the "Thirty-one miscellaneous pieces of harness, trappings, sandals, leather bindings etc." (Carter & Newberry, 1904: 38) from chamber 3. At one side is "11." written on it in ink.

Description

A plaited piece of red leather thongs with the plaiting (over one, under one) visible on one side (figure A, B). The other side consists of two loops, one at the top and the other at the bottom, that secures this object around a handle or strut of some type.

Description

A plaited leather binding for securing the blade of an axe or adze (here most likely an axe), forming an oval (figure A, B). The verso shows signs of being cut with a knife or sward. Some of the upper most surface of the leather is worn away on the recto; more abraded areas faces on the verso.

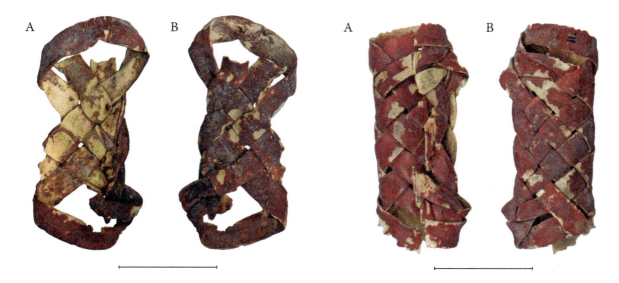

Cat. No. 26, JE 97824. Overviews.

Cat. No. 26, JE 97825. Overviews.

CATALOGUE NUMBER 27

Id. No.	SR 3365 (CG 46115).
Object	Scabbard.
Measurements	Length: 243. Width maximum: 30.2. Thickness top: 6.1. Thickness bottom: 11.7.
Remarks	Inside "10" is written in ink and "18" or "81" (?) in ink or pencil (faint). Found in room 3. Carter & Newberry (1904: 38).

Description

A scabbard (for a knife or dagger), or spear tip cover of leather (figure A, B). It takes the form of a long, thin, elongated leaf and is made of one piece of patterned (criss-cross, see below) leather that is folded over (figure C, D) and closed by means of sailor stitch that is made of sinew at the verso. The stitching is only preserved at the very tip of the object (figure C). The top of the recto is curved (figure E) and the patterning and decoration is a combination of impression and light incision. The top of the verso is torn off, but it probably was not curved and ended a bit below the level of the recto originally, making it easier to gain access to its contents.

The barely visible decoration of the recto is formed by an impressed, or more likely moulded, frame that follows the contour of the object. A central rib, moulded, runs down the piece; on top it opens up into a stylized papyrus plant, which is enhanced by vertical zigzag lines. The recto has a base patterning of tiny squares, which on the verso became fused lozenges.

Cat. No. 27, SR 3365. *E) Top of the recto with incised zigzag motif. Scale bar is 10 mm. The overviews and more details can be found on the next page.*

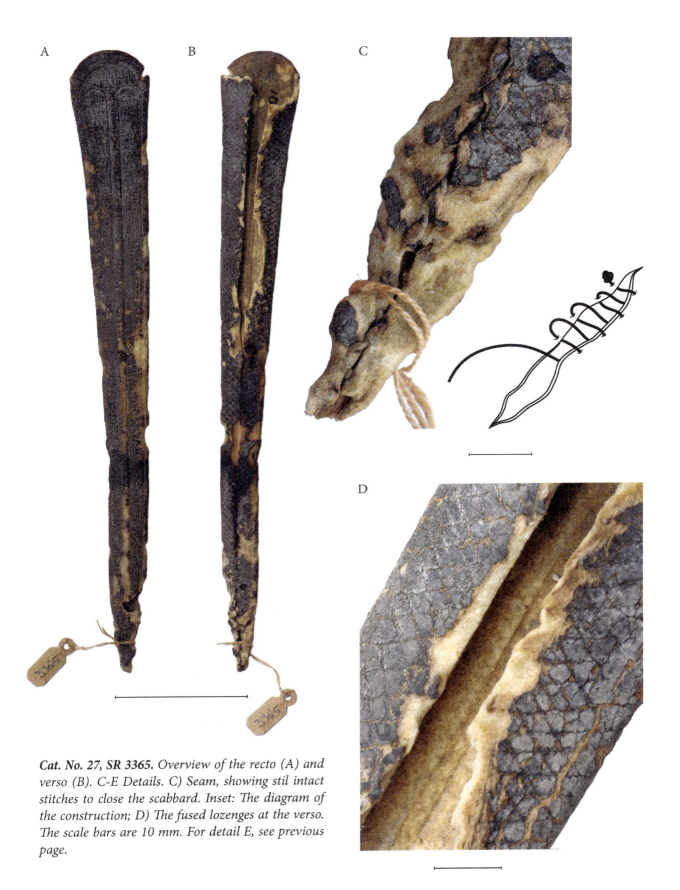

Cat. No. 27, SR 3365. Overview of the recto (A) and verso (B). C-E Details. C) Seam, showing stil intact stitches to close the scabbard. Inset: The diagram of the construction; D) The fused lozenges at the verso. The scale bars are 10 mm. For detail E, see previous page.

TOMB OF AMENHOTEP III

CATALOGUE NUMBER 28

Collection　Metropolitan Museum of Art (New York).
Id. No.　MMA 24.8.D.
Object　Fragment of siding frame(?); Littauer & Crouwel (1985: 73).
Provenance　Gift Howard Carter.
Measurements　Length (bent): 277. Diameter: 12.8 x 13.3.

Description
A long rod of wood is clad with red leather (figure A, B). This is punctuated by bands of green leather (width: 17 mm), flanked by narrow red strips, with a thin red band going over the centre of the green. These three green accents are spaced approximately 70 mm apart (width: 3 mm; figure D, E). One end (the bottom one in figure A) has a green piece added as well, the edge of which is convex – the underlying red seems to have been cut away. The leather is secured, along one length, by a green leather thong that is laced through itself (back stitch; figure E-G), a technique not uncommon in ancient Egypt (also in fibre objects) but not known from other chariot leather.

Cat. No. 28, MMA 24.8.D. *A) Overview from aside; B) Overview from above; the wooden top has not been included in the photograph; C, D) Details of the green decorative bands (note the fastening, see also figure E-G). Scale bar C, D is 10 mm.*

E F G

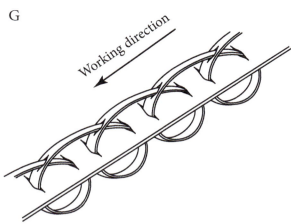

Cat. No. 28, MMA 24.8.D. *E-G) Details of the fastening of the leather cladding and the green decorative bands; G) Diagram of the construction. Scale bars are 10 mm.*

CATALOGUE NUMBER 29

Collection	Metropolitan Museum of Art (New York).
Id. No.	MMA 24.8.A-C.
Object	Unknown.
Provenance	Gift Howard Carter.
Measurements	A & C) Length: appr. 4150. Width: 15.2 - 33.2 - 39.2 - 35.9.
	B) Length: 21.6. Width: 36.3 - 31.5 - 26.5.
Remarks	The three fragments fit together. Conservation work undertaken in 1982, including the attachment of the three pieces.

Description
Three fragments of leather that fit together (figure A, B, D, E), with applied decoration (in stair-step fashion) in green, white and red. The condition of the fragment is fairly good, but the edge is not entirely complete in places. Fortunately, the beginning of the strip is still there, allowing for the identification of some additional constructional methods previously not noticed. The colour is not equally well preserved. The description is made from a horizontal perspective, with the overlap facing upwards.
The stair-step decoration (figure C, F) starts with a green strip (width: 1-1.5 mm), followed by a lengthwise folded, white strip (width: 1 mm) on top of which is a green strip (width: 2.5 mm). Next follows another

folded white strip (width: 1 mm) with a green strip on top (width: 2 mm). The second and third green strips actually started as one: the terminal end of the beginning of the strip is visible showing that it was cut lengthwise after which the white strip was inserted in between (arrow in figure G). These five strips are secured together with widely spaced running stitches than are stitched through the lower half of the cut green strip. A wide, red strip follows (width: 5-5.5 mm), on top of which a narrow green strip is applied (width: 1 mm; secured with widely spaced running stitches) that borders a band of zigzag motif in green (width: 3 mm). It leaves a small band of red leather visible at the top. The zigzag lines are cut, rather than being made of a long strip that is folded around the corner. They are secured with horizontal stitches at each corner (examples are encircled in figure G, H) rather than at an angle as seen, for example in MMA 24.8.H (Cat. No. 33). A green strip (width: 1.5-2 mm) borders the zigzag motif on the other side, followed by a lengthwise folded white strip (width: 1 mm) and again a green strip (width: 2 mm). The widely spaced running stitches that runs through it also secures the previous two layers. Next follows a wide white strip (width: 6 mm; in contrast to the other white applications, this layer is of single thickness) on top of which is secured a narrow green strip (width: 1 mm; leaving a small band of white visible) that borders a band with green zigzag motifs (width: 3.5-4 mm). It is secured with widely spaced running stitches. This motif is also cut, as was the previous one, and secured in the same way. A green strip borders it at the other side (width: 2 mm), followed by a folded white strip (1-1.5 mm). The next strip is a wide green one (width: 7 mm): the widely spaced running stitching that runs through it also secures the previous two strips. Lengthwise through the centre of this green strip is a narrow red strip attached (width: 1 mm), again by means of widely spaced running stitching. The last strip is a lengthwise folded white one (width: 1-1.5 mm), which is, in contrast to the rest, orientated with its fold towards the bottom, as to finish the construction. The foundation is slightly narrower than the applied decoration (figure F, H). All stitching is done with sinew, which seems slightly twisted Z-wise. Note the hole in the terminal end of one fragment (figure G, H) that might have been used to attach the fragment (with a split pin?) to another object.

Cat. No. 29, MMA 24.8.A-C. A-B) Overview of the recto of fragment A & C (A) and verso (B).

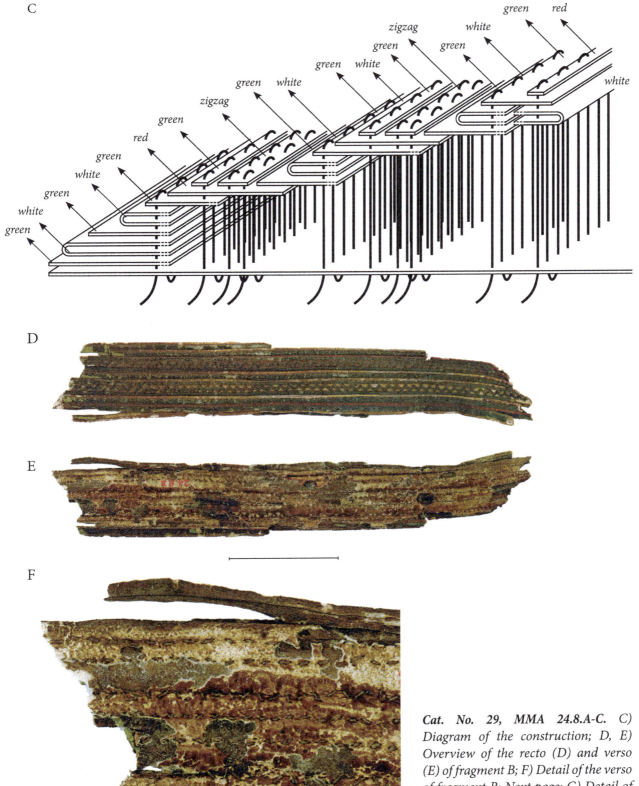

Cat. No. 29, MMA 24.8.A-C. C) Diagram of the construction; D, E) Overview of the recto (D) and verso (E) of fragment B; F) Detail of the verso of fragment B; Next page: G) Detail of the recto of fragment A, C. Note the cut (arrow) to divide the green strip. Some stitches that secure the zigzag motif are encircled; H) Detail of the verso of fragment A, C. Scale bars are 10 mm.

CATALOGUE NUMBER 30

Collection Metropolitan Museum of Art (New York).
Id. No. MMA 24.8.E.
Object Unknown.
Provenance Gift Howard Carter.
Measurements Length: 178. Width total: 23.8-43.2. Width green strip: 15.1.

Material Leather.
Colour Red, green.
Description
Piece of thin, red leather to which is glued two fragments of green leather.
Collection Metropolitan Museum of Art (New York).

Cat. No. 30, MMA 24.8.E. Overview of the recto (A) and verso (B).

CATALOGUE NUMBER 31

Id. No. MMA 24.8.F.
Object Shoe's upper fragment.
Provenance Gift Howard Carter.
Measurements Width: 185. Height: 58.8. Circular appliqué, overall dimensions: 51.1 x 78 and 52.4 x 73. Width green outer ring: 11.9 and 10.6. Width white ring: 4.5 and 4.2. Diameter inner ring: 25 x 41.9 and 26.5 x 40.9.
Material Leather.
Colour Red, green, brown, white.
Remarks Conservation work undertaken in 1982. See Veldmeijer (2009a) for a detailed discussion.

Description
Part of the red ventral lower upper of a so-called curled-toe ankle shoe (figure A, B; *cf.* Veldmeijer, 2009a, here figure H). A small scrap of the red strip, connecting the lower upper to the sole, still adheres below one of the appliqués. The outer, visible surface consists of two joined pieces (secured with large whip stitches; figure G), but the seam is not visible at the outer side of the upper as it is enhanced with two circular appliqués. These consists of three layers: a dark brown inner circle that is bordered with a narrow white and, finally, a wider green edge. The appliqué is secured at the outer edge with whip stitches of sinew (figure C, E, F). In addition, there is an occasional stitch through the green layer, close to the edge with the white leather. Note the drawstring running through the leather close to the connection of the two uppers and through one of the decorative patches (figure D).

Collection Metropolitan Museum of Art (New York).

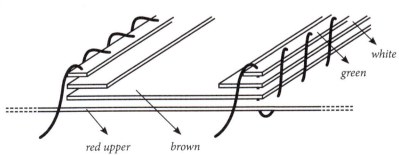

Cat. No. 31, MMA 24.8.F. *Overview of the recto (A) and verso (B). C) Diagram of the construction of the appliqué.*

Cat. No. 31, MMA 24.8.F. *D) Recto, showing a piece of drawstring and the whip stitching attaching the ventral upper with the dorsal upper (now lost). Note the attachment area of the appliqué; E) Outside, showing drawstring and stitching of the appliqué; F) Verso, showing the whip stitching that secures the appliqué; G) The attachment area of the two pieces that make the ventral upper. Scale bars are 10 mm.*

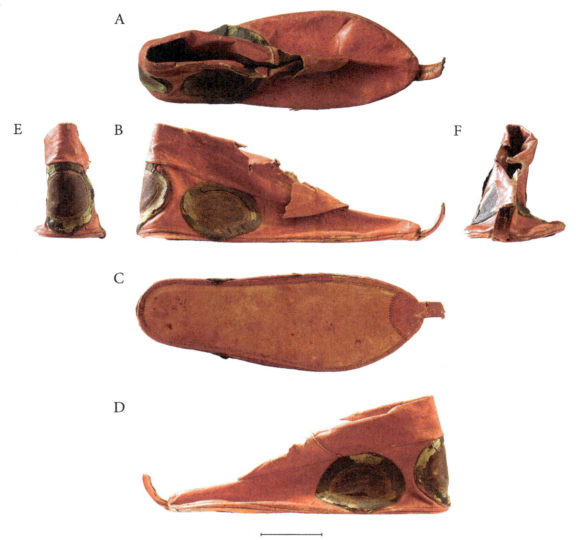

H) Left shoe of the pair SR 5174/5175 in the Egyptian Museum (Cairo). A) Dorsal; B) Medial; C) Ventral; D) Lateral; E) Posterior and F) Anterior views.

CATALOGUE NUMBER 32

Id. No.   MMA 24.8.G.
Object   Unknown.
Provenance   Gift Howard Carter.
Measurements   Length: 164 - 60.5 - 107.5 - 18.7.
Width: 44-8 - 49. Width appliqué: 23.7.
Material   Leather.
Colour   Red, green.
Description

A rectangular piece of leather (figure A, B), decorated at one side with appliqué work. Both ends curl backwards: one end is broken off nearly square whereas the other end terminates in two long protrusions at either side. The stiffness of the object prohibits unfolding it. Overall, the fragment is in fairly good condition, although suffering from discoloration (especially evident by looking at the layers beneath the oval appliqué). However, this has occurred far less with the oval appliqué. Unfortunately, the details of the stitching are obscure.

The red recto has lengthwise applied, 18 narrow strips of green leather (figure C-E; width: 1 mm) that are secured with widely spaced running stitches of sinew. At either side, the decoration is completed by an edge binding (figure F, H), consisting of a green strip, also secured with widely spaced running stitches of sinew. In both cases there is uncertainty about the twist of the thread, but it seems not to have been plied.

One end of the recto has an oval appliqué (figure C, E-G) that consists of a green centre part, covering, in stair-step fashion, a red and green strip respectively. These red and green strips are folded lengthwise (width: 2.5-3.5 mm). At least the topmost green centre part and the green strip below (arrows in figure C) are secured with seemingly interlocking running stitching (probably sinew of the same composition as the previously described stitching), but, as the verso could not be studied, it is not clear if this is truly interlocking stitching or that the appliqué was attached in a second stage by using the interstitch spaces (double running stitch). The red strip is secured with regular running stitches in sinew thread.

The opposite end shows no signs that the other part (if there was any) of the oval appliqué was attached to it, thus securing the object.

Collection   Metropolitan Museum of Art

A   B

Cat. No. 32, MMA 24.8.G. *Overview of the recto (A) and verso (B).*

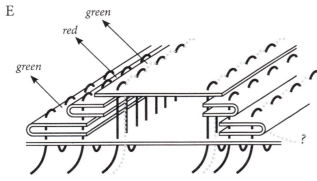

Cat. No. 32, MMA 24.8.G. *C-D) Detail of the appliqué; E) Diagram of the construction of the oval appliqué; F) Diagram of the construction of the appliqué. Scale bars C-D are 10 mm.*

CATALOGUE | 297

Cat. No. 32, MMA 24.8.G. G) Detail of the attachment of the oval appliqué; H) Detail of the red recto. Scale bars are 10 mm.

CATALOGUE NUMBER 33

	(New York).
Id. No.	MMA 24.8.H.
Object	Unknown.
Provenance	Gift Howard Carter.
Measurements	138 x 93.5 - 121.9. Width one end: 23.6.
Material	Leather.
Colour	Red, green and white.
Description	

A U-shaped band of leather enhanced (figure A, B) by applying strips of leather of different colour in stair-step fashion. All stitching is done with sinew. Both ends of the fragment show discolouration (figure D) as well as stitch holes that suggest that it once was covered with something. The layers are described from a horizontal perspective (figure C, D, F, G), with the overlap facing upwards. A green binding (figure E; width: 1.5 mm), extending relatively far at the verso (5-7 mm), is covered with a lengthwise folded white strip (width: 1.5 mm) and a single green one (total width: 6 mm; visible width at this side: 2.5 mm). These three are secured in a second stage by using the interstitch spaces (double running stitch), resulting in seemingly interlocking running stitching at the recto, but running stitching at the verso of the object. On top of this wide green strip, close to the edge furthest away from the edge of the fragment proper, is added a set consisting of a single red strip (width: 3 mm) with a narrower single green one (width: 1.5 mm) lengthwise down the centre. This set is attached with running stitching, which also further secures the wide green strip. The green zigzag motif, sewn onto a white foundation, which is the extension of the first folded white layer seen from the edge, is secured with single stitches at each point but at right angles rather than horizontally as seen in MMA 24.8.A-C (Cat. No. 29). The zigzag motif is cut out, rather than formed by a strip that is folded at the points. The other edge of the zigzag band is bordered by a green strip (width: 1.5 mm), followed by a lengthwise folded white band (width: 2 mm). The next green strip (total width: 7 mm; visible width at this side: 3 mm) is secured in two steps, using the interstitch space of the running stitches to secure the pre-constructed set to the undersurface, which also fixes the previous green and white strips. A set comprised of a red strip (width: 2.5 mm) with a green one (width: 1 mm) on top, running lengthwise down the centre, is added to this wide green strip, using running stitching. The wide green band underneath slightly protrudes at the other side, but here, the fragment is much damaged. Comparable to MMA 24.8.O (Cat. No. 37).

Collection   Metropolitan Museum of Art

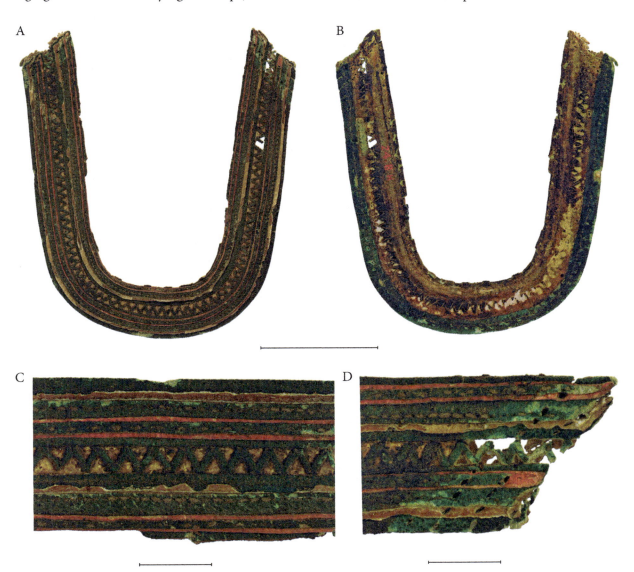

Cat. No. 33, MMA 24.8.H. *Overview of the recto (A) and verso (B). C, D) Details of the recto. Note the discoloration at the terminal end (D). Scale bars C, D are 10 mm.*

Cat. No. 33, MMA 24.8.H. E) Detail of the verso, showing the diagonal stitching of the zigzag motif and the large overlap of the green binding; F) Cross section, showing the way the appliqué is added; G) Diagram of the construction. Scale bars E, F are 10 mm.

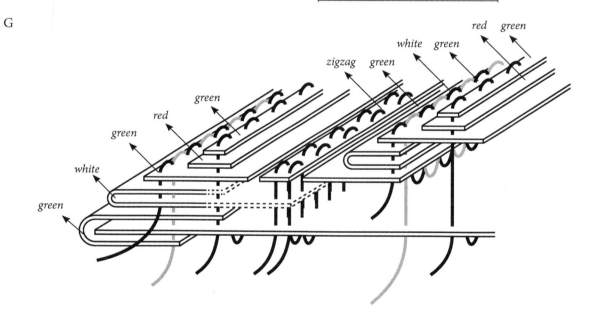

CATALOGUE NUMBER 34

Id. No.	MMA 24.8.I.
Object	Unknown.
Provenance	Gift Howard Carter.
Measurements	Length: 270. Width halfway: 21.4. Width curved end: 28.1. Diameter bosses: 9.5 x 10.4.
Material	Leather, bronze and gold foil.
Colour	Red, green and white.
Remarks	Conservation work undertaken in 1982.

Description
Fragment, whose shape resemble a question mark (figure A-C), consisting of two layers of leather (figure F). At the convex edge, the red layer that makes op the verso, is folded underneath to form a sort of edge binding (width: 1.5 mm; figure C). At the recto, this is further enhanced with a green strip (width: 3.5-4 mm) that is applied in stair-step fashion. It is probably secured in two phases, securing the set first with running stitches and using the interstitch spaces for adding it to the undersurface with another set of running stitches (double running stitch). This strip lies close to the green strip that makes up the centre of the fragment (the recto), but in some cases it runs over it and protrudes from the appliqué that was intended to cover it.

This appliqué consists of a single white bottom strip (width: 4.5 mm) on top of which is applied, lengthwise through the centre, a narrower single green one (width: 1.5 mm). This set seems to be secured with the same stitching as seen with the edge binding and includes the green strip to which it is applied. Next to this covering set of strips, and placed onto the central green band, are 11 bronze bosses (figure D, G), which are enhanced with gold foil. Split pins secure them at the back (figure E). At the opposite side, this band of bosses is bordered by a set of single white and green strips; the green one (width: 2 mm) runs lengthwise down the centre of the slightly wider bottom one (width: 5 mm). It covers the edge of the edge binding and is secured with comparable stitches as seen in the rest of the fragment; it also secures the binding. This edge binding is a strip of green leather, which is folded over the two layers. All stitching is made with sinew, consisting of two threads that are twisted S-wise.

At the verso, a small fragment of red leather (arrow in figure H), secured with whip stitching to the green edge binding, suggests that originally the verso was covered to protect the surface to which the object was attached from the split pins or the entire object was secured to a foundation of red leather.

Collection Metropolitan Museum of Art (New York).

Cat. No. 34, MMA 24.8.I. *Overview of the recto (A) and verso (B).*

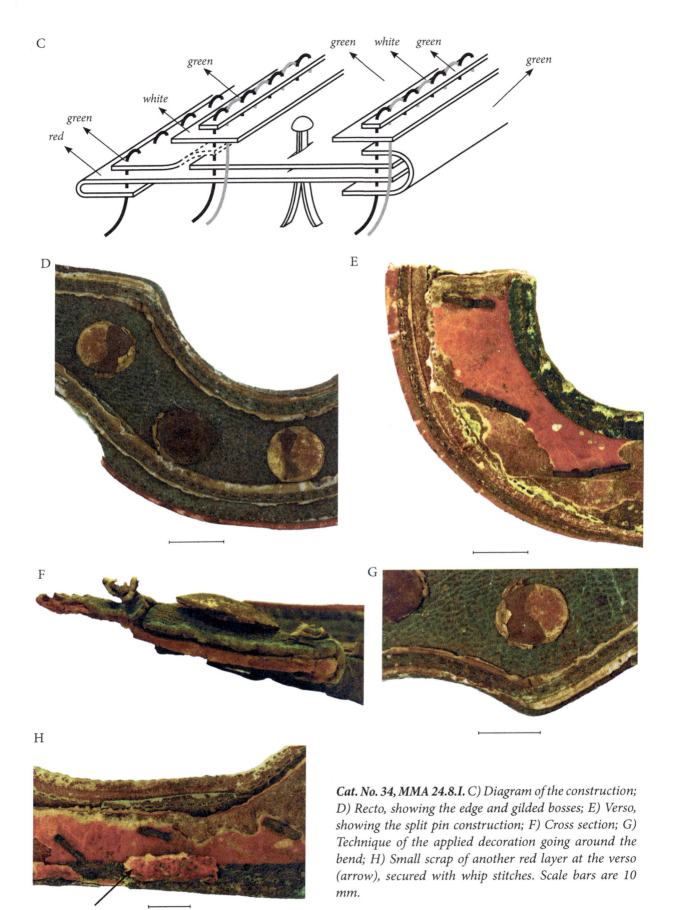

Cat. No. 34, MMA 24.8.I. C) Diagram of the construction; D) Recto, showing the edge and gilded bosses; E) Verso, showing the split pin construction; F) Cross section; G) Technique of the applied decoration going around the bend; H) Small scrap of another red layer at the verso (arrow), secured with whip stitches. Scale bars are 10 mm.

CATALOGUE NUMBER 35

Id. No.	MMA 24.8.J & K.
Object	Unknown.
Provenance	Gift Howard Carter.
Measurements	Length total: 105. Width: 27.5 - 33.9 - 22.3.
Material	Leather.
Colour	Green.
Remarks	Conservation work undertaken in 1982.

Description
Two small fragments of green leather that were cut (figure A, B). They have been re-attached in modern times. A row of empty stitch holes indicates that the fragment is incomplete.

Collection Metropolitan Museum of Art (New York).

Id. No.	24.8.L.
Context	Gift Howard Carter.
Measurements	73.5 x 39.5 - 40.1.
Material	Leather.
Colour	Greyish brown.

Description
Thick, irregularly shaped piece of leather (figure A, B). One end has an oval slit that looks much like the slits in some sandals for the reception of the front strap. A row of empty stitch holes is visible at one side.

Collection Metropolitan Museum of Art (New York).

Cat. No. 35, MMA 24.8.J & K. *Overview of the recto (A) and verso (B).*

Cat. No. 35, MMA 24.8.L. *Overview of the recto (A) and verso (B).*

CATALOGUE NUMBER 36

Id. No.	(New York). MMA 24.8.M.
Object	Unknown.
Provenance	Gift Howard Carter.
Measurements	Length: 79. Width maximal: 40.6. Width decoration strip: 14.2.
Material	Leather.
Colour	Red, green and white.

Description

Irregularly-shaped fragment, consisting of two layers (figure A-B). One edge is more or less intact; it is made up of the white verso that is folded over (width: approximately 2 mm; figure C, D). It is covered, in stair-step fashion, by a single green strip (width: approximately 4 mm), both of which are secured by a row of widely spaced running stitches of sinew. The sinew that secures the decoration in the centre (see below) is not twisted or plied. Possibly, but this could not be observed with certainty, the whole fragment is sewn with comparable sinew thread. Next follows, again in stair-step fashion, a white leather strip of which the outer edge is folded under (width: 1 mm). On top of this, also in stair-step fashion, is applied a wide single strip of green leather (width: approximately 6 mm) which has attached on top of it, lengthwise through the centre, a narrow strip of red leather (width: 1 mm). The green strip is secured, as is the red strip, with widely spaced running stitches of the same composition as the stitching that secures the edge binding. Note that this edge is slightly elevated despite the fact that the white strip is the extension of the central part of the object.

The white centre shows an elaborate pattern of stitch holes (figure E, G) of which only a small part of the decoration itself is preserved, in the form of a narrow green strip (width: 1 mm) picking out a floral motif. It is attached with widely spaced running stitches, most likely of sinew. Note that all stitching penetrates all layers (figure C, F).

Collection Metropolitan Museum of Art

Cat. No. 36, MMA 24.8.M. *Overview of the recto (A) and verso (B).*

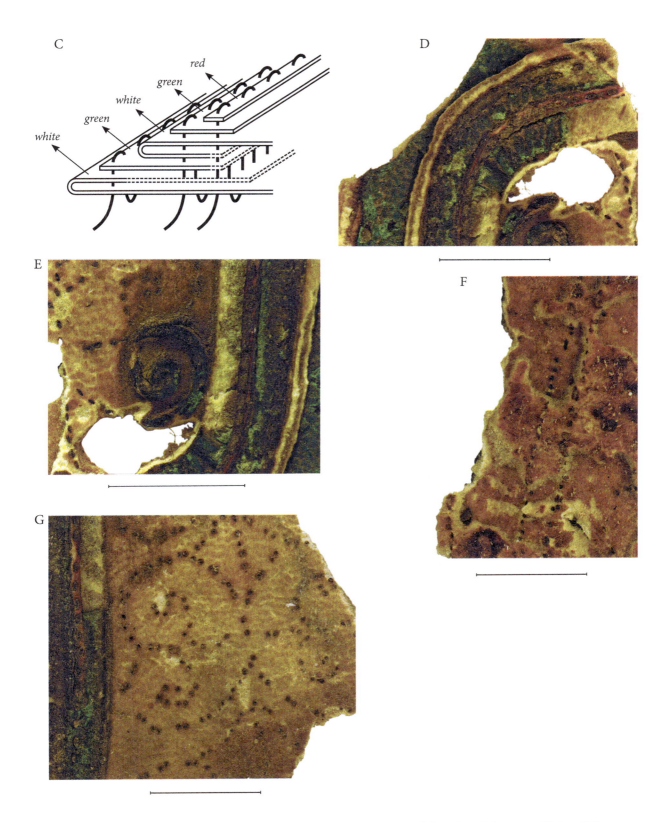

Cat. No. 36, MMA 24.8.M. *C) Diagram of the construction; D) Detail of the edge of the recto; E) Small fragment of the applied decoration of the recto in situ; F) Detail of the edge of the verso; G) Detail of the stitch holes at the recto of the, now lost, applied decoration. Scale bars are 10 mm.*

CATALOGUE NUMBER 37

Id. No.	(New York). MMA 24.8.O.
Object	Unknown.
Provenance	Gift Howard Carter.
Measurements	117.3 x 60.5 - 100. Width one end: 10.9.
Material	Leather.
Colour	Red, green and white.

Description

A U-shaped band of enhanced leather made by applying strips of leather of different colour in stair-step fashion (figure A, B) to create a striped effect. The thread for the stitching is made of sinew. Both ends show discolouration (and one end also stitch holes; figure C) that suggests that it once was covered. The description of the layers is made from a horizontal perspective, with the overlap facing upwards (figure D, E, G). A green binding (figure F; width: 2-3 mm), extending relatively far at the verso (4-5 mm), is covered with a lengthwise folded white strip (width: 1.5 mm) and a single green one (total width: 7 mm; visible width at this side: 3.5 mm). These three are sewn together with running stitching and secured to the undersurface with running stitching, using the interstitch space of the recto (double running stitch). Exactly which layers are included in the first set of stitching is not clear. On top of this wide green strip, close to the opposite edge, is added a set consisting of a single red strip (width: 2.5 mm) with a narrower single green one (width: 1.5 mm) lengthwise down the centre. This set is secured with comparable stitching as to the other side, which also further secures the wide green strip. Comparable to MMA 24.8.H (Cat. No. 33), but less complete.

Collection Metropolitan Museum of Art

Cat. No. 37, MMA 24.8.O. *Overview of the recto (A) and verso (B).*

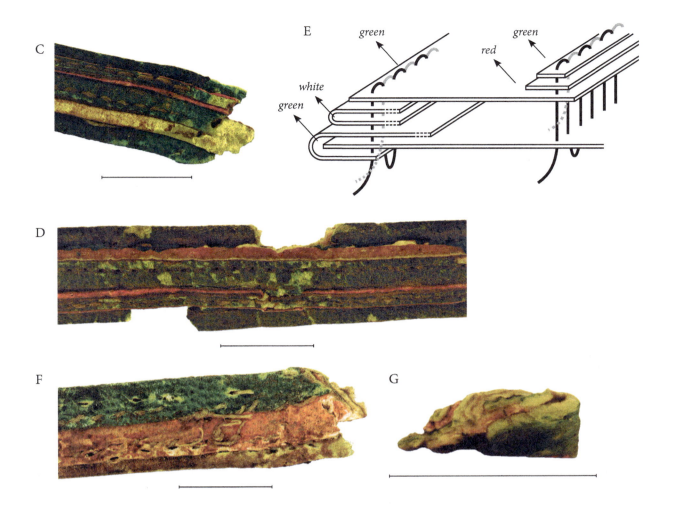

Cat. No. 37, MMA 24.8.O. *C, D) Details of the recto. Note the discoloration and the stitch holes at the terminal end (C); E) Diagram of the construction; F) Overview of the verso; G) Cross section showing the way the appliqué is added. Scale bars are 10 mm.*

CATALOGUE NUMBER 38

Id. No.	MMA 24.8.P.
Object	Unknown.
Provenance	Gift Howard Carter.
Measurements	Outer diameter: 88.7 x 90.4. Inner diameter: 72 x 73.1. Width strip: 8.6.
Material	Leather.
Colour	Red, green and white.

Description

Open circular object (figure A, B), consisting of a lengthwise folded, white layer that makes up the outermost band (width: 8 mm). On top of this is fixed, in stair-step fashion, a wide green strip (width: 7 mm). This strip, in its turn, has a red strip (width: 3 mm) on top of which is attached, lengthwise through the centre, a narrow green strip (width: 1 mm; figure C-E). Although there seems to be stitch holes visible at the verso, nothing can be seen at the recto, which suggests that the applied decoration was attached with glue. Note, at the verso, the points where the two ends of the first white layer meet (figure F).

Collection   Metropolitan Museum of Art (New York).

Cat. No. 38, MMA 24.8.P. *Overview of the recto (A) and verso (B).*

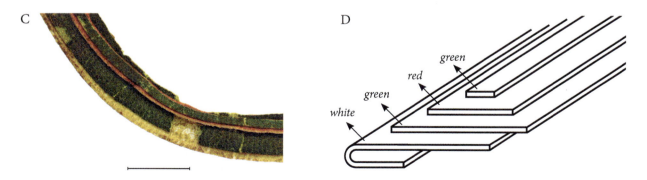

Cat. No. 38, MMA 24.8.P. *C) Detail of the edge of the recto; D) Diagram of the construction. Although there seems to be stitch holes, the elements were most likely glued as no thread is visible. Scale bar is 10 mm.*

Cat. No. 38, MMA 24.8.P. *E) Detail of the edge of the verso; F) Detail of the edge of the verso showing the attachment area. Scale bars are 10 mm.*

CATALOGUE NUMBER 39

	(New York).
Id. No.	MMA 24.8.Q & R.
Object	Unknown.
Provenance	Gift Howard Carter.
Measurements	Q) Length: 60.
	R) Length: 50 (both measurements according to museum archive).
Material	Leather.
Colour	Red, green.

Description
Two lengthwise folded strips of leather. The green one still has remnants of a stitch attached.

Collection   Metropolitan Museum of Art

Cat. No. 39, MMA 24.8.Q & R. *Overview. Scale bar is 10 mm.*

CATALOGUE NUMBER 40

Id. No.	MMA 24.8.S.
Object	Unknown.
Provenance	Gift Howard Carter.
Measurements	Length: 133 (measurements according to museum archive).
Material	Leather.
Colour	Red, green and white.

Description

From bottom to top, the torn fragment (figure A, B) starts with a band of zigzag motif in green (figure C-E; width: approximately 3 mm) on a white surface. The motif is a cut-out rather than a folded strip, and secured with stitching at the tips (the sinew thread is largely intact on the verso). It is bordered by a narrow strip of green (width: 1 mm). It seems that the white foundation protrudes from it; the set (foundation with zigzag and border) overlaps in stair-step fashion, a set of single green upper (width: 3 mm) and lengthwise folded red lower strips (width: 1 mm). Two further sets of single green upper, but white, lengthwise folded lower strips (width: 2 and 1 mm respectively), also overlapping in stair-step fashion, follows. The fragment seems to have consisted of more layers, but the exact composition can no longer be determined.

Collection Metropolitan Museum of Art (New York).

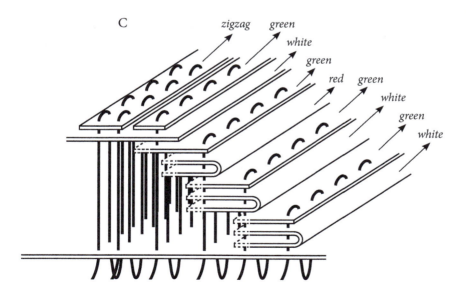

Cat. No. 40, 24.8.S. *Overview of the recto (A) and verso (B); C) Diagram of the construction.*

Cat. No. 40, MMA 24.8.S. D) *Detail of the recto;* E) *Detail of the verso. Scale bars are 10 mm.*

CATALOGUE NUMBER 41

	(New York).
Id. No.	MMA 24.8.T.
Object	Unknown.
Provenance	Gift Howard Carter.
Measurements	Length: 78.2. Width: 11.2 - 25.5.
Material	Leather.
Colour	Red, green and white.

Description

An incomplete fragment of decorated leather (figure A, B). The remnants of a green strip, which would have bordered the now-lost topmost zigzag motif, is followed by a lengthwise folded white strip (width: 1 mm) and a single green strip (width: 3 mm). The widely spaced running stitches, most of which are lost, secure the three layers. These are made, like all other stitching in the object, of sinew. Next follows a wide, white strip (in contrast to the other white applications, this layer is of single thickness) on top of which is secured a narrow green strip (width: 1 mm), leaving a small band of white visible, that borders a band with green zigzag motifs. It is secured with widely spaced running stitches. This zigzag motif is cut rather than made with a folded strip, and secured with single stitches at the corners. A green strip borders it at the other side (width: 2 mm), followed by a white, folded strip (width: 1 mm) that overlaps it in stair-step fashion. The sides of this wide strip seem to be folded under, rather than being folded lengthwise. The next strip is a wide, single green one (width: 7 mm): the widely spaced running stitching that runs through it also secures the previous two strips. Lengthwise through the centre of this green strip is a narrow red strip (width: 1 mm) attached by means of widely spaced running stitching. The last band is a lengthwise folded white one, largely incomplete, which seems the other side of the previous strip.

Collection Egyptian Museum (Cairo).

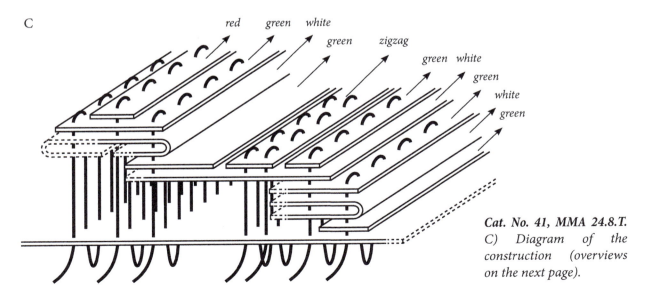

Cat. No. 41, MMA 24.8.T. C) *Diagram of the construction (overviews on the next page).*

Cat. No. 41, MMA 24.8.T. Overview of the recto (A) and verso (B).

CATALOGUE NUMBER 42

Id. No.	SR 4/10676 (TR 6 3 25 4).
Object	Unknown.
Measurements	A) Width total: 16.
	B) 42 x 75.
Remarks	Both pieces have the same identification number. "Amenhetep III" is written in ink on the back of A.

Description

A) A long piece of leather (figure A, C) consisting of green and white sets of leather strips. There are four sets (figure B) of a thin, folded white strip of leather with a green one lengthwise down the centre. In one set, the protruding layer is red. The white and red at either side are folded over (figure D). The layers are secured with running stitches of sinew, many of which protrudes from the stitch holes (figure E).

B) A triangular piece, consisting of a relatively thick, red leather foundation with an applied elaborate decoration of different coloured strips (overlapping in stair-step fashion) and zigzag motifs (figure A-C). Starting at the edge with a green binding (width: 2 mm; figure F), a lengthwise folded strip of white leather follows (width: 1.5 mm) and a wider but single green one (width: 3 mm). These strips, like all other strips (not the zigzag motifs, see below), are secured with running stitches of sinew, suggesting that none of the sets were pre-fabricated. A lengthwise folded red strip is next in line (width: 1 mm), followed by a wider but single green one (width: 3 mm); these two are secured with stitching. A wide, white strip, which functions as foundation for the following decoration, follows. Exactly how far it extends is not clear, but it includes at least the green layer at the opposite of the zigzag pattern (minimal width: 9 mm). The edge of this white layer is folded; shortly inwards from the edge is a narrow, single green strip (width: 1 mm) that borders a band of zigzag motif (width: 3 mm; figure E). The motif is cut from a long narrow strip (width: 1 mm); it is secured at the corners with a single stitch. At the opposite side, the zigzag is bordered by a narrow, single green strip (width: 1.5-2 mm). A comparable wide white strip (as with the previous one, it is not clear how far it extended, but is at least 7 mm wide) overlaps the green border of the previous set. About 1 mm inwards from this white strip's edge is attached a narrow green strip (width: 1 mm), which is stitched so that it includes the previous white, green and white layers too. The green strip borders a second band of zigzag motif of the same dimensions and construction as the previous one (figure E). Finally, two wide green strip borders the zigzag motif at the opposite side (width: 4-6.5 mm); one has stitch holes lengthwise down the centre. At the top, a red leather strip is stitched through the layers (figure D). A green strip is attached to it a right angles, but this seems coincidental.

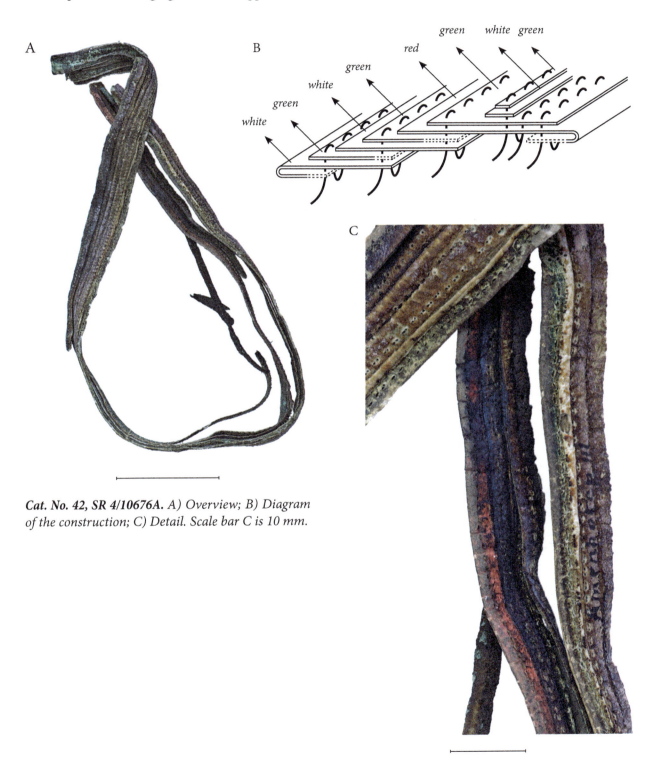

Cat. No. 42, SR 4/10676A. A) Overview; B) Diagram of the construction; C) Detail. Scale bar C is 10 mm.

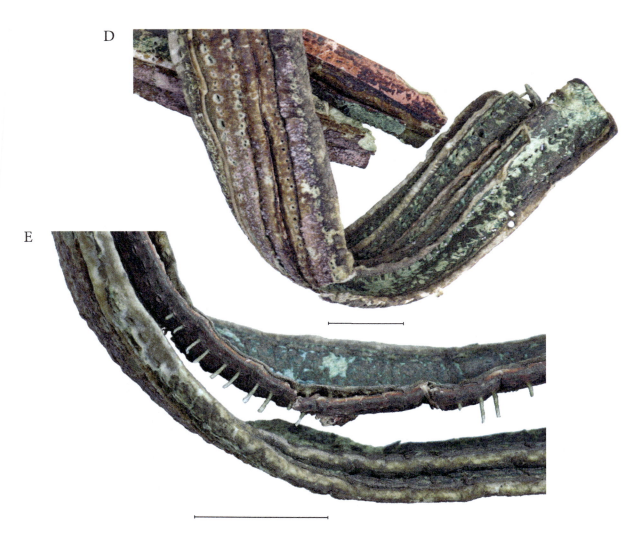

Cat. No. 42, SR 4/10676A. *D) Detail of the verso; E) Detail of the fine sinew stitching. Scale bars are 10 mm.*

Cat. No. 42, SR 4/10676B. *Overview of the recto (A) and verso (B).*

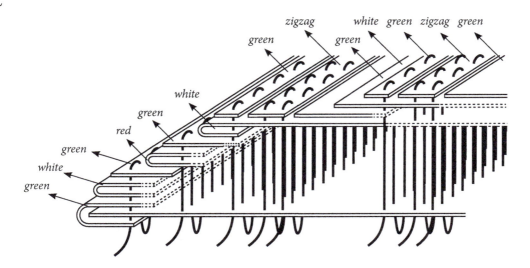

Cat. No. 42, SR 4/10676B. *C) Diagram of the construction; D) Detail of the recto. Scale bar is 10 mm.*

***Cat. No. 42, SR 4/10676B.** E) Detail of the recto; F) Detail of the verso, showing the diagonal stitching that secures the zigzag motif and the green edge binding. Scale bar is 10 mm.*

TANO LEATHER
MAIN CASING

CATALOGUE NUMBER 43

Id. No.   L3 #001.

Measurements   Overall dimensions: Length: 255. Width: 90. Thickness: 0.7 (both, red and green layers).

Description

A slightly curved, rectangular fragment consisting of two layers, one red and the other green, stitched together on the flesh side; thus, the coloured sides face outwards (figure A, B). The red layer is enlarged with a slight overlap (arrow in figure A, see figure C), the two parts being secured with whip stitches that are made of flax (inset), as indicated by remnants of the thread. The two layers are attached to a tube of red leather, the seam of which faces the green side, and is secured with running stitches (figure D-H) that are made of sinew zS_2 thread. The stitch holes are in pairs and circular.

The tube, whose width varies, is lengthened by having another piece overlapping it (figure I), but in contrast to other pieces with tubes, such as L1 #016 (Cat. No. 73), it is not secured with stitches. No drawstring remains, but originally, one existed. The edge opposite the connection of the piece with the tube is decorated with bands of green and red strips of leather (figure J-M), suggesting that this side would be facing outwards on the chariot. However, comparable parts (see L3 #004, Cat. No. 46) show also impression of the wood on this green side, suggesting it was facing inwards, and the red outwards. The outermost strip of green leather is an edge binding. It is secured at the red side (recto) with whip stitches over the edge (figure C, M). It extends relatively far (10 mm) and partially covers the stitching of the remaining part of the decorative edge that is visible at the verso of the object. The edge of the binding is folded, at the verso, towards the green surface. The fold (width: 9 mm) abuts the first strip of red leather (figure M). Originally, it would have overlapped, in stair-step fashion, the next strip of red leather (width: 1.6 mm), which is folded lengthwise. However, as it is pulled, the green binding is very tight on the red surface, and is pulled away from the rest of the decoration. This is also evidenced at the recto, where the edge of the binding is stretched at the stitches, due to the stress of the tightness. The next green band (width: 3.7 mm), which is partly overlapped by the red strip in stair-step fashion, lies with its edge against the previous red strip. Although visibility is limited because the edge is mostly complete, it is probable that this is an individual piece. It overlaps, again in stair-step fashion, the last strip, which is a single red one (width: 3.4 mm). It rests immediately on top of the green surface of the piece. The edge binding is, at the verso, secured with running stitches (zS_2 threads made of flax) that pierce through all layers. The green and last red strips are also secured to the object, at the edge of the red one, with rows of running stitches. The stitches that pierce the red strip, however, are more widely spaced and are slightly shorter than those that pierce the green one (and further secure the red). Broken areas in L3 #003 (Cat. No. 45) suggests that the green strip was secured to the red one first before the set was added to the object: the stitches are not visible at the recto.

Cat. No. 43, L3 #001. Overview of the recto (A) and verso (B); C) The seam resulting from the extension of the body's red layer (recto). The inset shows the diagram of the seam. Scale bar C is 10 mm.

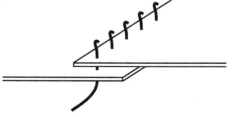

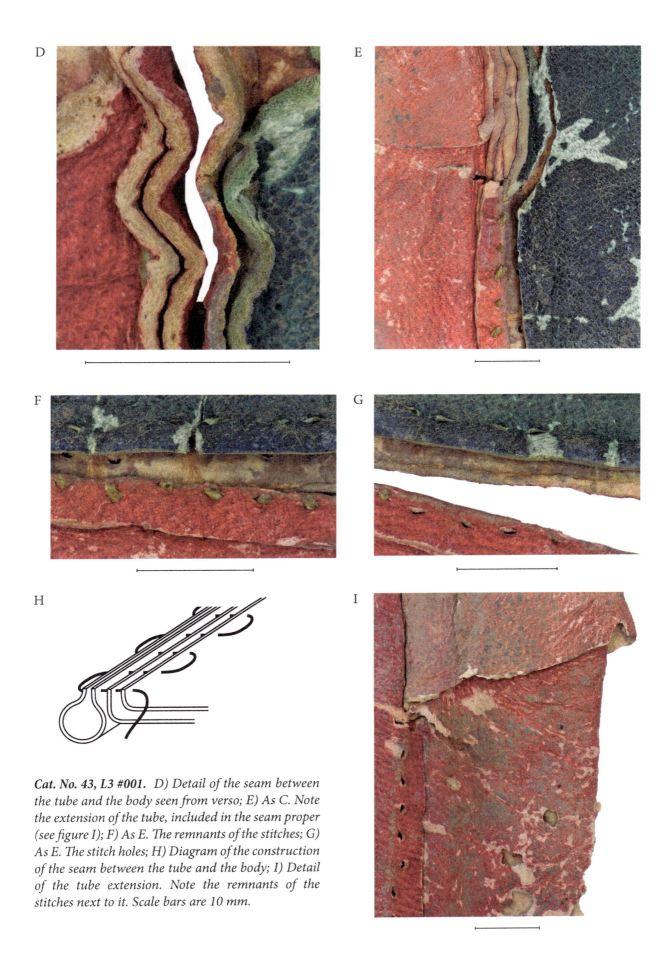

Cat. No. 43, L3 #001. *D) Detail of the seam between the tube and the body seen from verso; E) As C. Note the extension of the tube, included in the seam proper (see figure I); F) As E. The remnants of the stitches; G) As E. The stitch holes; H) Diagram of the construction of the seam between the tube and the body; I) Detail of the tube extension. Note the remnants of the stitches next to it. Scale bars are 10 mm.*

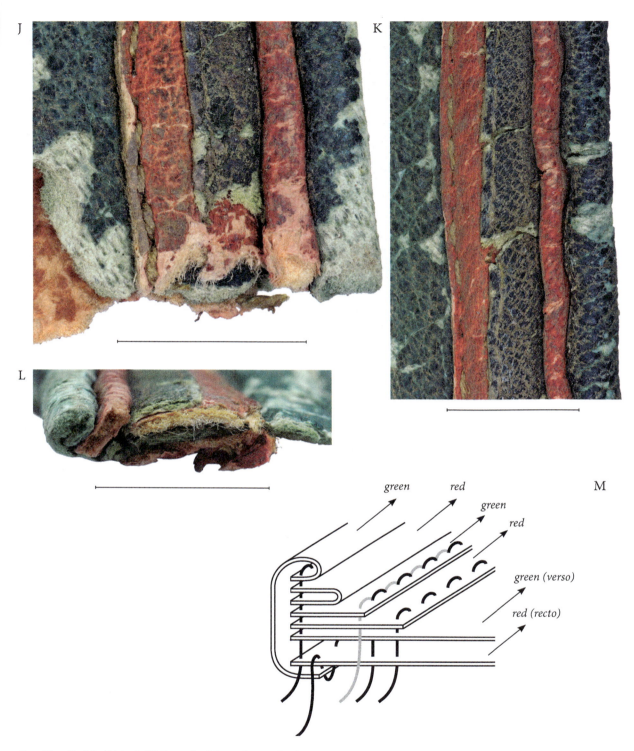

Cat. No. 43, L3 #001. *J, K) Detail of the enhanced edge, including the binding, seen from verso; L) As J, K but seen in cross section; M) Diagram of the construction of the enhanced edge seen in J, K. Scale bars are 10 mm.*

CATALOGUE NUMBER 44

Id. No. L3 #002.
Measurements Width: 220. Height: 95-180. Thickness: 0.7.

Description
A roughly rectangular piece, with a triangular protrusion in the centre of one long edge (figure A, B). The piece is actually made of two layers of green leather that is secured with the flesh side facing each other. It fits perfectly with L3 #003 (Cat. No. 45; * in figure A), which shows, as does the verso of L3 #002 (and the recto but far less distinctly), an impression of the rod of the wooden body of the chariot.

The verso has an elaborate border that edges three of the sides of the piece (figure C-E, N). The outermost strip of green leather is an edge binding. Most likely it is secured at the verso with running stitches (but these are not visible), after which it is pulled both over itself and the edge of the object; at the recto it is secured with whip stitches. It extends about 9.5 mm and only covers its own row of stitching. The edge of the binding is folded, at the verso, towards the surface, the fold (width: 4 mm) abutting the first strip of red leather (folded lengthwise; width: 2.2 mm) in several spots rather than overlapping it. Originally, it would have overlapped, in stair-step fashion, this strip along its entire length, but due to tightly pulling the green binding, it is pulled away from the rest of the enhancement. However, stress on the stitching is not visible at the recto, in contrast to L3 #001 (Cat. No. 43). The next strip is green and has a width of 4.5 mm. It is partially overlapped by the previous red strip in stair-step fashion. Although visibility is limited because the edge is largely intact, most likely this green band is an individual band that was, as in L3 #001 (Cat. No. 43), secured to the underlying red strip first, before being added to the object (hence double running stitching). It overlaps, again in stair-step fashion, this last, single red strip (width: 2 mm), which rests immediately on top of the verso. The last green and red bands are secured (most likely besides the running stitching that also secures the edge binding) to the verso with a row of running stitches at the edge using the interstitch spaces (double running stitches). Broken areas in L3 #003 (Cat. No. 45) suggest that the green strip was secured to the red one first before the pre-stitched set was added to the object (arrow in figure N). However, these first row of stitches are not visible at the recto.

A curious feature of the innermost red strip of the decoration of the verso is that at the corners (figure F-M) the strip pierces the object and emerges at the recto. The strip of the short, incomplete side and the strip of the long side with protruding triangle are both pulled through at the corner of the most incomplete edge (figure I). At the other corner, by contrast, the strip that is part of the short, but intact side and that of the long side with protruding triangle is one strip (figure H). At the recto, the end is stitched back, forming a toggle (figure K). The appliqué is pulled through because at the verso, it does not continue along the lower border but the opposite is true for the recto: is has no enhanced border except for the lower edges (figure K). Here it is just the continuation of the decoration pulled through from the other side. The verso has the same green binding as the recto (*cf.* figure K). At the verso, in the triangular, protruding part, the innermost red strip is simply folded to fit the shape, showing creases (figure F-H). The other strips that make up the decorative band follow the outline of the edge without being crumpled, which might suggest that these were cut to shape before being applied. The lower edge, facing the intact short side, is intact and shows a green binding at the verso.

Cat. No. 44, L3 #002. Overview of the recto (A) and verso (B); C) Detail of the enhanced edge, including the binding, seen from verso; D) As C but seen in cross section. Scale bars C, D are 10 mm.

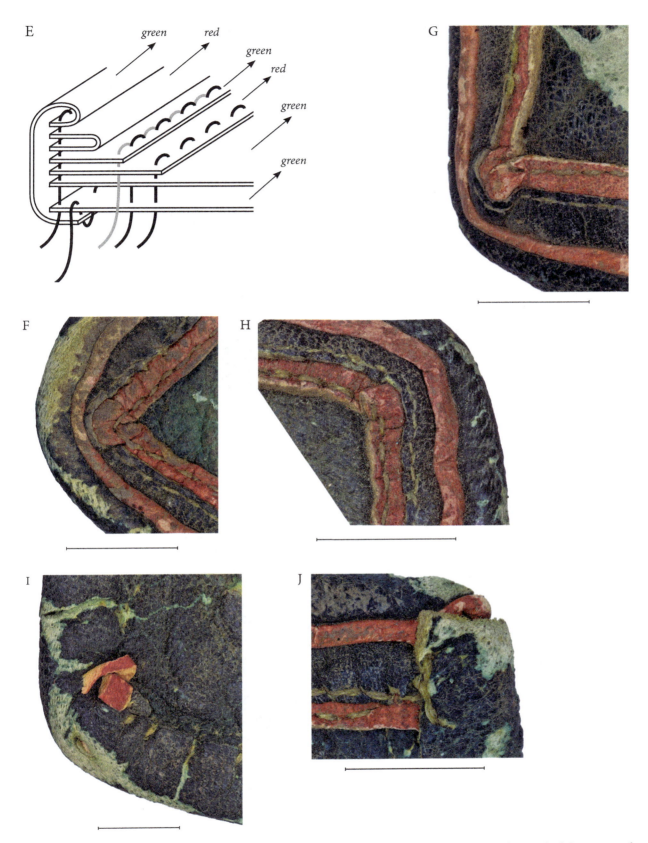

Cat. No. 44, L3 #002. *E) Diagram of the construction of the enhanced edge seen in C, D; F) Detail of the centre of the enhanced edge seen from verso; G) Detail of the left corner of the enhanced edge seen from verso; H) Detail of the right corner of the enhanced edge seen from recto; I) As H but seen from recto; J) As F but seen from recto. Scale bars are 10 mm.*

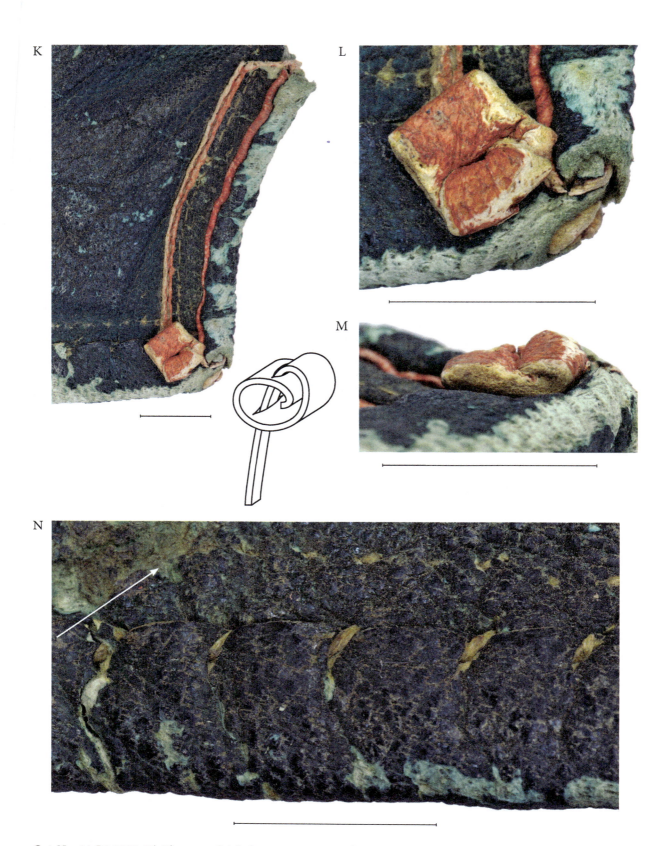

Cat. No. 44, L3 #002. *K) Close up of right lower corner, seen from recto. Inset: Diagram of the toggle. Cf. L3 #004A, C at. No. 46; L) Detail of the toggle at the recto; M) as L but seen from aside; N) Detail of the edge binding and stitching seen from the recto (see figure F). The arrow points to the second series of running stitches that secures the appliqué by using the interstitch spaces of the first set of running stitches (double running stitch). Scale bars are 10 mm.*

CATALOGUE NUMBER 45

Id. No.   L3 #003.
Measurements   Length: 424. Width: 140-74-83. Thickness: 1.

Description

A long, roughly rectangular, band of leather made of two pieces (red and green), which are sewn together (figure A, B). The piece flares out at either end (one end more than the other) and is narrowest in the centre. The two layers face each other with the flesh side. Both long sides are edged by a band of alternating red and green strips (figure C-H), which also serves to secure the two surfaces together. Fragment L3 #002 (Cat. No. 44), fits to the top of the piece (* in figure A), whereas the bottom edge has a perfect fit with L3 #004C (Cat. No. 46; # in figure A).

The red side clearly shows the impression of the rod of the wooden framework of the chariot body and was thus facing inward most of the time (arrow in figure B). It is, therefore, referred to as the verso. The recto, however, shows a comparable feature albeit less distinctly (arrow in figure A). The band of decoration is identical to that on L3 #001 (Cat. No. 43), including the stitching: the outermost strip of green leather is an edge binding. Most likely it is secured at the recto with running stitches, after which it is pulled both over itself and the edge of the object; at the verso it is secured with whip stitches. It extends about 8.6 mm and only covers its own row of stitching. The edge of the binding is folded, at the recto, towards the surface, the fold (width: 5 mm) overlapping, in stair-step fashion, the first strip of red leather (folded lengthwise; width: 2.2 mm). The next green strip has a width of 3.2 mm and is partially overlapped by the red strip in stair-step fashion. This green strip is secured to the underlying red one (width: 1 mm), in stair-step fashion, with flax, before being added to the object. The red strip rests immediately on top of the verso. The final green and red bands are further secured to the object (most likely besides the running stitching that also secures the edge binding) with a row of running stitches at the edges, using the interstitch spaces (double running stitch).

At the verso an overlapping layer of green leather is attached to one of the short ends, which is secured with whip stitches of sinew (figure I; there is no indication of a comparable attachment to the other short end). Note the damage in the middle, which might have been caused by folding (anciently?). As seen throughout the fragments, spots that ones were covered with edging shows a distinctly darker colour.

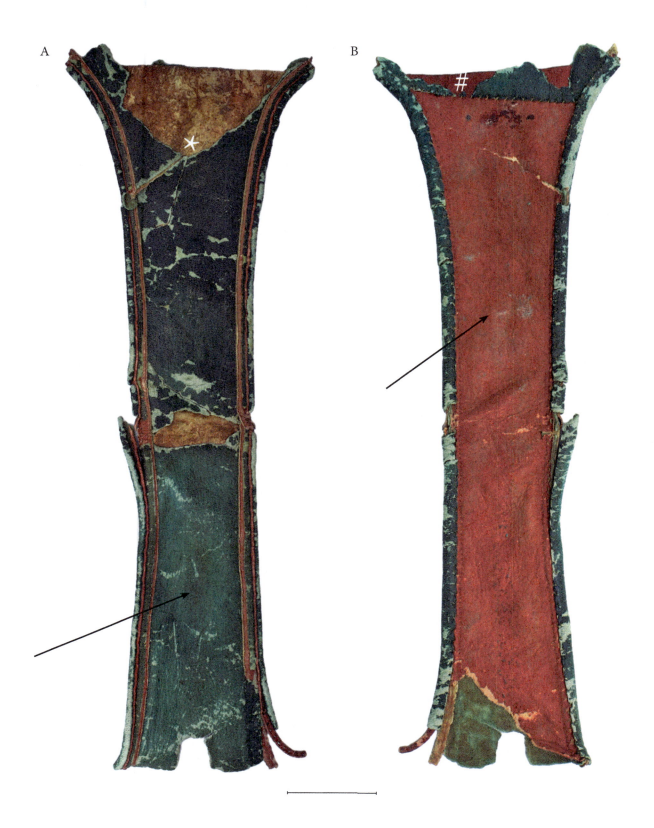

Cat. No. 45, L3 #003. *Overview of the recto (A) and verso (B). Note the slight impression and discolouration that is caused by the rod to which the fragment was secured (arrows). The * and # indicate the fit with L3 #002 (Cat. No. 44) and L3 #004C (Cat. No. 46) respectively.*

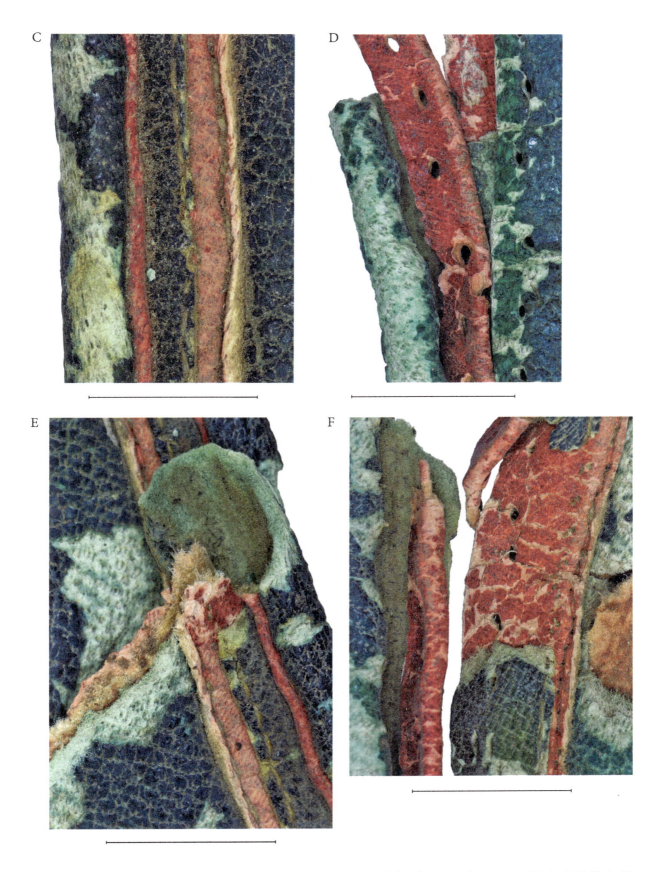

Cat. No. 45, L3 #003. *Details. C) Close up of the enhanced edge with binding seen from recto; D) As C; E-F) As D. Scale bars are 10 mm.*

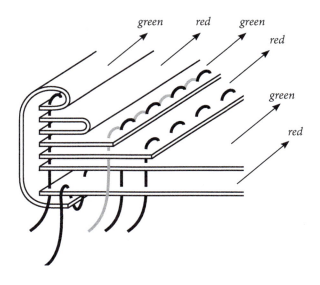

Cat. No. 45, L3 #003. Details. G) Detail of the enhanced edge, seen from verso. Note the two lines of stitch holes; H) Diagram of the construction of the enhanced edge; I) Detail of the whip stitching, securing the extension of the red verso with green. The inset shows the diagram of the seam. Scale bars are 10 mm.

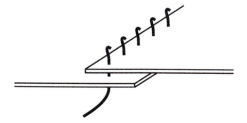

CATALOGUE NUMBER 46

Id. No. L3 #004A-F.
Description: General
Six large pieces of red and green leather (figure A), with various appliqué decoration. Although several fit with each other (and previously described fragments) the pieces are described independently but with one catalogue number. Measurements of the various fragments are included in the specific descriptions.

A

Cat. No. 46, L3 #004. *Overview of the various fragments before they were separated, consolidated/conserved and joined. For details of the various fragments (L3 #004A-F) see pp. 330-345).*

Id. No.   L3 #004A.

Measurements   Length: 410. Width: 95-210. Thickness: 1. For measurements of the decoration *cf.* L3 #001-003 (Cat. No. 43-45).

Description

L-shaped fragment of two pieces (red and green) sewn together (figure A, B). Since the fragment is part of the main casing (it fits with L3 #004B, described below, * in figure B), of which it has been established that the red surface faced inwards (see L3 #003, Cat. No. 45), this side will be referred to as 'verso'.

The two layers of the fragment face each other with their flesh side. Approximately three quarters of the length of the bottom edge is connected to a tube (secured with running stitches of zS_2 sinew; figure C): the seam faces the green side. Part of the drawstring is still present. There is no sign of a (decorative) cover of the seam. The edge of the vertical extension has a binding of alternating red and green strips, which also serves to secure the two surfaces together (figure D-F; for a detailed description of the edge binding see L3 #001, Cat. No. 43). At the short, horizontal edge of this extension, the green binding as well as the first red strip, which the green binding overlaps in stair-step fashion, continue towards the concave edge. The two innermost layers, *i.e.* the green and final red one, however, overlap the comparable elements of the vertical edge (arrow in figure D). This construction supports the previous suggestion that these two elements of the enhanced binding were secured together before being applied to the main piece. At the concave edge, the binding reverses, the band of alternating red and green strips facing the green recto. On the verso the green strip is pulled over the edge and secured with tiny whip stitches. The outer half of the vertical extension is covered with a piece of green leather, which is secured in the middle with whip stitches (sinew zS_2; figure I) and, at the edge, included in the binding (figure D). The terminal, torn off end of the horizontal part shows the extension by means of another piece of red leather, which is secured with sinew zS_2 whip stitches (figure G). It overlaps the attached part by approximately 10 mm (see L3 #004B, below). In the lower corner between the horizontal and vertical parts, *i.e.* opposite the concave edge, the edge is diagonal with a small, shallow, decorative protrusion in the centre. The corner between this part and the vertical edge itself has a hole (thus it is positioned in the green area of the mainly red verso) and reinforced with a relatively thick, red leather ring, which is secured at either edge with running stitches of sinew (zS_2; figure H). The hole, used to secure the casing to the wooden framework of the body of the chariot, is distorted due to pulling.

As described for L3 #002 (Cat. No. 44), at the corners of the vertical part, the decorative strip pierces the object and emerges at the verso. One of these is a toggle; the other is broken but nonetheless was, most likely, not a toggle (figure J).

D

Cat. No. 46, L3 #004A. D) *Close up of green/red terminal part seen from verso. Note the opposite finishing of the edges. The arrow points to the overlap in part of the enhanced edge (the inner two elements), where the other part (the other two elements) continue around the corner. Scale bar is 10 mm.*

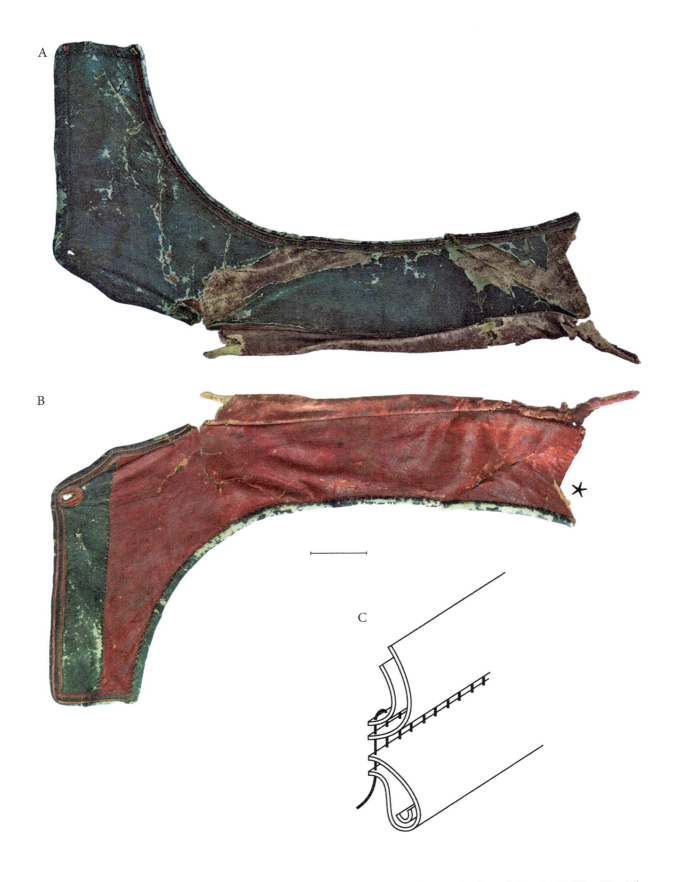

Cat. No. 46, L3 #004A. *Overview of the recto (A) and verso (B); The * indicates the fit with L3 #004B (Cat. No. 45); C) Diagram of the construction between the tube and the body.*

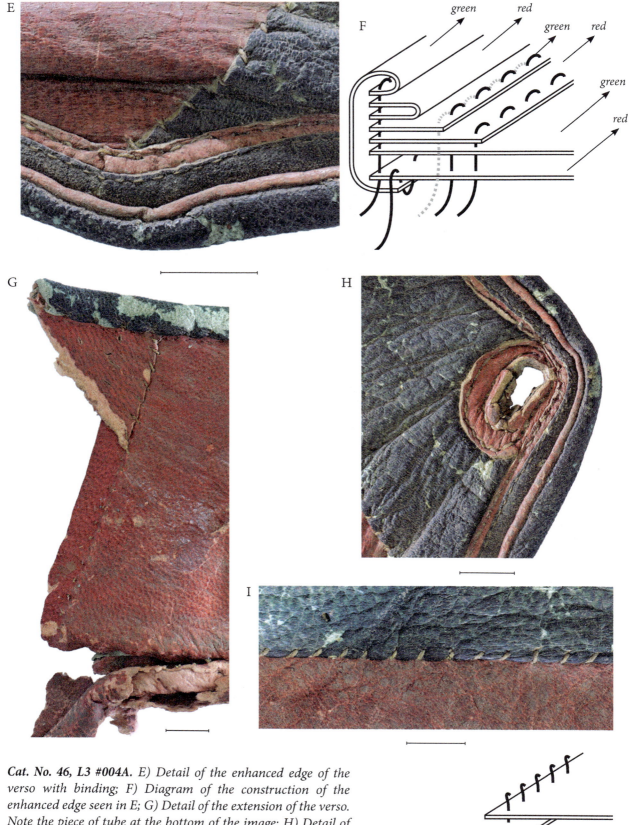

Cat. No. 46, L3 #004A. *E) Detail of the enhanced edge of the verso with binding; F) Diagram of the construction of the enhanced edge seen in E; G) Detail of the extension of the verso. Note the piece of tube at the bottom of the image; H) Detail of the reinforced hole in the corner (seen from verso); I) Detail of the seam between the green and red parts. The inset shows the diagram of the seam. Scale bars are 10 mm.*

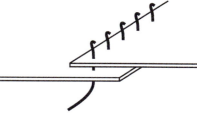

***Cat. No. 46, L3 #004A.** J) Detail of the toggles, which are made by pulling through the edge decoration and stitching it back in itself (cf. L3 #002, Cat. No. 44, figure K). Scale bar is 10 mm.*

Id. No.	L3 #004B.
Measurements	Length: 310. Width: 110. Thickness: 1. For measurements of the decoration *cf.* L3 #001-003 (Cat. No. 43-45).

Description

Two pieces (red and green) are sewn together, flesh sides facing each other (figure A, B). Since the fragment is part of the main casing (it fits with L3 #004C, see below; # in figure A, and L3 #004A, see above; * in figure A), with the green surface facing outwards, this side will be referred to as the 'recto'. The bottom edge is connected to a tube (figure C-E), which is secured with running stitches of zS_2 sinew; the seam faces the green side. Part of the drawstring is still present. There is no sign of a (decorative) cover of the seam.

The recto has a binding of alternating red and green strips (figure F-H), which also serves to secure the two surfaces together. For a detailed description of the edge binding see L3 #001 (Cat. No. 43). The recto shows the extension with another piece of green leather (figure I), which is secured with zS_2 whip stitches of sinew. Interestingly, the stitches have a clear green hue suggesting that staining of the leather was done after the two pieces were attached. However, there is no green visible at the binding and red. At the uncoloured backside of the verso, the overlap of the attachment of an extension described with L3 #004A (see above), is visible by means of a discoloration of about 10 mm wide (arrow in figure B). The two pieces show that extensions of the two layers at the same spot were avoided.

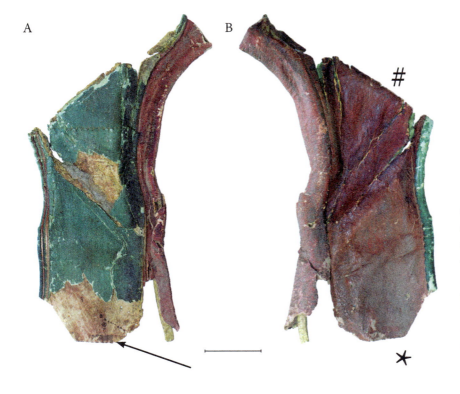

***Cat. No. 46, L3 #004B.** Overview of the recto (A) and verso (B). The edge marked with * connects to L3 #004A (see above) and the one marked with # to L3 #004C (see below). The arrow points to the overlap of an extension of the body leather.*

CATALOGUE | 333

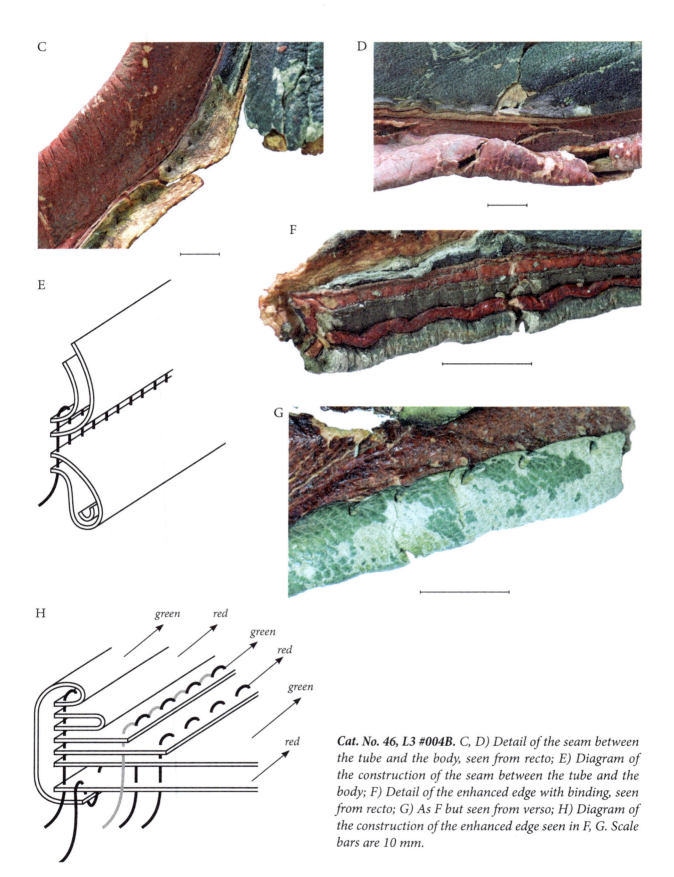

Cat. No. 46, L3 #004B. C, D) Detail of the seam between the tube and the body, seen from recto; E) Diagram of the construction of the seam between the tube and the body; F) Detail of the enhanced edge with binding, seen from recto; G) As F but seen from verso; H) Diagram of the construction of the enhanced edge seen in F, G. Scale bars are 10 mm.

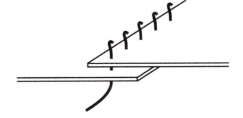

***Cat. No. 46, L3 #004B.** I) Detail of the extension of the recto. Note the discolouration of the stitches. The inset shows the diagram of the seam. Scale bar is 10 mm.*

Id. No.	L3 #004C & E.
Measurements	Length: 635. Width: 220 (central part). Diameter cut-out circle: 75. Thickness: 1. For measurements of the decoration *cf.* L3 #001-003 (Cat. No. 43-45).

Description

Tripartite fragment (figure A, B) consisting of two pieces of leather (red and green) sewn together. The fragment is the central element of the main casing (L3 #002, Cat. No. 44 fit at the vertical element, * in figure B on the next page; L3 #004D, described below to the left, + in figure B; L3 #004E, described below, to the right, # in figure B). The red surface shows the most distinct impression of the wooden framework and is therefore referred to as verso. The diamond shaped fragment at the short end is L3 #004E but it is attached by the conservator of the project, as is the small triangular, unnumbered piece in between L3 #004E and L3 #004C (figure B). Note that L3 #004E itself consists of two fragments. The description will focus on these three fragments together. The bottom edge has a small piece of tube, as described for L3 #004A (see below; figure C). Most of the tube, however, is missing. Opposite the central, vertical element, there is a semi-circular cut-out to accommodate the axle tree. The tube with drawstring would go underneath. The cut-out has a simple edge binding of a lengthwise folded, green leather strip that is secured with whip stitches, the fold facing away from the edge (figure D).

The green recto has a binding of alternating red and green strips, which also serves to secure the two surfaces together (figure E-H). For a detailed description of the edge binding see L3 #001 (Cat. No. 43).

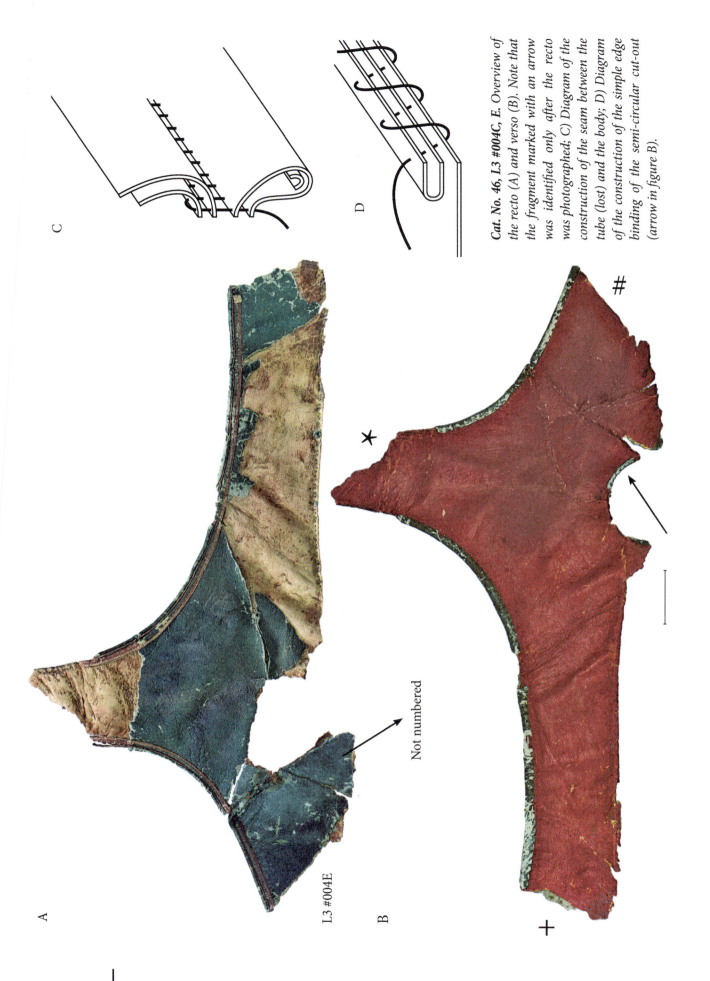

Cat. No. 46, L3 #004C, E. Overview of the recto (A) and verso (B). Note that the fragment marked with an arrow was identified only after the recto was photographed; C) Diagram of the construction of the seam between the tube (lost) and the body; D) Diagram of the construction of the simple edge binding of the semi-circular cut-out (arrow in figure B).

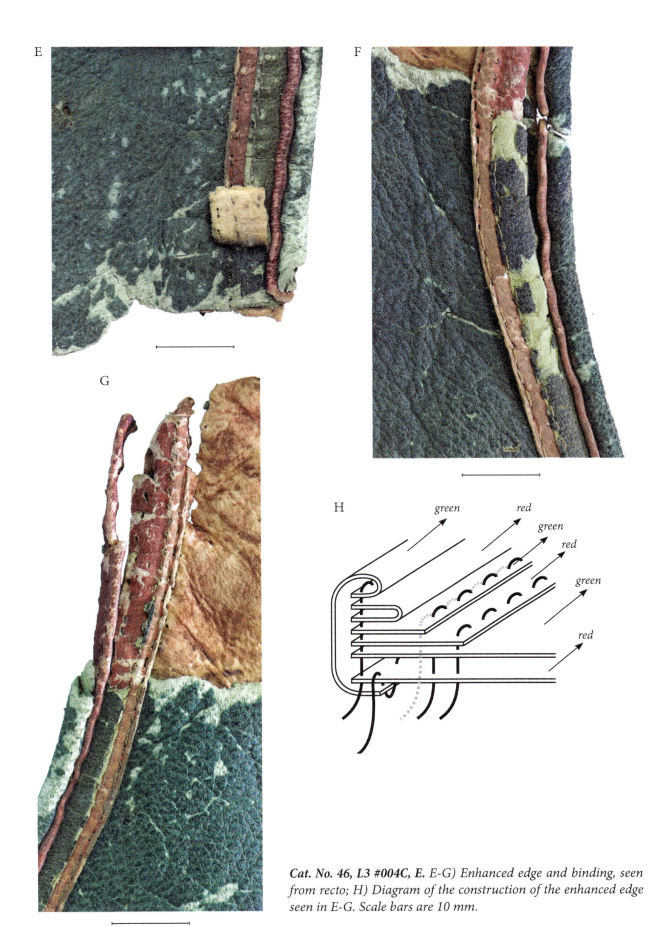

Cat. No. 46, L3 #004C, E. *E-G) Enhanced edge and binding, seen from recto; H) Diagram of the construction of the enhanced edge seen in E-G. Scale bars are 10 mm.*

CATALOGUE | 337

Id. No.   L3 #004D.
Measurements   Length: 250. Width: 230. Thickness: 1. For measurements of the decoration *cf.* L3 #001-003 (Cat. No. 43-45).

Description

For the description of L3 #004D, reader is kindly referred to L3 #004A (see above).

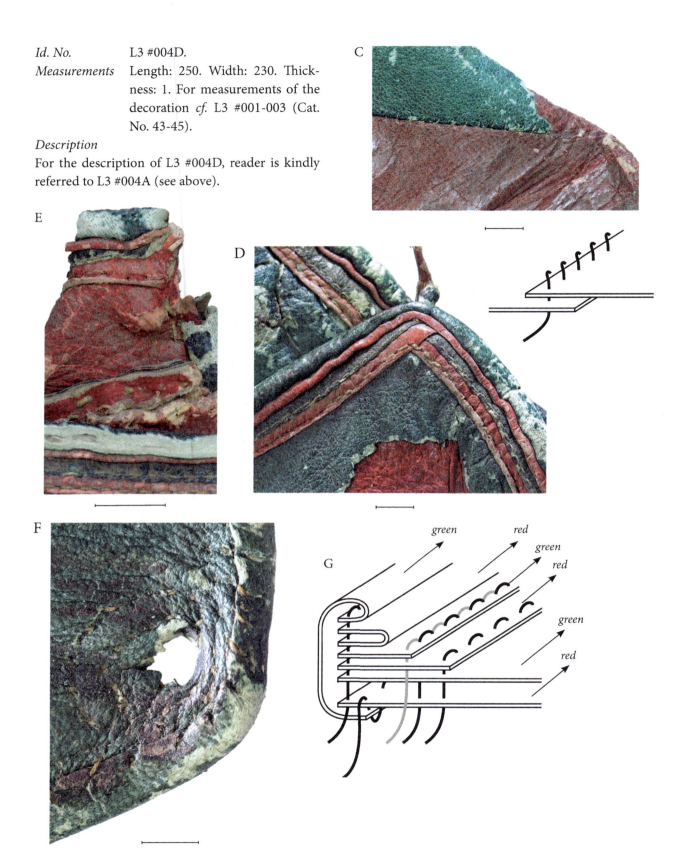

Cat. No. 46, L3 #004D. C) *Detail of the extension of the verso. The inset shows the diagram of the seam; D, E) Details of the enhanced edge of the verso; F) Detail of the edge binding seen at the recto; G) Diagram of the construction of the enhanced edge seen in D & E. Scale bars are 10 mm.*

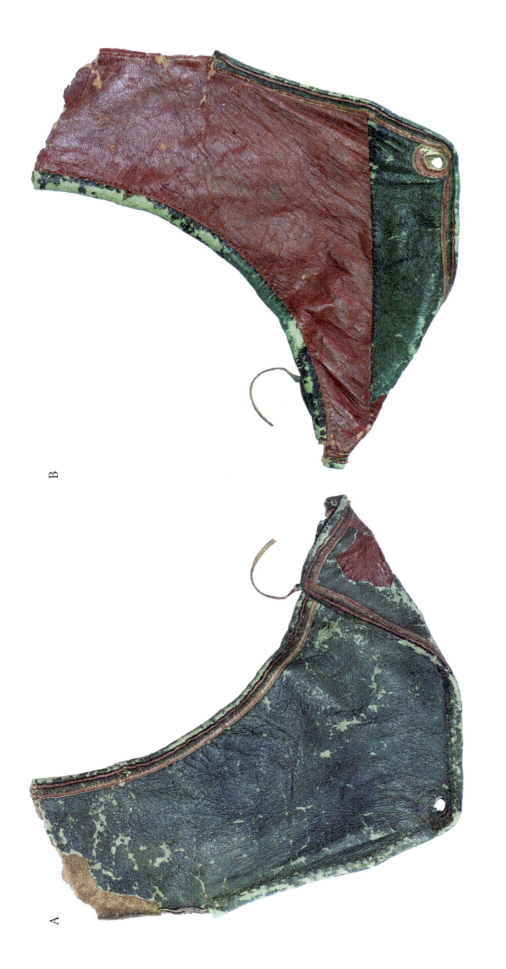

Cat. No. 46, L3 #004D. Overview of the recto (A) and verso (B).

CATALOGUE | 339

Id. No.   L3 #004F.
Object   Holder(?)
Measurements   Overal: 465 x 500 (along folded edge). Width appliqué: 63 - 22.7 - 40.6. Diameter roundel: 62.7 x 63.2. Thickness: 9 (at enhanced edge with binding).

Description

Roughly isoceles triangular shaped fragment (figure A, B) that is made of red leather, enhanced with green. The red sides both face outwards. One edge of the fragment is straight and is finished by folding the outer layer, sandwiching a third layer in between (* in figure A). The opposite edge is concave and enhanced with a binding of strips of differently coloured leather. It shows, from outside in, strips, alternating red and green, which partially overlap in stair-step fashion (figure C, D) and is comparable to previously described fragments in design. The first strip after the green binding (which overlaps it) is red, lengthwise folded and narrow (width: 1 mm); it is placed on top of the lower, green one in stair-step fashion (width: 2.5 mm) which is probably of single thickness. The red one is kept in place by the stitching of the binding (see below); the green one, however, has a line of double running stitch in flax (zS_2). It is placed in stair-step fashion on a single(?) red one (width: 2 mm), which, as the green one, extends most likely until the edge of the object proper. The red one partially overlaps another green one (width: 1-1.5 mm) in stair-step fashion, but this strip does not seem to extend until the edge of the object but about halfway the width of the overlapping strip. It is, in contrast to the other green strip, folded lengthwise. It is held in position by the row of running stitches that also keeps the overlapping red strip secured. It cannot be determined through which layers these stitches are sewn (as with the stitching mentioned above), but no stitching is visible at the verso except for the running stitches that secures the binding proper. Probably, as in the previously described fragments, part of the decoration was stitched together before being added to the object by using double running stitching. The edge of the fragment, including the decoration, is bound by a strip of green leather (width: 3 mm). At the recto, it is folded inwards and stitched, most likely, with running stitches through all layers except the binding at the verso. Here, the binding is secured with whip stitches to the verso only (though possibly and the stitches include one or two more layers accidentally). Sinew is used to secure the binding. The binding of the concave edge overruns the binding of the short end of the element described below (figure H). Note that, rather than forming a concave edge at the other side of the enhanced element, a small piece of decorated edge suggests a entirely different construction (arrow in figure C). However, since it is torn off, this portion of the object cannot be dependably reconstructed.

One short edge is also torn off, possibly from the opposite side, in which case the object was a tube with open ends at either side. One end is an integral part of the complete object (arrow in figure A), but at the side of the folded edge, the decoration sticks out of the edge (dashed arrow in figure A). This element, running from one edge to the other, is enhanced by applied decoration in green, bordered by alternating strips of red and green (figure E-J). The decoration is stuffed, creating a pleasing relief (figure F-J). The elongated part is trapezoidal in shape. The central appliqué is like a tall bouquet of three stacked lilies with a vegetal top, made of green leather. It consists of a diamond compartment, with a short stub at the top and bottom. Curling tendrils flank these diamond-shaped compartments. The whole terminates in tendrils with a central element extended to the narrow edge. At the other end, the motif ends in three narrow leaves or stylised lilies flanked by outwards curling tendrils. The central part (width: 3 mm) extends towards the far opposite end of this element; roughly at the junction between the trapezoidal element and the bridging, narrow part to the other terminal(?) end, the extended central leave(?) is joint at either side by flaring, narrow lines in green (arrow in figure E). These three lines are cut together from one piece of leather and separate from the design to which they attach at either end. The flaring lines are flanked by an edge that follows their contour. From outside in, it consists of a wide strip of green (folded inwards at either side(?) and secured with stiches of flax at either edge; width: 4.5 mm) that overlap a single red strip (width: 3 mm) in stair-step fashion (which is included in the stitching of the green wider strap but also with an aditional row of stitches at the opposite edge, which include also the next and last lengthwise folded green strip; width: 1 mm).

The opposite terminal end is distinctly smaller. The edges toward it flare gently outwards into the trapezoidal part, which is enhanced with one small circular compartment with double tendrils at either side (figure E-G). At the end, facing the previously-described terminal end, are three narrow leaves or stylised lilies. The other end of the compartment extends into a line towards the edge proper. The decoration is applied with regular running stitching of flax at either side (with very short interstitch spaces). Note at the extended corners the cuts in the red edge (encircled in figure G).

A special feature is seen next to this described element: a circular appliqué (figure A, K-M). It consists of three concentric circles of diminishing size (wide green [width: 3.5 mm] which are folded lengthwise; a faded red one [width: 7 mm] on top of which is secured a narrow green one [width: 1.5 mm], approximately leaving 1 mm wide red visible at the other side). The outermost ring is attached in such a way that the fold, which faces outwards, is lifted off slightly from the undersurface, a feature also seen in part of the harness (such as #40 & #41, Cat. No. 96). The central wheel-like motif, attached on top of the faded red, has eight spokes with a central line, arising from a central circle. The total diameter of the roundel is 60 mm.

The verso shows an element of comparable width with green edge binding. It is not entirely clear what its relation is to the overall piece; it is in bad condition, probably because it seems to have been attached with glue. At the verso of the smaller terminal end, a strip of beige leather, torn off short (figure F), comparable to BI-003 (Cat. No. 85) is attached by several stitches at the edge.

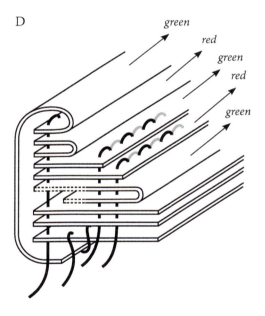

Cat. No. 46, L3 #004F. C) Detail of the edge opposite the concave, intact edge, suggesting a different construction. The arrow refers to the small fragment of this part; D) Diagram of the construction of the concave edge with binding (shown in the top half of figure C; the diagram of the construction of the edge to the left lower corner is shown in figure J. Scale bar is 10 mm. Overviews of L3 #004F on the next page.

CATALOGUE | 341

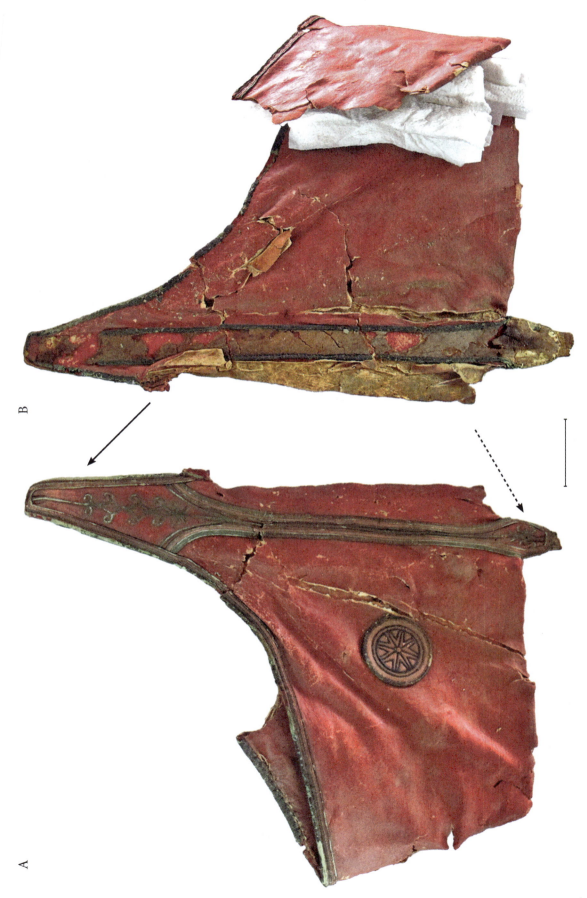

Cat. No. 46, L3 #004F. *Overview of the recto (A) and verso (B). The arrow indicates the end which is integral of the complete object; the dashed arrow indicates the opposite end where the decoration sticks out (see also figure C).*

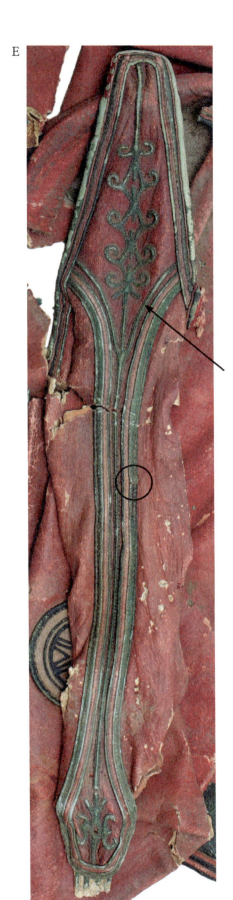

Cat. No. 46, L3 #004F. Details. E) The elongated element enhanced with appliqué. The arrow points to the two lines at either side of the central appliqué motif. The encircled part is shown in detail in figure I; F) The torn off fragment of strap coming from the elongated central element; G) The terminal end, showing the cuts of the red strip (encircled). Note the central strip of the decoration, which drops short of the appliqué at the trapezoidal part. Scale bars F, G are 10 mm.

Cat. No. 46, L3 #004F. Details. H) The enhanced edge with binding runs over the central appliqué; I) The appliqué. Note the cut of the green strip; J) Diagram of the construction of the central appliqué motif seen in figure I. Scale bars are 10 mm.

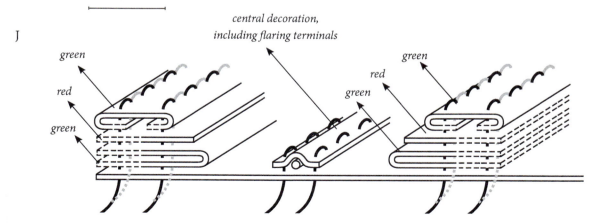

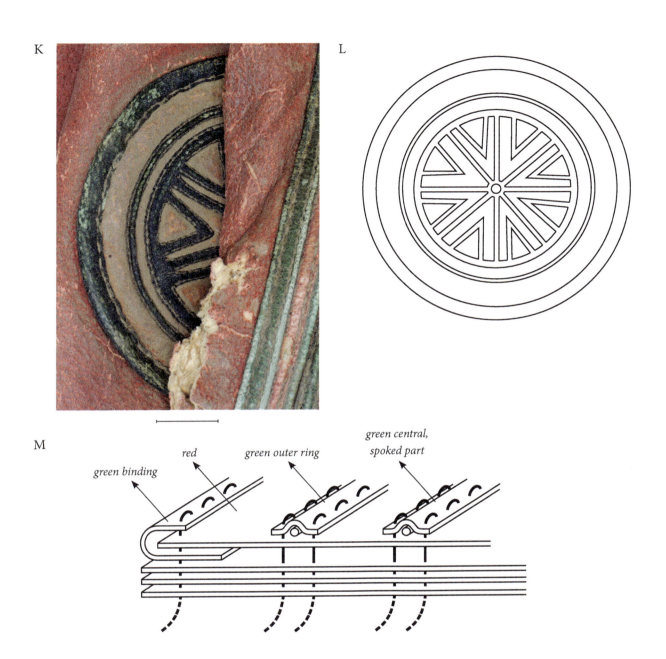

Cat. No. 46, L3 #004F. *Details. K) The roundel (only partially visible here as the object was still folded over at time of photographing, but* cf. *figure A); L) Diagram of the roundel. M) Diagram of the construction of the roundel. Scale bar is 10 mm.*

CATALOGUE NUMBER 47

Id. No. L1 #011.
Object Body part of holder(?).
Measurements Length: 220. Width: 100-220. Thickness edge: 11.5.

Description

A tapering piece of red leather (figure A, B) that is folded over (figure G). The edge opposite the folded edge is decorated with attached bands of alternating red and green. Both surfaces are lined. The only other object that consists of folded leather comparable to L1 #011 (including the design of the binding) is the possible holder L3 #004F (Cat. No. 46).

The decoration is applied to the recto (figure C-D, F, H). It shows, from outside in, alternating red and green strips, which partially overlap in stair-step fashion. The first strip is red, lengthwise folded and narrow (width: 1 mm). It is placed on top of the next, green one in stair-step fashion (width: 2.5-3 mm) which is probably of single thickness. The red one is kept in place by the stitching of the binding (see below); the green one, however, has a line of stitching in flax (zS_2). It is placed in stair-step fashion on a single red one (width: 1 mm), which, as is the case with the green one, extends until the edge of the object proper. The red one partially overlaps another green one (width: 1.5 mm) in stair-step fashion, but this strip does not extend until the edge of the object, but about halfway the width of the overlapping strip. It is, in contrast to the other green strip, folded lengthwise. It is held in position by the row of running stitches that also keeps the overlapping red strip secured. It cannot be determined through which layers these stitches are sewn (as with the stitching mentioned above), but no stitching is visible at the verso except for the running stitching that secures the binding (figure E). The interstitch space is used to attach the strips to the undersurface (double running stitch). The edge of the object, including the decoration, is bound by a strip of green leather (width: 4-5 mm). At the recto, it is folded inwards and stitched, most likely, with running stitches through all layers except the binding at the verso. Here, the binding is secured with whip stitches to probably the verso only or,

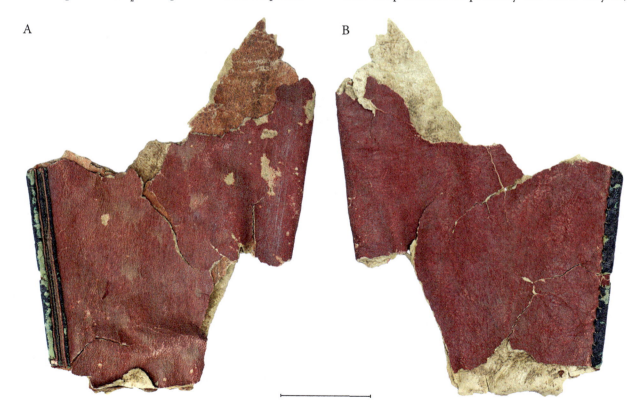

Cat. No. 47, L1 #011. *Overview of the recto (A) and verso (B) respectively.*

possibly and if so, accidentally, one or two more layers. Sinew is used to attach the binding. The intact condition makes it difficult to identify details; the broken edge in L1 #034 (Cat. No. 120) probably is the same.

The recto shows, parallel to the folded edge, two slightly impressed lines (figure I), which might be accidental.

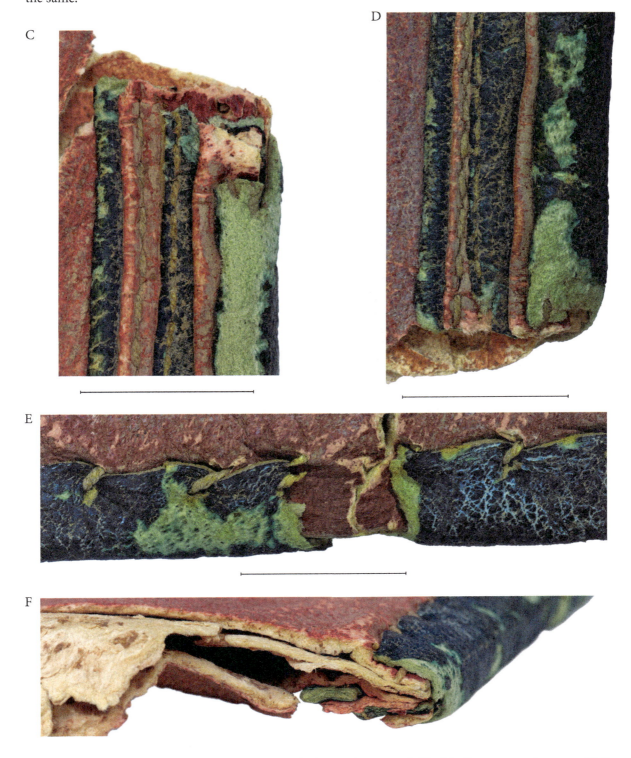

Cat. No. 47, L1 #011. *C-D) Details of the enhanced edge at the recto; E) The binding seen at the verso; F) Cross section of the enhanced edge. Scale bars C-F are 10 mm.*

CATALOGUE | 347

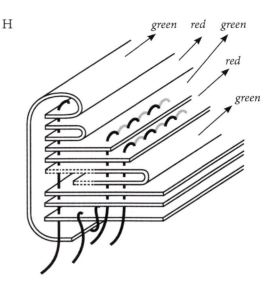

Cat. No. 47, L1 #011. G) Cross section of the folded edge; H) Diagram of the construction of the edge decoration; I) Impressed lines at the recto. Scale bars are 10 mm.

CATALOGUE NUMBER 48

Id. No. L5 #009.
Object Fragment of holder(?).
Measurements Length: 3. Width: 2.3. Thickness: 5.
Description

Edge piece from a larger leather object (figure A, B), which originates, judging the lining, from the possible holder (L3 #004F, Cat. No. 46). The recto shows, from outside in, lengthwise folded strips, alternating red and green, which partially overlap in stair-step fashion (figure C, D). The first strip is narrow and red, folded lengthwise (width: 1.5 mm); it is placed on top of the lower, green one, in stair-step fashion (width: 2.5-3 mm). The red one is kept in place by the stitching of the binding (see below); the green one, however, has a line of running stitches in flax (zS_2). It is placed in stair-step fashion on a red one (width: 2.5-3 mm), which, as the green one, extends until the edge of the object proper. The red one partially overlaps another green one (width: 2 mm) in stair-step fashion, but this strip, folded lengthwise, does not extend until the edge of the object but only about to halfway the width of the overlapping strip. It is held in position by the row of running stitches that also keeps the overlapping red strip secured. It cannot be determined through which layers these stitches are sewn (as with the stitching mentioned above), but no stitching is visible at the verso except for the running stitching that secures the binding. The edge of the object, including the decoration, is bound by a strip of green leather (width: 4.5 mm). At the recto, it is folded inwards and stitched, most likely, with running stitches through all layers except the binding at the verso. Here, the binding is secured with whip stitches to probably the verso only or, possibly and if so, accidentally, one or two more layers. Sinew is used to attach the binding.

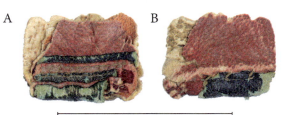

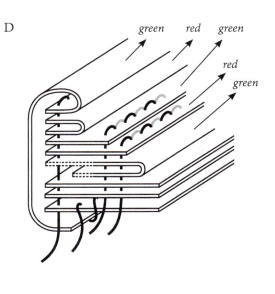

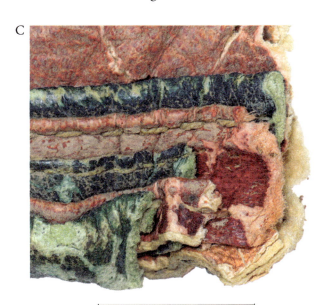

Cat. No. 48, L5 #009. *Overview of the recto (A) and verso (B); C) Detail of the enhanced edge (recto); D) Diagram of the construction of the edge decoration. Scale bar C is 10 mm.*

CATALOGUE NUMBER 49

Id. No.   L1 #022.
Object   Fragment of holder(?).
Measurements   102 x 135. Thickness: 1.
Description
Brittle, crumpled piece of red leather that is folded over.

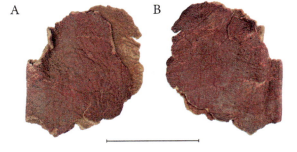

Cat. No. 49, L1 #022. *Overview of the recto(?; A) and verso(?; B).*

SIDING FILL

CATALOGUE NUMBER 50

Id. No.   L1 #001.
Measurements   Overall dimensions: 310 x 375. Thickness: 0.4. Width of tube: 28. Width green decoration strips: 4. Width red decoration strip: 4.5.

Description

A roughly oval piece of leather that was broken off from a larger object (figure A, B). The catalogue number also includes two small, featureless scraps, which are not numbered separately. The piece is severely worn due to use (hands gripping the railing around which the leather was tied; figure L, M), visible by the discolouration close to the tube (edge of the casing; figure E-I) as well as flaking off of the topmost surface layer.

One edge consists of a tube (figure C, D, K), containing a matching red drawstring that is folded lengthwise, the fold of which faces away from the tube's attachment to the body of the piece. The tube is made of one piece of leather that is folded and secured at one side, the seam of which attaches it to the large body of the piece as well. Although the seam is obscured due to the folding of the piece, one can establish that it is secured with running stitches, most likely made of sinew. A connection between two pieces of tube is visible at approximately one-fifth of its length (arrow in figure J). Here, one tube is inserted into the other; empty stitch holes suggests that the two pieces were secured with stitching.

At the recto, the seam between the two edges of the tube and the body of the object is hidden by a band that is made of two green strips flanking a central red one (figure E-K). The three elements were stitched together before being attached to the piece, which means that only the rows of stitches at the outer edges of the band secure the band to the casing. In all cases, the sewing was done using zS_2 threads of flax using whip stitch. Note the distinctly redder colour of the leather beneath the decoration band. An interesting feature is visible on the verso: a corner that sticks out of the body has an irregularly shaped piece of creamy leather attached to it (figure N, O). Because no stitches are visible, it is plausible that it is glued onto the body of the piece proper. It might have served as reinforcement of some kind.

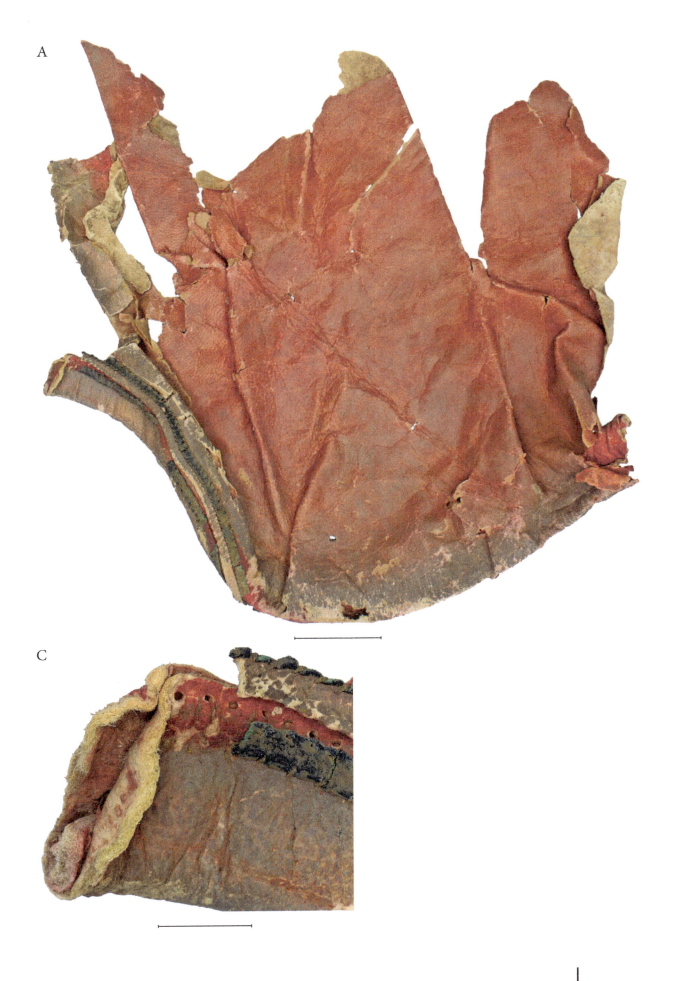

B

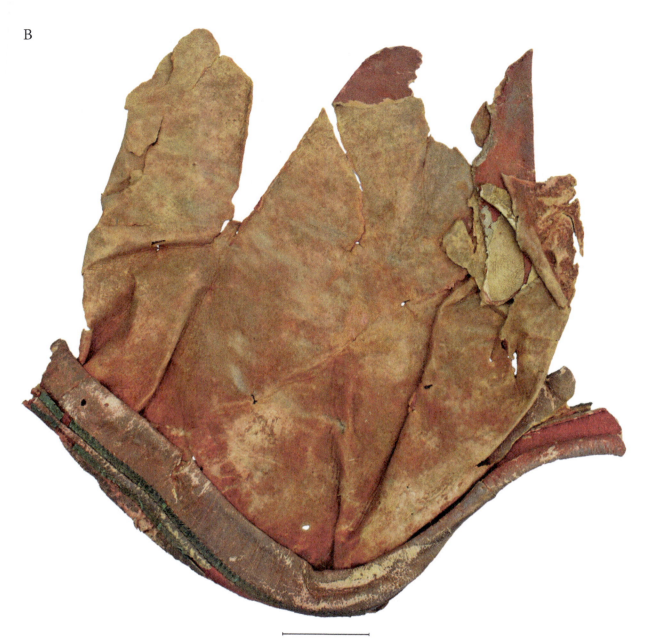

D

Cat. No. 50, L1 #001. *Overview of the recto (A) and verso (B); C) Detail of the tube with drawstring and remnants of the tripartite band that covers the seam between the tube and body; D) Detail of the seam between the tube and body. Scale bars C, D are 10 mm.*

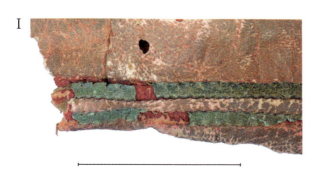

Cat. No. 50, L1 #001. Details of the recto. E-J) The tripartite band that obscures the seam between the tube and the body. Note the distinct darker colour of the leather beneath this decoration. The arrow indicates the connection of two pieces of tube.

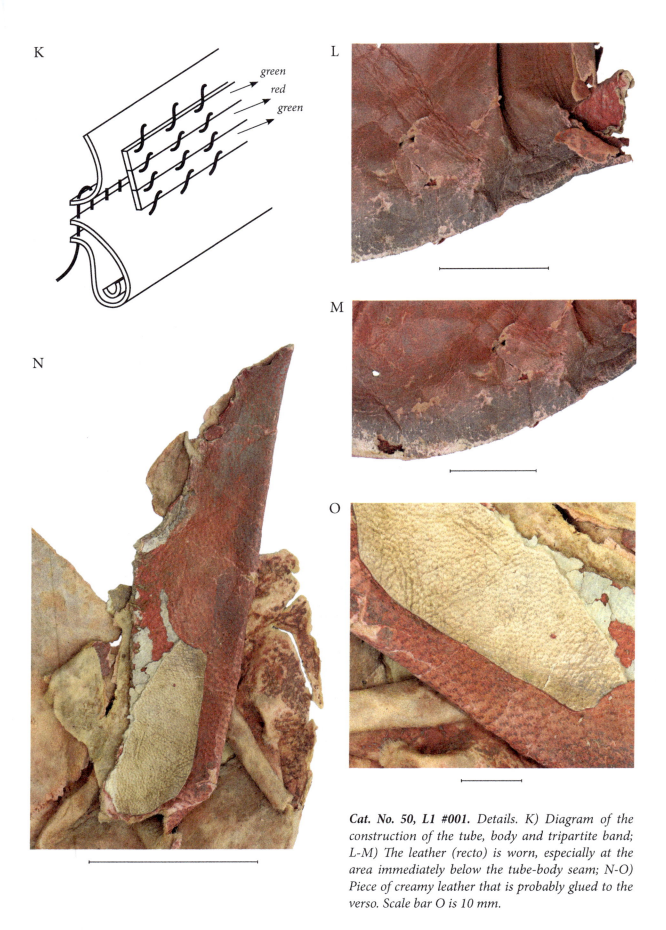

Cat. No. 50, L1 #001. Details. K) Diagram of the construction of the tube, body and tripartite band; L-M) The leather (recto) is worn, especially at the area immediately below the tube-body seam; N-O) Piece of creamy leather that is probably glued to the verso. Scale bar O is 10 mm.

CATALOGUE NUMBER 51

Id. No. L1 #002.

Measurements Overall dimensions: 240 x 240. Thickness: 0.6. Width with tube: 94. Width without tube: 65. Length tube: approximately 260. Width tube: 28. Thickness tube's leather: 0.7.

Description

An irregularly-shaped piece, with one crescent-shaped and one straight edge. The latter has a tube attached to it (figure A-C). The verso is pink (figure G-I) and has not been coloured at all. Wear is visible at the some places comparable to L1 #001 (Cat. No. 50), but it is less severe, suggesting that the piece was part of the casing that was not touched or abraded as much as others.

The tube (figure I, J) is made of one piece of leather that is folded and secured at one side, the seam of which attaches it to the large body of the piece as well. It includes a lengthwise folded drawstring, the fold of which faces away from the attachment of the tube to the body of the piece. At the recto, a band of decoration that is made of two green strips flanking a central red strip obscures the seam (figure G, H, J). These three narrow strips were secured before being attached to the piece, which means that only the rows of stitches at the outer edges of the three strips secure the band to the casing. In all cases, the sewing was done with whip stitching using zS_2 threads of flax. At about one-third of its length, the tube is torn in two (rather than an intended connection as seen, for example, in L1 #001, Cat. No. 50), although the drawstring is still intact (figure K). One end of the tube has, running at its edge, a decoration of two green strips flanking a central red strip, similar to the band that obscures the seam at the recto (figure L, M). The outermost green strip is secured over the edge of the tube with whip stitches (mostly lost). This seems to indicate that this is the end of the tube.

The concave edge of the body of the fragment is enhanced by a green edge binding (figure D-F). This is, at the edge/verso, attached by whip stitches (probably sinew) after which the strip is folded over itself and secured with running stitches at the recto (long, but with short interstitch spacing). Here, it overlaps a red strip in stair-step fashion, which, in its turn, overlaps a lengthwise folded strip of green leather. These latter two are secured with running stitches (long, but with short interstitch spacing). This stitching is done with zS_2 flax thread.

D

E

Cat. No. 51, L1 #002. Details. D) The enhanced edge at the recto; E) The edge seen from the verso. Scale bars are 10 mm. Overviews at the next page.

Cat. No. 51, L1 #002. Overview of the recto (A) and verso (B); C) Two small fragments, the top one being part of the tripartite band that obscures the seam between tube and body.

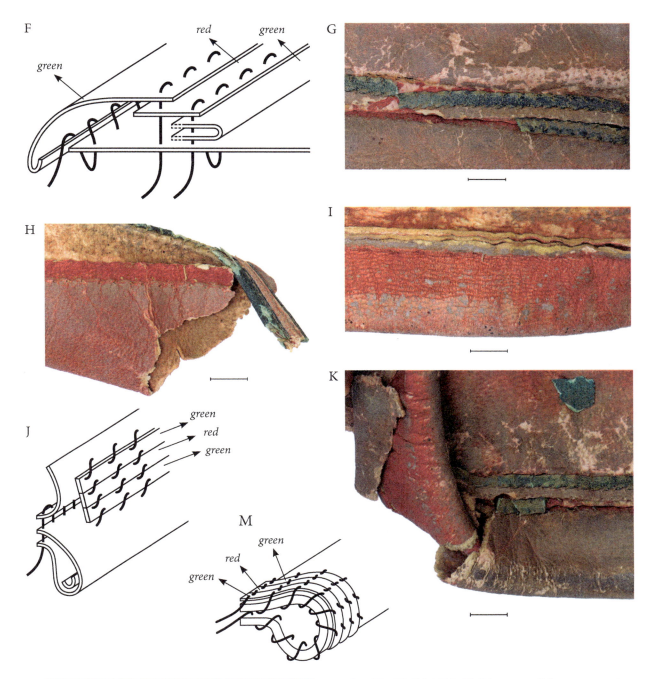

Cat. No. 51, L1 #002. *F) Diagram of the construction of the enhanced edge with binding (see D, E); G, H) Detail of the tripartite band that covers the seam between the tube and the body. Note the distinct darker, original colour of the leather beneath this decoration; I) Detail of the seam (recto) between the tube and the body; J) Diagram of the construction of the tube, body and tripartite band, seen in G, J, K; K) The tube is torn in two; L) Detail of the edge binding of the end of the tube; M) The diagram of the construction of the end of the tube, seen in L. Scale bars are 10 mm.*

CATALOGUE | 357

CATALOGUE NUMBER 52

Id. No. L1 #003.
Measurements Overall dimensions: 130 x 102. Thickness: 1. Total width edge: 6.7 (from edge to body: 3.2 - 2.5 - 1.0 respectively).

Description
Roughly triangular (due to tearing) piece of red leather of which the decorated edge is concave (figure A, B). The verso is the natural beige shade of the leather. The colour of the leather is, as usual, applied to the grain side. A green edge binding is, at the edge/verso, attached by whip stitches (figure C-H), made of sinew (indicated by its glazed appearance) and including the red strip that is part of the edge decoration at the recto. After this, the strip is folded over itself and secured with running stitches at the recto (long, but with short interstitch spacing). Here, it overlaps a red strip in stair-step fashion, which, in its turn, overlaps a lengthwise folded strip of green leather. This green leather strip is considerably thinner than the red and could, therefore, easily be folded. These latter two are secured with running stitches (long, but with short interstitch spacing). This stitching is done with zS_2 flax thread.

At one corner, the green strip shows a diagonal cut (arrow in figure C) at the outwards facing fold; a second cut(?) is seen slightly away towards the centre of the piece at the edge that faces the edge of the foundation (double arrow in figure C). The former cannot be indentified at the back of the piece; the latter, however, is visible on the verso.

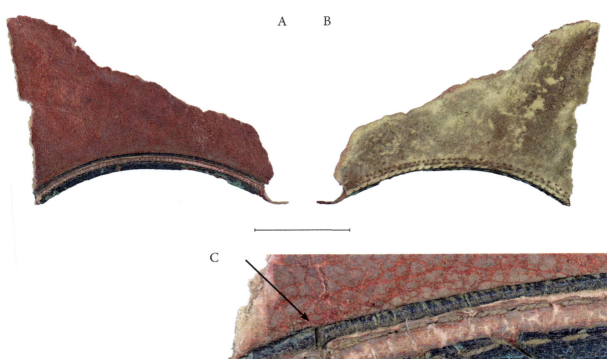

Cat. No. 52, L1 #003. *Overview of the recto (A) and verso (B); C) Enhanced edge with binding seen at the recto (see figure E). The arrows are explained in the description. Scale bar C is 10 mm.*

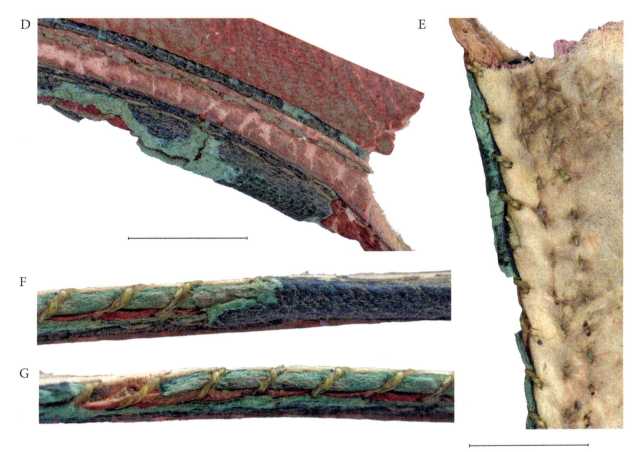

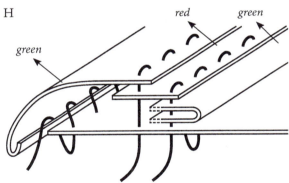

Cat. No. 52, L1 #003. Details. D) Enhanced edge with binding seen at the recto (see figure E). Note the original red colour under the binding; E) The binding at the verso; F, G) Binding, clearly showing the sinew zS_2 whip stitching (glazed appearance); H) Diagram of the edge construction. Scale bars C-E are 10 mm.

CATALOGUE NUMBER 53

Id. No.   L1 #018.
Measurements   Length tube: 150. Width tube: 28. Circumference tube: 54. Thickness tube's leather: 0.7. Attached leather: 150 x 6 - 18. Thickness: 0.5-0.6.

Description
A leather tube that was part of a larger piece but is broken off at either side (figure A, B). The large flat piece is torn off too (figure C). At one end of the object, a small piece of worn leather is attached, with whip stitches in sinew, to the first element that connects with the tube (arrow in figure A). This might, however, be a repair rather than part of the original construction. Alternatively, it might be remnants of the stitches that attached the decoration that once hid the seam at the obverse (see below). The elements are of red leather and stitched together with

running stitches that are made of what has tentatively been identified as sinew.

The tube is made of one piece of leather that is folded and secured at one side (figure C-E) – the seam attaches the torn off piece as well. There is no passepoil. Originally, it must have been covered by another strip of leather as is suggested by stitch holes and difference in coloration. Probably this would have been done with a band of green-red-green strips of leather, as seen in L1 #001 and L1 #002 (Cat. No. 50 and 51; dashed in figure F). Inside the tube, at the side opposite the seam, is a red leather drawstring, which is slightly thicker than the rest. It is folded lengthwise with the fold facing away from the seam. It is not secured. The piece of leather that is attached to the tube shows, at the recto, signs of stress, approximately 11 mm away from the seam: it is distressed and discoloured. Also one end of the tube is discoloured.

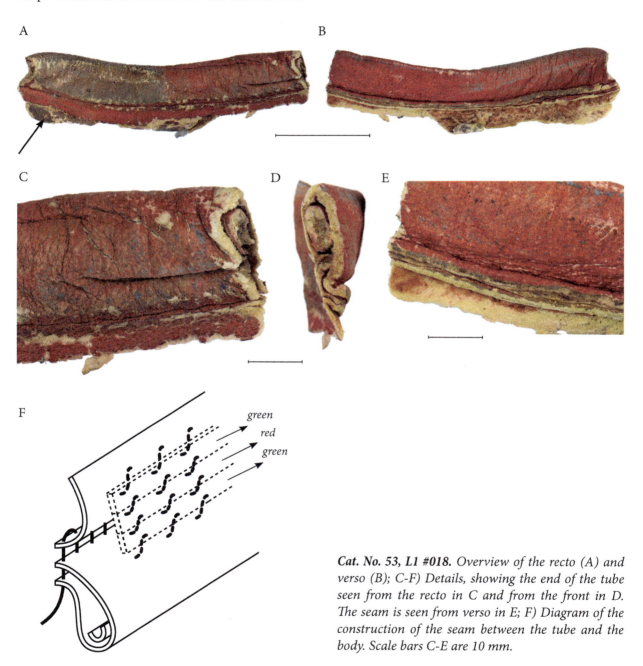

Cat. No. 53, L1 #018. *Overview of the recto (A) and verso (B); C-F) Details, showing the end of the tube seen from the recto in C and from the front in D. The seam is seen from verso in E; F) Diagram of the construction of the seam between the tube and the body. Scale bars C-E are 10 mm.*

CATALOGUE NUMBER 54

Id. No. L1 #023.

Measurements Length tube: 530. Diameter tube: 30. Thickness tube's leather: 1. Larger piece attached to tube: appr. 10 x 53 (folded). Thickness: 0.5.

Description

A large, irregularly shaped and partially folded fragment (figure A, B), consisting of a tube of leather that was part of a larger piece, but broken off now. The tube (figure F, G) is connected to a much larger piece of red leather, which is torn off too. The elements are secured with running stitches of sinew. The tube contains a lengthwise folded strip of red leather, which acted as a drawstring. Note the connection between the two components which form the tube in order to obtain the required length: one part is pushed inside the other, the junction of which is secured with whip stitches (figure H).

At the outer, visible surface (recto), a set of three strips of leather, two green (width: 7.5 mm) flanking a red one (width: 5 mm), covers the seam with one of the outer green ones placed directly on top of the seam (figure C-E). These are secured to each other as well as to the object with whip stitches of zS_2 flax thread. They were stitched together before being applied to the object, which is evidenced by the fact that the stitches that secure the inner edges do not pierce the leather of the object, in contrast to the two rows of stitches at either side of the set. Note the distinct redder colour beneath the decoration as opposed to the exposed leather, which has faded. At one point, the lower strip of green shows the end of one and start of an additional piece, one end slightly overlapping the other (arrow in figure C).

The flat piece of leather that is attached to the tube is pierced by at least four slits (see arrow in figure A) that are oriented parallel to the tube's length. Each is about 17 mm in length. The area above these slits (figure I) is much darker in hue with gray spots of wear, suggesting that it was covered by another piece of leather, secured through these slits either with a series of individual lashings or extensions emerging from the piece of leather covering.

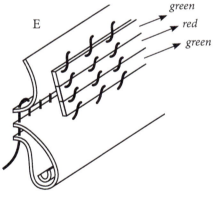

Cat. No. 54, L1 #023. *C, D) Detail of the tripartite decoration that obscures the seam between the body and the tube. Note the connection of the two pieces of green strip in C (arrow); E) Diagram of the construction of the seam between the tube and the body. Scale bars are 10 mm. The overviews can be found on the next page.*

Cat. No. 54, L1 #023. *Overview of the recto (A) and verso (B). Clearly visible is the area that ones was covered and thus protected from fading and wear.*

F

G

H

Cat. No. 54, L1 #023. F) *Seam seen from verso; note the regular, circular shape of the stitch holes, suggesting pre-pricking;* G) *Detail of the seam seen from recto; the remnants of the stitches that secured the tripartite enhancement are still partially in place;* H) *The tube consists of two parts that are secured with whip stitching (inset);* I) *Detail of the discoloured part above the slits. Note the distinct darker hue of red, suggesting it used to be covered and protected from sunlight. Scale bars F-H are 10 mm.*

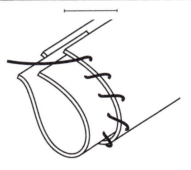

I

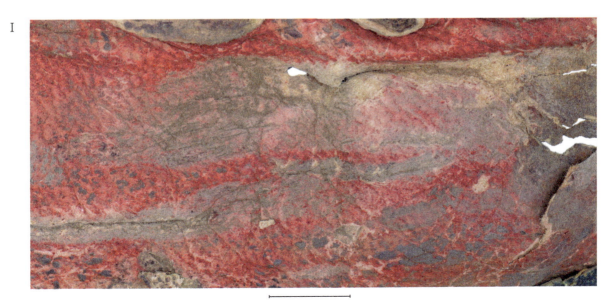

CATALOGUE NUMBER 55

Id. No.   L2 #002.
Measurements   Length: 330. Width: 120. Width tube: 30. Thickness: 0.7. Thickness tube's leather: 0.4.

Description
A crumpled piece of leather (figure A, B). One edge consists of a red tube, containing a matching red drawstring that is folded lengthwise, the fold of which faces away from the tube's attachment to the red body of the piece. The tube is made of one piece of leather that is folded and secured at one side with running stitches made of sinew (figure F, G), the seam of which includes the large body of the piece as well.

At the recto, the seam between the two edges of the tube and the body of the object is covered with a band made of two green strips (width: 5 mm) flanking a central red one (figure C-E, G; width: 4.6 mm). The three elements are stitched together before being attached to the piece. The stitching was done using zS_2 threads of flax (whip stitch). Note the distinct redder colour of the leather beneath the decoration band, where it has not faded.

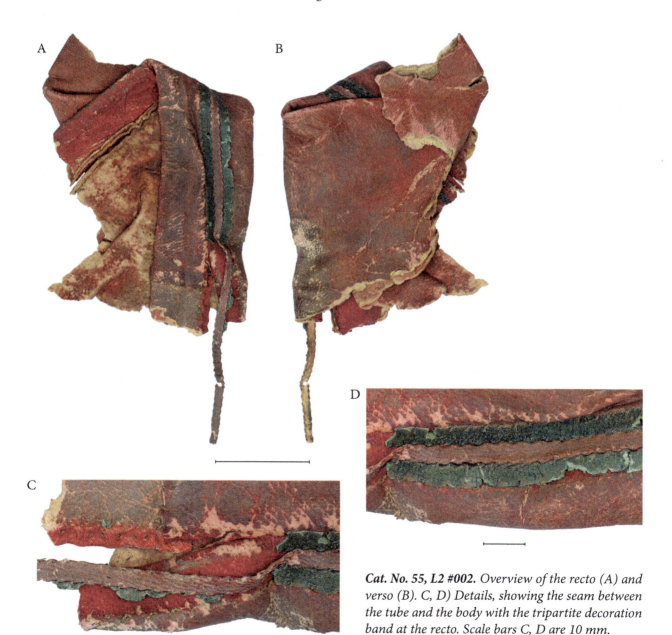

Cat. No. 55, L2 #002. *Overview of the recto (A) and verso (B). C, D) Details, showing the seam between the tube and the body with the tripartite decoration band at the recto. Scale bars C, D are 10 mm.*

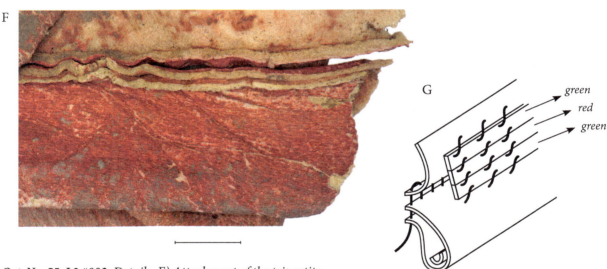

Cat. No. 55, L2 #002. Details. E) Attachment of the tripartite enhancement at the recto; F) Seam between the tube and the body seen from the verso; G) Diagram of the construction of the seam between the tube and the body. Scale bars are 10 mm.

CATALOGUE NUMBER 56

Id. No.	L2 #008A-C.
Measurements	(As shown in figure A). Length: 330. Width: 120. Width tube: 30. Thickness: 0.7. Thickness tube's leather: 0.4.

Description: General

Initially, this entry was thought to be a single piece, but is actually three fragments (figure A-D). The leather is crumpled and torn in places but fragment L2 #008A is in fairly good shape. A small black spot roughly in the centre of the visible surface clearly is the start of decay due to moisture (causing gelatinisation of the collagen) and is the reason that the two layers of the fragment remain stuck together.

Description: L2 #008A

The object (figure B, C) is described with the tube at the top. The edges of the red leather tube, which contains a lengthwise folded strip of comparable leather that acts as a drawstring (figure D, H) are secured with widely spaced running stitches of zS_2 thread made of sinew. In doing this, it secures a

A

Cat. No. 56, L2 #008A-C. *Overview before conservation (L2 #008C is not visible as this featureless fragment is sandwiched between the other two fragments and not further described/depicted).*

B

***Cat. No. 56, L2 #008A.** B, C [next page]) Overviews (the red surface is the recto; the creamy beige surface is the verso). The * refers to the break that fits with L6 #007 (Cat. No. 57).*

C

large piece of thin red leather, with various interesting features and shapes (see below). The interstitch space is slightly larger than the length of the stitches themselves. Due to this the stitch holes are in pairs (figure F).

One end of the tube is torn off, but might have been connected originally to the torn off end of the tube in fragment L2 #008B. The intact end of the tube, showing a slightly protruding piece of drawstring, is enhanced with a set of three strips of leather (figure H, I) – two green (width: 5 mm), flanking a red one (width: 5 mm). The strips have been stitched together with whip stitches of zS_2 threads of flax before adding them to the edge of the tube. The one closest to the edge of the tube is secured with whip stitches that runs over the edges of the tube's leather. The green strip at the other side of the set is secured to the tube's leather with whip stitches as well. In both cases, the number of whip stitches is far less than those that attach the three elements to each other. One isolated stitch, at a right angle to the length of the decorative band (arrow in figure H), further secures them to the seam of the tube with the leather of the body. Next to the intact end of tubing the leather of the body continues and shows a rounded top, beyond which, at the far end, it continues to form a corner. At the verso, the rounded edge shows evidence of whip stitches (figure J), which are the stitches that secures the tripartite decoration (comparable to the above-described edge decoration of the tube; figure K) that obscures the seam between the tube and the body of the pieces a bit further on the recto. Shortly below the rounded edge and approximately centred to it, is a horizontal, man-made slit (figure L), showing stress from a strip of approximately the same width that was pulled through it at its top edge. The edges of the slit are not reinforced. Below the tube and opposite the corner, is a concave edge, which is part of a fairly large circular cutaway (figure M-P). It has a green binding that is enhanced with alternating red and green strips of leather (figure N-P). The edge binding starts with a wide strip of green leather (width: 4 mm) that is set against the edge of the red leather and secured with whip stitches after which it is folded over the stitching, as well as the edge of the red leather. At the recto, it overlaps, in stair-step fashion, a red strip of leather (width: 3 mm). These two are secured with a row of long, but shortly-spaced running stitches; here, it is certain that it did not include the green strip that follows (this is not always visible; it might also be the case in, for example, L1 #002, Cat. No. 51). The red strip overlaps, also in stair-step fashion, a lengthwise folded strip of green leather (width: 1 mm), which is secured with comparable stitching. All stitching of this edge decoration is done with zS_2 flax thread.

Attached to the vertical side, at right angle to this rounded corner, is a second piece of red leather. This piece is folded over the other and is stuck to it due to the circular deteriorated spot mentioned previously. Originally, it was attached to the bigger piece with a slight overlap (average of 5 mm) and secured with whip stitches of flax zS_2 thread at the edges of both pieces (figure Q-T), thus showing two rows of stitches. As with the other part, it shows a concave edge, which is part of a comparable cutaway, but less of it is preserved. This one too has an edge binding and two-strip enhancement, like the previously described circular cut-out.

D

Cat. No. 56, L2 #008A. D) *Overview of the tube-body seam with drawstring.*

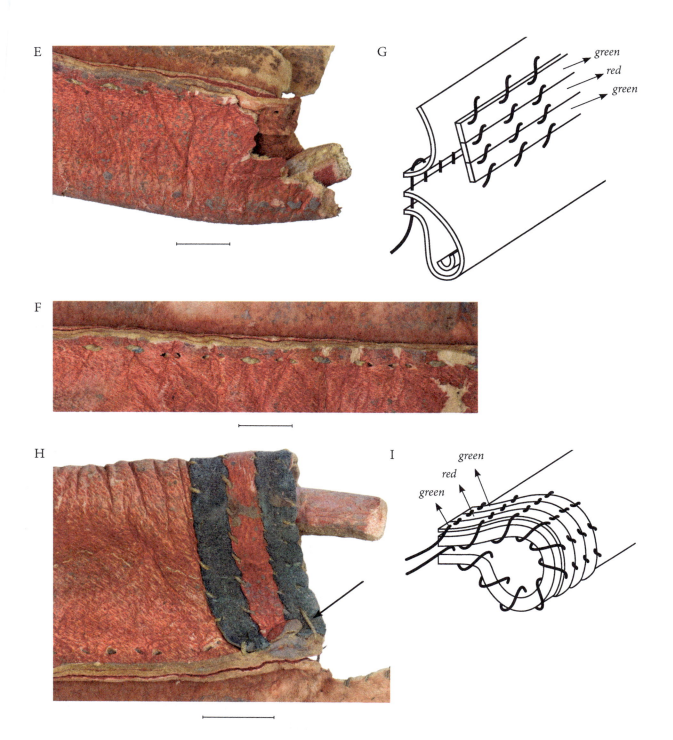

Cat. No. 56, L2 #008A. *E, F) Detail of the seam between the tube and the body (verso); G) Diagram of the construction of the tube/body seam shown in E, F; H) Detail of the intact end of the tube with the tripartite enhancement (the arrow is explained in the text); I) Diagram of the construction of the tube-end, shown in H. Scale bars are 10 mm.*

▷ ***Cat. No. 56, L2 #008A.*** *J) Detail of the edge of the rounded top next to the tube (seen from verso); K) Diagram of the construction of the edge shown in J; L) Detail of the slit (seen from verso); M) Close up of the edge of the circular opening; N) Detail of the edge, seen from recto, shown in M; O) Detail of the edge, seen from verso, shown in M; P) Diagram of the edge construction. Scale bars J, L, N, O are 10 mm.*

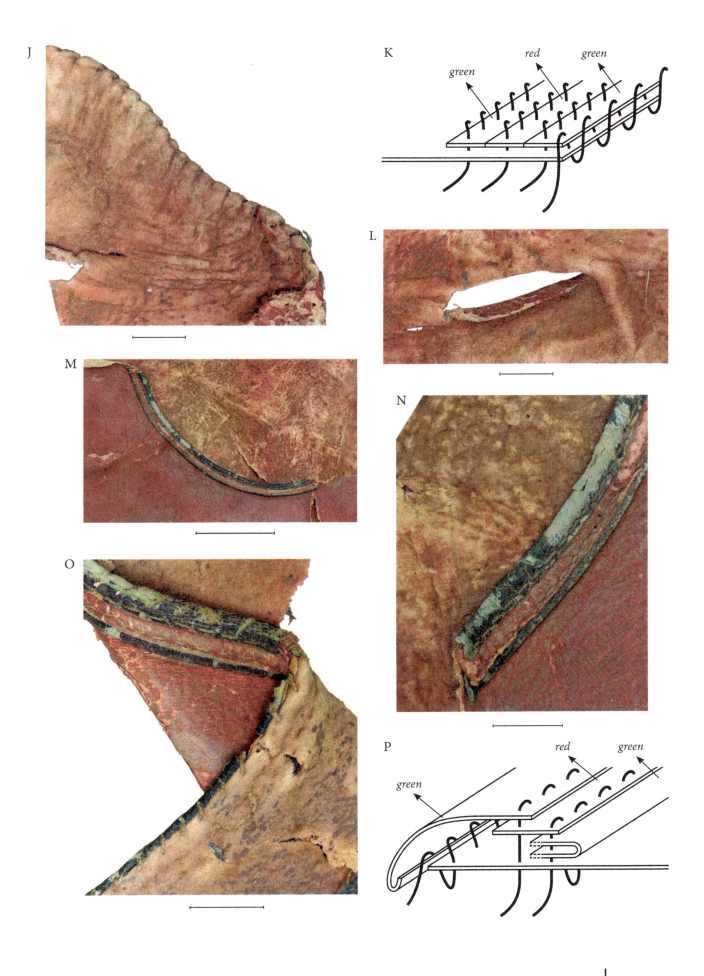

CATALOGUE | 371

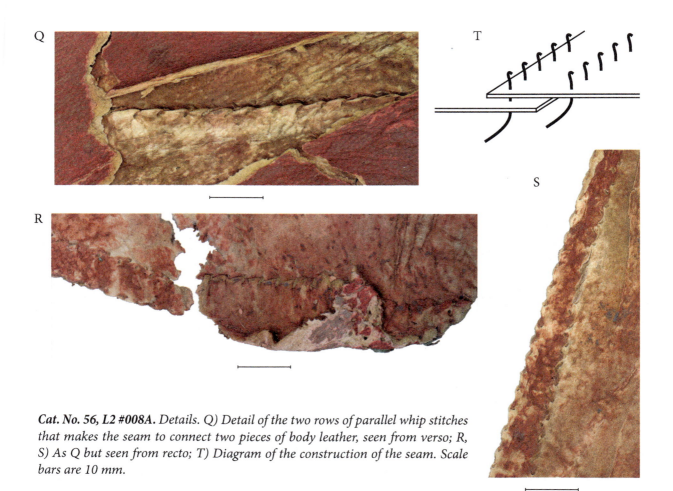

***Cat. No. 56, L2 #008A.** Details. Q) Detail of the two rows of parallel whip stitches that makes the seam to connect two pieces of body leather, seen from verso; R, S) As Q but seen from recto; T) Diagram of the construction of the seam. Scale bars are 10 mm.*

Description: L2 #008B

This fragment is described with the tube at the top (figure A). The edges of the red leather tube (figure B, C), which contains a lengthwise folded strip of comparable leather that act as a drawstring, is mostly detached from the bigger piece of thin red leather. The drawstring, folded lengthwise, survives. At about one quarter of the length, two elements of the tube are disconnected, but the brighter red colour of the smaller piece clearly shows that, originally, it was inserted into the other tube part in order to obtain the required length (arrow in figure A). Remnants of two green strips (width: 5 mm) flanking a red strip of leather (width: 5 mm) suggest that the seam was covered at the recto. Remnants of edge binding and/or enhancement of the ends of the tube are all that are left of it, prohibiting identification of the exact construction. Note the horizontal slit (figure D), which is manmade and shows stress of a strip having been pulled through. Although this strap is now lost, the discoloration of the leather, especially clear at the tube (double arrow in figure A), indicates a strap was used to further secure the leather to the framework of the chariot body.

To one side of the tube, the leather of the body shows a smaller oval-like, concave cut-out (dashed arrow in figure A; figure E-G) relative to the previously-described ones. It ends in a narrow protrusion that has a green, lengthwise folded binding at either edge. This binding runs along the round edge of the concave cut-out and seemingly continues at the straight, vertical edge (double dashed arrow in figure A), where, at the lowest preserved piece, a scrap of red leather is still attached at the other side. The cut-out seems to be the grip close to the upper railing of the chariot that is so often seen in two-dimensional art. This suggests that, at least at this vertical edge, the binding functioned as a passepoil (figure H, I), with the fold facing to the red surface (recto). The green edge binding/passepoil is secured with whip stitches, made of zS_2 threads of flax, which makes it extraordinary: passepoils are almost always secured with running stitches.

Cat. No. 56, L2 #008B. A) Overview of the recto. The fragment was, at time of study, too fragile to turn over to photograph the verso. The arrow points to the attachment area of the two pieces of tube. The dashed arrow indicate the handgrip whereas the double, dashed arrow indicates the double arrow indicates discoloration of the tube. The double arrow indicate the handgrip whereas the double, dashed arrow indicates the passepoil.

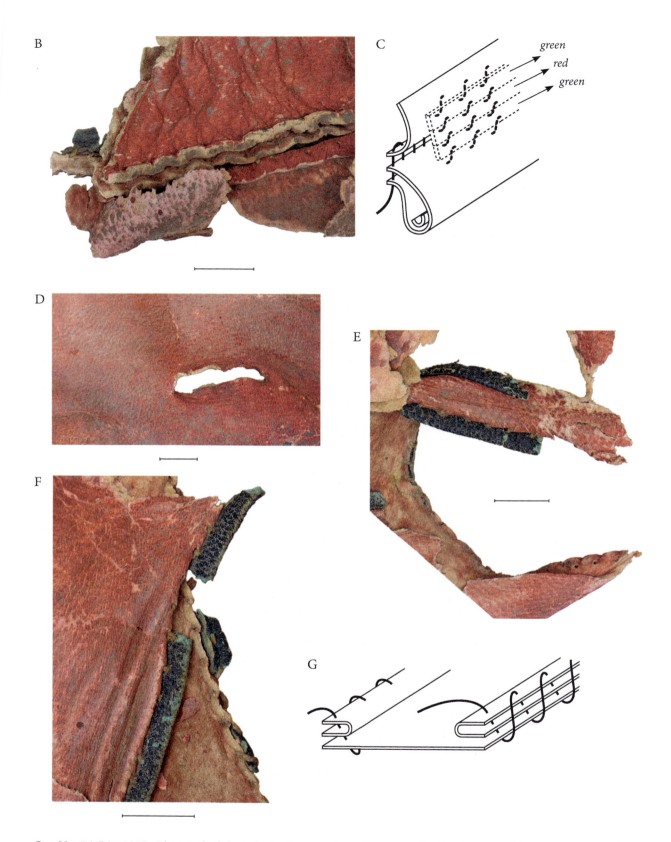

Cat. No. 56, L2 #008B. *B) Detail of the tube-body seam (seen from verso); C) Diagram of the construction of the tube/body seam shown in B; D) Detail of the secondary slit. Note the slight discolouration due to a strap that was pulled through; E) Detail of the edge binding of the small, oval cut-out (handgrip) with a green binding at both edges; F) As E; G) Diagram of the construction of the binding of the cut-out, shown in E, F. Scale bars are 10 mm.*

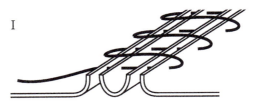

Cat. No. 56, L2 #008B. Details. H) The vertical seam with green passepoil (possible extension of the cut-out); I) Diagram of the construction of the seam with passepoil. Scale bar is 10 mm.

CATALOGUE NUMBER 57

Id. No.   L6 #007.
Measurements   Width: 60-160. Height: 110. Thickness: 0.7.

Description
A piece of red leather, which is folded over on two sides (figure A, B). One edge is enhanced with a band comprised of red and green strips (figure C-F). A green edge binding extends a bit beyond the edge of the red piece. At the verso it is stitched in place with zS_2 threads of sinew, after which it is pulled over the edge of the piece and secured at the recto with wide, but closely spaced running stitches made of zS_2 sinew(?). The green binding (width: 32 mm) overlaps, in stair-step fashion, a single red strip, the width of which extends to the edge of the object proper (visible width: 36 mm), which is secured at one edge with the same stitching that secures the binding. This red strip, in its turn, overlaps in stair-step fashion another green strip (width: 16 mm). The furthest edge of the green one is folded towards the red leather of the body, the extent of which cannot be determined. Note the end of one strip and the beginning of another (arrow in figure C).

The fragment fits with L2 #008A (the break is marked with * in figure A of L2 #008A, Cat. No. 56, and figure A of the presently described fragment).

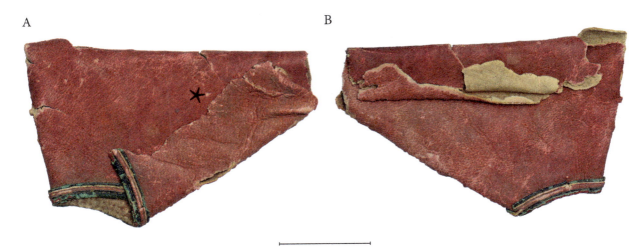

*Cat. No. 57, L6 #007. Overview (A, B) of the folded piece with visible recto of the folded sides. The * indicates the break that fits with L2 #008A (Cat. No. 56).*

C

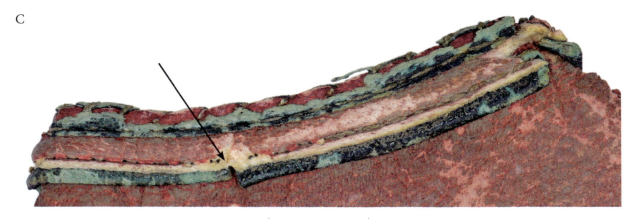

D

E

F

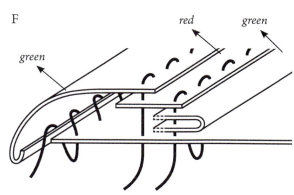

Cat. No. 57, L6 #007. *C) Close up of the enhanced edge. The arrow points to the adding of a new strip of green; D) Detail of the enhanced edge, showing the stitching, seen from the recto; E) As D but seen at the verso; F) Diagram of the construction of the edge. Scale bars are 10 mm.*

CATALOGUE NUMBER 58

Id. No. L4 #013.
Measurements Length: 57. Width: 8 - 25. Thickness: 0.9.

Description
A roughly triangular (with one curving and one straight edge) piece of red leather (figure A, B). It was, at both long sides, a green, lengthwise folded edge binding (width: 3.8 mm) that is secured with whip stitches over the edge (figure C). The stitches are made of zS_2 threads of sinew(?). The fragment probably fit with L2 #008B (Cat. No. 56).

A

B

C
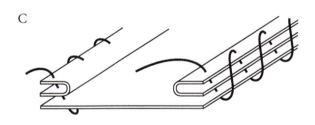

Cat. No. 58, L4 #013. *Overview of the recto (A) and the verso (B). C) Diagram of the construction of the edges. Scale bar is 10 mm.*

CATALOGUE NUMBER 59

Id. No. L6 #002.
Measurements Length: 270. Width: 260. Thickness: 0.7.

Description
A large, very crumpled and folded piece of red leather (figure A) that is extremely fragile, and is pierced by insect holes. One edge shows the addition of a second piece by securing the relatively wide overlap at both edges with whip stitches (zS_2, flax?; figure B, C). Possibly, this is a comparable seam to that of L2 #008A, B. (Cat. No. 56). As the piece is folded, it forms a triangle. In this triangular part, shortly below the edge, are two holes that insert diagonally in the leather (arrow in figure B) in between which the impression of the element that was pulled through them is vaguely visible.

Cat. No. 59, L6 #002. *A) Overview. The other side could not be photographed due to the fragile condition; B) Detail of the seam (the other row of stitching is folded towards the other side). The arrow points to the two diagonally inserting holes in the approximate centre of the triangle; C) Diagram of the construction. Scale bar B is 10 mm.*

CATALOGUE NUMBER 60

Id. No. L6 #001.

Measurements Overall dimensions: 415 x 280. Thickness: 0.7. Length horizontal tube: 335. Width horizontal tube: 36. Thickness horizontal tube: 0.7. Length vertical tube: 115. Width vertical tube: 32. Thickness vertical tube: 0.7. Width drawstring: appr. 4. Thickness drawstring: appr. 2.

Description

A large piece of red leather to which a tube of red leather is attached along the long side, with running stitches (figure A, B). The tube (figure C, D; marked with # in figure B) contains a lengthwise folded drawstring, the fold of which faces away from the seam. In contrast to previously described fragments with tubes, this tube is attached to the main piece by means of a green passepoil (lengthwise folded, the fold of which faces the recto). Note the extension to obtain the required length by slightly overlapping two tubes and securing them with whip stitches, judging by the stitch holes and the malformed shape of the edge over the overlapping piece (stitches itself are not preserved; figure E). The red colour of the shorter piece of tube (which inserts into the other) is much more intact that the rather worn other piece. This seems to be due to a repair rather than being positioned in an area of the framework that was less subject to wear. One end of both tubes is intact; the presence of empty stitch holes suggests that originally there was a simple binding here (figure C) and not a tripartite finishing, as seen in other examples (*e.g.* L2 #008A, Cat. No. 56). The edge of the body of the leather next to this intact end of the tube shows empty stitch holes as well (arrow in figure B), indicating that this edge is intact, except for the binding (which was probably the same as described for the vertical edge below). It runs to another piece of tubing, but at nearly a right angle. The attachment of the vertical tube (marked by * in figure B) to the main piece of red leather is also made with running stitches of sinew and it also includes a lengthwise folded drawstring, but it does not include a passepoil (figure F-H). At the recto, the seam was obscured, judging by the remnants and the distinctly darker hue of the red underneath. Without a doubt it was covered with a tripartite band of green strips flanking a red one, but only remnants of a green one are still *in situ*. However, an isolated piece of band is included in this entry (length: 109 mm; width green 5 & 5.2 mm; width red: 4-5.3 mm), but since it was lying loose on the piece, it might originate from another fragment altogether. The edge of the main piece between the intact end of the tube of the horizontal side and the end of the tube of the vertical side has a lengthwise folded green binding with the fold facing away from the edge of the tube (*i.e.* it faces the recto; dashed arrow in figure A, see figure I-K). It is secured with widely spaced, but short running stitches (that are possibly made of sinew). However, this clearly is a repair, as the edge proper shows the diagonal impressions and the empty stitch holes of the original whip stitches (arrow in figure I).

A tear-shaped slit is visible in the corner of the tubes (arrow in figure F), inserted in the main piece of the object. A faint impression of a strap directed towards the tube is visible. It must have been used to fasten the leather to the framework of the body. The fragment is a corner piece with the vertical tube running down with one of the vertical rods at the back of the wooden framework.

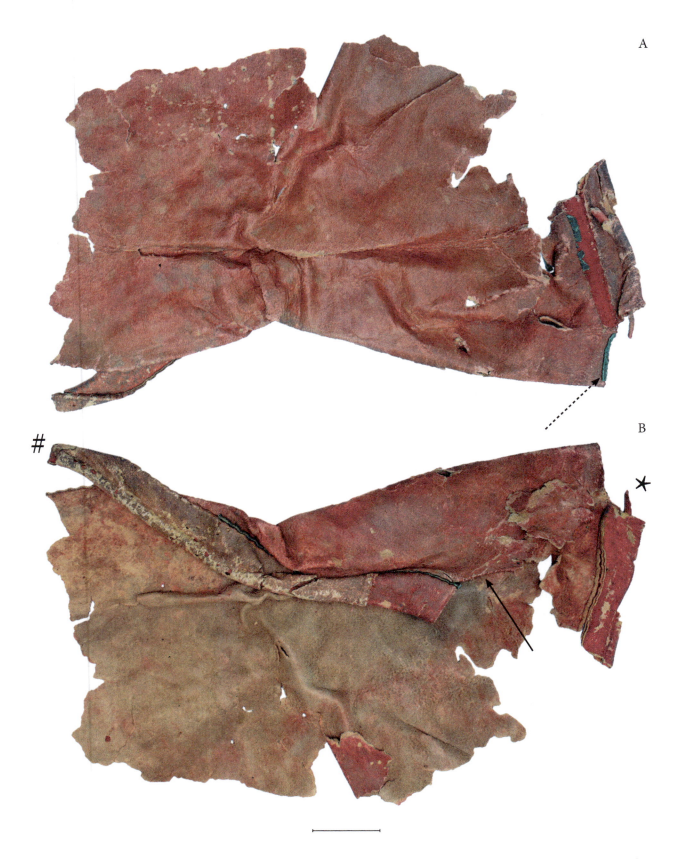

Cat. No. 60, L6 #001. *Overview of the recto (based on the major part of the folded fragment); A) and the verso (B). # refers to the long tube with passepoil (figure C-E) whereas * refers to the vertical tube without a passepoil (figure F-H). The arrow points to empty stitch holes; the dashed arrow to the edge binding.*

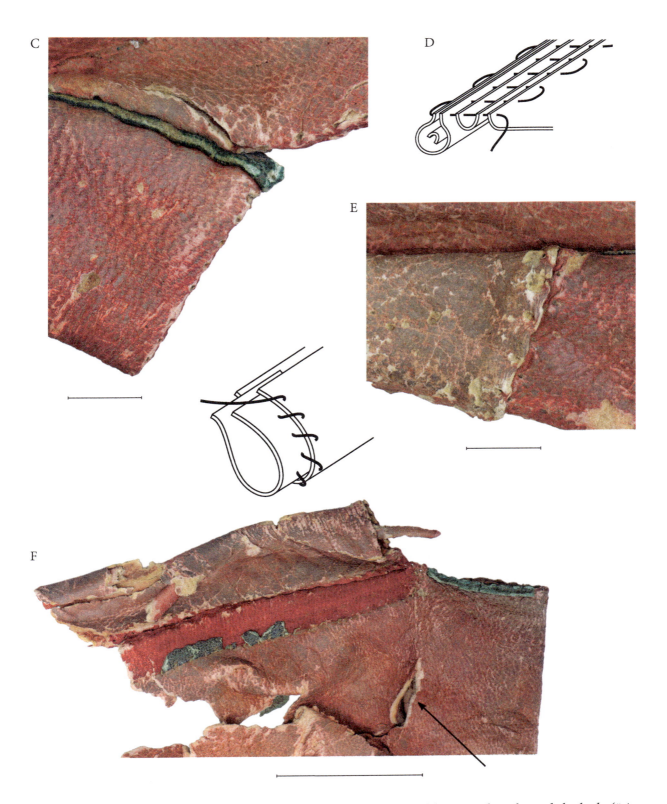

Cat. No. 60, L6 #001. *C) Detail of the green, lengthwise folded passepoil between the tube and the body (# in figure B). Note the empty stitch holes at the tube's end, suggesting the attachment of an edge binding, now lost; D) Diagram of the construction of the attachment of the tube and the body including a passepoil, shown in C; E) Detail of the attachment area of two pieces of tube (inset). Note the difference in condition (much worn versus less so); F) Overview of the vertical tube (* in figure B), seen from recto. Note the distinct darker colour of the area beneath the tripartite enhancement, suggesting it fell of in modern times. Scale bars C, E are 10 mm.*

G

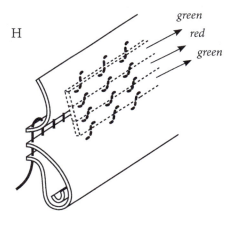

H

I

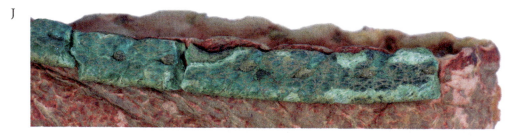

J

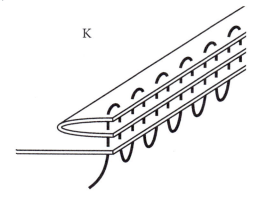

K

Cat. No. 60, L6 #001. *G) Detail of the seam between the vertical tube and the body, seen from recto; H) Diagram of the construction of the tube/body seam shown in F, G; I, J) Detail of the green edge binding next to the tube (dashed arrow in figure A). The arrow points to the impressions of the original whip stitches of the edge binding; K) Diagram of the construction of the green binding shown in I, J. Scale bars I, J are 10 mm.*

CATALOGUE NUMBER 61

Id. No.   L6 #003.
Measurements   Length: Appr. 555. Width: 212. Thickness: 0.7.

Description
A large semi-circular piece of red leather, faded and worn to a dingy grey-green in places (figure A, B). It is folded along the curving side, the edge of which is folded also, hinting at a seam to attach a tube comparable to for example L1 #002 (Cat. No. 51; figure C, D). This edge was once enhanced with a band, the vestiges of which remain in two spots (width of the green strip: 4.2 mm; width of the red one: 5.2 mm). In other examples, this band was made up of two green strips flanking a red one, which were secured with flax whip stitches and attached to the red piece, thus covering the seam at the recto. Judging from the width of the distinct darker colour of the once-covered area, one might conclude that there were only two strips (one red, one green) instead of three. However, since only part of the red leather where the third strip once would have been is faded, and other areas suggest by their width that there was originally a tripartite band here, it suggests that the third strip, *viz.* the one closest to the seam, must have fallen off while the leather object was still in use and never replaced.

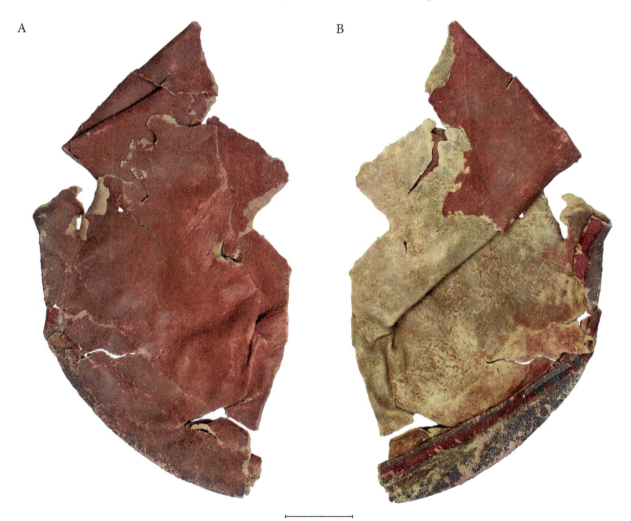

Cat. No. 61, L6 #003. *Overview of the recto (A) and verso (B).*

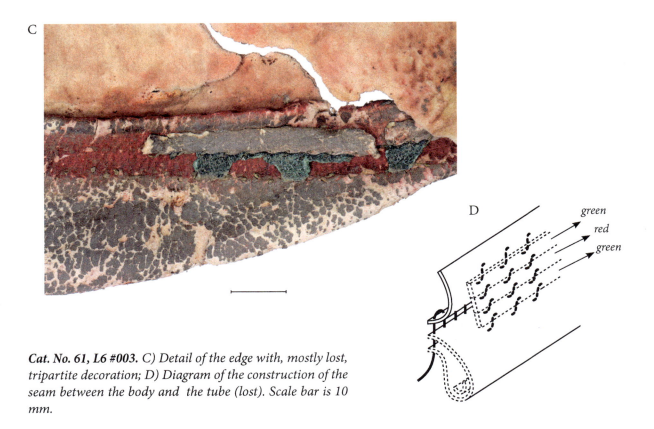

Cat. No. 61, L6 #003. *C) Detail of the edge with, mostly lost, tripartite decoration; D) Diagram of the construction of the seam between the body and the tube (lost). Scale bar is 10 mm.*

CATALOGUE NUMBER 62

Id. No. L6 #004.
Measurements Length: 110. Width: 32. Thickness: 0.5.

Description
A lengthwise folded piece of red leather, once secured on one side forming a tube (figure A, B). It contains a drawstring of a folded strip of red leather. Note that one side of the tube is faded; the other still bright red, clearly indicating which side was exposed to the sun and which not.

Cat. No. 62, L6 #004. *Overview of the recto (A) and verso (B). Scale bar is 10 mm.*

CATALOGUE NUMBER 63

Id. No. L6 #027.
Measurements Length: 262. Width: 34. Thickness: 0.7.

Description
A tube of red leather (figure A, B) that is made by folding over a strip of leather and securing the edge with running stitches of zS_2 sinew thread. It contains a narrow red drawstring (figure C). One of the short ends is wrinkled due to stress placed on it (arrow in figure B).

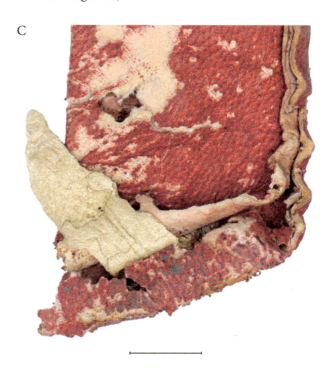

Cat. No. 63, L6 #027. *Overview of the recto (A) and verso (B). The arrow points to the wrinkled area, which is due to stress; C) Detail of the drawstring and seam. Scale bar C is 10 mm.*

CATALOGUE NUMBER 64

Id. No. L4 #014.
Measurements Length: 18 - 42. Width: 15 - 40. Thickness: 0.8. Width folded edge: 3.5 - 3.8.

Description
A small piece of red leather with one folded edge, which is pierced with stitch holes (no remnants of the stitches remain) reminiscent of the seams in tubes (see for example L1 #001, Cat. No. 50). The upper part of the recto retains its bright red colour, while the lower part seems to lack the uppermost surface of the leather. Note that the change occurs with the remnants of a row of zS_2 whip stitches (of sinew?) parallel to the folded edge, which suggests another layer of leather was attached to it, most likely a tripartite band of green and red strips of leather.

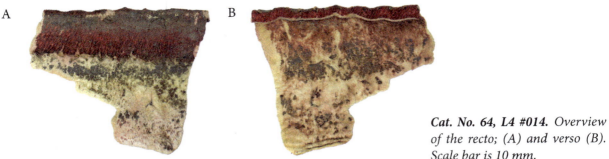

Cat. No. 64, L4 #014. *Overview of the recto; (A) and verso (B). Scale bar is 10 mm.*

CATALOGUE NUMBER 65

Id. No.   L4 #018.
Measurements   Length: 128. Width as folded: 7.5. Thickness single: 1.7.

Description
A strip of red leather (figure A, B), unevenly folded lengthwise, identified as piece of drawstring like those found in for example L1 #016 (Cat. No. 73).

Cat. No. 65, L4 #018. *Overview. Obverse (A) and reverse (B).*

CATALOGUE NUMBER 66

Id. No.   L4 #003.
Measurements   Length: 70. Width: 40. Thickness: 0.7.

Description
A small piece of tube, made of a folded piece of red leather (figure A, B). The edges were stitched together, but nothing remains save the stitch holes. The tube contains a narrow red leather drawstring, which is folded lengthwise. Remnants of green leather at the edge, with one whip stitch *in situ*, are still visible (arrow in figure A), suggesting the seam at the recto was covered originally with a tripartite band of green and red strips (see for example L2 #008A, Cat. No. 56).

Cat. No. 66, L4 #003. *Overview of the recto (A) and verso (B). The arrow points to the whip stitch.*

CATALOGUE NUMBER 67

Id. No. L4 #001.
Measurements Length: 80. Width: 30 - 40. Thickness: 0.6 - 0.8.

Description
A small piece of slightly curving red tube without a drawstring. This might have been there, but has fallen away. Some insect damage.

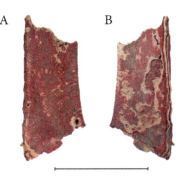

Cat. No. 67, L4 #001. *Overview of the recto (A) and verso (B).*

CATALOGUE NUMBER 68

Id. No. L1 #005.
Measurements 470 x 120. Thickness total: 0.7. Width green strip: 2.5. Length green strip: 32.

Description
A piece of red leather, slightly crumpled, and stained in some places (figure A, B). At one side, part of an edge made up of a lengthwise folded strip of green leather is stitched into place with whip stitches (figure C, D). It is an edge binding that is comparable to those seen in, for example, L4 #013 (Cat. No. 58). An interesting detail is the stitching at the corner (arrow in figure C): here, one stitch is placed at right angle to the usual diagonal course, suggesting that it is the start of the stitching. Note also the overhand stopper knot (encircled), suggesting that the thread was broken in ancient times and knotted to prevent it from slipping. The opposite edge is folded, but the object does not seem to be closed (and thus consisting of a double thickness).

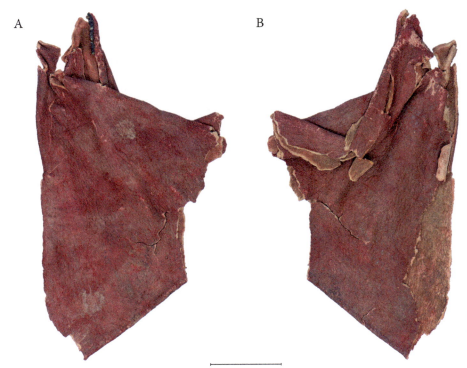

Cat. No. 68, L1 #005. *Overviews. Obverse (A) and (B) reverse.*

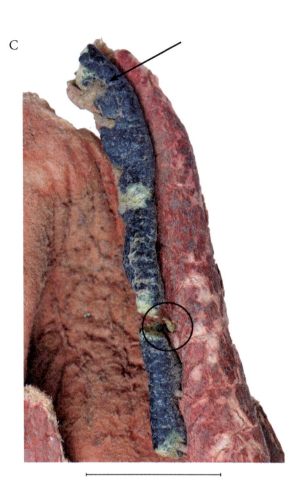
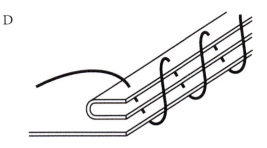

Cat. No. 68, L1 #005. *C) Detail of the edge binding. The arrow points to the possible start of the stitching; the circle indicates the stopper knot to prevent the broken thread from slipping; D) Diagram of the construction of the edge binding. Scale bar is 10 mm.*

CATALOGUE NUMBER 69

Id. No.	L1 #008A, B.
Measurements	A) 91 x 23. Thickness: 0.7.
	B) Measurements: 110 x 40. Thickness: 0.8.

Description
This entry includes a tiny, featureless scrap that is not numbered separately.

Description: L1 #008A
Small, roughly rectangular piece of leather that is stitched to a second piece (which is largely torn off) by means of a thin, lengthwise folded passepoil. It is secured with running stitches, possibly of sinew.

Description: L1 #008b
Small piece, roughly diamond-shaped, without features.

▷ ***Cat. No. 69, L1 #008A, B.*** *Overview of the recto (A) and verso (B).*

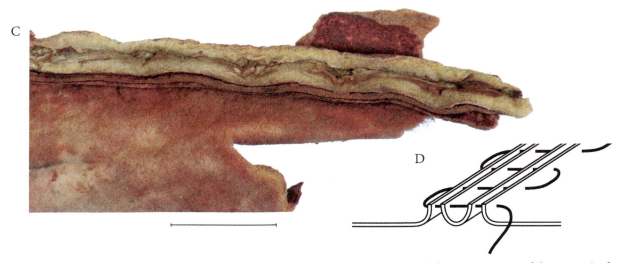

Cat. No. 69, L1 #008B. C) *Detail of the verso, showing the seam; D) Diagram of the construction of the seam. Scale bar is 10 mm.*

CATALOGUE NUMBER 70

Id. No. L1 #010A, B.
Measurements A) 260 x 65. Thickness: 1. With green strip following on passepoil: 3.1. Width subsequent red strip: 1.2. Width next green strip: 1.2.
B) Length: 26.0. W: 8. W passepoil: 1.

Description: L1 #010A

An irregularly shaped fragment consisting of two pieces of red leather stitched together by means of a red, lengthwise folded passepoil (figure A, B). An extraordinary construction without parallels in the Tano material, as a further edging extends along part of the opposite piece. It follows onto the passepoil, consisting of a green strip, which is most likely of single thickness (figure C-E). It partially overlaps, in stair-step fashion, a band of red leather that is a folded extension of one 'body-piece' that are attached by means of the seam. This, in its turn, overlaps in the same way a lengthwise folded strip of green leather. The first green, as well as the red strip are secured with running stitches of zS_2 flax thread; the stitches that secure the red strip also include the final green strip. The two layers, the edging as well as the passepoil are, at the reverse, stitched with running stitches of sZ_2 sinew thread (figure D).

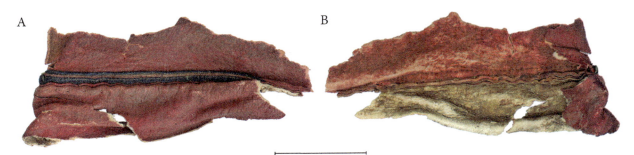

Cat. No. 70, L1 #010A. *Overview of the recto (A) and verso (B).*

C

D

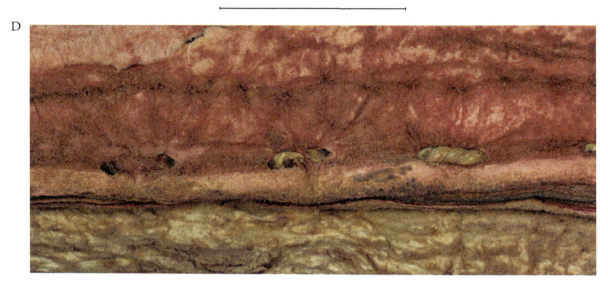

E

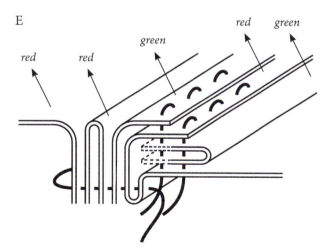

Cat. No. 70, L1 #010A. C) *Detail of the seam seen from recto;* D) *Detail of the seam seen from verso;* E) *Diagram of the extraordinary construction of the seam. Scale bars are 10 mm.*

Description: L1 #010B

A small, roughly rectangular piece of leather that is stitched to a second piece (both are torn off; figure A, B) by means of a thin, lengthwise folded passepoil (figure C). It is secured with running stitches, possibly of sinew.

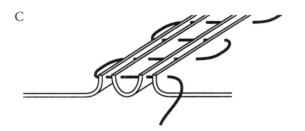

Cat. No. 70, L1 #010B. *Overview of the recto (A) and the verso (B); C) Diagram of the construction of the seam.*

CATALOGUE NUMBER 71

Id. No. L1 #012.
Measurements 112 x 170. Thickness: 0.8.
Description
Irregularly-shaped piece of red leather (figure A, B). The colour has faded and flaked off at several spots. A row of holes in pairs that punctuate one of the edges is indicative of stitching; the wavy appearance suggests running stitches (figure C, D) pulled tight.

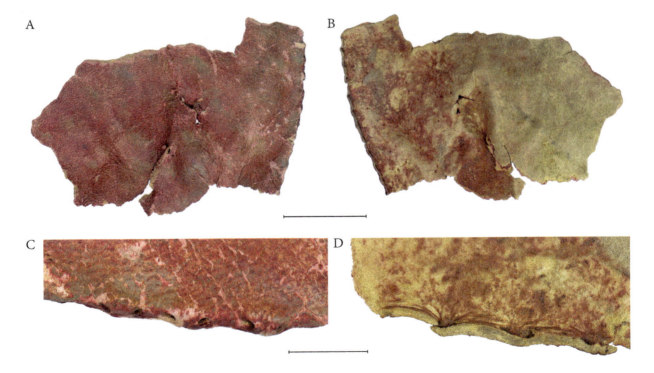

Cat. No. 71, L1 #012. *Overview of the recto (A) and verso (B); C) Detail of the stitch holes seen from the recto; D) Detail of the stitch holes seen from the verso. Scale bars C, D are 10 mm.*

CATALOGUE NUMBER 72

Id. No. L1 #014.
Measurements Tube length: 146 x 33. Attached element: 60 x 30. Thickness: 0.6. Width drawstring inside tube: 7.6.

Description
Irregularly-shaped fragment (figure A, B) consisting of a tube that was connected to a larger piece of which only a fragment survives. The two elements are made of red leather and are secured with a lengthwise folded passepoil in green, the folded edge of which faces outwards (figure D-F). The tube is made of one piece of relatively thick leather that is secured with running stitches of s-twisted sinew(?) thread. Inside the tube, at the side opposite to the seam, is a lengthwise folded drawstring (the fold facing away from the seam). It is thicker than the leather of the rest of the fragment. As usual, the drawstring was not secured inside the tube.

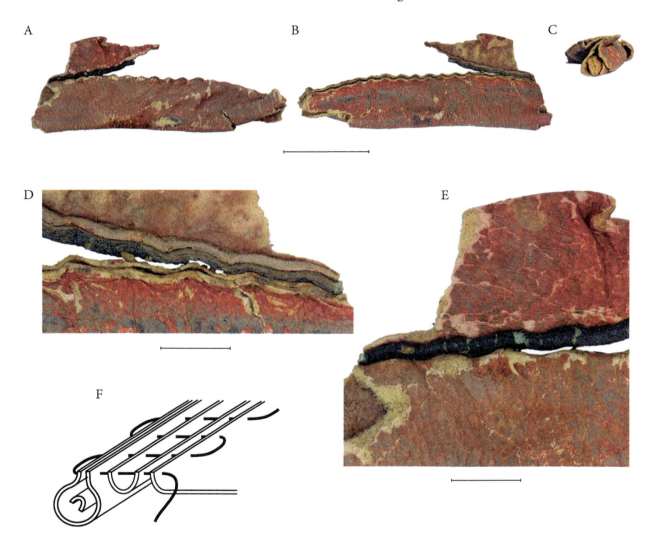

Cat. No. 72, L1 #014. *Overview of the recto (A) and verso (B); C) Tube end seen from aside; D) Detail of the seam seen from the verso; E) Detail of the seam seen from the recto; F) Diagram of the construction of the seam. Scale bars D-E are 10 mm.*

CATALOGUE NUMBER 73

Id. No. L1 #016.
Measurements Length: 246. Width: 140. Thickness: 0.8. Length tube: 268 (215 & 53). Width tube: 29. Width edge binding: 4.5. Length drawstring: 156. Width drawstring: 15. Thickness drawstring: 3-4. Toggles: 16.3 x 13.8 & 15.3 x 15.0. Width strip: 15-24.

Description
An irregularly shaped fragment of leather consisting of a tube that is connected to a much larger piece which is torn off (figure A, B). The two elements are made of red leather and are secured with a lengthwise folded passepoil in green, the folded edge of which faces outwards (verso; figure C-E). The tube is made of one piece of thicker leather that is folded and stitched together at one side, the seam of which attaches the torn off thinner piece as well. Another tube is attached to this in order to provide the required length, by inserting it into the other, and stitching it into place (figure F-H). Although the stitches itself are mostly lost, the way the leather is deformed suggests that it was secured with whip stitches. Note the discolouration of the tube's leather compared to that of the main piece (recto). The tube has one intact end, which has a green edge binding (figure I, J, L). This lengthwise folded green edge binding is not folded around the edges of the red leather but placed with the edges parallel to the edges of the tube's leather and secured with whip stitches.

At the side opposite the seam, the tube contains a drawstring. It consists of a lengthwise folded strip of red stained leather (the fold facing away from the seam) that is thicker than the attached, single layer. The end terminates in a toggle (figure I, K) that is made of green leather which tightly encircles the red strip four times. It is secured by stitching the end of the strip through itself. Attached to this terminal end of the drawstring is a portion of a comparable element that is pulled through a slit in the main drawstring, close to its toggle.

▷ **Cat. No. 73, L1 #016.** *Overview of the recto (A) and verso (B).*

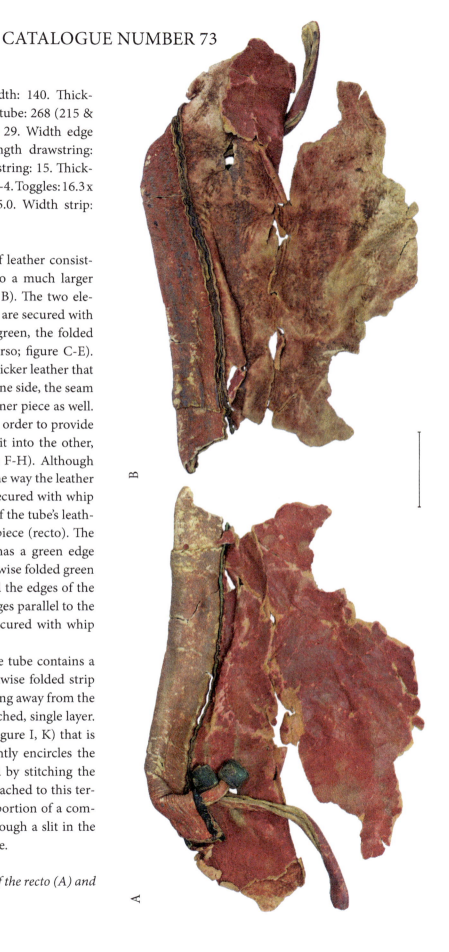

CATALOGUE | 393

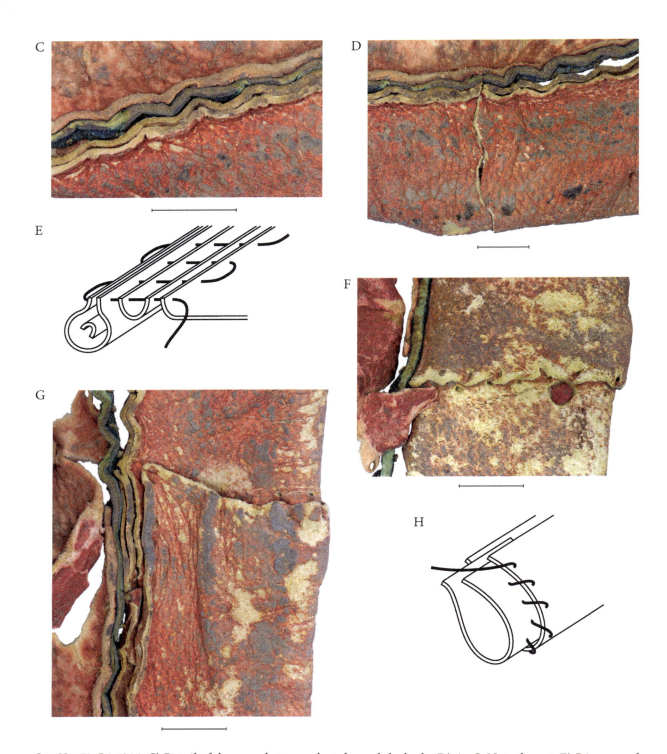

Cat. No. 73, L1 #016. C) Detail of the seam between the tube and the body; D) As C. Note the cut; E) Diagram of the construction of the seam; F) Detail of the extension of the tube seen from the recto; G) As F but seen from the verso; H) Diagram of the construction of the extension of the tube. Scale bars are 10 mm.

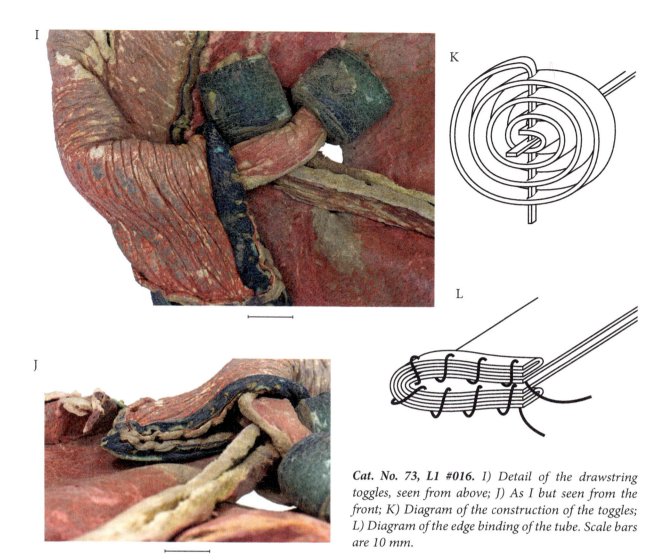

Cat. No. 73, L1 #016. I) Detail of the drawstring toggles, seen from above; J) As I but seen from the front; K) Diagram of the construction of the toggles; L) Diagram of the edge binding of the tube. Scale bars are 10 mm.

CATALOGUE NUMBER 74

Id. No. BI-034.

Measurements Length total: 158. Length one strip (incl. toggle): 92. Length other strip (incl. toggle): 116. Width strips: 12. Thickness strips: 2.8. Diameter toggles: 14.8 & 15.4. Length slit: 51.

Description

A pair or fairly thick, red leather strips (stained at one side only; these are pieces of drawstring; figure A) terminating as cores in green leather toggles. The toggles (figure B, C) are made by a green strip of leather that are coiled around the tip of the red one; the end is stitched through the toggle and the tip of the red leather strip, thus keeping it all together. Just before becoming the core of the toggle, one of the red leather strips has a slit through which the other toggle is pulled.

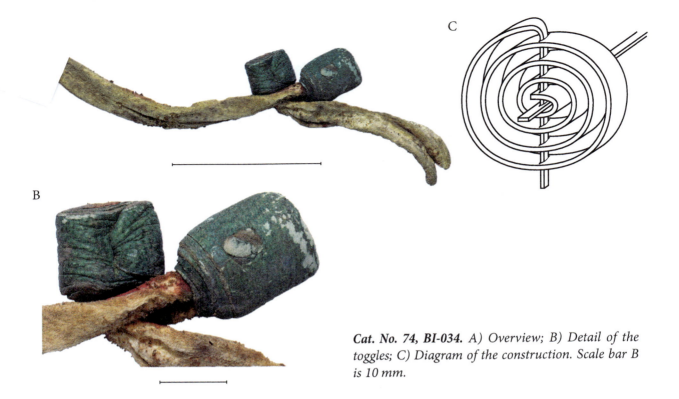

Cat. No. 74, BI-034. A) Overview; B) Detail of the toggles; C) Diagram of the construction. Scale bar B is 10 mm.

CATALOGUE NUMBER 75

Id. No. L1 #020.

Measurements Length tube: 203. Diameter tube: 30-35. Thickness tube's leather: 0.7. Edge binding intact corner: 4.2. Larger piece attached to tube: 120 x 145. Thickness: 0.5-0.9. Width passepoil: 0.7 (height: 2.2).

Description

An irregularly shaped fragment (figure A, B) consisting of a tube that was connected to a larger piece, which is torn off. The two elements are made of red leather (note that the recto is bright red, but the verso is only slightly coloured, which is due to the colour of the recto that seeped through) and are secured including a lengthwise folded passepoil in green, the folded edge of which faces outwards (verso; figure C-E).

The tube is made of one piece of leather that is folded and secured at one side, of whose seam includes the larger fragment as well. It is secured with running stitches that are made of s-twisted sinew. Due to the fact that the seam is loosened at one side, a clear view of the stitch holes is possible (figure D). These are nearly perfectly circular, suggesting that they were pre-pricked. Inside the tube, at the side opposite the seam, is a drawstring, which is thicker than the rest. The way it lies and is slightly creased suggests that it was once folded lengthwise. It is not secured. The tube has one intact end (figure F-H), which has a green edge binding (width: 4.2 mm). This lengthwise folded strip is not folded around the edges of the red leather but placed with the edges parallel to the edges of the red leather and secured with whip stitches of sinew.

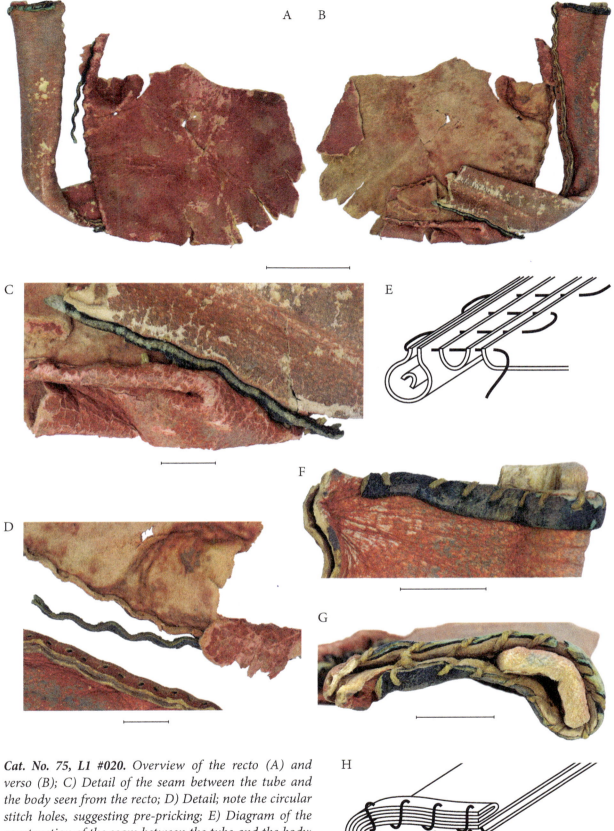

Cat. No. 75, L1 #020. *Overview of the recto (A) and verso (B); C) Detail of the seam between the tube and the body seen from the recto; D) Detail; note the circular stitch holes, suggesting pre-pricking; E) Diagram of the construction of the seam between the tube and the body; F) Detail of the edge binding of the tube seen from above; G) As F, but seen from the front; H) Diagram of the edge binding of the tube. Scale bars C, D, F, G are 10 mm.*

CATALOGUE NUMBER 76

Id. No.   L4 #002.
Measurements   Length: 81. Width: 40. Thickness: 0.7. Width drawstring: 0.8.

Description
A small piece of tube made of red leather (figure A, B). The tube is made by folding and the edges are secured with running stitches (sinew?). The edge has a lengthwise folded, green strip (width: 3.5 mm) included in the stitching of the tube's edges (figure C, D). Most likely it is a passepoil, as for example seen in L1 #020 (Cat. No. 75), but the leather at the other side is torn off. The tube has a lengthwise folded drawstring whose folded edge faces towards the seam of the tube.

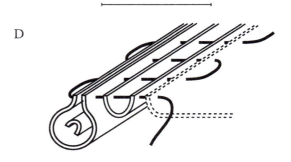

Cat. No. 76, L4 #002. *Overview of the recto (A) and verso (B); C) Detail of the seam between the tube and the body; D) Diagam of the construction of the seam between tube and body. Scale bar C is 10 mm.*

CATALOGUE NUMBER 77

Id. No.   L6 #017.
Measurements   Length: 190. Width: 37. Thickness: 0.7. Width drawstring: 18-20. Thickness drawstring: 2.3. Width edge binding: 2.5.

Description
A tube made of a piece of folded red leather that is sewn together at one edge (figure A, B). One end is nearly intact (figure C, D); the other is torn off. It contains a drawstring consisting of a narrow, lengthwise folded strip of red leather, whose fold faces the seam. The tube is affixed to another piece of red leather, which is torn off, with a green lengthwise folded passepoil, and is secured, in turn, with running stitches (sinew?; figure E). The fold of the passepoil faces the recto.

The near-intact end of the tube was once finished with a green edge binding, secured with whip stitches that are made of flax (zS_2?). Only a small scrap and empty stitch holes (see arrow in figure D) survive (figure F).

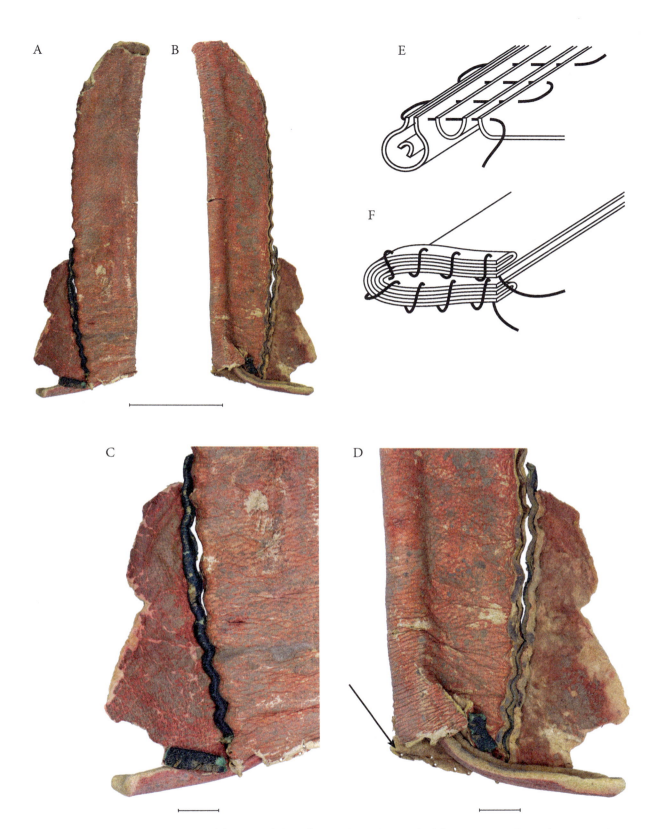

Cat. No. 77, L6 #017. *Overview of the recto (A) and verso (B); C) Detail of the seam seen from the recto; D) As C but seen from the verso. The arrow points to the empty stitch holes for the lost edge binding (see F); D) Diagram of the construction of the seam between the tube and the body; F) Diagram of the probable construction of the tube's edge binding. Scale bars C, D are 10 mm.*

CATALOGUE NUMBER 78

Id. No. L4 #006.
Measurements Length: 205. Width: 111. Thickness: 0.6. Width green binding: appr. 3.

Description
A large crumpled piece of red leather (figure A, B). In a couple of places, strips of green leather binding are visible that are secured with whip stitches (figure C, D). The cut strips of green leather have been secured onto the edge of the red leather with two whip stitches (one at the corner). The sewing thread (zS_2, flax) at one end of the small green fragment is knotted (overhand knot; arrow in figure C) and, together with the fact that the end of the green strip proper is inserted in the red leather, marks the start (or end) of the attachment. In continuation of the smallest of the bindings, at the other end of the knotted end, the edge of the red leather shows empty stitch holes. At the other side of the smallest fragment of binding is another small piece of green binding, which is secured with running stitches. In the figure, top right to the latter (dashed arrow in figure C) the edge has stitch holes with, in some, remnants of whip stitches still *in situ*. Possibly, the green strip is not a binding, but rather a passepoil, as seen, for example, in L1 #024 (Cat. No. 120; possibly, the two pieces fit together).

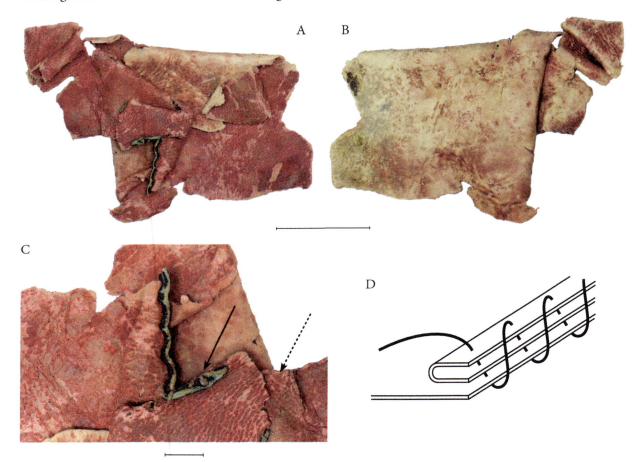

Cat. No. 78, L4 #006. *Overview of the recto (A) and verso (B); C) Detail of the seam; the arrow points to the S-overhand stopper knot; the dashed arrow to the empty stitch holes; D) Diagram of the construction of the possible edge binding. Scale bar C is 10 mm.*

CATALOGUE NUMBER 79

Id. No. L2 #001.
Measurements 280 x 280. Thickness: 0.8.
Description
A very roughly circular piece of red leather (figure A, B) that has broken off from a larger bit. It is slightly crumpled and extremely fragile. The wear, including the fading colour, suggests this was an exterior part of the casing.

Cat. No. 79, L2 #001. *Overview of the recto (A) and verso (B).*

CATALOGUE NUMBER 80

Id. No. L5 #003.
Measurements 71 x 21. Thickness: 0.8. Width passepoil: 2.
Description
A piece of red leather (figure A, B), broken away from something larger (tube?) that has remnants of a green, lengthwise folded passepoil (figure C). This is secured with running stitches of zS_2 sinew thread.

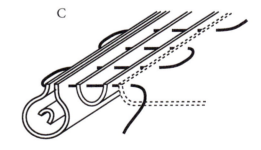

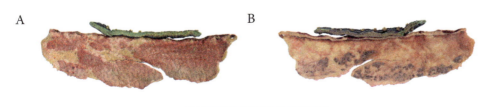

Cat. No. 80, L5 #003. *Overview of the recto (A) and verso (B); C) Diagram of the construction of the incomplete seam.*

SUPPORT STRAPS

CATALOGUE NUMBER 81

Id. No. BI-001.
Measurements Rectangular element: Length: 165. Width: 60. Thickness: 3.5-4. Loop: Length: 68. Width: 8. Thickness: 2.5. Width green decoration: 4.4.

Description

A rectangular piece of beige leather from which emanate two long bands of leather that taper at the ends (figure A), enhanced by green leather. The rectangular element is comprised of two pieces of beige leather which are secured at the edges by means of whip stitching (made of sinew) that include the green edge binding (5 mm wide at the recto; figure B-D). At the recto, this binding is secured with running stitches of flax thread, including a beige (width: 2.2 mm) and lengthwise folded strip of green leather (seen from top to bottom; this lowest green strip is 1.2 mm wide), which overlap in stair-step fashion. The beige and lower green strip together are secured separately as well (running stitching, flax thread). This decoration follows three edges, as the fourth edge is devoid of decoration where the two rectangular bands are inserted between the two layers (figure E, F).

Lengthwise down the centre, and continuing underneath the edge decoration of the short end, runs a decorative pattern consisting of one wide green strip of leather of which the long sides are folded inwards (figure C, D). This technique is seen more often. However, it cannot be entirely ruled out, as the piece is intact and thus portions invisible, that the lowest green consists of two separate and lengthwise folded strips. On top and lengthwise down the centre, leaving a strip of 1.8 mm of green visible at either side, follows a less wide beige strip, which is secured at either side with running stitches of flax. Lengthwise down the centre of this beige strip is a narrow green strip of leather that is secured at either side with flax running stitches. It leaves a strip of beige visible of 3.4 mm at either side; the green top band is 3.5 mm wide.

At the free end of the rectangular element there was once a narrow strip of leather attached at either side by stitching, forming two small loops (figure E; BI-006, Cat. No. 82). One became detached but is still present; the other is detached and not found with this piece. It consists of a piece of thick, beige leather with another piece of green leather sewn onto it lengthwise down the centre. It is secured with one row of running stitches of zS_2 flax thread going lengthwise and slightly off centre.

The two long, narrow bands consist of a wide strip of thick, beige leather of which the long sides are folded towards the recto (figure G-J). The recto is decorated with applied green and beige leather bands, thus obscuring and securing the folded sides of the foundation. At both sides, the decoration starts with a lengthwise folded strip of green (width: 0.8 mm), followed by a wide strip of beige (width: 1.5 mm) that runs lengthwise over the two green bands; these are secured together. On top of the beige are two narrow strips of green (width: 3.1 mm), leaving visible a central beige strip (width: 3.5 mm). Both green top bands are secured at both edges with running stitches of zS_2 flax thread (all other stitches are made of flax too). Note that the decoration of these bands faces the opposite side (verso) of the decorated rectangular element. The end of the bands are very curly due to desiccation and probably also due to use, prohibiting detailed description, but clearly they taper (*cf.* BI-013, Cat. No. 83). Remnants (slit) of a toggle closure are visible (arrow in figure A). The last 230 mm (approximately) is undecorated. The two bands are secured to the rectangular element with sinew running stitches, applied in a triangle (figure E), which also serves to reinforce this section.

Cat. No. 81, BI-001. A) Overview; B-C) Detail of the rectangular element. The arrow points to the remnant of a toggle closure. Scale bars B, C are 10 mm.

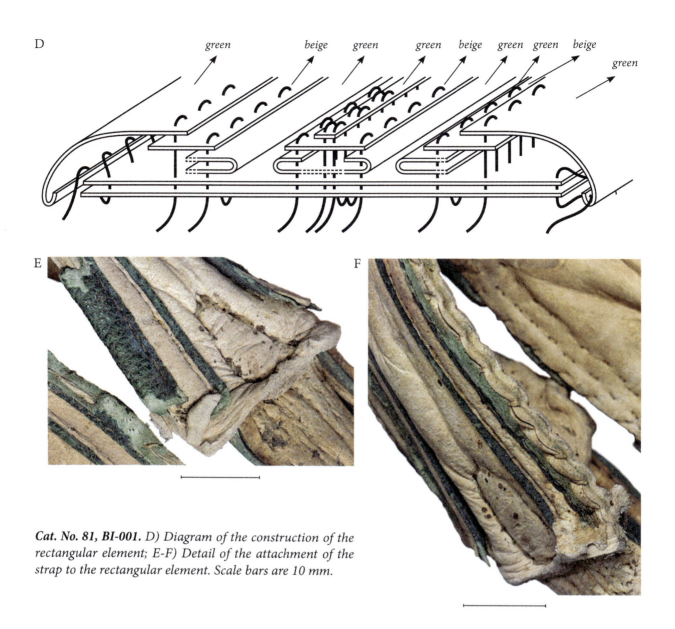

Cat. No. 81, BI-001. D) Diagram of the construction of the rectangular element; E-F) Detail of the attachment of the strap to the rectangular element. Scale bars are 10 mm.

Cat. No. 81, BI-001. Detail of the straps (recto) with appliqué. Scale bar is 10 mm.

H

I

J
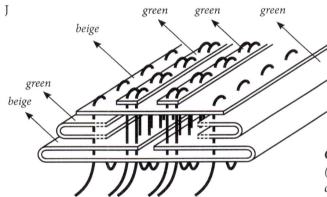

Cat. No. 81, BI-001. H-I) Details of the straps (verso and side view respectively; J) Diagram of the construction of the strap. Scale bars are 10 mm.

CATALOGUE NUMBER 82

Id. No. BI-006.

Measurements Band: Length: 748. Width: 23. Thickness: 3.5. Rectangular element: Length: 173. Width: 55. Thickness: 4. Loop: 33 and 37. Width: 9. Thickness: 2.5. The measurements of the decoration are comparable to BI-001 (Cat. No. 81). The fragments described under Cat. No. 83, 84 and 86 belong to BI-006.

Description

Identical to BI-001 (Cat. No. 81) although one of the long bands is missing (figure A-C). Probably, BI-004 (Cat. No. 86) is the missing strap. Two loops are visible on the verso of the rectangular element (figure G). The loops are made of one piece of leather, but tacked down in the middle to make two loops. It is decorated with a strip of green leather that runs lengthwise down the centre. The end of the top green strip of the centre decoration of the rectangular element (figure D-F), is, at the short end that accommodates the two long rectangular bands, inserted through the leather as a way of finishing.

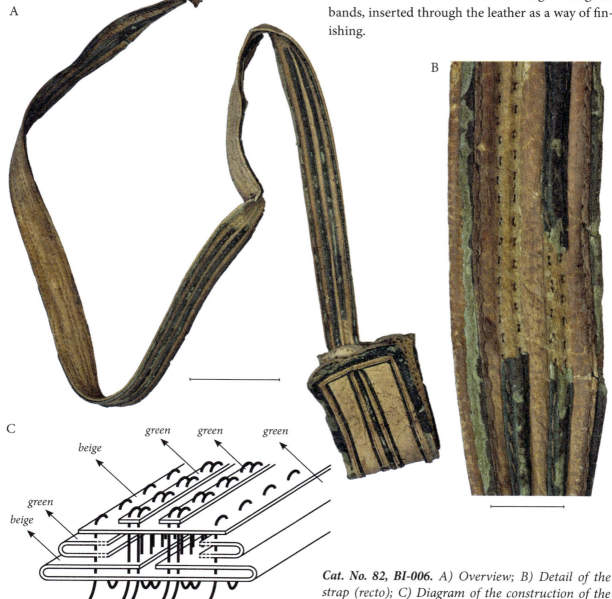

Cat. No. 82, BI-006. A) Overview; B) Detail of the strap (recto); C) Diagram of the construction of the strap. Scale bar B is 10 mm.

Cat. No. 82, BI-006. D-E) Details of the rectangular element; D shows the part with the loops at the back (see figure G); E shows the part to which the straps are secured; F) Diagram of the construction of the rectangular element; G) The loops and attachment area of the straps. Scale bars are 10 mm.

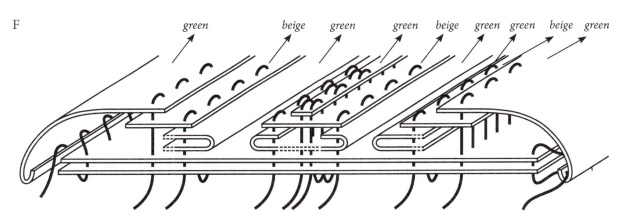

green   beige   green   green   beige   green   green   beige   green

CATALOGUE | 407

CATALOGUE NUMBER 83

BI-013.

...surements Length: 1034. Width: 2.6 - 12.8 - 17.6 - 19.4 - 22.1. Thickness: 3. The measurements of the decoration are comparable to BI-001 (Cat. No. 81). It belongs to BI-006 (Cat. No. 82).

Description

A long band of beige leather that starts wide and ends narrow (figure A, B), as it is rolled up to form a very tight and narrow cord (figure C, D), closed with whip stitches. The bands consist of a wide strip of thick, beige leather of which the long sides are folded towards the recto. The recto is decorated with applied green and beige leather strips (figure E-H, J), thus obscuring and securing the folded sides of the foundation. At both sides, the decoration starts with a lengthwise folded strip of green, followed by a wide strip of beige that runs lengthwise down the centre over the two green ones, which are secured together. On top of the beige are two narrow strips of green, leaving visible a centre beige strip; both green top strips are secured at either edges with running stitches of zS_2 flax, as are all other stitches. The two centre strips are made from one strip (figure I): shortly before the beige strip is rolled up, the pointed joined start of the two is clearly visible. The start of the outer two green strips joins with the start of the rolling up of the beige leather (figure C): the centre beige strip that partially overlaps the green is inserted in the rolled up terminal end, thus obscuring the start of the green and securing it.

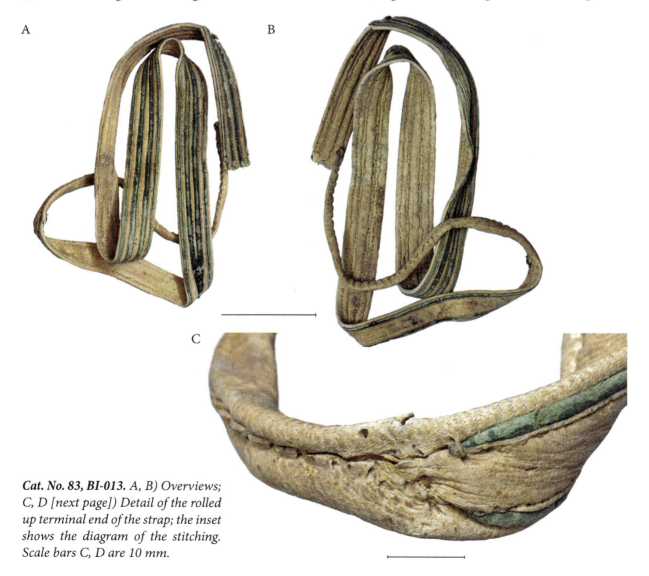

Cat. No. 83, BI-013. A, B) Overviews; C, D [next page]) Detail of the rolled up terminal end of the strap; the inset shows the diagram of the stitching. Scale bars C, D are 10 mm.

Cat. No. 83, BI-013. E, G, H) Details of recto; F) Detail of the verso. Scale bars are 10 mm.

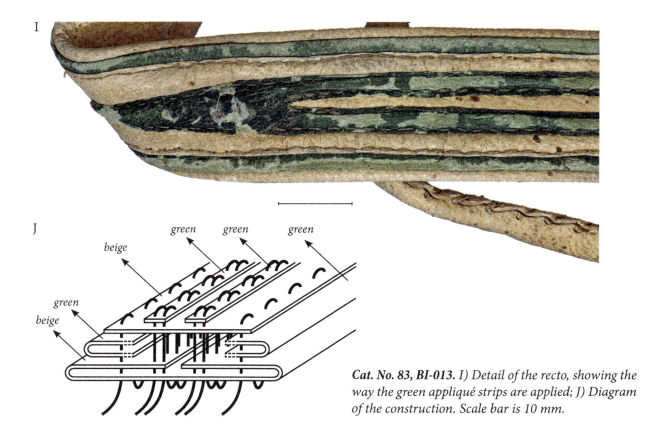

Cat. No. 83, BI-013. *I) Detail of the recto, showing the way the green appliqué strips are applied; J) Diagram of the construction. Scale bar is 10 mm.*

CATALOGUE NUMBER 84

Id. No. BI-026.
Measurements Length: appr. 770. Width: 13.1 - 19.4. Thickness: 3.5. The measurements of the decoration are comparable to BI-001 (Cat. No. 81).

Description
Fragment, much twisted into itself, consisting of several decorated strips of leather (figure A, B). The foundation consists of a beige strip of leather of which the long edges are folded inwards (towards the recto). The recto is decorated with applied green and beige leather strips (figure C, D), thus obscuring and securing the folded sides of the foundation. At both sides, the decoration starts with a lengthwise folded strip of green, followed by a wide strip of beige that runs lengthwise down the centre of the two green; these green and beige strips are secured together with running stitches of flax. Two narrow strips of green are sewn onto the top of the beige, leaving a central beige strip exposed. The green strips are secured with two rows of running stitches of flax (zS_2), as are all other stitches along either edge. One end of the fragment shows the beginning of the central green applied strips, indicating they originate from one wide strip that was slit down its centre (*cf.* BI-013, Cat. No. 83). It belongs to BI-006 (Cat. No. 82).

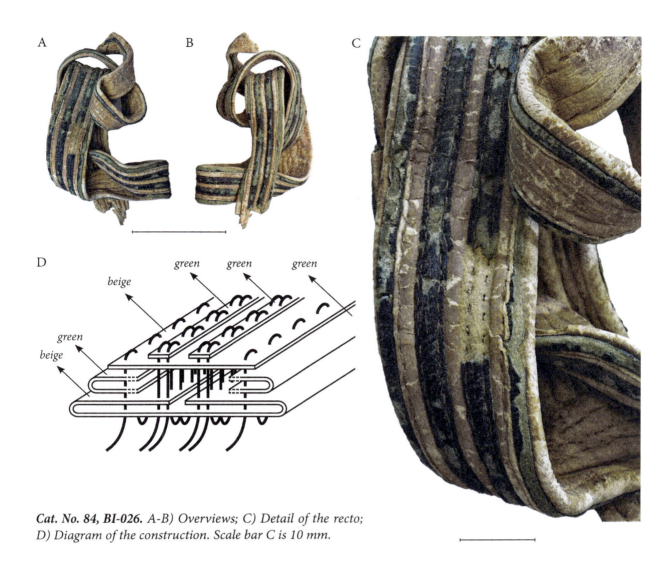

Cat. No. 84, BI-026. *A-B) Overviews; C) Detail of the recto; D) Diagram of the construction. Scale bar C is 10 mm.*

CATALOGUE NUMBER 85

Id. No.   BI-003.
Measurements   Length: 156. Width: 19.8 - 11.5 - 10.3. Thickness: 3.5. Length added pieces: 107 and 90.

Description
A fragment, which is comparable to BI-006 (Cat. No. 82) but probably not part of it. However, BI-003 consists of several decorated strips of leather (figure A, B). The foundation consists of a beige strip of leather of which the long edges are folded inwards (towards the recto). The recto is decorated with applied green and beige leather strips, thus obscuring and securing the folded sides of the foundation (figure C, E). At both sides, the decoration starts with a lengthwise folded strip of green (width visible strip at either side of the fragment 2 and 1.8 mm respectively), followed by a wide strip of beige that runs lengthwise through the centre of the two green ones (width 2.5 mm at both sides); these green and beige strips are secured together with running stitches of flax. On top of the beige are two narrow strips of green, leaving visible a centre beige strip (width 2.2 mm; the two green top strips have a width of 3.1 and 2.7 mm respectively). These green strips are secured with two rows of running stitches of flax along the edges.

At the verso two narrow pieces of decorated leather strips are attached by means of coarse leather thong stitches (figure D). It is not clear whether these were sewn together before being added, but most probably not. The decoration differs, as there are only four rows of stitches visible at their verso. This suggests that the decoration of the verso of these added pieces consists of (from outside to inside) green, lengthwise folded strips at either side, on top of which is applied a beige, wide piece; these are secured together to the foundation. This, in its turn, has a green strip lengthwise down the centre that seems to be secured with two rows of stitching at the edges. Probably, the edges of the foundation are also folded inwards (towards the recto), being obscured by the applied decoration.

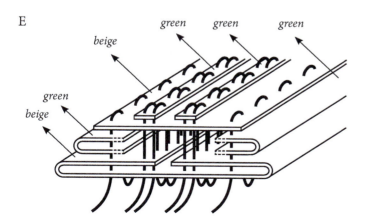

Cat. No. 85, BI-003. Overview of the recto (A) and verso (B); C) Detail of the recto; D) Detail of the verso; E) Diagram of the construction. Scale bars C, D are 10 mm.

CATALOGUE NUMBER 86

Id. No. BI-004.
Measurements Length: 1100. Width: 12-20. Thickness: 2.8. The measurements of the decoration are comparable to BI-001 (Cat. No. 81).

Description
A long, narrow band (figure A, B) consisting of a wide strip of thick, beige leather of which the long sides are folded towards the recto (figure C-F). The recto is decorated with applied green and beige leather strips, thus obscuring and securing the folded sides of the foundation. At both sides, the decoration starts with a lengthwise folded strip of green, followed by a wide strip of beige leather that runs lengthwise down the centre of the two green ones; these are secured together. On top of the beige are two narrow strips of green, leaving a centre beige strip visible; both green top strips are secured at both edges with running stitches of flax (all other stitches are done with flax thread too). The end of the bands are very curly, only allowing for a tentative description of how the pattern terminates: the inner two green strips are clearly connected close to the terminal end of the band, indicating that both the strips were cut from one single wider strip of leather, rather than separately (*cf.* BI-013, Cat. No. 83). The outer two green strips might have been made in a comparable way, but the beige centre strip runs over the terminal end and therefore prohibits visibility of this part of the decoration. Probably, this strap is the missing one of BI-006 (Cat. No. 82).

Cat. No. 86, BI-004. *D) Detail of the recto; E) Detail of the verso. Scale bars are 10 mm. See next page for figure A-C, F.*

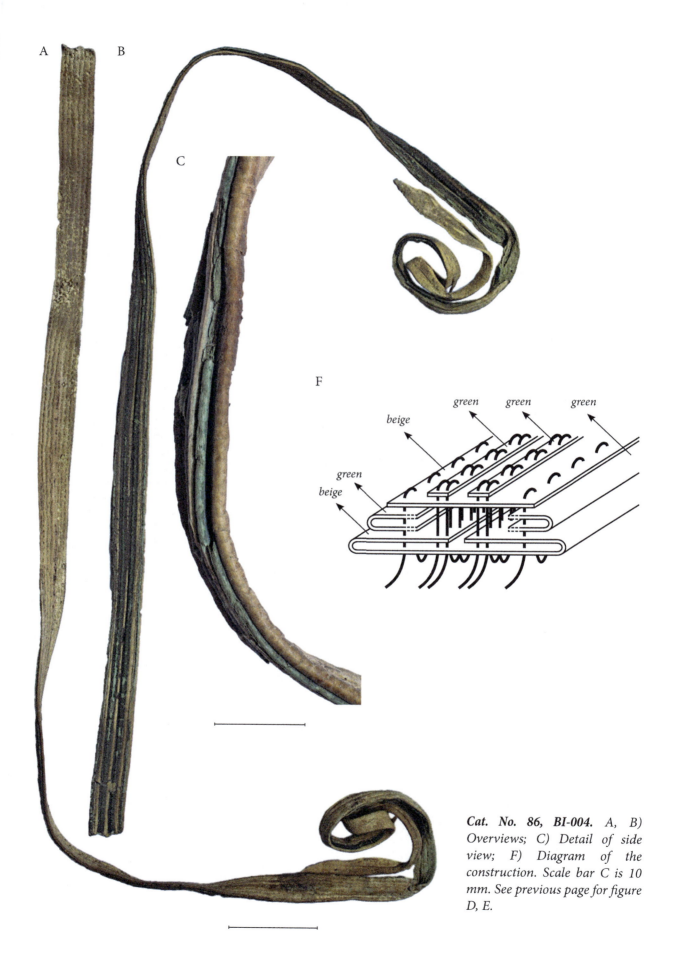

Cat. No. 86, BI-004. A, B) Overviews; C) Detail of side view; F) Diagram of the construction. Scale bar C is 10 mm. See previous page for figure D, E.

CATALOGUE NUMBER 87

Id. No. BI-011.
Measurements Length: 108. Thickness: 3.5 - 4 - 5.5.

Description
A long piece of beige leather (figure A, B) that is rolled in on itself lengthwise and secured with whip stitches of flax (figure D, E). The square terminal end suggests that it was cut from a longer piece. This end is knotted into a half knot, followed by a half hitch (figure C). The part that is broken off contains a piece of green leather that was doubtless connected to the rest of the leather piece. It compares well with the rolled up end of BI-013 (Cat. No. 83), which is part of the support strap; it might thus belong to BI-006 (Cat. No. 82).

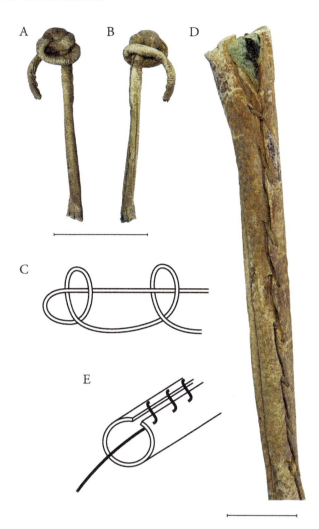

Cat. No. 87, BI-011. *A, B) Overviews; C) Diagram of the knots in the fragment (hitch and half knot); D) Detail of the seam with whip stitching; E) Diagram of the stitching. Scale bar D is 10 mm.*

NAVE HOOP

CATALOGUE NUMBER 88

Id. No. #33 & #34.

Measurements #33: Length: 180. Diameter: 80-120. Thickness: 2.3-3.1. Tab: 11.3 x 15.5. Thickness tab: 2;
#34: Length: 180. Diameter: 80-125 (but squashed). Tab: *cf.* #33.

Description

Two nave hoops (figure A-G), made of beige leather with a green edge binding at either side (width: 4.5 mm one side but only 2.2 mm wide at the other). This binding (figure L-O) is secured at the inner side by means of whip stitching of sinew (figure J), folded over it and secured at the outer side of the hoop with running stitches. Only at the wide (= inner) end does it include, at the outer side and in stair-step fashion, a beige (width: 3.2 mm) and a lengthwise folded green strip (width: 3.3 mm) respectively (figure H, I, K, N). A lengthwise folded strip of green leather (width: 2.4 mm) is included between the two ends that meet along the length to close the cylinder (figure L, N, O), acting as a passepoil. Possibly, it is sewn with interlocking stitching, the only time this is encountered in the Tano leather (but see IV.1.1. 'Glue, Stitching and Seams'). Close to the wider end a tab is included in the longitudinal edge (figure P, Q), with an edge binding in green (width: 2.4 mm; figure Q) consisting of a folded strip that is secured with whip stitches of zS_2 flax thread. It has a vegetal motif appliqué, which is secured with closely spaced running stitches of zS_2 flax thread, consisting of a central, vertical element that is flanked by curling tendrils (*fleur de lys*). It is made of green leather that might be padded to create high relief. However, it cannot be ruled out that the relief is created by deliberate bulging of the green leather itself, as seen in, *e.g.*, the bow-case (#30, Cat. No. 91).

The nave hoop has the shadow of a strap that was fixed in place, as is attested by a strategically placed hole (arrow in figure D). The width of the strap impression is 25.6 mm. The ends of the strap were rounded (see BI-023 & BI-025, Cat. No. 89 & 90).

Cat. No. 88, #34. *G) Side view. Overviews and details of #33 can be found on the following pages.*

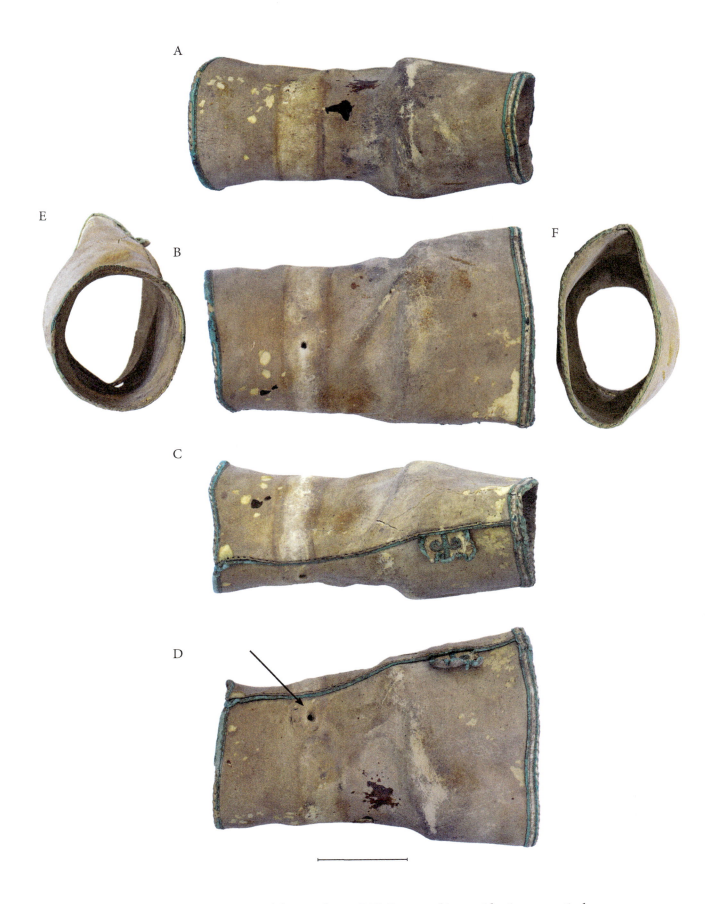

Cat. No. 88, #33. *A-D) Various views of the nave hoop; E-F) Outer and inner side view respectively.*

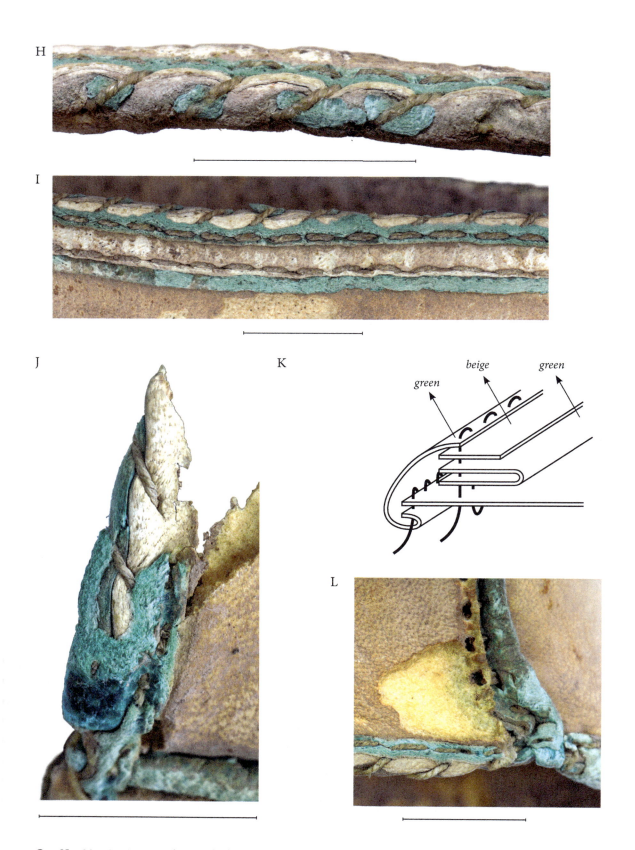

Cat. No. 88, #33 & #34. H) *Detail of the edge of the widest (= inner) side seen from the front. The green binding is damaged, showing the whip stitches underneath; I) As H but seen from aside; J) Detail of the binding, which is secured with sinew thread; K) Diagram of the construction shown in H-J; L) Detail of the crossing of the edge binding at the narrower end (see figure M) and the seam lengthwise (figure O). Scale bars are 10 mm.*

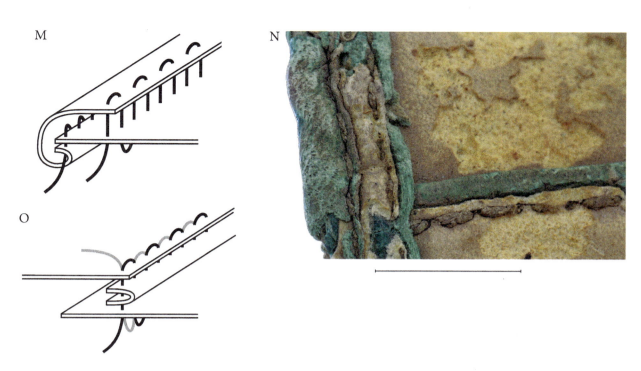

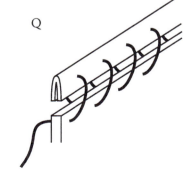

Cat. No. 88, #33 & #34. M) Diagram of the construction of the edge binding shown in figure L; N) Detail of the seam to close the hoop. At the left is just visible the elaborate edge binding of the wider (= inner) end; O) Diagram of the construction of the seam, shown in figure N; P) Detail of the tab with fleur de lys motif; Q) Diagram of the binding of the motif shown in figure P. Scale bars are 10 mm.

CATALOGUE NUMBER 89

Id. No.   BI-023.
Object   Strap to secure the nave hoop.
Measurements   Length: 63. Width: 14.8-17.8-22.1. Thickness: 1.4. Diameter hole: 3.6.

Description
Rounded end of a beige strap with green edge binding (figure A, B). At the verso, the binding is folded towards the recto (figure C-E), abutting the edge, and secured with whip stitching after which it is folded over itself and the edge of the beige foundation. At the recto (width: 3 mm) it is secured with running stitches. Lengthwise down the centre a green strip of leather is applied (width: 3.3 mm); it is secured at either side with running stitching. It terminates shortly before the drop-shaped hole in the rounded end. All stitching is done with flax zS_2 thread. The fragment fits with BI-025 (Cat. No. 90) resulting in a complete strap.

Cat. No. 89, BI-023. *Overview of the recto (A) and verso (B); C) Detail of the recto; D) Detail of the verso; E) Diagram of the construction. Scale bars are 10 mm.*

CATALOGUE NUMBER 90

Id. No. BI-025.
Object Strap to secure the nave hoop.
Measurements Length: 190. Width: 22.2. Thickness: 1.2-1.5;
Remarks Cf. BI-023 (Cat. No. 89) for detail images and diagram of the construction.

Description
A sturdy strap made of beige leather that is rounded at one end and broken off at the other (figure A). At the verso, the green edge binding is folded towards the recto, abutting the edge, and secured with whip stitching after which it is folded over itself and over the edge of the beige foundation. At the recto (width: 3.4 mm) it is secured with running stitch. Lengthwise down the centre is applied a green strip of leather (width: 2.7 mm) that is secured at either side with running stitching. All stitching is done with flax zS_2 thread. At the torn off end, a circular hole is introduced through the central green strip decoration. At the rounded end a 'lace' (roundish piece in section) of beige leather has been introduced beneath the central strip of green and protrudes out at the end. Presumably it broke off but would originally have been used to tie the strap. The fragment fit with BI-023 (Cat. No. 89), resulting in a complete strap.

Cat. No. 90, BI-025. *A, B) Overviews. Scale bar is 10 mm.*

BOW-CASE

CATALOGUE NUMBER 91

Id. No. #30.
Object Top.
Measurements Length: 120. Width: 66 - 110. Thickness: 8 - 10. Additional measurements in description.

Description

A small 'u-shaped' container of red leather with a horizontal strap on top that extends beyond its mouth (figure A-D). The top surface of the leather has rubbed away in several places, particularly around the outer edges of the piece. There are also small breaks in the leather of the sides. The top left side (seen from the recto) is torn off. However, there is no obvious evidence for an extension of the mouthpiece on this side as there is on the right. The right side is also damaged at the point where the mouthpiece joins the body of the object.

The recto is the most elaborately decorated (figure E, F, I-L; see the numbers in figure B; see esp. figure K). There is a band on top that was probably originally used to secure the mouth or attach it to another part of the object (figure E, R, S). This mouthpiece (1), which has a lining (2), was made separately and attached to the main body of this piece. It consists of a wide green strip (3; width: 3.6 mm) that secures this section to the main body of the object, using a running stitch of flax zS_2 thread; the bottom of the strip is also affixed using a comparable running stitch. The edges at either side are possibly tucked under the strip. The lining is stitched under this strip. A narrow red strip of thick leather (4; width: 2.7 mm) is stitched lengthwise down the centre, using running stitch of flax zS_2 thread on either side. This piece of leather has been pushed together so it stands in relief (figure I, J). This is followed by a band containing applied zigzag decoration in green (5; width band: 7.1 mm; width strip: 2.2 mm). This shape was cut out of the leather in one piece (figure I) and is affixed to the main backing that makes up the body of the mouthpiece with running stitches along both edges. This is followed by another strip of green leather (6; width: 1.2 mm), the edges of which are probably folded under, which is secured at the top edge with a row of running stitches of zS_2 flax thread. Another piece of thick red leather (7; width: 2.5 mm), is secured on the top of this strip. The end of the mouthpiece extends beyond the perimeter of the piece and folds over part of the verso (figure R, S). Its terminus is reinforced by further decoration. This consists, from in to out, of a folded strip of green leather (8; width: 1.8 mm) followed by one strip of red leather (9; width: 2.8 mm) that is secured to the green strip by a row of running stitches (flax zS_2 thread) along its centre. This seam also serves to anchor the green strip. Another green strip (10; width: 3-3.2 mm) lies over the far edge of the red strip; the two are secured together by running stitch (flax zS_2 thread). The penultimate edge is formed by the continuation of the red leather (11) that edges the pendentive triangles, resembling icicles/petals, of the body of the piece (see below). The lower edge of the mouthpiece's extension and its terminus is finished by a green binding (12) that parallels the construction of the edge of the body of the piece (see below). A lengthwise folded strip of red leather (13; width: 1.2 mm) constitutes the next strip, running across the mouth of the object where the mouthpiece is attached; *i.e.* it helps to connect the mouthpiece with the body. Beneath this red strip lies a strip of red leather upon which is secured, with flax (zS_2?) running stitches, a band of green leather consisting of narrow, thin pendentive icicles/petals (14; width: 4 mm; figure J). The same set, red strip with green pendentive icicles/petals, borders the edges of the body (15). The inner edge of these sets has a green strip attached, which probably is an edge binding of the red strip (16; width: 2.3 mm; figure E). It is attached by flax thread in running stitch (zS_2?). Probably, this stitching secures this decorative band to the red surface of the recto. From the beginning at the right-corner (figure E), the green edge binding runs across the mouth towards the other corner where it curves around and runs downwards (figure F), following the outline of the body until it terminates at right angles to the beginning, short of the mouth section. The outer edges of the decoration of the main body of the object is finished with a folded red strip (11; width: 1.5 mm; figure E), which seems to start on the left side, follows the body's edge and forms a connection to the mouth, continuing along part of its edge. It is included in the same running stitches (made of sinew) that fix the green edge binding (12; width: 2.6 mm). After this stitching, the binding is pulled over it and the edge of the object, and secured at the verso (figure G). At this side the binding is also secured with running stitches (of sinew) and pulled over itself, rather than with whip stitches as is usually seen in this kind of binding. Lengthwise down the centre, *i.e.* at the edge of the object proper, this green binding is enhanced with a narrow strip of red leather (width: 1.7 mm), affixed at either side with whip stitching of flax thread. Possibly, although the object is too complete to be certain, it is this strip that further secures the two pieces of binding.

The middle section of the verso of the piece (figure D; 1) is reddish-pink, and is bound by a wide strip of green (2; width: 2.2-3.2 mm; figure M, N), which runs to the edge of the object. It is secured to it by a series of running stitches of flax thread (zS_2). It is followed by a lengthwise folded piece of red leather (3; width: 1.8-2 mm) that runs from right to left along the mouth of the object, and then turns downward, following the edge of the object. It terminates on the right side, extending beyond the mouth and overlapping at its point of origin. Although the section that shows in the decoration is very narrow, the actual piece of leather is wide, as it is included in the stitching of the edge binding (see above). At the mouth, the border is completed by a wide green strip (4; width: 7.1 mm; figure T) that is secured by running stitching of zS_2 flax thread.

Seemingly the two elements ('recto' and 'verso') are connected by the mouthpiece (figure U) and the green-red-green binding at the edge. However, possibly the running stitching goes through all layers, but visibility is obscured hence the dashed lines in figure G.

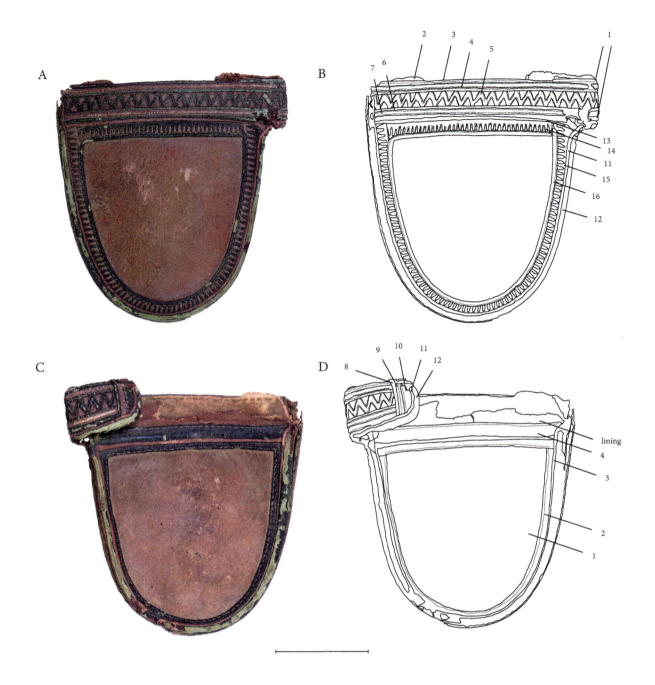

Cat. No. 91, #30. *Overview of the recto (A) and verso (C) of the top of the bow-case; B, D) Sketches, with the various parts that are described in the text, indicated.*

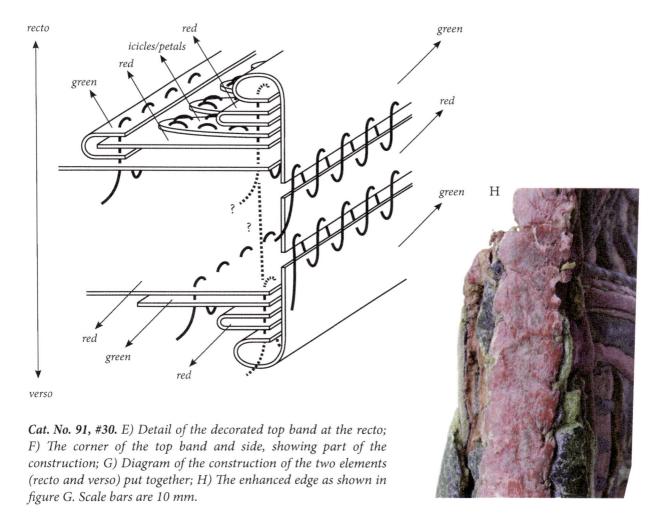

Cat. No. 91, #30. *E) Detail of the decorated top band at the recto; F) The corner of the top band and side, showing part of the construction; G) Diagram of the construction of the two elements (recto and verso) put together; H) The enhanced edge as shown in figure G. Scale bars are 10 mm.*

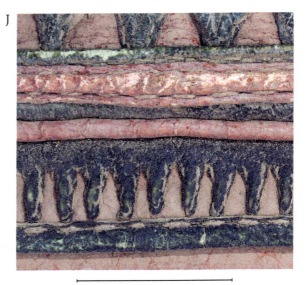
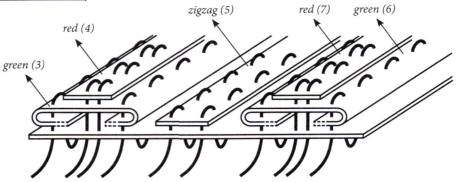

Cat. No. 91, #30. *I) Detail of the zigzag motif of the decorative top band that connects the body and the edge (recto); J) Detail of the pendentive icicles/petals that borders the part beneath the top band on the recto; K) Diagram of the construction top band shown in figure I. The numbers are explained in the description and figure A-D; L) Detail of the enhanced edge at the recto; M) As L but shown at the verso. Scale bars are 10 mm.*

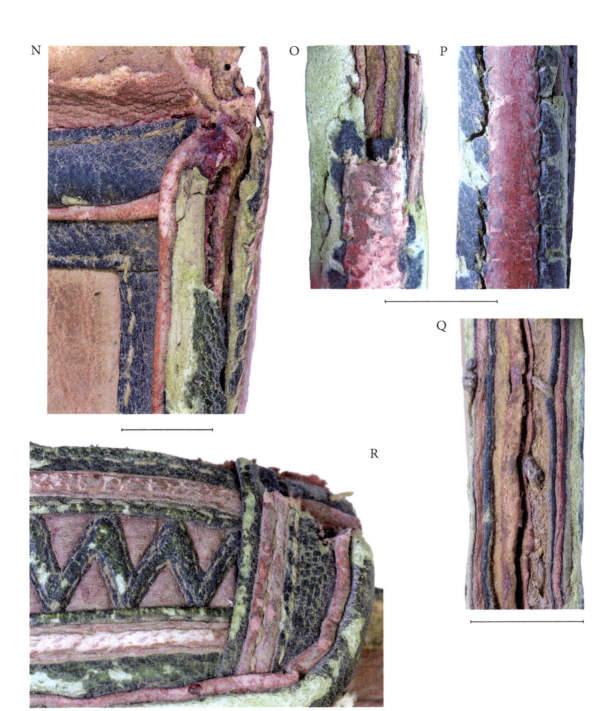

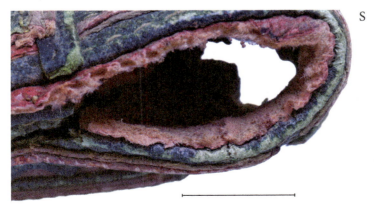

Cat. No. 91, #30. N) Verso, detail of the corner of the edge and the top; O-P) Details of the side of the object, which is finished by the green bindings and a central red strip; Q) Inside view of the various layers; R) The tip of the terminus of the extension, seen from recto; S) As R but seen from the top. Scale bars are 10 mm.

Cat. No. 91, #30. T) Detail of the connection between the top band and the body, seen from verso; U) Detail of the mouthpiece seen from above. Scale bars are 10 mm.

CATALOGUE NUMBER 92

Id. No. #31.
Object Bottom part.
Measurements Length: 208-242. Width: 70-116-140. Thickness: 32. Thickness leather: 5-7. Additional measurements in description.

Description

A 'U'-shaped portion of a red leather container, lined with another layer of leather (figure A-E). It is decorated with red and green strips of leather. The top edge has been torn off. On the verso, the upper zone shows wear or tearing that reveals the lining. The lower zone has been eaten through by insects in places, resulting in (large) holes. The strap that runs through the transverse band, and the absent lower oval feature was ripped off (figure O, S). The edge is abraded, particularly at the lower end, perhaps due to use. The recto is much better preserved, showing little insect activity. However, the edges, including the areas with the pendentive icicle/petal decoration, are abraded. The recto (figure F-K) is more elaborately decorated than the verso (see the numbers in figure B; see also figure I). There is a band on top that was probably originally used to secure the mouth or attach it to another part of the object. This mouthpiece (1), which has a lining (2), was made separately and attached to the main body of this piece. It consists of a wide green strip (3; width: 5-6 mm) that secures this section to the main body of the object, using a running stitch of flax zS_2 thread; the bottom of the strip is also affixed using a comparable running stitch. The edges at either side are possibly tucked under the strip. The lining is stitched under this strip. A narrow red strip of thick leather (4; width: 2 mm) is stitched lengthwise down the centre, using running stitch of flax zS_2 thread on either side. This piece of leather has been pushed together so it stands in relief. This is followed by a band containing applied zigzag decoration in green (5; width band: 6.4 mm). This shape was cut out of the leather in one piece and is affixed to the main backing that makes up the body of the mouthpiece with running stitches that runs along both edges. This is followed by another strip of green leather, probably folded at either edge (6; width: 5-6 mm), which is secured at the top edge with a row of running stitches of zS_2 flax thread. On top of this strip is secured another piece of thick red leather (7; width: 2 mm), as it is on the top. A lengthwise folded strip of leather (8; width: 1.2 mm) constitutes the next strip, running across the top of the object where the mouthpiece is attached, *i.e.*, it helps to connect the mouthpiece to the body and is an independent strip opening (a comparable strip runs along the edge of the body of the bottom, 14, see below). In this upper part, the red strip also forms the top edge for a series of green pendentive icicles/petals (9). These pendentive icicles/petals, that also surround the edge of the piece (10; width: 5 mm), are secured onto a red leather strip along the edges (11; width: 6 mm). The strip has a green binding (12; width: 2 mm), which is secured at its lower edge using running stitches, but which is continuous, starting and finishing at the top right edge (8). Some of the icicles/petals are attached by one or more whip stitches at the tip and/or sides rather than with running stitching, which seems a repair.

The folded red leather strip running along the entire lower edge of the bow-case (13; width: 1 mm), ultimately crosses over, together with the tripartite edge decoration, and secures the top to the mouth (7). It is also a key piece in the sides of the object (see below).

The sides are formed by a series of leather pieces that are coloured red and green. These are affixed by sinew. The previously mentioned red leather strip (13; width: 1.2 mm) forms the outer edge of the pendentive icicle/petal strip on the recto (9; width 5 mm) and also forms the edge of this side. This might be similar on both sides, being affixed with the strong, big sinew stitching, and comparable to the top part of the bow-case (#30, Cat. No. 91), but due to the fact that it is so complete and well preserved it is not possible to be certain. A green strip of leather (14; width: 4 mm) is sewn onto the red, with sinew. It is first sewn on one edge, and then pulled over tightly and seems to stop halfway along the side. Here, the band of strips (see below) would connect and secure them, which, if this is true, is again comparable to #30 (Cat. No. 91). Strips of alternating red and green leather (15; width each: appr. 4.5 mm) have been affixed using a whip stitch (flax) on top of the whole side. At one end there is evidence that the strips were not single, but run in a boustrephon pattern (figure H). In some places strain can be detected on the leather and its stitching, due both to the method of construction, what the object once contained and, possibly, how it was used.

Beyond the torn upper edge of the verso (figure M-T; see the numbers in figure D), the opening is edged with green (1; width: 4 mm). The bulging of the stitching of the lower edge suggests that it is secured with running stitching and pulled over this; the strip is again folded at the top and secured, visibly, with running stitches as well (zS_2, flax thread). The following red strip (2; width: 2-2.5 mm), which is overlapped in stair-step fashion by the green, is folded lengthwise and secured with the stitches that secure the first green strip. Possibly this red is not a strip proper, but the fold of the visible red part at the top and its lining. The red element overlaps the next strip, green (4; width: 3 mm), in stair-step fashion. In contrast to the construction of the top of the bow-case, where this element is a single strip, here it seems to be a true edge binding of the red (3), secured with zS_2, flax thread running stitches. This is suggested by the small part of it that protrudes from under the centre portion (5; arrow in figure M).

The central area of the verso is divided into two zones by an applied transverse undulating band of red leather (6; maximum height: 53 mm; figure O-R) edged by a single(?) strip of green leather (7; width: 1.5-2.4 mm; the entire width of this strip is 6.3 mm). The red leather overlaps the green in stair-step fashion and is secured with short running stitches of zS_2 flax thread. A transverse compartment, running down the centre of the undulating strip, is created by stitching at either side (running stitching with zS_2 flax thread). It is pierced by three holes; a large one in the centre and two slits at either end. It contains some kind of plain, thick leather strap (8; width: 20 mm) that is visible through the holes. The strap is made of thick leather that is folded over and secured by four lines of stitching, probably running stitch, not unlike straps such as BI-033 (Cat. No. 114). The central prominence of the strap is covered by a rectangular piece of folded green leather (9; 19.3 x 27 mm), which is secured by whip stitches of flax thread. Probably this is a repair or reinforcement; it already shows a distinctly abraded area in the centre.

In the zone above the undulating transverse division (the top of the band is 67.5 mm below the top edge; the bottom of the band is 80.5 mm above the bottom edge), on the right side, an oval piece of red leather (10: 36 x 21.7 mm; figure S, T) has been secured onto the centre part using running stitches (zS_2, flax thread) all along its edge. It is pierced on the top and bottom by two slits (11; length: 11.3 and 11.5 mm) through which a strap, consisting of a red and a green layer, is pulled. The red layer lies below the green and is wider than it: it is folded over. The straps are secured along the outer edges of the slits with a series of running stitches, creating a slight bulge at either end of the oval. This was presumably repeated below the undulating transverse band, roughly parallel to this oval (12). Now only the shadow of the oval remains, outlined by the empty pairs of stitch holes (figure T).

▷ **Cat. No. 92, #31.** *Overview of the recto (A) and verso (C) of the bottom of the bow-case; B, D) Sketches, with the various parts that are described in the text, indicated.*

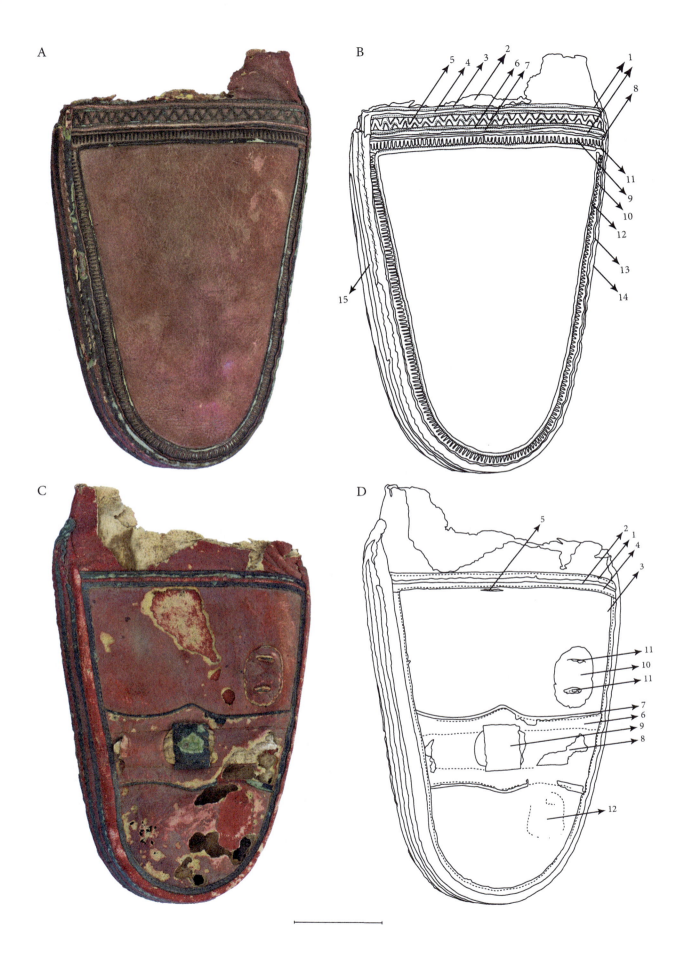

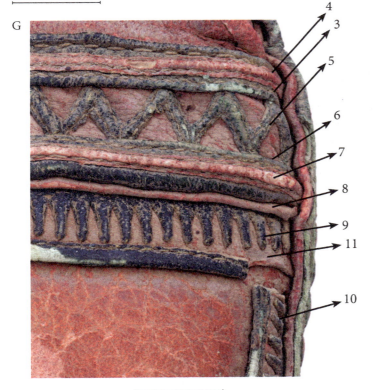

Cat. No. 92, #31. *E) Side view; F) Detail of the right top and side, seen from the recto; G) Detail of the left top and side, seen from the recto, with the numbers added that are used in the description (see figure A, B); H) The start of the decorative strips of the edge. Scale bars are 10 mm.*

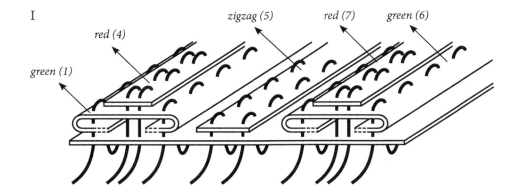

Cat. No. 92, #31. Details. I) Diagram of the construction of the top edge (recto). The numbers refer to the description and figure A, B; J) The edge including part of the pendentive icicles/petals of the recto; K) The enhanced edge of the recto; L) The mouth, showing the various layers of the piece (including the lining). Scale bars are 10 mm.

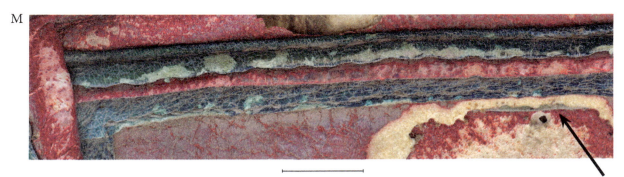

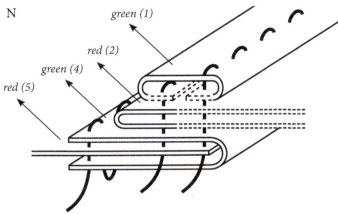

Cat. No. 92, #31. M) Top of the piece with the edge binding (arrow: see text); N) Diagram of the construction shown in figure M (the numbers refer to the description, see figure D; O) The undulating transverse attachment area; P) Detail of the green lining of the area seen in O (see also figure R). Scale bars are 10 mm.

CATALOGUE | 433

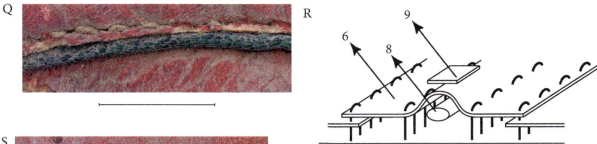

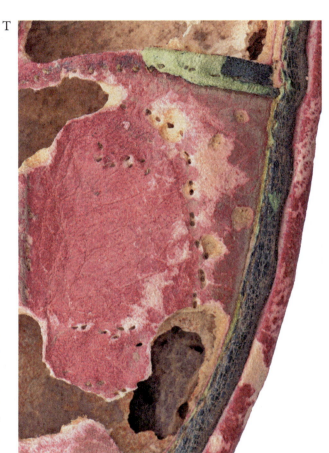

Cat. No. 92, #31. *Q) Detail of the green lining of the area seen in O, showing the edge intact; R) Diagram of the construction of the attachment area (the numbers refer to the description, see figure D); S) The intact oval, additional attachment area at the verso; T) The empty stitch holes idicative of another oval attachment area as seen in S, but now lost. Scale bars are 10 mm.*

CATALOGUE NUMBER 93

Id. No. L1 #015.
Object Flap.
Measurements Width: 232. Height: 106. Thickness: 2.

Description

An elaborate semi-circular flap that was connected to a larger piece of red leather (figure A, B). The flap is made of two pieces of leather that are stitched together along all edges with binding and decoration in the usual alternating colours and in stair-step fashion. An additional band of decoration, also in alternating red-green strips that (partially) overlap each other, bisects the flap, running perpendicular to the straight edge.

On the recto (figure C, E-I), the edging of the rounded side consists (described from outside in) of a wider green edge binding (width: 2.7-3 mm) that partially overlaps the next narrower red strip. On this side, the binding is secured with zS_2 flax running stitches after which it is folded around the edge of the object and secured with zS_2 whip stitches at the verso. The decoration's narrow red strip (width: 1 mm) is folded lengthwise and extends to the edge of the object proper. It too is held in place by the aforementioned running stitches of the binding. The next strip is green and much wider (width: 2.7-3.1 mm). It is folded lengthwise but it could not be identified whether it was folded in the middle or only at the innermost edge. It is secured with closely spaced running stitches (seemingly only spun) in flax. Probably, it also secures the next strip, which is red and narrower at its outermost edge (width: 2 mm). This strip, folded lengthwise, is secured with closely spaced flax running stitches (in addition to the stitches of the overlapping green strip), which secures the last strip (green and narrow) too. The length of these stitches is larger than those securing the former described strips. This last strip is, as all others except for the edge binding, folded lengthwise (width: 2.8-3 mm), which is extraordinary since usually enhanced edges include non-folded strips too. The verso (figure D, J, K) only shows the green edge binding, which is secured with whip stitches and only the innermost row of stitching, suggesting that some strips were premade (*cf.* L3 #001, Cat. No. 43). The straight edge is enigmatic, and due to the torn off red strip that covers it, it was not possible to exactly determine its composition (figure L-N). At the verso, a green strip (arrow in figure I) is folded over the edge of a red strip, the fold facing towards the curved edge. Close to this fold, it is secured with tiny but widely spaced, flax running stitches. Possibly, the red strip (about 12 mm wide) is folded at the edge backwards over the green strip. It is fixed at the edge of the object with widely spaced, running stitches of zS_2 sinew. At the cross section another red and green layer are visible, whose origin cannot be determined. At the corner, a small piece protrudes. Clearly visible is the aforementioned green sandwiching strip. However, the other edge of the red strip has a small fragment of green leather attached in opposite orientation (dashed arrow in figure I). It is attached to the red strip with running stitches at its intact edge, facing the terminal edge of the green binding, and thus creating a 'band' of the red strip because it is not covered. At the verso, the entire edge is obscured by a torn off piece of red leather (double arrow in figure I), which is secured with widely spaced running stitches of zS_2 sinew that also secure the construction at the recto. The torn off strip is pulled over the edge, away from the object. The cross section (figure L-N) shows another layer of red leather underneath, the origin of which could not be identified.

The additional decoration at the recto, running vertical down the centre from the convex to the straight edge (figure C-E) consists of a wide strip of green leather (width: 15 mm), which is folded at either side. The extent of these folds cannot be observed as the decoration is intact. However, since the strip is firstly only fastened with a row of stitches lengthwise down the middle (see below), it seems obvious that the edges overlap each other slightly so that both could be included in the stitches, a technique not seen in other fragments. On top of this strip is a wide strip of red leather (but narrower than the green strip; width 12 mm) that is not folded. Stitched to it, lengthwise through the centre, is a narrow green strip (width: 12 mm) that is not folded either. The topmost narrow green strip is attached at either side with closely spaced flax running stitches. These four rows of stitches, however, do not show at the verso (figure D). Here are only three rows of stitches visible, which allows for reconstructing the application of the decoration. The lower green strip was applied first by means of a row of stitches that run lengthwise down the centre: these show only at the verso as it is covered on the recto by the set of red-with-green strips. The topmost green strip was applied to the red one before being attached to the object: these two rows of stitches do not show at the reverse. It is attached to the green with the stitches at either side, thus securing the lower green strip too. Note the cuts or breaks of the green leather close to the straight edge (arrow in figure C).

Emerging roughly from the centre of the rounded edge of the verso are three narrow strips of leather that are folded lengthwise (figure O-Q), the edges of which are secured with whip stitches of flax: two red ones that flank a green one. They are inserted in the edge proper, slightly away from the centre, and most likely in such a way that they are secured with the stitching that fixes the decoration of the edge itself (figure P). They run semi-horizontal towards the centre of the convex edge where they are attached to a red leather strip (also folded lengthwise) that is at a right angle to them. This element is fastened to the edge of the object in the same way as described for the horizontal ones, *i.e.* inserted in the edge and included in the stitching of the edge binding and decoration. Seemingly, the small stubs that are inserted in the edge are cut out of the strip of leather as is the blade of a key. The red horizontal elements are inserted into slits in this reinforcement-element; the green one, however, is pierced itself, through which the reinforcement-element is pulled. After this connection, the elements continue and are, much closer to this side of the reinforcement-element than at the other side, re-inserted into the edge of the object in the same way. They protrude beyond the edge binding, and are finally securely stitched to the verso of the flap. The end of the reinforcement-element terminates in a small green toggle of leather (detached; figure Q). The short stub of leather that protrudes from it at the other side shows that the edges of the strips are secured with whip stitches in flax. This object was a flap that was closed with this construction. Possibly, the construction served for the reception of (a) toggle(s).

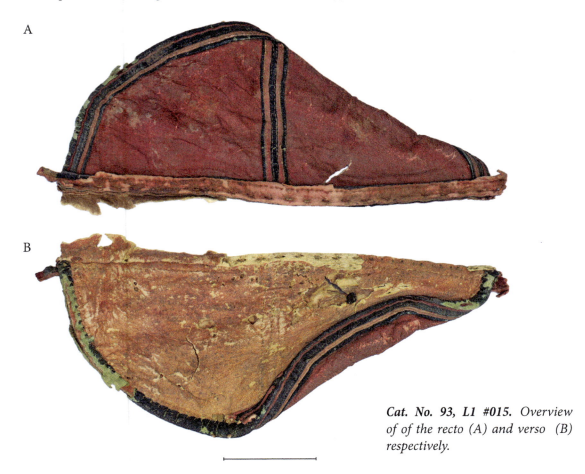

Cat. No. 93, L1 #015. Overview of of the recto (A) and verso (B) respectively.

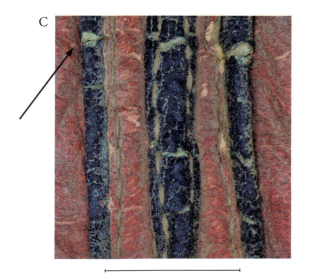
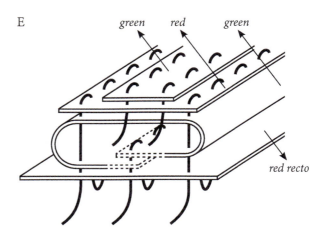

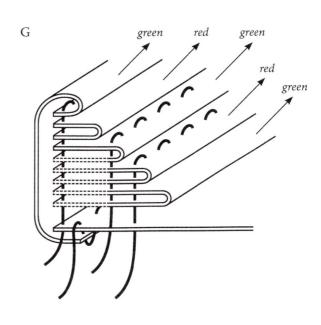

Cat. No. 93, L1 #015. C) Detail of the applied decoration vertical from the convex to the straight edge (recto). The arrow is explained in the text; D) As C, but seen from verso; E) Diagram of the construction of the applied decoration seen in C, D; F) Detail of the enhanced edge; G) Diagram of the construction of the edge decoration seen in F. Scale bars are 10 mm.

CATALOGUE | 437

Cat. No. 93, L1 #015. H) Corner, seen from the verso); I) Opposite corner, seen from the recto (see figure K). The arrows are explained in the text; J) The binding of the enhanced edge (see figure F, G), seen from the verso. Scale bars are 10 mm.

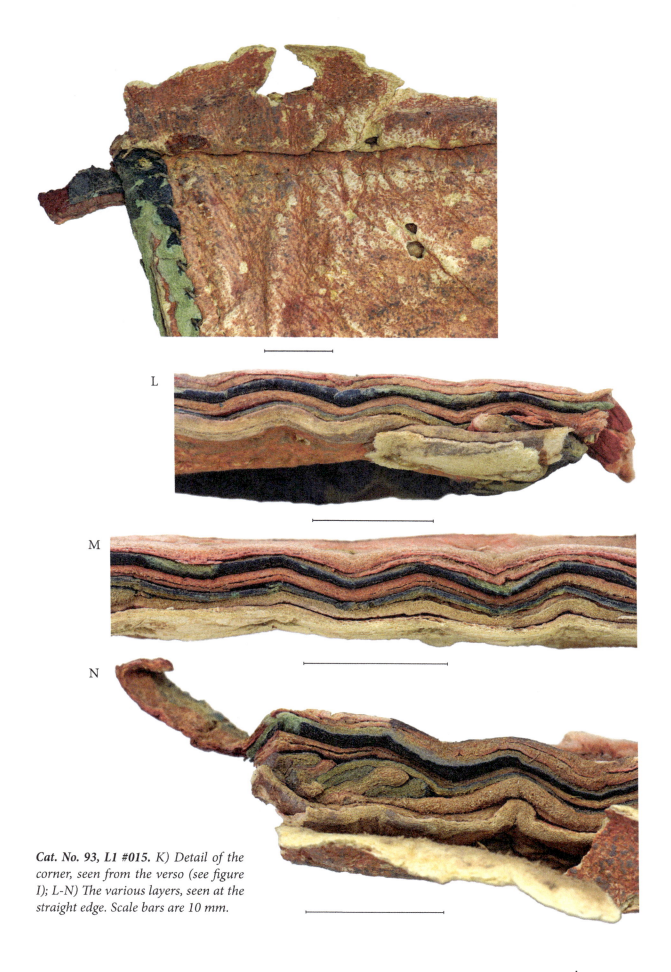

Cat. No. 93, L1 #015. *K) Detail of the corner, seen from the verso (see figure I); L-N) The various layers, seen at the straight edge. Scale bars are 10 mm.*

Cat. No. 93, L1 #015. O) Detail of the edge with remnants of the closing system, seen from recto/edge; P) As O but seen from verso/edge; Q). Detail of the detached toggle. Scale bars are 10 mm.

CATALOGUE NUMBER 94

Id. No. L5 #034.
Object Element of closing system bow-case flap.
Measurements Length: 10. Diameter loop: 7.5 x 11. Thickness: 0.7.

Description
A loop of red leather (figure A, B), made to receive (fasten) a toggle. It passed through a larger piece of green leather. The size suggests a close link to the closing system of what has been identified as the bow-case flap (L1 #015, Cat. No. 93).

Cat. No. 94, L5 #034. *Overview of loop of the closing system of the bow-case flap. Scale bar is 10 mm.*

CATALOGUE NUMBER 95

Id. No. L5 #035.
Object Element of closing system bow-case flap.
Measurements Length: 17.5. Diameter red strip: 1.5. Diameter toggle: 5.4.

Description
A tiny green toggle that is attached to a narrow strip of red leather (figure A), which is made by coiling it lengthwise and secure it with whip stitches (zS_2, flax thread). The end of the red leather probably provides the bulk of the attachment area of the toggle proper, which itself is made of green leather, stitched over the end of the red strip. The object equals the one found at the flap of the bow-case.

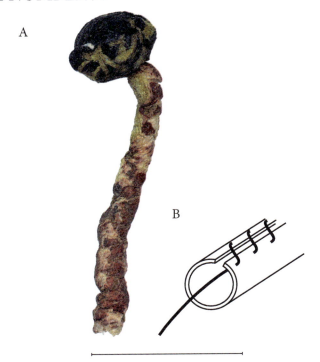

Cat. No. 95, L5 #035. *A) Overview of the toggle of the closing system of the bow-case flap. Scale bar is 10 mm; B) Diagram of the coiled part.*

CATALOGUE | 441

HARNESS

CATALOGUE NUMBER 96

Id. No. #40 & 41.
Object Girth.
Measurements #40: Length: 646. Width: 60-65-70. Thickness undecorated part: 2.5-3.1. Thickness decorated end: 6.1-6.7;
#41: Length: 20. Width: 6.5 - 6.7. Thicknesses: *cf*. #40.

Description
Both #40 and #41 (figure A, B, H-J) are broken parts of a strong belt that is made of thick beige leather. It is identified as the backing element (girth), the belt that runs underneath the body of the horse, immediately posterior of the front limbs. Both pieces terminate in an area that is reinforced by a piece of appliqué, with a circular hole that is integrated into the design.

The decoration of the ends of the belt fragments consists of a symmetrical appliqué in beige leather that is outlined in green leather (length in #40 approximately 147 mm; in #41 approximately 146 mm; figure E-G, M). The green strip that makes this outline is folded lengthwise (width in #40: 1.4 mm; in #41: 1.4 mm); the beige leather that makes up the centre of the motif is padded to create high relief (figure G, N-P). It emanates from the terminal area that includes the circular hole and can be described as lily-like tripartite motif but instead of a motif in a diamond compartment, as seen for example in #36 (Cat. No. 97), a short stub is visible. Curling tendrils flank the diamond-shaped compartment. The whole terminates in three narrow leaves or stylised lily flanked by outwards curling tendrils. Below the compartment are tendrils as well, which emanates from the basis that covers the terminal end. The hole (diameter #40: 16.4 mm; #41: 19.5 mm) is lined with a green strip of leather (width #40: 3.5 mm; #41: 3.7 mm; figure N), including a narrow leaf(?) that points towards the vegetal design just described. It is flanked with curling tendrils.

All applied decoration is secured with closely spaced running stitching of zS_2 flax thread. The edge of the terminal end has a binding that is secured at the verso with whip stitches (figure C, D, K, L) after which it is pulled over it and secured with running stitches at the recto (width: 2.5 mm; figure C), including in stair-step fashion a beige (width: 3 mm) and a lengthwise folded green strip (width: 1.5 mm) respectively. These are secured with running stitches of zS_2 flax thread (figure C).

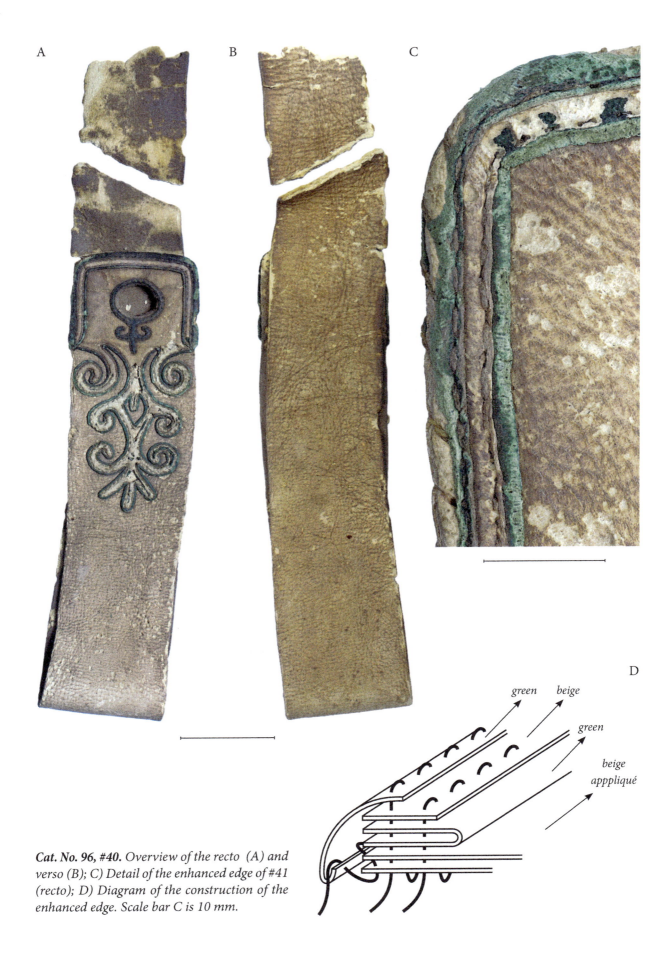

Cat. No. 96, #40. *Overview of the recto (A) and verso (B); C) Detail of the enhanced edge of #41 (recto); D) Diagram of the construction of the enhanced edge. Scale bar C is 10 mm.*

CATALOGUE | 443

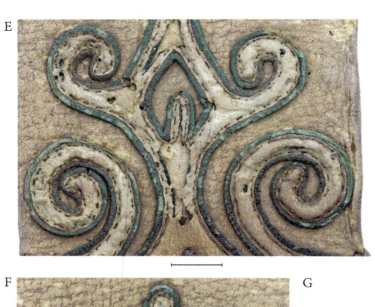

Cat. No. 96, #40. E-F) *Details of the appliqué;* G) *Diagram of the construction of the appliqué; Overview of the side* (H), *recto* (I) *and verso* (J) *respectively;* K) *Detail of the appliqué and the edge. Scale bars E, F, K are 10 mm.*

444 | CHARIOTS IN ANCIENT EGYPT

Cat. No. 96, #41. *L) Detail of the enhanced edge; M) Stitching pattern visible at the verso; N) Detail of the hole and its reinforcement/enhancement; O-P) Detail of the appliqué at the recto. Clearly visible is the stuffing of the motif in P. Scale bars L-P are 10 mm.*

CATALOGUE NUMBER 97

Id. No. #35 & #36.
Object (?).
Measurements #35: Decorated piece: Length: 945. Width: 92-115.
#36: Length: 635 and 800. Width: 100-120. Width at end of vegetal motif: 104. Thickness: 4.5;
#35: Plain piece: Length: 470. Width: 90-94. Thickness: 2.8-3.6.

Description
Long and tapering belts made of beige leather, both of which are broken in parts (figure A-C, E, F, O-R). One side is folded inwards partially (beyond the end with the applied decoration). Close to one end, which is squared off by being cut, is a vegetal motif that is appliqué in beige leather, outlined in green (total length of motif in #35 is 180 mm; width: 34.5-71.2-81.2 mm). The objects are too intact to be sure about the construction of the outlining of the design, but it is assumed that the construction is comparable to #40 and #41 (Cat. No. 96); *i.e.* consisting of lengthwise folded strip at either side of the beige 'filling' (figure D, I, J-N). The beige 'filling' include a core to create relief working in the decoration (not seen in the basis of the motif). The material of the core cannot be ascertained here as it is intact, but parallels #41 (and also from Amarna; Veldmeijer, 2011b: 26, 137-138) suggests that string was used for padding. The beige leather is stitched to the foundation together with the green lining with running stitches of zS_2 flax thread.

The vegetal motif is not centred (figure B, O); when viewed with the green line as a horizontal basis (this strip of green leather has a width of 11.5-11.7 mm; figure H, T), it lies to the right of the centre. It is missing some of the original green lining at the right side. The motif emanates from the horizontal green strip and can be described as a lily-like tripartite motif within a diamond. This is repeated. Curling tendrils flank the diamond. The whole terminates in three narrow leaves, reminiscent of a stylised lily, flanked by outwards curling tendrils. The decoration is secured at either side with running stitching of zS_2 flax thread; note that in #36, the spacing of both rows of stitching differs distinctly.

On the left side of the applied motif in #36 only, a loop has been stitched on top of the green strip (length: 49.5 mm; width: 8.5 mm; thickness: 2.5 mm; figure S, T). It is secured not only with stitches on the top of the green strip, but also with three stitches that cause it to lie on the thickness of the belt. Both belts have relatively big stitch holes (some still containing remnants of sinew stitches) in the thickness of the leather that favours the appliqué (*i.e.* the opposite side to the edge with the loop just described; figure G, U). Putting these edges together, the appliqué 'fits', resulting in an overall symmetrical design. In ancient Egypt, symmetry was very important and asymmetry is extremely rare in decoration, suggesting that these two pieces were, originally, attached to each other.

On the verso of #36, some 18-20 mm from the stitches that secure the green strip, is a vertical green smudge (not visible in the photographs). It might be due to metal rather than green dye. The verso also shows, from the cut end to the far edge of the stitching for the green strip, a discoloured or worn away area with a few shiny bits. It suggests as if something else had been attached to it by glue, perhaps.

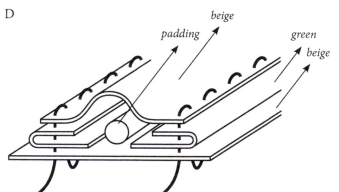

Cat. No. 97, #35. Overviews of side (A), recto (B) and verso (C) respectively; D) Diagram of the construction of the padded appliqué.

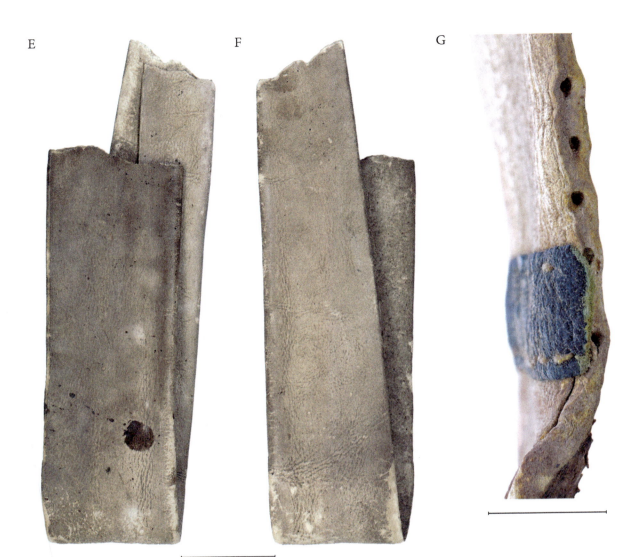

Cat. No. 97, #35. E-F) Overviews of the second piece; G) Detail of the side view; H) Detail of the appliqué strip, which is the basis of the vegetal motif; I) Detail of the edge of the appliqué. Scale bars G-I are 10 mm.

***Cat. No. 97, #35.** J-N) Details of the appliqué (recto). Scale bars are 10 mm.*

Cat. No. 97, #36. O-P) Overview of the recto and verso; Q-R) Overview of the additional, undecorated fragment.

450 | CHARIOTS IN ANCIENT EGYPT

Cat. No. 97, #36. S, T) *Detail of the loop;* U) *Detail of the edge. Scale bar is 10 mm. Indication of scale for S, T: the thickness of the leather is between 2.8-3.6 mm.*

CATALOGUE NUMBER 98

Id. No. #42.
Object Piece of strap *cf.* #35 & #36 (Cat. No. 97).
Measurements Length: 670. Width: 53.5-59. Thickness: 3.2-3.9.

Description
Undecorated part of a strap that is made of thick beige leather. It is broken at both ends (figure A, B).

▽ *Cat. No. 98, #42. Overviews.*

A

B

CATALOGUE NUMBER 99

Id. No. #43.
Object Piece of strap *cf.* #35 & #36 (Cat. No. 97).
Measurements Length: 740. Width: 38.6-54.2. Thickness: 2.2-3.

Description
Undecorated part of a strap that is made of thick beige leather. It is broken at both ends (figure A, B).

A B

Cat. No. 99, #43. *Overviews.*

CATALOGUE NUMBER 100

Id. No. #44.
Object Piece of strap *cf.* #35 & #36 (Cat. No. 97).
Measurements Length: 174. Width: 11.5-21.7-26. Thickness: 1.5-2.2.

Description
Undecorated, tapering part (two pieces that fit; figure A, B) of a strap that is made of thick beige leather. Both ends are broken.

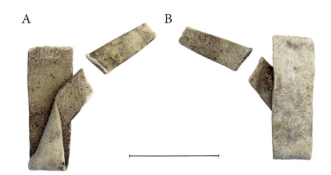

***Cat. No. 100, #44.** Overviews.*

CATALOGUE NUMBER 101

Id. No. #45.
Object Piece of strap *cf.* #35 & #36 (Cat. No. 97).
Measurements Length: 242. Width: 39-43.7-46.4. Thickness: 1.6-2.

Description
Fragment of undecorated strap of thick beige leather (figure A, B).

***Cat. No. 101, #45.** Overviews.*

CATALOGUE NUMBER 102

Id. No. #46.
Object Pieces of strap *cf.* #35 & #36 (Cat. No. 97).
Measurements A) Length: 103. Width: 51.2.
B) Length: 144. Width: 33.5-37.1.
C) Length: 73. Width: 30-32.
D) Length: 80. Width: 49.4.
E) Length: 47. Width: 48.7.
F) Length: 73. Width: 48.8.

Description
Six small fragments of undecorated strap of thick beige leather.

Cat. No. 102, #46. Fragment A-F in overview.

CATALOGUE NUMBER 103

Id. No. #37 & #39.
Object Neckstraps.
Measurements #37: Length: 730. Width: 110. Thickness total: 5.4. Thickness centre: 2.5-3.1. Thickness edge: 5.2. Width tie: 22. Thickness tie: 6.5.

#39: Length wide part: 600. Length tie: 125 & 730. Width: 16.9-22.5. Thickness total: 4.3. Thickness tie: 4.9. Thickness connection: 7.8.

Description

Two broad straps of thick, beige leather that has a lining of thinner beige leather; these layers are secured along the edges with running stitches of sinew (figure A-E). The two ends of the straps terminate in narrow, reinforced ties – in #37, one has a short piece still *in situ* whereas the other one has broken off at the attachment to the belt proper. One tie in #39 is still substantial in length, whereas the other one is also broken off. Object #39 is tied around a rectangular piece of wood, which is of recent date as is the textile band (striped grey, white, light and dark blue) that is used to secure the leather loosely to the wood.

The applied motif of beige leather (#37: length: 155 mm; width: 23-80 mm; #39: length: 150 mm; width: 24-70-96 mm; figure M, N, S, T), outlined in green, emanates from the passage between strap and neckstrap proper and can be described as a lily-like tripartite motif – the first is situated within a 'triangular' compartment and the second within a diamond. The triangular compartment has curling tendrils on top; the diamond is flanked by comparable motifs. The whole terminates in three narrow leaves or stylised lily flanked by outwards curling tendrils. The beige 'filling' overlap the green lining and include a core to create relief working in the decoration (figure N, S, T). The material of the core cannot be ascertained here as it is intact, but parallels (#35 & #36, Cat. No. 97; #40 & #41, Cat. No. 96); also from Amarna; Veldmeijer, 2011b: 26, 137-138) suggests that string was used for padding. The beige leather is attached to the foundation together with the green lining with running stitches of zS_2 flax thread.

The triangular part opposite the end with the applied decoration that forms the passage of the neckstrap proper into the narrow ties (figure F, P) has a separate lining (arrow in figure F), that is fixed in a comparable way to the other lining, but has an additional row of stitching lengthwise down the centre (figure G, H, P, Q, R). A row of big stitch holes is visible at the horizontal edge (figure I); probably, this triangular lining was secured together with the lining of the rest of the belt.

At the concave sides of the belt-strap transition, the lining is folded over the recto and includes a lengthwise folded green strip in stair-step fashion, which is thus sandwiched (dashed arrow in figure F, P). The edge is secured with three rows of running stitching of sinew zS_2 thread. The folded part of the lining extends over the narrow ties itself in such a way that the one coming from one side overlaps the one from the other side (figure J, P). One row of stitching follows the edge, crossing each other in front of the applied decoration (arrow in figure P): the middle row of the five rows of stitching that secures the ties starts at this junction (figure O). The ties are folded twice (figure K, L), and might, especially at the attachment to the belt proper, include two cores (possibly one folded lengthwise) but it is not clear whether these are separately inserted elements or extensions of the leather of the belt itself.

Both neckstraps show slits that are inserted lengthwise in the centre of the ties (best visible in #39; figure O), close to the wider part of the neckstrap. These slits (length: 24 mm) have reinforcement stitching (running stitching of probably flax zS_2 thread) round them.

Cat. No. 103, #37. Overview of the recto (A), side view (B) and verso (C).

Cat. No. 103, #37. D-E) Overviews of the recto (D) and verso (E).

CATALOGUE | 457

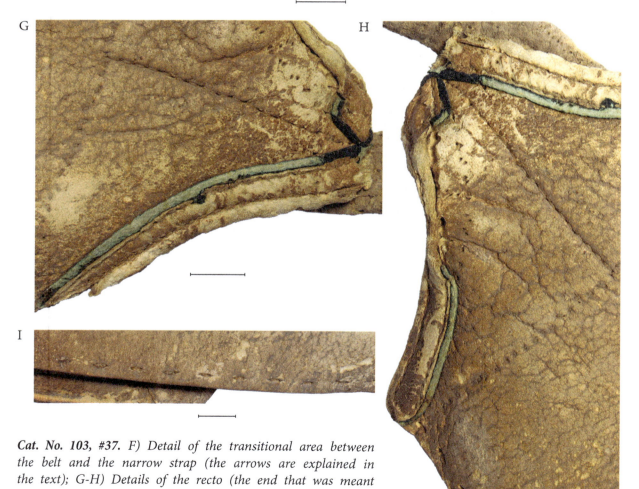

Cat. No. 103, #37. *F) Detail of the transitional area between the belt and the narrow strap (the arrows are explained in the text); G-H) Details of the recto (the end that was meant not to be seen as it was secured in between the horse span); I) Detail of the edge. Scale bars are 10 mm.*

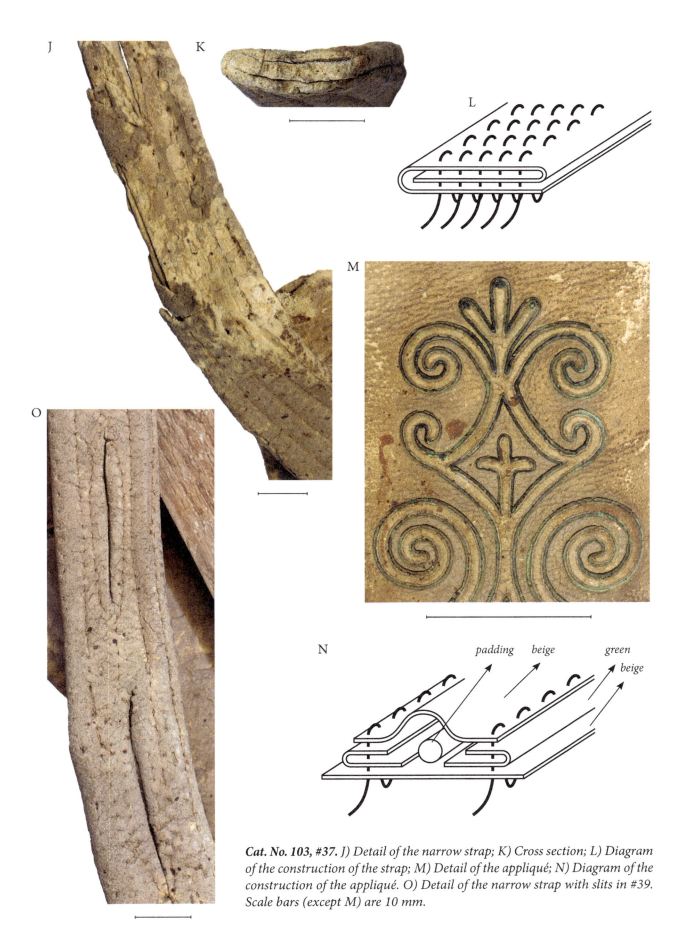

Cat. No. 103, #37. *J) Detail of the narrow strap; K) Cross section; L) Diagram of the construction of the strap; M) Detail of the appliqué; N) Diagram of the construction of the appliqué. O) Detail of the narrow strap with slits in #39. Scale bars (except M) are 10 mm.*

CATALOGUE | 459

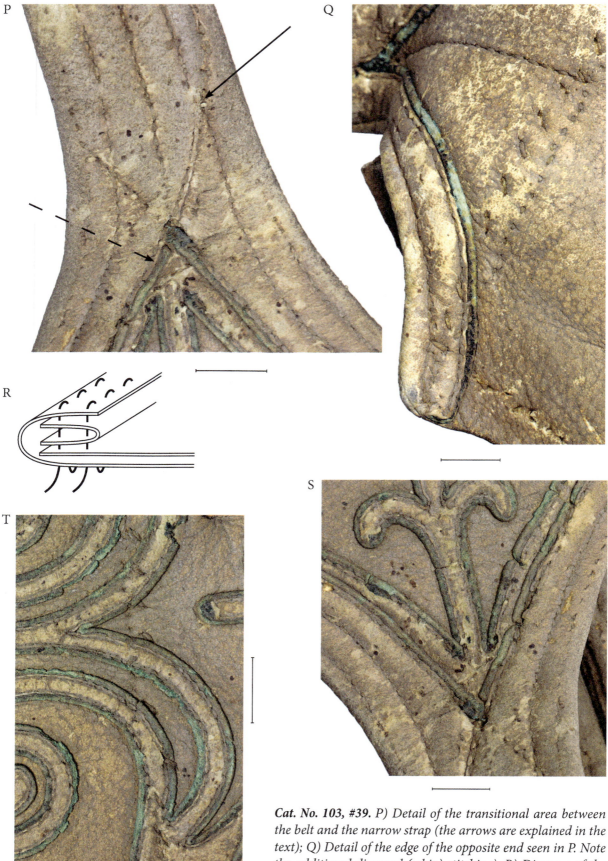

Cat. No. 103, #39. P) Detail of the transitional area between the belt and the narrow strap (the arrows are explained in the text); Q) Detail of the edge of the opposite end seen in P. Note the additional diagonal (whip) stitching; R) Diagram of the construction of the edge seen in Q; S, T) Details of the applied decoration. Scale bars are 10 mm.

CATALOGUE NUMBER 104

Id. No. BI-005.
Object Strap.
Measurements Length total: 1038. Width: 15.6 - 85.6 (but folded). Thickness: 1.8 - 3 - 4.3. Thickness overlap: 4.8.

Description
Two pieces of band that fit together. They are made from beige leather (figure A, B). These band fragments are broken off from longer pieces. Both differ slightly in thickness. Fragment A consists of two pieces that are secured together by overlapping (figure C-E). The overlapping area (50 x 52 mm) is secured by running stitches along the length but with whip stitches along the width (zS_2 sinew). At one side, after this connection, the leather is folded lengthwise. Fragments A and B are inequal in width and fragment B, the one without the overlapping attachment area, tapers distinctly.

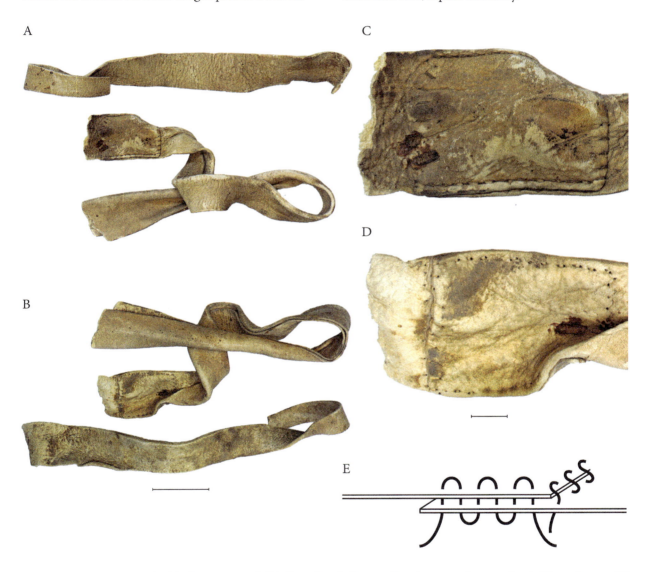

Cat. No. 104, BI-005. *A, B) Overviews; C-D) Details of the overlapping attachment (recto(?) and verso(?) respectively); E) Diagram of the construction of the overlapping attachment, showing combined running and whip stitching. Scale bars C, D are 10 mm.*

CATALOGUE NUMBER 105

Id. No. BI-007.
Object Strap.
Measurements Length: 283. Width: 26-30. Thickness: 2.5. Width: 23.

Description
A beige piece of band, which is incomplete, consisting of two parts that are secured together where they overlap. The overlapping area (45 x 23 mm) is secured by running stitches along the length but with whip stitches along the width (zS_2 sinew).

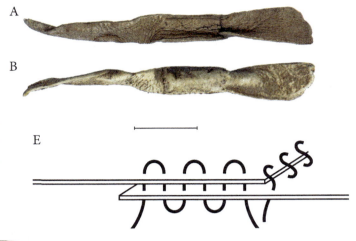

Cat. No. 105, BI-007. *Overview of the recto(?; A) and verso(?; B); C-D) Details of the overlapping attachment (recto(?) and verso(?) respectively); E) Diagram of the construction of the overlapping attachment, showing combined running and whip stitching. Scale bars C, D are 10 mm.*

CATALOGUE NUMBER 106

Id. No. BI-008.
Object Strap.
Measurements Length: 398. Width: 9.9-13-19.2. Thickness: 2.5.

Description
Two narrow bands of beige leather (figure A, B) that overlap where they are secured together, forming a rectangle (figure C-E). One side is torn off just at the joint with the overlapping part. The other end is intact, terminating in a slightly convex edge. The overlapping area (43 x 28 mm) is secured by running stitches along the length but with whip stitches along the width (zS_2 sinew).

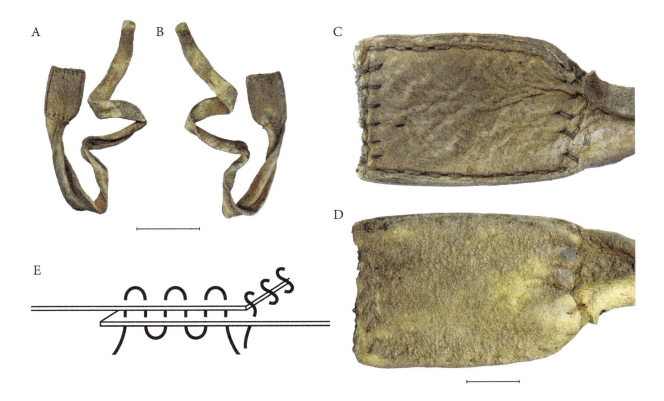

Cat. No. 106, BI-008. *A-B) Overviews; C-D) Details of the overlapping attachment area (recto(?) and verso(?) respectively); E) Diagram of the construction of the overlapping attachment, showing combined running and whip stitching. Scale bars C, D are 10 mm.*

CATALOGUE NUMBER 107

Id. No. BI-014.
Object Strap.
Measurements Length: 842. W: 42-54. Thickness: 2.2-2.5-3.2.

Description
Two straps that are attached by means of an overlapping part, forming a rectangle (62 x 46 mm). It is secured with running stitches along the length and with whip stitches along the width. Both ends are broken off.

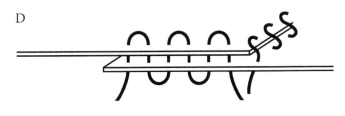

Cat. No. 107, BI-014. A-B) Overviews; C) Detail of the overlapping attachment (verso(?)); D) Diagram of the construction of the overlapping attachment, showing combined running and whip stitching. Scale bar C is 10 mm.

CATALOGUE NUMBER 108

Id. No. BI-039.
Object Strap.
Measurements Length: 30. Width: 28. Thickness: 1.2-1.5.

Description
A small, nearly-square fragment of beige leather that has broken off from a larger strap (figure A, B).

Cat. No. 108, BI-039. Overviews. Scale bar is 10 mm.

CATALOGUE NUMBER 109

Id. No. BI-012.
Object Part of neckstrap(?).
Measurements Length: 368. Width: 17.6-22.2. Thickness: 4.2-6.

Description
Beige piece of narrow strap (figure A, B) that is folded lengthwise twice and sewn into place with running stitches of sinew at either side as well as lengthwise down the centre (figure C, D). One terminal end is rounded. Near the other end is a large slit (length: 20.9 mm) that is reinforced with stitching (made of sinew) around its edge (figure E, F); it is deformed due to use. Note, however, that at the end that contains the slit the edges of two layers are turned upwards. The end is broken off shortly after the slit, showing the complexity of this end of the band: another, very thin strip of leather was introduced within the fold of the main piece (arrow in figure F). Another piece of leather, of slightly darker colour and incompletely preserved, was wrapped on top of it and secured on the long edges, which might have acted as reinforcement.

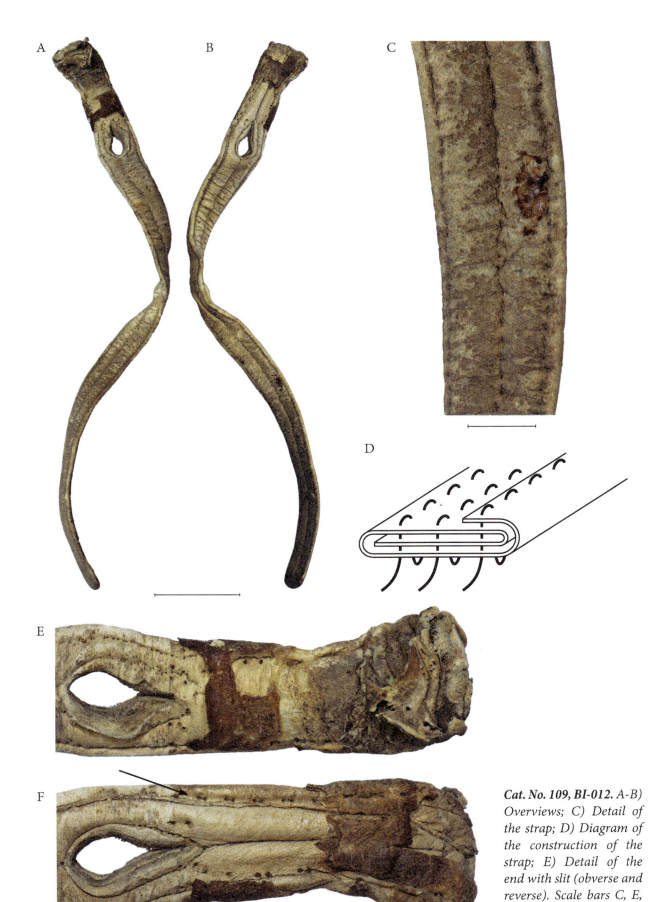

Cat. No. 109, BI-012. A-B) Overviews; C) Detail of the strap; D) Diagram of the construction of the strap; E) Detail of the end with slit (obverse and reverse). Scale bars C, E, F are 10 mm.

CATALOGUE NUMBER 110

Id. No. BI-009.
Object Part of neckstrap(?).
Measurements Length: 500. Width: 14.4-15.6. Thickness: 4.5-4.7.

Description
Beige piece of narrow strap (figure A), consisting of a strip that is folded lengthwise twice and secured into place with running stitches at either side as well as lengthwise down the centre (sinew?; figure B-D). Towards a broken end another piece of leather that has been introduced into the fold is visible (width: 0.48 cm; thickness: 1.5 mm). This end has also a slit (length: 26.7 mm; figure E) that is reinforced by stitching only. The layout of the strap is comparable to the narrow extension in the neckstrap (#37 & #39, Cat. No. 103).

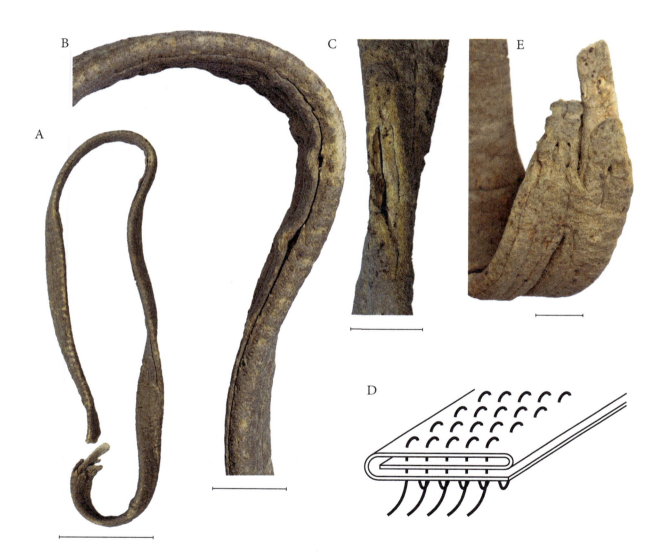

Cat. No. 110, BI-009. *A) Overview; B-C) Side views; D) Diagram of the construction of the strap; E) Detail of the terminal end with slit. Scale bars B, C, E are 10 mm.*

CATALOGUE NUMBER 111

Id. No. #38.
Object Part of neckstrap(?).
Measurements Length: 294. Width: 20. Thickness: 4.5-7.2.

Description
Reinforced strap, which is broken at both ends (figure A, B). It is pierced by a slit lengthwise down the centre (length: 24.3 mm), which is reinforced with running stitching of zS_2 sinew thread. The strap consists of a strip that is folded lengthwise twice and secured with a row of closely spaced running stitches of zS_2 sinew thread at either side and one row lengthwise down the centre (figure C-E). The layout of the strap is comparable to the narrow and short strap BI-012 (Cat. No. 109).

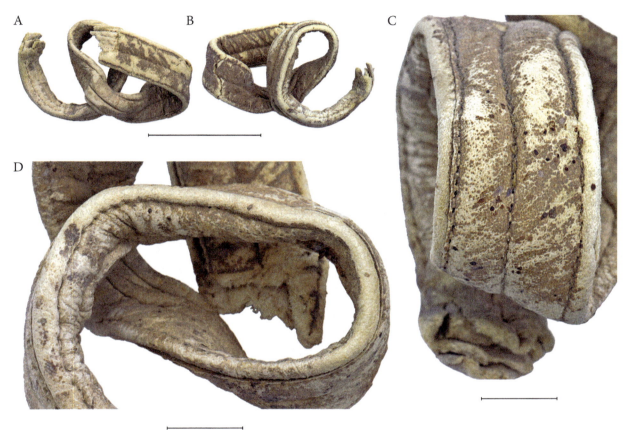

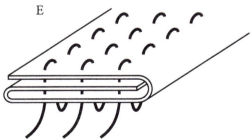

Cat. No. 111, #38. *A-B) Overviews; C-D) Details of the strap; E) Diagram of the construction of the strap. Scale bars C, D are 10 mm.*

CATALOGUE NUMBER 112

Id. No. BI-020.
Object Strap.
Measurements Length: 110. Width: 11.6. Thickness: 2.6.

Description

A strip of beige leather, rather damaged at especially the verso (eaten by insects; figure A, B). Both edges of the beige leather are folded towards the recto and covered by applied decoration (figure C-F), consisting of lengthwise folded green strips at either side (width: 2 mm). This, in its turn, is covered in stair-step fashion by a wide strip of beige leather, which is secured with running stitches of zS_2 flax thread that also secures the green strips and the folded edges of the beige foundation layer. A green strip (width: 2.7 mm) runs lengthwise down the centre of the beige strip. It is secured at either edge with comparable stitching. Note that, in contrast to other fragments with comparable decoration (identified as support straps, Cat. No. 78-84), here the beige foundation does not protrude from the first green strips of leather.

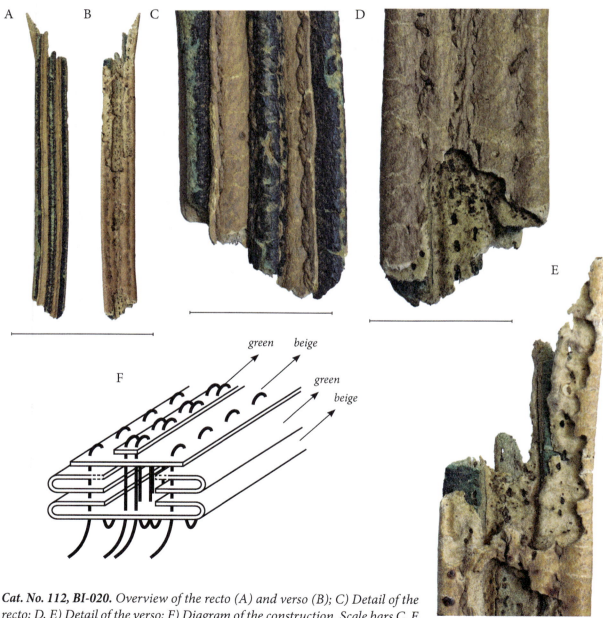

Cat. No. 112, BI-020. *Overview of the recto (A) and verso (B); C) Detail of the recto; D, E) Detail of the verso; F) Diagram of the construction. Scale bars C, E are 10 mm.*

CATALOGUE NUMBER 113

Id. No. BI-022.
Object Strap.
Measurements Length: 212. Width: 14.8 - 15.3. Thickness: 4.2-5.8.

Description
A well made narrow, thick strap of beige leather that is rounded at one end and broken off at the other end (figure A, B). The fragment is much worn due to use. It is folded lengthwise twice; the open edge is seemingly tucked in too and secured with whip stitches (figure C). These are entirely lost but indicated by the characteristic diagonal impression and slight discoloration of the beige leather. The three layers are secured with two rows of tightly sewn running stitches along the edge. Two additional rows of tightly sewn running stitches run lengthwise down the centre and terminate distinctly before the rounded end (approximately 53 mm). The stitches are made with threads of zS_2 sinew(?).

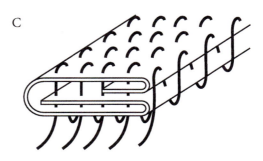

Cat. No. 113, BI-022. *A-B) Overviews; C) Diagram of the construction.*

CATALOGUE NUMBER 114

Id. No. BI-033.
Object Strap.
Measurements Length: 342. Width: 14-17. Thickness: 3.5.

Description
A piece of narrow strap that is folded lengthwise twice and secured into place with running stitches (zS_2, sinew?) at either side, as well as lengthwise down the centre (figure A-D). The two middle rows of stitching drop short of the rounded intact end by running sideways towards the edges (figure E, F); the opposite end of the strap is broken off. Possibly, the open edge is tucked in and secured with whip stitches, remnants of which are visible at the thickness.

Cat. No. 114, BI-033. *A-B) Overviews.*

Cat. No. 114, BI-033. C) Side view; D) Diagram of the construction; E) Detail of the recto; F) Detail of the verso. Scale bars C, E, F are 10 mm.

CATALOGUE NUMBER 115

Id. No. BI-021.
Object Strap.
Measurements Length: 188. Width: 12.6. Thickness: 2.4.

Description
A strip of beige leather that is folded lengthwise at least one time, but possibly twice (figure A, B). It is enhanced with a strip of green of slightly smaller width (3.1-7-9 mm), which is secured at either side with running stitches of zS_2 sinew thread (figure C-F). This green strip tapers at one end. Note the start of the stitching, which is secured with an overhand knot (figure C).

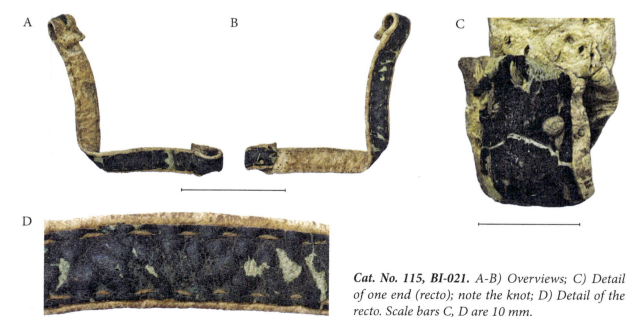

Cat. No. 115, BI-021. A-B) Overviews; C) Detail of one end (recto); note the knot; D) Detail of the recto. Scale bars C, D are 10 mm.

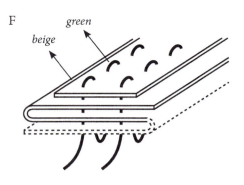

Cat. No. 115, BI-021. E) Detail of the verso; F) Diagram of the construction. Scale bar E is 10 mm.

CATALOGUE NUMBER 116

Id. No. BI-024.
Object Strap.
Measurements Length: 760. Width: 2.6-8-14.7-18.6-21.8. Thickness: 1.8-3. Thickness at rolled end: 2.6.

Description
A long piece of beige leather, the edges of which are folded inward upon itself towards the recto (figure A, D). The fold is not always equal; sometimes one fold is wider than the other (figure B, C). A piece of green leather (width: 7.5-16 mm) covers the seam (figure E, F) and is secured at either side with widely spaced running stitches of zS_2 flax thread. However, the interstitch spacing is distinctly smaller than seen in BI-021 (Cat. No. 115). Note that the construction of BI-021 differs from BI-024: the edges of the beige strip are not folded inward upon itself. Still, the appearance equals BI-024. The thread also secures the fold of the beige leather. At one end, the beige swallows up the green, which tapers dramatically (figure B). From here until the tip of the piece, where the beige leather ultimately rolls itself up lengthwise, the edges are now secured together by means of whip stitches (figure D; mostly lost, so it is not certain if they are of flax or sinew).

Possibly, BI-024 connects to BI-028 (Cat. No. 117); it resembles BI-021 (Cat. No. 115).

Cat. No. 116, BI-024. A) Overview.

CATALOGUE

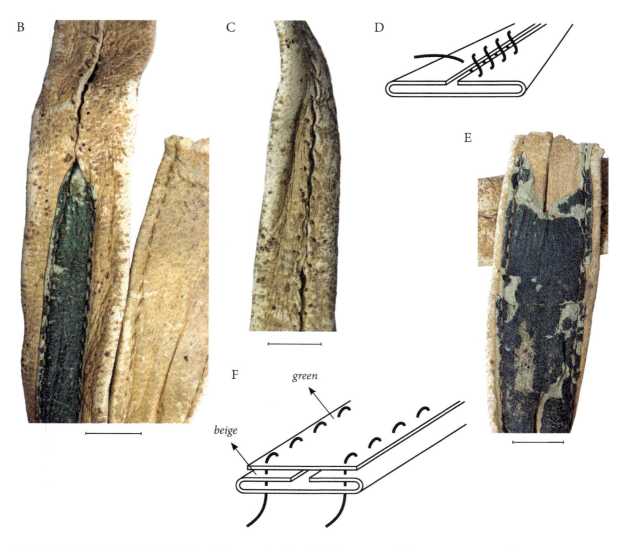

Cat. No. 116, BI-024. *B-C) Details of the terminal end; D) Diagram of the construction of the terminal end; E) Detail of the recto; F) Diagram of the construction of the strap. Scale bars B, C, E are 10 mm.*

CATALOGUE NUMBER 117

Id. No.	BI-028.
Object	Strap with toggle.
Measurements	Length: 160. Width: 18.5. Thickness: 2-3.5. Diameter toggle: 24.6 x 32.2.

Description
A beige leather strap of which the sides are folded inwards (figure A, B, F-H). Added to this surface, and obscuring the folds of the beige leather, is a green strip of leather, which is secured with running stitches of zS_2 flax thread. This also secures the folded parts. This strap is lead through a ball (figure C-E), the outer side of which is made of red leather with green leather strips at the top, centre and bottom (width strips at either side: 6.3 and 5.2 mm; width centre strip: 5.6 mm; secured with whip stitches of flax thread). A circular, red leather stopper piece has been strung onto one end (diameter: 17.6 mm; figure C). The construction of the toggle is impossible to determine without taking it apart. Possibly, connecting to BI-028 (Cat. No. 117); it resembles BI-021 (Cat. No. 115).

Cat. No. 117, BI-028. *Overview of the recto (A) and verso (B); C-E) Details of the toggle; F) Diagram of the construction of the strap; G) Detail of the recto; H) Detail of the verso. Scale bars C-E, G, H are 10 mm.*

CATALOGUE NUMBER 118

Id. No. BI-029.
Object Strap.
Measurements Length: 146. Width: 2-13. Thickness: 2.7-3.

Description
A fragment of a longer piece of beige leather that tapers to a point. The piece has been folded over and is secured with whip stitches, made of zS_2 flax thread. The whole has been rather flattened.

Cat. No. 118, BI-029. *A-B) Overviews; C) Detail of the sewing; D) Diagram of the construction. Scale bar C is 10 mm.*

CATALOGUE NUMBER 119

Id. No. BI-038.
Object Strap.
Measurements Length: 70. Diameter: 3-4.

Description
Tiny piece of beige leather that has been broken off from a longer piece. A strip of leather has been folded inward and is secured with whip stitches of zS_2 flax thread.

Cat. No. 119, BI-038. *A-B) Overviews; C) Diagram of the construction.*

UNIDENTIFIED

CATALOGUE NUMBER 120

Id. No. L1 #024.
Object ?
Measurements Length: 395. Width: 70-141. Thickness: 0.7.

Description

A heavily torn piece of red leather (figure A, B), with a broad decorative band of alternating strips of green and red leather that enhances one edge (figure C-F). The opposite edge, showing the initial width of the piece that might have been rectangular originally, has a green binding. As usual, the red strips are narrower than the green ones. The green edge binding is secured at the verso with whip stitches after which it is folded over both it and the edge of the red leather.

At the obverse, the edge is folded towards the red leather, overlapping in stair-step fashion a red, lengthwise folded strip (width: 1.5 mm). Here, the green strip (width: 3.7 mm) is secured with running stitches. These stitches are mostly invisible due to the folding of the green strip over its own edge. The fold of the green binding and the red strip underneath is, in its turn, placed on top of a wide green strip that protrudes from it (width: 3.8 mm), its far edge being folded towards the red leather of the main piece. Shortly before this far edge, a strip of red leather (width: 2.3 mm) is attached on it, its running stitches including the folded edge of the wide green strip as well; this protrudes from the red leather strip on the other side (width: 1.5 mm). Shortly before the red strip, a row of running stitches secures the wide green strip. The running stitches are relatively small and distinctly spaced, although both, the short as well as the more widely spaced stitching is seen throughout the entire Tano corpus. The stitches are made of zS_2 flax thread, except for the edge binding, which is made of sinew. Despite the seeming differences in the enhanced edge (only in the present object the edge is broken, allowing for clear vision) it is highly probable that the edge equals those of L3 #004F (Cat. No. 46) and L1 #011 (Cat. No. 47).

The edge opposite the elaborately enhanced edge has a green binding (figure G, H), which is folded lengthwise, and secured to the red leather by means of whip stitches of zS_2 threads made of flax. The edge of the red leather looks as if it were folded as well, but this is only due to the relative heavy binding.

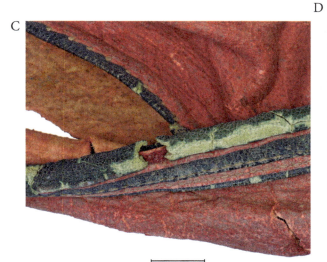

Cat. No. 120, L1 #024. *Overviews can be found on the next page. C, D) Details of the enhanced edge. Scale bars are 10 mm.*

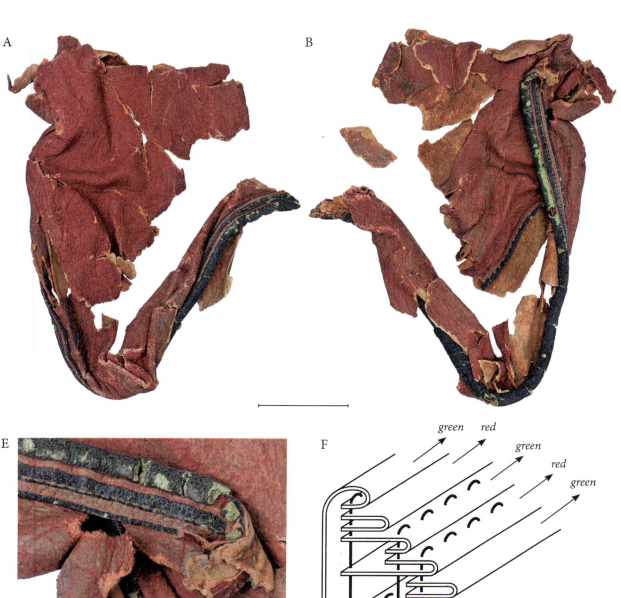
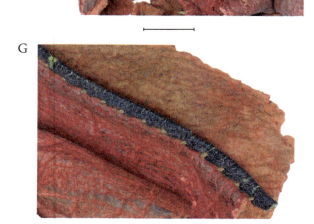
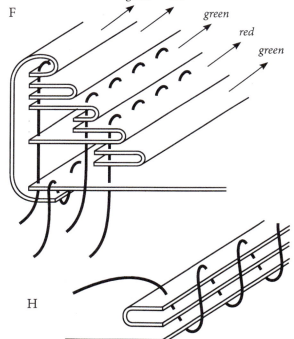

Cat. No. 120, L1 #024. *C, D see previous page. Overviews of the obverse (recto?; A) and reverse (verso?; B); E) Detail of the enhance edge; F) Diagram of the construction of the enhanced edge; G) Detail of the edge with binding; H) Diagram of the construction of the edge with simple binding. Scale bars are 10 mm.*

CATALOGUE NUMBER 121

Id. No.	L1 #009.
Object	?
Measurements	Width recto: 152. Length recto: 83. Thickness recto: 9. Width verso: 156. Length verso: 53. Thickness verso: 9. Holes: 26 - 22 - 27. Width green binding: 13.

Description

A rectangular piece of leather with one long edge and an opposite, rounded edge, made of two fairly thick layers of leather (figure A-D). These were either originally one piece folded over and stitched into place or two individual thicknesses put together, but as it is broken now, it is impossible to say. One side (recto) is larger than the other (verso) but its colour is faded. The fading might be due to the fact that this surface was on the exterior and thus exposed to the sun. Note the wrinkles than run horizontally from one short edge to the other on the recto. The verso shows, perpendicular to the long edges and slightly off centre, a narrow, lengthwise impression (figure H) with a black (perhaps once green?) surface. This seems to have been caused by being tied tightly to a corresponding element, whose shape was then impressed in the leather.

The two sides are secured with their flesh side facing inwards, and two horizontal rows of relatively large stitch holes (roughly in pairs), starting at about two centimetre from their curved edges. Tiny remnants of running stitches are preserved, probably made of sinew. At this point, another comparably thick piece of leather is sandwiched between the recto and verso, and all three are secured at the far edge (figure D). This reinforced section is pierced with three large oval holes (figure E-G), which are orientated horizontally and situated between the row of stitch holes. The edges of these holes that face the curved edge of the object clearly show that they were used to tie the object to something else, probably by means of a strip of leather or rawhide of about equal width to the length of the holes. This also explains the additional layer that reinforces the slits. It is remotely possible that the reverse had an additional hole, but due to the incompleteness of the piece, this is impossible to determine with confidence.

The short edges have an edge binding (figure I-N), consisting of a strip of green leather that is secured with whip stitches of flax thread (zS_2?) to the recto. It is folded over the whip stitching towards the verso, where it would have been secured. Since the layer is largely lost, it is not certain how it was secured, but most likely with running stitching as seen in several other fragments. Note the small fragment of a green leather strip, at a right angle to the green binding at the verso (figure M-N), whose purpose is not certain; there is no evidence that a green strip ran from one short edge of the object to the other. Possibly, it is the terminal end of the edge binding, folded back and protruding from the edge binding itself.

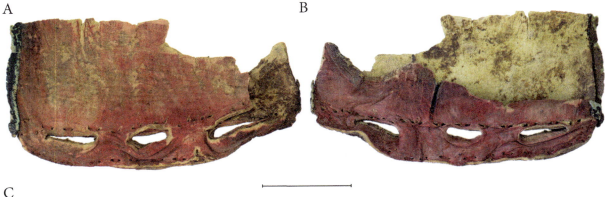

Cat. No. 121, L1 #009. *A) Overview of the recto; B) Overview of the verso; C) Side view.*

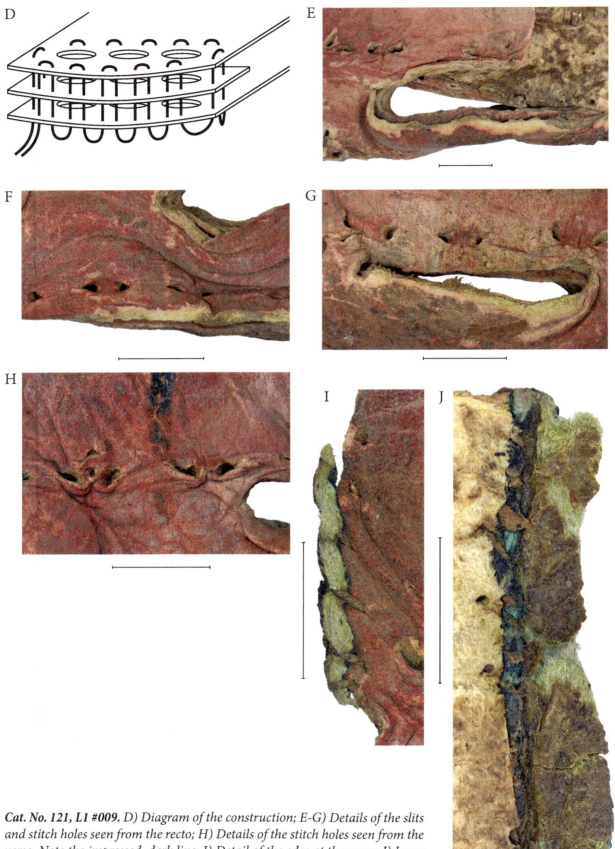

Cat. No. 121, L1 #009. D) Diagram of the construction; E-G) Details of the slits and stitch holes seen from the recto; H) Details of the stitch holes seen from the verso. Note the impressed, dark line; I) Detail of the edge at the verso; J) Inner view of the edge seen from verso. Scale bars are 10 mm.

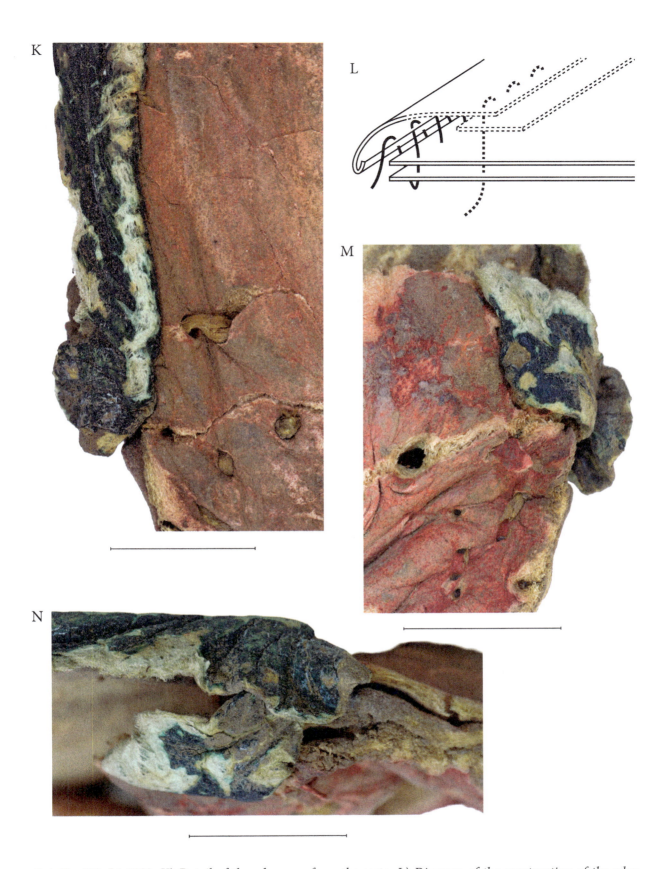

Cat. No. 121, L1 #009. K) *Detail of the edge seen from the recto;* L) *Diagram of the construction of the edge binding;* M) *Detail of the small piece of green strip seen from the verso;* N) *As M but seen from aside. Scale bars are 10 mm.*

CATALOGUE NUMBER 122

Id. No. L1 #019.
Object ?
Measurements 104 x 56. Thickness: 1.2. Width green binding: 6.2.

Description
Piece of roughly trapezoidal red leather (figure A, B) with a fragment of green edge binding still *in situ* at one edge (figure C-E). It is folded over, with whip stitches securing it at one side.

At the opposite side of the bound edge, a short impressed line is visible, comparable to the one described for L1 #009 (Cat. No. 121). This, together with the edge binding, suggests that the two pieces belonged together.

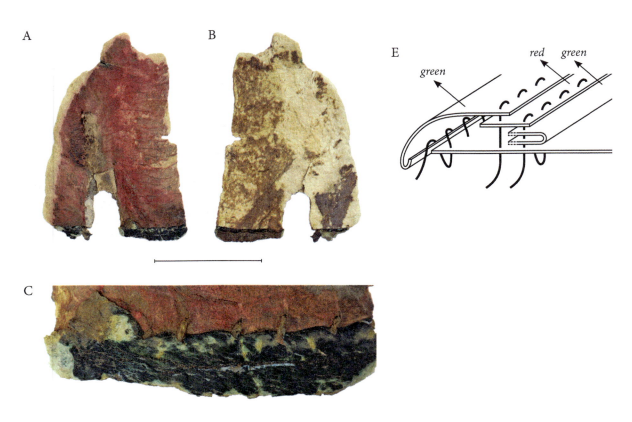

Cat. No. 122, L1 #019. *Overview of the recto (A) and verso (B); C) Detail of the edge binding seen from the recto; D) Detail of the edge binding seen from the verso; E) Diagram of the construction. Scale bars C-D are 10 mm.*

CATALOGUE NUMBER 123

Id. No. L5 #001.
Object Fragment of the horizontal edge of the bow-case flap?
Measurements Length: 85. Width: 12. Thickness: 2.8.

Description

A torn off fragment of edge decoration that has separated from the main body of red leather of the piece (figure A, B). The fragment consists of alternating coloured strips of leather (figure C-E). A green strip (width: 1.3 mm), folded lengthwise, is overlapped in stair-step fashion, by a red strip (width: 2.4 mm). These layers are secured with fairly thin and long running stitches of zS_2 flax thread. This is covered, again in stair-step fashion, by a wider green strip (width: 4 mm), which is secured with running stitches of zS_2 flax thread. These stitches are shorter than those in the previous row of stitches. The final strip is a lengthwise folded piece of red leather (width: 0.6 mm), which appears to have been secured to the main piece. The big sinew stitches for affixing it are still visible.

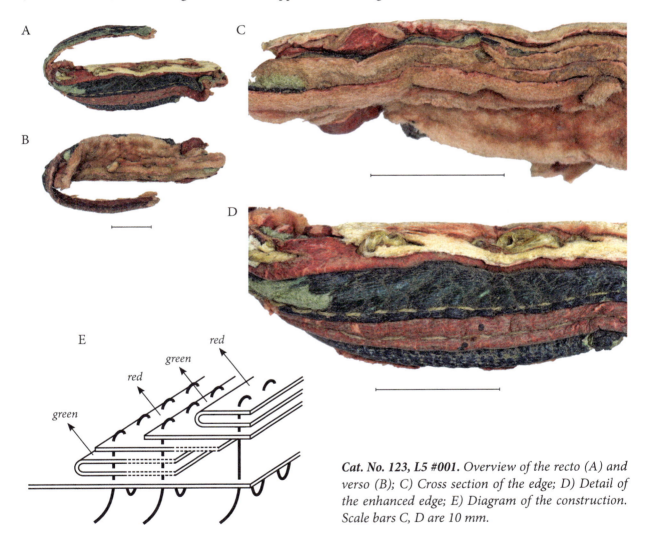

Cat. No. 123, L5 #001. *Overview of the recto (A) and verso (B); C) Cross section of the edge; D) Detail of the enhanced edge; E) Diagram of the construction. Scale bars C, D are 10 mm.*

CATALOGUE NUMBER 124

Id. No.   L5 #002.
Object   ?
Measurements   Length: 38. Width: 15. Thickness: 1.

Description
Roughly triangular fragment of green leather (figure A, B). One edge shows a row of empty, slightly oval stitch holes, with the leather edge extending slightly beyond them.

Cat. No. 124, L5 #002. *Overview of the recto (A) and verso (B). Scale bar is 10 mm.*

CATALOGUE NUMBER 125

Id. No.   L5 #004.
Object   Decoration band of tube attachment.
Measurements   Length: 68. Width: 12.5. Thickness: 0.7.

Description
Fragment of decorative band that consists of a strip of red leather (width: 4 mm), flanked by two strips of green leather (width: 4 and 4.4 mm respectively; figure A, B). The strips are secured with whip stitches (zS_2, flax).

Cat. No. 125, L5 #004. *Overview of the recto (A) and verso (B). Scale bar is 10 mm.*

CATALOGUE NUMBER 126

Id. No.   L5 #006.
Object   Decoration band of tube attachment.
Measurements   Length: 55.6. Width total: 10. Thickness: 0.8.

Description
Fragment of decorative band that consists of a strip of red leather (width: 4.1 mm), with attached a strip of green leather (width: 3.6 mm; figure A, B). The strip is secured with whip stitches (zS_2, flax).

Cat. No. 126, L5 #006. *Overview of the recto (A) and verso (B). Scale bar is 10 mm.*

CATALOGUE NUMBER 127

Id. No.   L5 #007.
Object   Probably a fragment of tripartite element of the main casing. *Cf.* L3 #002 (Cat. No. 44).
Measurements   Length: 43. Width: 2.8. Thickness: 0.7.

Description
Fragment of the edge of an object that is made of two layers of green leather which are folded over (figure A, B). The fold is enhanced, at the recto, with alternating red and green strips of leather (figure C). The first red strip is folded lengthwise (width: 15 mm) and is followed by a set of red (width: 2.4 mm) and green bands (width: 3.7 mm). Stitching of the red and green is done with zS_2 flax thread in running stitches. Note that the stitching that secures the red material is slightly bigger in diameter.

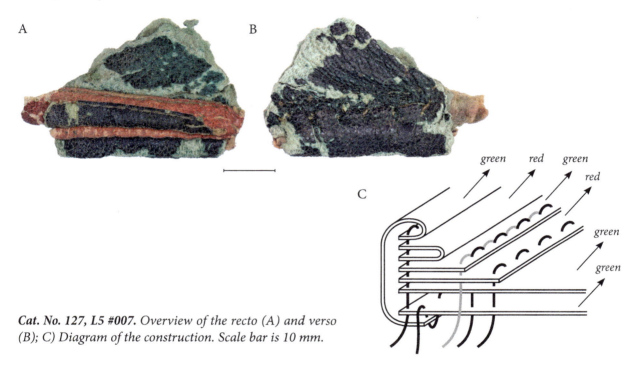

Cat. No. 127, L5 #007. *Overview of the recto (A) and verso (B); C) Diagram of the construction. Scale bar is 10 mm.*

CATALOGUE NUMBER 128

Id. No.   L5 #011.
Object   Toggle?
Measurements   Length: 17.5. Width: 16.8. Thickness: 7.9. Length band: 10.7. Width band: 11.4. Thickness band: 1.

Description
A toggle(?) attached to a strip of leather (figure A-D). It consists of pieces of leather that are covered over by a wide green strip of leather. These strips are secured together on the open sides. The toggle(?) is attached to a band that is made of three strips of leather, one of which appear to be folded. Uncoloured strips (that might have been coloured once) are added to the green ones. The exact pattern, however, cannot be determined. The back of the band shows evidence for some solid bits of leather but is much destroyed. It is sewn together with zS_2 flax thread using running stitches.

Cat. No. 128, L5 #011. Overviews of the side (A), recto(?; B), opposite side (C) and verso(?; D). Scale bar is 10 mm.

CATALOGUE NUMBER 129

Id. No. L5 #017.
Object ?
Measurements 32 x 19. Thickness: 0.8.
Description
A small green fragment that consist of two parts that are secured with tiny whip stitches (figure A, B).

Cat. No. 129, L5 #017. Overview of the recto (A) and verso (B). Scale bar is 10 mm.

CATALOGUE NUMBER 130

Id. No. L5 #020.
Object ?
Measurements 35 x 23. Thickness: 0.6 (1.6 of leather and rawhide).
Description
A roughly trapezoidal fragment of red leather (figure A, B). A thin, red-brown piece of rawhide(?) is attached to the red recto, probably by glue. This glue slightly discoloured it. At a right angle, remnants of stitches are visible, although not on the verso.

Cat. No. 130, L5 #020. Overview of the recto (A) and verso (B). Scale bar is 10 mm.

CATALOGUE NUMBER 131

Id. No. L5 #031.
Object ?
Measurements 29 x 12. Thickness total: 0.8-1.
Description
A nearly rectangular fragment of red leather (figure A, B). At one of the long edges of the recto two pieces of thin, red-brown rawhide(?) are visible, which must have been glued to the red leather. Possibly, the added piece is discoloured due to glue.

Cat. No. 131, L5 #031. *Overview of the recto (A) and verso (B). Scale bar is 10 mm.*

CATALOGUE NUMBER 132

Id. No. L5 #022.
Object ?
Measurements Length: 37.8. Width: 16.5. Thickness: red: 0.5; green: 1.7.
Description
A fragment of red leather (figure A, B) to which is attached a lengthwise folded, green edge binding with zS_2 sinew thread (figure C). The fold faces the recto of the red piece.

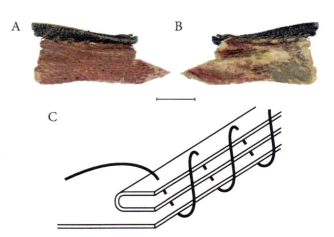

Cat. No. 132, L5 #022. *Overview of the recto (A) and verso (B); C) Diagram of the construction of the binding. Scale bar is 10 mm.*

CATALOGUE NUMBER 133

Id. No. L5 #032.
Object ?
Measurements Length: 42. Width: 10.8. Thickness: 0.5.
Description
A fragment of red leather (figure A, B) to which is whip stitched (sinew, zS_2) a lengthwise folded(?), green strip of leather. The fold faces the recto of the red piece.

Cat. No. 133, L5 #032. *Overview of the recto (A) and verso (B). Scale bar is 10 mm.*

CATALOGUE NUMBER 134

Id. No. #32.
Object ?
Measurements Length: 494. Width: 110-126. Thickness: 1.9.

Description
A roughly long rectangular (but folded over) piece of red leather (figure A, B) whose ends are rounded. The piece is assymetrical throughout. It is pierced by three holes (approximately the same diameter, *viz.* 24 mm) – one at either end, and the third in the centre. The holes are connected by an impressed line (figure D) that also encircles the two holes at either end. Note the dark discoloration of the edge (figure C), which might have been caused by glue. A comparable discolored band is visible transversely and shortly before the central hole (arrow in figure A) as well as at the long edges.

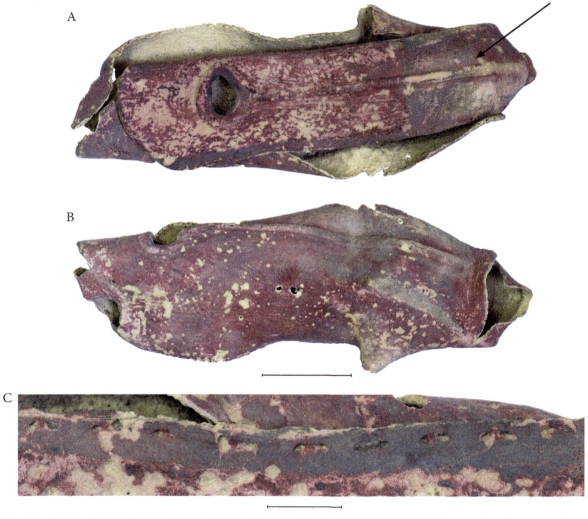

Cat. No. 134, #32. *A-B) Overviews; C) Detail of the edge, showing the stitch holes and discoloured edge; D) Detail of the hole with impression. Scale bars C, D are 10 mm.*

CATALOGUE NUMBER 135

Id. No. L1 #017.
Object Strap.
Measurements Length: 380. Width strip: 8. Thickness strip: 0.8.

Description
A long piece of narrow, red leather thong (figure A), that might have been used as a tie or lace.

***Cat. No. 135, L1 #017.** Overview.*

CATALOGUE NUMBER 136

Id. No. L1 #021.
Object ?
Measurements A) Length: 140. Width: 27; B) Length: 142; C) Width: 14. Thickness: 0.9; D) Length: 130. Width: 13. Thickness: 1.2. E) Length: 72. Width: 5.2.

Description
Part of a longer leather object made up of several strips of red and green leather (figure A, B). One strip (A), is a long piece of green leather whose side folds over to enclose a piece of red leather (B; figure C, D). The other side is bound with another piece of green leather (E) that is secured with whip stitches (figure E). A diagonal strip of red leather (C), punctuated by holes, is attached to (B). Another small strip of red leather (D) is located above (C). It seems that (C) and (D) are secured to (B) with leather lashings, some of which might also penetrate (A).

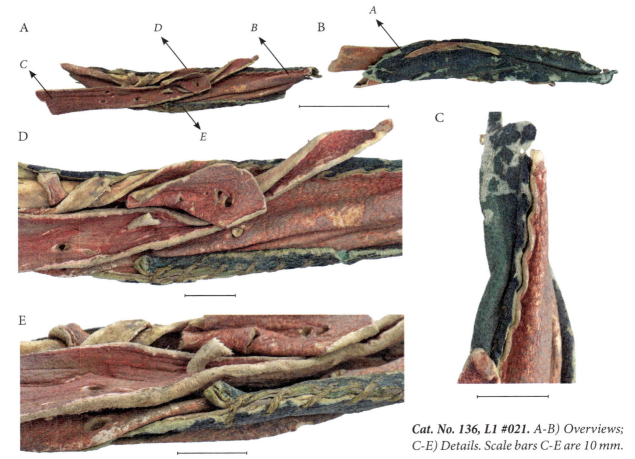

***Cat. No. 136, L1 #021.** A-B) Overviews; C-E) Details. Scale bars C-E are 10 mm.*

CATALOGUE NUMBER 137

Id. No. L2 #007.
Object Decoration band of tube attachment.
Measurements Length: 890. Width: 14.8. Thickness: 0.7.

Description

Part of decorative strip that is separated from its main body (figure A). It consists of two long strips of leather, one green (width 6.1 mm) and one red (width: 7.2 mm), which are attached at one of their edges by means of whip stitches of flax zS_2 thread.

The other edge of the red strip seems not to have been attached, based on several intact parts showing no stitch holes. This could indicate that it was part of the background to which the green strip was attached (*cf.* for example L1 #001, Cat. No. 50) but the opposite edge of the green strip shows a comparable condition. Thus it seems that, originally, the fragment indeed consisted of these two strips only. Note the beige background at some parts, which suggest that the decoration was glued onto a surface (before being applied to a body?).

A

B

Cat. No. 137, L2 #007. *A) Overview; B) Detail. Scale bar B is 10 mm.*

CATALOGUE NUMBER 138

Id. No. L4 #004.
Object ?
Measurements Length: 93. Width: 18-30. Thickness red layer: 0.8. Thickness green layer: 0.5.

Description

A tapering piece of leather (figure A, B) comprised of two pieces of leather (one red and one green). At one long edge they are secured to each other with a lengthwise folded, green edge binding, the fold of which faces away from the edge of the object proper (figure C). It is attached to the red surface. The other long side does not have a binding and only a short distance of the widest end of the object shows the characteristic wavy appearance of running stitches. Despite that, however, remnants of whip stitching are visible too, but these seem only to be attached to the red layer. Possibly, it has been repaired.

At the narrower end are several small (1 mm diameter) holes, 7.5 mm apart. These pierce both sides, and might be deliberate or the result of damage.

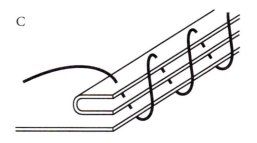

Cat. No. 138, L4 #004. *Overview of the recto (A) and verso (B); C) Diagram of the edge binding.*

CATALOGUE NUMBER 139

Id. No.   L4 #005.
Object   ?
Measurements   Length: 78. Width: 9.5. Thickness green: 0.5. Thickness plain leather: 0.4.

Description
A fragile, narrow strip of green leather (figure A, B), secured onto a three-times, lengthwise folded uncoloured leather strip (figure C). The layers are secured with short, widely spaced running stitches (zS_2 thread) that are made of flax. They run lengthwise along either side of the piece. *Cf.* BI-021 (Cat. No. 115).

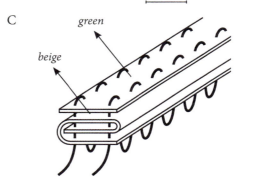

Cat. No. 139, L4 #005. *A-B) Overviews; C) Diagram of the construction. Scale bar is 10 mm.*

CATALOGUE NUMBER 140

Id. No. L4 #008.
Object ?
Measurements Length: 162. Width: 18-appr. 60. Thickness: 1.2. Width green 'lashing': 3.4. Thickness green binding: 1.1.

Description
A band of red leather, currently (folded) roughly the shape of a 'J' (figure A, B). One end is expanded. A binding in green leather once pierced either side (length) of the piece, until the bend in the 'J', where stitching in flax or sinew served to secure the piece to something else.

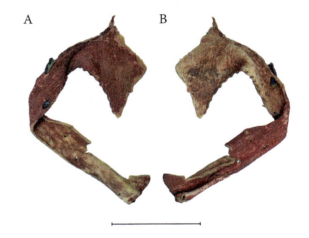

Cat. No. 140, L4 #008. A, B) Overviews.

CATALOGUE NUMBER 141

Id. No. L4 #010.
Object ?
Measurements Length: 38. Width: 23. Thickness: 0.7. Width green binding at the verso: 12.

Description
A roughly rectangular piece of red leather with a green edge binding at one of the short sides. The binding is secured with whip stitches that are made of zS_2 sinew; the fold faces away from the edge of the red piece. Note the isolated running stitch at the binding. One of the long sides as well as the opposite side of the edge-with-binding has stitch holes at their edges. Those at the adjacent long side, however, extend to the short edge with the green binding. The verso shows, at the same edge as the green binding, a larger piece of unfolded green leather that is secured at the edge of the piece with the same whip stitches as the edge binding.

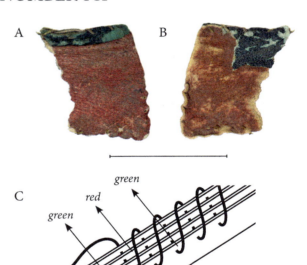

Cat. No. 141, L4 #010. Overview of the recto (A) and verso (B); C) Diagram of the construction.

CATALOGUE NUMBER 142

Id. No.   L4 #011.
Object   ?
Measurements   Length: 98. Width: 8-10. Thickness: 0.6. Width green binding: 3.8.

Description

A tapering strip of red leather (figure A, B). A narrower, lengthwise folded green strip of leather is stitched on one side lengthwise (binding; figure C). The broken stitch holes at this edge seemingly are those from the whip stitches that secured the binding. The red strip seems to have been secured at the other long sides, judging the stitch holes with remnants of stitches made of sinew.

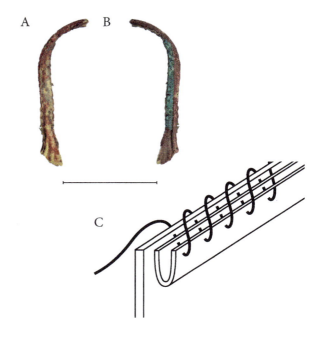

Cat. No. 142, L4 #011. A-B) Overviews; C) Diagram of the construction.

CATALOGUE NUMBER 143

Id. No.   L4 #012.
Object   Strips.
Measurements   Length: appr. 33-50. Width: 2.5-3.5. Thickness: 0.7.

Description

A group of thin, very narrow strips of leather that are coiled in such a way as to suggest that they were wound around a pole or something similar (figure A). As strips of leather to secure parts have not been attested among the finds, it seems unlikely they have or would have been used for that purpose.

Cat. No. 143, L4 #012. Overviews.

CATALOGUE NUMBER 144

Id. No.   L4 #015.
Object   ?
Measurements   Length: 45. Width red leather: 3.2. Width total green: 7.5. Thickness green: 0.8. Thickness red: 1.

Description
A wide strip of green leather (figure A, B) that is folded under at one edge and attached to a narrow strip of lengthwise folded red leather. The fold of this red strip faces upwards. These were part of an elaborate edge decoration or, more likely, the red is a passepoil used to connect two pieces of leather. The green leather shows signs of being joined in order to lengthen it: there is a slight overlap of the two elements, but no signs of securing the two. The unattached edge is ruched due to having been sewn.

Cat. No. 144, L4 #015. Overviews. Scale bar is 10 mm.

CATALOGUE NUMBER 145

Id. No.   L4 #016.
Object   ?
Measurements   Length: 50-170. Width: 7-9. Thickness: 1.6.

Description
A selection of narrow strips of red leather of unknown purpose (figure A). Might be pieces of the drawstrings that are found in tubes.

Cat. No. 145, L4 #016. Overview.

CATALOGUE NUMBER 146

Id. No.   L4 #017.
Object   ?
Measurements   Length: 158. Width: 6.8-9.4. Thickness: 1.2.

Description
A long curving strip of green leather (figure A, B), one side of which is slightly turned in where it was secured onto another piece. Note the oval shape of the stitch holes as opposed to the pre-pricked circular ones seen in the attachments of several pieces, such as the tubes and leather body.

Cat. No. 146, L4 #017. Overview of the recto (A) and verso (B).

CATALOGUE NUMBER 147

Id. No. L4 #020.
Object ?
Measurements Length: appr. 120. Width: 5.8-10. Thickness green: 0.5.

Description
A green strip of leather that is lengthwise, on both sides, secured onto a thinner piece of uncoloured (beige) leather (figure A, B). This beige layer is folded at least twice.

Cat. No. 147, L4 #020. *Overview verso and recto respectively.*

CATALOGUE NUMBER 148

Id. No. L6 #009.
Object Piece of siding fill(?).
Measurements Length: 126. Width: 110. Thickness: 0.7.

Description
An irregularly-shaped piece (broken in two) of red leather that is cut with the top undulating (figure A, B). There is a deliberate, oval slit (eyelet) on one side of the top. The two long sides are pierced by holes, indicative of stitching.

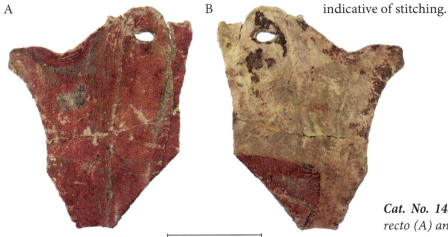

Cat. No. 148, L6 #009. *Overview of the recto (A) and verso (B).*

CATALOGUE NUMBER 149

Id. No. L6 #010.
Object ?
Measurements 63 x 51. Thickness: 0.7. Glued piece: 5.2-5.7. Thickness: 0.3.

Description
A small 'L'-shaped piece of red leather that has (remnants of) stitch holes (slits rather than holes) at its long side (figure A, B). The horizontal edge has a strip of uncoloured leather glued to the recto that slightly protrudes beyond its edge.

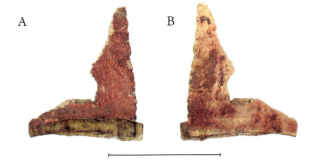

Cat. No. 149, L6 #010. *Overview of the recto (A) and verso (B).*

CATALOGUE NUMBER 150

Id. No.   L6 #014.
Object   ?
Measurements   70 x 40. Thickness: 0.8-0.9. Diameter hole: 8.

Description
A small, roughly rectangular piece of red leather, the top of which is folded (figure A, B). It has stitch holes at the intact, long edge (the other edge being torn off). One of the small edges is reinforced with a glued strip of leather, which is beige/brown in colour (figure C, D). The edge-with-stitch holes and the corner of this edge with the reinforcement has tiny, dark patches that might be remnants of a green binding. There appears to be a deliberate hole in the leather, 21.5 mm from edge opposite the reinforced edge.

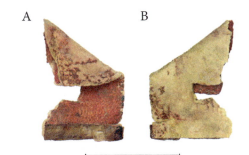

▷ **Cat. No. 150, L6 #014.** *Overview of the recto (A) and verso (B); C, D) Detail of the edge. Scale bars C, D are 10 mm.*

CATALOGUE NUMBER 151

Id. No.   L6 #019.
Object   ?
Measurements   67 x 106. Thickness: 0.7. Length glued strip: 58. Width glued strip: 5.5-8. Diameter hole: 9.5 x 13.

Description
An irregularly-shaped piece of red leather, one edge of which is reinforced with a strip of beige/brown leather that is glued on its recto (figure A, B). Shortly above this edge, there is a rectangular hole that seems deliberate.

Cat. No. 151, L6 #019. *Overview of the recto (A) and verso (B).*

CATALOGUE NUMBER 152

Id. No.   L6 #028.
Object   ?
Measurements   81 x 105. Thickness: 0.9.
Description
An irregularly-shaped, crumpled piece of red leather to which another piece of red leather, partly broken, was once attached (empty stitch holes).

▷ ***Cat. No. 152, L6 #028.*** *Overview of the recto (A) and verso (B).*

CATALOGUE NUMBER 153

Id. No.   L6 #030.
Object   ?
Measurements   115 x 345. Thickness: 0.7. Width binding: 3.4.

Description
An irregularly-shaped piece of red leather that is folded over but not deliberately (figure A, B). At one side, along the top, a green binding (lengthwise folded strip, the fold of which faces away from the edge; figure C, D) is secured by means of whip stitches (zS_2 thread that is made of flax).

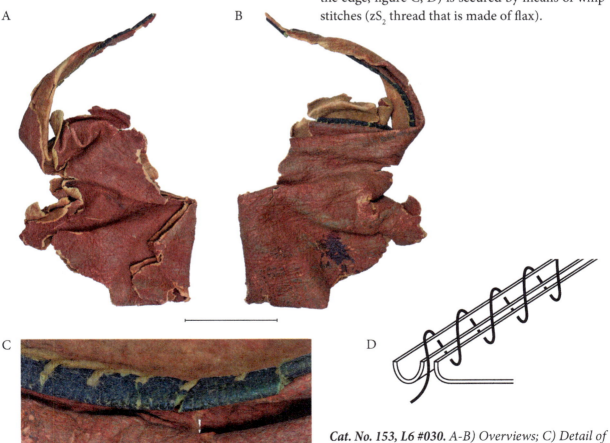

Cat. No. 153, L6 #030. *A-B) Overviews; C) Detail of the enhanced edge; D) Diagram of the construction. Scale bar C is 10 mm.*

CATALOGUE NUMBER 154

Id. No. BI-018.
Object ?
Measurements Length: 30.7. Width: 19.1. Thickness total: 1.3.

Description
A small piece of red leather that is broken off from a larger piece (figure A, B). At one end a green leather circle (diameter: 10.8 mm) has been stitched on with flax thread (zS_2?). From its centre two small bits of red leather protrude - part of a bigger 'string'? This 'string' does not go through the red leather.

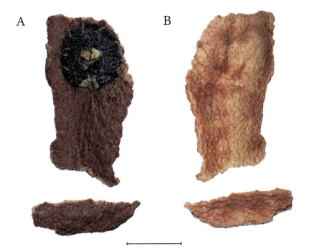

▷ **Cat. No. 154, BI-018.** *Overview of the recto (A) and verso (B). Scale bar is 10 mm.*

CATALOGUE NUMBER 155

Id. No. BI-002.
Object ?
Measurements Length: 400. Width: 3-5-15-19.6. Thickness: 2.

Description
A tapering strip of thick, beige leather.

▷ **Cat. No. 155, BI-002.** *Overview.*

CATALOGUE NUMBER 156

Id. No. BI-010.
Object ?
Measurements Length: 72. Width: 9.5-11.7 Thickness: 1.7.

Description
A brittle small strip of beige leather (figure A, B) that has a strip of green leather affixed to it. Possibly, the beige leather is folded lengthwise, but this cannot be determined with certainty. Both long edges have a green edge binding that is secured with whip stitches and running stitches at the other side(?).

Cat. No. 156, BI-010. *A, B) Overviews.*

CATALOGUE NUMBER 157

Id. No. BI-015.
Object ?
Measurements Length: 540. Width: 7-22-24.
Thickness: 1.
Description
Thin strap of faded red leather. It tapers towards one end (figure A).

▷ ***Cat. No. 157, BI-015.** Overview.*

CATALOGUE NUMBER 158

Id. No. BI-016.
Object ?
Measurements Length: 488. Width: 23.3-24.
Thickness: 0.8.
Description
Long strip of thin, faded red leather that is of approximately equal width throughout (figure A, B).

▷ ***Cat. No. 158, BI-016.** A, B) Overviews.*

CATALOGUE NUMBER 159

Id. No. BI-017.
Object ?
Measurements Length: 320. Width: 23-25-26.
Thickness: 0.8-0.9.
Description
Thin piece of red leather that is of approximately equal width throughout (figure A, B).

▷ ***Cat. No. 159, BI-017.** A, B) Overviews.*

CATALOGUE NUMBER 160

Id. No. BI-019.
Object ?
Measurements Length: 44.6. Width: 25.8. Thickness: 2.8.

Description
A strip of fairly thick leather, which is broken off from a bigger piece (figure A, B). The long sides have a green edge binding (width: 5.2-5.4 mm). Scored lines, lengthwise following the edges as well as sets of three scored lines transversely in between them, enhance the recto. It is possible that the scored part is a thin piece of leather put on top of the thicker fragment. There is insect damage. The verso looks as if some glue or varnish was used on it; the concentric motifs look very much like (ancient?) finger impressions. The object is unlike the rest of the Tano leather.

Cat. No. 160, BI-019. *Overviews of the recto (A) and verso (B).*

CATALOGUE NUMBER 161

Id. No. BI-027.
Object Coiled strap – lashing.
Measurements Length: 168. Diameter overall: 80. Width of the strip: 12. Thickness of the strip: 2.6.

Description
A long strip of fairly thick leather, dyed red on one side (figure A-D). It is coiled over upon itself lengthwise (here, the strip of leather is folded lengthwise) after which it was wrapped by itself transversely. At either side obstructions are made to prevent the construction from slipping.

Cat. No. 161, BI-017. *A-D) Various overviews.*

CATALOGUE NUMBER 162

Id. No. BI-031.
Object ?
Measurements Length: 155. Width: 16. Thickness: 1.8-2.1.

Description
A tapering strip of beige leather that has broken off from a longer piece.

▷ *Cat. No. 162, BI-031. A, B) Overviews.*

CATALOGUE NUMBER 163

Id. No. BI-032.
Object Drawstring fragment(?)
Measurements Length: 123. Width: 10-11-13. Thickness: 1.8.

Description
A strip of red leather (only one side is coloured) that has broken off from a longer piece. Relatively thick.

▷ *Cat. No. 163, BI-032. Overview of the recto (A) and verso (B).*

CATALOGUE NUMBER 164

Id. No. BI-036.
Object ?
Measurements Length: 73. Width: 8.8. Thickness: 1.

Description
A strip of beige leather with, at one side, a score mark lengthwise down the centre. Both edges are dyed green. The edges of the green bits show holes indicative of being secured onto something else. One end the beige leather is pierced and a narrow strip of green leather is secured to it.

Cat. No. 164, BI-036. Overview of the recto (A) and verso (B).

CATALOGUE NUMBER 165

Id. No. BI-037.
Object Decoration band of tube attachment.
Measurements Length: 70. Width: 3. Thickness: 0.9.

Description
An incomplete, decorative band of slightly curved leather (figure A, B) that is made up of three strips that are secured with whip stitches (flax zS_2 thread). The central strip is red (width: 0.41 cm), flanked by green strips (width: 4.3 & 4.5 mm). Bands as these are seen in various fragments as part of the decoration of the tube area.

Cat. No. 165, BI-037. *Overview of the recto (A) and verso (B).*

CATALOGUE NUMBER 166

Id. No. BI-040.
Object ?
Measurements Length: 20. Diameter: 12. Width strip: 2.5-3.5.

Description
An obstruction made of beige leather, consisting of a lengthwise folded strip of leather (secured with zS_2 flax thread) that is coiled around itself (figure A).

Cat. No. 166, BI-040. *Overview.*

CATALOGUE NUMBER 167

Small Scraps	Shape (as in the photograph)/Colour	Further Description	Measurements
L1 #004	Irregular/red	Broken piece of leather (foundation), coloured red at its obverse. One edge is folded but not deliberately.	41.4 (incl. folded edge) x 18.5. Thickness: 0.8
L1 #006	Triangular/red	One edge is folded over accidentally.	14.3 (incl. folded edge) x 10. Thickness: 0.7
L1 #007	Irregular/red	One edge is folded over accidentally.	14.4 (incl. folded edge) x 10.3. Thickness: 0.7
L1 #013	Square/red	Several abrasion spots (indication of wear due to use).	16.3 x 13.2. Thickness: 0.7
L2 #003	Irregular/red	Accidentally folded.	19 x 18. Thickness: 0.7
L2 #004	Strip/red	Accidentally folded at either end.	Length: 25. Width: 0.6-2.2. Thickness: 0.7
L2 #005	Triangular/red	Accidentally folded.	15 x 11.2. Thickness: 0.6
L2 #006	Strip/red	Irregular. Folded accidentally.	Length: 87. Width: 1.2-3.8. Thickness: 0.7
L4 #007	Irregular/red	-	13.5 x 12. Thickness: 0.7
L4 #009	Irregular/red	-	11 x 8.5. Thickness: 0.7
L4 #019	Irregular/red	-	7 x 5.5. Thickness: 0.7
L4 #021	Triangular/red	-	
L4 #022	Irregular/red	One edge has empty, circular stitch holes reminiscent of running stitches. The verso shows a red band at the edge with the stitch holes. The other side of this band is sewn with whip stitches.	

Small Scraps	Shape (as in the photograph)/Colour	Further Description	Measurements
L4 #023	Rectangular/red	Folded? One edge of one side shows a darker red band, either side of which has stitch holes with in some remnants of whip stitches (zS_2, flax).	-
L4 #024	Irregular/red	Folded. Note slightly darker band at either side of the leather at one edge.	-
L4 #025	Irregular/red	Dark red band at one of the edges, showing stitch holes at either side.	-
L4 #026	Triangular/green	One row of tiny, closely spaced stitch holes at the straight edge, some of which includes remnants of stitches.	-
L4 #027	Irregular/red	-	-
L4 #028	Rectangular/red	Folded.	-
L4 #029	Irregular/red	Folded.	-
L4 #030	Rectangular/red	-	-
L4 #031	Irregular/red	-	-
L4 #032	Irregular/red	-	-
L4 #033	Square/red	-	-
L4 #034	Rectangular/red	Folded.	-
L4 #035	Irregular/red	-	-
L4 #036	Irregular/red	One of the long edges has stitch holes, the other side of the piece shows a darker red band. The other edge is sewn with whip stitches.	-

Small Scraps	Shape (as in the photograph)/Colour	Further Description	Measurements
L4 #073	Trapezoid/red	-	-
L4 #074	Triangular/red	-	-
L4 #075	Triangular/red	Folded, the opposite edge being sewn.	-
L4 #076	Strip/red	Colour extremely faded.	-
L4 #077	Irregular/red	-	-
L4 #078	Various/red	5 tiny scraps.	-
L4 #079	Various/red	5 tiny scraps.	-
L4 #080	Various/red	5 tiny scraps.	-
L4 #081	Irregular/red	Two small pieces sewn together in slight overlap with two rows of whip stitches (zS_2, flax) at either edge.	-
L4 #082	Various/red	6 tiny scraps.	-
L4 #083	Various/red	5 tiny scraps.	-
L4 #084	Various/red	5 tiny scraps.	-
L4 #085	Various/red	3 tiny scraps.	-
L4 #086	Various/red	8 tiny scraps.	-
L4 #087	Various/red	8 tiny scraps.	-
L4 #088	Various/34 red & 6 green	40 tiny scraps.	-
L4 #089	Irregular/red	Two small pieces, which might be sewn together in slight overlap with two rows of whip stitches at either edges.	-

Small Scraps	Shape (as in the photograph)/Colour	Further Description	Measurements
L5 #008	Irregular/green	Fragment of edge binding (not illustrated).	-
L5 #010	Rectangular/green	Piece of passepoil.	-
L5 #012	Irregular/red	Stitch holes at one edge.	-
L5 #013	Irregular/red	Glued?	-
L5 #014	Rectangular/red	Accidentally folded. Stitch holes.	-
L5 #016	Square/red	Purposely cut?	-
L5 #018	Irregular/red	Several empty stitch holes.	-
L5 #019	Irregular/red	Small scrap of green secured with whip stitches.	-
L5 #021	Triangular/red	Note black spots at edge of recto. Empty stitch holes.	-
L5 #023	Irregular/red	-	-
L5 #024	Triangular/red	-	-
L5 #025	Tapering/red	Sinew whip stitches at either side (intact at one edge).	-
L5 #026	Triangular and rectangular/red	Stitch holes with remnants of stitches.	-
L5 #027	Irregular/red	Two emtpy stitch holes.	-
L5 #028	Irregular/red	-	-
L5 #029	Irregular/red	-	-
L5 #030	Rectangular/red	Several layers.	-
L5 #033	Square/red	Several empty stitch holes.	-
L5 #037	Rectangular/red	Small piece of strap(?)	-

Small Scraps	Shape (as in the photograph)/Colour	Further Description	Measurements
L5 #038	Irregular/red	4 scraps.	-
L5 #039	Strip/red	19 fragments of strips.	-
L6 #005	Irregular/red	Broken.	14.7 x 5 - 11.8. Thickness: 0.07
L6 #006	Irregular/red	-	15.7 x 1 - 8. Thickness: 0.07
L6 #008	Irregular/red	-	8 x 11. Thickness: 0.1
L6 #011	Rectangular/red	Folded ones.	14.8 x 5.2 - 6. Thickness: 0.1
L6 #012	Irregular/red	Folded and sandwiching other piece of red.	8.1 x 6.3. Thickness: 0.7
L6 #013	Irregular/red	Torn off.	7 x 9. Thickness: 0.7
L6 #015	Irregular/red	Accidentally folded and broken off.	5.7 x 8.5. Thickness: 0.7
L6 #016	Irregular/red	Crumpled.	9.2 x 11.5. Thickness: 0.7
L6 #018	Irregular/red	-	4.8 x 7.2. Thickness: 0.9
L6 #020	Rectangular/red	Accidentally folded, cracked.	7.8 x 11. Thickness: 0.7
L6 #021	Triangular/red	Cracked.	8.7 x 10.7. Thickness: 0.9
L6 #022	Irregular/red	-	11.4 x 13.4. Thickness: 0.7 - 0.8
L6 #023	Irregular/red	Accidentally folded and crumpled.	11 x 15. Thickness: 0.6
L6 #024	Irregular/red	Accidentally folded and crumpled.	11 x 24. Thickness: 0.7
L6 #025	Irregular/red	Almost broken in two.	23 x 23.5. Thickness: 0.7 - 0.8
L6 #026	Triangular/red	-	8.5 x 10. Thickness: 0.7

Small Scraps	Shape (as in the photograph)/Colour	Further Description	Measurements
L6 #029	Irregular/red	Large, crumpled and folded. The colour suggests that a portion had once been covered in antiquity.	18.5 x 37. Thickness: 0.5 - 0.7

L1 #004.

L1 #006.

L1 #007.

L1 #013.

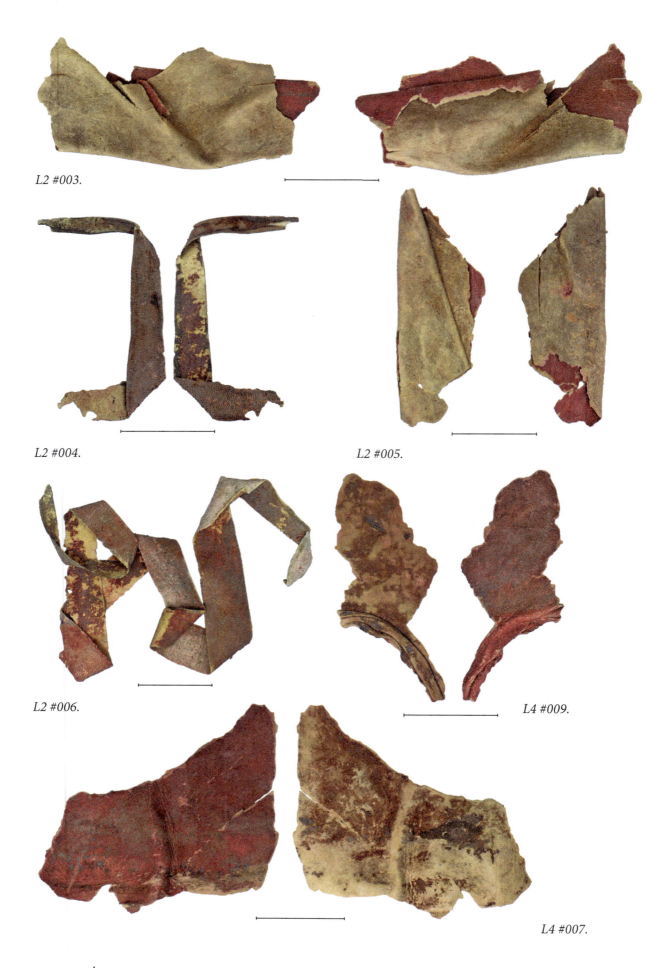

L2 #003.

L2 #004.

L2 #005.

L2 #006.

L4 #009.

L4 #007.

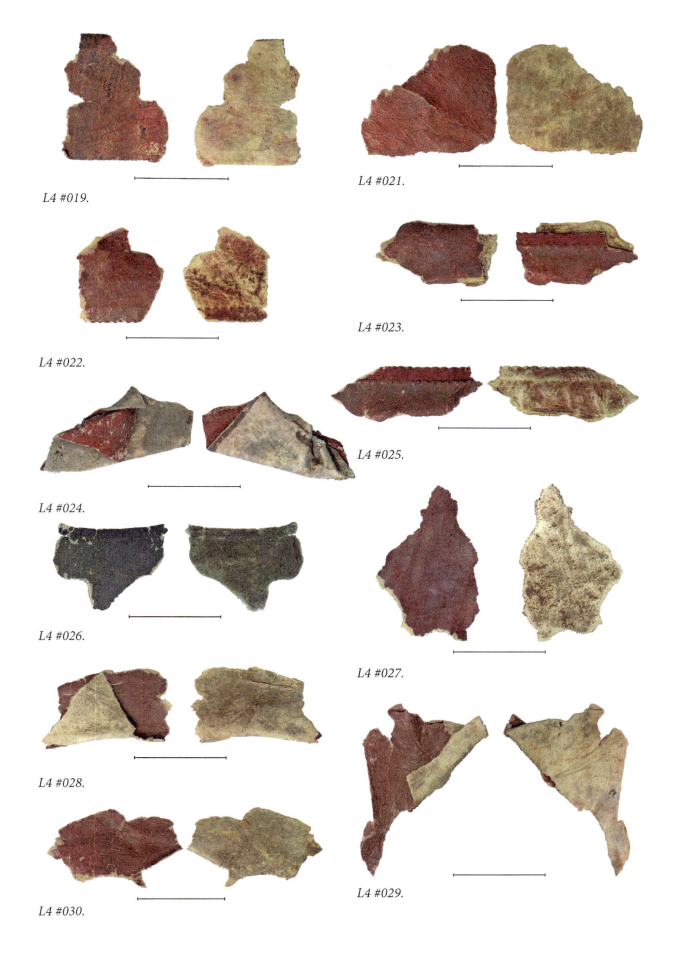

L4 #019.

L4 #021.

L4 #022.

L4 #023.

L4 #025.

L4 #024.

L4 #026.

L4 #027.

L4 #028.

L4 #029.

L4 #030.

CATALOGUE | 511

L4 #031.

L4 #032.

L4 #033.

L4 #034.

L4 #035.

L4 #036.

L4 #037.

L4 #039.

L4 #038.

L4 #040.

L4 #041.

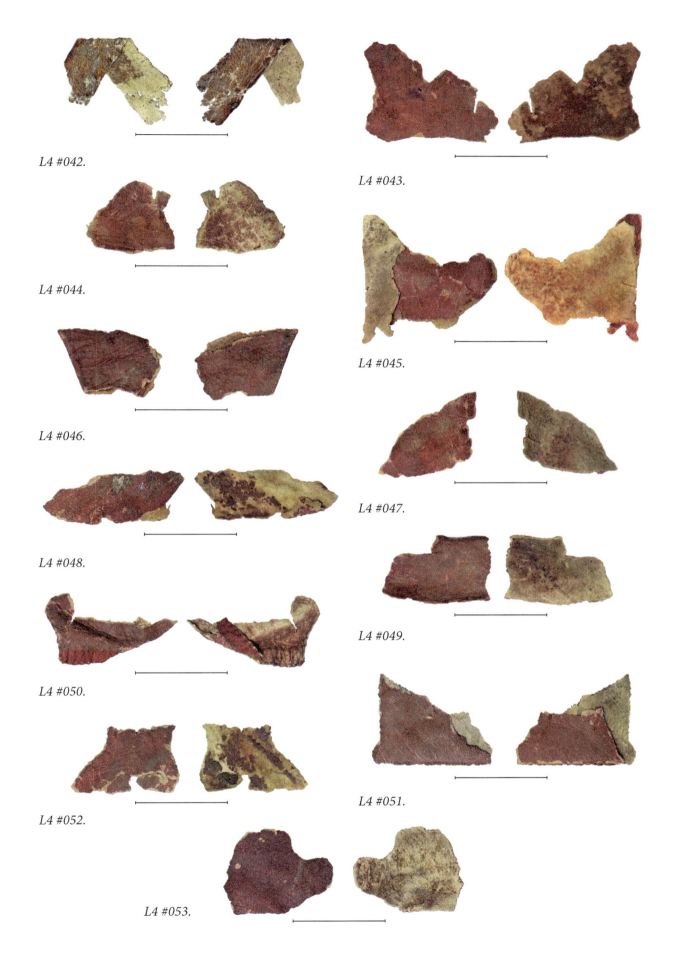

L4 #042.

L4 #043.

L4 #044.

L4 #045.

L4 #046.

L4 #047.

L4 #048.

L4 #049.

L4 #050.

L4 #051.

L4 #052.

L4 #053.

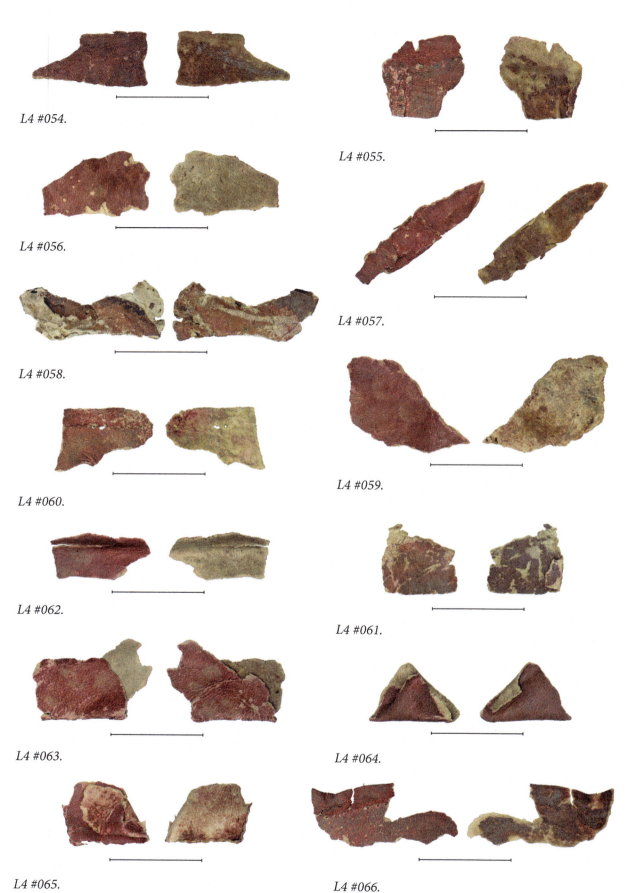

L4 #054.

L4 #055.

L4 #056.

L4 #057.

L4 #058.

L4 #059.

L4 #060.

L4 #061.

L4 #062.

L4 #063.

L4 #064.

L4 #065.

L4 #066.

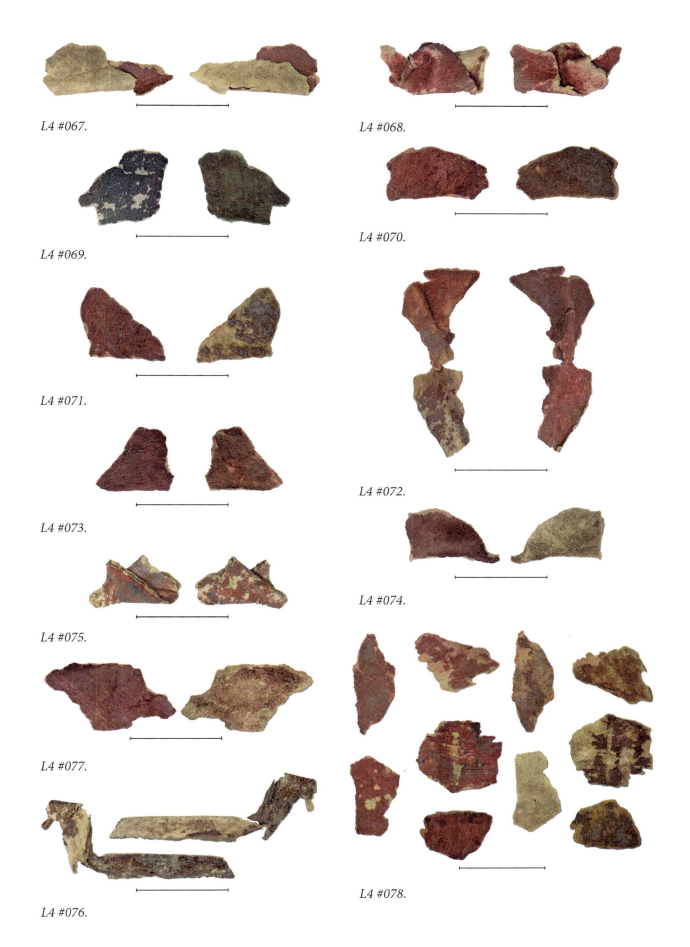

L4 #067.

L4 #068.

L4 #069.

L4 #070.

L4 #071.

L4 #072.

L4 #073.

L4 #074.

L4 #075.

L4 #076.

L4 #077.

L4 #078.

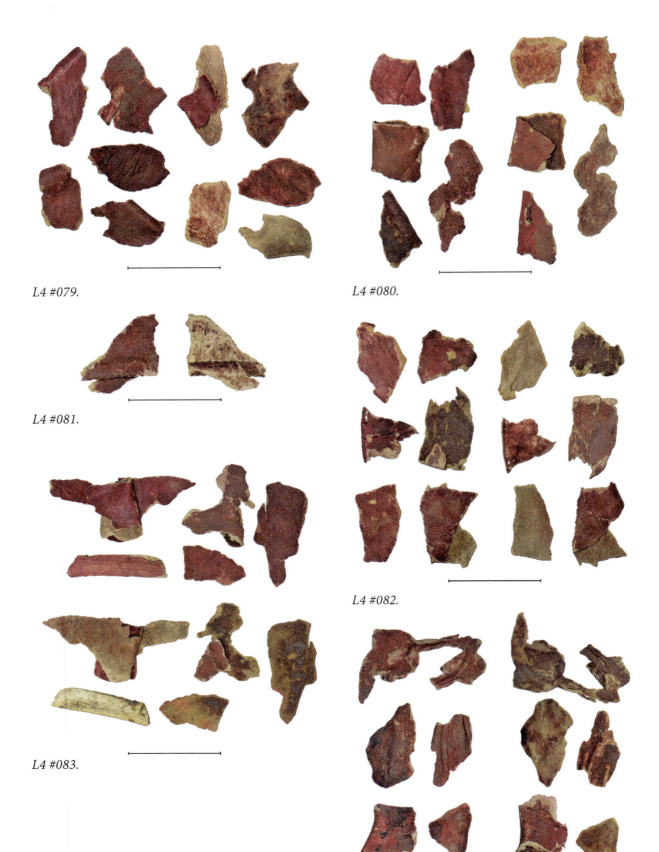

L4 #079.

L4 #080.

L4 #081.

L4 #082.

L4 #083.

L4 #084.

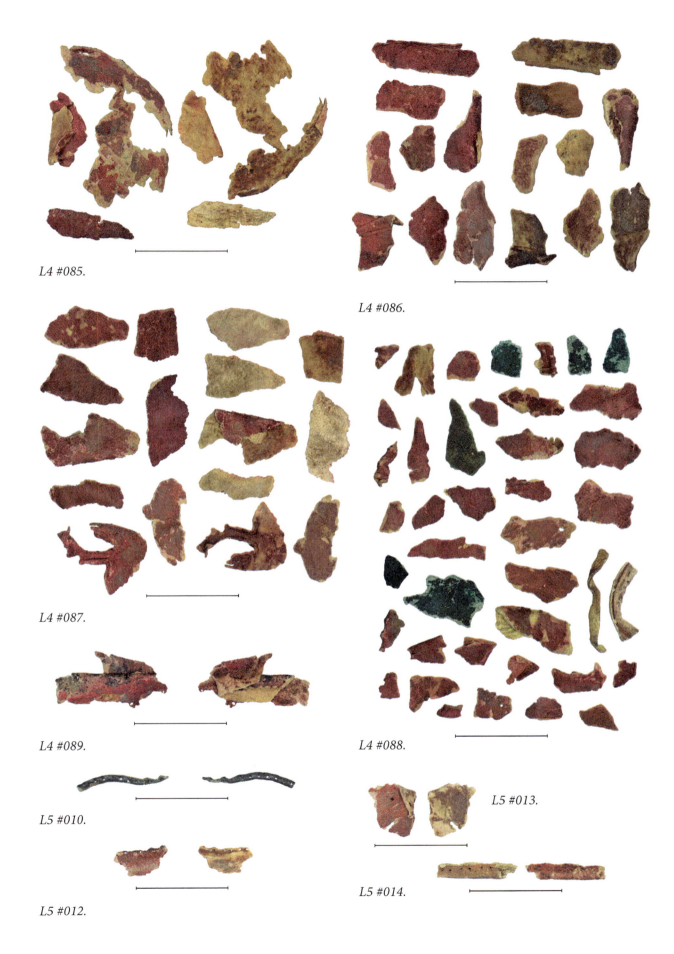

L4 #085.

L4 #086.

L4 #087.

L4 #089.

L4 #088.

L5 #010.

L5 #013.

L5 #012.

L5 #014.

CATALOGUE | 517

L5 #016. Scale bar is 10 mm.

L5 #018. Scale bar is 10 mm.

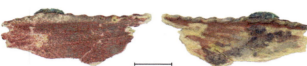

L5 #019. Scale bar is 10 mm.

L5 #021. Scale bar is 10 mm.

L5 #023. Scale bar is 10 mm.

L5 #024. Scale bar is 10 mm.

L5 #025. Scale bar is 10 mm.

L5 #026. Scale bar is 10 mm.

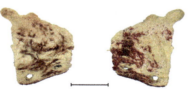

L5 #027. Scale bar is 10 mm.

L5 #028. Scale bar is 10 mm.

L5 #029. Scale bar is 10 mm.

L5 #030. Scale bar is 10 mm.

L5 #033. Scale bar is 10 mm.

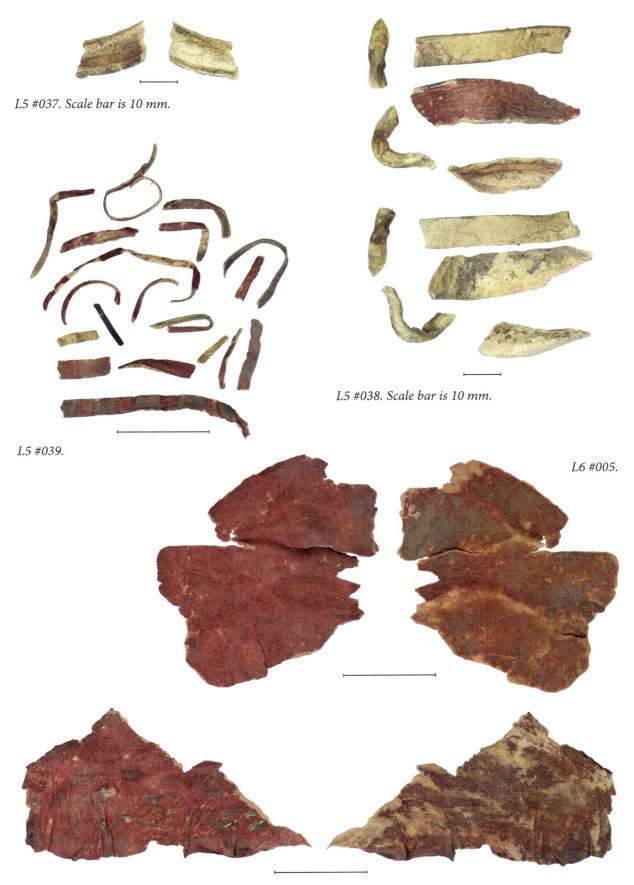

L5 #037. Scale bar is 10 mm.

L5 #038. Scale bar is 10 mm.

L5 #039.

L6 #005.

L6 #006.

CATALOGUE | 519

L6 #008.

L6 #011.

L6 #012.

L6 #013.

L6 #015.

L6 #016.

L6 #018.

L6 #020.

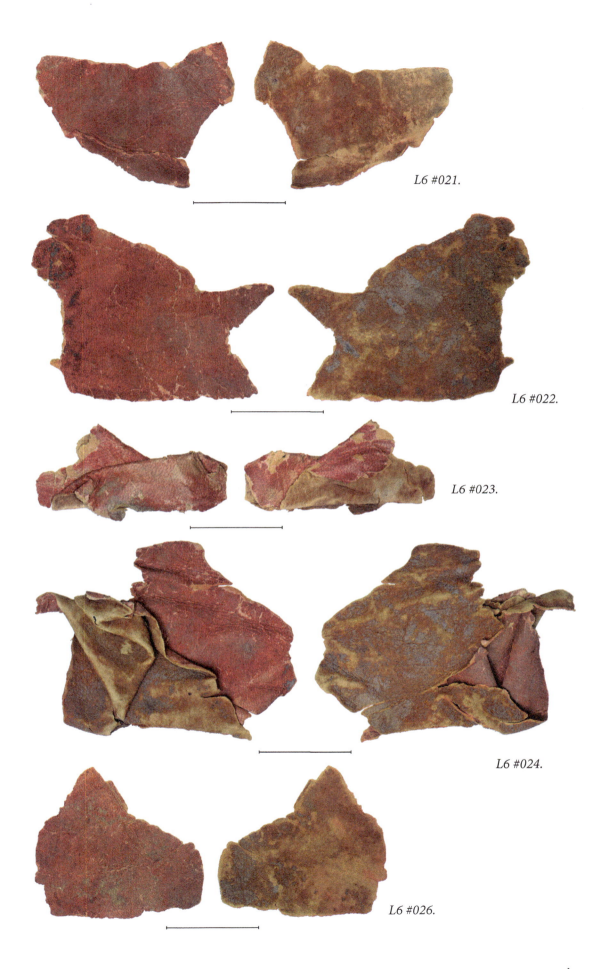

L6 #021.

L6 #022.

L6 #023.

L6 #024.

L6 #026.

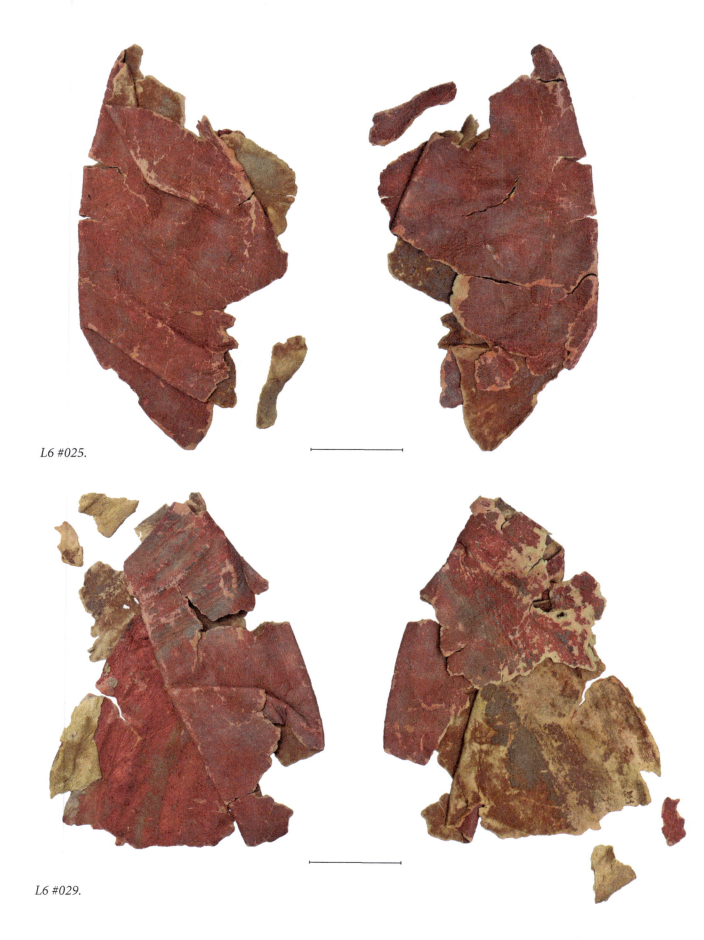

L6 #025.

L6 #029.

APPENDIX I: CONCORDANCE
CATALOGUE NUMBER/PROVENANCE

Catalogue Number	Provenance	Object Identification	Museum Number (other than EM)	Specialist Number	Journal d'Éntree (JE)	Catalogue General	Special Registry	Temporary Number
1	Amenhotep II	container (bow-case/quiver)	-	-	96912A	24151	2502A	-
1	Amenhotep II	container (bow-case/quiver)	-	-	96912B	24151	2502B	-
1	Amenhotep II	container (bow-case/quiver)	-	-	96912C	24151	2502C	-
1	Amenhotep II	container (bow-case/quiver)	-	-	96912D	24151	2502D	-
1	Amenhotep II	container (bow-case/quiver)	-	-	96912E	24151	2502E	-
1	Amenhotep II	container (bow-case/quiver)	-	-	96912F	24151	2502F	-
1	Amenhotep II	container (bow-case/quiver)	-	-	96912G	24151	2502G	-
1	Amenhotep II	container (bow-case/quiver)	-	-	96912H	24151	2502H	-
1	Amenhotep II	container (bow-case/quiver)	-	-	96912I	24151	2502I	-
1	Amenhotep II	container (bow-case/quiver)	-	-	96912J	24151	2502J	-
1	Amenhotep II	container (bow-case/quiver)	-	-	96912K	24151	2502K	-
1	Amenhotep II	container (bow-case/quiver)	-	-	96912L	24151	2502L	-
1	Amenhotep II	container (bow-case/quiver)	-	-	96912M	24151	2502M	-
1	Amenhotep II	container (bow-case/quiver)	-	-	96912N	24151	2502N	-
1	Amenhotep II	container (bow-case/quiver)	-	-	96912O	24151	2502O	-
1	Amenhotep II	container (bow-case/quiver)	-	-	96912P	24151	2502P	-

Catalogue Number	Provenance	Object Identification	Museum Number (other than EM)	Specialist Number	Journal d'Éntree (JE)	Catalogue General	Special Registry	Temporary Number
1	Amenhotep II	container (bow-case/quiver)	-	-	96912Q	24151	2502Q	-
1	Amenhotep II	container (bow-case/quiver)	-	-	96912R	24151	2502R	-
1	Amenhotep II	container (bow-case/quiver)	-	-	96912S	24151	2502S	-
1	Amenhotep II	container (bow-case/quiver)	-	-	96912T	24151	2502T	-
1	Amenhotep II	container (bow-case/quiver)	-	-	96912U	24151	2502U	-
1	Amenhotep II	container (bow-case/quiver)	-	-	96912V	24151	2502V	-
1	Amenhotep II	container (bow-case/quiver)	-	-	96912W	24151	2502W	-
2	Amenhotep II	container (bow-case/quiver)	-	-	32509A	24150	2505A	-
2	Amenhotep II	container (bow-case/quiver)	-	-	32509B	24150	2505B	-
2	Amenhotep II	container (bow-case/quiver)	-	-	32509	24150	2505C	-
2	Amenhotep II	container (bow-case/quiver)	-	-	32509	24150	2505D	-
2	Amenhotep II	container (bow-case/quiver)	-	-	32509	24150	2505E	-
3	Amenhotep II	container (bow-case/quiver)	-	-	32435A	24149	2506C	-
3	Amenhotep II	container (bow-case/quiver)	-	-	32435B	24149	2506A	-
3	Amenhotep II	container (bow-case/quiver)	-	-	32435C	24149	2506B	-
3	Amenhotep II	container (bow-case/quiver)	-	-	32435D	24149	2506G	-
3	Amenhotep II	container (bow-case/quiver)	-	-	32435[-]	24149	2506H	-
3	Amenhotep II	container (bow-case/quiver)	-	-	32435[-]	24149	2506I	-
4	Amenhotep II	bow-case flap	-	-	32513	24147	2500	-
5	Amenhotep II	quiver (tube-shaped)	-	-	32400A	24148	2507A	-
5	Amenhotep II	quiver (tube-shaped)	-	-	32400B	24148	2507B	-
6	Amenhotep II	axe binding	-	-	32559	24155	2508	-
7	Amenhotep II	bridle boss	-	-	32625	24145	2501	-
8	Amenhotep II	blinker	-	-	32506	24144	2504	-
9	Amenhotep II	support strap	-	-	32435D	24149	2506E	-

Catalogue Number	Provenance	Object Identification	Museum Number (other than EM)	Specialist Number	Journal d'Entrée (JE)	Catalogue General	Special Registry	Temporary Number
10	Amenhotep II	unidentified	-	-	-	24152	2503A	-
10	Amenhotep II	unidentified	-	-	-	24152	2503B	-
10	Amenhotep II	unidentified	-	-	-	24152	2503C	-
11	Amenhotep II	unidentified	-	-	32435	24149	2506F	-
12	Thutmose IV	bridle boss	-	-	97801	46106	3367	-
13	Thutmose IV	support strap	-	-	97803	-	3369	21 3 21 3
14	Thutmose IV	support strap	-	-	97802	46109	3368	-
15	Thutmose IV	unidentified	-	-	-	-	3385	21 3 21 10
16	Thutmose IV	unidentified	-	-	-	46108	3386	-
17	Thutmose IV	wrist guard(?)	-	-	97827	-	3388	21 3 21 2
18	Thutmose IV	unidentified	-	-	97827	-	3394	21 3 21 7
19	Thutmose IV	unidentified	-	-	-	46110	3375	-
20	Thutmose IV	unidentified	-	-	97809	46111	3389	-
21	Thutmose IV	unidentified	-	-	97826	-	3393	21 3 21 8
22	Thutmose IV	pouch flap	-	-	97820	46103	3376	-
23	Thutmose IV	wrist guard	-	-	-	-	3387	21 3 21 4
24	Thutmose IV	wrist guard	-	-	-	46112	3374	-
25	Thutmose IV	wrist guard	-	-	-	46113	3390	-
26	Thutmose IV	axe binding	-	-	97824	-	3391	21 3 21 6
26	Thutmose IV	axe binding	-	-	97825	-	3392	21 3 21 5
27	Thutmose IV	scabbard	-	-	-	46115	3365	-
28	Amenhotep III	unidentified	24.8.D	-	-	-	-	-
29	Amenhotep III	unidentified	24.8.A-C	-	-	-	-	-
30	Amenhotep III	unidentified	24.8.E	-	-	-	-	-
31	Amenhotep III	upper of shoe	24.8.F	-	-	-	-	-
32	Amenhotep III	unidentified	24.8.G	-	-	-	-	-
33	Amenhotep III	unidentified	24.8.H	-	-	-	-	-
34	Amenhotep III	unidentified	24.8.I	-	-	-	-	-
35	Amenhotep III	unidentified	24.8.J	-	-	-	-	-
35	Amenhotep III	unidentified	24.8.J	-	-	-	-	-
35	Amenhotep III	unidentified	24.8.L	-	-	-	-	-
36	Amenhotep III	unidentified	24.8.M	-	-	-	-	-
37	Amenhotep III	unidentified	24.8.O	-	-	-	-	-
38	Amenhotep III	unidentified	24.8.P	-	-	-	-	-
39	Amenhotep III	unidentified	24.8.Q	-	-	-	-	-
39	Amenhotep III	unidentified	24.8.R	-	-	-	-	-
40	Amenhotep III	unidentified	24.8.S	-	-	-	-	-
41	Amenhotep III	unidentified	24.8.T	-	-	-	-	-
42	Amenhotep III	unidentified	-	-	-	-	4/10676A	6 3 25 4
42	Amenhotep III	unidentified	-	-	-	-	4/10676B	7 3 25 4
43	Tano	main casing	-	L3 #001	88962	-	14530	-
44	Tano	main casing	-	L3 #002	88962	-	14530	-
45	Tano	main casing	-	L3 #003	88962	-	14530	-

Catalogue Number	Provenance	Object Identification	Museum Number (other than EM)	Specialist Number	Journal d'Entrée (JE)	Catalogue General	Special Registry	Temporary Number
46	Tano	main casing	-	L3 #004A	88962	-	14530	-
46	Tano	main casing	-	L3 #004B	88962	-	14530	-
46	Tano	main casing	-	L3 #004C	88962	-	14530	-
46	Tano	main casing	-	L3 #004D	88963	-	14531	-
46	Tano	main casing	-	L3 #004E	88962	-	14530	-
46	Tano	holder(?)	-	L3 #004F	88962	-	14530	-
47	Tano	holder(?)	-	L1 #011	88962	-	14530	-
48	Tano	holder(?)	-	L5 #009	88962	-	14530	-
49	Tano	bow-case	-	L1 #022	88962	-	14530	-
50	Tano	siding fill	-	L1 #001	88962	-	14530	-
51	Tano	siding fill	-	L1 #002	88962	-	14530	-
52	Tano	siding fill	-	L1 #003	88962	-	14530	-
53	Tano	siding fill	-	L1 #018	88962	-	14530	-
54	Tano	siding fill	-	L1 #023	88962	-	14530	-
55	Tano	siding fill	-	L2 #002	88962	-	14530	-
56	Tano	siding fill	-	L2 #008A	88962	-	14530	-
56	Tano	siding fill	-	L2 #008B	88962	-	14530	-
56	Tano	siding fill	-	L2 #008C	88962	-	14530	-
57	Tano	siding fill	-	L6 #007	88962	-	14530	-
58	Tano	siding fill	-	L4 #013	88962	-	14530	-
59	Tano	siding fill	-	L6 #002	88962	-	14530	-
60	Tano	siding fill	-	L6 #001	88962	-	14530	-
61	Tano	siding fill	-	L6 #003	88962	-	14530	-
62	Tano	siding fill	-	L6 #004	88962	-	14530	-
63	Tano	siding fill	-	L6 #027	88962	-	14530	-
64	Tano	siding fill	-	L4 #014	88962	-	14530	-
65	Tano	siding fill	-	L4 #018	88962	-	14530	-
66	Tano	siding fill	-	L4 #003	88962	-	14530	-
67	Tano	siding fill	-	L4 #001	88962	-	14530	-
68	Tano	siding fill	-	L1 #005	88962	-	14530	-
69	Tano	siding fill	-	L1 #008A	88962	-	14530	-
69	Tano	siding fill	-	L1 #008B	88962	-	14530	-
70	Tano	siding fill	-	L1 #010A	88962	-	14530	-
70	Tano	siding fill	-	L1 #010B	88962	-	14530	-
71	Tano	siding fill	-	L1 #012	88962	-	14530	-
72	Tano	siding fill	-	L1 #014	88962	-	14530	-
73	Tano	siding fill	-	L1 #016	88962	-	14530	-
74	Tano	siding fill	-	BI-034	88962	-	14530	-
75	Tano	siding fill	-	L1 #020	88962	-	14530	-
76	Tano	siding fill	-	L4 #002	88962	-	14530	-
77	Tano	siding fill	-	L6 #017	88962	-	14530	-
78	Tano	siding fill	-	L4 #006	88962	-	14530	-
79	Tano	siding fill	-	L2 #001	88962	-	14530	-

Catalogue Number	Provenance	Object Identification	Museum Number (other than EM)	Specialist Number	Journal d'Entrée (JE)	Catalogue General	Special Registry	Temporary Number
80	Tano	siding fill	-	L5 #003	88962	-	14530	-
81	Tano	support strap	-	BI-001	88962	-	14530	-
82	Tano	support strap	-	BI-006	88962	-	14530	
83	Tano	support strap	-	BI-013	88962	-	14530	-
84	Tano	support strap	-	BI-026	88962	-	14530	-
85	Tano	support strap	-	BI-003	88962	-	14530	-
86	Tano	support strap	-	BI-004	88962	-	14530	-
87	Tano	support strap	-	BI-011	88962	-	14530	-
88	Tano	nave hoop	-	#33	88962	-	14530	-
88	Tano	nave hoop	-	#34	88962	-	14530	-
89	Tano	nave hoop	-	BI-023	88962	-	14530	-
90	Tano	nave hoop	-	BI-025	88962	-	14530	-
91	Tano	bow-case	-	#30	88962	-	14530	-
92	Tano	bow-case	-	#31	88962	-	14530	
93	Tano	bow-case	-	L1 #015	88962	-	14530	-
94	Tano	bow-case	-	L5 #034	88962	-	14531	-
95	Tano	bow-case	-	L5 #035	88962	-	14530	
96	Tano	girth	-	#40	88962	-	14530	-
96	Tano	girth	-	#41	88962	-	14530	-
97	Tano	harness	-	#36	88962	-	14530	-
97	Tano	harness	-	#35	88962	-	14530	-
98	Tano	harness	-	#42	88962	-	14530	-
99	Tano	harness	-	#43	88962	-	14530	
100	Tano	harness	-	#44	88962	-	14530	-
101	Tano	harness	-	#45	88962	-	14530	-
102	Tano	harness	-	#46	88962	-	14530	-
103	Tano	neckstrap	-	#37	88962	-	14530	-
103	Tano	neckstrap	-	#39	88962	-	14530	
104	Tano	harness	-	BI-005	88962	-	14530	-
105	Tano	harness	-	BI-007	88962	-	14530	-
106	Tano	harness	-	BI-008	88962	-	14530	
107	Tano	harness	-	BI-014	88962	-	14530	-
108	Tano	harness	-	BI-039	88962	-	14530	
109	Tano	harness	-	BI-012	88962	-	14530	-
110	Tano	harness	-	BI-009	88962	-	14530	
111	Tano	harness	-	#38	88962	-	14530	-
112	Tano	harness	-	BI-020	88962	-	14530	
113	Tano	harness	-	BI-022	88962	-	14530	-
114	Tano	harness	-	BI-033	88962	-	14530	
115	Tano	harness	-	BI-021	88962	-	14530	
116	Tano	harness	-	BI-024	88962	-	14530	
117	Tano	harness	-	BI-028	88962	-	14530	-
118	Tano	harness	-	BI-029	88962	-	14530	

Catalogue Number	Provenance	Object Identification	Museum Number (other than EM)	Specialist Number	Journal d'Entrée (JE)	Catalogue General	Special Registry	Temporary Number
119	Tano	harness	-	BI-038	88962	-	14530	-
120	Tano	unidentified	-	L1 #024	88962	-	14530	-
121	Tano	unidentified	-	L1 #009	88962	-	14530	-
122	Tano	unidentified	-	L1 #019	88962	-	14530	-
123	Tano	unidentified	-	L5 #001	88962	-	14530	-
124	Tano	unidentified	-	L5 #002	88962	-	14530	-
125	Tano	unidentified	-	L5 #004	88962	-	14530	-
126	Tano	unidentified	-	L5 #006	88962	-	14530	-
127	Tano	unidentified	-	L5 #007	88962	-	14530	-
128	Tano	unidentified	-	L5 #011	88962	-	14530	-
129	Tano	unidentified	-	L5 #017	88962	-	14530	-
130	Tano	unidentified	-	L5 #020	88962	-	14530	-
131	Tano	unidentified	-	L5 #031	88962	-	14530	-
132	Tano	unidentified	-	L5 #022	88962	-	14530	-
133	Tano	unidentified	-	L5 #032	88962	-	14530	-
134	Tano	unidentified	-	#32	88962	-	14530	-
135	Tano	unidentified	-	L1 #017	88962	-	14530	-
136	Tano	unidentified	-	L1 #021	88962	-	14530	-
137	Tano	unidentified	-	L2 #007	88962	-	14530	-
138	Tano	unidentified	-	L4 #004	88962	-	14530	-
139	Tano	unidentified	-	L4 #005	88962	-	14530	-
140	Tano	unidentified	-	L4 #008	88962	-	14530	-
141	Tano	unidentified	-	L4 #010	88962	-	14530	-
142	Tano	unidentified	-	L4 #011	88962	-	14530	-
143	Tano	unidentified	-	L4 #012	88962	-	14530	-
144	Tano	unidentified	-	L4 #015	88962	-	14530	-
145	Tano	unidentified	-	L4 #016	88962	-	14530	-
146	Tano	unidentified	-	L4 #017	88962	-	14530	-
147	Tano	unidentified	-	L4 #020	88962	-	14530	-
148	Tano	unidentified	-	L6 #009	88962	-	14530	-
149	Tano	unidentified	-	L6 #010	88962	-	14530	-
150	Tano	unidentified	-	L6 #014	88962	-	14530	-
151	Tano	unidentified	-	L6 #019	88962	-	14530	-
152	Tano	unidentified	-	L6 #028	88962	-	14530	-
153	Tano	unidentified	-	L6 #030	88962	-	14530	-
154	Tano	unidentified	-	BI-018	88962	-	14530	-
155	Tano	unidentified	-	BI-002	88962	-	14530	-
156	Tano	unidentified	-	BI-010	88962	-	14530	-
157	Tano	unidentified	-	BI-015	88962	-	14530	-
158	Tano	unidentified	-	BI-016	88962	-	14530	-
159	Tano	unidentified	-	BI-017	88962	-	14530	-
160	Tano	unidentified	-	BI-019	88962	-	14530	-
161	Tano	unidentified	-	BI-027	88962	-	14530	

Catalogue Number	Provenance	Object Identification	Museum Number (other than EM)	Specialist Number	Journal d'Entrée (JE)	Catalogue General	Special Registry	Temporary Number
162	Tano	unidentified	-	BI-031	88962	-	14530	-
163	Tano	unidentified	-	BI-032	88962	-	14530	-
164	Tano	unidentified	-	BI-036	88962	-	14530	-
165	Tano	unidentified	-	BI-037	88962	-	14530	-
166	Tano	unidentified	-	BI-040	88962	-	14530	-
167	Tano	unidentified	-	L1 #004	88962	-	14530	-
167	Tano	unidentified	-	L1 #006	88962	-	14530	-
167	Tano	unidentified	-	L1 #007	88962	-	14530	-
167	Tano	unidentified	-	L1 #013	88962	-	14530	-
167	Tano	unidentified	-	L2 #003	88962	-	14530	-
167	Tano	unidentified	-	L2 #004	88962	-	14530	-
167	Tano	unidentified	-	L2 #005	88962	-	14530	-
167	Tano	unidentified	-	L2 #006	88962	-	14530	-
167	Tano	unidentified	-	L4 #009	88962	-	14530	-
167	Tano	unidentified	-	L4 #007	88962	-	14530	-
167	Tano	unidentified	-	L4 #019	88962	-	14530	-
167	Tano	unidentified	-	L4 #021	88962	-	14530	-
167	Tano	unidentified	-	L4 #022	88962	-	14530	-
167	Tano	unidentified	-	L4 #023	88962	-	14530	-
167	Tano	unidentified	-	L4 #024	88962	-	14530	-
167	Tano	unidentified	-	L4 #025	88962	-	14530	-
167	Tano	unidentified	-	L4 #026	88962	-	14530	-
167	Tano	unidentified	-	L4 #027	88962	-	14530	-
167	Tano	unidentified	-	L4 #028	88962	-	14530	-
167	Tano	unidentified	-	L4 #029	88962	-	14530	-
167	Tano	unidentified	-	L4 #030	88962	-	14530	-
167	Tano	unidentified	-	L4 #031	88962	-	14530	-
167	Tano	unidentified	-	L4 #032	88962	-	14530	-
167	Tano	unidentified	-	L4 #033	88962	-	14530	-
167	Tano	unidentified	-	L4 #034	88962	-	14530	-
167	Tano	unidentified	-	L4 #035	88962	-	14530	-
167	Tano	unidentified	-	L4 #036	88962	-	14530	-
167	Tano	unidentified	-	L4 #037	88962	-	14530	-
167	Tano	unidentified	-	L4 #038	88962	-	14530	-
167	Tano	unidentified	-	L4 #039	88962	-	14530	-
167	Tano	unidentified	-	L4 #040	88962	-	14530	-
167	Tano	unidentified	-	L4 #041	88962	-	14530	-
167	Tano	unidentified	-	L4 #042	88962	-	14530	-
167	Tano	unidentified	-	L4 #043	88962	-	14530	-
167	Tano	unidentified	-	L4 #044	88962	-	14530	-
167	Tano	unidentified	-	L4 #045	88962	-	14530	-
167	Tano	unidentified	-	L4 #046	88962	-	14530	-
167	Tano	unidentified	-	L4 #047	88962	-	14530	-

Catalogue Number	Provenance	Object Identification	Museum Number (other than EM)	Specialist Number	Journal d'Entrée (JE)	Catalogue General	Special Registry	Temporary Number
167	Tano	unidentified	-	L4 #048	88962	-	14530	-
167	Tano	unidentified	-	L4 #049	88962	-	14530	-
167	Tano	unidentified	-	L4 #050	88962	-	14530	-
167	Tano	unidentified	-	L4 #051	88962	-	14530	-
167	Tano	unidentified	-	L4 #052	88962	-	14530	-
167	Tano	unidentified	-	L4 #053	88962	-	14530	-
167	Tano	unidentified	-	L4 #054	88962	-	14530	-
167	Tano	unidentified	-	L4 #055	88962	-	14530	-
167	Tano	unidentified	-	L4 #056	88962	-	14530	-
167	Tano	unidentified	-	L4 #057	88962	-	14530	-
167	Tano	unidentified	-	L4 #058	88962	-	14530	-
167	Tano	unidentified	-	L4 #059	88962	-	14530	-
167	Tano	unidentified	-	L4 #060	88962	-	14530	-
167	Tano	unidentified	-	L4 #061	88962	-	14530	-
167	Tano	unidentified	-	L4 #062	88962	-	14530	-
167	Tano	unidentified	-	L4 #063	88962	-	14530	-
167	Tano	unidentified	-	L4 #064	88962	-	14530	-
167	Tano	unidentified	-	L4 #065	88962	-	14530	-
167	Tano	unidentified	-	L4 #066	88962	-	14530	-
167	Tano	unidentified	-	L4 #067	88962	-	14530	-
167	Tano	unidentified	-	L4 #068	88962	-	14530	-
167	Tano	unidentified	-	L4 #069	88962	-	14530	-
167	Tano	unidentified	-	L4 #070	88962	-	14530	-
167	Tano	unidentified	-	L4 #071	88962	-	14530	-
167	Tano	unidentified	-	L4 #072	88962	-	14530	-
167	Tano	unidentified	-	L4 #073	88962	-	14530	-
167	Tano	unidentified	-	L4 #074	88962	-	14530	-
167	Tano	unidentified	-	L4 #075	88962	-	14530	-
167	Tano	unidentified	-	L4 #076	88962	-	14530	-
167	Tano	unidentified	-	L4 #077	88962	-	14530	-
167	Tano	unidentified	-	L4 #078	88962	-	14530	-
167	Tano	unidentified	-	L4 #079	88962	-	14530	-
167	Tano	unidentified	-	L4 #080	88962	-	14530	-
167	Tano	unidentified	-	L4 #081	88962	-	14530	-
167	Tano	unidentified	-	L4 #082	88962	-	14530	-
167	Tano	unidentified	-	L4 #083	88962	-	14530	-
167	Tano	unidentified	-	L4 #084	88962	-	14530	-
167	Tano	unidentified	-	L4 #085	88962	-	14530	-
167	Tano	unidentified	-	L4 #086	88962	-	14530	-
167	Tano	unidentified	-	L4 #087	88962	-	14530	-
167	Tano	unidentified	-	L4 #088	88962	-	14530	-
167	Tano	unidentified	-	L4 #089	88962	-	14530	-
167	Tano	unidentified	-	L5 #008	88963	-	14531	-

Catalogue Number	Provenance	Object Identification	Museum Number (other than EM)	Specialist Number	Journal d'Entrée (JE)	Catalogue General	Special Registry	Temporary Number
167	Tano	unidentified	-	L5 #010	88962	-	14530	-
167	Tano	unidentified	-	L5 #012	88962	-	14530	-
167	Tano	unidentified	-	L5 #013	88962	-	14530	-
167	Tano	unidentified	-	L5 #014	88962	-	14530	-
167	Tano	unidentified	-	L5 #016	88962	-	14530	-
167	Tano	unidentified	-	L5 #018	88962	-	14530	-
167	Tano	unidentified	-	L5 #019	88962	-	14530	-
167	Tano	unidentified	-	L5 #021	88962	-	14530	-
167	Tano	unidentified	-	L5 #023	88962	-	14530	-
167	Tano	unidentified	-	L5 #024	88962	-	14530	-
167	Tano	unidentified	-	L5 #025	88962	-	14530	-
167	Tano	unidentified	-	L5 #026	88962	-	14530	-
167	Tano	unidentified	-	L5 #027	88962	-	14530	-
167	Tano	unidentified	-	L5 #028	88962	-	14530	-
167	Tano	unidentified	-	L5 #029	88962	-	14530	-
167	Tano	unidentified	-	L5 #030	88962	-	14530	-
167	Tano	unidentified	-	L5 #033	88962	-	14530	-
167	Tano	unidentified	-	L5 #037	88962	-	14530	-
167	Tano	unidentified	-	L5 #038	88962	-	14530	-
167	Tano	unidentified	-	L5 #039	88962	-	14530	-
167	Tano	unidentified	-	L6 #005	88962	-	14530	-
167	Tano	unidentified	-	L6 #006	88962	-	14530	-
167	Tano	unidentified	-	L6 #008	88962	-	14530	-
167	Tano	unidentified	-	L6 #011	88962	-	14530	-
167	Tano	unidentified	-	L6 #012	88962	-	14530	-
167	Tano	unidentified	-	L6 #013	88962	-	14530	-
167	Tano	unidentified	-	L6 #015	88962	-	14530	-
167	Tano	unidentified	-	L6 #016	88962	-	14530	-
167	Tano	unidentified	-	L6 #018	88962	-	14530	-
167	Tano	unidentified	-	L6 #020	88962	-	14530	-
167	Tano	unidentified	-	L6 #021	88962	-	14530	-
167	Tano	unidentified	-	L6 #022	88962	-	14530	-
167	Tano	unidentified	-	L6 #023	88962	-	14530	-
167	Tano	unidentified	-	L6 #024	88962	-	14530	-
167	Tano	unidentified	-	L6 #026	88962	-	14530	-
167	Tano	unidentified	-	L6 #025	88962	-	14530	-
167	Tano	unidentified	-	L6 #029	88962	-	14530	-

APPENDIX I: CONCORDANCE
OBJECT IDENTIFICATION

Object Identification	Catalogue Number	Provenance	Museum Number (other than EM)	Specialist Number	Journal d'Éntrée (JE)	Catalogue General	Special Registry	Temporary Number
axe binding	6	Amenhotep II	-	-	32559	24155	2508	-
axe binding	26	Thutmose IV	-	-	97824	-	3391	21 3 21 6
axe binding	26	Thutmose IV	-	-	97825	-	3392	21 3 21 5
blinker	8	Amenhotep II	-	-	32506	24144	2504	-
bow-case	49	Tano	-	L1 #022	88962	-	14530	-
bow-case	91	Tano	-	#30	88962	-	14530	-
bow-case	92	Tano	-	#31	88962	-	14530	-
bow-case	93	Tano	-	L1 #015	88962	-	14530	-
bow-case	94	Tano	-	L5 #034	88962	-	14531	-
bow-case	95	Tano	-	L5 #035	88962	-	14530	-
bow-case flap	4	Amenhotep II	-	-	32513	24147	2500	-
bridle boss	7	Amenhotep II	-	-	32625	24145	2501	-
bridle boss	12	Thutmose IV	-	-	97801	46106	3367	-
container (bow-case/quiver)	1	Amenhotep II	-	-	96912A	24151	2502A	-
container (bow-case/quiver)	1	Amenhotep II	-	-	96912B	24151	2502B	-
container (bow-case/quiver)	1	Amenhotep II	-	-	96912C	24151	2502C	-
container (bow-case/quiver)	1	Amenhotep II	-	-	96912D	24151	2502D	-
container (bow-case/quiver)	1	Amenhotep II	-	-	96912E	24151	2502E	-
container (bow-case/quiver)	1	Amenhotep II	-	-	96912F	24151	2502F	-
container (bow-case/quiver)	1	Amenhotep II	-	-	96912G	24151	2502G	-
container (bow-case/quiver)	1	Amenhotep II	-	-	96912H	24151	2502H	-
container (bow-case/quiver)	1	Amenhotep II	-	-	96912I	24151	2502I	-
container (bow-case/quiver)	1	Amenhotep II	-	-	96912J	24151	2502J	-

Object Identification	Catalogue Number	Provenance	Museum Number (other than EM)	Specialist Number	Journal d'Entrée (JE)	Catalogue General	Special Registry	Temporary Number
container (bow-case/quiver)	1	Amenhotep II	-	-	96912K	24151	2502K	-
container (bow-case/quiver)	1	Amenhotep II	-	-	96912L	24151	2502L	-
container (bow-case/quiver)	1	Amenhotep II	-	-	96912M	24151	2502M	-
container (bow-case/quiver)	1	Amenhotep II	-	-	96912N	24151	2502N	-
container (bow-case/quiver)	1	Amenhotep II	-	-	96912O	24151	2502O	-
container (bow-case/quiver)	1	Amenhotep II	-	-	96912P	24151	2502P	-
container (bow-case/quiver)	1	Amenhotep II	-	-	96912Q	24151	2502Q	-
container (bow-case/quiver)	1	Amenhotep II	-	-	96912R	24151	2502R	-
container (bow-case/quiver)	1	Amenhotep II	-	-	96912S	24151	2502S	-
container (bow-case/quiver)	1	Amenhotep II	-	-	96912T	24151	2502T	-
container (bow-case/quiver)	1	Amenhotep II	-	-	96912U	24151	2502U	-
container (bow-case/quiver)	1	Amenhotep II	-	-	96912V	24151	2502V	-
container (bow-case/quiver)	1	Amenhotep II	-	-	96912W	24151	2502W	-
container (bow-case/quiver)	2	Amenhotep II	-	-	32509A	24150	2505A	-
container (bow-case/quiver)	2	Amenhotep II	-	-	32509B	24150	2505B	-
container (bow-case/quiver)	2	Amenhotep II	-	-	32509	24150	2505C	-
container (bow-case/quiver)	2	Amenhotep II	-	-	32509	24150	2505D	-
container (bow-case/quiver)	2	Amenhotep II	-	-	32509	24150	2505E	-
container (bow-case/quiver)	3	Amenhotep II	-	-	32435A	24149	2506C	-
container (bow-case/quiver)	3	Amenhotep II	-	-	32435B	24149	2506A	-
container (bow-case/quiver)	3	Amenhotep II	-	-	32435C	24149	2506B	-

Object Identification	Catalogue Number	Provenance	Museum Number (other than EM)	Specialist Number	Journal d'Éntree (JE)	Catalogue General	Special Registry	Temporary Number
container (bow-case/quiver)	3	Amenhotep II	-	-	32435D	24149	2506G	-
container (bow-case/quiver)	3	Amenhotep II	-	-	32435[-]	24149	2506H	-
container (bow-case/quiver)	3	Amenhotep II	-	-	32435[-]	24149	2506I	-
girth	96	Tano	-	#40	88962	-	14530	
girth	96	Tano	-	#41	88962	-	14530	-
harness	97	Tano	-	#36	88962	-	14530	-
harness	97	Tano	-	#35	88962	-	14530	-
harness	98	Tano	-	#42	88962	-	14530	-
harness	99	Tano	-	#43	88962	-	14530	-
harness	100	Tano	-	#44	88962	-	14530	-
harness	101	Tano	-	#45	88962	-	14530	-
harness	102	Tano	-	#46	88962	-	14530	-
harness	104	Tano	-	BI-005	88962	-	14530	-
harness	105	Tano	-	BI-007	88962	-	14530	-
harness	106	Tano	-	BI-008	88962	-	14530	
harness	107	Tano	-	BI-014	88962	-	14530	-
harness	108	Tano	-	BI-039	88962	-	14530	-
harness	109	Tano	-	BI-012	88962	-	14530	-
harness	110	Tano	-	BI-009	88962	-	14530	
harness	111	Tano	-	#38	88962	-	14530	-
harness	112	Tano	-	BI-020	88962	-	14530	-
harness	113	Tano	-	BI-022	88962	-	14530	-
harness	114	Tano	-	BI-033	88962	-	14530	
harness	115	Tano	-	BI-021	88962	-	14530	-
harness	116	Tano	-	BI-024	88962	-	14530	-
harness	117	Tano	-	BI-028	88962	-	14530	-
harness	118	Tano	-	BI-029	88962	-	14530	-
harness	119	Tano	-	BI-038	88962	-	14530	
holder(?)	46	Tano	-	L3 #004F	88962	-	14530	-
holder(?)	47	Tano	-	L1 #011	88962	-	14530	-
holder(?)	48	Tano	-	L5 #009	88962	-	14530	-
main casing	43	Tano	-	L3 #001	88962	-	14530	
main casing	44	Tano	-	L3 #002	88962	-	14530	-
main casing	45	Tano	-	L3 #003	88962	-	14530	-
main casing	46	Tano	-	L3 #004A	88962	-	14530	-
main casing	46	Tano	-	L3 #004B	88962	-	14530	-
main casing	46	Tano	-	L3 #004C	88962	-	14530	-
main casing	46	Tano	-	L3 #004D	88963	-	14531	-
main casing	46	Tano	-	L3 #004E	88962	-	14530	-
nave hoop	88	Tano	-	#33	88962	-	14530	

Object Identification	Catalogue Number	Provenance	Museum Number (other than EM)	Specialist Number	Journal d'Entrée (JE)	Catalogue General	Special Registry	Temporary Number
nave hoop	88	Tano	-	#34	88962	-	14530	-
nave hoop	89	Tano	-	BI-023	88962	-	14530	-
nave hoop	90	Tano	-	BI-025	88962	-	14530	-
neckstrap	103	Tano	-	#37	88962	-	14530	-
neckstrap	103	Tano	-	#39	88962	-	14530	-
pouch flap	22	Thutmose IV	-	-	97820	46103	3376	-
quiver (tube-shaped)	5	Amenhotep II	-	-	32400A	24148	2507A	-
quiver (tube-shaped)	5	Amenhotep II	-	-	32400B	24148	2507B	-
scabbard	27	Thutmose IV	-	-	-	46115	3365	-
siding fill	50	Tano	-	L1 #001	88962	-	14530	-
siding fill	51	Tano	-	L1 #002	88962	-	14530	-
siding fill	52	Tano	-	L1 #003	88962	-	14530	-
siding fill	53	Tano	-	L1 #018	88962	-	14530	-
siding fill	54	Tano	-	L1 #023	88962	-	14530	-
siding fill	55	Tano	-	L2 #002	88962	-	14530	-
siding fill	56	Tano	-	L2 #008A	88962	-	14530	-
siding fill	56	Tano	-	L2 #008B	88962	-	14530	-
siding fill	56	Tano	-	L2 #008C	88962	-	14530	-
siding fill	57	Tano	-	L6 #007	88962	-	14530	-
siding fill	58	Tano	-	L4 #013	88962	-	14530	-
siding fill	59	Tano	-	L6 #002	88962	-	14530	-
siding fill	60	Tano	-	L6 #001	88962	-	14530	-
siding fill	61	Tano	-	L6 #003	88962	-	14530	-
siding fill	62	Tano	-	L6 #004	88962	-	14530	-
siding fill	63	Tano	-	L6 #027	88962	-	14530	-
siding fill	64	Tano	-	L4 #014	88962	-	14530	-
siding fill	65	Tano	-	L4 #018	88962	-	14530	-
siding fill	66	Tano	-	L4 #003	88962	-	14530	-
siding fill	67	Tano	-	L4 #001	88962	-	14530	-
siding fill	68	Tano	-	L1 #005	88962	-	14530	-
siding fill	69	Tano	-	L1 #008A	88962	-	14530	-
siding fill	69	Tano	-	L1 #008B	88962	-	14530	-
siding fill	70	Tano	-	L1 #010A	88962	-	14530	-
siding fill	70	Tano	-	L1 #010B	88962	-	14530	-
siding fill	71	Tano	-	L1 #012	88962	-	14530	-
siding fill	72	Tano	-	L1 #014	88962	-	14530	-
siding fill	73	Tano	-	L1 #016	88962	-	14530	-
siding fill	74	Tano	-	BI-034	88962	-	14530	-
siding fill	75	Tano	-	L1 #020	88962	-	14530	-
siding fill	76	Tano	-	L4 #002	88962	-	14530	-
siding fill	77	Tano	-	L6 #017	88962	-	14530	-
siding fill	78	Tano	-	L4 #006	88962	-	14530	-
siding fill	79	Tano	-	L2 #001	88962	-	14530	-

Object Identification	Catalogue Number	Provenance	Museum Number (other than EM)	Specialist Number	Journal d'Éntrée (JE)	Catalogue General	Special Registry	Temporary Number
siding fill	80	Tano	-	L5 #003	88962	-	14530	-
support strap	9	Amenhotep II	-	-	32435D	24149	2506E	-
support strap	13	Thutmose IV	-	-	97803	-	3369	21 3 21 3
support strap	14	Thutmose IV	-	-	97802	46109	3368	-
support strap	81	Tano	-	BI-001	88962	-	14530	-
support strap	82	Tano	-	BI-006	88962	-	14530	
support strap	83	Tano	-	BI-013	88962	-	14530	-
support strap	84	Tano	-	BI-026	88962	-	14530	-
support strap	85	Tano	-	BI-003	88962	-	14530	-
support strap	86	Tano	-	BI-004	88962	-	14530	-
support strap	87	Tano	-	BI-011	88962	-	14530	-
unidentified	10	Amenhotep II	-	-	-	24152	2503A	-
unidentified	10	Amenhotep II	-	-	-	24152	2503B	-
unidentified	10	Amenhotep II	-	-	-	24152	2503C	-
unidentified	11	Amenhotep II	-	-	32435	24149	2506F	-
unidentified	15	Thutmose IV	-	-	-	-	3385	21 3 21 10
unidentified	16	Thutmose IV	-	-	-	46108	3386	-
unidentified	18	Thutmose IV	-	-	97827	-	3394	21 3 21 7
unidentified	19	Thutmose IV	-	-	-	46110	3375	-
unidentified	20	Thutmose IV	-	-	97809	46111	3389	-
unidentified	21	Thutmose IV	-	-	97826	-	3393	21 3 21 8
unidentified	28	Amenhotep III	24.8.D	-	-	-	-	-
unidentified	29	Amenhotep III	24.8.A-C	-	-	-	-	-
unidentified	30	Amenhotep III	24.8.E	-	-	-	-	-
unidentified	32	Amenhotep III	24.8.G	-	-	-	-	-
unidentified	33	Amenhotep III	24.8.H	-	-	-	-	-
unidentified	34	Amenhotep III	24.8.I	-	-	-	-	-
unidentified	35	Amenhotep III	24.8.J	-	-	-	-	-
unidentified	35	Amenhotep III	24.8.J	-	-	-	-	-
unidentified	35	Amenhotep III	24.8.L	-	-	-	-	-
unidentified	36	Amenhotep III	24.8.M	-	-	-	-	-
unidentified	37	Amenhotep III	24.8.O	-	-	-	-	-
unidentified	38	Amenhotep III	24.8.P	-	-	-	-	-
unidentified	39	Amenhotep III	24.8.Q	-	-	-	-	-
unidentified	39	Amenhotep III	24.8.R	-	-	-	-	-
unidentified	40	Amenhotep III	24.8.S	-	-	-	-	-
unidentified	41	Amenhotep III	24.8.T	-	-	-	-	-
unidentified	42	Amenhotep III	-	-	-	-	4/10676A	6 3 25 4
unidentified	42	Amenhotep III	-	-	-	-	4/10676B	7 3 25 4
unidentified	120	Tano	-	L1 #024	88962	-	14530	-
unidentified	121	Tano	-	L1 #009	88962	-	14530	-
unidentified	122	Tano	-	L1 #019	88962	-	14530	-
unidentified	123	Tano	-	L5 #001	88962	-	14530	-

Object Identification	Catalogue Number	Provenance	Museum Number (other than EM)	Specialist Number	Journal d'Entrée (JE)	Catalogue General	Special Registry	Temporary Number
unidentified	124	Tano	-	L5 #002	88962	-	14530	-
unidentified	125	Tano	-	L5 #004	88962	-	14530	-
unidentified	126	Tano	-	L5 #006	88962	-	14530	
unidentified	127	Tano	-	L5 #007	88962	-	14530	-
unidentified	128	Tano	-	L5 #011	88962	-	14530	-
unidentified	129	Tano	-	L5 #017	88962	-	14530	-
unidentified	130	Tano	-	L5 #020	88962	-	14530	-
unidentified	131	Tano	-	L5 #031	88962	-	14530	-
unidentified	132	Tano	-	L5 #022	88962	-	14530	-
unidentified	133	Tano	-	L5 #032	88962	-	14530	-
unidentified	134	Tano	-	#32	88962	-	14530	-
unidentified	135	Tano	-	L1 #017	88962	-	14530	-
unidentified	136	Tano	-	L1 #021	88962	-	14530	
unidentified	137	Tano	-	L2 #007	88962	-	14530	-
unidentified	138	Tano	-	L4 #004	88962	-	14530	-
unidentified	139	Tano	-	L4 #005	88962	-	14530	-
unidentified	140	Tano	-	L4 #008	88962	-	14530	-
unidentified	141	Tano	-	L4 #010	88962	-	14530	
unidentified	142	Tano	-	L4 #011	88962	-	14530	-
unidentified	143	Tano	-	L4 #012	88962	-	14530	
unidentified	144	Tano	-	L4 #015	88962	-	14530	
unidentified	145	Tano	-	L4 #016	88962	-	14530	-
unidentified	146	Tano	-	L4 #017	88962	-	14530	
unidentified	147	Tano	-	L4 #020	88962	-	14530	-
unidentified	148	Tano	-	L6 #009	88962	-	14530	-
unidentified	149	Tano	-	L6 #010	88962	-	14530	-
unidentified	150	Tano	-	L6 #014	88962	-	14530	-
unidentified	151	Tano	-	L6 #019	88962	-	14530	
unidentified	152	Tano	-	L6 #028	88962	-	14530	-
unidentified	153	Tano	-	L6 #030	88962	-	14530	
unidentified	154	Tano	-	BI-018	88962	-	14530	-
unidentified	155	Tano	-	BI-002	88962	-	14530	-
unidentified	156	Tano	-	BI-010	88962	-	14530	
unidentified	157	Tano	-	BI-015	88962	-	14530	-
unidentified	158	Tano	-	BI-016	88962	-	14530	-
unidentified	159	Tano	-	BI-017	88962	-	14530	-
unidentified	160	Tano	-	BI-019	88962	-	14530	-
unidentified	161	Tano	-	BI-027	88962	-	14530	
unidentified	162	Tano	-	BI-031	88962	-	14530	-
unidentified	163	Tano	-	BI-032	88962	-	14530	-
unidentified	164	Tano	-	BI-036	88962	-	14530	-
unidentified	165	Tano	-	BI-037	88962	-	14530	-
unidentified	166	Tano	-	BI-040	88962	-	14530	

Object Identification	Catalogue Number	Provenance	Museum Number (other than EM)	Specialist Number	Journal d'Éntrée (JE)	Catalogue General	Special Registry	Temporary Number
unidentified	167	Tano	-	L1 #004	88962	-	14530	-
unidentified	167	Tano	-	L1 #006	88962	-	14530	-
unidentified	167	Tano	-	L1 #007	88962	-	14530	-
unidentified	167	Tano	-	L1 #013	88962	-	14530	-
unidentified	167	Tano	-	L2 #003	88962	-	14530	-
unidentified	167	Tano	-	L2 #004	88962	-	14530	-
unidentified	167	Tano	-	L2 #005	88962	-	14530	-
unidentified	167	Tano	-	L2 #006	88962	-	14530	-
unidentified	167	Tano	-	L4 #009	88962	-	14530	-
unidentified	167	Tano	-	L4 #007	88962	-	14530	-
unidentified	167	Tano	-	L4 #019	88962	-	14530	-
unidentified	167	Tano	-	L4 #021	88962	-	14530	-
unidentified	167	Tano	-	L4 #022	88962	-	14530	-
unidentified	167	Tano	-	L4 #023	88962	-	14530	-
unidentified	167	Tano	-	L4 #024	88962	-	14530	-
unidentified	167	Tano	-	L4 #025	88962	-	14530	-
unidentified	167	Tano	-	L4 #026	88962	-	14530	-
unidentified	167	Tano	-	L4 #027	88962	-	14530	-
unidentified	167	Tano	-	L4 #028	88962	-	14530	-
unidentified	167	Tano	-	L4 #029	88962	-	14530	-
unidentified	167	Tano	-	L4 #030	88962	-	14530	-
unidentified	167	Tano	-	L4 #031	88962	-	14530	-
unidentified	167	Tano	-	L4 #032	88962	-	14530	-
unidentified	167	Tano	-	L4 #033	88962	-	14530	-
unidentified	167	Tano	-	L4 #034	88962	-	14530	-
unidentified	167	Tano	-	L4 #035	88962	-	14530	-
unidentified	167	Tano	-	L4 #036	88962	-	14530	-
unidentified	167	Tano	-	L4 #037	88962	-	14530	-
unidentified	167	Tano	-	L4 #038	88962	-	14530	-
unidentified	167	Tano	-	L4 #039	88962	-	14530	-
unidentified	167	Tano	-	L4 #040	88962	-	14530	-
unidentified	167	Tano	-	L4 #041	88962	-	14530	-
unidentified	167	Tano	-	L4 #042	88962	-	14530	-
unidentified	167	Tano	-	L4 #043	88962	-	14530	-
unidentified	167	Tano	-	L4 #044	88962	-	14530	-
unidentified	167	Tano	-	L4 #045	88962	-	14530	-
unidentified	167	Tano	-	L4 #046	88962	-	14530	-
unidentified	167	Tano	-	L4 #047	88962	-	14530	-
unidentified	167	Tano	-	L4 #048	88962	-	14530	-
unidentified	167	Tano	-	L4 #049	88962	-	14530	-
unidentified	167	Tano	-	L4 #050	88962	-	14530	-
unidentified	167	Tano	-	L4 #051	88962	-	14530	-
unidentified	167	Tano	-	L4 #052	88962	-	14530	-

Object Identification	Catalogue Number	Provenance	Museum Number (other than EM)	Specialist Number	Journal d'Entrée (JE)	Catalogue General	Special Registry	Temporary Number
unidentified	167	Tano	-	L4 #053	88962	-	14530	-
unidentified	167	Tano	-	L4 #054	88962	-	14530	-
unidentified	167	Tano	-	L4 #055	88962	-	14530	-
unidentified	167	Tano	-	L4 #056	88962	-	14530	-
unidentified	167	Tano	-	L4 #057	88962	-	14530	-
unidentified	167	Tano	-	L4 #058	88962	-	14530	-
unidentified	167	Tano	-	L4 #059	88962	-	14530	-
unidentified	167	Tano	-	L4 #060	88962	-	14530	-
unidentified	167	Tano	-	L4 #061	88962	-	14530	-
unidentified	167	Tano	-	L4 #062	88962	-	14530	-
unidentified	167	Tano	-	L4 #063	88962	-	14530	-
unidentified	167	Tano	-	L4 #064	88962	-	14530	-
unidentified	167	Tano	-	L4 #065	88962	-	14530	-
unidentified	167	Tano	-	L4 #066	88962	-	14530	-
unidentified	167	Tano	-	L4 #067	88962	-	14530	-
unidentified	167	Tano	-	L4 #068	88962	-	14530	-
unidentified	167	Tano	-	L4 #069	88962	-	14530	-
unidentified	167	Tano	-	L4 #070	88962	-	14530	-
unidentified	167	Tano	-	L4 #071	88962	-	14530	-
unidentified	167	Tano	-	L4 #072	88962	-	14530	-
unidentified	167	Tano	-	L4 #073	88962	-	14530	-
unidentified	167	Tano	-	L4 #074	88962	-	14530	-
unidentified	167	Tano	-	L4 #075	88962	-	14530	-
unidentified	167	Tano	-	L4 #076	88962	-	14530	-
unidentified	167	Tano	-	L4 #077	88962	-	14530	-
unidentified	167	Tano	-	L4 #078	88962	-	14530	-
unidentified	167	Tano	-	L4 #079	88962	-	14530	-
unidentified	167	Tano	-	L4 #080	88962	-	14530	-
unidentified	167	Tano	-	L4 #081	88962	-	14530	-
unidentified	167	Tano	-	L4 #082	88962	-	14530	-
unidentified	167	Tano	-	L4 #083	88962	-	14530	-
unidentified	167	Tano	-	L4 #084	88962	-	14530	-
unidentified	167	Tano	-	L4 #085	88962	-	14530	-
unidentified	167	Tano	-	L4 #086	88962	-	14530	-
unidentified	167	Tano	-	L4 #087	88962	-	14530	-
unidentified	167	Tano	-	L4 #088	88962	-	14530	-
unidentified	167	Tano	-	L4 #089	88962	-	14530	-
unidentified	167	Tano	-	L5 #008	88963	-	14531	-
unidentified	167	Tano	-	L5 #010	88962	-	14530	-
unidentified	167	Tano	-	L5 #012	88962	-	14530	-
unidentified	167	Tano	-	L5 #013	88962	-	14530	-
unidentified	167	Tano	-	L5 #014	88962	-	14530	-
unidentified	167	Tano	-	L5 #016	88962	-	14530	-

Object Identification	Catalogue Number	Provenance	Museum Number (other than EM)	Specialist Number	Journal d'Éntree (JE)	Catalogue General	Special Registry	Temporary Number
unidentified	167	Tano	-	L5 #018	88962	-	14530	-
unidentified	167	Tano	-	L5 #019	88962	-	14530	-
unidentified	167	Tano	-	L5 #021	88962	-	14530	-
unidentified	167	Tano	-	L5 #023	88962	-	14530	-
unidentified	167	Tano	-	L5 #024	88962	-	14530	-
unidentified	167	Tano	-	L5 #025	88962	-	14530	-
unidentified	167	Tano	-	L5 #026	88962	-	14530	-
unidentified	167	Tano	-	L5 #027	88962	-	14530	-
unidentified	167	Tano	-	L5 #028	88962	-	14530	-
unidentified	167	Tano	-	L5 #029	88962	-	14530	-
unidentified	167	Tano	-	L5 #030	88962	-	14530	-
unidentified	167	Tano	-	L5 #033	88962	-	14530	-
unidentified	167	Tano	-	L5 #037	88962	-	14530	-
unidentified	167	Tano	-	L5 #038	88962	-	14530	-
unidentified	167	Tano	-	L5 #039	88962	-	14530	-
unidentified	167	Tano	-	L6 #005	88962	-	14530	-
unidentified	167	Tano	-	L6 #006	88962	-	14530	-
unidentified	167	Tano	-	L6 #008	88962	-	14530	-
unidentified	167	Tano	-	L6 #011	88962	-	14530	-
unidentified	167	Tano	-	L6 #012	88962	-	14530	-
unidentified	167	Tano	-	L6 #013	88962	-	14530	-
unidentified	167	Tano	-	L6 #015	88962	-	14530	-
unidentified	167	Tano	-	L6 #016	88962	-	14530	-
unidentified	167	Tano	-	L6 #018	88962	-	14530	-
unidentified	167	Tano	-	L6 #020	88962	-	14530	-
unidentified	167	Tano	-	L6 #021	88962	-	14530	-
unidentified	167	Tano	-	L6 #022	88962	-	14530	-
unidentified	167	Tano	-	L6 #023	88962	-	14530	-
unidentified	167	Tano	-	L6 #024	88962	-	14530	-
unidentified	167	Tano	-	L6 #026	88962	-	14530	-
unidentified	167	Tano	-	L6 #025	88962	-	14530	-
unidentified	167	Tano	-	L6 #029	88962	-	14530	-
upper of shoe	31	Amenhotep III	24.8.F	-	-	-	-	-
wrist guard	23	Thutmose IV	-	-	-	-	3387	21 3 21 4
wrist guard	24	Thutmose IV	-	-	-	46112	3374	-
wrist guard	25	Thutmose IV	-	-		46113	3390	
wrist guard(?)	17	Thutmose IV	-	-	97827	-	3388	21 3 21 2

APPENDIX II: CHARIOT LEATHER FROM AMARNA

FACSIMILE

DECORATED LEATHER
(CAT. NOS. 31-49)

Cat. No.	**31**
Specialist No.	ÅM AM 013b-d
Group	ÅM AM 013a-e
Year	1911/1912
Find No.	Uncertain: 1602?
Context	Uncertain: house P 49, 2?
Measurements	(b) l: 95.0 (folded); l: 180.0 (unfolded); w: 37.8 - 68.2; t: 4.5;
	(c) l: 36.0; w: 30.3; t: 3.5;
	(d) l: 19.2; w: 20.8; t: 3.7
Material	Leather
Colour	(b) Dark brown, black;
	(c) Brown, green, red
Remarks	(a), (e) See 'Straps, Belts, Cordage etc.' (Cat. No. 67). Although identified as 1602, this is highly unlikely as the description "*Riemengeflecht*" does not match the objects. ÅM AM 057 (Cat. No. 59) has this number as well and is indeed an axe lashing.

Description

(b) Folded fragment with a system of stitched decorative strips, comparable to ÅM AM 074 (Cat. No. 43). Although the fragment's condition is better than ÅM AM 074 (Cat. No. 43), still the visibility is largely obscured due to poor preservation. Moreover, in contrast to ÅM AM 074, there are no excavation photographs of this object. The 'top' of the object tapers and terminates in a rounded end. The perimeter has a set of decorative strips, possibly followed more inwards by a band of zigzag appliqué work and, finally, a set of two strips of leather (as the outermost set consisting of a wider lower and narrower upper strip). The object is made of two layers of leather. Parallels in the Metropolitan Museum of Arts, New York, dated to Amenhotep III, suggests that the stitching in the centre once fastened appliqué work of narrow strips of leather. Remnants of red colour suggest the use of green and red to decorate the leather.

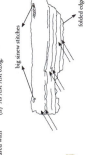

(c) Two pieces of leather secured by means of green and red decorative strips. The lower green strip (7 mm wide) lies close to the edge of the second layer and is secured at the edge of the edge. Small appliqué, green leather lilies are secured against the opposite edge with one stitch in the central leaf (slightly overlapping the green strip), and a stitch in the top of the side leaf. A narrow (1.2 mm wide) red strip is secured lengthwise down the centre of the green strip. All stitches are running stitches with sinew. The stitches on the back side are largely obscured by adhering dirt.

(d) Small fragment, which possibly consists of two strips stitched to a surface. Another layer is attached on the reverse side. It is uncertain whether the features are artificial or not.

ÅM AM 013b. Obverse and reverse. Cf. ÅM AM 074 (Cat. No. 43).

ÅM AM 013d. Obverse and reverse.

ÅM AM 013c. Obverse and reverse. Scale bar is 30 mm. Right: Line drawing. Stitches indicated in dashed line.

Detail. Note the small green lilies. Indication of scale: the width of the red strip is only 1.2 mm.

Cat. No.	**32**
Specialist No.	ÅM AM 026a-h
Year	1912/1913
Find No.	333
Context	House Q 47, 7
Measurements	(a) l: 54.2; w: 14.1; t: 2.6;
	(b) l: 47.8; w: 15.1; t: 2.6;
	(c) l: 37.4; w: 16.8; t: 3.1;
	(d) l: 67.7; w: 16.4; t: 2.9;
	(e) 32.4 x 31.9;
	(f) l: 45.9 (curved); w: 15.4; t: 2.8;
	(g) l: 21.3; w: 16.2; t: 3.1;
	(h) l: 24.5; w: 16.2; t: 3.4
Material	Leather
Colour	Light brown, red on one side, dark brown and black on the other, green

Description

General: Layers of coloured leather arranged alternatively green and red, although often the colour cannot be distinguished throughout anymore (for example, the lowest two narrow 'red' strips in ÅM AM 026a is referred to as 'faded red' but may not have been red at all but light brown [= original colour of the leather?]). The layers are secured with small sinew threads in running stitch on a very thin foundation. The threads are placed in such a way that they are obscured by the next layer, but sometimes the overlap is too short to cover the stitches.

(a) Seven layers of coloured leather. Note that the green colour flakes; this contrasts with the red colour, which seems to have been 'absorbed' by the leather.

(b) Seven layers of alternating strips of green and red leather.

(c) Seven layers of alternating layers of green and red leather. Here, the layers are secured at the edges, showing the stitches rather than being obscured by a partly overlapping next layer.

(d) Seven layers of differently coloured leather. Stitches are visible.

(e) Irregularly-shaped, badly 'melted' blackened piece without visible features.

(f) Seven layers (note that the distinction between the first and second layer is not visible) in a crescent shape.

(g) Small fragment of seven layers. Clearly visible sinew stitches.

(h) As ÅM AM 026g.

Top left: ÅM AM 026a. Obverse and reverse. Bottom left: Detail. The decorated surface showing the green, flaking colour. Note the sinew stitch. Scale bar is approximately 5 mm. Top right: Line drawing showing the sets of layers (dashed arrows). Bottom right: Construction drawing. Not to scale.

APPENDIX | 543

ÄM AM 026b. Obverse and reverse.

Details of obverse, showing the overlapping strips, and the reverse of the fragment, showing the foundation. Note the sinew stitches. Scale bars are approximately 5 mm.

ÄM AM 026c. Obverse and reverse.

ÄM AM 026d. Obverse and reverse.

ÄM AM 026d. Details. Top and centre: Obverse. The overlapping layers obscure the stitches. Bottom: Reverse. Note the folded edge on the foundation. Scale bar is 30 mm.

ÄM AM 026e. Obverse and reverse.

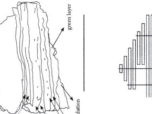

f   g   h

Left and middle: ÄM AM 026f e-g. Right: ÄM AM 026h. Obverse and reverse.

Cat. No.	33
Specialist No.	ÄM AM 030k, l
Group	ÄM AM 030a-l
Year	1911
Find No.	227
Context	House N 50, 8
Measurements	(k) l: 38.7; w: 25; t: 3.4; (l) l: 85.0; w: 13.0; t: 2.5; l: 60.3; w: 14.0; t: 4.9 (largest fragment)
Material	Leather
Colour	(k) Black, red, green, yellow brown; (l) Black, red
Remarks	(a), (b), (d) – (f), (i) See 'Sandals' (Cat. No. 13); (c), (g) See 'Unidentified' (Cat. No. 96); (h) See 'Weaponry' (Cat. No. 53); (j) See 'Straps, Belts, Cordage etc.' (Cat. No. 72). Several small, featureless scraps are not described/illustrated.

Description

(k) Nearly square fragment of layers of coloured leather. One set of strips, the bottom one slightly wider and thus protruding from the top one, is overlapped by the next set of overlapping strips. This set, however, is much wider than the first set. The top one has a narrow set of strips placed close to one edge of the top strip. These two sets of strips are secured with sinew running stitches lengthwise down the centre of the topmost, narrowest strip. The lower set, however, is also secured with running stitches through them at the first edge. The strips are stitched on a green layer of leather, which, in its turn, is attached to a foundation.

ÄM AM 030k. Obverse and reverse. Right: Line drawing (top) showing the sets of overlapping layers in stair-step fashion (dashed arrows); the dotted arrow marks the layers that are stitched entirely onto the previous layer). Scale bar is 25 mm.

Left: Detail. Clearly visible are the overlapping leather strips. Note the clearly visible running stitches. See overview for indication of scale. Right: Construction drawing. Not to scale.

(l) Three fragments of badly preserved decorated leather. One fragment is broken in two; the other is concreted to a rawhide strip (not illustrated). The fragments are too badly preserved to be sure what construction it is, but on one side there are five rows of tiny running stitches visible which run lengthwise. The middle part of this side has a red colour.

Left: ÄM AM 030l. Obverse and reverse. Note the packing paper adhering to the obverse. Right: Detail. Foundation, showing the stitching. Scale bar is approximately 30 mm.

Cat. No.	34
Specialist No.	ÄM AM 031a, b, e-g
Group	ÄM AM 031a-g
Year	1911
Find No.	227
Context	House N 50, 8
Measurements	(a) l: 107.6; w: 40.5 – 49.0; t: 5; (b) l: 75.0; w: 67.0; t: 20.0; (e) l: 18.6; w: 18.7; t: 3.1; (f) l: 135.0; w total: 71.0, topmost strip: 29.0; (g) l: 34.2; w: 23.2; t: 16.5
Material	Leather
Colour	(a) Yellow brown, brown, dark brown; (b) Black, red; (e) Black; (f) Yellow brown, black
Remarks	(c), (d) See 'Unidentified' (Cat. No. 97). Several featureless scraps and few pieces of rawhide strips not described/illustrated.

Description

(a) Rectangular fragment with one rounded end. At this rounded end, slightly off centre, is a large hole, which is original. Note the cut marks on one corner as well as at the rounded end itself. One layer of light brown leather is folded and stitched on top of one surface of which at least two thin layers of (now) dark brown leather are stitched. The two thicker layers are secured with the decorative thin leather along the perimeter with three rows of tiny stitches and lengthwise down the centre with two rows. Note that the stitches in the centre do not extend all the way to the rounded end. All stitches are running stitches of sinew. Two small, thin separate fragments of light brown leather are detached from ÄM AM 031a and show rows of stitch holes.

(b) Small fragment of leather, as described with ÄM AM 031a, to which a small fragment of 'melted' sandal (area of the slit for the reception of the front strap) is 'glued' (arrow). Also 'glued' are remnants of thin red leather to which no function can be assigned.

(e) Small, almost square piece consisting of five layers that are stitched in overlap. This number of layers differs throughout the fragment, which is likely due to the incompleteness of the fragment. No colours can be identified. Stitched onto a foundation with running stitches of sinew.

(f) Two rectangular fragments concreted together. The topmost one is of its original width and runs diagonally over the lower one; the lower one, however, is only part of the original width. Both

fragments show three lines of running stitches on the edge and lengthwise down the centre. In this way, they are comparable to ÄM AM 031a. However, there is no indication of the thin layer covering it (probably because it is lost). The top fragment has two lines of tiny running stitches on the edges. Concreted to the two is a black, highly 'melted' piece of leather, the rectangular extension of which has folded edges.

(g) Two edges(?) secured on either side with leather(?) thong whip stitches. No further details visible due to the bad state of preservation. Note the packing paper still adhering to the fragment.

Seven pieces and few small scraps of one and the same object, which is decoratively made with various overlapping layers of, according to the find card, coloured leather. Because the fragments are the only pieces with this type of decoration, it is certain that they are the remnants of the objects seen in the excavation photographs. However, it cannot be ascertained with certainty exactly which part of the object the seven fragments belong to and hence a general description is presented.

If seen with the circular decoration facing upwards, the decoration starts with strips of leather of which the lower part is cut into circular shapes, but still attached to the strip itself. Some fragments show that the closed edge is covered with a set of strips (comparable to the next rows with the circular decoration, see below). However, none of them are completely enough preserved to be sure about the nature of this cover, but note the paired stitch holes. It is certain that the stitching was done through the covered part. This strip is one of a set.

The top strip with the circular openwork motif is set back from the bottom one. It was probably of a different colour, as it shows in the open central part of the circles. Immediately below the circles, but well before the end of the second layer, is a narrow strip, which is used to stitch the layers. This set overlaps the next set, of which the top one is set back from the bottom one (in stair-step fashion). This set, in its turn, overlaps a same set of strips, which overlaps a band with circular openwork decoration, the composition of which is comparable to the previously-described one. Again two sets of strips follow, one overlapping the other. Finally, there is a strip with circular openwork decoration, which is with certainty the last one, as it lacks the narrow strip to stitch it to the foundation. Instead, the leather is folded around the edge.

ÄM AM 032e are small pieces concreted together. These lack the circular openwork decoration, but the composition of the overlapping sets of strips as well as the nature of preservation suggests they belong to the same objects.

Cat. No. 35

Below: ÄM AM 031a. Obverse and reverse. See the excavation photograph of the object shortly after recovery (illustrated with ÄM AM 075, Cat. No. 44). Stitching in the drawing is indicated in dashed lines.

ÄM AM 031e. Obverse and reverse. Right: ÄM AM 031g. Obverse and reverse. Note adhering packing paper, hindering visibility. Scale bars are 30 mm.

ÄM AM 031f. Obverse and reverse. Possibly, this fragment forms, together with ÄM AM 031a, a comparable object as seen in the excavation photograph (illustrated with ÄM AM 075, Cat. No. 44). Other fragments with specialist number ÄM AM 031 might originate from this object too.

Specialist No.	ÄM AM 032a–g
Year	1911
Find No.	336
Context	House N 50, 13
Measurements	(a) w: 51.3; h: 29.7; t: not measured, see remarks;
	(b) w: 39.9; h: 35.3; t: 3.6;
	(c) w: 41.0; h: 29.1; t: 3.0;
	(d) w: 45.7; h: 30.7; t: 3.8;
	(e) w: 42.3; h: 21.1; t: 3.9;
	(f) w: 41.8; h: 21.5; t: 3.7;
	(g) w: 25.3; h: 34.1; t: 3.2
Material	Leather
Colour	Black
Remarks	The thickness of ÄM AM 032a has not been measured due to its fragile condition.

ÄM AM 031b. Obverse and reverse.

ÄM AM 032. Excavation photograph shortly after recovery. Courtesy of the Ägyptisches Museum und Papyrussammlung, Berlin.

APPENDIX | 545

the top of the object (assuming it was directed with the tapering point downwards) and has three original edges preserved. The outer band of this edge consists of a set of two overlapping strips, the top one being set back from the bottom one in stair-step fashion. Next is a band of decorative zigzag appliqué work, but it is not certain if this band overlaps the previous set or vice versa. The appliqué work only occurs at the straight top edge of the fragment: one (or both?) of the corners of which are overlapped by the side edges. Following onto the zigzag appliqué decoration is a set of overlapping strips (as usual the top one set back from the bottom one), which overlaps the lower edge of the band with decoration. The lower edge of this set of strips, in its turn, is overlapped with another set of strips. A single strip obscures the lower edge of this set, which is the last component of the top edge of the object.

Top left: ÄM AM 032e. Obverse and reverse of accumulation of fragments. Top right and left: ÄM AM 032f & g respectively. Obverse and reverse.

Cat. No.	36
Specialist No.	ÄM AM 034
Year	?
Find No.	?
Context	House N 50, 1
Measurements	126.0 x 131.7 and 88.0 x 77.5; w band with edge complete: 16.0; w band with zigzag appliqué work: approximately 4
Material	Leather
Colour	Black
Remarks	Still attached to paper and cotton wool.

Description

Extremely badly preserved piece. As with all other decorative leatherwork, we can safely assume the use of different colours, which unfortunately cannot be identified anymore. The larger of the two (included in the number are also several smaller fragments) is

ÄM AM 034. Decorated surface of the badly 'melted' object.

ÄM AM 032a-d. Obverse and reverse.

Top right: Line drawing, showing the sets of overlapping layers in stair-step fashion (dashed arrows), and the construction drawing (left). Not to scale.

Top left: ÄM AM 034. Excavation photograph shortly after recovery. Courtesy of the Ägyptisches Museum und Papyrussammlung, Berlin. Top right: Line drawing, showing the sets of overlapping layers in stair-step fashion (dashed arrows), and the construction drawing (bottom). Not to scale.

The side edges are made, seen from the edge inwards, of two sets of overlapping strips, which start slightly inwards from the edge of the object proper. There are big, leather thong whip stitches at the side edges, the function of which is unclear. Possibly, they were used to attach the object to a foundation, which might be the second leather layer visible at the centre of the object. Note that there is a series of slits (about 8.5 mm long) close to the side edge, parallel to the edge with the appliqué zigzag decoration (but also one in the smaller fragment). Judging by the malformation of the slits, a rather thick item was pulled through (possibly a thick leather/rawhide strap?). As seen in other, comparable fragments, there is a raised line running lengthwise down the centre, which is most prominent at the top of the object.

Cat. No.	37
Specialist No.	ÄM AM 035
Year	?
Find No.	?
Context	House N 50, 1
Measurements	203.0 x 70.0 – 140.0, w edge complete: 18.5; w band with slits: approximately 5
Material	Leather
Colour	Black
Remarks	From "Buchkasten A." Still attached to paper and cotton wool.

Description

Extremely badly preserved piece, which makes a detailed analysis impossible. It is clear that the edge of the object consists of layers of (undoubtedly once coloured) leather. Assuming the tapering end should face downwards, the top edge starts most likely with a set of overlapping strips, which are now lost. It is followed by a band that consists of vertical 'bars,' which is bordered on both long edges by a narrow leather strip through which the stitching (running stitches) is done. This band is also the first horizontal decoration that can be recognised in the excavation photographs. The lower one obscures the long edge of a set of overlapping strips (as usual, the top one being set back from the bottom one in stair-step fashion),

which, in their turn, overlap another and final set of strips. The corners of this top edge are overlapped by the side edges. The convex curving side edges are made in exactly the same way as the top edge. Small damaged parts, however, show that the 'band of bars'

is an openwork strip of leather. The sides seem to consist, from inside out, of two sets of two strips, one isolated strip bordering the openwork strip (comparable to the top one) and possibly a comparable layout at the other side of this openwork strip.

Left: ÄM AM 035. Line drawing, showing the sets of overlapping layers in stair-step fashion (dashed arrows). Below: Construction drawing. Not to scale.

Left: ÄM AM 035. Excavation photograph shortly after recovery. Courtesy of the Ägyptisches Museum und Papyrussammlung, Berlin. Right: The decorated surface of the badly 'melted' object nowadays.

Cat. No.	38
Specialist No.	ÄM AM 053
Year	1911
Find No.	584
Context	House M 50, 11
Measurements	104.5 x 103.0 (folded) and 120.0 (total) x 5.3
Material	Rawhide and leather
Colour	Brown, beige, red

Description

Square-circular object, which consists of two rather thick (about 2 mm) layers of leather, both of which are coloured red on the outer surfaces. The dorsal surface has another layer of leather, dark in colour and much thinner. Along the edges, but not exactly following the perimeter, are stitched sets of strips of leather: the lower one is slightly wider than the top one (9.1 and 7.0 mm respectively, but the strips vary in width). The bottom one is red; the top one has a dark colour. Most likely the dark colour is decayed green. Diagonal from one 'corner' to the other, is stitched a comparable set of strips (width varies from 7.5 and 4.1 mm for the bottom and top strip respectively at one end to 9.8 and 6.8 mm at the other end). This set does not touch the edges of the perimeter set. All sets are secured on the edges of the top one through all layers, with running stitches of sinew. However, the diagonal one is at its widest end secured with stitches on both edges but towards the smallest end, the rows join in the middle. There are also several leather thong stitches; these are repairs of the original stitching. One end of this thong is finished with an overhand stopper knot. Note that the perimeter strips are a little too long and are either folded over the edge of the object or folded back.

ÄM AM 053. Obverse and reverse.

Centre and right: ÄM AM 053. Details. Stitches and details of the strip decoration at the obverse. Far right: Reverse. Detail of the stitches. Scale bars are 5 mm; scale bar far right and far right 30 mm.

ÄM AM 065c. Obverse and reverse of biggest fragment.

ÄM AM 068c. Obverse and reverse. Note the strip that is folded around the edges and secured with running stitches.

Cat. No.		
39	Specialist No.	ÄM AM 065c
	Group	ÄM AM 065a-c
	Year	1911/1912
	Find No.	1624
	Context	House O 49, 20
	Measurements	l: 31.6 and 71.0, w: 17.6 and 51.4; t: 4.5 and 4.1
	Material	Leather
	Colour	Black
	Remarks	(a), (b) See 'Sandals' (Cat. No. 25). Note that the list only mentions "2 *Sandalen*." The group includes several small, unnumbered scraps, some with empty stitch holes, which are not described/illustrated.

Description

Two black, 'melted' fragments. The biggest shows, albeit vaguely, a rectangular shape. The fragments are pieces of decorative leather; the various strips are partly visible on the bigger fragment. Both fragments have vegetable material concreted to them.

Cat. No.		
40	Specialist No.	ÄM AM 068c
	Group	ÄM AM 068a-g
	Year	1911
	Find No.	149?
	Context	House N 50, 5
	Measurements	93.8 x 100.0; t: 5.2 (all measurements as folded)
	Material	Leather
	Colour	Dark brown, red, green
	Remarks	(a), (b), (f), (g) See 'Sandals' (Cat. No. 27); (d), (e) See 'Unidentified' (Cat. No. 107). There is one entry in the list from this house, which mentions "*Sack*."

Description

Pieces of red leather, consisting of one layer. It is folded two, but possibly three times. One of the long edges is intact; the other, however, is incomplete. The intact edge shows a nearly 90-degree angle, in the corner of which is a hole that might have been used to attach the leather to a surface. Due to the folding it is not possible to get definite information about the opposite side, but if the third fold does exist, the leather tapers and terminates in a rounded end. The intact edges of the object show that a strip of leather was folded around it (extending about 3.5 mm, but with variations), thus sandwiching it. It is secured with running stitches of sinew. Note that many, but not all, stitch holes are in pairs. Looking at the corner, the edges have a row of stitches inwards of the edge binding (about 4 mm inwards) following the edges around the corner. Parallel to the one on the short edge, at right angles to the row of stitches on the long edge and with a distance of about 28 mm (thus close to the fold) are four more rows of stitches, separated from each other differently. They show a pattern characteristic for decorative sets of overlapping strips of leather. This suggestion seems to be confirmed by the relatively wide lines that are impressed into the surface: these might be the remnants of these decorative sets of strips, now lost.

A small strip with three running stitches can only be identified close to the corner(?) and its strip at right angles.

(b) Little can be said about this fragment; the surface is badly eroded and no details are visible.

(c) This fragment clearly shows four wide overlapping strips of leather (total w: 15.6; w top set: 8.0?); the two lower ones also show the remnants of a second strip. As usual in this type of leatherwork the top one is being set back from the bottom one in stair-step fashion (approximately 1 mm).

(d) Small fragment with a piece lying at right angle to a second fragment. Note that the two are still connected on one side. Several sets of strips are identified, including overlapping of the two. Shallow bumps indicate the running stitches.

(e) Nearly square fragment, showing two overlapping sets of leather strips (total w 11.2; w top set: 7.6). Dents and bumps indicate the stitching in the lower of the two sets.

(f) Badly preserved, showing only two overlapping leather strips. No signs of sets of decorative strips, but this is probably due to its poor state of preservation.

The excavation photograph proved again extremely useful. The straight edge, which is assumed to be the top of the object, consists of an openwork strip ('bars'), which is covered at both edges with a single

Cat. No.		
41	Specialist No.	ÄM AM 072a-f
	Year	1911
	Find No.	?
	Context	House N 51, 3
	Measurements	(a) 62.5 x 64.3;
		(b) 98.7 x 62.7;
		(c) 45.7 x 36.8;
		(d) 67.9 x 36.1;
		(e) 27.4 x 26.5;
		(f) 41.4 x 34.4
	Material	Leather
	Colour	Black
	Remarks	All fragments are badly deteriorated ('melted') and concreted to the packing paper and cotton wool; therefore, only one surface could be studied. Smaller fragments have not been numbered/discussed.

Description

(a) Most likely a corner fragment. It consists of several overlapping sets of leather strips. Two rows of horizontal openwork, vertical 'bar' decoration (cf. ÄM AM 035, Cat. No. 37) are visible too. Possibly, a row of openwork geometric figures can be seen close to the second band of openwork vertical 'bar' decoration but this is uncertain because these are not visible in the old photograph. In between, and above and below these bands, overlapping layers are visible but the exact composition cannot be identified.

strip. This strip also covers the first (i.e. topmost) set of partial overlapping strips in stair-step fashion. At least one more set follows with possibly another set, but this is uncertain. Lengthwise, the object is asymmetrical, in contrast to most other comparable objects: it has a convex left side edge, but a strong concave right edge, both of which have a comparable layout as the top edge. More towards the top, this latter edge is overrun by five sets of overlapping strips in the usual, stair-step fashion. This object too has a raised line, lengthwise down the centre. Little can be noted of the stitching, but we can assume it is stitched as seen with the other, comparable objects.

ÄM AM 072. Decorated surface of the badly 'melted' object.

Right: Excavation photograph shortly after recovery. Courtesy of the Ägyptisches Museum und Papyrussammlung, Berlin.

▶ *Left: Line drawing, showing the sets of overlapping layers in stair-step fashion (dashed arrows).*

▶ *Right: Construction drawing. Not to scale.*

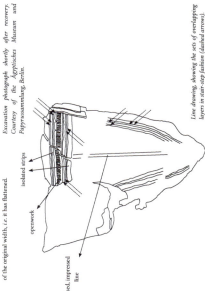

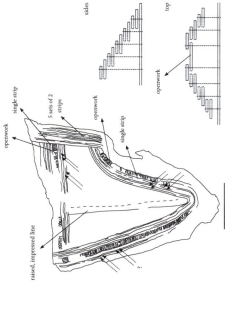

Cat. No.	42	
Specialist No.	ÄM AM 073a-f	
Year	1911	
Find No.	29?	
Context	House N 51, 3	
Measurements	(a) 57.4 x 42.7;	
	(b) 54.6 x 47.3;	
	(c) 30.1 x 29.3;	
	(d) 47.1 x 28.2;	
	(e): approximately 175.0; w: 143.0;	
	(f) 42.7 x 15.5. According to excavation records a total length of 18 cm.	
Material	Leather	
Colour	Black	
Remarks	If the identification is correct, then this object can only be the find no. 29, the entry of which reads: "Oberteil einer Bogenfutterals mit aufgenähten farbigen Mustern."	
Description		

Badly preserved object (severely 'melted' and concreted to the packing paper and cotton wool). Immediately after excavation, this object was largely intact and colourful; its photograph is used for the description. It tapers from a square edge to a pointed lower(?) part. On one corner at the straight edge is a large trapezoidal addition, which might be a repair. The structures in the photograph along the edge of this addition are tentatively identified as stitching; one stitch hole is identified on fragment ÄM AM 073d. The object in the Berlin collection consists of six fragments, of which ÄM AM 073a, b, c & d could be identified in the old photograph. The position of fragment ÄM AM 073f and an almost invisible piece, adhering to fragment ÄM AM 073e, could not be identified. The top of the object (i.e. the square edge) has an elaborate system of rows of decoration, which were most likely coloured in red and green originally. From top to bottom, there are two sets of two strips and, finally, a single strip (total width is 8.2 mm). The second set partly overlaps the first set of strips. A set in itself also consists of two overlapping strips in such a way that the top one is being set back from the bottom one in stair-step fashion. The second set is overlapped on its lower edge by a strip, which on its other side overlaps a band of vertical, openwork vertical 'bars' (about 5.8 mm high). Below this band is again a set of strips, which overlaps it. Here, an isolated strip covering the lower edge of the openworked strip lack, which seems accidental, judging the fact that it is there at the other edge (as well as in all other comparable objects). The second set overlaps the first and finally, a strip overlaps the second set on its lower edge (total width is 9.2 mm). This means that, rather than working symmetrically, the sets are attached in the same direction, which probably is accidental too. Moreover, the single strip, covering the second set and the top edge of the band of 'bars', is secured with one row of running stitches in the top half; in the lower half, however, this strip is secured with two rows of running stitches.

ÄM AM 073. Decorated surface of the badly 'melted' object.

Inset: sketch, showing the identified parts.

Left: Construction drawings. Not to scale.

Rows of decoration also adorn the sides. On one spot, about halfway down, a piece of leather seems to have been folded over the edge (see construction drawing). On one side of this fragment, two layers of leather are visible, which suggests that the object may have consisted (partly) of more than one layer; likely two comparable fragments. The connection of this part to the sets of decorative strips is not clear: there are two sets, but the lowest one (i.e. the one closest to the centre) might be the edge of the folded strip. No measurements could be taken due to its poor condition. An impressed line runs lengthwise down the centre, which appears in relief on the visible surface. It is approximately 3 mm wide. Nowadays on this object this line does not appear in relief, but rather as two tiny raised lines on each side of the original width, i.e. it has flattened.

Excavation photograph shortly after recovery. Courtesy of the Ägyptisches Museum und Papyrussammlung, Berlin.

Line drawing, showing the sets of overlapping layers in stair-step fashion (dashed arrows).

Cat. No.	43	
Specialist No.	ÄM AM 074a-c	
Year	1911	
Find No.	31?	
Context	House N 51, 3	
Measurements	(a) 114.7 x 108.0;	
	(b) 110.9 x 74.7;	
	(c) 92.2 x 73.0.	
Remarks	Find number uncertain. The list mentions "2 Laschen von Wagenteilen(?) mit aufgenähten farbigen Ornamenten", which could be the fragments. The list mentions for house N 51, 3 the year 1911; the labels say 1910/1911.	

APPENDIX | 549

Additional: "*Aus Buchkasten A*". Furthermore, the objects are the same as photographed with ÄM AM 077 (Cat. No. 46), a decorated piece excavated from house N 50, 1. The fact that these were photographed together suggests that they were found together, or at least in close association. Because the context of AM 077 (Cat. No. 46) is certain and the description as given for ÄM AM 074 is not in the list, it is assumed that the context given for ÄM AM 074a-c too. The measurements are approximate.

Material Leather
Colour Black

Description

Three fragments of extremely poorly preserved, decorated leather. Note that ÄM AM 074b is a group of concreted fragments rather than one that is isolated from the original objects. Due to the condition, the shape could not be identified with certainty. Details were not visible either. This is made worse due to packing paper adhering to the surface (the visible surface is the back of the object). Fortunately, the objects can be identified in the excavation photographs and the description be completed with the aid of these images.

(a) Fragment ÄM AM 074a shows an edge of about 15 mm wide, suggested by two, possibly three rows of stitch holes on one side. An indication of such an edge is shown on the other side too, but the stitch holes are far less clear. A horizontal, rather wide strip (varying in width, but the left side is about 20 mm wide) lies across the object. The right end can barely be identified, but the left half of a big slit is still visible.

(b) Fragment ÄM AM 074b shows a small part of the decoration, but the width could not be established, let alone details.

(c) Fragments of decorated edges, showing several overlapping layers. The terminating strip (4.8 mm wide) is clearly visible, which overlaps the previous set of strips with one edge. The other long edge does not overlap and is itself not overlapped by other decoration either.

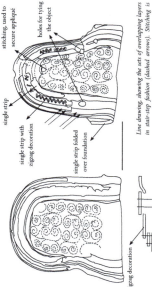

A horizontal row of shallow bumps suggests running stitches. There are two sets of strips of the usual layout: overlapping in stair-step fashion, leaving a narrow strip of the lower of the two strips visible. The total width is about 18 mm. Another fragment is part of a decorated edge. The terminating strip as well as two sets(?) of strips are tentatively identified.

The excavation photographs are more informative. The two objects are longer than they are wide. One end is rounded and towards the straight opposite end, which is bent towards the back of the object, it widens. The objects were meant to be tied to something, which is suggested by the straps on the back and the attachments of these at the front. Fragment ÄM AM 074b is the better preserved one. A thicker piece of leather serves as foundation. A strip of much thinner thickness is folded around the edge. The first part of the decorated edge might be a set of two strips but if so, the lower one protrudes only very slightly. The second set of strips, as usual with the top one being set back from the bottom one in stair-step fashion, is placed entirely on the previous and is thus less wide. A single strip with zigzag appliqué decoration partly overlaps this second set. An overlapping, thin single strip of leather follows. The other edge of this strip is covered with the centre fragment, which does not seem to overlap the previously mentioned single strip, but is rather placed with its edge against it or, perhaps, running underneath it. It seems to show decorative stitching, which would have been a unique feature in ancient Egyptian leatherwork, but better preserved examples of leatherwork from the tomb of Amenhotep III (housed in the Metropolitan Museum of Arts, New York and currently under study) shows that the stitching once held

appliqué decoration. Note that this stitching covers the entire surface except the edge, which is undecorated for a few millimetres. Several stitches can be identified, suggesting running stitches. Although the object itself does not give any information, it seems unlikely that these stitches would have been made of anything other than sinew. This stitching is, seemingly, not visible on the back and thus prefabricated. This contrasts with the stitches on the edge, securing the decorative strips, which are visible on the back of the object. The edge strip is secured with one row of running stitches, together with the first set of strips. The second set of strips is secured with at least one row of running stitches; perhaps, but most likely not, it is also included in the running stitches of the strip with the appliqué zigzag decoration. Besides these stitches, the strip is secured with stitches at the corner of the zigzag motif

(*cf.* text figure 11). The single strip following onto this one is secured with two rows of running stitches, neither of which go through other strips. The centre part is secured with the 'decorative' stitching, which are all running stitches. The strap on the back in ÄM AM 074b uses the original fastenings of leather thong and thus this narrow strap is original. In ÄM AM 074a, however, a wider one, terminating in a point with a slit, is stitched to the object, which therefore is regarded as a repair. From the photograph, the construction and decoration in ÄM AM 074a is the same, although it is not as clearly visible as in the other object. On the opposite side of the narrow, rounded end, a slit(?) is visible with the remnants of leather thong in it, the function of which is not clear. The exact attachment to the object is uncertain.

Line drawing, showing the sets of overlapping layers in stair-step fashion (dashed arrows). Stitching is indicated in dashed line.

Left: Construction drawing. Not to scale.

Cat. No.	44
Specialist No.	ÄM AM 075
Year	1911
Find No.	226
Context	House N 50, 8
Measurements	109.5 × 119.4; t. 2.8
Material	Leather
Colour	Black, red, green, greyish brown
Remarks	The object did not have a label. However, because it is photographed by the excavators together with ÄM AM 031a, it seems safe to assume a comparable context. The list mentions an "*ovaler Schild mit aufgenähten Streifen*," which perfectly suits the object. The fragment, which is attached to the object now, can be seen in the excavation photograph in its original

ÄM AM 074. Decorated surface of the badly 'melted' object.

▲ *Excavation photographs of the objects (obverse and reverse) shortly after recovery. Courtesy of the Ägyptisches Museum und Papyrussammlung, Berlin.*

Description

Tapering object, with slightly convex sides, which is elaborately decorated with stitched-on strips of leather of different colour originally, in describing the object, the tapering end is facing downwards. The applied decoration is secured with sinew, running stitches with a total width of 28.8 mm. It consists of two layers: the first is a foundation, seen in other decorated objects as well. The second layer is a coloured layer, which seems to be folded upwards at the edge, thus serving as the wider of the first set of strips (width 4.5 mm). This layer might be the same as the layer visible at the centre of the object (thus inside the edge decoration), even though on the edge its colour is red with green inside. The second set (width 4 mm) overlaps the first partly, leaving small strips visible. This second set is partly overlapped by a set which consists of a wider strip (width 6.3 mm) onto which is stitched a narrow single strip and a wide strip (width 4.8 mm) with zigzag appliqué work. This motif is secured on the corners (text figure 11). Note that, although it is stitched onto a separate strip, the zigzag decoration is stitched through all layers, which indicates that it was applied after the strip was added to the object rather than before. Strips are secured through the topmost one of the set; here, the row of stitches is situated just under the decoration. Following onto this, and overlapping the zigzag motif is a single strip (width 2 mm), which is secured together with the following set of strips (width 3.7 mm), the single strip slightly overlapping, and, again, followed by another set of strips. Finally, a more elaborate set of four strips follows (width 8.3 mm), as usual, overlapping the previous one in stair-step fashion. This last set consists of a wide strip onto which a narrower is placed. On the innermost edge are two much narrower strips (width 3.9 mm): the top one again narrower than the bottom one. In contrast to the previous sets, where the lower strip only protrudes from one of the edges of the top strip because the other edge is obscured by the next set of strips, here the top strips are placed lengthwise on the centre of the lower one, which therefore protrudes on both sides. The two narrower top strips are situated slightly inwards from the edge of the bottom two, thus creating a four-tier layer. The attachment, however, is uncertain.

nal position, i.e. as part of the long edges of the oval object. The separate piece in the excavation photograph does not belong to ÄM AM 075 (see also text figure 3).

ÄM AM 075. Obverse and reverse respectively.

Left: Construction drawing. Not to scale.

Details A-F: The elaborately decorated surface at various spots. G & H: The stitching on the reverse (foundation layer). Note the zigzag stitching. Scale bars are 10 mm.

Excavation photograph of the object, with at the right hand corner ÄM AM 075 (for other objects see ÄM AM 031a & j, Cat. No. 34; the object with the floral motif is currently housed in the Egyptian Museum, Cairo [10678]), the description of which will be published in the final analyses of Amarna's leatherwork) shortly after recovery. Courtesy of the Ägyptisches Museum und Papyrussammlung, Berlin.

APPENDIX | 551

Cat. No.	45
Specialist No.	ÄM AM 076a-ac
Year	1910-1911
Find No.	29-42
Context	House N 50, 1/N 51, 3
Measurements	(a) 49.0 x 28.2 x 5.0; (b) 41.3 x 22.7 x 4.1; (c) 74.7 x 25.4 x 3.6; (d) 97.0 x 23.2 x 4.8; (e) 23.0 x 30.2 x 4.0; (f) 68.6 x 50.2 - 78.6 x 47.0; (g) 16.5 x 56.4 x 4.1; (h) 31.6 x 49.9 x 2.9; (i) 15.2 x 38.5 x 3.8; (j) 21.0 x 33.4 x 4.0; (k) 31.0 x 71.8 x 4.6; (l) 50.4 x 31.0 x 4.1; (m) 27.9 x 43.9 x 3.2; (n) 46.4 x 39.9 x 3.9; (o) 22.6 x 78.5; t: 4.0; (p) 18.7 x 43.8 x 5.0; (r) 58.6 x 42.1 x 2.8; (r) 49.4 x 72.5 x 7.3; (s) 18.4 x 38.7 x 4.5; (t) 23.6 x 103.0 x 3.4; (u) 23.6 x 44.2 x 4.2; (v) 22.8 x 57.5 x 2.5; (w) 40.7 x 48.0 x 1.0; (x) 36.5 x 37.0 x 2.3; (y) 36.2 x 38.2 x 4.4; (z) 29.4 x 40.7 x 1.1; (aa) 21.2 x 39.0 x 2.6; (ab) 21.4 x 44.4 x 2.9; (ac) not measured
Material	Leather
Colour	Brown, green, red, black
Remarks	Two find cards accompanied this group of objects, suggesting two different house numbers. The point of one of the short edges of ÄM AM 076o was broken off after excavation and glued; it fits with ÄM AM 076j. See also text figure 11.

Description

(a) Corner piece, with stitched decoration of sets of strips clearly distinguishable on one end. The horizontal edge consists of two overlapping layers of four sets (consisting of two overlapping layers, as usual the top one being set back from the bottom one in stair-step fashion), each of which overlaps the next one (seen from outer to inner ones; total width: 15.5 mm). Stitched with sinew, running stitch. The vertical edge shows this type of decoration too, the exact composition of which cannot be identified (width 9.6 mm). It might be different in layout than the horizontal edge. On the outer edge of the decoration a small piece of decoration is still visible. This suggests that the decoration is placed over it: one wonders if the original edge was damaged and the decoration repaired. Note the bright green colour on the surface inside the two edges.

(b) Rectangular fragment, of which the strips of decorative leather are visible as lengthwise orientated bumps. Exact composition not possible to determine: there might be five sets of overlapping strips of leather, stitched on a foundation. One, however, might be a set of strips in which a narrow top strip runs lengthwise down the centre of a wider bottom one, the latter of which is therefore visible at both long edges of the top strip, as seen in other fragments. This set is secured without stair step overlap on top of the others.

(c) Complete width of decorated leather. On both long edges the foundation is sandwiched with a narrow strip of leather, which is, at least on the back side, included in the first row of stitches. The first set of strips (4.1 mm wide) overlaps the folded edge strip partly but is, on its other edge, partly overlapped by the second set of strips (width 3.7 mm). On the other edge of the object, the situation is the same: strip folded around the edge, followed by two overlapping sets of strips. This means that the overlap on both halves is directed towards the edges. In the middle is a seemingly single strip (width 6.2 mm), but it might be a set as described for ÅM AM 076b. Broken pieces of this centre strip, however, show that the strips did not meet edge to edge, but rather run over each other. Undoubtedly, the strips were coloured differently, but nothing remains of the colour anymore. All stitches are sinew running stitches.

(d) Like fragment ÅM AM 076c. Here, the topmost 'strip' clearly is a set of strips, the bottom one slightly wider than the top one. Note the remnant of green colour under the central strip.

(e) Roughly rectangular fragment with, on one of the short edges, four sets of strips. Inside this band of decoration are remnants of other decorative elements. Too little is preserved to give a detailed description, but circular forms are visible, which give the impression that this fragment might be comparable to ÅM AM 076h, q & x. Note that the surface upon which this decoration is stitched, is green.

ÅM AM 076d. Obverse and reverse.

Left: Line drawing, showing the sets of overlapping layers in stair-step fashion (dashed arrows). Right: Construction drawing. Not to scale.

ÅM AM 076e

(f) Larger, sturdy piece of leather onto which is stitched, on its edge, decoration consisting of a narrow strip folded around the edge of the foundation (cf. for example ÅM AM 076c & d), with a strip on top in the usual way. This is followed by a set of two overlapping strips. All are secured with sinew running stitches through the top layer. Note the diagonal, ill-defined red line across the surface. Close to the edge on the other side is a small piece of leather, which is secured with one leather stitch and is visible on the other side. From here downwards, with a length of about 22.5 mm, are several relatively large holes, which are stitch holes; remnants of the leather stitches are still in situ.

(g) Rectangular piece but slightly curving. The system and overall techniques are the same as the others. The width of the fragment seems incomplete, but starting from the convex edge, there are two overlapping sets of each two strips, followed by a wider strip (10.7 mm) and thicker strip with U-shaped decoration in high relief, i.e. the leather that surrounded the decoration is scraped away. Possibly, the strip with relief decoration is part of a set, but this cannot be identified with certainty. The relief decoration is the reason of the thickness of this strip. The fragment is broken off beneath this layer. The strip with the decoration is secured with sinew running stitches along its edges.

(h) Fragment, broken in the middle but glued together. Along the long edge of the relatively thick

ÅM AM 076f. Obverse and reverse.

Top left: ÅM AM 076g. Obverse and reverse. Top right: Line drawing, showing the sets of overlapping layers in stair-step fashion (dashed arrows). Left: Detail. Decoration in relief by scraping away the surrounding surface. Scale bar is 10 mm. Right: Construction drawing. Not to scale.

Far left: ÅM AM 076c. Obverse and reverse. Left: Line drawing, showing the sets of overlapping layers in stair-step fashion (dashed arrows).

Details: The edge of the obverse. Left: The single, big stitch at the reverse. Scale bars are 10 mm.

Top left: ÅM AM 076h. Obverse and reverse. Top right: Line drawing, showing the sets of overlapping layers in stair-step fashion (dashed arrows). Stitching in dashed lines. Left: Detail. Edge of the fragment, showing the layers and the stitching. Scale bar is 10 mm. Right: Construction drawing. Not to scale.

▼ ÅM AM 076c. Obverse and reverse. Bottom left: Line drawing, showing the sets of overlapping layers in stair-step fashion (dashed arrows). Bottom right: Construction drawing. Not to scale.

APPENDIX | 553

foundation is a set of leather strips, but the two are rather narrow. Overlapping this set, bringing the total width at 12.5 mm, is a set of three strips (total width of 10.1 mm), narrowing in width from bottom to top. It is secured with two rows of running stitches along the edges of the upper strip, and with stitches in the upper strips of the first set of strips. The strips vary in colour: the lower and upper ones are both green, whereas the middle one is red. On one end additional decoration is visible beneath the triple edge decoration. A set of strips runs from the edge band diagonally down the bottom of the fragment. It seems that the narrower, top strip is recessed a little from the bottom one at only one edge. It is secured along both edges of the narrow upper strip. In the corner below this diagonal strip are remnants of circular appliqué work, which also seem to consist of two layers. The semi-circle (the other half is missing) is secured with a row of tiny running stitches of sinew.

(j) Rectangular, incomplete fragment, missing part of its width. The remaining intact edge shows a foundation, which is sandwiched by two sets of leather. This is followed by two sets of overlapping leather strips. The third set has (almost) complete edges, showing that this was a centre strip and not overlapped. It thus resembles other fragments, such as ÄM AM 076c & d. The stitching as usual goes through the top layers: the folded strip is included in the stitching of the first set whereas with the centre set, rows of stitches are situated on both edges of the upper strip.

(k) Broken but glued fragment, consisting of a foundation, on which several layers are stitched: the first element seems to be a remnant of, probably, a set of strips: on the back, it is clear that this element is not the foundation. Following onto this is a set of strips (total width 3.8 mm) overlapped by a wider strip (about the same width). This, in its turn, is overlapped with a wider strip (8.5 mm wide), which is decorated, in high relief, with geometrical figures (running spirals). Possibly, the top edge of this strip has been left out as well when scraping away the leather. On its other edge it is overlapped with a set of strips (2.9 mm), which is in turn overlapped on the other side with a second set (4.1 mm; see also the description of fragment ÄM AM 076m). This second set, finally, is overlapped with a strip (6.2 mm wide) upon which a narrow strip of leather (width smaller than 1 mm) is stitched in zigzag, with stitches on the corners. This strip seems to have two narrow strips along both edges, but this could not be clearly identified: it might be in high relief, due to scraping away the surface on which the appliqué is applied. It can be assumed that the sets are secured as always through the upper strip. Stitches, however, have not been observed, except for the ones holding the zigzag appliqué decoration in place (cf. text figure 11).

(l) Roughly triangular piece, but broken in two. Two sets of strips are stitched onto the surface, partly overlapping each other. In contrast to most examples, where the overlap faces the edge, here the overlap is done away from the edge. The wide strip of leather, which sandwiches the edge of the leather, now includes the edge of the second set too. As always, secured through the upper strip with running stitches (sinew?) but no stitches have been identified at the folded strip. Moreover, there seems to be an extra row of stitches going through the edge of the widest strip of the first set, overlapping the second set.

ÄM AM 076i. Obverse and reverse. Right: Line drawing, showing the sets of overlapping layers in stair-step fashion (dashed arrows).

ÄM AM 076j. Obverse and reverse. Right: Line drawing, showing the sets of overlapping layers in stair-step fashion (dashed arrows).

ÄM AM 076k. Obverse and reverse. Glued at the crack.

Left: Line drawing, showing the sets of overlapping layers in stair-step fashion. Right: Detail of obverse. Scale bar is 10 mm.

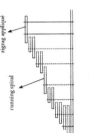

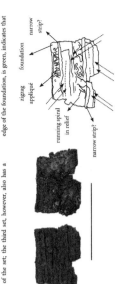

ÄM AM 076l. Obverse and reverse.

Left: Line drawing, showing the sets of overlapping layers in stair-step fashion (dashed arrows). Stitching in dashed lines. Right: Construction drawing. Not to scale.

(m) Rectangular fragment with the same decoration as fragment ÄM AM 076k, but in worse condition. However, the sinew stitches of the second row below the row with geometrical figures (i.e. the row overlapping the zigzag appliqué work) are better visible, showing that the stitches are very close to each other, and might have been made with double thread (straight stitching).

(n) Irregularly-shaped fragment with remnants of decorative strips. From the edge onwards, there are three (3.1, 3.5 and 7.0 mm wide). The third, however, has a green strip on top, which is narrower (3.8 versus 6.0 mm) and positioned at the lower edge, so that only the upper edge protrudes from it. All rows are secured with sinew running stitches through the upper strip of the set; the third set, however, also has a row of stitches lengthwise down the centre of the third, green strip. Two layers on top of each other, close to the edge, are overlapping almost entirely. The upper one is broken, at the break of which is a single stitch, which suggests a repair.

(o) Rectangular fragment, in layout like ÄM AM 076c & d. Clearly visible are the edges of the two sets, which meet beneath the central set; these do not touch but rather run over each other.

(p) Although this rectangular fragment is rather compacted, the layers are clearly visible and show that the central strip consists of one layer, which is secured at the edges with rows of running stitches of sinew. This layer is green. The fact that the strip, which is folded around the edge of the foundation, is green, indicates that

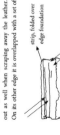  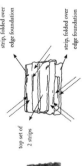

ÄM AM 076m. Obverse and reverse. Note the barely visible band with geometrical motifs (cf. ÄM AM 076k). Stitching in dashed lines.

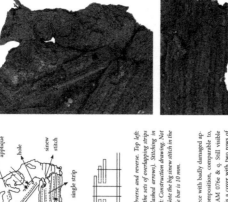

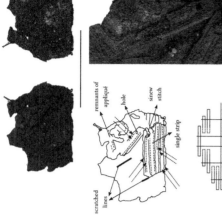

ÅM AM 076n. Obverse and reverse. Right: Line drawing, showing the sets of overlapping layers in stair-step fashion (dashed arrows). Stitching in dashed lines. Right: Construction drawing. Not to scale.

ÅM AM 076o. Obverse and reverse. Left: Line drawing, showing the sets of overlapping layers in stair-step fashion (dashed arrows). Stitching in dashed lines.

ÅM AM 076p. Obverse and reverse. Note the bright green colour of the foundation layer (reverse). Detail: Cross-section, showing the construction of the layers. Top right: Line drawing, showing the sets of overlapping layers in stair-step fashion (dashed arrows). Stitching in dashed lines. Right: Construction drawing. Not to scale.

in the sets, the lower one is green. Most likely the upper one is red, as this is the usual colour combination. Moreover, red might turn into very dark brown/black over time. In this fragment, the strip folded around the edge of the foundation acts as the lower strip of a set; in the comparable fragments, it did not act as lower layer but the next layer is a set of strips instead. The foundation has a green colour.

(q) Roughly rectangular piece with a appliqué decoration more inwards from the edge. The edge consists, from outside to inside, of two sets of strips, each one overlapping in stair-step fashion (total width 14.2 mm). This is finished with a single, green strip over the edge of the second strip, thus obscuring not only the edge, but also the joint between it and the set of strips preserved. At the other side of the central strip, there is only one set of strips coming from the other side. All are secured with sinew running stitches through their upper row: the central strip, however, is secured with a row of running stitches on either side. Inside the edge decoration, on a green foundation, is geometrical appliqué work, which is secured along both edges with running stitches of sinew. There might have been a core as in ÅM AM 076e. A diagonal strip (4 mm wide), seemingly borders this decoration; in it, close to the attachment of it with the edge decoration, is a relatively large stitch hole. Next to it, in the edge decoration, is a piece of sinew stitch sticking out; most likely it was inserted in the now-empty stitch hole in the diagonal strip. Possibly these were used to attach the leather to an object as the stitches are much bigger than those used to attach the decoration. At a roughly 35-degree angle to the diagonal strip are two parallel lines about 5.5 mm apart, scratched into the foundation.

(r) Large and thick, triangular piece. It seems to consist of three layers, but it is not certain if the top layer is an original feature of the leather object; it might be concreted on to it. Looking at the fragment with the intact short edge left, from top to bottom, two sets of strips follow onto each other, partly overlapping in such a way that the opening faces the edge. The sets as

well as the individual strips are rather close to each other, resulting in only slightly protruding edges. The second one is overlapped by a single, green strip, which on its other edge covers the upper edge of the row of openwork, vertical 'bar'-decoration (total width of these two sets and the single strip is about 5.2 mm; the 'bar'-decoration is about 3.1 mm wide). This vertical 'bar' decoration basically is a strip, which has been cut into the openwork pattern and inserted. The other edge is covered, again, with a single strip followed by a set of strips (total width about 4.8 mm), with the overlap facing the edge of the fragment. The lower edge covers a single strip (about 3.3 mm wide), which borders the next row with its lower edge. This row has a narrow leather thong (width 1 mm), which is stitched in zigzag with a stitch on the corners (cf. text figure 11). Against it and the top set overlapping the edge, are two sets of strips, partly overlapping each other in such a way that the opening faces the edge. A third and final set follows, consisting of three strips, the top one of which is a green strip that covers the edge of the lower strip (total width: 7.7 mm). The vertical edge is in bad condition. Possibly it consists of a set of strips, facing the horizontal decoration. More towards the outer side, dirt (and a third layer?) adheres to it, obscuring clear vision.

(s) Rectangular piece of incomplete width. In construction it is comparable to fragment ÅM AM 076g.

(t) Long rectangular fragment, but broken in two. Close to the current break is an older one, which has been repaired (post-excavation). In composition the same as e.g. fragment ÅM AM 076c & d.

(u) Rectangular fragment like ÅM AM 076c, d etc. The width is only partly complete.

(v) Badly preserved fragment, with much dirt adhering to the decorated surface. Although this seriously hindered identification, the band of zigzag appliqué work is clearly visible, which is made with a narrow strip of leather (cf. for example ÅM AM 076r).

(w) Featureless fragment, save for some parallel running folds and two stitch(?) holes.

Top: ÅM AM 076q. Obverse and reverse. Top left: Line drawing, showing the sets of overlapping strips in stair-step fashion (dashed arrows). Stitching in dashed lines. Bottom left: Construction drawing. Not to scale. Right: Details. Note the big sinew stitch in the second photograph. Scale bar is 10 mm.

(x) Roughly square piece with badly damaged appliqué work. In composition, comparable to, for example, ÅM AM 076e & q. Still visible on ÅM AM 076x is a cover with two rows of stitch holes, which are the remnants of a decoration of geometrical figures. This decoration is secured with rows of sinew running stitches along their edges. At the Y-junction of this decoration, short fragments of relatively thick fibre threads can be seen. They run under the appliqué decoration but are not used to attach the decoration to the surface. As the figures are stitched on their edges (as in for example ÅM AM 076q). However, the decorations bulge as a result of the thread underneath them, which

APPENDIX | 555

ÄM AM 076r. Obverse and reverse.

Left: Line drawing, showing the sets of overlapping strips in stair-step fashion (dashed arrows). Right: Construction drawing. Not to scale.

single strip / *openwork* / *openwork* / *appliqué* / *appliqué* / *set of 3(?) strips* / *stitches at corner zigzag motif*

Details. Note the complex decoration of the top of the fragment, consisting of vertical 'bars' and zigzag appliqué work. Scale bars are 10 mm.

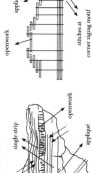

ÄM AM 076t. Obverse and reverse. The fragment is glued.

Below: ÄM AM 076t. Construction drawing. Not to scale.

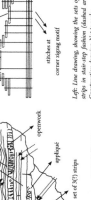

ÄM AM 076u. Obverse and reverse. The fragment equals, among others, ÄM AM 076t (see right for the construction drawing).

ÄM AM 076v. Obverse and reverse.

ÄM AM 076w. Obverse and reverse. Undecorated fragment.

suggests that, in order to let the decoration protrude from the surface proper ('relief'), the threads were included. It is uncertain if (and if so, how) these threads were secured, but likely they were just held in place by the stitching on each side of the leather strips.

(y) Largely incomplete, tapering fragment with appliqué work, which compares well with ÄM AM 076x. The intact edge has a small strip (3.7 mm wide), which is added just inwards of the fragment's edge proper. It is secured with a row of sinew running stitches along both edges. An empty area follows (about 5 mm; one wonders if something is missing as it seems hard to believe that this was the intended layout). What follows is a band of zigzag appliqué decoration (about 6.5 mm wide). The condition of the object does not allow definite identification, but it seems that there are two layers, the top one of which has

set of 2(?) strips, top one with U-motif in relief

the decoration stitched on (note that no stitches could be identified, again, due to the fragment's condition). Overlapping this band, the opening facing the edge, is a set(?) of two strips (about 4.3 mm wide). This set does not overlap; instead the upper one is somewhat smaller and positioned lengthwise down the centre on the lower one. A comparable set of strips is at an angle of about 45 degree, thus leaving a triangular central area.

(z) Like ÄM AM 076w, but without features.

(aa) Rectangular fragment in bad condition and with much dirt adhering. Comparable to ÄM AM 076c, d etc.

(ab) Badly preserved with plaster; comparable to ÄM AM 076c.

(ac) Pieces of wood with plaster; uncertain about the association with the leather pieces.

ÄM AM 076x. Obverse and reverse. Right: Construction drawing of the padded appliqué work. Not to scale.

ÄM AM 076y. Obverse and reverse.

ÄM AM 076aa. Obverse and reverse. Undecorated.

ÄM AM 076ab. Obverse and reverse. Badly preserved.

Cat. No.		
46		

Specialist No.	ÄM AM 077	
Year	1911	
Find No.	35	
Context	House N 50, 1	
Measurements	l: 120.0; w: 95.2 – 112.7; t: 1.5	
Material	Rawhide, black leather	
Colour	Red brown and black	

Description

One rounded end, the opposite end of which has broken off. The concave surface has a palmate motif, which is secured with widely-spaced running stitches of sinew along its perimeter. There are three rows of stitch holes along the perimeter of the object (respectively 5.2, 10.0 and 14.2 mm inwards from the edge), the stitch holes of which are grouped in pairs. Several intact sinew stitches clearly show that these were not used to attach the object to a surface: on the back side they are intact, and do not show that inclusion of any kind in them. The outer row, however, on the front, does show material included in the stitches, thus suggesting that it might have been attached to another surface in such a way

ÄM AM 076ac. Obverse and reverse of associated wood with plaster.

Excavation photograph of ÄM AM 077 (right; for the objects to the left see ÄM AM 074, Cat. No. 43) shortly after recovery. Courtesy of the Ägyptisches Museum und Papyrussammlung, Berlin.

ÄM AM 077. Left: Obverse. Top: Drawing of the obverse. Note the big stitches at the bottom. Drawing by M.H. Krick.

that the other material (i.e. to which the object was stitched) overlapped the edges on the surface with the decoration. Note the larger leather thong stitches at the bottom (arrow): these are broken on the back. The surface is red, the palmate motif was most likely green originally.

Cat. No.		
47		

Specialist No.	ÄM AM 078a-t	
Year	1911/1912	
Find No.	584?	
Context	House M 50, 11	
Measurements	(a) l: 51.8; w: 17.0 – 63.8;	
	(b) 39.1 x 46.4 x 3.0;	
	(c) l: 30.2; w: 38.4; t: 3.2;	
	(d) l: 37.7; w: 37.3; t: 4.1;	
	(e) l: 49.7; w: 28.8; t: 4.5;	
	(f) 30.1 x 29.3 x 4.1;	
	(g) 22.5 x 16.1 x 2.4;	
	(h) 25.0 x 20.2 x 3.1;	
	(i) 24.0 x 24.5 x 2.9;	
	(j) 26.2 x 19.5 x 1.6;	
	(k) l: 27.2; w: 14.9; t: 3.0;	
	(l) l: 27.7; w: 25.0; t: 4.6;	
	(m) l: 27.7; w: 12.2; t: 3.3;	
	(n) l: 27.4; w: 12.3; t: 3.9;	
	(o) 22.4 x 11.4 x 1.2;	
	(p) l: 24.7; w: 15.8; t: 4.2;	
	(r) 21.6 x 10.2 x 4.7;	
	(r) 17.0 x 11.3 x 3.8;	
	(s) l: 15.1; w: 9.4; t: 3.0;	
	(t) 13.4 x 8.0 x 2.4	
Material	Rawhide and leather	
Colour	Brown, red, green	
Remarks	According to the accompanying label, it "lag bei 11/12. 584." This object is described here with specialist number ÄM AM 053 (Cat. No. 38). Fragment ÄM AM 078a has been published by Van Driel-Murray (2000: 311-312). She refers to the object as coming from House N 50, 1, but this is unlikely. Several featureless scraps are not numbered/described. The decoration of the fragments equals the one seen in ÄM AM 079 (Cat. No. 48), but they do not originate from this, nearly intact, object. This suggests a second specimen comparable to ÄM AM 079.	

Description

(a) Roughly shaped like a quarter of a circle, but bent through the middle. It consists of a red foundation on which a lily-decoration is secured with running sinew stitching on both

ÄM AM 078a. Obverse and reverse. Lily motif cf. ÄM AM 079 (Cat. No. 48). Left: Line drawing showing the sets of overlapping layers in stair-step fashion (dashed arrows). Top: Construction drawing. Not to scale.

APPENDIX | 557

sides along the lily's perimeter (width varying from 5.7 to 6.3 mm). Some areas of the lily shape show a heightened central part. Most likely the leather of the figure covers a thread, as seen in, for example, fragment AM AM 076x. It seems that the rounded edge is sandwiched with a strip of leather but the visibility is poor and does not allow confident statements. However, ÄM AM 078d has such a construction. It is certain that there is a set of strips, partly overlapped with a second set, the opening of which faces the edge. The top strip of the second set runs a little further, leaving space for a narrow strip, which is placed on top in such a way that both edges of the upper strip of the set are visible.

(b) Diamond-shaped fragment. One surface shows remnants of the lily motif as seen in ÄM AM 078a. This fragment, however, is substantially thinner.

(c) Roughly rectangular fragment like AM AM 078a, but with only the remnants of the coiled extension of the lily motif. It is a piece of edge, suggested by the remnant of the edge decoration (cf. ÄM AM 078a).

(d) T-shaped fragment with intact edge and coil of the lily motif. This shows the same composition as described for ÄM AM 078a. Note that the fragment clearly shows the strip of leather, folded around the edge of the foundation layer. A small fragment of edge (length of 13 mm) adheres at right angle to the intact edge, including a 7 mm scrap of lily motif; it is not stitched to it and is interpreted as concreted rather than original.

(e) Triangular fragment of edge, including a remnant of the coils of two lily motifs. Adhering packing paper obscures visibility of the edge, but enough remains to be certain of the composition, which is the same as AM AM 078a.

(f) Small, rather damaged fragment; therefore, certainty about its composition is not possible. For certain there is a single strip, secured with running stitches lengthwise on both sides and overlapping another layer(?) on both sides, one of which might be a set of strips.

(g) Small quarter-of-a-circle-shaped fragment with remnants of appliqué decoration.

(h) Small, roughly rectangular fragment with remnants of appliqué decoration (cf. ÄM AM 078b).

(i) Irregularly-shaped fragment with remnants of appliqué decoration. Much dirt adhering to this fragment.

(j) Small irregularly-shaped fragment with scrap of appliqué decoration.

(k) Rectangular fragment of edge. The width is incomplete, which is why it is not certain if it belongs to the other described fragments. The upper strip is green.

(l) Irregularly-shaped fragment with edge, the width of which is intact. Remnants of three partly overlapping sets of strips are visible.

(m) Small, rectangular fragment which differs from the fragments described thus far, as it consists of a green edge (not certain if this is the original edge), and a band of green zigzag appliqué decoration (arrow), made of narrow leather thong. It is not certain if one overlaps the other or not. The other edge, however, overlaps a strip of leather (most likely there are a set. These two overlap at least one other layer (most likely a set too).

(n) Fragment of edge, the width of which is incomplete. Still remaining are two sets of partly overlapping strips as well as the edge, consisting of a strip that is folded around the foundation's edge. The colour is still visible: the upper strips are green, the lower strips of the sets are red and the folded strip is green too.

(o) Roughly triangular, incomplete fragment. Possibly a layer (and the remnants of another?) of an edge. Two rows of stitch holes are visible, suggesting running stitches.

(p) Big lump of 'melted' leather. Vaguely visible, however, are lengthwise structures, suggesting it is a part of an edge.

(q) Small rectangular piece of edge(?).

(r) Small rectangular piece of edge, showing remnants of overlapping layers.

(s) Small, roughly rectangular fragment, consisting of a set(?) of green on red(?) strips, overlapped partially by another set. This latter set, however, differs because the upper strip is much narrower (about 1.5 mm versus at least 6 mm for the upper strip of the lower set). The extremely fine sinew running stitches are largely intact.

(t) Scrap with one intact and several incomplete stitches (sinew, running stitch).

ÄM AM 078p-t. Obverse and reverse.

Cat. No.	
48	
Specialist No.	AM AM 079
Year	?
Find No.	Z 4420
Context	?
Measurements	Approximately 235 x 120
Material	Leather
Colour	Brown
Remarks	AM AM 079 is described on the basis of the excavation photograph, as at present the object is too fragile to study without consolidation first. Due to the discovery of the excavation photographs, the object could be identified as an Amarna find (Veldmeijer & Endenburg, 2007: 36)

Description

Tapering object with straight edge (assuming this is the top edge) and slightly convex side edges. The decorated edges equal the edges in ÄM AM 035 (Cat. No. 37), to which the reader is referred for a detailed description. Lengthwise down the centre, dividing the object into two compartments, is a relatively wide (about 20 mm) strip of leather. Clearly visible on both vertical edges of this strip is that there are at least two sets of partly overlapping strips, which overlap each other in the familiar, stair-step fashion. It seems that in the middle of these, with four sets altogether, is a central, single strip. This vertical strip runs under the edge decoration.

In the top half of both compartments are circular appliqué decorations where four lilies are arranged, coming together in the centre of the circle. The lily appliqué equals those described for ÄM AM 078a; although it is tempting to assume a comparable layout for the edge of the circle too, this cannot be identified in the photograph nor on the object in its present state. Attached(?) to it is a fragment with the most elaborately stitched edge thus far described, but still within the familiar designs and techniques. Note that it cannot be identified in the photograph whether the horizontal decoration indeed consists of partly overlapping sets, but there is no reason to assume otherwise: single overlapping strips have not been registered and the pattern is comparable to other finds. The stitches, however, can clearly be seen in the excavation photograph. From top to bottom there are three sets of strips, a band with zigzag appliqué decoration, several (two?) sets of strips, which are followed by a band with the vertical openwork 'bar'-decoration. As seen in ÄM AM 035, the attachment of this latter is finished with a narrow strip on both edges. Again several (exact number unknown) partly overlapping sets of strips follow as well as a band of zigzag appliqué decoration. Beneath this band, the decoration with sets of strips seems to continue. To the left is a vertical edge with decoration, running over the horizontal decoration just described, the layout of which is uncertain. Note the small triangular piece with vertical 'bar'-decoration at the top of the main object, the origin of which is uncertain.

measurements are taken from the photograph and are only a very rough indication of size.

Description
Large, elliptically-shaped object with decorated edges. The object is severely worn, which has caused a big hole in the centre, undecorated part. The decorated edges largely are lacking the decoration, so a description of the edge cannot be made. There is at least one strip with appliqué zigzag decoration. On the back of the object is a coarse textile fabric, but the type of fabric nor the type of fibre can be identified. Moreover, although it seems that the leather was stitched to the textile fabric by means of the relatively coarse, widely-spaced leather thong running stitches at the edges, certainty on the basis of the photograph is impossible. The vertical strip of leather, stitched over the wide decorated edge, might be a repair. Note the cut on the edge, which must have been done with a knife or other cutting device.

Top and right: Line drawing, showing the sets of overlapping layers in stair-step fashion (dashed arrows). Stitching is indicated in dashed lines. Left: Construction drawing of the edge, untill the 'bar'-decoration, only. Not to scale.

Specialist No.	ÄM AM not numbered
Year	?
Find No.	?
Context	?
Measurements	350 x 150
Material	Leather, textile
Colour	?

Remarks
This object has not been recognised among the material in the Berlin Museum. However, this does not mean that it is not there; it might have fallen apart into small fragments of which the origin cannot be determined with certainty. The

◀ *ÄM AM 079. Top: Decorated surface of the fragile object. Although fragile, fortunately this object did not suffer from 'melting' as most of the other decorated leather. Below: Excavation photograph of the object shortly after recovery. Courtesy of the Ägyptisches Museum und Papyrussammlung, Berlin.*

▲ *ÄM AM not numbered. Large piece of decorated, but badly worn leather, which has not been recognised among the material in the Berlin Museum. Courtesy of the Ägyptisches Museum und Papyrussammlung, Berlin.*

APPENDIX | 559

DECORATED LEATHER
(CAT. NOS. 276-278)

Cat. No. 276	
Collection	Petrie Museum of Egyptian Archaeology UCL
Inventory No.	UC 35939 (original find no. 30/744)
Specialist No.	UC 35939a-g
Year	Early expeditions?
Context	North City House U 25, 7
Measurements	(a) 54.7 x 133.2; (b) 51.5 x 115.3; w edge: approximately 22.7; (c) 60.4 x 114.1; w edge: approximately 21.3; (d) 49.3 x 55.5; w edge: approximately 22.5; (e) 28.8 x 54.1; w edge: approximately 25.5; (f) 21.1 x 65.0; w edge: approximately 24.8; (g) 16.7 x 47.3
Material	Leather
Colour	Black, dark reddish brown, green, red
Remarks	Originally distributed to Wellcome Historical Medical Museum (Frankfort & Pendlebury, 1933: 119), but in the 1960s moved to the Petrie Museum of Egyptian Archaeology UCL (Christopher Hilton and Stephen Quirke, personal communication September 2008). Several small unnumbered, featureless scraps (not described/illustrated). Note the melting process, resulting in the black, resinous appearance.

Description

The decoration, consisting of sets of partially overlapping strips in different colour, still shows most of the bright green colour; remarkably, most of the red colour has disappeared though patches can still be seen. From the edge onwards, the decoration consists of one strip that is folded over the edge, onto which follow two sets of overlapping strips, in stair-step fashion. The next set consists also of two overlapping layers, but the top one has an additional, red strip onto which a narrow strip of leather is stitched in zigzag. It cannot be excluded entirely that the lowest of the three strips is folded over the edge of the second, next to which is the narrowest, red strip onto which the appliqué work is attached. The zigzag appliqué is secured in the corners with single stitches (cf. text figure 11) that run at the back of the foundation from one corner of the decoration to the other. This set with appliqué work is overlapped with the fourth and last set of two strips. All stitching is done with sinew. Note the resinous condition of the top layer in (c).

Cat. No. 277	
Year	1933
Find No.	33/297
Context	Central City, The Police Barracks, House R 42, 10, from south rooms in the west section
Measurements	?
Material	Leather
Remarks	Pendlebury (1951: 136) mentions "Fragments of coloured leather collars, &c." No details given, but green and red colour visible. Distributed to the Manchester Museum and the Egyptian Museum, Cairo.

Cat. No. 278	
Year	1933
Find No.	33/304
Context	Central City, The Police Barracks, House R 42, 10, from the south rooms in the central court
Measurements	?
Material	Leather
Remarks	Pendlebury (1951: 136) mentions "Fragments of coloured leather

UC 35939a. Obverse and reverse. Top right and right: Details obverse. Much of the colour is still preserved. Note, however, the resinous patch, which is due to the 'melting' of the leather. Bottom and right: Details reverse. The zigzag appliqué work is secured in the corner (cf. text figure 11), the sinew of which runs at the back of the foundation (arrow). Scale bar details is 10 mm. Courtesy of the Petrie Museum of Egyptian Archaeology UCL.

UC 35939b. Obverse and reverse. Right and below right: Details of obverse. The edge with appliqué work, showing colour. Scale bar details is 10 mm. Courtesy of the Petrie Museum of Egyptian Archaeology UCL.

UC 35939c. Obverse and reverse. Courtesy of the Petrie Museum of Egyptian Archaeology UCL. Line drawing showing the sets of overlapping layers in stair-step fashion (dashed arrows). Stitching is indicated in dashed lines.

UC 35939c. Detail obverse. The edge with appliqué work, showing colour. Scale bar is 10 mm. Courtesy of the Petrie Museum of Egyptian Archaeology UCL.

UC 35939c. Detail reverse. The foundation, showing the stitching of the appliqué work. Note the fold around the edge with the first layer of the decoration. Scale bar is 10 mm. Courtesy of the Petrie Museum of Egyptian Archaeology UCL.

UC 35939d. Obverse and reverse. Courtesy of the Petrie Museum of Egyptian Archaeology UCL.

UC 35939f. Obverse and reverse. Courtesy of the Petrie Museum of Egyptian Archaeology UCL.

UC 35939g. Obverse and reverse. Courtesy of the Petrie Museum of Egyptian Archaeology UCL.

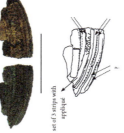

UC 35939e. Obverse and reverse. Courtesy of the Petrie Museum of Egyptian Archaeology UCL. Line drawing, showing the sets of overlapping layers in stair-step fashion (dashed arrows). Stitching is indicated in dashed lines. Left: Detail of the reverse. Several stitches are still complete. Scale bar is 10 mm. Courtesy of the Petrie Museum of Egyptian Archaeology UCL.

collars." Most likely this refers to the fragment in the photograph marked by the arrow. Indeed, there might be more fragments of coloured, decorated leather in the photograph, but these cannot be identified with certainty. Pendlebury, however, does not mention any of the other leather objects, most of which cannot be identified from the rather poor quality photograph. Distributed to the Manchester Museum and the Egyptian Museum, Cairo.

33/304. Only the coloured leather 'collars' are mentioned by Pendlebury (arrow). Unfortunately the quality of the photograph is too bad to describe most of the other fragments. Some comments, however, are made about the other numbered fragments. Courtesy of the Egypt Exploration Society.

APPENDIX | 561

APPENDIX III: WHAT'S IN A STITCH

FACSIMILE

Newsletter 34   September 2011

What's in a stitch?

by **André J. Veldmeijer**

Introduction

The study of leatherwork from ancient Egypt, and in particular the decorated leatherwork that is associated with chariotry, has shown that seemingly minor details are potentially of great importance for mapping technological development over time and possibly in space/location. Interpretation of the differences, however, is often less straightforward: should the use of different types of stitching (or of a different material for this stitching) be seen, for example, as the result of different traditions that evolved elsewhere? And if so, where is this 'elsewhere': foreigners that brought their tradition with them to Egypt? Or is it simply that the entire object was imported, rather than that craftsmen themselves came from abroad? Perhaps the differences are on a more regional scale, i.e. between various workshops. Another possibility is a learning process: things that break easily are being made in a different way or with different materials. Alternatively, the availability of certain materials changes, and thus alternatives are sought for by the leatherworker. In this work, I will present one such problem and discuss possible solutions. I hope, however, that a discussion arises from it that will shed more light on the questions at hand.

The Egyptian Museum Chariot Project (EMCP) is part of a bigger project on ancient Egyptian leatherwork (see www.leatherandshoes.nl for more information). The focus of the EMCP is on finds housed in the Egyptian Museum in Cairo, dating to the reigns of Thutmosis IV (Carter & Newberry, 1904), Amenhotep II (Daressy, 1902) & III (Littauer & Crouwel, 1985: 68, 87). Since they are of similar date, finds from Amarna (predominantly housed in the Ägyptisches Museum und Papyrussammlung, Berlin: Veldmeijer, 2010) are also included.

Stitching

The problem

By far the most common type of stitching in Pharaonic leatherwork is the so-called running stitch: a thread is inserted through the leather in a serpentine fashion (Fig.1a and b). Consequently, the stitch hole is used only once. This stitch is used constructionally and also to secure

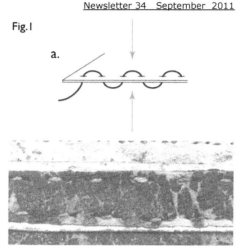

Fig.1
a.

b. Example of the stitching of an object from a chariot assemblage of Thutmosis IV.

decoration. Sinew, either slightly 'spun' or, more often in the chariot leather, 'spun-and-twisted' into a two-level string, is used rather than linen thread. Usually, but not exclusively, the stitching is very regular in stitch-length as well as inter-stitch spacing. This type of stitch results in opposite features one each side of the layer: where there is a stitch on the *recto*, there is a space on the *verso* and *vice versa* (arrows in Fig.1a).

Fig.2
a.

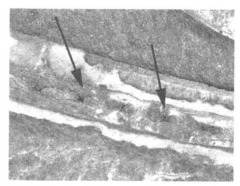

b. Detail of the stitching on an object from a chariot assemblage that is thought to have belonged to Amenhotep III.

Various fragments that the EMCP has studied, however, show different types of stitching. Whereas on the *verso* spaced stitching is still visible, on the *recto* the stitching seems continuous - the stitch hole is used twice (arrows in Fig.2b). This would not occur with ordinary running stitch, as Fig.2a demonstrates. A few fragments show this kind of stitching nearly everywhere, but most fragments have it only on one or two rows. No clear pattern has been observed thus far, although one thing stands out: if this stitching is used, it always includes several layers of leather that have been secured together. Thus far, it has been identified in the leatherwork from Thutmosis IV (ca. 1400-1390 BC) and Amenhotep III (ca. 1390-1352 BC).

Explanations

There are several possibilities that might explain these features. Fig.3 shows stitching that, theoretically, is executed diagonally through the leather in order to return through the same stitch hole after emerging on the *verso*. The stitch on the *verso* is shorter than on the *recto*, although the more slanting the stitching, the longer the stitches on the *verso* will be. This stitch might work well with thick leather, as there is enough space in its thickness to cross, but it is very unlikely it would have worked on

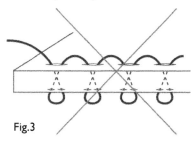

Fig.3

the thin leather where it is found. A comparable method of stitching is the so-called "closely-spaced running stitch" found at Amarna (Veldmeijer, 2010: 21), although in this case the stitching would be equally spaced on both sides of the leather.

However, as noted above, continuous stitching is only used where several layers needed to be secured. During stitching the layers are separate, which makes diagonal stitching easier (Fig.4) and suggests that even in thin leather this might be possible. Nevertheless, it is not the most convenient way of securing applied decoration.

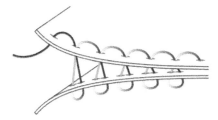

Fig.4

Another way of explaining this feature is that the stitch holes on the applied decoration might have been pre-pricked. The large slits could easily accommodate two stitches (Fig.5). However, stitch holes have not been pre-pricked in surfaces to which decoration was attached and one can see two stitch holes (as in running stitching proper). It seems strange that only the applied leather was pre-pricked and not the surface to which it was attached; at the moment I am not able to explain this way of working, if indeed the pre-pricked hypothesis is true.

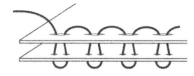

Fig.5

A better explanation is perhaps shown in Fig.6. It has been suggested that several elements of the decoration were pre-fabricated (Veldmeijer, 2010: 31). Suppose this was indeed the case,[1] then it would have been secured using running stitch. If, in the next stage, the assembly were attached to another object, again a running stitch might be used, but now applied in such a way that the inter-stitch space of the applied decoration was used to attach it to the object (gray line in figure 6). In this way, the stitch hole of the applied decoration is used twice (and might have been pre-pricked in order to better accommodate the stitching). The *verso* of the surface to which it was applied was not pre-pricked, as only one thread goes through it. The problem with this theory is that it cannot be verified without seeing the *verso* of the applied decoration, and this would mean destroying it. Hence it has not been done.

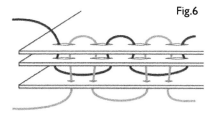

Fig.6

Conclusion

The painstaking, systematic mapping of even the smallest of details provides the archaeologist with much extra information that potentially provides strong indicators of manufacturing technology and its development. The lack of finds and/or research, both from Egypt and elsewhere, is a problem and does seriously hinder comparisons and therefore interpretation. But this may well be temporary, since scientific interest in leather is clearly increasing. The intention of this contribution to the Archaeological Leather Group Newsletter is to see if there is any experience with comparable problems as well as to show the potential of such research. Any suggestions, remarks or questions are therefore very welcome.

I thank Martin Moser and Salima Ikram for the inspiring discussions; Salima also checked the English. Erno Endenburg is thanked for turning working drawings into proper publishing format and Ibrahim el Gawaad is thanked for his wonderful collaboration. The Supreme Council of Antiquities as well as the Egyptian Museum Authorities are acknowledged for allowing the study of the material. I am grateful to the Metropolitan Museum of Art, New York for allowing me to publish Fig.2b; the Supreme Council of Antiquities is thanked for permission to publish Fig.1b. Both photographs are by the author.

Note

1. The isolated strips of decoration from the tomb of Amenhotep III might be such a pre-fabricated element for application onto another piece of leather. Note that this type of strip might also have been applied independently as decoration (i.e. without being attached to a larger piece of leather first), as seen on the chariot from Yuya and Tuiu.

Literature

Carter, H. & Newberry, P.E. (1904) *Catalogue Général des Antiquités Égyptiennes du Musée du Caire. The tomb of Thoutmôsis IV,* Westminster, Archibald Constable and Co.

Daressy, M.G. (1902) *Catalogue Général des Antiquités Égyptiennes du Musée du Caire. Fouilles de la Vallée des Rois,* Le Caire, Institut Francais d'archégologie orientale

Littauer, M.A. & Crouwel, J.H. (1985) *Chariots and Related Equipment from the Tomb of Tutankhamun,* Oxford, Griffith Institute (Tutankhamun's Tomb Series VIII)

Veldmeijer, A.J. (2010) *Amarna's Leatherwork. Part I. Preliminary Analysis and Catalogue,* Norg, Drukware.

Chariot conference

In 2012, a two-day conference on ancient Egyptian chariotry will be held at the Netherlands-Flemish Institute in Cairo (NVIC). The first announcement was made in August and exact dates in November will be announced later this year, together with detailed information on the objectives of the meeting.

The conference is a direct consequence of the Egyptian Museum Chariot Project, which is a detailed study of chariot leatherwork (see http://www.leatherandshoes.nl/ancient-egyptian-leatherwork-project-aelp/).

Key-note speaker: Prof. Dr. J.H. Crouwel (University of Amsterdam)

ABBREVIATIONS

AELP
Ancient Egyptian Leatherwork Project.

EM
Egyptian Museum, Cairo.

EMCP
Egyptian Museum Chariot Project.

GSL
Gardiner (1957: 438-548) Sign List of hieroglyphs.

KV
King's Valley, indicating tombs in the Vally of the Kings in Luxor. This abbreviation is followed by a number.

o (e.g. oEdinburgh)
'o', followed by a name, stands for 'Ostraca', pot sherds or stone chips that were used as writing material.

P. (e.g. P. Anastasi)
'P.' stands for 'Papyrus'.

T (e.g. T3)
'T' followed by a number stands for 'Tomb' (*e.g.* T3 is 'Tomb 3', the El Kab tomb of Paheri).

TT (e.g. TT 95)
TT, followed by a number, stands for 'Theban Tomb' (*e.g.* TT95 is 'Theban Tomb 95', the tomb of Mery). See for a complete list: http://www.ucl.ac.uk/museums-static/digitalegypt/thebes/tombs/thebantomblist.html.

WV
West Valley, indicating tombs in this part of the Valley of the Kings in Luxor. This abbreviation is followed by a number.

GLOSSARY

Alum tawing
Potash alum is a double salt of aluminium and potassium sulfate, occurring naturally, particularly in warm climates, as a weathering product of aluminous shales (Reed, 1972). When used in combination with water, salt, flour and maybe egg yolk it can be used to turn skin into leather. The aluminium salt can be washed out if the leather gets wet; hence the term 'tawing' rather than 'tanning' is used. The product of alum tawing is a soft white type of leather, which was commonly used in Medieval Europe for the production of high-quality gloves and bookbindings.

Appliqué
"A decoration or ornament, as in needlework, made by cutting pieces of one material [here: leather] and applying them to the surface of another [here: leather]" (www.thefreedictionary.com, visited 20 September 2017). In the present work, three types are distinguished: 'straight appliqué' or 'appliqué', simply consisting of cutting out pieces applied to an under surface; 'relief appliqué' which is the deliberate bulging or manipulating the appliqué as to create appliqué that is substantially higher than usual. In stuffed appliqué, material is inserted between the appliqué and the under surface to create high relief.

Axle (see figure below)
"A rod passing underneath the vehicle floor, with the wheels revolving on it, or it revolving with them" (Littauer & Crouwel, 1985: 5)

Back stitch
A stitch that is sewn backwards to the working direction. This can be in one line, resulting in an unbroken line of stitches, or diagonally.

sewing direction

Blinker (see figure below)
"An element attached to the cheekstrap [...] of the headstall [...] covering the horse's eyes and enabling him to see ahead but not to the side. In antiquity it probably also served to protect the eye in battle and/or prevent harnessed stallions from bickering with their team mates or with other stallions abreast of them" (Littauer & Crouwel, 1985: 5).

Body (of the chariot) (see figure below)
Floor and superstructure of the vehicle.

Bridle boss (see figure below)
The bridle is "a means of controlling the horse by the head; composed of headstall [...], with or without bit [...], and reins [...]" (Littauer & Crouwel, 1985: 5). The bridle boss is the element that secures the cheeckstraps to the headstall.

Butt seam or butted seam
Join made by placing the two edges together and sewing from the leather's surface through the thickness of the edges and through to the surface of the adjoining leather, often know as being sewn edge/flesh (split closing); the seam is invisible on the reverse side.

Central rod (see figure below)
Vertical thin wooden rod in the centre of the front view of the body. Not present in all chariots.

Cheekstrap (see figure below)
"The side straps of the headstall [...], attached to the cheekpieces [...] of the bit, and serving to hold them in place; in antiquity commonly branched to take the cheekpiece" (Littauer & Crouwel, 1985: 5).

Double running stitch
A running stitch is made by a single thread that follows a serpentine course in and out of the material. In the present work, the term 'double running stitch' is used if the interstitch space of the running stitch is used to apply the object with another running stitch. This should not be confused with the Holbein Stitch, where one thread makes up the first row of running stitch and comes back to fill the interstitch space. On the problems with interlocking running stitch (which is made with two threads simultaneously but in opposite direction) see Appendix II. With thanks to Lena Sadek.

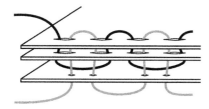

(Edge) binding
A strip of leather whip-stitched (or other types of stitching) to the edge of a piece of leather in order to finish it off neatly and reinforce the leather.

Girth (see figure below)
The strap that encircles the horse's thorax. It can act as backing element "that transmits backward movement (as opposed to the usual forward movement) of the draught animals to the vehicle" (Littauer & Crouwel, 1985: 5). This girth is attached either to both lower ends of the yoke saddles or to the lower end of their outer leg and to the pole in front of the yoke. With thanks to Joost Crouwel.

Headstall (see figure below)
"Part of the bridle [...], made of straps or rope and designed to hold a controlling bit or noseband in place. It comprises [among others] a crownpiece [...], crossing the crown of the head behind the ears [and] cheekstraps [...] running down from this to the noseband and/or bit" (Littauer & Crouwel, 1985: 6).

Housing (see figure below)
"A protective or decorative covering for the body of the horse" (Littauer & Crouwel, 1985: 6).

Interlocking running stitch (referred to in some work on ancient Egyptian leather as 'continuous running stitching)'. Two threads are used simultaneously but in opposite direction, resulting in an uninterrupted line of stitching (Grew & De Neergaard, 1988: 101).

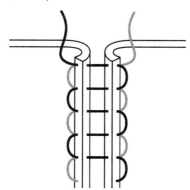

Knot
Terminology on knots follows Veldmeijer (2006).

Leathering
Leathering is a term first used by the leather chemist Covington (2009) to describe processes such as alum tawing and oil dressing/curing. Leathering processes produce a leather-like material with many properties similar to tanned leather. However, leathering does not significantly improve the thermal stability of raw skin (Ts) and may be reversed by washing out, unlike tanned leather.

Linch pin
"A toggle pin passing through the end of the axle to prevent the wheel from slipping off" (Littauer & Crouwel, 1985: 6).

Main casing (see figure below)
The main casing, *i.e.* the cover of the wooden frame of the body of the chariot, follows the lower part of the body, going upwards at the corners as well as the in the centre at the front. This can be narrow to a bit more substantial, but never covers the larger areas of the sides. The remaining area is covered sometimes with the siding fill, which usually has several apertures.

Nave (see figure below)
"The inner cylindrical element of a wheel, in which the inner ends of the spokes [...] are secured, and through which the axle [...] passes" (Littauer & Crouwel, 1985: 6).

Nave hoop (see figure below)
The covers "on the outer ends of the naves [which] would have given protection against wear caused by friction with the linch pins, and would have helped to prevent the nave from splitting" (Littauer & Crouwel, 1985: 76).

Neckstrap (see figure below)
"A strap passing around the neck and attached at either end to the lower ends of the yoke saddles or to the yoke itself. Its purpose is to hold the yoke in place" (Littauer & Crouwel, 1985: 6).

Oil tanning (after Covington, 2009)
Oil tanning involves the introduction of unsaturated fats such as fish oil to a dehaired and defleshed skin. By staking the treated skin, the action of friction and heat, causes oxidation to take place, fixing the oils to the collagen and making the hide imputrescible. Oil tanning, as opposed to oil dressing, cannot easily be removed from a processed skin by washing, and creates a soft and durable leather. However, oil tanning does not greatly improve the thermal stability (Ts) of skin.

Passepoil
Small strip of leather (usually) folded lengthwise and sewn in a seam that joins two pieces of leather. It reinforces the seam.

Pole (see figure below)
"In antiquity, the element that connected the vehicle to the yoke [...] of the draught animals" (Littauer & Crouwel, 1985: 6).

Running stitch
See 'Double running stitch'.

Sailor stitch
Stitch used to close cuts by going over and under the edge alternatively due to which the edges are, when the thread is pulled, drawn together tightly and the crack closed.

Sewing
See 'Stitching'.

Siding fill
See 'Main casing'.

Stamping/Impressing
In the present work, no distinction is made between stamping and impressing.

Stitch hole
The hole in the leather through which the thread passes. Often stitch holes are pre-pricked with an awl.

Stitching
In literature, difference is sometimes made between 'sewing' and 'stitching', the former defined as "when the awl, and subsequently the thread, pass partially through the thickness of the leather", the latter as "when the awl, and subsequently the thread, pass straight through the thickness of the leather" (Goubitz, 2001: 322-323). Here, the two terms are used without distinction – since sewing, as defined, is rare in Egyptian leather, it is specifically mentioned if the threads pass through the thickness partially.

Top railing (see figure below)
The wooden rod going round at the upper side of the body of the chariot.

(Vegetable) tanning (after Covington, 2009)
Tanning describes the process of converting raw animal skin into a durable and imputrescible material known as leather. Extracted from vegetal materials – for example, oak bark or *Vachellia nilotica* seed pods – vegetable tannins can be used to tan hides through reactions between the phenolic compounds in the tannins, and the protein collagen.

Whip stitch
The overcast stitch used to sew on reinforcement pieces, edge bindings. It wraps around in S-shape, as a whip would do, hence the reference.

Yoke (see figure below)
"The wooden element running across the necks of two or more draught animals and connecting them with the draught pole" (Littauer & Crouwel, 1985: 7).

Yoke saddle (see figure below)
"An element for adapting the yoke to the conformation of equids. Of inverted Y shape, its 'handle' was lashed to the yoke and its 'legs' lay along the animal's shoulders" (Littauer & Crouwel, 1985: 7).

Yoke saddle pad (see figure below)
"A piece of leather or fabric [or a combination of the two], lying beneath the yoke saddle" (Littauer & Crouwel, 1985: 7).

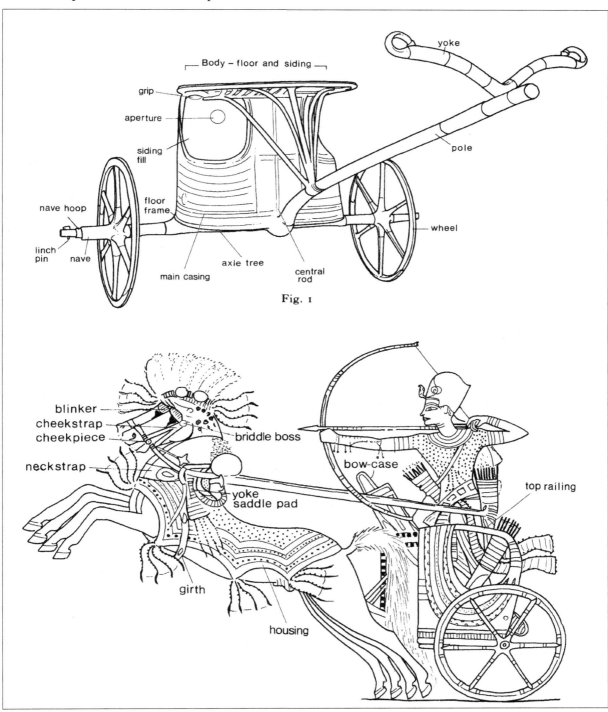

Chariot terminology. Adapted from Littauer & Crouwel (1985: 4).

CHRONOLOGY OF EGYPT

(WITH A FOCUS ON THE PERIOD AFTER THE ADVENT OF CHARIOTS)

PREDYNASTIC PERIOD (5000-3000)

Horus or Throne name	Personal Name	Regnal Dates (estimated)

ARCHAIC PERIOD (3050-2663; Dynasties 1-2)
OLD KINGDOM (2663-2195; Dynasties 3-6)
FIRST INTERMEDIATE PERIOD (2195-2066; Dynasties 7-mid-11)
MIDDLE KINGDOM (2066-1650; Dynasties mid-11 to 13)
SECOND INTERMEDIATE PERIOD (1650-1549; Dynasties 14-17)

Dynasty XIV
Unclear; possibly located in the Delta and precursor of Hyksos

Dynasty XV (Hyksos)

Maaibre	Sheshi	1650-
Meruserre	Yakobher	
Seuserenre	Khyan	
Nebkhepeshre/ Aqenenre/Auserre	Apophis	1585-1545
?	Khamudy	1545-1535

Dynasty XVI

?

Dynasty XVII (Theban)

Sekhemre-wahkhau	Rahotep	1650-
Sekhemre-smentawi	Djehuty	
Sankhenre	Mentuhotep VII	
Swedjenre	Nebiriau I	
Neferkare	Nebiriau II	
Sekhemre-shedtawi	Sobkemsaf I	
Sekhemre-wepmaat	Inyotef V	
Nubkheperre	Inyotef VI	
Sekhemre-heruhirmaat	Inyotef VII	
Sekhemre-wadjkhau	Sobkemsaf II	
Senakhtenre	Taa I	-1558
Seqenenre	Taa II	1558-1553
Wadjkheperre	Kamose	1553-1549

NEW KINGDOM (1549-1069; Dynasties 18-20)
Dynasty XVIII

Nebpehtire	Ahmose	1549-1524
Djeserkare	Amenhotep I	1524-1503
Akheperkare	Thutmose I	1503-1491
Akheperenre	Thutmose II	1491-1479
Menkheper(en)re	Thutmose III	1479-1424
Maatkare	Hatshepsut	1472-1457
Akheperure	Amenhotep II	1424-1398
Menkheperure	Thutmose IV	1398-1388
Nebmaatre	Amenhotep III	1388-1348
Neferkheperure-waenre	Amenhotep IV/Akhenaten	1352-1336
Ankhkheperure	Smenkhkare (coregent)	?
Neferneferuaten	(coregent & sole ruler)	?
Nebkheperre	Tutankhamun	?-1325
Kheperkheperure	Ay	1333-1328
Djeserkheperure-setpenre	Horemheb	1328-1298

Dynasty XIX

Menpehtire	Ramesses I	1298-1296
Menmaatre	Seti I	1296-1279
Usermaatre-setpenre	Ramesses II	1279-1212
Banenre	Merenptah	1212-1201
Userkheperure	Seti II	1201-1195
Menmire-setpenre	Amenmesse	1200-1196
Sekhaenre/Akheperre	Siptah	1195-1189
Sitre-merenamun	Tawosret	1189-1187

Dynasty XX

Userkhaure	Sethnakhte	1187-1185
Usermaatre-meryamun	Ramesses III	1185-1153
User/Heqamaatre--setpenamun	Ramesses IV	1153-1146
Usermaatre-sekheperenre	Ramesses V/Amenhirkopshef I	1146-1141
Nebmaatre-meryamun	Ramesses VI/Amenhirkopshef II	1141-1133
Usermaatre-setpenre-meryamun	Ramesses VII/ Itamun	1133-1125
Usermaatre-akhenamun	Ramesses VIII/Sethhirkopshef	1125-1123
Neferkare-setpenre	Ramesses IX/Khaemwaset I	1123-1104
Khepermaatre-setpenre	Ramesses X/Amenhirkopshef III	1104-1094
Menmaatre-setpenptah	Ramesses XI/Khaemwaset II	1094-1064
Hemnetjertepyenamun	Herihor	1075-1069

THIRD INTERMEDIATE PERIOD (1064-656; Dynasties 21-25)
Dynasty XXI

Hedjkheperre-setpenre	Smendes	1064-1038
Neferkare-heqawaset	Amenemnesu	1038-1034
Kheperkhare-setpenamun	Pinudjem I	1049-1026
Akheperre-setpenamun	Psusennes I	1034-981
Usermaatre-setpenamun	Amenemopet	984-974

Akheperre-setpenre	Osokhor	974-968
Netjerkheperre-meryamun	Siamun	968-948
Tyetkheperure-setpenre	Psusennes II	945-940

Dynasty XXII

Hedjkheperre-setpenre	Shoshenq I	948-927
Sekhemkheperre-setpenre	Osorkon I	927-892
(Heqakheperre-setpenre	Shoshenq II	895-895
Hedjkheprre-setpenre	Takelot I	892-877
Usermaatre-setpenamun	Osorkon II	877-838
Usermaatre-setpenre	Shoshenq III	838-798
Hedjkheperre-setpenre	Shoshenq IV	798-786
Usermaatre-setpenamun	Pimay	786-780
Akheperre	Shoshenq V	780-743

Theban Dynasty XXIII

Hedjkheperre-setpenamun	Harsiese	867-857
Hedjkheperre-setpenre	Takelot II	841-815
Usermaatre-setpenamun	Pedubast I	830-805
?	Iuput I	815-813
Usermaatre-setpenamun	Osorkon III	796-769
Usermaatre	Takelot III	774-759
Usermaatre-setpenamun	Rudamun	759-739
?	Iny	739-734
Neferkare	Peftjauawybast	734-724

Dynasty XXIII

Sehetepibenre	Pedubast II	743-733
Akheperre-setpenamun	Osorkon IV	733-715

Dynasty XXIV

Shepsesre	Tefnakhte	735-727
Wahkare	Bokkhoris	727-721

Dynasty XXV

Seneferre	Piye	752-721
Neferkare	Shabaka	721-707
Djedkare	Shabataka	707-690
Khunefertumre	Taharqa	690-664
Bakare	Tanutamen	664-656

SAITE PERIOD (664-525; Dynasty 26)
Dynasty XXVI

Wahibre	Psammetikhos I	664-610
Wehemibre	Nekho II	610-595
Neferibre	Psammetikhos II	595-589
Haaibre	Apries	589-570
Khnemibre	Amasis	570-526
Ankhka(en)re	Psammetikhos III	526-525

LATE PERIOD (525-332; Dynasties 27-31)

Dynasty XXVII (Persian)

Mesutire	Kambyses	525-522
Setutre	Darius I	521-486
?	Xerxes I	486-465
?	Artaxerxes I	465-424

Dynasty XXVIII

?	Amyrtaios	404-399

Dynasty XXIX

Baenre-merynetjeru	Nepherites I	399-393
Usermaatre-setpenptah	Psamuthis	393
Khnemmaatre	Akhoris	393-380
?	Nepherites II	380

Dynasty XXX

Kheperkare	Nektanebo I	380-362
Irimaatenre	Teos	365-360
Senedjemibre-setpenanhur	Nektanebo II	360-342

Dynasty XXXI (Persian)

Artaxerxes III	
Okhos	342-338
Arses	338-336
Darius III	335-332

Ptolemaic Dynasty (332-30)

ROMAN PERIOD (30 BC- AD 395)
BYZANTINE PERIOD (395-640)
ARAB PERIOD (640-1517)
OTTOMAN PERIOD (1517-1805)

BIBLIOGRAPHY

Albright, W.F. 1934. The Vocalization of the Egyptian Syllabic Orthographie. – New Haven, American Oriental Society 5.

Aldred, C. 1969. The 'New Year' Gifts to the Pharaoh. – Journal of Egyptian Archaeology 55: 73-81.

Aldred, C. 1973. Akhenaten and Nefertiti. – New York, The Brooklyn Museum.

Aldred, C. 1988. Akhenaten King of Egypt. – London, Thames & Hudson.

Assmann, J. 1991. Das Grab des Amenemope. – Mainz, Philipp von Zabern.

Assmann, J. 2001. Death and Salvation in Ancient Egypt. – Ithaca, Cornell University Press.

Bács, T.A. 2009. A Name with Three (?) Orthographies: The Case of the 'King's Son, Overseer of Southern Foreing Lands, Penre'. – Sudan & Nubia 13: 30-37.

Baillargeon, M. 2010. North American Aboriginal Hide Tanning: The Act of Transformation and Tevival. – Quebec, Canadian Museum of Civilization Corporation.

Baines, J. 2001. The Dawn of the Amarna Age. In: O'Connor, D & E. Cline. Eds. Amenhotep III: Perspectives on His Reign. – Ann Arbor, University of Michigan Press: 271-312.

Barakat, A. 1981. The Temple of Kha'-'Akhet in Western Thebes. – Mitteilungen des Deutschen Archäologischen Instituts, Abteilung Kairo 37: 29-33.

Beinlich-Seeber, C. & A.H. Shedid. 1987. Das grab des Userhat (TT 56). – Mainz, Philipp von Zabern.

Berlandini, J. 1998. Bès en aurige dans le char du dieu-sauveur. In: Clarysse, E. Ed. Egyptian Religion. The Last Thousand Years. – Leuven, Peeters: 31-55.

Binder, S. 2008. The Gold of Honour in New Kingdom Egypt. – Oxford, Aris and Phillips.

BLMRA, 1957. Hides, Skin and Leather Under the Microscope. – Surrey, The British Leather manufacturers' Research Association.

Bondi, J.H. 1886. Dem hebräisch-phönisischen Sprachzweige angehörige Lehnwörter hieroglyphischen und hieratischen Texten. – Leipzig, Breitkopf & Härtel.

Borchardt, L. 1911. Ausgrabungen in Tell el-Amarna 1911. – Mitteilungen der Deutschen Orientgesellschaft zu Berlin.

Borchardt, L. & H. Ricke. 1980. Die Wohnhäuser in Tell El-Amarna. – Berlin, Mann.

Boulos, L. 1999. Flora of Egypt. Vol. I. – Cairo, Al Hadara Publishing.

Brack, A. & A. Brack. 1980. Das Grab des Haremheb Theben Nr. 78. – Mainz, Philipp von Zabern.

Brand, P. 2004-2005. The Karnak Hypostyle Hall Project: Field Report 2004-2005: 1-8 (www.memphis.edu/hypostyle/links-and-ref/report_2004-2005.pdf).

Breasted, J.H. 1903. The Battle of Kadesh: A Study in the Earliest Known Military Strategy. – Chicago, The University of Chicago Press.

Brock, E. 2013. A Possible Chariot Canopy for Tutankhamun. In: Veldmeijer, A.J. & S. Ikram. Eds. Chasing Chariots: Proceedings of the First International Chariot Conference (Cairo 2012). – Leiden, Sidestone Press: 29-44 (online reading: https://www.sidestone.com/books/chasing-chariots).

Brugsch-Bey, E. 1889. Tente funéraire de la princesse Isimkheb, provenant de la trouvaille de Déir el-Bahari. – Le Caire.

Brunner, H. 1983. Sched. In: Helck, W. & E. Otto. Eds. Lexikon der Ägyptologie. Vol. V. – Wiesbaden, Otto Harrassowitz: 547-549.

Bruyère, B. 1926. Deir el Médineh. – Le Caire, Fouilles de l'Institut Francais d'Archaeologie Orientale du Caire.

Bryan, B. 2009. Memory and Knowledge in Egyptian Tomb Painting. In: Cropper, E. Ed. Dialogue in Art History for Mesopotamia to Modern: Readings from a New Century. – Washington, National Gallery of Art: 19-39.

Burchardt, M. 1909. Die altkanaanäischen Fremdworte und Eigennamen in Ägyptischen. – Leipzig, J.C. Hinrichs'sche Buchhandlung.

Calvert, A.M. 2013. Vehicle of the Sun: The Royal Chariot in the New Kingdom. In: Veldmeijer, A.J. & S. Ikram. Eds. Chasing Chariots. Proceedings of the First International Chariot Conference (Cairo 2012). – Leiden, Sidestone Press: 45-71 (online reading: https://www.sidestone.com/books/chasing-chariots).

Caminos, R.A. 1954. Late-Egyptian Miscellanies. – London, Oxford University Press.

Caminos, R.A. 1977. A Tale of Woe. P. Pushkin 127. – Oxford, Griffith Institute.

Campbell, C. 1910. Two Theban Princes. – Edinburgh/London, Oliver and Boyd.

Carter, H. 1903. Report on General Work Done in the Southern Inspectorate. – Annales du Service des Antiquités de l'Égypte 4: 46-47.

Carter, H. 1904 [and 2002]. Introduction. In: Davis, Th.M. The Tomb of Thoutmosis IV. – London, Archibald Constable & Co. [London, Gerald Duckworth & Co.]: vii-xi.

Carter, H. 1927 [and 2001]. The Tomb of Tut.ankh.Amen. The Burial Chamber. – London, Cassel & Company [London, Gerald Duckworth & Co.].

Carter, H. 1933 [and 2000]. The Tomb of Tut.ankh.Amen. The Annexe and Treasury. – London, Cassel & Company [London, Gerald Duckworth & Co.].

Carter, H. & A.C. Mace. 1923 [and 2003]. The Tomb of Tut.ankh.Amen. Search, Discovery and Clearance of the Antechamber. – London, Cassel & Company [London, Gerald Duckworth & Co.].

Carter, H. & P.E. Newberry. 1904 [and 2002]. Catalogue of the Antiquities found in the Tomb. In: Davis, Th.M. The Tomb of Thoutmosis IV. – London, Archibald Constable & Co. [London, Gerald Duckworth & Co.]: 1-144.

Černý, J. 1929. P. Salt 124 (Brit. Mus. 10055). – The Journal of Egyptian Archaeology: 243-258.

Černý, J. 1930. Ostraca Hiératiques (Catalogue Général des antiquités égyptiennes du Musée du Caire) Deuxième fascicule, Nos. 25501-25538. – Le Caire, Institut Français d'Archéologie Orientale.

Černý, J. 1939. Late Ramesside Letters. – Bruxelles, Fondation Égyptologique Reine Élisabeth.

Chenciner, R. 2003. Madder Red: A History of Luxury and Trade. – London, Routledge Curzon.

Cooney, J. 1965. Amarna Reliefs from Hermopolis in American Collections. – New York, The Brooklyn Museum.

Cotterell, A. 2004. Chariot: The Astounding Rise and Fall of the World's First War Machine. – London, Pimlico.

Covington, A.D. 2009. Tanning Chemistry: The Science of Leather. – Cambridge, RSC Publishing.

Coyat, J. & P. Montet. 1912. Les Inscriptions hiéroglyphiques et hiératiques du Ouâdi Hammâmât. – Le Caire, Institute Francais d'Archéologie Orientale du Caire.

Crouwel, J.H. 2013. Studying the Six Chariots from the Tomb of Tutankhamun. – An Update. In: Veldmeijer, A.J. & S. Ikram. Eds. Chasing Chariots. Proceedings of the First International Chariot Conference (Cairo 2012). – Leiden, Sidestone Press: 73-93 (online reading: https://www.sidestone.com/books/chasing-chariots).

Chassinat, M. 1904-1905. Appendix. – Egypt Exploration Fund Archaeological Reports.

Clutton-Brock, J. Ed. 1989. The Walking Larder Patterns of Domestication, Pastoralism, and Predation. – London, Unwin Hyman.

Covington, A.D. 2006. The Chemistry of Tanning Materials. In: Kite, M. & R. Thomson. Eds. Conservation of Leather and Related Materials. – Amsterdam etc., Butterworth-Heinemann: 22-35.

Covington, A. D. 2011. Tanning Chemistry. The Science of Leather. – Cambridge, CPI Group UK (Ltd).

Daniels, V.D. 1993. Evaluation of a Test for Tannins in Leather. – British Museum Conservation Research Section Report 1993/1: 1-6.

Daniels, V., T., Devièse, M. Hacke & C. Higgitt. 2014. Technological Insights Into Madder Pigment Production in Antiquity. – British Museum Technical Bulletin, 8: 13-17.

Daressy, G. 1898. Notes et Remarques. – Receuil de Travaux 20: 72-86.

Daressy, G. 1902. Fouilles de la Vallée des Rois 1898-1899. – Le Caire, Institute Français d'Archéologie Orientale.

Darnell, J.C. 1986. The Harried Helper. pPushkin 127: 4, 15-16. – Göttinger Miszellen 92: 17-21.

Darnell, J.C. & C. Manassa. 2007. Tutankhamun's Armies. Battle and Conquest During Ancient Egypt's Late 18th Dynasty. – Hoboken, John Wiley & Sons.

Davies, N. de Garis. 1902. The Rock Tombs of Deir el Gebrawi I. – London, Egypt Exploration Fund.

Davies, N. de Garis. 1903. The Rock Tombs of El Amarna. Part I. The Tomb of Meryra. – London, Egypt Exploration Fund.

Davies N. de Garis. 1905a. The Rock Tombs of El Amarna. Part II. The Tombs of Panehesy and Meryra II. – London, Egypt Exploration Fund.

Davies, N. de Garis. 1905b. The Rock Tombs of El Amarna. Part III. The Tombs of Huya and Ahmes. – London, Egypt Exploration Fund.

Davies, N. de Garis. 1906. The Rock Tombs of El Amarna. Part IV. The Tombs of Penthu, Mahu and Others. – London, Egypt Exploration Fund.

Davies, N. de Garis. 1908a. The Rock Tombs of El-Amarna, Part V. Smaller Tombs and Boundary Stelae. – London, Egypt Exploration Fund.

Davies, N. de Garis. 1908b. The Rock Tombs of El Amarna. Part VI. The Tombs of Parennefer, Tutu and Ay. – London, Egypt Exploration Fund.

Davies, de Garis. 1913. Five Theban Tombs (Being Those of Mentuherkhepeshef, User, Daga, Nehemawäy and Tati). – London, Egypt Exploration Fund.

Davies, N. de Garis. 1922-1923. The Tomb of Puyemre at Thebes. Vol. I-II. – New York, Metropolitan Museum of Art.

Davies, N. de Garis. 1923. The Tombs of Two Officials of Tuthmosis the Fourth. – London, Egypt Exploration Society.

Davies, N. de Garis. 1930. The Tomb of Ken-Amun at Thebes. Vol. I-II. – New York, Metropolitan Museum of Art.

Davies, N. de Garis. 1933a. The Tombs of Menkheperrasonb, Amenmose, and Another (Nos. 86, 112, 42, 226). – London, Egypt Exploration Society.

Davies, N. de Garis. 1933b. The Tomb of Neferhotep at Thebes. Vol. II. Plates in Folio. – New York, Publications of the Metropolitan Museum of Art.

Davies, N. de Garis. 1934-1935. The Work of the Graphic Branch of the Expedition. – Metropolitan Museum of Art Bulletin 30: 46-57.

Davies, N. de Garis. 1963. Scenes from Some Theban Tombs. Private Tombs at Thebes IV. – Oxford, Griffith Institute.

Davies, N.M. 1962. Tutankhamun's Painted Box. – Oxford, Griffith Institute.

Davies, N.M. & N. de G. Davies. 1926. The Tomb of Huy: Viceroy of Nubia in the Reign of Tutankhamun. – London, Egypt Exploration Society.

Davies, N.M. & N. de G. Davies. 1941. Syrians in the Tomb of Amunedjeh. – Journal of Egyptian Archaeology 27: 96-98.

Davies, N.M. & N. de G. Davies. 1940. The Tomb of Amenmose (No. 89) at Thebes. – Journal of Egyptian Archaeology 26: 131-136.

Davies, N. & A.H. Gardiner. 1936. Ancient Egyptian Paintings. Vol. I-II. – Chicago, University of Chicago Press.

Davis, Th. M. 1904 [and 2002]. The Tomb of Thoutmosis IV. – London, Archibald Constable & Co. Ltd. [London, Gerald Duckworth & Co.].

Davis, Th. M. 1907. The Tomb of Iouiya and Touiyou. – London, Archibald Constable & Co. Ltd.

Davis, Th. M. 1912. The Tombs of Harmhabi and Toutankhamanou. – London, Archibald Constable and Company & Co.

Dawson, W.R. & T.E. Peet. 1933. The So-Called Poem on the King's Chariot. – Journal of Egyptian Archaeology 19: 167-174.

Decker, W. 1971. Die Physische Leistung Pharaos. – Köln, Philosophischen Fakultät der Universität zu Köln.

Decker, W. 2006. Pharao und Sport. – Mainz, Philipp von Zabern.

Der Manuelian, P. 1987. Studies in the Reign of Amenophis II. – Hildesheim, Gerstenberg Verlag.

Desroches-Noblecourt, C. 1950. Un petit Monument Commémoratif du Roi Athléte. – Revue d'Égyptologie 7: 37-46.

Desroches Noblecourt, C., S. Donadoni & E. Edel. 1971. Grand Temple d'Abou Simbel: La Bataille de Qadech. – Cairo, Centre d'Études et de Documentation sur l'ancienne Égypte.

Dodson, A.M. & S. Ikram. 2008. The Tomb in Ancient Egypt. – London, Thames & Hudson.

Drenkhahn, R. 1976. Die Handwerker und ihre Tätigkeiten im alten Ägypten. – Wiesbaden, Otto Harrassowitz.

Dziobek, E. & M. Abdel Raziq. 1990. Das Grab des Sobekhotep: Theban Nr. 63. – Mainz, Philipp von Zabern.

Eastaugh, N., V. Walsh, T. Chaplin & R. Siddall. 2012. Pigment Compendium: A Dictionary of Historical Pigments. – London, Routledge.

Eaton-Krauss, M. 1983. Tutanchamun als Jäger. – Göttinger Miszellen 61: 49-50.

Eaton-Krauss, M. 2016. The Unknown Tutankhamun. – London, Bloomsbury.

Edel, E. 1953. Die Stelen Amenophis II aus Karnak und Memphis: mit dem Bericht uber d. asiatischen Feldzuge des Konigs. – Zeitschrift des Deutschen Palästina-Vereins 69, 2: 97-176.

Edel, E. 1983. Kleinasiatische und Semitische Namen und Wörter aus den Texten der Qadeššchlacht in Hieroglyphischer Umschrift. In: Görg, M. Ed. Fontes Atque Pontes - Eine Festgabe für Hellmut Brunner. – Wiesbaden, Otto Harrassowitz: 90-105.

Edwards, I.E.S. 1978. Tutankhamun. His Tomb and Its Treasures. – New York, Metropolitan Museum of Art.

Elnaggar, A., M. Leona, A. Nevin & A. Heywood. 2016. The Characterization of Vegetable Tannins and Colouring Agents in Ancient Egyptian Leather from the Collection of the Metropolitan Museum of Art. – Archaeometry 28 April 2016: 1-15.

Emiliozzi, A., A. Romualdi & F. Cecchi. 2000. Der currus aus dem >>Tumulo dei Carri<< von Populonia. In: Cecchi, F., M. Egg, A. Emiliozzi, R. Lehnert, A. Romualdi & M. Schönfelder. 2000. Zeremonialwagen: Statussymbol eisenzeitlicher Eliten. – Mainz am Rhein, Verlag des Römisch-Germanischer Zentralmuseum.

Erman, A. 1911. Die mit dem Zeichen geschriebenen Worte. – Zeitschrift für Ägyptische Sprache und Altertumskunde 48: 31-47.

Erman, A. & H. Grapow. 1971. See 'Wörterbuch'.

Ertman, E. 1998. Akhenaten's Use of Bound Foreign Prisoners in Chariot Scenes: A Commemoration of Specific Events or the King Victorious? – Annales du Service des Antiquités de l'Égypte 73: 51-60.

Faulkner, R.O. 1946. The Euphrates Campaign of Thutmose III. – Journal of Egyptian Archaeology 32: 39-42.

Faulkner, R.O. 2002. A Concise Dictionary of Middle Egyptian. – Oxford, Griffith Institute.

Fischer-Elfert, H.-W. 1983. Die Satirische Streitschrift des P. Anastasi I. Textzusammenstellung. – Wiesbaden, Otto Harrassowitz.

Fischer-Elfert, H.-W. 1986. Die Satirische Streitschrift des P. Anastasi I. Übersetzung und Kommentar. – Wiesbaden, Otto Harrassowitz.

Forbes, R.J. 1957. Studies in Ancient Technology. Vol. V. – Brill, Leiden.

Frankfort, H. & J.D.S. Pendlebury. 1933. The City of Akhenaten. Part II. The North Suburb and the Desert Altars. The Excavations at Tell el Amarna during the Seasons 1926-1932. – London, Egypt Exploration Society.

Freed, R. 1999. Pharaohs of the Sun. – Boston, Museum of Fine Arts.

Gaballa, G. 1969. Minor War Scenes of Ramesses II at Karnak. – Journal of Egyptian Archaeology 55: 82-88.

Gabolde, L. 1989. Les temples "mémoriaux" de Thoutmosis II et Toutânkhamon. – Bulletin de l'Institut Français d'Archéologie Orientale 89: 127-178.

Gabolde, L. 2009. Monuments décorés en bas relief aux noms de Thoutmosis II et Hatchepsout à Karnak. – Le Caire, l'Institut Français d'Archéologie Orientale.

Gardiner, A. H. 1911. Egyptian Hieratic Texts. – Leipzig, Hinrichs.

Gardiner, A.H. 1931. The Library of A. Chester Beatty. Description of a Hieratic Papyrus with a Mythological Story, Love-Songs and other Miscellanous Texts. – London, Emery Walker.

Gardiner, A.H. 1932. Late Egyptian Stories. – Bruxelles, Fondation Égyptologique Reine Élisabeth.

Gardiner, A.H. 1935. Hieratic Papyri in the British Museum. Third Series. Chester Beatty Gift. – London, British Museum Press.

Gardiner, A.H. 1937. Late Egyptian Miscellanies. – Bruxelles, Fondation Égyptologique Reine Élisabeth.

Gardiner, A.H. 1947. Ancient Egyptian Onomastica. Vol. I. – Oxford, Oxford University Press.

Gardiner, A.H. 1957. Egyptian Grammar. Being an Introduction to the Study of Hieroglyphs. 3rd Edition, Revised. – Oxford, Griffith Institute.

Gardiner, A.H. & T.E. Peet. 1952. The Inscriptions of Sinai. Second Edition revised and Augmented. Part I: Introduction and Plates. – London, Egypt Exploration Society/Geoffrey Cumberlege.

Gardiner, A.H. & T.E. Peet. 1955. The Inscriptions of Sinai. Part II: Translations and Commentary. – London, Egypt Exploration Society.

Grajetzki, W. 2001. Das Grab des Kii-iri in Saqqara. – Jaarbericht Ex Oriente Lux 37: 111-125.

Gauthier, H. 1925. Dictionnaire des noms geographiques contenus dans les textes hieroglyphiques. Vol. II. – Le Caire, Société Royale Géographie d'Égypte.

Glanville, S.R.K. 1932. Records of the Royal Dockyard of the Time of Thutmose III: P. British Museum 10056. – Zeitschrift für Ägyptische Sprache und Altertumskunde 68: 7-41.

Gohary, J. 1992. Akhenaten's Sed-Festival at Karnak. –London, Kegan Paul.

Goldwasser, O. 2002. Prophets, Lovers and Giraffes: Wor(l)d Classification in Ancient Egypt. – Wiesbaden, Otto Harrassowitz.

Goubitz, O. 2001. Glossary of Footwear Terms from Early Medieval Times Until 1800. In: Goubitz, O., C. van Driel-Murray & W. Groenman-van Waateringe. 2001. Stepping Through Time. Archaeological Footwear from Prehistoric Times Until 1800. – Zwolle, Stitching Promotie Archeologie: 317-324.

Grew, F. & M. de Neergaard. 1988. Shoes and Pattens. Medieval Finds from Excavations in London. – London, Boydell Press.

Groddek, D. 2000. Ist das Etymon von wrry.t "Wagen" gefunden? – Göttinger Miszellen 175: 109-111.

Guidotti, M.C. Ed. 2002. Il carro e le armi del museo Egizio di Firenze. – Firenze, Giunti Gruppo Editoriale.

Habachi, L. 1972. The Second Stela of Kamose and His Struggle Against the Hyksos Ruler and His Capital. – Glückstadt, J.J. Augustin.

Hagen, F. & K. Ryholt. 2016. The Antiquities Trade in Egypt 1880-1930. The H.O. Lange Papers. – Copenhagen, Det Kongelige Danske Videnskabernes Selskab.

Haines, B.M. 1981. The Fibre Structure of Leather. – Northampton, Leather Conservation Centre.

Haines, B.M. 2006a. Collagen: The Leathermaking Protein. In: Kite, M. & R. Thomson. Eds. Conservation of Leather and Related Materials. – Amsterdam etc., Butterworth-Heinemann: 4-10.

Haines, B.M. 2006b. The Fibre Structure of Leather. In: Kite, M. & R. Thomson. Eds. Conservation of Leather and Related Materials. – Amsterdam etc., Butterworth-Heinemann: 11-21.

Haines, B.M. & J.R. Barlow. 1975. Review: The anatomy of Leather. – Journal of Material Science 10: 525-538.

Hall, H.R. 1913. Catalogue of Egyptian Scarabs, Etc., in the British Museum. Vol. I. – London, British Museum.

Hallman, S. 2006. Die Tributszenen des Neuen Reiches. – Wiesbaden, Otto Harrassowitz.

Hanasaka, T. 2004. Archaeological Investigations. South Area. In: Kawanishi, H. & S. Tsujimura. Eds. Preliminary Report Akoris 2003. – Tsukuba, Institute of History and Anthropology, University of Tsikuba: 4-10.

Hansen, K. 1992. Collection in Ancient Egyptian Chariot Horses. – Journal of the American Research Center in Egypt 29: 173-179.

Hari, R. 1964. Horemheb et la Reine Moutnedjemet ou la Fin d'une Dynastie. – Genève, Imprimerie La Sirène.

Hartwig, M. 2007. A Vignette Concerning the Deification of Thutmose IV. In: D'Auria, S. Ed. Servant of Mut. Studies in Honor of Richard A. Fazzini. – Leiden, Brill: 120-124.

Harvey, S.P. 1998. The Cults of King Ahmose at Abydos. – Ph.D. Dissertation, University of Pennsylvania.

Hayes, W. C. 1953. The Scepter of Egypt. – New York, Harper & Brothers.

Heagren, B. 2010. An Analysis of the Tactical, Logistic, and Operational Capabilities of the Egyptian Army (Dynasties XVII-XX). – Ph.D. Dissertation, University of Auckland.

Healey, E. 2012. The Decorative Program of the Amarna Rock Tombs: Unique Scenes of the Egyptian Military and Police. In: Knoblauch, C. &

J. Gill. Eds. Egyptology in Australia and New Zealand. – Oxford, BAR Publishing.

Heinz, S. 2001. Die Feldzugsdarstellengun des Neuen Reichs. Eine Bildanalyse. – Vienna, Österreichischen Akademie der Wissenschaften.

Helck, H.W. 1955. Urkunden der 18. Dynastie. Heft 17: Historische Inschriften Thutmose' III und Amenophis' II. – Berlin, Akademie Verlag.

Helck, H.W. 1957a. Urkunden der 18. Dynastie. Heft 19: Historische Inschriften Thutmose' IV. und biographische Inschriften seiner Zeitgenossen. – Berlin, Akademie Verlag.

Helck, H.W. 1957b. Urkunden der 18. Dynastie. Heft 20: Historische Inschriften Amenophis' III. – Berlin, Akademie Verlag.

Helck, H.W. 1961. Urkunden der 18. Dynastie. Übersetzung zu den Heften 17-22. – Berlin, Akademie Verlag.

Helck, H.W. 1971. Die Beziehungen Ägyptens zu Vorderasien im 3. und 2. Jahrtausend. – Wiesbaden, Otto Harrassowitz.

Helck, H.W. 1977. Das Verfassen einer Königsinschrift. In: Assmann, J., E. Feucht & R. Grieshammer. Eds. 1977. Fragen an die altägyptische Literatur. – Wiesbaden, Ludwig Reichert: 241-256.

Helck, H.W. 1978. Ein indirekter Beleg für die Benutzung des leichen. – Journal of Near Eastern Studies 37: 337-340.

Hepper, F.N. 2009. Pharaoh's Flowers: The Botanical Treasures of Tutankhamun. – London, KWS Publishers.

Herold, A. 2003. Ein Puzzle mit zehn Teilen - Waffenkammer und Werkstatt aus dem Grab des Ky-jrj in Saqqara. In: Kloth, N., K. Martin & E. Pardey. Eds. 2003. Es Werde Niedergelegt als Schriftstück. Festschrift für Hartwig Altenmüller zum 65. Geburtstag. – Hamburg, Helmut Buske Verlag: 193-202.

Herold, A. 1999. Streitwagentechnologie in der Ramses-Stadt. Bronze and Pferd und Wagen. – Mainz, Philipp von Zabern.

Herold, A. 2006. Streitwagentechnologie in der Ramses-Stadt. – Mainz, Philipp von Zabern.

Herslund, O. 2011. Suns, Branding Irons and the White Cloth. Ancient Egyptian Classification of Material Culture. – Ph.D. Dissertation, University of Copenhagen.

Herslund, O. 2013. Chariots in the Daily Life of New Kingdom Egypt: A Survey of Production, Distribution and Use in Texts. In: Veldmeijer, A.J. & S. Ikram. Eds. Chasing Chariots. Proceedings of the First International Chariot Conference (Cairo 2012). – Leiden, Sidestone Press: 123-129 (online reading: https://www.sidestone.com/books/chasing-chariots).

Hoch, J. E. 1994. Semitic Words in Egyptian Texts of the New Kingdom and Third Intermediate Period. – Princeton, Princeton University Press.

Hodel-Hoenes, S. 1991. Life and Death in Ancient Egypt. – Ithaca/London, Cornell University Press.

Hofmann, U. 1989. Fuhrwesen und Pferdehaltung im alten Ägypten. – Bonn, Rheinischen Friedrich-Wilhelms-Universität Bonn.

Hoffmeier, J.K. 1988. The Chariot Scenes of Akhenaten at Karnak. In: Redford, D.B. Ed. Akhenaten Temple Project. Vol. II. Rwd-mnw and Inscriptions. – Toronto, University of Toronto Press: 35-45.

Hölscher, U. 1929. Medinet Habu 1924-1928. II. The Architectural Survey of the Great Temple and Palace of Medinet Habu (season 1927-28). – Chicago, University of Chicago Press.

Houlihan, P.F. 1986. The Birds of Ancient Egypt. – Warminster, Aris and Phillips.

Hulit, T. 2002. Late Bronze Age Scale Armour in the Near East: An Experimental Investigation of Materials, Construction, and Effectiveness, With a Consideration of Socio-Economic Implications. – Ph.D. Dissertation, University of Durham.

Hulit, T. 2006. Tut'Ankhamun's Body Armour: Materials, Construction, and the Implications for the Military Industry. In: Dann, R.J. Ed. Current Research in Egyptology 2004. Proceedings of the Fifth Annual Symposium. – Oxford, Oxbow Books: 100-111.

Hulit, T. & T. Richardson. 2007. The Warriors of Pharaoh: Experiments with New Kingdom Scale Armour, Archery and Chariots. In: Molloy, B. Ed. Cutting Edge. Studies in Ancient and Medieval Combat. – Stroud, Tempus: 52-63.

Ikram, S. 1995. Choice Cuts: Meat Production in Ancient Egypt. – Leuven, Peeters.

Ikram, S., G. Tallet & N. Warner. 2018. A Mineral for All Seasons: Alum in the Great Oasis. In:

Warfe, A., J. Gill, C. Hamilton, A. Pettman & D. Stewart. Eds. Studies on Ancient Egypt in Honour of Colin A. Hope. – Leuven, Peeters.

Iskander, S. & O. Goelet. 2015. The Temple of Ramesses II in Abydos. Vol. I. Wall Scenes. Part 1. Exterior Walls and Courts. – Atlanta, Lockwood Press.

Iwaszczuk, J. 2011. Unique Temple of Thutmose I. Annual Report. – Warsaw, Polish Academy of Sciences: 22-25.

Iwaszczuk, J. 2012. The Temple of Tuthmosis I Rediscovered. – Warsaw, Polish Archaeology in the Mediterranean 21: 269-277.

Jaeger, B. 1982. Essai de Classification et Datation des Scarabées Menkhéperrê. – Editions Universitaires Fribourg Suisse.

James, T.G.H. 2000. Tutankhamun: The Eternal Splendor of the Boy Pharaoh. – Cairo, American University in Cairo Press.

Janssen, J.J. 1975. Commodity Prices from the Ramesside Period. An Economic Study of the Village of Necropolic Workmen at Thebes. – Leiden, Brill.

Janssen, J.J. 1991. Late Ramesside Letters and Communications. – London, British Museum Press.

Janssen, J.J. 2005. Donkeys at Deir el-Medina. – Leiden, Nederlands Instituut voor het Nabije Oosten.

Janssen, R. M. & J.J. Janssen. 1990. Candlewick Coverlets. – Discussions in Egyptology 16: 53-61.

Janzen, M. 2013. The Iconography of Humiliation: The Depiction and Treatment of Bound Foreigners in New Kingdom Egypt – Ph.D. Dissertation, University of Memphis.

Jéquier, G. 1922. Matériaux pour servir à l'établissement d'un Dictionnaire d'Archéologie Égyptienne. – Bulletin de l'Institut Français d'Archéologie Orientale 19: 1-271.

Johnson, W. 1992. An Asiatic Battle Scene of Tutankhamun from Thebes: A Late Amarna Antecedent of the Ramesside Battle Narrative Tradition. – Ph.D. Dissertation, University of Chicago.

Johnson, W. 2009. Tutankhamen-Period Battle Narratives at Luxor. – KMT 20, 4: 20-33.

Kakosy, L.1977. Bark and Chariot. – Studia Aegyptiaca 3: 57-65.

Kemp, B. 2006. Ancient Egypt: Anatomy of a Civilization. Second Edition. – London, Routledge.

Kemp, B. 2008. Amarna's Ancient Roads. – Horizon 3: 8.

Kemp, B. 2012. The City of Akhenaten and Nefertiti. Amarna and Its People. – London, Thames & Hudson.

Kitchen, K.A. 1975. Ramesside Inscriptions. Historical and Biographical I. – Oxford, Blackwell.

Kitchen, K.A. 1979. Ramesside Inscriptions. Historical and Biographical II. – Oxford, Blackwell.

Kitchen, K.A. 1980. Ramesside Inscriptions. Historical and Biographical III. – Oxford, Blackwell.

Kitchen, K.A. 1982. Ramesside Inscriptions. Historical and Biographical IV. – Oxford, Blackwell.

Kitchen, K.A. 1983. Ramesside Inscriptions. Historical and Biographical V. – Oxford, Blackwell.

Kite, M. 2006. Collagen Products: Glues, Gelatine, Gut Membrane and Sausage Casings. In: Kite, M. & R. Thomson. Eds. Conservation of Leather and Related Materials. – Amsterdam etc., Butterworth-Heinemann: 192-198.

Knew, E. 1947. A Note on the Native Tanner of the Sudan and Some Proposed Production Developments. – The Sudan Government Pamplet 10/47.

Köpp-Junk, H. 2008. Weibliche Mobilität: Frauen in Sänften und auf Streitwagen. In: Peust, C. Ed. 2008. Miscellanea in honorem Wolfhart Westendorf. – Göttinger Miszellen Beiheft 3: 34-44.

Köpp-Junk, H. 2013. The Chariot as a Mode of Locomotion in Civil Contexts. In: Veldmeijer, A.J. & S. Ikram. Eds. Chasing Chariots. Proceedings of the First International Chariot Conference (Cairo 2012). – Leiden, Sidestone Press: 131-142 (online reading: https://www.sidestone.com/books/chasing-chariots).

Köpp-Junk, H. 2015a. Ikonographische und Textliche Belege für Frauen auf Streitwagen in der Amarnazeit. In: Huyeng, C. & A. Finger. Eds. Amarna in the 21st Century. – Kleine Berliner Schriften zum Alten Ägypten: 102-149.

Köpp-Junk, H. 2015b. Reisen im Alten Ägypten. Reisekultur, Fortbewegugns- und Transportmittel in pharaonischer Zeit. – Wiesbaden, Otto Harrassowitz.

Kuckertz, J. 2006. Schuhe aus der persischen Militärkolonie von Elephantine, Oberägypten, 6.-5. Jhdt. v. Chr. – Mitteilungen der Deutschen Orient-Gesellschaft zu Berlin 138: 109-156.

Lamb, M.J. 1981. The Hausa Tanners of Northern Nigeria and the Production of Sokoto Tanned Goatskins. – The New Bookbinder: 58-62. Available at: https://www.harmatan.co.uk/about/Hausa Tanners.pdf (Accessed: 7 August 2017).

Larsen, R. 2008. The Chemical Degradation of Leather. – CHIMIA Chimia Chemische Gesellschaft 62: 899-902.

Larsen, R. 2012. Transformation of Collagen Into Gelatine in Historical Leather and Parchment Caused by Natural Deterioration and Moist Treatment. Proceedings: 5th Freiberg Collagen Symposium, September 04-05, 2012. – Freiberg, Alte Mensa: 121-128.

Larsen, R., D.V. Poulsen, M. Odlyha, J. de Groot, Q. Wang, T. Wess, J. Hiller, C. Kennedy, F. Juchauld, H. Jerosch, C. Theodorakopoulos, G. Della Gatta, E. Badea, A. Maši, S. Boghosian & D. Fessas. 2005. Damage Assessment of Parchment: Complexity and Relations at Different Structural Levels. – The Hague, Preprints of the 14th Triennial Meeting of ICOM-CC (May 2014): 199-208.

Larsen, R., M. Vest, M. & U.B. Kejser. 1994. STEP Leather Project: Evaluation of the Correlation Between Natural and Artificial Ageing of Vegetable Tanned Leather and Determination of Parameters for Standardization of an Artificial Ageing Method. – Royal Danish Academy of Fine Arts & European Commission, Protection and Conservation of European Cultural Heritage 1.

Lauffray, J. 1979. Karnak d'Égypte: Domaine du divin. – Paris, Editions du Centre National de la Recherche Scientifique.

Lichtheim, M. 1976. Ancient Egyptian Literature. Vol. II. The New Kingdom. – Berkeley, University of California Press.

Leach, B. 1995. Tanning Tests for Two Documents Written on Animal Skin. – Journal of Egyptian Archaeology 81: 241-242.

Leblanc, C. & A. Sesana. 2006. Ippolito Rosellini. Monuments de l'Egypte et de la Nubie. – Paris, Bibliothèque des Introuvables.

Leclant, J. 1960. Astarté à cheval d'après les representations égyptiennes. – Syria 37.1-2: 1-67.

Leona, M. 2009. Microanalysis of Organic Pigments and Glazes in Polychrome Works of Art by Surface-Enhanced Resonance Raman Scattering. – Proceedings of the National Academy of Sciences of the United States of America 106, 35: 14757-14762.

Lesko, L. & B.S. Lesko 1982. A Dictionary of Late Egyptian. Vol. 1-5. – Berkeley, B.C. Scribe Publications.

Littauer, M.A. & J.H. Crouwel. 1979. Wheeled Vehicles and Ridden Animals in the Ancient Near East. – Leiden, Brill.

Littauer, M.A. & J.H. Crouwel. 1985. Chariots and Related Equipment from the Tomb of Tutankhamun. – Oxford, Griffith Institute.

Loschwitz, N. 2009. Am Ende ist es Gelatine. Eingeschränkte Möglichkeiten der Restaurierung bei versprödeten Lederobjecten. In: Peltz, U. & O. Zorn. Eds. Restaurierung Archäologischer Schätze an den Staatlichen Museen zu Berlin. – Main, Philipp von Zabern: 192-195.

Lucas, A. 1927. The Chemistry of the Tomb. In: Carter, H. 1927 [also 2001]. The Tomb of Tut.ankh.Amen. The Burial Chamber. – London, Cassel & Company [London, Gerald Duckworth & Co.].

Lucas, A. & J. Harris. 2012. Ancient Egyptian Materials and Industries. – New York, Dover Publications Inc.

Malek, J. 1989. An Eighteenth Dynasty Monument of Sipair from Saqqara. – Journal of Egyptian Archaeology 75: 61-76.

Manassa, C. 2002. Two Unpublished Memphite Relief Fragments in the Yale Art Gallery. – Studien zur Altägyptischen Kultur 30: 255-267.

Manassa C. 2003. The Great Karnak Inscription of Merneptah: Grand Strategy in the 13th Century BC. – New Haven, Yale Egyptological Seminar.

Manassa C. 2013. The Chariot that Plunders Foreign Lands: "The Hymn to the King in His Chariot". In: Veldmeijer, A.J. & S. Ikram. Eds. Chasing Chariots. Proceedings of the First International Chariot Conference (Cairo 2012). – Leiden, Sidestone Press: 143-156 (online reading: https://www.sidestone.com/books/chasing-chariots).

Markowitz, Y. 1999. String of Eye Beads. In: Freed, R., Y. Markowitz & S. D'Auria. Eds. Pharaohs of the Sun. – Boston, Museum of Fine Arts: 261.

Martin, G. 1976. Excavations at the Memphite Tomb of Horemheb, 1976: Preliminary Report. – Journal of Egyptian Archaeology 63: 13-19.

Martin, G. 1987. Corpus of Reliefs of the New Kingdom from the Memphite Necropolis and Lower Egypt. – London, KPI.

Martin, G. 1989. The Memphite Tomb of Horemheb, Commander-in-Chief of Tut'ankhamun. – London, Egypt Exploration Society.

Martin, G. 1991. The Hidden Tombs of Memphis. – London, Thames & Hudson.

Martin, G. 1997. The Tomb of Tia and Tia: A Royal Monument of the Ramesside Period in the Memphite Necropolis. – London, Egypt Exploration Society.

Martinez, P. 2012. Notes d'épigraphie Ramesside (II): Dieu est dans les détails. Dapour et la transfiguration de Ramsès II. – Memnonia XXIII: 181-207.

Meeks, D. 1997. Les emprunts Égyptiens aux langues sémitiques durant le Nouvel Empire et la Troisième Période Intermédiaire. Les aléas du comparatisme. – Bibliotheca Orientalis 54, 1/2: 32-62.

McLeod, W. 1982. Self Bows and Other Archery Tackle from the Tomb of Tutankhamun. – Oxford, Griffith Institute.

Merrillees, R.S. 2003. The Tano Family & Gifts from the Nile to Cyprus. – Lefkosia, Moufflon Publications.

Michel, A. 2014. Skin Deep: An Outline of the Structure of Different Skins and How it Influences Behaviour in Use. In: Harris, S. & A.J. Veldmeijer. Eds. Why Leather? The Material and Cultural Dimensions of Leather. – Leiden, Sidestone Press: 23-40 (online reading: https://www.sidestone.com/books/?q=why+leather).

Michel, A. & R. Daniels. 2009. Technology. Variations Within Hides and Skins. Part 1: The Influence of the Fibre Structure. – World Leather Magazine October/November 2009: 40-41.

Moran, W.L. 1987. Les Lettres D'El-Amarna. Correspondance Diplomatique du Pharaon. – Paris, Les Éditions du Cerf.

Morkot, R.G. 2007. War and Economy: The International 'Arms Trade' in the Late Bronze Age and After. – In: Schneider, T. & K. Szpakowska. Eds. Egyptian Stories: A British Egyptological Tribute to Alan B. Lloyd on the Accasion of His Retirement. Münster. – Münster, Ugarit-Verlag: 169-195.

Müller, H.W. 1989. Der „Armreif" des Königs Ahmose und der Handgelenkschutz des Bogenschutzen im Alten Ägypten und Vorderasien. – Mainz, Philipp von Zabern.

Murnane W.J. & C.C. van Siclen III. 1993. The Boundary Stelae of Akhenaten. – New York, Routledge, Chapman & Hall Inc.

Naville, E., D.N. Belaieff, G. Jéquier. 1930. Details releves dans les ruines de quelques temples égyptiens. – Paris, Geuthner.

Newman, R. & M. Serpico, 2000. Adhesives and Binders. In: Nicholson, P.T. & I. Shaw. Eds. Ancient Egyptian Materials and Technology. – Cambridge, Cambridge University Press: 475-494.

Ockinga, B. 1997. A Tomb from the Reign of Tutankhamun at Akhmim. – Warminster, Aris and Phillips.

O'Connor, D. 1988. Demarcating the Boundaries: An Interpretation of a Scene in the Tomb of Mahu, El-Amarna. – Bulletin of the Egyptological Seminar 9: 41-52.

O'Connor, D. 1990. The Nature of Tjemhu: (Libyan) Society in the Later New Kingdom. In: Leahy, A. Ed. Libya and Egypt c. 1300-750 BC. – London, Society for Libyan Studies: 29-113.

O'Connor, D. 1994. Beloved of Maat. The Horizon of Re. The Royal Palace in New Kingdom Egypt. In: O'Connor, D. & D. Silverman. Eds. Ancient Egyptian Kingship. – Leiden, Brill: 263-299.

O'Connor, D. 2001. The City and the World: Worldview and Built Forms in the Reign of Amenhotep III. In: O'Connor, D. & E. Cline. Eds. Amenhotep III Perspectives on His Reign. – Ann Arbor, University of Michigan Press: 125-172.

Oddy, A. & D.A. Scott. 2002. Copper and Bronze in Art: Corrosion, Colorants, Conservation. – Studies in Conservation 47, 4: 277.

Odegaard, N., S. Carroll & W.S. Zimmt. 2000. Material Characterization Tests for Objects of Art and Archaeology. – London, Archetype.

Orsenigo, C. & P. Piacentini. Eds. 2004. La Valle dei Re Riscoperta, I giornali di scavo Vitor Loret (1898-1899) e altri inediti. – Milan, Skira.

Orsenigo, C. 2016. La Tombe de Maiherpri (KV 36). – Milan, Bianca & Volta.

Osing, J. 1976. Die Nominalbildung im Ägyptischen. 2 Bde. – Mainz, Philipp von Zabern.

oEdinburgh 916. Dawson, W.R. & T.E. Peet. 1933. The So-Called Poem on the King's Chariot. – Journal of Egyptian Archaeology 19: 167-174.

oTurin 9588. Dawson, W.R. & T.E. Peet. 1933. The So-Called Poem on the King's Chariot. – Journal of Egyptian Archaeology 19: 167-174.

P. Anastasi I. Fischer-Elfert, H.-W. 1983. Die Satirische Streitschrift des P. Anastasi I. Textzusammenstellung. – Wiesbaden, Otto Harrassowitz.

P. Anastasi II. Gardiner, A.H. 1937. Late Egyptian Miscellanies. – Bruxelles, Fondation Égyptologique Reine Élisabeth.

P. Anastasi III. Gardiner, A.H. 1937. Late Egyptian Miscellanies. – Bruxelles, Fondation Égyptologique Reine Élisabeth.

P. Anastasi IV. Gardiner, A.H. 1937. Late Egyptian Miscellanies. – Bruxelles, Fondation Égyptologique Reine Élisabeth.

P. Bologna 1094. Gardiner, A.H. 1937. Late Egyptian Miscellanies. – Bruxelles, Fondation Égyptologique Reine Élisabeth.

P. Chester Beatty I. Gardiner, A.H. 1931. The Library of A. Chester Beatty: Description of a Hieratic P. with a Mythological Story, Love-Songs and other Miscellaneous Texts. – London, Emery Walker.

P. Chester Beatty III. Gardiner, A.H. 1935. Hieratic Papyri in the British Museum. Third Series: Chester Beatty Gift. – London, British Museum.

P. d'Orbiney. Gardiner, A.H. 1932. Late Egyptian Stories. – Bruxelles, Fondation Égyptologique Reine Élisabeth.

P. Harris 500. Gardiner, A.H. 1932. Late Egyptian Stories. – Bruxelles, Fondation Égyptologique Reine Élisabeth.

P. Lansing. Gardiner, A.H. 1937. Late Egyptian Miscellanies. – Bruxelles, Fondation Égyptologique Reine Élisabeth.

P. Koller. Gardiner, A.H. 1937. Late Egyptian Miscellanies. – Bruxelles, Fondation Égyptologique Reine Élisabeth.

P. Pushkin 127. Caminos, R.A. 1977. A Tale of Woe. P. Pushkin 127. – Oxford, Griffith Institute.

P. Turin B (Catalogue number 1881). Gardiner, A.H. 1937. Late Egyptian Miscellanies. – Bruxelles, Fondation Égyptologique Reine Élisabeth.

Parkinson, R. 2008. The Painted Tomb Chapel of Nebamun: Masterpieces of Ancient Egyptian Art in the British Museum. – Cairo, American University in Cairo Press.

Peet, T. & C. Woolley. 1923. The City of Akhenaten. Part I. – London, Egypt Exploration Society.

Partridge, R.B.1996. Transport in Ancient Egypt. – London, Rubicon Press.

Pelt, van, W. 2013. Revising Egypto-Nubian Relations in New Kingdom Lower Nubia: From Egyptianization to Cultural Entanglement. – Cambridge Archaeological Journal 23, 3: 523-550.

Pendlebury, J.D.S. 1951. The City of Akhenaten. Part III. The Central City and the Official Quarters. The Excavations at Tell el-Amarna during the Seasons 1926-1927 and 1931-1936. – London, Egypt Exploration Society.

Petrie, W.M.F. 1896. Six Temples at Thebes. – London, Bernard Quartich.

Pinch-Brock, L. 2001. The Tomb of Khaemhat. In: Weeks, K.R. Ed. Valley of the Kings: The Tombs and the Funerary Temples of Thebes West. – Vercelli: WhiteStar/Cairo, American University in Cairo Press: 364-375.

Popko, L. 2012a. oEdingburgh 916, Streitwagenhymnus. – Retrieved July 31st, 2017, from: http://aaew.bbaw.de/tla/servlet/OTPassport?u=herslund&f=0&l=0&oc=536&db=0.

Popko, L. 2012b. oTurin CG 57365. – Retrieved July 31st, 2017, from: http://aaew.bbaw.de/tla/servlet/OTPassport?u=herslund&f=0&l=0&oc=538&db=0.

Porter, B. & R. Moss. 1960. Topographical Bibliography of Ancient Egyptian Hieroglyphic Texts, Reliefs, and Paintings. Vol. I: The Theban Necropolis. Part I: Private Tombs. – Oxford, Griffith Institute.

Porter, B. & R. Moss. 1972. Topographical Bibliography of Ancient Egyptian Hieroglyphic Texts, Reliefs, and Paintings. Vol. II: Theban Temples. Second Edition. – Oxford, Oxford University Press.

Porter, B. & R. Moss. 1974. Topographical Bibliography of Ancient Egyptian Hieroglyphic Texts, Reliefs, and Paintings. Vol. III: Memphis. Second Edition. – Oxford, Oxford University Press.

Quack, J.F. 1994. Die Lehren des Ani. Ein neuägyptischer Weisheitstext in seinem kulturellen Umfeld. – Freiburg, Vandenhoeck & Ruprecht.

Quibell, J.E. 1908. The Tomb of Yuyaa and Thuiu. Catalogue Générale des Antiquitiés Égyptiennes de Musée du Caire. Nrs. 51001-51191. – Le Caire, l'Institut français d'archéologie orientale.

Quibell, J. E. 1912. Excavations at Saqqara (1908-9, 1909-10) - The monastery of Apa Jeremias. – Le Caire, l'Institut français d'archéologie orientale.

Quibell, J. & A. Hayter. 1927. Teti Pyramid, North Side. – Le Caire, l'Institut français d'archéologie orientale.

Radwan, A., 1969. Die Darstellungen des regierenden Königs und seiner Familienangehörigen in den Privatgräbern der 18. Dynastie. – Berlin, Bruno Hessling.

Raedler, C. 2007. Geräte aus Keramik in der spätbronzezeitlichen Ramsesstadt. Die Schaber der Werkstätten des Grabungsplatzes Q I. In: Pusch, E.B & M. Bietak. Eds. Die Keramik des Grabung-splatzes Q I. Teil 2. Schaber - Scherben - Marken. Forschungen in der Ramses-Stadt 5. – Hildesheim, Gerstenberg Verlag: 14-266.

Randall-Maciver, D. & C. L. Woolley. 1911. Buhen. Text. – Philadelphia, The University Museum Philadelphia.

Raulwing, P. 1994. Ein indoarischer Streitwagenterminus im Ägyptischen? - Kritische Bemerkungen zur Herleitung der Wagenbezeichnung wrrjj.t aus einem für das indoarische Sprachcorpus erschlossenen Nomen wrta 'Streitwagen'. – Göttinger Miszellen 140: 71-79.

Raulwing, P. Ed. 2002. Selected Writings on Chariots, Other Early Vehicles, Riding and Harness. By M.A. Littauer & J.H. Crouwel. – Leiden, Brill.

Raven, M. & R. van Walsem. 2014. The Tomb of Meryneith at Saqqara. – Turnhout, Brepols.

Raven, M., R. van Walsem, B. Aston, L. Horáčková & N. Warner. 2007. Preliminary Report on the Leiden Excavations at Saqqara, Season 2007: The Tomb of Ptahemwia. – Jaarbericht Ex Oriente Lux 40: 19-39.

Redford, D.B. 1967. History and Chronology of the Eighteenth Dynasty of Egypt. – Toronto, University of Toronto Press.

Redford, D. 1976. Akhenaten Temple Project. Vol. I: Initial Discoveries. – Toronto, University of Toronto Press.

Redford, D.B. 1984. Akhenaten the Heretic King. – Princeton, Princeton University Press.

Redford, D. B. 1988. The Akhenaten Temple Project. Vol. 2: Rwd-Mnw and Inscriptions. – State College, Akhenaten Temple Project.

Redford, D.B. 1994. The Concept of Kingship during the Eighteenth Dynasty. In: O'Connor, D. & D. Silverman. Eds. Ancient Egyptian Kingship. – Leiden, Brill: 157-184.

Reed, R. 1972. Ancient Skins, Parchments and Leathers. – London/New York, Seminar Press.

Reed, C. & D. Osborn. 1978. Taxonomic Transgressions in Tutankhamun's Treasures. – American Journal of Archaeology 82, 3: 273-283.

Reeves, C.M. 1990. Valley of the Kings. The Decline of a Royal Necropolis. – London/New York, Kegan Paul International.

Reeves, C.M. & R.H. Wilkinson. 1996. The Complete Valley of the Kings. – Cairo, American University in Cairo Press.

Ricke, H., G. Hughes & E. Wente. 1967. The Beit el-Wali Temple of Ramesses II. – Chicago, University of Chicago Press.

Ritner, R. 1993. The Mechanics of Ancient Egyptian Magical Practice. – Chicago, Oriental Institute of the University of Chicago Press.

Ritter, T. 1990. Dr.wt: Der Speichenkranz des Wagenrades. – Zeitschrift für Ägyptische Sprache und Altertumskunde 117: 60-62.

Roode, van, S.M. & A.J. Veldmeijer. 2005. Leatherwork from Qasr Ibrim: Preliminary Notes of the First Season. In: Roode, van, S.M. Ed. The PalArch Foundation's Proceedings of the annual Flemish-Netherlands Egyptologists Meeting 2004. – Amsterdam, PalArch Foundation: 4-5.

Romano, J. 1979. Catalogue: The Luxor Museum of Ancient Art. – Cairo, American Research Center in Egypt.

Romano, J. 1983. A Youthful Archer from El Amarna. In: De Moulenaere, H. & L. Limme. Eds. Artibus Aegypti: Studia in Honorem Bernardi

V. Bothmer. – Bruxelles, Musées Royaix d'Art et d'Histoire: 129-135.

Romano, J. 1991. A Prince or a God at El Amarna. – Amarna Letters. Vol. I.: 86-93.

Rommelaere, C. 1991. Les chevaux du nouvel empire Égyptien. Origines, races, harnachement. – Bruxelles, Connaissance de l'Égypte Ancienne.

Ryder, M. 1958. Follicle Arrangements in Skin from Wild Sheep, Primitive Domestic Sheep and in Parchment. – Nature 182: 781-783.

Ryder, M. 1973. Hair. – London, Edward Arnold Ltd (Studies in Biology 41).

Ryder, M.L. 1984 Skin, Hair and Cloth Remains from the Ancient Kerma Civilization of Northern Sudan. – Journal of Archaeological Science 11, 6: 477-482.

Sa'ad, R. 1975. Fragments d'un monument de Toutânkhamon retouvés dans le IXe pylone de Karnak. – Karnak 5: 93-109.

Sabbahy, L. 2013. Depictional Study of Chariot Use in New Kingdom Egypt. In: Veldmeijer, A.J. & S. Ikram. Eds. Chasing Chariots: Proceedings of the First International Chariot Conference (Cairo 2012). – Leiden, Sidestone Press: 191-102 (online reading: https://www.sidestone.com/books/chasing-chariots).

Sabbahy, L. 2016. The King Sitting Backward in his Chariot: A Ramesside Icon of Victory. – Journal of the American Research Center in Egypt 52: 321-328.

Saleh, M. & H. Sourouzian. 1987. Official Catalogue. The Egyptian Museum Cairo. – Mainz, Philipp von Zabern.

Sandor, B.I. 2013. Chariots' Inner Dynamics: Springs and Rotational Inertias. In: Veldmeijer, A.J. & S. Ikram. Eds. Chasing Chariots. Proceedings of the First International Chariot Conference (Cairo 2012). – Leiden, Sidestone Press: 257-271 (online reading: https://www.sidestone.com/books/?q=chasing+chariot).

Sauneron, S. 1963. Le temple d'Esna. Tome II (Nos 1-193). – Le Caire, l'Institut Français d'Archéologie Orientale.

Säve-Söderbergh, T. 1957a. Four Eighteenth Dynasty Tombs. – Oxford, Griffith Institute.

Säve-Söderbergh, T. 1957b. Private Tombs at Thebes. – Oxford, Griffith Institute.

Säve-Söderbergh, T. 1958. Eine Gastmahlsszene im Grabe des Schatzhausvorstehers Djehuti. – Mitteilungen des Deutschen Archäologischen Instituts, Abteilungen Kairo 16: 280-291.

Schiaparelli, E. 1887. Museo Archaeologico di Firenze. – Roma, Antichità.

Schneider, H.D. 1977. Shabtis. An Introduction to the History of Ancient Egyptian Funerary Statuettes with a Catalogue of the Collection of Shabtis in the National Museum of Antiquities at Leiden. – Leiden, Rijksmuseum van Oudheden.

Schneider, H.D. & M.J. Raven. 1981. De Egyptische Oudheid. – Leiden, Staatsuitgeverij.

Schneider, T. 1999. Zur Herkunft der ägyptischen Bezeichnung wrry.t "Wagen". Ein Indiz für den Lautwert von <r> vor Beginn des Neuen Reiches. – Göttinger Miszellen 173: 155-158.

Schneider, T. 2008. Fremdwörter in der Militärsprache des Neuen Reiches und ein Bravourstück des Elitesoldaten (P. Anastasi I 23, 2-7). – Journal of the Society for the Study of Egyptian Antiquities 35: 181-205.

Schulman, A. 1986. The So-Called Poem on the King's Chariot Revisited. – Journal of the Society for the Study of Egyptian Antiquities 16: 28-35, 39-44.

Schwarz, S. 2000. Altägyptisches Lederhandwerk. – Frankfurt etc., Peter Lang.

Schwarz, S. 2002. Leathercraft in the Mid-18th Dynasty. In: Audoin-Rouzeau, F. & S. Beyries. Eds. Le travail du cuir de la Préhistoire à nos jours. XX11e rencontres internationales d'archeologie et d'histoire d'Antibes. – Antibes, Editions APDCA: 481-493.

Schweinfurth, G. 1900. Neue Thebanische Gräberfunde. – Sphinx III: 103-107.

Sethe, K. 1906a. Urkunden der 18. Dynastie. Abteilung IV. Band I. Heft 1-4: Historisch-biographische Urkunden. – Leipzig, J C. Hinrichs'sche Buchhandlung.

Sethe, K. 1907. Urkunden der 18. Dynastie. Abteilung IV. Band III. Heft 9-12: Historisch-biographische Urkunden. – Leipzig, J.C. Hinrichs'sche Buchhandlung.

Sethe, K. 1961 [1927]. Urkunden der 18. Dynastie. Vol. I-III. – Berlin, Akademie-Verlag.

Settgast, J.1963. Untersuchungen zu Altägyptischen Bestattungsdarstellungen. – Glückstadt, J.J. Augustin.

Sharphouse, J.H. 1985. Theory and Practice of Modern Chamois Leather Production. – Journal of the Society of Leather Technologists and Chemists 69: 29-43.

Shaw, I. 1999 [1991]. Egyptian Warfare and Weapons. – Buckinghamshire, Shire Egyptology.

Simon, Z. 2010. Hethitisch-luwische Fremdwörter im Ägyptischen? – Göttinger Miszellen 227: 77-92.

Skinner, L.-A. 2007. A Visit to a Traditional Leather Tannery in Central Sudan, Sudan and Nubia. – Bulletin of the Sudan Archaeological Research Society 11: 125-127.

Skinner, L.-A. 2011. Traditional Leather Tanning in Central Sudan. In: Thomson, R. & Q. Mould. Eds. Leather Tanneries: The Archaeological Evidence. – London, Archetype Books: 49-57.

Skinner, L.-A. & A.J. Veldmeijer. 2015. Skin Deep: The Beautiful Leather of the Nubians at Hierakonpolis. – Neken News 27: 19-21.

Soldt, W. 1990. Fabrics and Dyes at Ugarit. – Leiden, Butzon & Bercker (Ugarit Forschungen 22): 321-357.

Spalinger, A. 2005. War in Ancient Egypt. The New Kingdom. – Oxford, Blackwell.

Speiser, E.A. 1933. Ethnic Movements in the Near East in the Second Millenium B. C. – Publications of the American schools of Oriental Research: 13-54.

Spiegelberg, W. 1928. Ein Gerichtsprotokoll aus der Zeit Tuthmosis' IV. – Zeitschrift für Ägyptische Sprache und Altertumskunde 63: 105-115.

Springuel, I. 2006. The Desert Garden: A Practical Guide. – Cairo, American University in Cairo Press.

Steinmann, F. 1980. Untersuchungen zu den in der handwerklich-künstlerischen Produktion beschäftigten Personen und Berufsgruppen des Neues Reichs. – Zeitschrift für Ägyptische Sprache und Altertumskunde 107: 137-158.

Sternberg-El Hotabi, H. 1999. Untersuchungen zur Überlieferungsgeschichte der Horusstelen I. – Wiesbaden, Otto Harrassowitz.

Strudwick, N. 2003. The Tomb of Amenemopet Called Tjanefer at Thebes (TT297). – Berlin, Achet Verlag.

The Epigraphic Survey. 1930. Medinet Habu. Vol. I. Earlier Historical Records of Ramses III. – Chicago, Oriental Institute of the University of Chicago Press.

The Epigraphic Survey. 1932. Medinet Habu. Vol. II. Later Historical Records of Ramses III. – Chicago, Oriental Institute of the University of Chicago Press.

The Epigraphic Survey. 1980. Tomb of Kheruef, TT 192. – Chicago, Oriental Institute of the University of Chicago Press.

The Epigraphic Survey. 1986. Reliefs and inscriptions at Karnak. Vol. IV. The Battle Reliefs of King Seti I. – Chicago, University of Chicago Oriental Institute Publications.

The Epigraphic Survey. 1994. Reliefs and Inscriptions at Luxor Temple. Vol. I. The Festival Procession of Opet in the Colonnade Hall. – Chicago, Oriental Institute of the University of Chicago Press.

Thomson, R. 2006a. Testing Leathers and Related Materials. In: Kite, M. & R. Thomson. Eds. Conservation of Leather and Related Materials. – Amsterdam etc., Butterworth-Heinemann: 58-65.

Thomson, R. 2006b. The Nature and Properties of Leather. In: Kite, M. & R. Thomson. Eds. Conservation of Leather and Related Materials. – Amsterdam etc., Butterworth-Heinemann: 1-3.

Thomson, R. 2006c. The Manufacture of Leather. In: Kite, M. & R. Thomson. Eds. Conservation of Leather and Related Materials. – Amsterdam etc., Butterworth-Heinemann: 66-81.

Trommer, B. Die Kollagenmatrix archäologischer Funde im Vergleich zu künstlich gealterten Ledermustern historischer Gerbverfahren (Dissertation). – Freiberg, Technischen Universität Bergakademie 2005 (https://fridolin.tu-freiberg.de/archiv/pdf/WerkstoffwissenschaftenTrommerBernhard923047.pdf).

Tuck, D.H. 1983. Oils and Lubricants Used on Leather. – Northampton, The Leather Conservation Centre.

Tylor, J.J. 1900. Wall Drawings and Monuments of El Kab. – London, Bernard Quaritch.

Tylor, J.J. & F. Ll. Griffith. 1894. The Tomb of Paheri at El Kab. – London, Egypt Exploration Fund.

Van Driel-Murray, C. 2000. Leatherwork and Skin Products. In: Nicholson, P.T. & I. Shaw. Eds. 2000. Ancient Egyptian Materials and Technology. – Cambridge, Cambridge University Press: 299-319.

Van Driel-Murray, C. 2002. Practical Evaluation of a Field Test for the Identification of Ancient Vegetable Tanned Leathers. – Journal of Archaeological Science 29: 17–21.

Veldmeijer, A.J. 2006. Knots, Archaeologically Encountered: A Case Study of the Material from the Ptolemaic and Roman Harbour at Berenike (Egyptian Red Sea coast). – Studien zur altägyptischen Kultur 35: 337-366.

Veldmeijer, A.J. 2009a. Studies of Ancient Egyptian Footwear. Technological Aspects. Part XV. Leather Curled-Toe Ankle Shoes. – PalArch's Journal of Archaeology of Egypt/Egyptology 6, 4: 1-21 (online at: www.PalArch.nl).

Veldmeijer, A.J. 2009b. Studies of Ancient Egyptian Footwear. Technological Aspects. Part XII. Fibre Shoes. – British Museum Studies in Ancient Egypt and Sudan 14: 97-129 (online at: www.britishmuseum.org/research/online_journals/bmsaes).

Veldmeijer, A.J 2009c. Studies of Ancient Egyptian Footwear. Technological Aspects. Part X. Leather Composite Sandals. – PalArch's Journal of Archaeology of Egypt/Egyptology 6, 9: 1-27.

Veldmeijer, A.J. 2010. Studies of Ancient Egyptian Footwear. Technological Aspects. Part XI. Sewn-Edge Plaited Sandals. – Jaarberichten Ex Oriente Lux 42: 79-124.

Veldmeijer, A.J. 2011a. With Contributions by: A.J. Clapham, E. Endenburg, A. Gräzer, F. Hagen, J.A. Harrell, M.H. Kriek, P.T. Nicholson, J.M. Ogden & G. Vogelsang-Eastwood. 2011. Tutankhamun's Footwear. Studies of Ancient Egyptian Footwear. – Leiden, Sidestone Press (republished 2010 volume; online reading: https://www.sidestone.com/books/tutankhamun-s-footwear).

Veldmeijer, A.J. 2011b. Amarna's Leatherwork. Part I. Preliminary Analysis and Catalogue. – Leiden, Sidestone Press (republished 2010 volume; online reading: https://www.sidestone.com/books/amarna-s-leatherwork). [The part on the chariot leather is included in the present work as Appendix II].

Veldmeijer, A.J. 2011c. What's in a Stitch? – Archaeological Leather Group Newsletter 34: 16-19. [This paper is included in the present work as Appendix III].

Veldmeijer, A.J. 2013. Studies of Ancient Egyptian Footwear. Technological Aspects. Part XVIII. Fibre Composite Sandals. – Jaarberichten Ex Oriente Lux 44: 85-115.

Veldmeijer, A.J. 2016. Leatherwork from Elephantine (Aswan, Egypt). Analysis and Catalogue of the Ancient Egyptian & Persian Leather Finds. - Leiden, Sidestone Press (online reading: https://www.sidestone.com/books/leatherwork-from-elephantine-aswan-egypt).

Veldmeijer, A.J. 2017. With Contributions by D. Polz & U. Rummel. Sailors, Musicians and Monks. The Leatherwork from Dra' Abu el Naga (Luxor, Egypt). – Leiden, Sidestone Press (online reading: https://www.sidestone.com/books/sailors-musicians-and-monks).

Veldmeijer, A.J. In Press. Ancient Egyptian Footwear Project. Phase I. Final Archaeological Analysis. – Leiden, Sidestone Press.

Veldmeijer, A.J. Submitted. Moreno García's (2017) "Leather Processing, Castor Oil and Desert/Nubian Trade at the Turn of the 3rd/2nd Millennium BC Some Speculative Thoughts on Egyptian Craftsmanship". - A Response. – Göttinger Miszellen.

Veldmeijer, A.J. & E. Endenburg. 2007. Amarna Leatherwork in Berlin. – Leiden, Egyptian Archaeology 31: 36-37.

Veldmeijer, A.J. & S. Ikram. 2009. Ancient Egyptian Leather Chariot Casing. – Archaeological Leather Group Newsletter 30: 8-9.

Veldmeijer, A.J. & S. Ikram. 2012a. With contributions by L. Skinner. Preliminary Report of the Egyptian Museum Chariot Project (EMCP). – Bulletin of the American Research Centre in Egypt: 7-11.

Veldmeijer, A.J. & S.Ikram. 2012b. Fit for a Pharaoh. Ancient Egyptian Chariot Leather. – World Archaeology 52: 36-38.

Veldmeijer, A.J. & S. Ikram. 2014. Why Leather in Ancient Egyptian Chariots? In: Harris, S. & A.J.

Veldmeijer. Eds. Why Leather? The Material and Cultural Dimensions of Leather. – Leiden, Sidestone Press: 115-122 (online reading: https://www.sidestone.com/books/?q=why+leather).

Veldmeijer, A.J. & L. Skinner. In Press. [The Harp's Related Skin Products]. In: Emerit, S. Ed. Dra' Abu el-Naga V: The Harps of Dra' Abu-el-Naga: Archaeological Studies. – Wiesbaden, Otto Harrassowitz.

Veldmeijer, A.J., S. Ikram & L. Skinner. 2013. Charging Chariots: Progress Report on the Tano Chariot in the Egyptian Museum Cairo. In: Veldmeijer, A.J. & S. Ikram. Eds. Chasing Chariots. Proceedings of the First International Chariot Conference (Cairo 2012). – Leiden, Sidestone Press: 257-271 (online reading: https://www.sidestone.com/books/?q=chasing+chariot).

Virey, Ph. 1891. Sept Tombeaux Thébains. – Paris, Ernest Leoux.

Vogelsang-Eastwood, G. 1993. Pharaonic Egyptian Clothing. – Leiden, Brill.

Vogelsang-Eastwood, G. 2000. Textiles. In: Nicholson, P. & I. Shaw. Eds. Ancient Egyptian Materials and Technology. – Cambridge University Press: 268-299.

Von Soten, W. 1965. Akkadisches Handwörterbuch. Bd. 1-3. – Wiesbaden, Otto Harrassowitz.

Ward, W.A. 1963. Notes on some Loanwords and Personal Names. – Orientalia 31: 413-436.

Ward, W.A. 1989. Egyptian txbs. A Hurrian Loan-Word in the Vernacular of Deir el Medina. – Göttinger Miszellen 109: 73-82.

Waterer, J.W. 1956. Leather. In: Singer, C.J. & R. Raper. Ed. History of Technology. – Oxford, Oxford University Press: 147-187.

Waterer, J.W. 1968. Leather Craftsmanship. – New York, Frederic A. Praeger.

Weber, A. 2012. Bead Chain with Udjat Eyes. In: Seyfried, F. Ed. In the Light of Amarna. – Berlin, Ägyptisches Museum und Papyrussammlung: 214-215.

Wegner, M. 1933. Stilentwickelung der Thebanischen Beamtengräber. – Mitteilungen des Deutschen Instituts für Ägyptische Altertumskunde in Kairo 4: 38-164.

Wente. F.E. 1967. Late Ramesside Letters. Studies in Ancient Oriental Civilization 33. – Chicago, University of Chicago Press.

Wente, F.E. & E.S. Meltzer. 1990. Letters from Ancient Egypt (Writings from the Ancient World). – Ann Arbor, Scholars Press.

Western, A.C. 1973. A Wheel Hub from the Tomb of Amenophis III. – Journal of Egyptian Archaeology 59: 91-94.

Westendorf, W. 1965-1977. Koptisches Handwörterbuch. – Heidelberg, C. Winter Universitätsverlag.

Westendorf, W. 1978. Beiträge zum Wörterbuch. – Göttinger Miszellen 29: 153-156.

Whitehouse, H. 2009. Egypt and Nubia in the Ashmolean Museum. – Oxford, Ashmolean Museum.

Wilson, J.A. 1969. An Egyptian Letter. In: Pritchard, J.B. Ed. Ancient Near Eastern Texts 'relating to the Old Testament'. – New Jersey, Princeton University Press: 475-479.

Wörterbuch I-V. Erman, A. & Grapow, H. 1971. Wörterbuch der ägyptische Sprache. Bd. I-V. – Berlin, Akademie-Verlag.

Wreszinski, W. 1915. Atlas zur altägyptischen Kulturgeschichte. – Leipzig, J.C. Hinrichs.

Yoyotte, J. & Lopez, J. 1969. L´Organisation de l´armée au Nouvel Empire. – Bibliotheca Orientalis 26: 3-19.

Yurco, F. 1986. Merneptah's Canaanite Campaign. – Journal of the American Research Center in Egypt 23: 189-215.

Zayed, A.H. 1985. Une representation inedited des campagnes d'Amenophis II. In: Posener-Kriéger, P. Ed. 1985. Melanges Gamal Eddin Mokhtar. Vol. I. – Le Caire, l'Institut Français d'Archéologie Orientale: 5-17, pl. II.

Zeidler, J. 2000. Zur Etymologie von wrr.yt 'Wagen'. – Göttinger Miszellen 178: 97-111.

Zimmern, H. 1917. Akkadische Fremdwörter als Beweis für babylonischen Kultureinfluss. – Leipzig, Hinrichs.

Printed by Printforce, United Kingdom